Aristotle on God's Life-Generating Power and on *Pneuma* as Its Vehicle

SUNY series in Ancient Greek Philosophy

Anthony Preus, editor

Aristotle on God's Life-Generating Power and on *Pneuma* as Its Vehicle

Abraham P. Bos

Cover art: "Genesis" painting courtesy of the artist Dr. Gerard P. Luttikhuizen.

Published by State University of New York Press, Albany

© 2018 State University of New York

All rights reserved

No part of this book may be used or reproduced in any manner whatsoever without written permission. No part of this book may be stored in a retrieval system or transmitted in any form or by any means including electronic, electrostatic, magnetic tape, mechanical, photocopying, recording, or otherwise without the prior permission in writing of the publisher.

For information, contact State University of New York Press, Albany, NY
www.sunypress.edu

Production, Ryan Morris
Marketing, Anne M. Valentine

Library of Congress Cataloging-in-Publication Data

Names: Bos, A. P., author.
Title: Aristotle on God's life-generating power and on pneuma as its vehicle / Abraham P. Bos.
Description: Albany, NY : State University of New York, 2018. | Series: SUNY series in ancient Greek philosophy | Includes bibliographical references and index.
Identifiers: LCCN 2017010328 (print) | LCCN 2017054041 (ebook) | ISBN 9781438468310 (ebook) | ISBN 9781438468297 (hardcover   ) | ISBN 9781438468303 (pbk.   )
Subjects: LCSH: Aristotle. | Religion. | God. | Soul. | Spirit.
Classification: LCC B491.R46 (ebook) | LCC B491.R46 B67 2018 (print) | DDC 185—dc23
LC record available at https://lccn.loc.gov/2017010328

10 9 8 7 6 5 4 3 2 1

Contents

1. God's Life-Generating Power and Its Transmission in Aristotle's Biology and Cosmology   1
2. The Dependence of All Nature upon God   11
3. The Natural Desire of All Things for God   21
4. God as Object of Erôs and Source of Attraction   41
5. God as Unmoved Principle of Motion and Source of Power   43
6. Reproduction: A Power Transmitted by the Begetter   63
7. Life Begins at the Moment of Fertilization   75
8. The Magnet as Model of a Mover at a Distance   87
9. God as Begetter of All Life According to *On the Cosmos*   97
10. *Pneuma* as the Vehicle of Divine Power in the Sublunary Region   131
11. Desire as a Form of Nostalgia for the Origin   237
12. Why Doesn't *Pneuma* Play an Important Role in Ancient and Modern Interpretations of Aristotle?   241
13. The Dubious Lines of *On the Soul* II 1, 412b1–4   245
14. Why Can't the Words *Sôma Organikon* in Aristotle's Definition of the Soul Refer to the Visible Body?   249
15. Collateral Damage of the Hylomorphistic Explanation of Aristotle's Psychology   255

16.	Resulting Damage to the Assessment of *On the Cosmos* and *On the Life-Bearing Spirit* (*De Spiritu*)	261
17.	Damage to the View of the Unity of Aristotle's Work	267
18.	Intellect, Soul, and Entelechy: The Golden Rope	271
19.	Aristotle on Life-Bearing *Pneuma* and on God as Begetter of the Cosmos: Brief Survey of Results	279
Bibliography		291
Index of Modern Names		321
Index of Ancient Names		325
Index of Texts		327

1

God's Life-Generating Power and Its Transmission in Aristotle's Biology and Cosmology

Is it possible that Aristotle presented three very different phases in his philosophy and that only one of these was scientifically important? Such was Werner Jaeger's claim in 1923, and still there is no alternative theory.

Is it likely that, during his lectures in the Peripatos, Aristotle talked about a vital *pneuma* connected with the soul as the principle of life, but that *pneuma* plays no role in his seminal work *On the Soul*?

Is it conceivable that he called God the "Great Leader" of the cosmos, but saw no divine governance in Nature?

These critical questions about the standard theory on Aristotle have spurred the author of this book to develop a perspective on Aristotle's philosophy that breaks with the accepted view.

A crucial part is assigned to *pneuma* as the vital principle in all that lives. *Pneuma* is the fine-material carrier of all psychic functions and is governed by the soul as entelechy. The soul is the principle that controls the activity of *pneuma* in a goal-oriented way (oriented, that is, to the form of the living being). The entelechy is a cognitive principle that acts on the vital *pneuma* and is active from the very beginning of life, as a kind of automatic pilot. In human beings, however, the entelechy can also be "awakened" to intellectuality. All entelechies of living beings, including those of the stars and planets, are actuated by the Power that proceeds inexhaustibly from the divine, transcendent Intellect.

This book also defends the authenticity of *On the Cosmos* (*De Mundo*), because this work does not present God as "Maker" but as "Begetter" of the cosmos. The same case is put for Aristotle's authorship of *On Pneuma* (*De Spiritu*), because Aristotle had to explain how there could be vital processes in plants and trees and in embryos and eggs, which do not possess respiration. Hence, he introduced *pneuma* as principle of vital heat, which is already present and active before the formation of lungs that enable breathing.

Many experts on Aristotle's work are in no doubt that he attributed a preeminent role to God in his philosophy of nature and cosmology. On the other hand there are authors who find it difficult to formulate the importance of God in Aristotle's analysis of everyday natural phenomena.[1] My intention is to describe how Aristotle held that nothing in the cosmos can exist independently of God, its ultimate Cause, whereas the existence of God depends on nothing external to him.

In this study I will first list some particulars about God's role in the Aristotelian system (in chapters 2–5). I will deal there with texts in which Aristotle talks about the dependence of the visible world on God and the degrees involved in this dependence. I will also discuss the structural desire for immortality and the condition of God in everything forming part of the cosmos, and the "love" (*erôs*) for God, which is a way in which this desire may also manifest itself.

I then explore how these particulars are related to one another and to other elements of Aristotle's philosophy, especially *to his theory of reproduction,* which I discuss in chapters 6 and 7.[2] In these chapters I consider how Aristotle came

---

1. W. D. Ross, *Aristotle's Metaphysics. A Revised Text with Introduction and Commentary.* II vols. (Oxford: Clarendon Press, 1924), vol. 1, cliii stated: "It is exclusively as first mover that a God is necessary to his system." Ross viewed *Metaphysics* Λ as the only specimen of Aristotle's "mature" theology; D. Frede, "Theodicy and Providential Care in Stoicism," in *Traditions of Theology. Studies in Hellenistic Theology*, ed. D. Frede, and A. Laks (Leiden: Brill, 2002), 86: "How little Greek philosophers thought of direct divine interference in worldly affairs at the end of the classical age is shown above all by Aristotle's Unmoved Mover whose thoughts are concerned exclusively with himself, because contact with inferior objects would mean a lessening of his perfection." S. Menn, "Aristotle's Theology," in *The Oxford Handbook of Aristotle*, ed. C. Shields (Oxford: Oxford University Press, 2012), 422 noted: "This way of thinking about Aristotle's theology is not entirely false, but it is badly misleading." I myself prefer the position taken by J. E. Whiting, "Locomotive Soul: The Parts of Soul in Aristotle's Scientific Works," *Oxford Studies in Ancient Philosophy* 22 (2002): 144: "the prime mover . . . can exist apart from all other things, none of which can exist apart from it."

2. For a diametrically opposite interpretation of Aristotle's theology, see R. Bodéüs, *Aristote et la Théologie des Vivants Immortels* (Québec: Éd. Bellarmin, 1992); Eng. ed. *Aristotle and the Theology of the Living Immortals* (Albany: State University of New York Press, 2000). He defends the remarkable position that Aristotle did hold a cosmic theology, closely attuned to traditional Greek conceptions, but not a meta-cosmic theology. According to Bodéüs, the notion of a transcendent Unmoved Mover, as proposed in *Metaphysics* Lambda, is not Aristotelian, but came to be attributed to Aristotle through the influence of the treatise *On the Cosmos* (*De Mundo*), which Bodéüs dates to the beginning of the Christian era—Eng. ed., 33–34.

to see the life of plants and trees and the vegetative, nutritive or reproductive function of animals and humans as the most general function of life in the sublunary sphere, and the first in the development of all living creatures. This function is essential to all mortal living entities, but does not depend on respiration or breath. It is already active before the birth of living creatures, from the moment of fertilization or conception. Focusing on this subject, Aristotle started to wonder how specific identity (the *eidos*) is determined for a new living being from the moment of fertilization, and what agency is responsible for producing the new being, since that agency cannot be an immaterial soul that enters a previously formed embryo from outside. This led Aristotle to draw up his entirely new theory of the soul as carrier of specific form and as entelechy of a pneumatic instrumental body. His radical new outlook on the genesis of life also led Aristotle to describe God's relationship with the cosmos caused by him in a very different way from his predecessors Plato and the Presocratics (chapter 9). For Aristotle, God is not an entity that produces the world as a Creator or Demiurge. He is, however, the cause of all things, such that Aristotle is convinced of a divine design of the cosmos. Aristotle's view of the cosmos is "teleological," because everything functions in the best possible way, not through an external entity that creates something as a producer, but through an internal power, in the same way that this works in a grain of wheat or in an embryo. God is the cause of the cosmos as the source of all order, structure and governance, which manifests itself in a material reality that is subservient to this order and structure.

In the theory developed here, Aristotle's concept of *pneuma* plays an important role. In other views on Aristotle his theory of *pneuma* seems strangely disconnected, as if scholars are at a loss what to do with it. The divine element, ether, and *pneuma* (in the sublunary sphere) are instruments functioning as bearers of the divinely emanating Power that brings about order and structure. All facets of *pneuma* as sublunary analogue of the astral element ether will be discussed in chapter 10. A number of important questions that often are neglected will be considered there:

> Can *pneuma* be a "natural body"?
> Does it have its own natural motion or its own natural place?
> Is *pneuma* an independent, sixth natural body alongside ether and the four sublunary elements?
> What does it mean that *pneuma* is an analogue of the astral element?
> Why can't it change into one of the sublunary elements and why doesn't it share any common matter with these elements?
> Is *pneuma* (infinitely) divisible?
> Is *pneuma* imperishable or can it be affected by old age and disease?

Should *pneuma* be regarded as an efficient cause, or is it also the material cause of living beings?

How is it possible that *pneuma* pervades other natural bodies?

Is this also the reason why *pneuma* is invisible?

How is "vital heat" related to *pneuma*?

And finally, as the most important question: How is the soul as entelechy the rei(g)ning principle of *pneuma*? If we succeed in understanding this, it is possible to fathom Aristotle's teleological view of nature.

This requires us to consider in a new way the question: What is the meaning of Aristotle's proposition: "In being soul there is sleep and waking"?[3]

In chapters 12–17 I try to show why an entirely unhistorical outlook on Aristotle's philosophy has become dominant since Antiquity from the time of the teaching and commenting activities of Alexander of Aphrodisias (2nd century CE), an outlook that cancels any connection between his theology and his doctrine of reproduction and life in the sublunary sphere.

Chapters 18–19 provide a summarizing overview of the problems discussed. Chapter 19 especially can be read as a short summary of the line of argument developed in this book.

My working hypothesis in this study is that Aristotle's philosophy proposed a drastic correction of Plato's views. The most fundamental correction was his rejection of Plato's doctrine of the soul and his own sharp distinction of intellect and soul instead of it. Aristotle did not view God as a perfect Soul and Demiurge, but as a pure, transcendent Intellect.

Distinguishing the Intellect from the Soul, Aristotle could not accept the three "parts" of the soul posited by Plato in his famous myth about the soul in the *Phaedrus*. Of the three parts, solely "the driver" of the team of horses remained as First Principle and Cause of everything. But an essential connection with the "psychic" components was maintained. To this "driver" Aristotle attributed a guiding influence, as a "Leader" (κοίρανος, στρατηγός, ἡγεμών, οἰκόνομος) and Chief Intelligence Officer. It was impossible that this driver could "strive" or "desire" or even "will." Nor could this driver be the Maker of the elements of the cosmos, as Plato had posited, because this would clash with the dogma of the unchangeability of the First Principle. Only intellect-principles or guiding principles can proceed from the divine Intellect.

---

3. Cf. *Anim.* II 1, 412a9–11; a19–28 and §10q below for a radical new interpretation of this crucial distinction.

They are the soul-principles, which Aristotle saw as representatives of God's procreative Working Power in all that lives, as guiding principles that are active in organization and production, clothed in a fine-material body consisting of ether or (in the sublunary sphere) *pneuma*. In order to understand Aristotle's theology, we must recognize that the guiding *Dynamis* of the Great Cosmic Helmsman is active in all entelechy-principles[4] in the cosmos with their instrumental bodies, as in the horses that draw the chariot containing the driver in Plato's famous comparison.

However, in talking about the cosmos Aristotle exchanged the metaphor of artisanal production (by a divine Demiurge) for the biotic metaphor of the transmission of life in reproduction.[5] His radically new insights into reproduction and his different outlook on "life" inspired him to speak about God as "Begetter" of all forms of life in the cosmos through the Power (*Dynamis*) proceeding from him, as a critique of Plato's concept of the Demiurge and the World Soul. What is vitalized by that divine Power is the *materies*, "the underlying," the female contribution to all what lives. This Working Power of God differs from God's Essence by manifesting itself in a natural body differentiated into a multitude of divine astral beings, who in turn are productive as efficient causes of countless life forms of mortal creatures, with the results of spontaneous generation and plants and trees as last and lowest species. In this view, unensouled bodies as "dead matter" are residual products of the unlimited fullness of life in which God's vitalizing Power displays itself.

The distinction that Aristotle drew between God's Essence and Power is grounded in the distinction between pure theoretical knowledge and guiding activity resulting in action and production. Plato had seen these as two facets of the one divine Intellect. Aristotle strictly separated the two, as Intellect on the one hand and Logos or Rational Soul on the other. The distinction involves an internal dialectic in Aristotle's system, the same kind of tension that was present in Plato's doctrine of the Demiurge. This dialectic is the basis of what in later systems, including the Gnostic world views, is often called "the split in the Deity."

Aristotle presented this philosophy to his contemporaries in the dialogues that he himself published during his lifetime, but also in the lectures that he gave at the Lyceum, of which most of the extant writings are the result.

---

4. In his surviving works Aristotle never explained what he means by the term *entelecheia*. In any case the standard exegetical tradition should be rejected. For an alternative, cf. §10q below.

5. His motivation for that was made clear by S. Broadie, "Why no Platonistic Ideas of Artefacts?" in *Maieusis: Essays in Ancient Philosophy in Honour of Miles Burnyeat*, ed. D. Scott (Oxford: Oxford University Press, 2007), 232–52.

In those lectures he could refer to his published works and he supposed his audience to be acquainted with them.

What are the advantages of this approach over the standard explanation of Aristotle's philosophy? It shows that Aristotle's philosophy was coherent and consistent, and was driven by new insights that forced him to reject Plato's doctrine of soul with all its consequences. It admits of an interpretation that makes it unnecessary to divide his work into three or more different developmental phases with very divergent positions, a division introduced by W. Jaeger in 1923.[6] It can give a meaningful and significant place to the splendid work *On the Cosmos (De Mundo)*[7] and it defends the authenticity of the treatise

---

6. W. Jaeger, *Aristoteles. Grundlegung einer Geschichte seiner Entwicklung* (Berlin: Weidmannsche Buchhandlung, 1923; repr. 1955). Eng. version: *Aristotle. Fundamentals of the History of his Development*, transl. with the author's corrections and additions by R. Robinson (Oxford: Oxford University Press, 1934; 2nd ed. 1948; repr. 1962). Cf. A. P. Bos, "'Development' in the Study of Aristotle" (Amsterdam, Free University, 2006); id., *The Soul and Its Instrumental Body. A Reinterpretation of Aristotle's Philosophy of Living Nature* (Leiden: Brill, 2003), 13–30. See also K. Oehler, "Der Entwicklungsgedanke als Heuristisches Prinzip der Philosophiehistorie," *Zeitschrift für Philosophische Forschung* 17 (1963): 606–15; repr. in id., *Antike Philosophie und Byzantinisches Mittelalter. Aufsätze zur Geschichte des Griechischen Denkens* (München: C. H. Beck, 1969), 38–47; W. C. Calder III, ed., *Werner Jaeger Reconsidered* (Atlanta: Scholars Press, 1992). M. Rashed, *L'Héritage Aristotélicien. Textes Inédites de l'Antiquité* (Paris: Les Belles Lettres, 2007), 9 expressed his criticism of W. Jaeger, F. Nuyens, J. Dumoulin nicely: "La génétique, en se focalisant sur la pierre, manque la cathédrale."

7. See G. Reale and A. P. Bos, *Il Trattato Sul Cosmo per Alessandro Attribuito ad Aristotele. Monografia Introduttiva, Testo Greco con Traduzione a Fronte, Commentario, Bibliografia Ragionata e Indici* (Milano: Vita e Pensiero, 1995); and A. P. Bos, *Aristoteles, Over de Kosmos. Ingeleid, Vertaald en van Verklarende Aantekeningen voorzien* (Meppel: Boom, 1989). Against their view: P. Moraux, *Der Aristotelismus bei den Griechen von Andronikos bis Alexander von Aphrodisias*, vol. 2 (Berlin: W. de Gruyter, 1984), 5–82; J. C. Thom, ed., *Cosmic Order and Divine Power. Pseudo-Aristotle, On the Cosmos. Introduction, Text, Translation, and Interpretive Essays* (Tübingen: Mohr Siebeck, 2014). Cf. my review in *Acta Classica* 58 (2015): 232–37. Arguments against Aristotle's authorship are often based on the traditional title of the treatise, differences from the *Meteorologica*, the references to Homer as "the Poet" and the use of the term *aiôn*. Support for the work's authenticity could be drawn from the designation of Alexander, to whom the work is dedicated, as *hègemôn*, the order in which the names of the planets are listed, the subtle references to *Iliad* 8, which is also cited in *Motu anim.*, the links with Thales of Miletus and *Gener. anim.* III 11, and the fact that the name of the city of Persepolis is not mentioned. These matters are mainly treated in chapter 9 below. The line of argumentation pursued in this book will be: the philosophy presented in *On the Cosmos* does not fit with any date proposed for the work's genesis. Nobody has plausibly explained how the work could have been written by anyone other than Aristotle. On the other hand, the theology of God as the "Begetter" of all living entities in the cosmos and the *pneuma* doctrine, as well as the citation of an Orphic line in 7, 401b2 on Zeus as male and female, fit remarkably well with Aristotle's view of how living creatures are generated. In the time after Aristotle's death his biological insights were seriously neglected.

On the Life-Bearing Spirit (*De Spiritu*)[8] as a work in which Aristotle treats a subject that he had to treat in any case because he had adopted an entirely new position on its central subject.

This view does more justice to Aristotle's insight that the beginning of a new living being is situated at the moment of fertilization, and not at the moment of birth. Aristotle therefore had to explain how the soul can be present at this point and how, through its instrumental body, the soul is able to produce the visible body with all its different parts (the heart being the first) as an individual exemplar of an intelligible species. This view also allows us to understand how Aristotle could talk about a great "Plan" or "Design" for the cosmos and could relate this to the divine Intellect, and how he could comprehend and present all vital phenomena in a teleological perspective.

My view is an alternative to the interpretation of Aristotle's psychology by Alexander of Aphrodisias, who left no room for a doctrine of *pneuma* in Aristotle's philosophy of living nature.[9] The ready acceptance of the standpoint put forward by Alexander of Aphrodisias fostered an image of Aristotle's philosophy in which *On the Cosmos* and *De Spiritu* could no longer be accommodated and his dialogues, too, were dismissed as irrelevant.

---

8. Aristotle was alone in having *a philosophical need* to write about the status of *pneuma*, on account of the fact that he had come to reject Plato's doctrine of breath as the dominant process in a living being, after reaching the insight that life does not begin at the moment of birth but at the moment of fertilization. This puts paid to the idea that an immaterial soul enters the body of a new living creature at birth and at the beginning of the process of respiration. He therefore concluded that the semen of animals and the seeds of fruits already contain the soul and its instrumental, pneumatic body (*Anim.* II 1, 412b25–7). The same view is defended by Aristotle in his *De Respiratione* and *Gener. anim.* In *De Motu Animalium* 10, 703a10, Aristotle himself also seems to indicate that he wrote a contribution on the very theme of *De Spiritu*. There was no longer much reason for such an argumentation fifty years after Aristotle's death. It is therefore unfortunate that the work was rejected as nongenuine by W. Jaeger, "Das *Pneuma* im Lykeion," *Hermes* 48 (1913): 29–74; repr. in *Scripta Minora* (Roma: Edizioni di Storia e Letteratura, 1960), 57–102. On his authority, it was long disregarded. See thereafter A. Roselli, [*Aristotele*] *De Spiritu* (Pisa: Ets. Editrice, 1992); P. Macfarlane, *A Philosophical Commentary on Aristotle's* De Spiritu (PhD thesis Duquesne University, 2007); A. P. Bos and R. Ferwerda, "Aristotle's *De Spiritu* as a Critique of the Doctrine of *Pneuma* in Plato and his Predecessors," *Mnemosyne* 60 (2007): 565–88 and *Aristotle, On the Life-Bearing Spirit (De Spiritu). A Discussion with Plato and his Predecessors on* Pneuma *as the Instrumental Body of the Soul. Introduction, Translation, and Commentary* (Leiden: Brill, 2008) have defended the authenticity of the small work. However, see now P. Gregoric, O. Lewis, M. Kuhar, "The Substance of *De Spiritu*," *Early Science and Medicine* 20 (2015): 101–24; P. Gregoric, O. Lewis, "Pseudo-Aristotelian *De Spiritu*: a New Case against Authenticity." *Classical Philology* 110 (2015): 159–67; O. Lewis, P. Gregoric, "The Context of *De Spiritu*," *Early Science and Medicine* 20 (2015):125–49. Their contribution emphasizes medical matters dealt with in the work. They date it after 270 BCE because an Aristogenes is mentioned in *Spir.* 2.

9. See especially chapters 12 ff. below.

The results achieved in this work can be summarized in nine points:[10]

1. The "instrumental body of the soul" of which Aristotle speaks in his definition of soul is ether in the superlunary sphere and *pneuma* in all that comes into being and passes away.

2. This *pneuma* is an essential component of semen and menstrual fluid.

3. The *pneuma* in semen is the carrier of a power (*dynamis*) that is the actual soul-principle (entelechy).

4. This entelechy is "asleep" when it works in plants and animals, and in human beings until the age of discretion. In human beings the entelechy may be "awakened" and may then itself take on a "guiding" role. For the soul or entelechy is always a "goal-pointing system" (G.P.S.). In its default mode it is always "asleep," but it "awakens" in a human being who has achieved intellectual liberation. This concept of "double entelechy" is the basis of Aristotle's teleological view of nature, which many believe he failed to anchor in his philosophical system.

5. Aristotle's new theory was necessary, because he rejected Plato's doctrine of the inhalation of the soul at the first breath. According to Aristotle, life starts at the moment of fertilization.

6. This point made it necessary for Aristotle to write the treatise *De Spiritu*, in which he argues that *pneuma* is present before respiration begins, and is therefore not identical with breath.

7. The guiding power inherent in all that lives derives from the Entelechy par excellence, the divine Intellect, and is compared by Aristotle with the power of a magnet. The notion of entelechy/guiding power follows from Aristotle's strict separation between the "charioteer" and his "two horses" in Plato's image of "the soul."

8. The designation of God as "Begetter" (γενέτωρ) and of his Power as the all-structuring and all-ordering Principle, as found in *On the Cosmos*, cannot have been defended by anyone other than the author of *Generation of Animals*.

---

10. For a fuller survey, cf. ch. 19 below.

9. Radically new interpretations of the following texts are proposed:

On the Soul	I 4, 408b14–5	(§ 10d)
	II 1, 412a22–6	(§ 10q)
	412b1–4	(§ 13)
	412b4–6	(§ 14)
	412b17–3a5	(§ 5; § 10e)
	413a8–9	(§ 10q)
	4, 415b7	(§ 3a; § 6)
	III 9, 433a4–6	(§ 10q)
De Caelo	I 1, 268a9–b10	(§ 3c)
Physics	VIII 2, 253a11–2	(§ 5d)
	6, 259b16–8	(§ 5e)
On the Cosmos	1, 391b5–8	(§ 9; § 9h)
On Sleep	1, 454a8–10	(§ 10e)

2

The Dependence of All Nature upon God

a. *On the Heavens* I 9, 279a28–30

Aristotle repeatedly asserts that the lower levels of life depend on higher agencies or one supreme principle. We find such a passage in *On the Heavens* I 9, 279a28–30:

> From it depend the being and life which other things enjoy, for some more clearly, for others only dimly noticeable

> ὅθεν καὶ τοῖς ἄλλοις ἐξήρτηται, τοῖς μὲν ἀκριβέστερον τοῖς δ' ἀμαυρῶς, τὸ εἶναί τε καὶ ζῆν.[1]

---

1. Cf. W. K. C. Guthrie, *Aristotle, On the Heavens with an English Translation* (London: William Heinemann, 1939; repr. 1960), 93: "In dependence on it all other things have their existence and their life, some more directly, others more obscurely"; O. Longo, *Aristotele, De Caelo. Introduzione, Testo Critico, Traduzione e Note* (Firenze: Sansoni, 1962), 75: "È di lassù che dipende, per gli uni più manifestamente, per gli altri meno visibilmente, anche l'essere e la vita di quant'altro esiste"; P. Moraux, *Aristote, Du Ciel. Texte établi et traduit* (Paris: Les Belles Lettres, 1965), 37: "C'est de là que, pour les autres êtres, dépendent, avec plus de rigueur pour les uns, d'une manière assez indistincte pour d'autres, l'être et la vie"; J. L. Stocks in *The Complete Works of Aristotle. The Revised Oxford Translation*, 2 vols., ed. J. Barnes (Princeton: Princeton University Press, 1984), vol. I, 463 translates: "From it derive the being and life which other things, some more or less articulately but others feebly, enjoy." A. Jori, *Aristoteles Über den Himmel, übersetzt und erläutert* (Darmstadt: Wissenschaftliche Buchgesellschaft, 2009), 44: "Davon hängen für die übrigen Dinge—für die einen in genauerer, für die anderen in weniger genauer Art—das Sein und das Leben ab." E. Diamond, *Mortal Imitations of Divine Life. The Nature of the Soul in Aristotle's De Anima. Rereading Ancient Philosophy* (Evanston: Northwestern University Press, 2015), 17, emphasizes the importance of this text.

We may leave aside what the agency is on which everything depends in this text.[2] But there is dependence, and this dependence displays *degrees*. We need to establish here whether Aristotle means that the dependence on supreme levels is "more clearly" noticeable for some living beings and "more vaguely" for others, or that the life and existence of the dependent levels are quite distinct in one case and only dimly recognizable in the other.[3]

As Aristotle here talks explicitly about the "life" that depends on the supreme Principle, we may conclude that the supreme Principle itself possesses life, but also that Aristotle identifies the "dependent" entities with all that lives and therefore possesses soul. And every soul is inextricably linked to a *sôma organikon*, according to Aristotle, *On the Soul* II 1, 412b5–6, and the *dynamis* of every soul has something of a more divine body than the four ordinary elements according to *Generation of Animals* II 3, 736b27 ff. (see § 10a below).

It is clear that the existence and life of levels of life beneath the outer celestial sphere are impossible without a principle of this existence and life. But it is not clear here how Aristotle saw the relation between the supreme Principle (or the multiplicity of transcendent principles) and the lower levels of life. In itself the term *to depend* (ἐξήρτηται) suggests a "connection," but it is used here in a very comprehensive sense. Perhaps it is meant as a metaphor or idea. The question is how we are to imagine "contact" with the Origin.[4]

---

2. It is either the outer celestial sphere or the totality of all transcendent substances "beyond" the outer celestial sphere. But in the former case the outer celestial sphere itself, in its turn, must depend on a supreme Principle. Cf. E. Martineau, "*Aiôn* chez Aristote 'De Caelo' 1.9: Théologie Cosmique ou Cosmo-théologie?," *Revue de Métaphysique et de Morale* 84 (1979): 32–69; id., "Réponse à M. Denis O'Brien (À propos d'Aristote, 'De Caelo' 1.9)," *Revue de Métaphysique et de Morale* 85 (1980): 519–28. See also D. O'Brien, "Aristote et l'Aiôn': Enquête sur un Critique Récente," *Revue de Métaphysique et de Morale* 85 (1980): 94–108; and a second reply in 87 (1982): 557–58. Later, "Life beyond the Stars: Aristotle, Plato, and Empedocles (*De Caelo* I 9, 279a11–22)," in *Common to Body and Soul. Philosophical Approaches to Explaining Living Behaviour in Greco-Roman Antiquity*, ed. R. A. H. King (Berlin: W. de Gruyter, 2006), 49–102, who clearly shows how many problems inhere in the final part of *Cael.* I 9 (pp. 49–66).

3. The description "for some more clearly, for others only dimly noticeable" (τοῖς μὲν ἀκριβέστερον τοῖς δ᾽ ἀμαυρῶς) must be taken to modify "depend" (ἐξήρτηται) and not "the being and life" (τὸ εἶναί τε καὶ ζῆν). But the fact that the "dependence" is "clearer" or "less evident" manifests itself in the quality of the being and life of these entities. One is a consequence of the other, as we will repeatedly see in the texts discussed below.

4. The same problem applies to the local reference "outside (or above) the outer circle," meaning, the sphere of the fixed stars. In *Cael.* I 9 Aristotle talks extensively about the eternal, perfect, and blissful life of beings "outside" the sphere of the fixed stars (I 9, 279a18–22). But it is difficult to talk about what is nonmaterial in terms of "above" or "outside." Yet Aristotle often does so. In *Phys.* VIII 10, 267b5–9 he "proves" that the Unmoved Mover is not situated in the center of the cosmos, but on the periphery. He also has no qualms about using the terminology *closer to* and *more distant from* in relation to God. In later times a solution to some of these

Aristotle also emphasized that "the beings outside the cosmos possess eternally the best and most self-sufficient life."[5]

We note here that, according to various scholars, the passage I 9, 279a19–b3 to which our text belongs is set apart from *On the Heavens* as a whole by a number of stylistic features. These seem to indicate a similarity to Aristotle's more literary and polished writings, his dialogues.[6] A suggestion often made is that we are dealing here with an extract from Aristotle's *On Philosophy*.[7]

b. *On the Heavens* I 2, 269b13–7

The theme of differences in quality of life connected with the theme of distance from the Origin is also found in *On the Heavens* I 2, 269b14–6, where Aristotle's argument for the necessity of a separate, special body distinct from the four elements concludes with the words:

> [O]n all these grounds, therefore, we may infer with confidence that there is something beyond the bodies that are about us on this earth, different and separate from them, and that the superior glory of its nature is proportionate to its distance from this world here.

---

problems was provided by the notion of the "omnipresence" of God in reality and of the soul in a living entity. But for Aristotle this way out was not yet passable. In *On the Cosmos* 6, he forcefully combats the notion of God's ubiquity. Plato talked in *Respublica* VI 509b about the Idea of the Good as ἐπέκεινα τῆς οὐσίας. Equally problematic is Aristotle's repeated localization of "the (immaterial) soul" "in the center" of a living being and his talk about the intellect "coming from outside" (*Gener. anim.* II 3, 736b28). The same goes for expressions such as the intellect's "being separate" from all corporeality (*Anim.* II 2, 413b26–7). The "limits" of the world of human experience also impose limits on what human beings can say. We constantly need to consider whether the occurrence of these problems indicates an improper separation of what is not separate but distinct. (Psychic phenomena are different but not "separate" from biotic ones.)

5. *Cael.* I 9, 279a21–2: "They continue through their entire lifetime unalterable and unmodified, living the best and most self-sufficient of lives [ἀναλλοίωτα καὶ ἀπαθῆ τὴν ἀρίστην ἔχοντα ζωὴν καὶ τὴν αὐταρκεστάτην διατελεῖ τὸν ἅπαντα αἰῶνα]."

6. Cf. W. Jaeger, *Aristoteles*, 316–20; M. Untersteiner, *Aristotele, Della Filosofia. Introduzione, Testo, Traduzione e Commento Esegetico* (Roma: Edizioni di Storia e Letteratura, 1963), 58–59 and 285–95; P. Moraux, *Aristote, Du Ciel* (1965), lxxv; A. Jori, *Aristoteles Über den Himmel* (2009), 145.

7. We should note here that interest in Aristotle's dialogues has sharply declined in recent years. Cf. W. Kullmann, *Aristoteles, Über die Teile der Lebewesen, übersetzt und erläutert* (Darmstadt: Wissenschaftliche Buchgesellschaft, 2007), 155. For an opposite view, see A. P. Bos, "Why Is Aristotle Treated so Differently from Other Greek Philosophers?" *Elenchos* 29 (2008): 145–65.

διόπερ ἐξ ἁπάντων ἄν τις τούτων συλλογιζόμενος πιστεύσειεν ὡς ἔστι τι παρὰ τὰ σώματα τὰ δεῦρο καὶ περὶ ἡμᾶς ἕτερον κεχωρισμένον, τοσούτῳ τιμιωτέραν ἔχον τὴν φύσιν ὅσῳπερ ἀφέστηκε τῶν ἐνταῦθα πλεῖον.[8]

The theme of degrees in quality of life of souls and quality of material body is crucial in *Generation of Animals* II 3, 736b29–7a7, which we will discuss in §10a. According to the passage in *On the Heavens* I 2, the highest quality of life is only possible at a great distance from the earthly vale of tears. The living beings on the moon, says *Generation of Animals* III 11, 761b13–22, will be higher in quality than human beings, quadrupeds, or fish on land and in the sea, because the lunar sphere forms the boundary for the element of fire, which occupies the fourth location, seen from the earth.

We add that Aristotle underpins his argument for the eternity and divinity of the astral sphere with a reference to general human experience. All people have an awareness of gods and they all point to the heavens as "the place"[9] for the gods whom they venerate. It follows that they consider the heavens to be eternal and divine and that "they suppose that immortal is linked with immortal [ὡς τῷ ἀθανάτῳ τὸ ἀθάνατον συνηρτημένον]."

c. *Metaphysics* Λ 7, 1072b13

In *Metaphysics* Λ 7, 1072b3–30 Aristotle uses the same basic idea that all forms of life in the cosmos "depend" on a First Principle (*Archè*). He formulates this as follows in 1072b13:

---

8. The term *separate* (κεχωρισμένον) mainly expresses the great difference in relation to earthly reality. Certainly the author did not mean that there was a vacuum between the ethereal sphere and the sublunary elements. *Mu.* 2, 392a34 calls the sphere of the perishable elements "continuous" (συνεχής) compared with the ether. Cf. also *Cael.* I 3, 270b20: "and so, implying that the primary body is different from earth, fire, air and water, they gave the highest place the name *aether* [ὡς ἑτέρου τινὸς ὄντος τοῦ πρώτου σώματος παρὰ γῆν καὶ πῦρ καὶ ἀέρα καὶ ὕδωρ, αἰθέρα προσωνόμασαν τὸν ἀνωτάτω τόπον]." See also *Mu.* 2, 392a5–10 with a9–10: "as a different element from the four elements, pure and divine" (J. C. Thom, ed., *Cosmic Order and Divine Power. Pseudo-Aristotle,* On the Cosmos. *Introduction, Text, Translation, and Interpretive Essays* [Tübingen: Mohr Siebeck, 2014]) (στοιχεῖον οὖσαν ἕτερον τῶν τεττάρων, ἀκήρατόν τε καὶ θεῖον) and *Gener. anim.* II 3, 736b30–1: ἑτέρου σώματος . . . καὶ θειοτέρου τῶν καλουμένων στοιχείων.

9. *Cael.* I 3, 270b5–9. But in *Cael.* I 9, 279a11–22 Aristotle goes on to argue that the God on whom the heavens "depend" cannot be in "a place," because only bodies can be in a place. However, this does not make Aristotle's God "utopian." See also *Mu.* 6, 400a15–6: "And all ages bear witness to this fact, and allot the upper region to God [συνεπιμαρτυρεῖ δὲ καὶ ὁ βίος ἅπας, τὴν ἄνω χώραν ἀποδοὺς θεῷ]" (D. J. Furley, 1955).

From such a Principle, then, depend the heavens and the world of nature.

ἐκ τοιαύτης ἄρα ἀρχῆς ἤρτηται ὁ οὐρανὸς καὶ ἡ φύσις.

It is natural to assume that Aristotle means that the celestial spheres depend on the supreme Principle, and so does Nature, but *via* the celestial spheres. This implies a "more or less" in the dependent relation of the heavenly spheres or nature to the highest Principle. In this passage, Aristotle says explicitly of the highest Principle that it is God and possesses Intellect and a perfect mode of existence, to which man can only attain, if at all, during single moments in his earthly life.[10]

Aristotle clarifies this "dependence" in the image of the *power* of "attraction" exercised by Eros.

d. *Metaphysics* Γ 2, 1003b16–7

In *Metaphysics* Γ 2, 1003b16–7 Aristotle is also looking for a first Principle "on which all other things depend":

But everywhere science deals chiefly with that which is primary, and on which the other things depend, and in virtue of which they get their names.

πανταχοῦ δὲ κυρίως τοῦ πρώτου ἡ ἐπιστήμη, καὶ ἐξ οὗ τὰ ἄλλα ἤρτηται, καὶ δι' ὃ λέγονται.

e. *Motion of Animals* 4, 699b32–700a6 and Homer's Motif of the Golden Rope

The notion of the "dependence" of all things on a first Principle is also underlined by Aristotle in *Motion of Animals* 4, 699b32–700a6, which ends with the words:

---

10. *Metaphysics* Λ 7, 1072b14: "Its life is such as the best which we enjoy, and enjoy for but a short time. For it is ever in that state [διαγωγὴ δ' ἐστὶν οἵα ἡ ἀρίστη μικρὸν χρόνον ἡμῖν. οὕτω γὰρ ἀεὶ ἐκεῖνο]." Cf. L. A. Kosman, *The Activity of Being. An Essay on Aristotle's Ontology* (Cambridge: Harvard University Press, 2013), 189.

if it depends from an Origin which is unmovable.

εἰ ἐξ ἀκινήτου ἤρτηται ἀρχῆς.

The subject of this work is motion, and specifically how living beings can possess locomotion. Aristotle introduces the remarkable idea that motion is possible only on condition that there be *something unmoved as principle of motion*. He then transposes this to Nature and the Cosmos. There must be an Unmoved Principle outside of the moving celestial spheres.

Like the previous text, this passage therefore emphasizes the "dependence" of all things on the first Principle. At the same time, Aristotle calls this first Principle the "Principle of Motion." And in chapters 3 and 4 he talks about the necessity that a Power (*Dynamis*) proceeds from such a Mover. We need to find out whether the idea that an unmoved first Principle may nevertheless possess and exercise Power was in fact defended by Aristotle and on what grounds.

The text of *Motion of Animals* 4 is also interesting for its intertextual connections with *On the Cosmos* 6, Theophrastus's *Metaphysics* 2, 5b10–7 and Homer's *Iliad*. Aristotle gives a striking quotation from Homer's *Iliad* 8, 20–22, thus suggesting that Homer had already well formulated how totally "dependent" all gods and people are on the supreme god Zeus:

Nay, ye would not pull Zeus, highest of all,
from the heavens to the ground, no not even if ye toiled right hard;
come, all ye gods and goddesses! Set hands to the rope.[11]

ἀλλ' οὐκ ἂν ἐρύσαιτ' ἐξ οὐρανόθεν πεδίονδε
Ζῆν' ὕπατον πάντων, οὐδ' εἰ μάλα πολλὰ κάμοιτε·
πάντες δ' ἐξάπτεσθε θεοὶ πᾶσαί τε θέαιναι.

---

11. *Motu anim.* 4, 699b32–700a6. Cf. M. C. Nussbaum, *Aristotle's De motu animalium* (Princeton: Princeton University Press, 1978), 320–21. See now also O. Primavesi and K. Corcilius, *Aristoteles* De Motu Animalium. *Kritische Neuedition des Griechischen Textes und Deutsche Übersetzung* (forthcoming). Eustathius, *Comm. in Hom. Iliadem* Y, ed. M. van der Valk (Leiden: Brill, 1976), vol. II, 515, 17, describes this as an allusion to the divine Monarchia. Cf. P. Lévêque, *Aurea Catena Homeri. Une Étude sur l'Allégorie Grecque* (Paris 1959), 53–54. A. Coles, "Animal and Childhood Cognition in Aristotle's Biology and the *Scala Naturae*," in *Aristotelische Biologie. Intentionen, Methoden, Ergebnisse*, ed. W. Kullmann; S. Föllinger (Stuttgart: Franz Steiner Verlag, 1997), 289, argues that the idea of the *scala naturae* is soundly Aristotelian and that A. O. Lovejoy, *The Great Chain of Being. A Study of the History of an Idea* (Cambridge: Harvard University Press, 1936) could have anchored his theme much more firmly in Aristotle's work.

In a passage[12] from *On the Cosmos*, a work addressed to Alexander of Macedonia (with whom Aristotle had read Homer's *Iliad* in Mieza, near the "Cave of the Nymphs"),[13] Aristotle compares the cardinal importance of God for the cosmos with that of the Persian Great King for his empire,[14] and in using the words *the supreme* and *on the highest peak* refers subtly to this text from *Iliad* 8, which Alexander must have relished. The author explains there that God dwells "on the highest peak" and is called "the supreme," because like a Persian king he does not personally administer the affairs in his realm, but effortlessly organizes all things in perfect governance through his all-pervasive Power. This means that the context of the reference to *Iliad* 8 in *On the Cosmos* is the same as that in *Motion of Animals* 4. It is significant that Theophrastus in his *Metaphysics* 2, 5b10–7 also quotes a line from Homer, *Iliad* 8 (in this case, line 24) in an enumeration of problems that could arise in a systematic philosophy of the kind developed by Aristotle, when he talks about the impact of the First Principle on the cosmos and its parts.[15]

Two facts here argue for attribution of *On the Cosmos* to Aristotle. (1) *On the Cosmos* 6, which deals with the all-pervasive Working Power that emanates from God, contains references to the same text in Homer, *Iliad* 8, which an imitator could not have added with such subtlety. (2) Theophrastus in his *Metaphysics* 5b13 proposes the option "because the power of the prime mover does not penetrate to them [ἢ ὡς οὐ διϊκνουμένου τοῦ πρώτου]," and thus seems clearly to refer to *On the Cosmos* 6, 397b33: ἐπὶ πᾶν διϊκνεῖσθαι.[16]

f. Plato's *Ion* on Iron Rings Suspended from a Magnet

To clarify the term that Aristotle used in the above passages on "dependence," we cite a text from Plato's *Ion*, in which Socrates explains that the poetic inspi-

---

12. This passage will be discussed below in §9c.
13. The World Congress, "Aristotle: 2400 Years," held in Thessaloniki in May 2016, convened in Mieza for one day.
14. Aristotle mentions Darius, Xerxes, and Cambyses, names from the remote past, but in doing so calls to mind the Persian wars, for which Alexander was determined to get even.
15. See M. C. Nussbaum (1978), 320–21; A. P. Bos, "'Notes on Aristotle's *De Mundo* Concerning the Discussion of Its Authenticity," *Philosophical Inquiry* 1 (1979): 149–52; M. van Raalte, *Theophrastus, Metaphysics, with an Introduction, Translation, and Commentary* (Leiden: Brill, 1993), 221–28; G. Reale and A. P. Bos (1995), 319–22.
16. For more on this, see §9a below.

ration of the rhapsodist Ion comes from something like the "divine power" residing in the stone of Magnesia or Heraclaia. "This stone not only attracts iron rings, but also imparts to them a similar power of attracting other rings; and sometimes you may see a number of pieces of iron and rings suspended from one another so as to form quite a long chain: and all of them derive their power of suspension from the original stone."[17]

That is to say, the magnet stays where it is and remains unmoved, but acts on the iron rings through the power proceeding from the magnet. This power penetrates the mass of the iron rings, creating a "chain reaction." In Antiquity this fascinating phenomenon started to attract attention and was considered exceptional, there being nothing comparable at the time. It was put on a par with "possession," "ecstasy," and the "holy disease," epilepsy, since these forms of inspiration were thought to come from the Muses or the gods.[18]

A salient point here is that Socrates, in his discussion with Ion, wants to show that "poetic inspiration," like possession and epilepsy, is a matter hard to reconcile with sense and intellect.[19] But the essence in Aristotle is that all levels of life depend somehow on God and the divine Intellect and are crucially connected with them for their existence and operation.

---

17. Plato, *Ion* 533d1-e5: "The gift which you possess of speaking excellently about Homer is not an art, but, as I was just saying, an inspiration; there is a divine power moving you like that in the stone which Euripides calls a magnet, but which is commonly known as the stone of Heraclaia. This stone not only attracts iron rings, but also imparts to them a similar power of attracting other rings; and sometimes you may see a number of pieces of iron and rings suspended from one another so as to form quite a long chain: and all of them derive their power of suspension from the original stone. In like manner the Muse first of all inspires men herself; and from these inspired persons a chain of other persons is suspended, who take the inspiration [Ἔστι γὰρ τοῦτο τέχνη μὲν οὐκ ὂν παρὰ σοὶ περὶ Ὁμήρου εὖ λέγειν, ὃ νῦν δὴ ἔλεγον, θεία δὲ δύναμις ἥ σε κινεῖ, ὥσπερ ἐν τῇ λίθῳ ἣν Εὐριπίδης μὲν Μαγνῆτιν ὠνόμασεν, οἱ δὲ πολλοὶ Ἡρακλείαν. Καὶ γὰρ αὕτη ἡ λίθος οὐ μόνον αὐτοὺς τοὺς δακτυλίους ἄγει τοὺς σιδηροῦς, ἀλλὰ καὶ δύναμιν ἐντίθησι τοῖς δακτυλίοις ὥστε δύνασθαι ταὐτὸν τοῦτο ποιεῖν ὅπερ ἡ λίθος, ἄλλους ἄγειν δακτυλίους, ὥστ' ἐνίοτε ὁρμαθὸς μακρὸς πάνυ σιδηρῶν [καὶ] δακτυλίων ἐξ ἀλλήλων ἤρτηται· πᾶσι δὲ τούτοις ἐξ ἐκείνης τῆς λίθου ἡ δύναμις ἀνήρτηται. Οὕτω καὶ ἡ Μοῦσα ἐνθέους μὲν ποιεῖ αὐτή, διὰ δὲ τῶν ἐνθέων τούτων ἄλλων ἐνθουσιαζόντων ὁρμαθὸς ἐξαρτᾶται]" (B. Jowett, 1871). See also *Ion* 536a1-b4. In *Timaeus* 80c2 Plato also talks about τῶν Ἡρακλείων λίθων.

18. Cf. Plato, *Ion* 534d2: "(in order that we who hear them may know them) to be speaking not of themselves, who utter these priceless words while bereft of reason, but that God himself is the speaker, and that through them he is addressing us [οὐχ οὗτοί εἰσιν οἱ ταῦτα λέγοντες οὕτω πολλοῦ ἄξια, οἷς νοῦς μὴ πάρεστιν, ἀλλ' ὁ θεὸς αὐτός ἐστιν ὁ λέγων, διὰ τούτων δὲ φθέγγεται πρὸς ἡμᾶς]." See also ἔνθεοι in *Ion* 533e6; 534b5 and θείη δύναμις in 533d3; 534c6.

19. Cf. Plato, *Phaedrus* 245 ff.

g. *Politics* VII 4, 1326a31–3

It is surprising that many authorities on Aristotle's oeuvre have problems with the notion of God's Working Power. P. Moraux believes that the theme first appeared in authors interested in allegorically explaining the Old Testament.[20] But in *Politics* VII 4, 1326a31–3 Aristotle talks freely about a divine Power "as holds together the universe."[21] There was no need for Aristotle to make this addition about "a Power as holds together the universe" if this had not been been a fundamental idea and belief for him. In fact, he is totally convinced that God's Working Power is "the cause that holds the world together," like the author of *On the Cosmos*.[22] It is incomprehensible that J. J. Duhot, who does refer to this text in *Politics* VII 4, insists that the author of *On the Cosmos* borrowed this notion from the Stoa.[23]

---

20. P. Moraux, *Der Aristotelismus bei den Griechen von Andronikos bis Alexander von Aphrodisias* (Berlin: W. de Gruyter, 1984), vol. 2, 41: "Merkwürdigerweise erscheint das Motiv der δύναμις θεοῦ, soweit uns bekannt, zuerst bei Autoren, die sich um eine allegorisierende Interpretation des Alten Testaments bemühten." See also 81.

21. "But a very great multitude cannot be orderly: to introduce order in such a number is the work of a divine power—of such a power as holds together the universe [ὁ δὲ λίαν ὑπερβάλλων ἀριθμὸς οὐ δύναται μετέχειν τάξεως· θείας γὰρ δὴ τοῦτο δυνάμεως ἔργον, ἥτις καὶ τόδε συνέχει τὸ πᾶν]."

22. *Mu.* 6, 397b9: Λοιπὸν δὲ δὴ περὶ τῆς τῶν ὅλων συνεκτικῆς αἰτίας κεφαλαιωδῶς εἰπεῖν. See also A. P. Bos, "La *Metafisica* di Aristotele alla Luce del Trattato *De Mundo*," *Rivista di Filosofia Neo-scolastica* 85 (1993): 448–49.

23. J. J. Duhot, "Aristotélisme et Stoicisme dans le Περὶ κόσμου pseudo-aristotélicien," *Revue de Philosophie Ancienne* 8 (1990): 195–98. Duhot describes the author on p. 225 as "un médiocre philosophe aristotélicien."

3

The Natural Desire of All Things for God

Besides the notion of the dependence of all things in nature on God, Aristotle's work also contains the concept of the "natural desire" which all that lives has for God. Important in this regard is the text in *On the Soul* II 4, which I will discuss below.

a. *On the Soul* II 4, 415a25–b3 on Desire for Eternity

In *On the Soul*, where Aristotle sets out his theory on the various possible activities of the soul in books II and III, he calls the nutritive function the first and most widely shared soul-power, in virtue of which all have life.[1] This vital activity is not just present in humans and animals, but also in fish and trees and plants.

In what sense is the nutritive soul-power the "first"? Clearly, Aristotle did not mean this in an evolutionist sense. He must be saying that the nutritive power represents the least complex form of life. He had already touched on this problem in *On the Soul* II 3, 414b19–5a1, in his comparison of the

---

1. *Anim.* II 4, 415a24–5: πρώτη καὶ κοινοτάτη δύναμίς ἐστι ψυχῆς, καθ' ἣν ὑπάρχει τὸ ζῆν ἅπασιν. The nutritive function is called "first" (πρώτη) here in a methodological sense. Cf. II 1, 412a14–5: "by 'life' I mean nutrition, growth and decay by itself" (ζωὴν δὲ λέγω τὴν δι' αὑτοῦ τροφήν τε καὶ αὔξησιν καὶ φθίσιν). For life in Aristotle, see also §3c below. E. Diamond, *Mortal Imitations of Divine Life. The Nature of the Soul in Aristotle's* De Anima (Evanston: Northwestern University Press, 2015), 79 calls *Anim.* II 4, 415a26–b8 "one of the most important passages of the whole treatise."

concept of "soul" with the concept of "figure." In the series of figures one can distinguish between a polygon, a square, and a triangle. A figure is never these three figures at the same time, but only one of the three. The triangle is the simplest of these. In the group of figures it would be called "the first." In our passage, Aristotle says that both the series of figures and that of souls (human, animal, or vegetable) potentially contain "the earlier" in the later (the more complex). The example he gives is: "the triangle exists potentially in the square, and the nutritive soul-part in the sensitive soul-part." He adds: "But we must also consider why they are thus arranged in a series."[2] It is by no means certain that Aristotle provides the answer to this question in *On the Soul* itself. Perhaps it was at the back of his mind that a final answer to this question can only be given by linking up with nonmaterial reality, and considering that the *scala naturae* should be seen as a succession, like the "chain" of iron rings, "the golden rope," or the activities of automata, when their winding mechanism has been released.[3] Each case involves the transmission of vital power, but to a decreasing degree.[4] Seen from this theological and metaphysical perspective, the nutritive soul-power and spontaneous generation are the last and lowest level on which the divine power of life manifests itself. Although plant life still produces a specific form that is knowable and recognizable, plants are incapable of knowing, a faculty that animals do possess (perception is a form of "knowing").[5] Hence, Aristotle holds that the degrees in quality of life in the sublunary sphere in the series man ==> animal ==> plant ==> product of spontaneous generation are the result of a devolution process, with the least complex life form as the last product. For Aristotle, the succession of levels of life is characterized by a succession of levels of knowing (in the sense of a reduction in cognitive level to zero and, as *On the Soul* III 12–13 shows, a reduction in quality of life from "the good life" to "life *tout court*." With it goes a material covering of the life principle that differs from not very to highly obstructive for the cognitive level of the living being. We find here evidence of the connection between Aristotle's biology and theology, a con-

---

2. *Anim.* II 3, 414b33–5a1: Διὰ τίνα δ' αἰτίαν τῷ ἐφεξῆς οὕτως ἔχουσι, σκεπτέον. W. D. Ross, *Aristotle, De Anima, Edited, with Introduction and Commentary* (Oxford: Clarendon Press, 1961), 224 refers to 415a1–11 and to III 12, 434a22–5b24. R. Polansky, *Aristotle's De Anima* (Cambridge: Cambridge University Press, 2007), 107, mentions *Anim.* III 12–13.

3. Cf. A. P. Bos, "Aristotle on the Differences between Plants, Animals, and Human Beings and on the Elements as Instruments of the Soul (*Anim.* II 4, 415b18)," *Review of Metaphysics* 63 (2010); 838–41; "Aristotle on God as Principle of Genesis," *British Journal for the History of Philosophy* 18 (2010): 363–77 and §§2e and 2f above; §9e below.

4. See especially Arist. *Mu.* 6, 397b27–8a1 and §§9a and 9f below.

5. Cf. *Gener. anim.* I 23, 731a29–b2.

nection deeply obscured by Alexander of Aphrodisias's dominant explanation of Aristotle's psychology.[6]

However, we will also have to emphasize Aristotle's insight that all living entities that come into being and pass away possess this nutritive or generative function as the "first" in the process of their individual development. This contains an important element of his criticism of Plato, who took the soul to be the principle of self-motion. For Aristotle, it became obvious that plants and trees, which do not possess locomotion, do have a soul-principle. It was also crystal-clear to him that an animal embryo, before it starts to breathe and move, has already developed and grown for a good while under the guidance of its soul-principle as entelechy. In §5d below I will discuss how Aristotle in *De Spiritu* 4–5 emphatically proves that the vegetative processes, such as pulsation and nutrition, precede respiration, and how he argues in *Physics* VIII 2 and 6 that the locomotion of a living being is only possible on the basis of prior vegetative functions. The most characteristic feature of life is not self-motion but metabolism and reproduction. This process makes visible the intelligible Form or Idea!

All that lives in the sublunary sphere has this basic nutritive soul-function. As specific activities of the vegetative or nutritive soul Aristotle goes on to mention reproduction and digestion.[7] This work is typical of all living entities in the sphere of coming-to-be and passing-away: "Its works are generating life and the assimilation of food. For this is the most natural of all works among living entities, provided that they have completed their natural development and are not deformed, and do not have spontaneous generation:[8] *viz.*, to make a new specimen like itself."[9] This also means: causing a new process of life that continues *under its own power*.

---

6. I disagree on this with K. Corcilius, in *Aristoteles-Handbuch: Leben, Werk, Wirkung*, ed. C. Rapp and K. Corcilus (Stuttgart: J. B. Metzler, 2011), 92, cited below.

7. Plants and trees have only this soul activity, that is, uncombined with perception or reasoning. In results of spontaneous generation this activity does not manifest itself in reproduction but only in production and feeding. See also §10d below.

8. "Spontaneous generation" is discussed by Aristotle in *Gener. anim.* III 11, 762a18–3a25. An essential factor is the presence of *pneuma* with its "psychic heat" (762a20). This theory is therefore presupposed in *Anim.* II 4. Cf. A. P. Bos, "Pneuma as Instrumental Body of the Soul in Aristotle's *De Anima* I 4," *Philotheos. International Journal for Philosophy and Theology* (Beograd) 13 (2013): 113–27.

9. *Anim.* II 4, 415a25–8, translation W. S. Hett (1936), 85–87, with changes: Ἥς ἐστιν ἔργα γεννῆσαι καὶ τροφῇ χρῆσθαι. Φυσικώτατον γὰρ τῶν ἔργων τοῖς ζῶσιν, ὅσα τέλεια καὶ μὴ πηρώματα ἢ τὴν γένεσιν αὐτομάτην ἔχει, τὸ ποιῆσαι ἕτερον οἷον αὐτό. . . . Cf. also *Gener. anim.* II 1, 735a17–9: "be they plants or animals, this, the nutritive, faculty is present in all of them alike (this also is the faculty of generating another creature like itself, since this is a function which belongs to every animal and plant that is perfect in its nature) [εἴτε γὰρ φυτὸν εἴτε ζῷον ὁμοίως τοῦτο πᾶσιν ὑπάρχει τὸ θρεπτικόν. τοῦτο δ' ἐστὶ τὸ γεννητικὸν ἑτέρου οἷον αὐτό. τοῦτο γὰρ παντὸς φύσει τελείου ἔργον καὶ ζῴου καὶ φυτοῦ]" (trans. A. L. Peck [1942]).

In passing, we find here that although Aristotle assigns two activities to the vegetative soul-part, namely, digestion and reproduction, his attention immediately shifts to the function of creating new life. For whereas all living entities necessarily have a digestive process, fewer than half are capable of begetting a new living specimen. The restriction of reproductive capability by the addition "provided that they have completed their natural development and are not deformed" should certainly be related to all female partners. They are unable to beget a new specimen because "the female" is always characterized by a lower degree of pneumatic heat, and menstrual fluid is a defective form of semen. This leads to the curious situation that "the female" is a "principle of generation" and necessary (*Gener. anim.* II 1, 732a1–3), but nonetheless a nonperfect product of nature.[10]

By using the terms *work* (*ergon*) and *make/produce* (another specimen), Aristotle transfers the natural activity of procreation and reproduction to the sphere of human labor and craft. The use of suitable instruments and the availability of material are matching notions here. Nature is thus presented as one huge workshop where life is produced.[11] And just as human artisanal production always takes place to fill a need, so natural production is regarded by Aristotle as an activity that is motivated by endeavor and supplies a need.

According to Aristotle, the underlying factor in all reproductive processes is *the desire (orexis) for the divine and the eternal*.[12] He introduces here, in a new form, a theme that also played an important role in Plato and that Plato had

---

10. In §3e and 3f, 6a and 9b below, we will note that Aristotle not only presents the male and the female as reciprocally oriented, but also that they are necessary in all that exists as Principles of Generation. Moreover, all genesis is understood to be effected by God himself, as a way of imparting a kind of eternity to what is not divine. Finally, we will see that Aristotle endorses an Orphic poem in *Mu.* 7, 401b2 in which Zeus is called "male" and "female." Although Aristotle always talks about the female as being lower in value than the male, he ultimately reduces this difference to the divine Origin itself.

11. See on this theme J. Morsink, *Aristotle on the Generation of Animals* (Washington, DC: Univerity Press of America, 1982), 150: "It is quite obvious that the form-matter hypothesis was suggested to Aristotle by the production of artifacts"; see also S. Broadie, "Nature and Craft in Aristotelian Teleology," in *Aristotle and Beyond. Essays on Metaphysical Ethics* (Cambridge: Cambridge University Press, 2007), 85–100. This may well be seen as a critique and correction of Plato's theological conception of the divine Demiurge. Plato had seen the genesis of the cosmos and all living beings as the work of the Demiurge, who materialized his intellectual labor in visible entities. Aristotle criticized Plato's theology of a divine World Former and introduced a separation between the divine Intellect as First Principle on the one hand and an Efficient Cause on the other. Yet he too continued to understand Nature as intelligible forms that are individualized in matter. He often ascribes demiurgic activity to "Nature" (e.g., *Gener. anim.* I 23, 731a24). See also M. Rashed, "La Préservation (σωτηρία) Objet des *Parva Naturalia* et Ruse de la Nature," *Revue de Philosophie Ancienne* 20 (2002): 50–59.

12. *Anim.* II 4, 415a29–b6. The use, twice, of τοῦ ἀεὶ καὶ τοῦ θείου is striking.

even combined with the motif of "becoming like God."[13] In itself, it is remarkable that producing "another like yourself" could play a part in "becoming like God." For this other will be just as mortal as the parents themselves. It is not immediately clear how the multiplication of mortal beings results from a desire for eternity, and it is extremely surprising that the activities of plants and animals, even on the simplest level, are explained as expressions of a striving for eternity and divinity, of which they cannot possibly have any knowledge. How could their ways of functioning ever be associated with a divine and eternal reality?[14]

What we find in *On the Soul* II 4, 415a25–b3 is therefore the perspective that all life in the sublunary part of the cosmos has an active desire (*orexis*) for immortality, and that this is the motor behind the urge to reproduce in living beings, even in plants:

> For this is the most natural of all functions among living entities, . . . : *viz.*, to produce a new specimen like itself . . . in order that they may have a share in the immortal and divine in the way they can; for every living entity strives for this, and for the sake of this performs all its natural functions." (translation W. S. Hett [1936], 85–87, with changes)[15]

---

13. Cf. L. Roig Lanzillotta, "A Way of Salvation: Becoming like God in Nag Hammadi," *Numen* 60 (2013): 71–102; E. Diamond, *Mortal Imitations of Divine Life. The Nature of the Soul in Aristotle's De Anima* (2015). In *Theaet.* 176a-b Plato associates the earthly region with evil and mortality; and the divine with the good and immortality. Therefore, mortals "ought to try to escape from here to yonder as quickly as possible." Plato alludes there to the famous text from *Iliad* 2, 140, where the Greeks are exhorted to leave Troy and return to their homeland. Plotinus, *Enn.* 1.6 [1] 8, 16 refers to this Platonic text when he mentions Odysseus's burning desire to escape from the witch Circe to Ithaca and Penelope (*Od.* i 29 and k 483–84. Plotinus may well have followed Aristotle here, who in the *Eudemus* compared human existence to Odysseus's wanderings.) In Plato's *Symposium* 207d–9e Diotima explains that all mortal things always desire, according to their capacity, to be everlasting and immortal. And in a certain sense this is made possible by procreation. In Plato there is a plausible explanation of the "desire" for eternity and the divine. For Plato holds, on the basis of his Orphic (mythical) view of life, that the human soul originally resided in the divine sphere and only later suffered a "fall" into transient reality. According to Plato, the soul still contains a "memory" of this period in which it dwelled in a higher sphere. (But this is therefore a memory of matters that the soul perceived in a prenatal period!) A "memory" of a prenatal situation would certainly have been rejected by Aristotle. For him, all memory is inextricably bound up with prior perceptions. At most, Aristotle allows room for a postmortal memory. Cf. his *Eudemus* fr. 5 Ross; 923 Gigon. However, the notion of a "desire for the divine" is just as a fundamental for him as for his teacher.

14. I will return to this problem in §10p and chapter 11 below.

15. Φυσικώτατον γὰρ τῶν ἔργων τοῖς ζῶσιν . . . τὸ ποιῆσαι ἕτερον οἷον αὐτό . . . ἵνα τοῦ ἀεὶ καὶ θείου μετέχωσιν ᾗ δύνανται· πάντα γὰρ ἐκείνου ὀρέγεται, καὶ ἐκείνου ἕνεκα πράττει ὅσα πράττει κατὰ φύσιν: text A. Jannone and E. Barbotin (1966). For this passage, cf. also M. R. Johnson, *Aristotle on Teleology* (Oxford: Clarendon Press, 2005), 65–69.

Plants and animals thus become the cause of the existence of new plants and animals, and of the survival of their own species, even though they are led by an entelechy that is the entelechy of nothing other than its own instrumental body! But how can this urge to reproduce and attain to immortality, inasmuch as this is within reach, be explained?

Aristotle takes a further step in *On the Soul* II 4, 415b1–3, where he says that *everything* that any living being does in nature can only be understood from the desire for eternity and divinity. Although Aristotle also looks at all processes in nature in their focus on smaller and narrower goals, he subsumes them under the comprehensive goal of a striving for eternity and divinity.[16]

In *On the Soul* II 4, 415b3–7, Aristotle gives his explanation for the continuity of the process of generation and decay. Something that is mortal cannot share in eternity and the divine as an individual entity. But there is another way. This possibility is that not the individual survives but the species (the *eidos*). In Aristotle's conception here, all material nature is aimed at realizing the eternity of the species, as an *imitation* of real eternity within the sphere of mortality. The reproductive process is a passing on of the specific form from one individual to another, as in a relay. And as we shall see in §3e, Aristotle reduces this perpetual process to God himself. There is a certain affinity here between Aristotle's philosophy and that of Plato.[17] Yet the differences should not be overlooked. There is a similarity between the intelligible specific forms and all the forms of corresponding living creatures. However, this imitation is not realized by the Ideas themselves, but by "efficient causes," that is, carriers of divine *dynameis*. The necessary intermediary for this is the eternal, divine element, ether (and its sublunary analogue, *pneuma*). The mediating role played

---

16. K. Corcilius, in *Aristoteles-Handbuch: Leben, Werk, Wirkung*, ed. C. Rapp and K. Corcilius, 92, remarks: "Es ist allerdings nicht klar, inwieweit diese metaphysischen Gesichtspunkte tatsächlich Eingang in Aristoteles' Theorie des Lebendigen finden." But the theme in question here is so often present in Aristotle and in such crucial places (see below) that we cannot simply wave it aside. In what follows I will show that in all that lives the body serving the soul as an instrument for realizing its production is itself of divine "descent." Cf. chapter 11 below.

17. Cf. *Metaph.* Λ 3, 1070a18: "And so Plato was not far wrong when he said that there are as many Forms as there are kinds of natural things (if there are Forms at all)—though not of such things as fire, flesh, head [διὸ δὴ οὐ κακῶς Πλάτων ἔφη ὅτι εἴδη ἔστιν ὁπόσα φύσει, εἴπερ ἔστιν εἴδη, ἀλλ' οὐ τούτων οἷον πῦρ σάρξ κεφαλή]." For Aristotle, however, the materialization of forms takes place exclusively in nature. All the forms produced by craft are of a different, secondary order, in which a craftsman imitates nature. The eternal specific form is realized in mortal specimens of living creatures through the instrumental body of the soul as *eidos* and entelechy, the soul that is connected with the Origin of all being and life through God's life-generating *dynamis*.

by the mathematical magnitudes in Plato's system was assigned by Aristotle to ether and *pneuma*.[18]

What agency carries out this reproductive process? Not the specific forms themselves—Aristotle rejects this idea—but the soul-principles. A soul-principle, as the vital principle of a living entity, first leads the individual living creature to its "purpose," that is to say, to the complex, mature condition of the specific form, and then produces, *via the "work" of procreation*, a new specimen of the same species, through fertilization, usually by means of the male semen.

Thus, like Plato, Aristotle drew an ontological distinction within all mortal living entities, but in a different way. Plato had distinguished in all humans and animals between the mortal (visible) body and the immortal (nonvisible) soul. The soul remains immortal, eternal, and divine, even though it comes to reside in a mortal environment. Aristotle makes a distinction between the specific form, which is eternal and which as a rationally working, efficient power is continually passed on to new specimens in the generative process of procreation, and the visible bodies produced thereby.

However, the carrier of the specific form (the *eidos*) is the soul, and Aristotle does not say anywhere that the soul is also immortal. The soul is the carrier of the *eidos*, which is eternal and imperishable, but the soul itself need not be immortal, according to Aristotle.[19]

How does the soul pass on the *eidos* of its species to a new specimen? In most cases the soul uses semen or the male seed.[20] This was also explicitly stated in the text of *On the Soul* II 4, immediately after the passage discussed above.[21]

---

18. Aristotle will explain in *Anim.* III 10, 433b19–21 that all "desire" (*orexis*) should be attributed not to the (immaterial) soul as entelechy, but to its material instrument. "Desire" is also a form of motion or activity, and as such not to be connected with an immaterial magnitude (see §10g below). In the present chapter II 4 Aristotle will already explain in 416b26–30 that digestion is a matter of vital heat (of the soul's instrumental body).

19. Aristotle argued in his dialogue *Eudemus* fr. 2 Ross; 58 Gigon that Plato's arguments for the immortality of the soul should rather be understood as arguments for the immortality of the intellect. In his *Phaedo* Plato had proved the immortality of the soul by claiming that the soul contemplates the Ideas. According to Aristotle, this is not a matter of the soul, but of the intellect. In *Timaeus* 41c–42d Plato not only distinguished an immortal part of the soul, which is supplied by the Demiurge, but also two mortal parts, which are necessary for the mortal bodies of humans.

20. Cf. *Gener. anim.* I 22, 730b19–23.

21. *Anim.* II 4, 415b6: "What persists is not the individual itself, but something in its image. <It is> identical not numerically but specifically. <*For that reason the seed of animals and plants is an instrument of their soul*>. It is the soul that is the cause and first principle of the living body" (trans. W. S. Hett [1936], 85–87, with changes). The sentence was probably deleted in the textual tradition after "body equipped with organs" had become the prevailing interpretation of the words σῶμα ὀργανικόν in Aristotle's definition of the soul. For more on this, see ch. 6 below.

b. Natural Desire in Degrees

The passage in *On the Soul* II 4, 415a25 ff. quoted above is striking for various reasons. Inasmuch as it deals with the vegetative function of the soul, we would expect all emphasis to lie on the digestive process as the core of all processes of growth and on the development from germ cell, grain of seed, *kyèma* to the mature, full-grown plant or the adult specimen of an animal species. Instead, Aristotle stresses that a mature plant or animal is characterized by its capacity to generate new life and reproduce. Although the soul is the principle of the being of that of which it is the soul, it is also, via its generative function, the principle of the being of another being.

Aristotle's explanation is: "in order that they may have a share in the immortal and divine in the way they can; for every living entity *strives by nature* for this, and for the sake of this performs by nature all its functions [πάντα γὰρ ἐκείνου ὀρέγεται, καὶ ἐκείνου ἕνεκα πράττει ὅσα πράττει κατὰ φύσιν]." Often the words *by nature* are only connected with πράττει, but there is good reason to link them to ὀρέγεται as well. The issue here is a "natural desire," of plants as well as of animals, and it is emphatically presented as a desire *that is not fulfilled*. A plant reproduces out of a desire for the divine, without reaching the divine. We could say that all natural cyclical processes are a form of "imitation" (*mimèsis*) of divine eternity.[22]

Other terms worth mentioning here are *strive* (ὀρέγεται) and *perform* (πράττει). The former cannot really apply to plants, because Aristotle always directly connects ὄρεξις with "perception" (II 2, 413b33; 3, 414b1) and plants do not possess power of perception, and he only associates "to perform" (πράττειν) in the proper sense with human beings, because "to perform" presupposes the possibility of choice and deliberation. But to the extent that Aristotle can talk about a work (ἔργον) of every soul (415a26), πράττειν may be taken to be used here in a comprehensive sense.

However, it is also significant that Aristotle writes in 415a29: "in the way they can [ᾗ δύνανται]." This seems to contain an allusion to the differences in value and quality of life between plants and animals, and between the various animal species among themselves.[23] Aristotle gives this extra emphasis in the words of 415b3–6:

---

22. Cf. D. Sedley, "*Metaphysics* Λ 10," in *Aristotle's* Metaphysics *Lambda*, ed. M. Frede and D. Charles (Oxford: Clarendon Press, 2000), 334–36; "Teleology, Aristotelian and Platonic," in *La Scienza e le Cause a Partire dalla Metafisica di Aristotele*, a cura di F. Fronterotta (Napoli: Bibliopolis, 2010), 317–22.

23. In *On Coming-to-Be and Passing-Away* II 10, 336b27–9 and *Generation of Animals* III 11, 761b14–22, Aristotle connects these differences with the distance to the Origin, as I will discuss in §3e below.

Since, then, they cannot share in the immortal and divine by continuity of existence . . . they share in these in the only way they can, some to a greater and some to a lesser extent.

ἐπεὶ οὖν κοινωνεῖν ἀδυνατεῖ τοῦ ἀεὶ καὶ τοῦ θείου τῇ συνεχείᾳ . . . ᾗ δύναται μετέχειν ἕκαστον κοινωνεῖ ταύτῃ, τὸ μὲν μᾶλλον τὸ δ' ἧττον.

For every living entity, the process of reproduction is the same. But the degree to which entities participate[24] in the eternal and divine differs. Some entities apparently share more in the divine than others.

c. What is the Ontological Scheme behind the Desire for the Divine and the Degrees in this Desire?

In chapter 2 above we saw that Aristotle makes the "life" and the "being" of all cosmic reality dependent on a supreme Principle. The preceding part of chapter 3 has shown that all life possesses an urge to procreate, which is explained from a desire for the divine. While this "desire" is more comprehensive than the human or animal desire for food, since this desire is also attributed to plants, it seems clear that the "desire" to procreate is in any case an aspect of all things possessing soul.

The question is: Why are ensouled creatures burdened with a desire for the "being" and the "life" of the Origin? As regards "being," we may perhaps assume that there is equivalence between the "being" of the Origin and the "being" of mortal "beings." Inasmuch as these "beings" exist, they may be considered to share in the "being" of the Origin. (This does raise the problem of whether "not being" is also something in which mortal things share.) The same applies to goodness and beauty, in which mortal things participate too.

But what about "life"? The Cause of all that lives in the cosmos must certainly also "live." Aristotle says as much in *Metaphysics* Λ 7, 1072b26: "the activity of Intellect is life [ἡ γὰρ νοῦ ἐνέργεια ζωή]."[25] However, in *On the Soul* II 1, 412a14–5, Aristotle had said: "by 'life' I mean nutrition, growth and

---

24. Aristotle's use of the term *participate*—μετέχειν—indicates his correction of Plato. It always points to the dependence of visible, living entities on the world of the transcendent Intellect and the immaterial entelechy-principles. Cf. *Anim.* II 4, 415a29; 1, 412a15; 2, 413b8; *Gener. anim.* II 1, 732a12; b29; II 3, 736b6.

25. Cf. also *Cael.* II 3, 286a9: "The activity of a god is immortality, that is, eternal life [Θεοῦ δ' ἐνέργεια ἀθανασία· τοῦτο δ' ἐστὶ ζωὴ ἀΐδιος]." On that topic cf. L. A. Kosman (2013), 238–54.

decay by itself."[26] This kind of life is most emphatically not connected with the Intellect. And yet the life of a plant or a tree must be explained from the life of the Intellect. This explanation is suggested by the leads in Plotinus's "On Contemplation." According to Plotinus, every form of life is a form of *theôria* (contemplation) and of *gnôsis*. But the Intellect realizes this activity in a perfect way. All other levels of life do so to a lesser extent, in degrees.[27] In all that lives, the souls are carriers of (lower) forms of *theôria*; they are *nous*-principles of a lower order, because they are connected with materiality.

Thus, a crucial difference between plants and animals stressed by Aristotle is that the latter possess perception. "Animals have a certain level of 'knowledge,' though for some kinds this is restricted to the lowest level of perception. This worthiness of only a form of perception may seem minimal in comparison with the human mind, but compared with the condition of a plant or a stone it is something astonishing."[28]

Every living being that possesses perception also has a natural desire to use this faculty (*Metaph.* A 1, 980a21–7). In human beings, this natural desire is expressed in a natural desire for knowledge (*Metaph.* A 1, 980a20). This must have to do with the fact that human beings have a potential for intellectuality. For the intellect in act itself is divine, but also separate from all materiality.[29] By actualizing this potential, a human being sometimes achieves the condition that God always possesses (*Metaph.* Λ 7, 1072b24–5).

God, the divine Intellect, as the source of Being, Goodness, Beauty, and Life, has no deficiency or want and therefore no "desire" for something he does not lack.[30] On the part of the caused, there is a "desire" (*orexis*),

---

26. *Anim.* II 1, 412a14–5: ζωὴν δὲ λέγω τὴν δι' αὐτοῦ τροφήν τε καὶ αὔξησιν καὶ φθίσιν. This sentence in this place could arouse suspicion. It can be missed without any problem and seems to have been added after the time of Alexander of Aphrodisias's reinterpretation of *On the Soul*. It is also contradicted by the passage slightly farther down in 2, 413a22 about the multiple meanings of "life," in which Aristotle mentions not only the vegetative function of life, but also the sensitive, motor, and intellective functions: "But the word living is used in many senses, and we say that a thing lives if any of the following is present in it [Πλεοναχῶς δὲ λεγομένου τοῦ ζῆν, κἄν ἕν τι τούτων ἐνυπάρχῃ μόνον, ζῆν αὐτὸ φαμεν]."

27. Plotinus, *Enneads* III 8 [30]. The scheme is: *theôria* → *technè* / *praktikos nous* → *aisthèsis* → *gennèsis* / *auxèsis* → spontaneous generation → lifeless bodies. In III 8 [30] 8. 15–6, Plotinus talks about ἡ μὲν φυτικὴ νόησις, ἡ δὲ αἰσθητική, ἡ δὲ ψυχική. Cf. A. P. Bos, *In de Greep van de Titanen. Inleiding tot een Hoofdstroming van de Griekse Filosofie* (Amsterdam: Buijten & Schipperheijn, 1991), 108–10. Cf. E. Diamond, *Mortal Imitations of Divine Life* (2015), x, 21–23.

28. *Gener. anim.* I 23, 731a30–b4. Cf. A. Coles, "Animal and Childhood Cognition in Aristotle's Biology and the *Scala Naturae*," in *Aristotelische Biologie. Intentionen, Methoden, Ergebnisse*, ed. W. Kullmann and S. Föllinger (Stuttgart: Franz Steiner Verlag, 1997), 297.

29. Cf. C. Cohoe, "Why the Intellect Cannot Have a Bodily Organ: *De Anima* 3.4," *Phronesis* 58 (2013): 347–77.

30. Cf. Arist. *Philos.* fr. 16 Ross; 30 Gigon.

because there is not the perfection that God possesses. For Aristotle, leaving the Fullness of theoretical thought implies a "distance" that results in a "lack" and a "deficiency."

Plato had used an ontological scheme in which dependent reality was the consequence of the "departure" (ἔκβασις) from the absolute One, through the Separation of the Negation (the not-One). The products of this separation were, first, the Numbers, then the Lines, then the Planes, and finally the three-dimensional Bodies. As a result of this process, the Bodies are farthest removed from the Origin and share least in the divine Fullness.[31] For Plato, this meant that he could regard the study of mathematical objects as a science alongside the ultimate science of dialectic.[32] In the *Timaeus*, too, he presented mathematical figures as the structural principles of the material elements earth,

---

31. Plato, *Leges* X 894a. Cf. Arist. *On the Heavens* I 1, 268b3: "The departure necessarily goes together with a decrease in being [ἀνάγκη γὰρ γίγνεσθαι τὴν ἔκβασιν κατὰ τὴν ἔλλειψιν]." In this text, Aristotle is engaged in formulating his fundamental disagreement with Plato in relation to material reality. Cf. J. Philip, "The 'Pythagorean' Theory of the Derivation of Magnitudes," *Phoenix* 20 (1966): 32–50. Aristotle's positive thesis is that the three-dimensional body shares in *all* (three, possible) dimensions. His negative thesis is that it is wrong to construct, as Plato did, a deduction of the three-dimensional as a process of "departure" (*ekbasis*) from the One by the not-One (or the unbounded). This process involves an increase in deficiency (*elleipsis*). And according to this Platonic method, the three-dimensional body can never become a "perfect" magnitude, but at most a "lack of substance." Here, and elsewhere, Aristotle consistently rejects Plato's deduction of one genus of being from another (*metabasis eis allo genos*). Cf. J. J. Cleary, *Aristotle and Mathematics. Aporetic Method in Cosmology and Metaphysics* (Leiden: Brill, 1995), 73: "Plato is the intended target of Aristotle's firm rejection of the transition (μετάβασις) into another genus that is involved in generating planes out of lines or bodies out of planes." This passage is usually explained very differently. For instance in P. Moraux, *Aristote, Du Ciel.* (1965), 2: "Voici, en revanche, un point qui est clair: il n'est pas possible de passer du corps à un autre genre de grandeur, comme on le fait pour aller de la ligne à la surface, puis de la surface au corps, car s'il permettait cette opération, le corps cesserait d'être une grandeur parfaite. De toute nécessité, en effet, le passage d'un genre supérieur ne peut avoir lieu que parce que quelque chose fait défaut au genre d'où l'on part; or il n'est pas possible que ce qui est parfait comporte quelque défaut: il est, en effet, totalement parfait." See also his Introduction, xxxiii–iv. Moraux reads this passage as an Aristotelian polemic against a phantom problem (the possibility of a four-dimensional magnitude). He is unaware that Aristotle here is offering one of his most fundamental refutations of Plato's deduction philosophy. Cf. A. P. Bos, *On the Elements. Aristotle's Early Cosmology* (Assen: Van Gorcum & Comp., 1973), 33–43. See also C. Wildberg, *John Philoponus' Criticism of Aristotle's Theory of Aether* (Berlin: Walter de Gruyter, 1988), 20: "there is no other magnitude besides these three," and "Aristotle wants to exclude the possibility of a fourth dimension"; C. Dalimier and P. Pellegrin (2004), 71: "le passage <du corps> à un autre genre <plus élevé> . . . ne serait plus parfaite"; D. O'Brien (2006) 71 n. 72: "The existence, and even the possibility, of a fourth dimension is explicitly discounted in . . . *De Caelo* (I 1, 268a9-b10)." See also A. Jori, *Aristoteles Über den Himmel* (2009), 22. On this problem, see further §10h below. I will argue there that if Aristotle had wanted to rule out a fourth dimension, he would have written ὡς in 268b1, and not ὥσπερ.

32. Cf. Plato, *Respublica* VI 506b2–11e4.

water, air, and fire. In fact, this led him basically to deny the existence of the material elements.[33]

Aristotle defended a much more positive approach to the Bodies, one in which they are "perfect" spatial magnitudes[34] and therefore ontologically "higher" than Lines and Planes, which he considers products of "abstraction." But in his doctrine of the distinction between God's Essence and his Power[35] he did accept that the departure of God's Power leads to a decrease in the effects of this Power. The cosmos is the arena of the productive association of God's Power with the matter used by this Power. Aristotle argued that there is continuity of the Power emanating from God. This Power manifests itself to a lesser or greater degree in the soul-principles (entelechies) of all living entities,[36] depending on the smaller or greater distance to the Source of Power. But Aristotle doubtless held that there is continuity in the *scala naturae* throughout the various species of living beings. There is an uninterrupted "chain of life." Nature does not proceed by leaps and bounds, and the order of the cosmos is not a loose series of episodes, as in a bad tragedy.[37] Aristotle directs this reproach against some of his predecessors and contemporaries.[38] They turn the cosmos into a hotch-potch of separate elements, each with its own principle. Aristotle's vigorous answer is: "The rule of many is not good; there is only one the Ruler [οὐκ ἀγαθὸν πολυκοιρανίη· εἷς κοίρανος]."[39] Although this means that God is no longer the Demiurge of the cosmos, he is most certainly the author and source of all order and structure.

That is to say that Aristotle assumes a desire for the divine on all levels in all natural reality, a desire that is the motor of all processes in nature. "Desire" in this sense functions as an "idea" in Aristotle's philosophy. We should see it as an ontological feature of all extra-divine reality. That is what Aristotle is referring to in *Physics* I 9, 192a16–9: "For admitting that there is something divine, good and desirable, we hold that there are two other principles, the one contrary to it, the other such as of its own nature to desire and yearn for it."[40]

---

33. Plato, *Tim.* 53c4–55c6.
34. Cf. *Cael.* I 1, 268a22: "body is the only complete magnitude [τὸ σῶμα μόνον ἂν εἴη τῶν μεγεθῶν τέλειον]." See also §3f below on Aristotle's more positive attitude to the physical world.
35. See §9a below.
36. Cf. §10q below.
37. Cf. *Metaph.* N 3, 1090b19; Λ 10, 1076a1. See also *Poetics* 9, 1451b34–5.
38. These certainly include Speusippus, as may be inferred from *Metaph.* Z 2, 1028b21–4.
39. *Metaph.* Λ 10, 1076a4, where he quotes Homer, *Iliad* 2, 204, but probably also adapts the line resolutely to his own purposes, by omitting the Homeric ἔστω. Aristotle was a convinced monarchianist. This made his view attractive to later Jewish authors such as Aristobulus and Philo of Alexandria.
40. *Phys.* I 9, 192a16–9: ὄντος γάρ τινος θείου καὶ ἀγαθοῦ καὶ ἐφετοῦ, τὸ μὲν ἐναντίον αὐτῷ φαμεν εἶναι, τὸ δὲ ὃ πέφυκεν ἐφίεσθαι καὶ ὀρέγεσθαι αὐτοῦ κατὰ τὴν αὐτοῦ φύσιν.

In 192a13–4 Aristotle characterizes this last principle as "a joint cause, with the form, of what comes to be—a mother as it were [Ἡ μὲν γὰρ ὑπομένουσα συναιτία τῇ μορφῇ τῶν γιγνομένων ἐστίν, ὥσπερ μήτηρ]."

The divine has no deficiency and therefore no striving or desire. However, according to Aristotle, the divine is also pure Intellect. And he regards striving or desire or will as matters of the soul. For this reason, too, no desire or striving can be attributed to God. But matter does desire, as the female desires the male (192a22–3). This must be connected with the proposition of *Generation of Animals* II 1, 732a1–3 that the female and the male always exist in what already exists, for the sake of *genesis*.[41]

However, from this perspective, it is undeniable that Aristotle draws a fundamental distinction between "the goal" of a living creature that comes into being and "the meaning" of this genesis and of all things in nature. Just as the divine Origin is the male *Archè geneseôs* of everything that comes into being, so there is just as necessarily a female principle of *genesis*, matter, which is structurally characterized by a deficiency of being and therefore "desires" structuration by the (male) form-principle.[42]

Plants do not have the possibility of participating in the divine through knowledge, but can only do so in a vegetative way, through reproduction. However, the vegetative desire for the eternal and the divine is structurally identical to the human desire for knowledge. It is just as much a manifestation of a lack of unity with the divine Origin, resulting in a lack of fullness of being and therefore leading to *orexis*.

d. *Generation of Animals* II 1, 731b24–2a3

Aristotle broaches the same theme of natural desire for the divine and immortality in *Generation of Animals* II 1, 731b24–2a3, where he draws an

---

41. Cf. A. P. Bos, "The Soul and Soul-'Parts' in Semen (*GA* II 1, 735a4–22)," *Mnemosyne* 62 (2009): 373–74. See §3d below. As *Anim.* II 4, 415a25–b7 shows, the desire for eternity through reproduction belongs indeed to the male specimens of mortal species as well. In the end, however, Aristotle explains this with reference to their participation in "matter." Although, for Aristotle, God is the ultimate principle of the generation of living beings in the cosmos, this is not the consequence of an *orexis* on his part. Nor can it be that a multitude of intellects achieve eternity through their succession.

42. We saw in §3a above that Aristotle characterizes the female as a failed product of nature (πήρωμα—cf. *Anim.* II 4, 415a27). "Desire" is therefore not a reciprocal relation between the male and the female. Cf. also Simplicius, *in de Caelo* 288, 28–289, 15 = Arist. *Philos.* fr. 16 Ross; 30 Gigon. On God's side there rather is ἀφθονία. Cf. *Metaph.* A 2, 983a2.

empirical distinction between the "eternal-and-divine beings"[43] and the changeable-and-mortal. Aristotle immediately goes on there to identify the "beautiful and divine" with the "eternal and divine entities" that he has mentioned. By virtue of their nature, they are the cause of "the better" for the noneternal beings.[44] For in the dependent sphere, too, we again find *degrees*: that which is not eternal may be but also not be, and may partake in "the worse or better."

Here, too, the idea is that all good things come "from above." But there are degrees to which the lower part partakes in the higher. For the lower living entities, eternity can only be achieved as eternity of the species, through reproduction. It is desirable for reproduction that there be a distinction between the male and the female factor.[45] And it is, in fact, better that these two exist separately. Aristotle adds that the male factor, which fertilizes, is "better and more divine in its nature."

e. *On Coming-to-Be and Passing-Away* II 10, 336b31-4 on the Distance to the Origin

Aristotle also discusses the theme of *orexis* for "the better" in *On Coming-to-Be and Passing-Away* II 10, in connection with his thesis that the cycle of generation and decay always continues. In II 10, 336b27-9 he says:

> for in all things, as we affirm, nature always strives after the better. Now being is better than not-being.
>
> ἐπεὶ γὰρ ἐν ἅπασιν ἀεὶ τοῦ βελτίονος ὀρέγεσθαί φαμεν τὴν φύσιν, βέλτιον δὲ τὸ εἶναι ἢ τὸ μὴ εἶναι.

---

43. *Gener. anim.* II 1, 731b24: "of the things which are, some are eternal and divine [τὰ ἀΐδια καὶ θεῖα τῶν ὄντων]." Aristotle makes no distinction there between the ethereal celestial gods and the Prime Unmoved Mover.

44. It is not wrong to discern here a kind of "*superabundantia boni*," which has an inner urge to share its goodness.

45. *Gener. anim.* II 1, 732a1-3: "But since the male and female are the first principles of these, they will exist in all beings for the sake of generation [Ἐπεὶ δὲ τούτων ἀρχὴ τὸ θῆλυ καὶ τὸ ἄρρεν ἕνεκα τῆς γενέσεως ἂν εἴη τὸ θῆλυ καὶ τὸ ἄρρεν ἐν τοῖς οὖσιν]." On this passage, see A. P. Bos (2009)—cited above—373-74, where I reject the correction <ἔχ>ουσιν by H. J. Drossaart Lulofs (1965), 47. Here it needs to be emphasized that the male represents "the higher and more divine" cause—732a2-6. In §3f below we shall see that Aristotle in *Physics* I 9 gives sexual differentiation an ontic function too, and in *On the Cosmos* 7, 401b2 even a theological function.

But in 336b27–7a7 he adds two remarkable details;

1. First, the fact that some things do not possess eternity has to do with the distance that separates them from the Origin:

   since they are too far removed from the Principle

   διὰ τὸ πόρρω τῆς ἀρχῆς ἀφίστασθαι[46]

2. Second, the statement that God himself *completed the cosmos by making the process of Coming-to-Be everlasting*:

   God therefore adopted the remaining alternative, and fulfilled the perfection of the universe by making coming-to-be uninterrupted; for the greatest possible coherence[47] would thus be secured to existence, because that coming-to-be should itself come-to-be perpetually is the closest approximation to eternal being. (transl. H. H. Joachim, 1922)[48]

Although the course of life is linear from birth, the linking of decay to generation makes this linear process of mortal life into a kind of cycle (336b34–7a7).

---

46. This theme is also important in *Gener. anim.* III 11, 761b13–23 for the difference in quality of sublunary living beings. Cf. 761b14–5: "the variations of quantity and distance make a great and amazing difference [τὸ δὲ μᾶλλον καὶ ἧττον καὶ ἐγγύτερον καὶ πορρώτερον πολλὴν ποιεῖ καὶ θαυμαστὴν διαφοράν]." See also *Cael.* II 12, 292b17–9: "to attain the ultimate end would be in the truest sense best for all; but if that is impossible, a thing gets better and better the nearer it is to the best [μάλιστα μὲν γὰρ ἐκείνου τυχεῖν ἄριστον πᾶσι τοῦ τέλους· εἰ δὲ μή, ἀεὶ ἄμεινόν ἐστιν ὅσῳ ἂν ἐγγύτερον ᾖ τοῦ ἀρίστου]" (in a discussion on the question why the outer celestial sphere carries out one single orbit, whereas the planets execute a multiplicity of orbits).

47. J. B. Skemp, "The Activity of Immobility," in *Études sur la Métaphysique d'Aristote* (Actes du VIe Symposium Aristotelicum), 1978, 232, comments on these words: "the words . . . represent something Aristotle may have believed but which he could not sustain so long as his πρῶτον κινοῦν is God and God is in all senses 'ἀκίνητον.' Aristotle uses the verb συνείρεται here. In *Mu.* 7, 401b9 the author connects the verb '*eirô*' with '*Heimarmenê*,' Fate, as the sequence or chain of all natural factors."

48. *Gener. corr.* II 10, 336b31–4: τῷ λειπομένῳ τρόπῳ συνεπλήρωσε τὸ ὅλον ὁ θεός, ἐνδελεχῆ ποιήσας τὴν γένεσιν. οὕτω γὰρ ἂν μάλιστα συνείρεται τὸ εἶναι διὰ τὸ ἐγγύτατα εἶναι τῆς οὐσίας τὸ γίνεσθαι ἀεὶ καὶ τὴν γένεσιν. Cf. T. Buchheim, *Aristoteles, Über Werden und Vergehen. Übersetzt und Erläutert* (Darmstadt: Wissenschaftliche Buchgesellschaft, 2010), 545: "Dem genannten aristotelischen Gott kommt, ohne Demiurg zu sein, eine alles in Richtung auf 'Gutsein' orientierende Funktion zu."

This passage is highly remarkable for saying that God "brings about" something (ποιήσας),[49] although Aristotle presented this in various other contexts as something suited to a figure such as Plato's Demiurge, or as a function of the celestial spheres, but not to God, who is perfectly transcendent Intellect. Moreover, what God brings about is the sphere of all generation and decay. But this is the sphere of the four sublunary elements in particular, since they are characterized by "opposites," which effect each other's destruction.[50] Although the text offers no further clarification, this means that God, as pure, transcendent Intellect, is conceived of as the Cause and "Effecter" of the world of (the operative principles in) the elementary bodies and all that is composed of them. In any case, this means that Aristotle did not view the extended, three-dimensional reality of the elementary bodies as purely negative and as not-being, but rather as "less perfect" than the sphere of the Intellect.

In some way or other Aristotle also attributed to God, the pure, theoretical Intellect, an operation in which the astral world, but even the world of mortal things, can be presented as necessary in God's plan and the natural bodies as "instruments" and serviceable material for soul-principles.

The closest we can get to an explanation is if we take into account the fact that Aristotle, in his discussion of the human motor system, presented will and desire as connected with the soul and as "materially characterized."[51] The will of a human being and desire (in animals) are not faculties of the immaterial soul as governing principle, but powers that must necessarily be material. In §9b we shall see that the theology of *On the Cosmos* also emphatically postulates two aspects of God as Intellect, to wit, God's Essence and his Power. And this Power manifests itself in material reality.

---

49. In *Cael.* I 4, 271a33 we find: "But God and nature create nothing that does not fulfil a purpose [ὁ δὲ θεὸς καὶ ἡ φύσις οὐδὲν μάτην ποιοῦσιν]." There, the verb might still be understood as appropriate to ἡ φύσις. But it is preferable to see everything that Nature does as a manifestation of the Working Power that proceeds from God and is clothed in natural materiality. Cf. also *Anim.* II 4, 415b17: "For just as mind acts with some purpose in view, so too does nature [ὥσπερ γὰρ ὁ νοῦς ἕνεκά του ποιεῖ, τὸν αὐτὸν τρόπον καὶ ἡ φύσις]."

50. Cf. *Cael.* I 3, 270a22: "because generation and destruction take place among opposites [ἐν τοῖς ἐναντίοις γὰρ ἡ γένεσις καὶ ἡ φθορά]."

51. Cf. *Anim.* III 10, 433b19: "The instrument by which appetite causes movement belongs already to the physical sphere [ᾧ δὲ κινεῖ ὀργάνῳ ἡ ὄρεξις, ἤδη τοῦτο σωματικόν ἐστιν]." See also *Motu anim.* 10, 703a5–6. This point has not been correctly dealt with by E. Diamond, *Mortal Imitations of Divine Life. The Nature of the Soul in Aristotle's De Anima* (2015), 236–37.

f. *Physics* I 9 and Aristotle's Moderate Dualism

In *Physics* I 9, Aristotle presents his own ontology as an alternative to Plato's views in the sense that Plato supposedly held an "extreme dualism," almost in Eleatic fashion, in which Being can only have a not-Being as its negation. In contrast, Aristotle describes his own concept of *hylè* not as a negation of Being but as typified by deficiency of being and desire for being. Aristotle does still have a dualism, but it is a "moderate dualism," in which the imperfect is characterized by "desire for" and "striving after" the divine and Being, just as the female desires the male (in the Aristotelian conception).

Plato, says Aristotle, was neglectful of the fact that between the Good and its negation there must be a third agency that functions for the form-principle as a kind of contributory cause of all that comes into being; *as a kind of mother figure*.[52] Aristotle calls this agency "matter" and "the underlying."[53]

Aristotle therefore specifies his own, moderately dualist, position in this important chapter by means of a formulation in which he interprets "form" and "matter" as a pair of reciprocally oriented principles: "For admitting that there is something divine, good and desirable, we hold that there are two other principles, the one contrary to it, the other such as of its own nature to desire and yearn for it."[54] The principle characterized by desire is *hylè*. It desires the divine and good and beautiful, just as the female desires the male and the ugly the beautiful.[55]

This is a fundamental choice of Aristotle, by which he tries to mitigate the radical dualism between a spiritual reality and a material reality. Where Plato in his dialogues did not just present the body as a "prison" and a "grave" of the soul, but also as an instrument and as something that the soul must

---

52. *Phys.* I 9, 192a12–4: "for he overlooked the other nature. For the one which persists is a joint cause with the form, of what comes to be—a mother as it were [τὴν γὰρ ἑτέραν παρεῖδεν. ἡ μὲν γὰρ ὑπομένουσα συναιτία τῇ μορφῇ τῶν γιγνομένων ἐστίν, ὥσπερ μήτηρ]."

53. *Phys.* I 9, 192a31: "For my definition of matter is just this—the first underlying of each thing [λέγω γὰρ ὕλην τὸ πρῶτον ὑποκείμενον ἑκάστῳ]." For Aristotle, there is always a sexual metaphor in the term *the subject, the underlying*. The Latin translation *materia, materies* has retained this connotation.

54. *Phys.* I 9, 192a16–9, cited above.

55. *Phys.* I 9, 192a22–3: "what desires the form is matter, as the female desires the male and the ugly the beautiful [τοῦτ' ἔστιν ἡ ὕλη, ὥσπερ ἂν εἰ θῆλυ ἄρρενος καὶ αἰσχρὸν καλοῦ]."

take care of, Aristotle develops the even more positive approach that corporeal reality serves as an "instrument" of the soul.

Against this background, it is understandable that *On the Cosmos* 7, 401b2 approvingly cites an Orphic poem with the remarkable words:

Zeus is a man, Zeus an immortal maid

Ζεὺς ἄρσην γένετο, Ζεὺς ἄμβροτος ἔπλετο νύμφη[56]

In the same work *On the Cosmos*, the author, who in any case wants to appear Aristotelian, has a strikingly positive appreciation of the conjunction of opposites. He sees it as evidence of the "harmonious community" (*homonoia*) in nature and the cosmos:

> It may perhaps be that nature has a liking for contraries and evolves harmony out of them and not out of similarities (just as she joins the male and the female together and not members of the same sex), and has devised the original harmonious community by means of contraries and not similarities. (E. S. Forster, in J. Barnes (1984) vol. 1, 633)[57]

The "natural desire" in all that lives in the cosmos, which we have discussed in this chapter 3, is an important component of Aristotle's philosophy and the result of his criticism of Plato's view. We encountered it in *Physics* I 9 as characteristic of "the underlying" in all things of nature, which Aristotle describes as "the maternal." This concept of "natural desire" also underlies Aristotle's teleological view of nature. I will talk about this at length in §10q.

Important too is Aristotle's view that all motion is proper to a body, and specifically to *pneuma*, as instrumental body of the soul. He emphatically rejects and marshals many arguments against Plato's view that motion is proper to the soul as "principle of motion" in *On the Soul* I 3–4 en III 9–10 (cf. §10g below).

---

56. Cf. L. Brisson, *Le Sexe Incertain: Androgynie et Hermaphrodisme dans l'Antiquité Gréco-romaine* (1997; 2me éd augmentée Paris: Les Belles Lettres, 2008), 90–91.

57. *Mu.* 5, 396b7–11: Ἴσως δὲ τῶν ἐναντίων ἡ φύσις γλίχεται καὶ ἐκ τούτων ἀποτελεῖ τὸ σύμφωνον, οὐκ ἐκ τῶν ὁμοίων, ὥσπερ ἀμέλει τὸ ἄρρεν συνήγαγε πρὸς τὸ θῆλυ καὶ οὐχ ἑκάτερον πρὸς τὸ ὁμόφυλον, καὶ τὴν πρώτην ὁμόνοιαν διὰ τῶν ἐναντίων συνῆψεν, οὐ διὰ τῶν ὁμοίων. Cf. J. C. Thom, ed., (2014), 39.

No doubt we should see this side of Aristotle's philosophy in connection with his theological conception, in which he introduced a more abstract notion of God than Plato had presented. In this concept any form of "willing" and "providential action" is denied to God (cf. §9h below). This has often been taken to mean that Aristotle had developed a less anthropomorphic image of God than Plato. But we should also note here that through his notion of "natural desire" and his teleological view of nature Aristotle did offer a more "anthropomorphic" outlook on nature!

Although "natural desire" is present throughout the cosmos, Aristotle strongly stressed the separation between the supralunary and the sublunary spheres. In this way he could present the region of the astral celestial beings as being entirely under God's governance, and the world of mortal beings as less perfect, because the elements of earth, water, air, and fire act prohibitively there as a kind of residual matter. This makes the sublunary sphere seem more directly dependent on the astral world than on the supreme divine principle, so that the later doxographical tradition could attribute the notion of a "limited" divine Providence to Aristotle.[58]

---

58. Cf. R. W. Sharples's Non Sublunary Providence theory; A. P. Bos, *Providentia Divina* (1976).

4

God as Object of Erôs and Source of Attraction

a. *Metaphysics* Λ 7, 1072b3

In *Metaphysics* Λ Aristotle demonstrates that there must exist a nonphysical substance that is separate from all materiality and unmoved.[1] This means that there must exist something that is not one of the basic elements or their composites, but cannot be described as soul either (since every soul as soul is connected with an instrumental body). In chapter 6 he focuses on this last principle. It must be the eternal ground of explanation for the continuous motion of the celestial sphere.

In Λ 7, 1072b3 we then find the famous words: "it produces motion by being loved, and through what is moved it moves the other things."[2] The *erôs* mentioned here is the *erôs* of the outer celestial sphere directed at God, the Intellect, as supreme Principle. This implies that the divine acts on the superlunary sphere of the divine beings via their rational souls.[3] (Love is different from "striving" or "desire." Plants do not have "love.")

Again, we have an indication here that God is not directly involved in the genesis and existence of things in the sublunary region. These are set in

---

1. *Metaph.* Λ 1, 1069a30–3.
2. *Metaph.* Λ 7, 1072b3: κινεῖ δὲ ὡς ἐρώμενον, κινουμένῳ δὲ τἆλλα κινεῖ (text W. Jaeger). Cf. L. A. Kosman (2013), 198–210.
3. A rational soul is explicitly attributed to the celestial beings in *Cael.* II 12, 292a18–b3. See also II 2, 285a29.

motion by causes closer to them. However, this does not mean that God has no influence whatsoever on the sublunary sphere. For Aristotle, it is God's Power that operates in the outer celestial sphere, as the efficient cause of the lower motions.

Finally, Aristotle argues that the first Principle cannot possess magnitude, because otherwise this Principle cannot possess infinite Power (*Dynamis*).[4]

---

4. *Metaph.* Λ 7, 1073a5–11, with a7: "but nothing finite has infinite power [οὐδὲν δ' ἔχει δύναμιν ἄπειρον πεπερασμένον]."

5

God as Unmoved Principle of Motion and Source of Power

Aristotle was critical of Plato on many points. But one point was at the center of this criticism: Plato's doctrine of Soul.[1] According to Aristotle, what Plato calls "soul" is a highly ambiguous concept, or even a bundle of contradictions, because what Plato considers the most important part of "soul" is not "soul" but "intellect." And what Aristotle calls "soul" is not in itself immaterial and immortal, as Plato said, but always inextricably bound up with a "natural body" and, in the case of animals and plants, mortal.[2] Just as Plato had distinguished within the comprehensive category of "Soul" between (1) the Demiurge who contemplates the Ideas and (2) the Demiurge who produces the visible world and connects the World Soul with it, and (3) the World Soul and (4) the souls of celestial beings and (5) the souls of human beings and (6) of animals (as second-rate and third-rate souls), so Aristotle had distinguished between (1) a supreme, immaterial Intellect and an extensive series of governing principles

---

1. See also chapter 7 below.
2. As Arist. *Philos.* fr. 27a-d Ross; 994–6 and T 18, 1 Gigon seems clearly to show, Aristotle argued that people have something of the astral element, which Cicero referred to as "*quinta essentia.*" This would imply that the covering of man's soul is *pneuma*, which can be purged of alien elements and transformed into pure ether, because it is of astral origin. This difference between humans beings and animals (and plants) is also the subject of *Anim.* II 1, 413a4–7, but since Antiquity this passage has usually been misinterpreted. After arguing in the first part of that chapter that the soul should be understood as the "first entelechy of a body that potentially possesses life and that serves the soul as an instrument" (412a27–b6), Aristotle then explains that the same applies to "the parts" (of the soul!) (412b17–3a3). The vegetative soul and the sensitive soul, too, are inextricably bound up with an instrumental body. The reason Aristotle brings up the eye in 412b18 is that he wants to show that *sight* is inextricably bound up with

of instrumental bodies, namely (2) rational souls of divine celestial beings, (3) rational souls of lunar beings, (4) entelechies of human beings, (5) of animals and (6) of plants and even (7) of products of spontaneous generation.[3] Only the

---

the "instrument for seeing," like the other senses. Cf. A. P. Bos, "Het Gehele Lichaam dat Waarnemingsvermogen Bezit (Aristoteles, *De Anima* II 1, 412b24–25)," *Algemeen Nederlands Tijdschrift voor Wijsbegeerte* 91 (1999): 112–28. Aristotle concludes from this that semen of animals and seeds of plants already contain the sensitive soul-*part* or the vegetative soul-part. These soul-parts are not added later, but are already present from the moment of fertilization, even if they have not yet been activated. In 413a4–5 Aristotle postulates: "It is quite clear, then, that neither the soul nor certain parts *of it*, if it has parts, can be separated from the body; for in some cases the entelechy is the entelechy of the parts themselves." Cf. ch. 15 below. The misinterpretation of the words *the parts* was a crucial factor in the misconception of the soul as the entelechy of a body equipped with instrumental parts! However, (this is not to say that no part of the soul occurs separately from its [instrumental] body, because) "there is nothing to prevent some parts being separated, because they are not the entelechy of any [instrumental] body [ὅτι μὲν οὖν οὐκ ἔστιν ἡ ψυχὴ χωριστὴ τοῦ σώματος, ἢ μέρη τινὰ αὐτῆς, εἰ μεριστὴ πέφυκεν, οὐκ ἄδηλον· ἐνίων γὰρ ἡ ἐντελέχεια τῶν μερῶν ἐστιν αὐτῶν. οὐ μὴν ἀλλ' ἔνιά γε οὐθὲν κωλύει, διὰ τὸ μηθενὸς εἶναι σώματος ἐντελεχείας]." What is the point of this brief passage? In my view, it is something said nowhere else in Aristotle's extant writings, namely, that the souls of plants and animals are inextricably bound up with their instrumental bodies, because they solely possess the functions of metabolism (in plants this is the only soul-function; plants therefore have a soul that cannot be subdivided into "parts") and perception, and these functions (or "parts" of the soul) are impossible without an instrumental body, to wit the vital *pneuma* that for animals also functions as the instrument of perception (σῶμα αἰσθητικόν: cf. *Anim.* II 1, 412b23–4). But there is one function of the soul, the intellect, that is not inextricably bound up with an instrumental body. This intellect, which occurs in only human beings among mortal creatures, is "a different genus of soul," as Aristotle says explicitly in *Anim.* II 2, 413b24–7. That is why this is not a soul as "first entelechy," but a "different kind of soul." Aristotle does not explain anywhere in *On the Soul* how this immortal "other soul" can be present in man as a mortal "living being." But because his *Eudemus* expressly characterized the human soul's bondage to a mortal body and to an instrumental body as a form of "penance" (τιμωρία) for a previous crime (cf. *Eudem.* fr. 6 Ross; 65 Gigon; and A. P. Bos, "Aristotle on the Etruscan Robbers: a Core Text of 'Aristotelian' Dualism," *Journal of the History of Philosophy* 41 [2003]: 289–306), we will have to assume that this view also applies to the psychology of *On the Soul*. That is in fact what Aristotle is referring to in the concluding sentence of *On the Soul* II 1 (413a8–9): "It is also uncertain whether the soul as entelechy has the same relation to the body as the sailor to the ship [Ἔτι δὲ ἄδηλον εἰ οὕτως ἐντελέχεια τοῦ σώματος ἡ ψυχὴ ὥσπερ πλωτὴρ πλοίου]." For in this way Aristotle alludes to the distinction he had made in I 3, 406a5–7. A sailor moves along with the motion of his ship as long as he is sailing on her. Of himself, however, the sailor has a different way of moving. In the same way a human being's intellect, once it is activated, can develop its own activity, independently of the motion of the instrumental body that made possible the vital activities of this human being on the level of metabolism and perception. However, on this text, see also H. J. Easterling, "A Note on *De Anima* 413a8–9," *Phronesis* 11 (1966): 159–62.

3. As we pointed out in §3f above, Aristotle emphatically argues in *Anim.* III 10, 433b13–21 and in *Motu anim.* 10, 703a4–6 that will and desire are not parts of the immaterial soul, but are material, and should therefore be assigned to the instrumental body of the soul. This is another clear indication that Aristotle leaves only the functions of knowing and guiding for the soul by itself, that is, the task of the charioteer in Plato's "charioteer and pair of horses."

Intellect itself is always oriented to its own thought as its goal. But everything in (living) nature is analogously goal-oriented, because the soul as entelechy controls the motion of its instrumental body in such a way that their combination always functions teleologically, too.[4] But as "first" entelechy, the soul does this not as a "waking" intellect but, as it were, "sleeping," like an automatic pilot.[5] And this soul-principle is already present at the moment of fertilization, as we will discuss further in chapter 7. This insight forced Aristotle to adopt his radically new approach, in which he also attributed "life" to plants and trees (which do not have locomotion like animals).

Aristotle was fundamentally critical of Plato's theory that the soul is the "principle of motion" and is itself in perpetual motion too. In *On the Soul* I 3, 405b31–6b25, Aristotle proves that the essence of soul *cannot possess motion*, but moves only accidentally with the body with which it is connected.[6] Aristotle's criticism of Plato's psychology links up here with the image of the charioteer and his pair of horses that Plato used in *Phaedrus* 246a. In this image the intellect is the charioteer who drives his horses while standing still in his chariot (*ochèma*).

For Aristotle, motion is motion of natural, elementary bodies (and their compositions). It is therefore intriguing that he nevertheless talks about the soul as "principle of motion";[7] but also, very emphatically, about God as the Principle of Motion. Aristotle does add: "Unmoved" Principle of Motion, but it remains hard to understand how God can be this principle. In my view, Aristotle could find a model for this in the sphere of magnetic phenomena. A magnet is not itself in motion but sets something else in motion and does

---

4. Cf. *Anim.* II 4, 415b15: "Clearly the soul is also the cause in the final sense. For just as mind acts with some purpose in view, so too does nature [Φανερὸν δ' ὡς καὶ οὗ ἕνεκεν ἡ ψυχὴ αἰτία· ὥσπερ γὰρ ὁ νοῦς ἕνεκά του ποιεῖ, τὸν αὐτὸν τρόπον καὶ ἡ φύσις]" (W. S. Hett). See also *Phys.* VIII 1, 252a11: "But that which holds by nature and is natural can never be anything disorderly; for nature is everywhere the cause of order [Ἀλλὰ μὴν οὐδέν γε ἄτακτον τῶν φύσει καὶ κατὰ φύσιν· ἡ γὰρ φύσις αἰτία πᾶσι τάξεως]" (R. P. Hardie and R. K. Gaye in *The Complete Works of Aristotle*, ed. J. Barnes). In 252a23 Aristotle blames the pre-Socratic philosophers for talking about "order" in nature but not identifying its cause. In book VIII Aristotle himself arrives at God as the cause of this order. See also *Cael.* I 4, 271a33: "But God and nature create nothing that does not fulfil a purpose [ὁ δὲ θεὸς καὶ ἡ φύσις οὐδὲν μάτην ποιοῦσιν]" (W. K. C. Guthrie).

5. Cf. *Anim.* II 1, 412a23–b7. On this, see §10q below.

6. In *Motu anim.* 6, 700b4–6 Aristotle again refers explicitly to this passage in *De Anima*. Cf. M. C. Nussbaum (1978) 331 and K. Corcilius and P. Gregoric, "Aristotle's Model of Animal Motion," *Phronesis* 58 (2013): 52–97.

7. *Anim.* I 3, 406b24–5: "In general the living creature does not appear to be moved by the soul in this way, but by some act of mind or will [Ὅλως δ' οὐχ οὕτως φαίνεται κινεῖν ἡ ψυχὴ τὸ ζῷον, ἀλλὰ διὰ προαιρέσεώς τινος καὶ νοήσεως]." He elaborates this in *Anim.* III 9–10.

so through a power that proceeds from the magnet and pervades the object that is moved.

a. Aristotle's Dual Physics and the Place of *Pneuma*

A characteristic feature of Aristotle's outlook on the cosmos and its parts is the doctrine of the four-plus-one elements presented in his book *On the Heavens* I 1–3. This doctrine involves a radical distinction between the four "ordinary,"[8] sublunary elements and the fifth element, ether. He states that the four elements are each others' "opposites" and reciprocally bring about each others' destruction (air may become water; water is evaporated by fire). But they also have a common "matter." Ether, on the other hand, is completely separate: this body falls outside the sphere of opposites and is therefore unchanging, timeless, eternal, and divine.[9]

However, this also means that the sublunary elements do not have any effect on ether. Conversely, ether does have an impact on the sublunary sphere. The revolution of the sphere of the fixed stars and that of the Zodiac and the planets have important consequences for meteorological phenomena, for the winds and the tides. Moreover, the revolution of the Sun is essential to the generation of life on Earth, because the heat of the Sun differs essentially from the heat of fire and it alone brings about vital heat in living entities. And owing to the fact that the circle of the Zodiac is oblique to the circle of the celestial equator, "the locomotion will produce generation perpetually by bringing near and then removing that which is life-generating."[10]

---

8. See on this topic especially A. Falcon, *Aristotle's Science of Nature. Unity without Uniformity* (Cambridge: Cambridge University Press, 2005), 113–18. Aristotle repeatedly calls them the "so-called" elements. See T. J. Crowley, "On the Use of *Stoicheion* in the Sense of 'Element,'" *Oxford Studies in Ancient Philosophy* 29 (2005): 367–94; "Aristotle's 'So-Called Elements,'" *Phronesis* 53 (2008): 223–42. Perhaps this addition "so-called" should be explained against the background of *Metaph*. Z 17, 1041b11–22. Cf. L. A. Kosman (2013), 26–27. The elements that are integrated into a living body are different from the building blocks of a house.

9. Cf. *On the Heavens* I 2–3. See especially I 3, 270a18–22: "There cannot be an opposite to the body under discussion, because there cannot be an opposite motion to the circular. It looks, then, as if nature had providently abstracted from the class of opposites that which was to be ungenerated and indestructible, because generation and destruction take place among opposites [εἰ δὴ τούτῳ μηδὲν ἐναντίον ἐνδέχεται εἶναι διὰ τὸ καὶ τῇ φορᾷ τῇ κύκλῳ μὴ εἶναι ἄν τιν' ἐναντίαν κίνησιν, ὀρθῶς ἔοικε ἡ φύσις τὸ μέλλον ἔσεσθαι ἀγένητον καὶ ἄφθαρτον ἐξελέσθαι ἐκ τῶν ἐναντίων· ἐν τοῖς ἐναντίοις γὰρ ἡ γένεσις καὶ ἡ φθορά]" (W. K. C. Guthrie). See also §10.1.

10. *Gener. corr.* II 10, 336a16–8: ἡ γὰρ φορὰ ποιήσει τὴν γένεσιν ἐνδελεχῶς διὰ τὸ προσάγειν καὶ ἀπάγειν τὸ γεννητικόν. C. J. F. Williams, *Aristotle's De Generatione et Corruptione, Translated with Notes* (Oxford: Clarendon Press, 1982) translates: "by bringing near and then removing the

In this way, Aristotle was the founder of a "dual physics," in which the physics of the astral sphere displays features of a doctrine of a World Soul. Although *On the Heavens* makes much more the impression of containing a general physics than Plato's cosmology, with its mythical theory about an all-pervasive and vitalizing World Soul, this is a façade concealing an equally fundamental division. In his great study on *The Mechanization of the World Picture*,[11] E. J. Dijksterhuis described at length how much effort it took to break out of this Aristotelian mould.

It is quite legitimate to say that, for Aristotle, the fundamental distinction in the cosmic world is the separation between the sphere of "organic physics" and that of "anorganic physics." The sphere of anorganic physics is the sphere of necessity, of lack of order and structure and of contingency. For him, the sphere of living nature is the sphere of "organic physics," that is, the sphere in which all natural bodies have been taken into service as *sôma organikon* by rational structural or psychic principles.[12] One could also refer to the sphere of living nature as the object of "psychico-physics." However, because Aristotle regularly characterizes the soul as the entity that is always connected "with a natural body,"[13] the sphere of living nature may even be described as the object of "meta-physics."

---

generating body." He identifies this body with the Sun (186). Cf. *Gener. corr.* II 10, 336b17: "we see that while the sun is approaching there is generation [ὁρῶμεν γὰρ ὅτι προσιόντος τοῦ ἡλίου γένεσίς ἐστιν]." See now also M. Rashed, *Aristote, De la Génération et la Corruption* Nouvelle édition (Paris: Les Belles Lettres, 2005). Aristotle sees the changing of the seasons as a cosmic coitus interruptus, with a central role for the Sun as "begetter." Indirectly, he thus returns to the notion of a fertilizing god, like Ouranos in Hesiod's *Theogony*. However, as in human and animal processes of procreation, the truly crucial role is played by the life-generating power (*dynamis*). In §3e we already discussed how the difference between the sphere of the eternal gods and the sublunary sphere of mortal creatures has to do with the difference in distance from the Origin. Aristotle connects the change within the sublunary sphere between the generation of new life and death with the difference in distance from the Sun.

11. E. J. Dijksterhuis, *The Mechanization of the World Picture* (Oxford: Oxford University Press, 1969); originally published as *De Mechanisering van het Wereldbeeld* (Amsterdam: Meulenhof, 1950). Cf. also J. Longrigg, "Elementary Physics in the Lyceum and Stoa," *Isis* 66 (1975): 214. See now D. Wootton, *The Invention of Science. A New History of the Scientific Revolution* (London: Allen Lane, 2015).

12. *Het Groot Woordenboek der Nederlandse Taal*, 10th edition, 2 vols., part 2 ('s Gravenhage: Martinus Nijhoff, 1976), 1744 gives the second sense of "organic" as: "equipped with, possessing organs or instruments," citing as an example: "the organic beings" (= plants and animals). It seems natural to conclude that this sense derives from the definition of "soul" given by Aristotle, but understood in its wrong interpretation by Alexander of Aphrodisias in the second century CE (see ch. 12 below). The same *Woordenboek* also mentions that "organic chemistry" was originally the discipline that studied the independencies occurring in the animal or vegetable organism, but is now "the chemistry of carbon compounds."

13. Cf. *Anim.* I 1, 403a16: μετὰ σώματος. 403a6: οὐθὲν ἄνευ σώματος.

b. Does *Pneuma* Belong to the Imperishable or the Perishable Part of the Cosmos?

Of course, this urges the question: *How are we to classify pneuma? Pneuma*, which Aristotle talks about so often, is a body in the sublunary sphere. At the same time, in this sphere, it is an analogue of the astral ether.[14] As far as I know, modern researchers have not addressed this question, but Aristotle does not explicitly discuss it either. Only once does he seem to allude to the problem when dealing with the question whether there is any place in the sphere of living beings where something perishable can be imperishable.[15] At first sight, this seems a totally eccentric question, but it becomes slightly less so when we consider that all living creatures in the sublunary sphere are mortal, despite being ensouled and therefore, according to the text of *Generation of Animals* II 3, 736b29–7a1, despite participating in "some body which is different from the so-called 'elements' and more divine than they are." For Aristotle, this warrants the question why all living beings, which are born thanks to their life-bearing *pneuma*, which is an analogue of the divine astral element, are doomed to die nonetheless. Aristotle cannot answer that death separates the immaterial soul from the material and perishable (visible) body, as Plato had claimed. For the souls of plants and the soul-parts of animals, but also the lower soul-parts of humans, are inextricably linked to an instrumental soul-body. This leads Aristotle to talk about a body that "has no opposite" and that he refers to as "the fire above" (τὸ πῦρ ἄνω) (*Long.* 3, 465b2–3). He goes on to argue that living creatures are not immortal, because although vital heat is not destroyed by water, it does have an "opposite" in another sense, and can be "extinguished." In my view, 'τὸ πῦρ ἄνω' there refers to vital heat, of which Aristotle has said in 6, 467a32 that it is present in the upper half of the human body.[16] If this is right,

---

14. Cf. *Gener. anim.* II 3, 736b29–7a7 and §10a below.

15. *De Longitudine et Brevitate Vitae* 2–3, with the question in 3, 465b1–3: ἆρ' ἔστιν οὗ ἄφθαρτον ἔσται τὸ φθαρτόν, οἷον τὸ πῦρ ἄνω, οὗ μή ἔστι τὸ ἐναντίον; Here Aristotle is talking in any case about a "fire" that is "above." *Cael.* II 2, 284b35 οἷον τὸ πῦρ ἄνω μόνον <κινεῖται> is about ordinary fire that moves upward.

16. *Long.* 6, 467a32–3: "and the warmth resides in the upper parts, and the cold in the lower [ἐν δὲ τῷ ἄνω τὸ θερμόν, καὶ τὸ ψυχρὸν ἐν τῷ κάτω]." See also Arist. *Resp.*15, 478a16: "the psychic fire [τὸ ψυχικὸν πῦρ]." *Gener. anim.* III 4, 755a20: "This is the handiwork of the soul-heat in the case of animals [δημιουργεῖ δὲ τοῦτο ἡ τοῦ ψυχικοῦ θερμοῦ φύσις ἐν τοῖς ζῴοις]" and *Hist. anim.* I 17, 496a4, which says that "the heart . . . lies above the lung [ἀνωτέρω τοῦ πλεύμονος]" and 496a17, where it is located "in the upper part of the chest" [ἐν τῷ ἄνω μέρει τοῦ στήθους]. On these places, see now also S. Zierlein, *Aristoteles, Historia Animalium Buch I und II, Übersetzt, Eingeleitet und Kommentiert* (Berlin: Akademie Verlag, 2013), 350. The fact that the source of vital heat (the heart) is situated in the upper part of the body explains why the lungs (which provide cooling) are also there.

it strongly suggests that *pneuma* corresponds to ether on the essential point that it cannot be grouped with the "opposites" (in the sense of the sublunary elements). However, this text has always been explained in a very different and, in my view, erroneous way. I therefore confine myself here to citing an earlier publication on this problem.[17] I will return to it in §§10b and 10k below.

On the other hand, Aristotle sees many things and bodies in the sublunary sphere that can have opposite properties. Such entities are always able to act on something else, but in turn suffer reactions from their environment.[18] The rule in this category is that anything that sets *physically* in motion is also moved itself.[19] That is to say, such entities set in motion while being (potentially) moved or in motion. They do this through "contact" (*thixis*).[20] But he immediately adds that not everything that sets in motion belongs to this category. "It is possible for a thing to cause motion, though it is itself incapable of being moved."[21] This setting in motion is presumably not purely physical.

c. A Metaphysical Principle Is the Origin of All Physical Motion: *Physics* VIII

In view of our discussion in the previous section, it is not surprising that the treatises of Aristotle, who is often called the founder of physics, regularly contain propositions that collide head-on with modern physics. A crucial thesis in this regard is that all motion in nature must be necessarily seen as caused by an indivisible principle without magnitude.[22] For in this way Aristotle grounds his entire physics in his metaphysics.

In this connnection, he asks: "Was there ever a becoming of motion . . . or are we to say that it . . . always was and ever will be? Is it in fact an immortal never failing property of things that are, a sort of life as it were to all naturally

---

17. A. P. Bos, "'Fire Above': The Relation of Soul to Its Instrumental Body in Aristotle's *De Longitudine et Brevitate Vitae 2–3*," Ancient Philosophy 22 (2002); 303–17; *The Soul and Its Instrumental Body* (2003), 183–209. My interpretation becomes less offensive if the work *De Spiritu* from the same *Parva Naturalia* collection can be accepted as authentically Aristotelian.

18. *Phys.* III 1, 201a23: "each of them will be capable at the same time of acting, and being acted upon [ἅπαν γὰρ ἔσται ἅμα ποιητικὸν καὶ παθητικόν]."

19. *Phys.* III 1, 201a23–4: "Hence, too, what effects motion as a natural agent can be moved [Ὥστε καὶ τὸ κινοῦν φυσικῶς κινητόν]."

20. *Phys.* III 2, 202a7; a8.

21. *Phys.* III 1, 201a27: ἔστι γάρ τι κινοῦν καὶ ἀκίνητον. See also VIII 5, 257b23: ἔτι οὐκ ἀνάγκη τὸ κινοῦν ἀντικινεῖσθαι.

22. *Phys.* VIII 6, 258b25; 10, 266a10: ἀμερές, 267a23: ἀμέγεθες.

constituted things?"[23] This motion, as the motion of all living beings, is always and universally goal-oriented.

This metaphysical principle of all motion in nature is therefore not just the cause of purely physical motion. As a metaphysical principle it can only be Intellect, in Aristotle's ontological scheme, and the motion sustained by the Power of this Principle can therefore be compared with what Anaxagoras said about the Intellect as the unmixed, pure principle of motion for all *"spermata."*[24]

It is therefore a goal-oriented motion, like that of an instrument used by a craftsman and like the motion transmitted by the begetter in all forms of reproduction. Precisely this shows once again how polyvalent the concept of "motion" is in Aristotle. For he states without hesitation that the principle of motion cannot have any potentiality for motion. This principle must exist entirely in act, just as the "motion" of reproduction can only have its beginning in the begetter, an adult specimen.[25]

His well-wrought argument in *Physics* VIII clearly shows how all the threads of his philosophy are drawn tight and interwoven here. For instance, all spontaneous, new kinetic impulses are possible only in living beings, such as animals and humans. These are therefore beings with a soul, that is to say, with a pneumatic soul-body controlled by an entelechy. But typical of Aristotle's anti-Platonist outlook on life is his insistence that spontaneity, impulsiveness, and the sudden transition from rest to motion in animals and humans are possible only *because they already possess life* and because of the vital dynamics of metabolism, respiration, and pulsation.[26] Aristotle rightly points out there that a human being who goes from rest to motion, or wakes from a deep sleep and sets to work, was not motionless like a corpse; even rest is a form of motion and this "coming into action" is possible only on the basis of processes that

---

23. *Phys.* VIII 1, 250b11–3: Πότερον δὲ γέγονέ ποτε κίνησις . . . ἤ . . . ἀεὶ ἦν καὶ ἀεὶ ἔσται, καὶ τοῦτ' ἀθάνατον καὶ ἄπαυστον ὑπάρχει τοῖς οὖσιν, οἷον ζωή τις οὖσα τοῖς φύσει συνεστῶσι πᾶσιν; (text H. Carteron vol. 2, 1956; trans. R. P. Hardie and R. K. Gaye, in J. Barnes [ed.], vol. 1).

24. *Phys.* VIII 5, 256b24–7: "So, too, Anaxagoras is right when he says that Mind is impassive and unmixed, since he makes it the principle of motion; for it could cause motion in this way only by being itself unmoved, and have control only by being unmixed [Διὸ καὶ Ἀναξαγόρας ὀρθῶς λέγει, τὸν νοῦν ἀπαθῆ φάσκων καὶ ἀμιγῆ εἶναι, ἐπειδήπερ κινήσεως ἀρχὴν αὐτὸν ποιεῖ εἶναι· οὕτω γὰρ ἂν μόνως κινοίη, ἀκίνητος ὤν, καὶ κρατοίη, ἀμιγὴς ὤν]." In *Anim.* I 2, 404a25–b6 and 405a13–9 Aristotle is less positive about Anaxagoras as regards the distinction between intellect and soul.

25. *Phys.* VIII 5, 257b10: "in general that which possesses the form begets [ὅλως γεννᾷ τὸ ἔχον τὸ εἶδος]."

26. See *Phys.* VIII 2, 253a7–21 and 6, 259b1–20. These texts rightly receive much attention in K. Corcilius and P. Gregoric, "Aristotle's Model of Animal Motion," 53 ff.

are *always* present and active in animals and man. "This, however, is false [that a living being is ever completely at rest]; for we observe that there is always some basic part of the animal in motion."²⁷ These "basic parts" thus react to the living being's environment.²⁸

Here Aristotle emphasizes again that the (voluntary) movement of muscles and sinews and limbs is a function anchored in the (involuntary) processes of metabolism and respiration. In 6, 259 b1–20 he clarifies his meaning: "There are other natural motions in animals, which they do not experience through their own agency, e.g. increase, decrease, and respiration."²⁹

This conclusion, that locomotion by human will or animal reaction to perception is always grounded in the underlying functions of metabolism together with reproduction,³⁰ fluid balance, and (in higher animals) respiration, had led Aristotle to attribute "life" and "soul" to plants and to see "the beginning" of life in the moment of fertilization and not in that of parturition. This was in fact the decisive reason why he dismissed Plato's psychology, but it also made him ask what principle was transmitted via the male seed in fertilization, the principle which from that moment governs the embryo's independent development. For this role, Aristotle introduced the (immaterial) soul as entelechy and as controlling/regulating factor of *pneuma* (i.e., the instrumental body of the soul), both of which are present in semen and subsequently in the embryo.³¹

At crucial places in Aristotle's work we encounter the distinction between (c) that which is moved; (b) that which sets in motion while being in motion itself, and (a) that which sets in motion but is not itself in motion.³² Wherever this distinction occurs, we are dealing with Aristotle's correction of Plato's doctrine of soul: his separation of the intellect or the guiding soul-principle as entelechy (a), from that which is the carrier of motion and conation (b) but is controlled by (a).

---

27. *Phys.* VIII 2, 253a11–2: Τοῦτο δ' ἐστὶ ψεῦδος. Ὁρῶμεν γὰρ ἀεί τι κινούμενον ἐν τῷ ζῴῳ τῶν συμφύτων.

28. *Phys.* VIII 2, 253a13; a16: "the environment" (τὸ περιέχον).

29. *Phys.* VIII 6, 259b8–9: ἔνεισι ἄλλαι κινήσεις φυσικαὶ τοῖς ζῴοις, ἃς οὐ κινοῦνται δι' αὐτῶν, οἷον αὔξησις φθίσις ἀναπνοή. In *Motu anim.* 11, Aristotle brings up the same distinction in his treatment of voluntary and involuntary movements (such as reflexes and the pulsation of blood). "Respiration" is ambivalent, in that we can vary it but not stop it.

30. Hence, Aristotle calls this function "the first" in *Anim.* II 4, 415a24. Cf. §3a above. It is the first function to be active in all living entities that come into being and pass away.

31. Cf. *Anim.* II 1, 412b25–7; *Gener. anim.* II 1, 735a4–22.

32. See *Anim.* III 10, 433b13–21; *Motu anim.* 10, 703a4–9; *Metaph.* Λ 7, 1072a21–b4.

d. Basic Parts that Always Move in a Living Being (*Physics* VIII 2 and 6)

A critical question remains to be asked about the passages from *Physics* VIII 2 and 6 discussed above. In chapter 6, Aristotle talks about increase and decrease and respiration as "natural motions" that are the precondition for locomotion. Yet in 2, 253a11–2 Aristotle spoke about processes of "basic parts" (τῶν συμφύτων) of the living being that are *always* present. However, respiration is not always present, but only starts after birth or after a chicken has hatched. A good while before respiration begins, there are already processes at work that enable the growth of the living being in the making, *and that also realize the formation of the lungs*!

Therefore, if we read in VIII 2, 253a11–12: "for we observe that there is always some basic part of the animal in motion," *then this cannot properly refer to the respiration* that Aristotle mentions in 6, 259b9.

What, then, did Aristotle mean by these "basic parts," of which he says in VIII 2, 253a12 that some part is always in motion? Really the only place where this is clearly explained is in the treatise *On the Life-Bearing Spirit* (*De Spiritu*), 4–5. The author shows there that *three* motions in the body of a living being need to be distinguished, viz. (1) the motion that supplies and assimilates the food; (2) pulsation, and (3) respiration.[33] He goes on to explain that (1) and (2) are present from fertilization, but (3) is not. For respiration only starts after birth.[34] So when Aristotle claims in *Physics* VIII 2, 253a11–2 that "some basic part of the living being is *always* in motion," he cannot be referring to the lungs that breathe. He cannot even be referring to the heart with its pulsation, because although the heart is the first "part" of the body to be formed, it does not yet exist at the moment of fertilization, since no part of the visible body is present in the male semen or the female menstrual fluid. The heart, too, must be formed as the first part by that which is the most basic component,[35] namely, *pneuma* (σύμφυτον πνεῦμα) under the guidance

---

33. *Spir.* 4, 482b14–6: "There are three movements of the air in the *artèria* [according to their theory], viz. respiration, pulsation, and thirdly the movement which supplies and assimilates the food [Ἐπεὶ δὲ τρεῖς αἱ κινήσεις τοῦ ἐν τῇ ἀρτηρίᾳ πνεύματος, ἀναπνοή, σφυγμός, τρίτη δ' ἡ τὴν τροφὴν ἐπάγουσα καὶ κατεργαζομένη]."

34. *Spir.* 5, 483a13–5: "For respiration only begins when separation has taken place from her who has borne the new living creature, and the supply and the food belong both to what is being formed and to what already exists [τὸ μὲν γὰρ ἀναπνεῖν ὅταν ἀπολυθῇ τῆς κυούσης, ἡ δ' ἐπιφορὰ καὶ ἡ τροφὴ καὶ ξυνισταμένου καὶ ξυνεστηκότος]."

35. I use the term *basic parts* here and not *innate components*, because Aristotle is emphatically talking about matters that are present before birth. Translations such as "innate" are therefore undesirable. Perhaps the *symphyton pneuma* could be best designated as a "sown" component. Etymologically speaking, "implanted" would also be attractive.

of its soul-principle. This is explained very precisely in *De Spiritu*, which is yet another reason to claim this work for Aristotle.

Aristotle restates this train of thought very clearly in *Physics* VIII 6, 259b14–6: "Therefore animals are not always in continuous motion by their own agency: it is something else that moves them, itself being in motion and changing as it comes into relation with each several thing that moves itself."[36] Aristotle is referring here to *pneuma* as that which reacts to perceptual images from outside and then conceives desire or aversion, fear or joy, and expands or contracts through these stimuli, and thus sets in motion the entire motor system of the living being.[37]

e. The Soul and Its Lever (*Physics* VIII 6)

But although *pneuma* sets in motion and is itself also set in motion in act, something else is the proper cause of the living being's self-motion, and this principle also moves itself, *but only accidentally*. This is the (immaterial) soul or entelechy, which Aristotle makes clear in *Physics* VIII 6, 259b16–8: "In all these (self-moving living beings) the first mover and cause of their self-motion is itself moved, though in an accidental sense."[38] The reason for this is that the soul changes its place, because the visible body that contains it moves,[39] like sailors on a ship. Aristotle had already demonstrated this distinction very plainly in *On the Soul* I 3, 405b31–6a12.[40] But Aristotle goes on to add seven

---

36. *Phys.* VIII 6, 259b14–6: διὸ οὐκ ἀεὶ κινοῦνται συνεχῶς ὑφ' αὐτῶν· ἄλλο γὰρ τὸ κινοῦν, αὐτὸ κινούμενον καὶ μεταβάλλον πρὸς ἕκαστον τῶν κινούντων ἑαυτά. See now S. Odzuck, *The Priority of Locomotion in Aristotle's Physics* (Göttingen: Vandenhoeck and Ruprecht, 2014), 53–67.

37. On this, the paper by T. K. Johansen, "The Soul as an Inner Principle of Change: The Basis of Aristotle's Psychological Naturalism," in: *Maieusis: Essays in Ancient Philosophy in Honour of Miles Burnyeat*, ed. D. Scott (Oxford: Oxford University Press, 2007), 276–99 is disappointing; see also the important article by K. Corcilius and P. Gregoric (2013). D. Blyth (2013), 49–51; L. A. Kosman (2013), 195–98. However, these authors identify the heart as the central sensitive organ and assign a subordinate role to *pneuma*.

38. *Phys.* VIII 6, 259b16–8: Ἐν πᾶσι δὲ τούτοις κινεῖται τὸ κινοῦν πρῶτον καὶ τὸ αἴτιον τοῦ αὐτὸ ἑαυτὸ κινεῖν ὑφ' αὑτοῦ, κατὰ συμβεβηκὸς μέντοι.

39. *Phys.* VIII 6, 259b18–9: "the body changes its place, so that that which is in the body and that moves itself by leverage, changes its place also [μεταβάλλει γὰρ τὸν τόπον τὸ σῶμα, ὥστε καὶ τὸ ἐν τῷ σώματι ὂν καὶ τὸ ἐν τῇ μοχλείᾳ κινοῦν ἑαυτό]."

40. Cf. *Anim.* I 3, 406a4–6: "But everything may be moved in two senses (directly and accidentally). We call movement accidental when a thing moves because it is in something which moves; for instance the sailors in a ship [Διχῶς δὲ κινουμένου παντός (ἢ γὰρ καθ' ἕτερον ἢ καθ' αὑτό· καθ' ἕτερον δὲ λέγομεν, ὅσα κινεῖται τῷ ἐν κινουμένῳ εἶναι, οἷον πλωτῆρες]." A reader from Antiquity familiar with Aristotle's *Eudemus* may have been reminded by this comparison of the splendid story about Odysseus, sleeping in the ship in which the Phaeacians took him to Ithaca.

words that have remained highly problematic for the traditional explanation of Aristotle's psychology. These are the words: καὶ τὸ ἐν τῇ μοχλείᾳ κινοῦν ἑαυτό, which can only be translated correctly by a sentence such as: "and that moves itself *by leverage*," in the sense of "moving itself by using a lever as instrument."

It is plain from H. Carteron's translation "en effet le corps change de lieu et par suite il en est de même pour l'automoteur, logé dans son corps comme dans le levier"[41] that he considers the visible body to be moved by the soul as self-moving principle. But this is a highly unusual and laborious mode of locomotion and completely fails to explain why the soul needs the visible body as a lever. The only possible interpretation is that the visible body is the lever of the soul in order for the soul to move itself. But Aristotle says constantly that the soul does not have a motion of its own.

Precisely in 259b15–20 it is obvious that Aristotle distinguishes two matters contained in the visible body, namely (1) a first mover that moves accidentally with the moving visible body, and (2) a moved mover that properly sets in motion the visible body and that is used by the soul (1) as a lever in order to move the visible body.[42] The soul uses this *pneuma* as its instrument/lever in order to propel arms and legs, and thus the entire visible body, through the levering *motion* (τῇ μοχλείᾳ) of this instrument.[43]

The "lever" plays an important role in the *Problemata Mechanica*. The title of that treatise might have been *On the Lever*, for with very few exceptions it explains all the mechanical questions discussed by reference to the principle of the lever. The treatise is generally attributed not to Aristotle himself, but to the peripatetic school, say 280 BC.[44]

---

41. H. Carteron, *Aristote, Physique, Texte Établi et Traduit* (Paris: Les Belles Lettres, vol. 1 (3e éd.) 1961; vol. 2 (2e éd.) 1956), vol. 2, 123. Likewise W. D. Ross, *Aristotle's Physics* (1936) 707. K. Corcilius and P. Gregoric (2013), 73, translate correctly "moving itself by leverage," but in their view Aristotle maintained "that animal bodies contain parts that exploit the leverage principle, so that the small mechanical impulse in the heart can produce large movements in the limbs." T. K. Johansen, *The Powers of Aristotle's Soul* (Oxford: Oxford University Press, 2012), 28–34 also has major problems here. D. Blyth (2013), 185–91 does not provide us with a convincing solution.

42. In *Physics* VIII 5, 256b14–5, Aristotle had emphatically formulated his well-known framework: "For there must be three things–the moved, the mover, and the instrument of motion [τρία γὰρ ἀνάγκη εἶναι, τό τε κινούμενον καὶ τὸ κινοῦν καὶ τὸ ᾧ κινεῖ]." See also *Anim.* III 10, 433b19 and *Motu anim.* 10.

43. Cf. A. P. Bos, *The Soul and Its Instrumental Body* (2003), 130–32.

44. Cf. A. G. Drachmann, T*he Mechanical Technology of Greek and Roman Antiquity. A Study of the Literary Sources* (Copenhagen: Munksgaard, 1963), 13.

f. The Power Emanating from the First Unmoved Mover

In *Physics* VIII 7, Aristotle emphasizes the role of the outer celestial sphere in the process of all generation and thus sidesteps his own objection to Plato: How can visible creatures come out of intelligible forms?

If the Power proceeding from the Intellect manifests itself in nature as a goal-oriented, form-realizing motion, then we understand straightaway why Aristotle always talks about nature in teleological terms. He can regard the soul as an entelechy because it is connected with the Intellect as source by means of a "golden rope" or "golden chain" in the chain reaction of vital phenomena.

An important aspect of *Physics* VIII 10 will be discussed in §8c. Here we emphasize that this chapter constantly talks about the Power (*Dynamis*) of the Prime Unmoved Principle of all motion. Time and again, Aristotle refutes propositions by predecessors or by fictitious opponents who wanted to identify a cosmic agency as the cause of all dynamics and life in reality, and he then shows that such an agency can never possess the "unlimited *dynamis*" that is required.[45] The Prime Unmoved Principle does have the ability to exercise such a Power. This Power is the only connection that ties the Origin, God, the divine Intellect, to the cosmos. This, too, follows from Aristotle's correction of Plato's doctrine of soul. The fundamental principle of Aristotle's philosophy is not a perfect Soul, but an Intellect. Aristotle denied to this principle any activity of the will and any conation or any creative activity and providence. Like Plato, however, he did assign to the supreme divine Principle the government of the cosmos, and interpreted the order and functionality in the cosmos as a consequence of the connection that ties the cosmos to its Leader, just as reins are the connection between a charioteer and his pair of horses.

g. The Soul as Principle of Motion in *Motion of Animals*

Aristotle opens his study *Motion of Animals* with the statement that he has already demonstrated in a different context that motions can be reduced in the first place to that which moves itself, and this in turn to an agency that is

---

45. Cf. *Physics* VIII 10, 266a24–5: "in no case is it possible for an infinite working power to reside in a finite magnitude [ὅλως οὐκ ἐνδέχεται ἐν πεπερασμένῳ μεγέθει ἄπειρον εἶναι δύναμιν]." Likewise, 266b5–6; 266b25–7; 267b12. Cf. I. M. Bodnár, "Movers and Elemental Motions in Aristotle," *Oxford Studies in Ancient Philosophy* 15 (1997): 113–17.

unmoved.[46] It is generally assumed that he is referring here to his expositions in *Physics* VIII, which I have described in §5c above. These were specifically focused on the everlasting motion of the outer celestial sphere and on the principle of this motion. In *Motion of Animals*, Aristotle follows the same starting points.

He offers interesting arguments about an arm that moves and can only do so because the upper arm on which it hinges does not move; and about how a ship can be pushed along from the waterside because it is possible to push off against the earth.

In chapter 3, Aristotle then inquires into the cause of motion of the entire celestial sphere. Can such a principle be characterized as unmoved and not forming part of the celestial sphere that is moved?[47] Aristotle repeatedly speaks there about the *dynamis*[48] that is needed to set or keep the globe in motion. In passing, Aristotle rejects proposals to the effect that the poles of the axis of the celestial sphere possess a power to move (699a20), or that the figure of the sky-supporting Atlas (standing on the pillars of Hercules [Gibraltar]) could be interpreted as a pivot which, through its power, causes the celestial body to turn.

At the end of chapter 4 he then reaches the conclusion discussed in §2e above: there must be an unmoved principle of motion that is situated outside the heavenly sphere and does not form part of it.[49] The great canopy of heaven is solely safeguarded against disintegration if it depends on such a principle.[50]

On the decisive point, Aristotle avoids saying how the transcendent, Unmoved Principle, which does not possess parts, can transmit the Power that

---

46. *Motu anim.* 1, 698a7–10: "Now we determined before . . . that the origin of other movements is that which moves itself, that the origin of this is unmoved, and that the first mover must necessarily be unmoved [Ὅτι μὲν οὖν ἀρχὴ τῶν ἄλλων κινήσεων τὸ αὐτὸ ἑαυτὸ κινοῦν, τούτου δὲ τὸ ἀκίνητον, καὶ ὅτι τὸ πρῶτον κινοῦν ἀναγκαῖον ἀκίνητον εἶναι, διώρισται πρότερον]" (text M. C. Nussbaum 1978).

47. *Motu anim.* 3, 699a12–4. Of a globe or sphere that moves, no part is nonmoving (699a17–9). Cf. also *Mu.* 2, 391b14–2a9.

48. Cf. *Motu anim.* 3, 699a21; a34; b8; b16. But the term *ischys* (ἰσχύς) is also used regularly: 699a33; a34; b5; b6; b16.

49. *Motu anim.* 4, 699b32–700a2.

50. *Motu anim.* 4, 700a3–6: "Herein lies the solution of the problem we mentioned some time before, the possibility or impossibility of the dissolution of the composition of the heavens, given that they depend on an unmoved origin [ὅθεν λύεται καὶ ἡ πάλαι λεχθεῖσα ἀπορία, πότερον ἐνδέχεται ἢ οὐκ ἐνδέχεται διαλυθῆναι τὴν τοῦ οὐρανοῦ σύστασιν, εἰ ἐξ ἀκινήτου ἤρτηται ἀρχῆς]" (M. C. Nussbaum). The passage suggests the image of iron rings coming apart when the magnet that kept them together is removed. It is due to this cohesive Power of the one Principle of Origin that reality is not a set of individual Lego blocks, or a hotch-potch, like a bad tragedy.

sustains the motion of the heavenly sphere.⁵¹ However, we should properly consider that, in Aristotle's view, *noèta* set something in motion by means of *orexis* for it.⁵²

The contact should therefore be seen as taking place in the *dianoia* of living beings (the celestial gods). The *dynamis* that proceeds from God as nonphysical transcendent being cannot be a purely physical *dynamis*. God's Working Power acts on the outer celestial sphere, but the latter consists of the divine element ether and is structurally ensouled. And the soul of the outer celestial sphere is a soul of the highest quality of life and therefore also has an instrumental body of the highest quality. This should prevent us from thinking in modern physicalist or mechanist terms here. Rather we will have to speak of an "intellectualist vitalism."

However, in chapter 6 Aristotle continues with the question how a living being is able to move: "It remains to consider how the soul moves the body, and what the origin is of an animal's motion."⁵³ To identify the soul here as the principle of locomotion, as Plato had argued in the *Phaedrus*, is incorrect, because Aristotle has expressly denied any form of motion to the soul in *On the Soul* I 3, as we have seen in the foregoing.⁵⁴

On the basis of his expositions in *On the Soul* he concludes: "Now we see that the movers of the animal are reasoning and *phantasia* and choice and wish and appetite. And all of these can be reduced to thought and desire."⁵⁵

This is a crucial point, also in connection with what Aristotle argues in *Motion of Animals* 10 and in *On the Soul* III 10. For there he constantly distances

---

51. See the criticial analysis in D. Lefebvre, "La Critique du Mythe d'Atlas *DMA*, 3, 699a27–b11," in *Aristote et le Mouvement des Animaux. Dix Études sur le* De Motu Animalium, ed. A. Laks and M. Rashed (Villeneuve d'Ascq: Presses Universitaires du Septentrion, 2004), 115–36.

52. Cf. *Metaph.* Λ 7, 1072a26: "And the object of desire and the object of thought move in this way, they move without being moved [κινεῖ δὲ ὧδε τὸ ὀρεκτὸν καὶ τὸ νοητόν· κινεῖ οὐ κινούμενα]." But see also *Motu anim.* 10 and ch. 4 above.

53. *Motu anim.* 6, 700b9–11: λοιπόν ἐστι θεωρῆσαι πῶς ἡ ψυχὴ κινεῖ τὸ σῶμα, καὶ τίς ἀρχὴ τῆς τοῦ ζῴου κινήσεως.

54. This is strongly reaffirmed by K. Corcilius and P. Gregoric (*art.* 2013).

55. *Motu anim.* 6, 700b17–9: ὁρῶμεν δὲ τὰ κινοῦντα τὸ ζῷον διάνοιαν καὶ φαντασίαν καὶ προαίρεσιν καὶ βούλησιν καὶ ἐπιθυμίαν. ταῦτα δὲ πάντα ἀνάγεται εἰς νοῦν καὶ ὄρεξιν and 700b23–5: "So that the first mover is the object of desire and also of thought; not, however, every object of thought, but the end in the sphere of things that can be done [ὥστε κινεῖ πρῶτον τὸ ὀρεκτὸν καὶ διανοητόν. οὐ πᾶν δὲ τὸ διανοητόν, ἀλλὰ τὸ τῶν πρακτῶν τέλος]" and 6, 701a4–6: "For the animal moves and progresses in virtue of desire or choice, when some alteration has taken place in accordance with sense-perception or *phantasia* [κινεῖται γὰρ καὶ πορεύεται τὸ ζῷον ὀρέξει ἢ προαιρέσει, ἀλλοιωθέντος τινὸς κατὰ τὴν αἴσθησιν ἢ τὴν φαντασίαν]."

himself from Plato's doctrine of soul by asserting that *phantasia* (imagination) is a matter of the sensitive soul, which records images of perceived data, and *nous* ("understanding," in this case, because it involves plans and projects that lead to action) is a matter of the rational soul-function. A perceptual image or a rational plan is therefore the trigger for action. But this action itself is not a matter of the soul (which is immaterial), but of the instrumental body with which the soul is connected. Aristotle states this explicitly both in *On the Soul* III 10, 433b19–20 and in *Motion of Animals* 10, 703a5–6.[56] So, according to Aristotle, ideas and images have an impact on the pneumatic soul-body of a human or an animal, because they pull a lever, so to speak, that activates the power of the mechanism of the soul-body. It is the motion of *pneuma* that is catalyzed by a mental or perceptual image, and naturally this impact does not affect just any ordinary elementary body, but only the soul-body: ether and (in the sublunary sphere) *pneuma*.

Thus, we find again that Aristotle presents the action of the unmoved mover as something that through its controlling power, via a kind of remote trigger, prompts the soul-body to perform a task of its own, just as a magnet uses its power to move iron rings purposefully, and a constructor activates an automaton through the power of a single cord that is wound up.[57]

h. Unmoved Mover and Moved Mover in Living Beings

While Aristotle therefore regards "the object of striving" and "the object of thought" as principles of motion, he distinguishes them from "willing and that which wills" and "striving and that which strives." These are "moved movers,"[58] which, according to Aristotle, must be something material.[59] This is because they

---

56. In *Motu anim.*7, 701b15 we should also read *pneuma* according to O. Primavesi. Cf. §10g below.

57. It may well be here that Aristotle associated the name of the "Titans" with "stretching," "extending," and thus linked the winding mechanism of the cosmos to the "Titans," who were "bound" by Zeus with the bond of the fine-material body, ether, and to "emotions" and all the "stress" these cause. Cf. Plutarch, *De Facie in Orbe Lunae* 942A: "the Titanic emotions and soul-movements are a kind of winding up [εἶναι δ' ἀνάτασιν τὰ τιτανικὰ πάθη καὶ κινήματα τῆς ψυχῆς]" (ed. H. F. Cherniss [1957]). In the *Politicus*, Plato had also assigned a role to the Titan Kronos as "winder up" of the cosmic system (see §9h below).

58. *Motu anim.* 6, 700b35: "desire and the faculty of desire impart movement while being themselves moved [ἡ δ' ὄρεξις καὶ τὸ ὀρεκτικὸν κινούμενον κινεῖ]." See also 10, 703a5: "desire is the middle, which imparts movement being moved [ἐστὶν ἡ ὄρεξις τὸ μέσον, ὃ κινεῖ κινούμενον]." For "will," cf. 700b17–9, which we quoted above.

59. *Motu anim.* 10, 703a5: "But in living bodies there must be some body of this kind [ἐν δὲ τοῖς ἐμψύχοις σώμασι δεῖ τι εἶναι σῶμα τοιοῦτον]." The entire work *Motion of Animals*

are a material substrate of the soul's guiding principle. They are material and physical, but at the same time psychically characterized as ἔμψυχος οὐσία and as ἔμψυχος θερμότης and σῶμα ὀργανικόν of an entelechy. In Aristotle's view, natural bodies primarily serve to give shape to the goal of an entelechy-principle.

In chapter 10, 703a11 it is clear that, for mortal living beings, this material substrate is "the implanted *pneuma*" (τὸ σύμφυτον πνεῦμα), which reacts to the guiding power of the unmoved principle of motion of the living being (10, 703a11–6).[60] The sharp distinction between the ordinary, sublunary elements and the divine ether plus its analogue *pneuma* should lead us to see Aristotle less as a modern physicalist and more as the one who introduced a special soul-body as intermediary between the world of the intellect and thought on the one hand and the lifeless bodies on the other. There is no reason to call Aristotle a "hylozoist." But certainly he is a "vitalist."

This also means that the concepts of "motion" and "power" are used by Aristotle in a very extended sense. We could also say that these terms are ambivalent, because they are used both for the "setting in motion" of the heavenly sphere by the transcendent, metaphysical Intellect and for the physical motion of pushing along a ship with a pole, etc.

Aristotle strongly emphasizes that all human and animal doings start with an act of perception or an act of thought, that is, with an activity of the soul as (immaterial) entelechy. This is essential to his criticism of Plato. The guiding principle (the entelechy) is the "motor" of all activity of the soul-body, which then moves the arms and legs of the visible body. However, man is not always conscious of the complexity of this operation, because human action, too, is often unreflected, "automatic."

i. The Intellect of the Supreme God and the Will of the Celestial Gods

In this way, Aristotle drew a sharp distinction between pure theoretical thought and all mental activity aimed at making and producing something. Although all human craft is directed at an object of thought as model, a product is only

---

is uninterpretable if the hylomorphistic psychology of Alexander of Aphrodisias is read into it. This led F. J. C. J. Nuyens, *Ontwikkelingsmomenten in de Zielkunde van Aristoteles. Een Historisch-Philosophische Studie* (Nijmegen/Utrecht: Dekker & Van de Vegt, 1939) to situate the work in a different ("instrumentalist") period of Aristotle's activity. But this does not really help us to gain a proper understanding of Aristotle's intentions.

60. This point is neglected in the valuable article by K. Corcilius and P. Gregoric (2013), which we have repeatedly mentioned.

formed when mental orientation to a model is accompanied by the *will* of the craftsman to realize the product in a concrete form. Aristotle says emphatically in *On the Soul* III 10 that this will cannot be understood as a "part" of the soul (as entelechy and immaterial principle), but that it must have a somatic constitution!

Whereas in Plato the Demiurge is focused on the reality of the Ideas, but is also the agency that *willed* to make the cosmos as similar as possible to the intelligible model,[61] Aristotle conceived of the divine Intellect as self-contained, theoretical thought. Yet he maintains the notion of the absolute dependence of the entire cosmos on God[62] by speaking about the life-generating Power emanating from God, which is clothed in a fine-material body, ether. Ether, as the material agency that represents the *will*, is aimed at producing a perfect and ordered cosmos, which is realized in matter consisting of the four coarse-material sublunary elements.

Thus, Aristotle's theology carried through the separation that he had introduced on every level, that between "intellect" and "soul." He presented as the absolute Origin of all things the purely divine theoretical Intellect, but as directly dependent on him the divine creative and productive thought of the ethereal heavenly beings, who represent a creative (artisanal) thought.

j. The Winding Mechanism as a Model for the Human Motor System

In *Motion of Animals* 7, Aristotle draws a comparison between human functioning and the action of a winding mechanism or *automaton*. This is highly significant, because we will see in §6b below that he uses the same model for the phenomenon of fertilization and in §10e below that the entire cosmos is presented in *On the Cosmos* as a winding mechanism.[63] In all three cases, ether

---

61. This means that we can call Plato's doctrine of principles "dialectical." His *Parmenides* is the most notable example of this. But it also means that Aristotle has a reasonable case when he criticizes Plato for denying the Demiurge the position of being the absolute unchanging foundation of all things. The Demiurge is the "principle of origin" for the cosmos (*Tim.* 28b6–7), but can only be so *after* introducing order into a matter that is *first* without order (Arist. *Cael.* I 10, 279b31–80a10).

62. Indeed, in *On Coming-to-be and Passing-away* II 10, 336b31–2, he identifies God as the orchestrator of the perfection of the cosmos!

63. For this theme, cf. also W. Spoerri, "Inkommensurabilität, Automaten und Philosophisches Staunen im Alpha der 'Metaphysik,'" in *Aristoteles, Werk und Wirkung. Paul Moraux gewidmet*, Bd. 1, ed. J. Wiesner (Berlin: W. de Gruyter, 1985), 262 ff. Regrettably, Spoerri ignores the text about a winding mechanism in *On the Cosmos* 6. See also J. de Groot, "*Dynamis* and the Science of Mechanics: Aristotle on Animal Motion," *Journal of the History of Philosophy* 46 (2008): 52 ff.

or *pneuma* (as the instrumental body of the soul) is put forward as the receiver of the Power of the transcendent Principle and as the agency that has stored this Power in itself, just as the winding mechanism also possesses power, even when it is completely at rest.

k. Summary of the Results So Far

In chapter 2, we saw that Aristotle boldly declares that everything in the cosmos exists and functions only by virtue of God. But we found it difficult to explain how he conceived of this dependence.

Next, we established in chapter 3 that Aristotle was equally convinced that everything in the cosmos has a "desire" for being and for the divine, including entities that will never attain it and do not even have knowledge of it. It was obvious here that Aristotle held this primal longing for divinity to be present in all that lives and has soul. According to Aristotle (and Plato too), this primal desire for divinity is the driving force behind (the perpetuation of mortality through) fertilization.

In chapter 5, we saw that Aristotle assigns to God the role of being the source of all life and motion through the Working Power (*Dynamis*) that proceeds from him. We underlined there that this cannot be a purely physical power, because God is extraneous to purely physical reality and because this Power mainly has a guiding and controlling effect on rational, ensouled beings, that is to say, on the astral heavenly beings. They are considered by Aristotle to be responsible for the process of generation and decay of mortal living beings.

Time and again, we have been led to conclude that Aristotle criticized Plato for his vagueness about the relation of intellect and soul, or theoretical thought and practical understanding. As a result, Aristotle came to embrace a different theology from Plato's, but also a different approach to the generation of living creatures and to the presence of soul in plants and trees. (In Aristotle's view, living creatures do not come into being because an immortal soul is breathed into them at birth, but because female menstrual fluid is fertilized—by male semen in most cases, as I will discuss in chapter 6.)

6

Reproduction

A Power Transmitted by the Begetter

Aristotle developed an important new view on the generation of new living beings. For him, as we will see more fully in chapter 7, the moment when a new life begins is not at birth, but before that, when fertilization takes place. The entire embryonic phase is the first, clearly distinguishable stage in the life of a new living being. That is why Aristotle had to pay much more attention to the role of semen and seed in the process of life being transferred. It also explains why he was so fascinated by the fact that the semen of a cat will never produce anything but a young cat and a grain of barley will never produce a wheat plant or rye stalk. An extra complication here was that although this life-principle is present in plant seed, it only becomes vitally active when the environmental conditions of temperature and moistness are suitable. The same factors play a role in the spontaneous generation of simple living beings.[1] However, Aristotle says emphatically of semen too that it is the "instrument of the soul,"[2] and contains soul, but it is not an ensouled living

---

1. In *Gen. anim.* III 11, Aristotle describes spontaneous generation as the begetting of simple living beings through the spontaneous formation of a soul-principle in *pneuma* that has gained a condition comparable with semen. Cf. §10d below.

2. *Anim.* II 4, 415b7; cf. *Gener. anim.* I 22, 730b19–23. Cf. A. P. Bos, "A Lost Sentence on Seed as Instrument of the Soul in Aristotle, *On the Soul* II 4, 415b7," *Hermes* 138 (2010): 276–87. The sentence in question is: "what persists is not the individual itself, but something in its image. <It is> identical not numerically but specifically. <For that reason the seed of animals and plants is an instrument of their soul>. It is the soul that is the cause and first principle of the living body"

creature. Hence, Aristotle considers it necessary in his definition of "soul" to talk about a "natural body" that "potentially" possesses life. For this he uses a comparison with a winding mechanism that already "possesses power" when it is wound up, but has not yet been set in motion.[3] In this way Aristotle took an important new step in relation to Plato, who talked about the soul as the principle of motion and of perpetual motion, but had no inkling of anything like "germinative dormancy" or "spontaneous generation."

Because he introduces such a new insight here, we will have to look closely at how he presents "reproduction," the generation of new life. He describes the process of reproduction in his great pivotal study *Generation of Animals* as the transmission (via semen, but in some small insects without any role for semen) of a working power (*dynamis*) from the father specimen to the menstrual fluid of the mother specimen.[4]

In his introductory chapter, he presents the entire book *Generation of Animals* as a discussion on the parts of the body that enable the reproductive process and on the cause of motion in the sphere of living nature. He suggests that he has said enough about the operation of the other three "causes"

(trans. W. S. Hett (1936), 85–87, with changes). The Greek text of 415b6–8 in the edition of A. Jannone and E. Barbotin (1966), 39, if we add the extra sentence, reads: καὶ διαμένει οὐκ αὐτὸ ἀλλ' οἷον αὐτό. Ἀριθμῷ μὲν οὐχ ἕν, εἴδει δ' ἕν <ἐστι. Διόπερ τὸ σπέρμα τῶν ζῴων καὶ φυτῶν ὄργανόν ἐστι τῆς ψυχῆς>. Ἔστι δὲ ἡ ψυχὴ τοῦ ζῶντος σώματος αἰτία καὶ ἀρχή, etc. The same idea is formulated in *Generation of Animals* I 22, 730b19–22: "In like manner, in the male of animals which emit semen, nature uses the semen as a tool and as possessing motion in actuality, just as tools are used in the products of any art [ὁμοίως δὲ καὶ ἡ φύσις ἡ ἐν τῷ ἄρρενι τῶν σπέρμα προϊεμένων χρῆται τῷ σπέρματι ὡς ὀργάνῳ καὶ ἔχοντι κίνησιν ἐνεργείᾳ, ὥσπερ ἐν τοῖς κατὰ τέχνην γιγνομένοις τὰ ὄργανα κινεῖται]" (ed. and trans. J. Barnes (1984), vol. 1, 1134). Consequently, Aristotle is also saying in *Anim.* II 1, 412b27 that semen and seed possess soul, including the instrumental body of the soul, and that therefore the soul with its instrumental body, which Aristotle talks about in his definition, is already present at this stage. So this instrumental body cannot possibly be the visible body of man or animal, as Alexander of Aphrodisias thought and scholars after him. Cf. §7b and §15a below. Precisely in view of the crucial importance that Aristotle was the first (!) to attribute to semen in the process of transferring life, it is remarkable that the passage in question has disappeared in a number of the manuscripts.

3. *Gener. anim.* II 1, 734b9–11. See §6b below.

4. Cf. J. G. Lennox, "Teleology, Change, and Aristotle's Theory of Spontaneous Generation," *Journal of the History of Philosophy* 20 (1982): 221; D. M. Balme, "Ἄνθρωπος ἄνθρωπον γεννᾷ. Human is Generated by Human" (1990), 23–24. See also the important section on Aristotle in J. Needham, *A History of Embryology* (1934; 2nd ed. Cambridge: Cambridge University Press, 1959), 37–60.

in the preceding *Parts of Animals*, but not yet about the "efficient cause."[5] By the "efficient cause" or "principle of motion" Aristotle means the male partner in the reproductive process.[6] The male partner uses his semen and the *pneuma* it contains to transfer the life-principle to the menstrual fluid of the female partner. The male partner is a living being made up of a form-principle and material components, but he only transfers a form-principle (a life-generating working power) on the material substrate of the menstrual fluid.[7]

Aristotle states emphatically that fertilization does not involve a mixture of seminal fluid with menstrual fluid, but the transmission of a vitalizing and goal-orientated structuring power.[8] However, this power in all living creatures is a force controlled from the beginning by a soul as entelechy. It contains the *logos* or the structural plan of the new living creature to be generated. This power is always carrying out a "work" of the soul by means of the soul's instrumental body. The crucial difference between this power and the forces that unensouled bodies exert on each other lies in its goal-oriented nature. In his biological writings Aristotle always talks on the one hand about matters that are organized in accordance with "the best," and on the other about matters that are as they are "by necessity."[9] This represents the division in the cosmos

---

5. D. M. Balme, *Aristotle's De Partibus Animalium I and De Generatione Animalium I* (1972), 127 reacts to this by remarking: "It is wrong to say that *P.A.* has dealt with only three of the four causes," and, "the writer probably means that nutritive soul is the source of both generation and growth." Balme has failed to recognize that "the efficient cause" refers specifically to the male principle and the *pneuma* that transmits the procreative power via the semen.

6. Cf. *Gener. anim.* II 1, 732a3–11; text H. J. Drossaart Lulofs (1965).

7. Aristotle's doctrine of reproduction comes very close to what he says about the life-generating Power that proceeds from God to the ether of the celestial sphere. See §§9a and 9b below.

8. *Gener. anim.* I 21, 729b4–8: "or does the physical part of the semen have no share nor lot in the business, only the *dynamis* and movement contained in it? This, anyway, is the active and efficient ingredient; whereas the ingredient which gets set and given shape is the remnant of the residue in the female animal [ἢ τὸ μὲν σῶμα οὐθὲν κοινωνεῖ τοῦ σπέρματος, ἡ δ' ἐν αὐτῷ δύναμις καὶ κίνησις· αὕτη μὲν γὰρ ἐστιν ἡ ποιοῦσα, τὸ δὲ συνιστάμενον καὶ λαμβάνον τὴν μορφὴν τὸ τοῦ ἐν τῇ θήλει περιττώματος λοιπόν]" (A. L. Peck [1942], 113). In II 3, 737a7–12 Aristotle emphasizes that the moist substance of semen disappears completely through evaporation. See in particular a11–2: "This physical part of the semen, being fluid and watery, dissolves and evaporates [τὸ σῶμα τῆς γονῆς διαλύεται καὶ πνευματοῦται φύσιν ἔχον ὑγρὰν καὶ ὑδατώδη]."

9. Cf. *Part. anim.* I 1, 642a1–3: "We have, then, these two causes before us, to wit, the 'Final' cause, and also Necessity, for many things come into being owing to Necessity [Εἰσὶν ἄρα δύ' αἰτίαι αὗται, τό θ' οὗ ἕνεκα καὶ τὸ ἐξ ἀνάγκης· πολλὰ γὰρ γίνεται, ὅτι ἀνάγκη]" (A. L. Peck [1937], 75). Cf. *Gener. anim.* II 1, 731b20–4.

of everything that is governed by the Vital Power that proceeds from God as Origin, and the necessary powers that remain where life ends.[10]

The big question is: How can Aristotle, who sees motion as a matter of elementary bodies (and their composites), and who presents God and the intellect and the soul-as-entelechy as nonmaterial, still talk about God as the (Unmoved) Principle of Motion and about the soul as the Principle of Motion? Aristotle's answer was that God is the unmoved source of working power just as a magnet is an unmoved source of a moving power, and that in analogous fashion the soul (the entelechy) is the unmoved source of the moving power of its instrumental body. L. A. Kosman, in his study on Aristotle's doctrine of Being, reduces all vital activity in the cosmos to the "activity of Being."[11] We need to observe that Aristotle rejected Plato's doctrine of the soul as "principle of motion," opting instead for the eternal activity (*energeia*) of divine thought (*theôrein*) as origin for the motion (*kinèsis*) of the ether of the astral beings and the *pneuma* (as analogue of ether) in mortal creatures, through the divine *energeia* manifesting itself in the receptive natural body whose motion reveals three-dimensionally the governance of the divine principle, just as the power (*dynamis*) of a winding mechanism executes the plan (the *logos*) of its constructor when the mechanism is running. The *energeia* of divine thought is not itself a *motion*, but a source of motion, as a kind of *kinèsis akinètos*.[12]

---

10. P.-M. Morel, *De la Matière à l'Action. Aristote et le Problème du Vivant* (Paris: J. Vrin, 2007), 42 n. 1 points out one important objection to the view of those who see *pneuma* as the "instrumental body" of the soul: "si le problème posé par la doctrine [sc. traditionelle, hylémorphique] est de savoir comment un principe incorporel (l'âme) peut mouvoir un corps, il faut alors admettre qu'il n'est que déplacé et transposé au rapport entre l'âme et le sc. [= souffle connaturel]." However, this point may be rebutted by stating that the soul does not "move" the *pneuma* or "*souffle connaturel*," but guides it. And this requires that *pneuma* be akin to the soul, adapted to the soul and suited to the soul. Cf. A. P. Bos, "The 'Instrumental Body' of the Soul in Aristotle's Ethics and Biology," *Elenchos* 27 (2006): 35–72. None of the four sublunary elements qualifies for this. Motion (*kinèsis*) is proper to *pneuma* as a natural body characterized by desire (*orexis*) for the perpetuity and divinity of the supreme Principle. The "guidance" of this motion is not itself a motion, but a power (*dynamis*). See further §§10.1 and 10.o below.

11. L. A. Kosman, *The Activity of Being. An Essay on Aristotle's Ontology* (Cambridge: Harvard University Press, 2013).

12. It is confusing to say, "In such cases, he suggests, the males does [*sic*] not actually transfer any semen, but only a potential," as A. M. Leroi, *The Lagoon* (2014), 191 has it. He continues on p. 192: "Aristotle's aim is clear: he is trying to show that the power of semen to direct development rests not on the transmission of seminal matter itself, but on something else. . . . To solve this problem Aristotle once again invokes that mysterious stuff, *pneuma*."

a. What Determines the Difference between Male and Female?

Aristotle is the philosopher of the genesis of life. His work *Generation of Animals* can be seen as the center of his philosophical reflections. For him, the genesis of life includes all variations of life in the world of flowers and plants, where new specimens arise through fertilization, but also through slipping, grafting, and the dividing of flower bulbs. In the sphere of living creatures, he distinguishes between species that multiply through sexual reproduction with or without semen and creatures that come into being through spontaneous generation.

Aristotle tried to understand all these generative forms in nature as variants of one and the same principle: the transfer of a goal-oriented motion by means of a "power," a goal-oriented motion that operates on material suitable to be formed into a new specimen.[13] According to Aristotle, this does not involve the mixture of two material contributions (one from the father specimen and one from the mother specimen), but the transfer of a goal-oriented controlling motion to a passive (but suitable, appropriate,[14] corresponding) material, which has a natural motion of its own.[15]

In all higher species of living creatures the goal-oriented power in the process of fertilization is transferred via semen. However, according to Aristotle, fertilization may also take place when a female specimen introduces a part of her body into the male and receives the goal-oriented motion via this prolonged contact. He devotes all of *Generation of Animals* I 21 to this crucial fact. Yet the thrust of this chapter only becomes truly clear when we realize that Aristotle

---

[13]. It is important to stress here that Aristotle has good reason to distinguish between "power" (δύναμις) and "motion" (κίνησις). Fertilization is the transmission of a guiding "power" to a "motion" of the menstrual fluid, so that this motion becomes a goal-orientated motion that can lead to the entire process of generation and existence of a new specimen.

[14]. Cf. E. Lesky, *Die Zeugungs- und Vererbungslehren der Antike und ihr Nachwirken* (Wiesbaden: Steiner, 1950), 125 ff. The necessity for the instrumental body to be appropriate, corresponding to the capacities of the user, is emphasized by Aristotle in *Anim.* I 3, 407b13–27. Aristotle thus also explains why copulation can only succeed between specimens of the same kind.

[15]. However, there is a problem here for Aristotle in the difference between the reproduction of animals and humans on the one hand and the multiplication of plants on the other. Fertilization always involves the transmission of a guiding power from a living and adult male specimen to the menstrual fluid of a female. The multiplication of plants takes place through seeds that are long dormant, until they germinate owing to an increase in the environmental temperature. Cf. *Gener. anim.* III 11, 762b14: "the seasonal heat present in their environment [ἡ τῆς ὥρας ἐν τῷ περιέχοντι θερμότης]." Cf. also *Probl.* X 13.

saw this "fact" *in relation to his theological views*.¹⁶ For although, according to Aristotle, God does not produce semen, he can be viewed as the Generator of Power (as he is in fact presented in *On the Cosmos*; see chapter 9 below).¹⁷

Indeed, we can only really understand the entire book I of *Generation of Animals* if we see the connections with Aristotle's ontology and theology, his talk about "form" and "matter" and about an unmoved principle of moving power. While we are used to talking about X chromosomes and Y chromosomes brought together by the partners in a fertilization process to form a new embryo with new genetic properties, Aristotle takes great pains to eradicate such a view. The contribution of the male differs structurally from that of the female.¹⁸ The female does not produce "seed" (729a20–1). The male does produce "seed" in many cases, but the important factor here is not the material substance of this semen, but only the working power (*dynamis*) that is thus transferred to the female's contribution. This power acts on the female's contribution to the process of copulation (just as a craftsman uses his tools to work his material) in order to produce all the parts of the new specimen from available food drawn from the environment. The result of the copulation is a living *kyèma*, as the composite substance¹⁹ of an *eidos*-bearing soul-principle (as entelechy) and an instrumental body that consists of the pneumatic residue of the female's menstrual fluid.

Aristotle often summarizes this insight in the slogan "A human being begets a human being." He does not say: "A man begets a male child." The begetter can pass on life, which results in a new specimen of the same species. But its sex is not thus determined. The soul as entelechy is bearer of the *eidos* of the species, but is neither female nor masculine. Both boys and girls are bearers of the *eidos* "human being." Sexual differentiation does not follow from the specific form, but from the quality of the *pneuma* that is the instrument of the soul!²⁰

---

16. E. Diamond, *Mortal Imitations of Divine Life* (2015), 79, speaks about "the ontological and theological significance of reproduction"! In his theological conception Plato had comparably expressed his reflections on generation in terms of craft.

17. The evangelist Luke talks about the divine generation of Jesus in the remarkable words: "the power of the Most High will overshadow you [δύναμις ὑψίστου ἐπισκιάσει σοι]" (1:35).

18. Cf. R. Mayhew, *The Female in Aristotle's Biology* (Chicago: University of Chicago Press, 2004), 114.

19. Cf. *Anim.* II 1, 412a15–6.

20. We saw earlier that, for Plato, the difference in quality of life of the souls on earth is determined by the quality of their knowledge of the Ideas. Cf. *Phaedrus* 248c-e. In *Timaeus* 90e Plato notes that the soul of a man who has led a cowardly and unjust life is converted (*metephyonto*) into a woman—as if these men had no mother. Cf. S. Broadie, "Why no Platonistic Ideas of Artefacts?" (2007).

Aristotle proves his ideas in I 21, 729b22–30a28 by referring to the behavior of certain insects. The males among these do not have seminal tubes and do not ejaculate in the body of the female, but instead the female makes contact with the male through a part of her body.[21] Through his vital heat and working power the male then has a vitalizing effect on the part of the female that contains the residue for reproduction (I 16, 721a13–4; 18, 723b19–24 and 21, 729b22–8).

In *Generation of Animals* II 1, Aristotle will go on to argue that higher animals have separate female and male specimens (732a3–11). This allows him to defend the "separateness" of the Origin of all vital power from everything that is begotten by this power. He presents here a special slant on the role of semen, because in his theology he only wants to talk about God as the source of Life through the Power proceeding from him. God produces life-generating Power that, clothed in ether (as instrumental body), operates throughout the cosmos as *logos spermatikos*.

From the world of birds and fish Aristotle believes that he can also derive the most convincing arguments[22] for his idea—crucial to all his philosophizing—that reproduction is a matter of transferring a power or motion, and not a substance (*Gener. anim.* I 21, 729b33–30a23). He gives the examples there of birds: "Supposing a hen bird is in process of producing wind-eggs, and then that she is trodden by the cock while the egg is still completely yellow and has not yet started to whiten: the result is that the eggs are not wind-eggs but fertile ones. And supposing the hen has been trodden by another cock while the egg is still yellow, then the whole brood of chickens when hatched out takes after the second cock" (trans. A. L. Peck, 1942, 117). According to Aristotle, specialist breeders apply this method deliberately and to particular ends.[23]

For Aristotle, life is a lifelong goal-oriented dynamics which *in a natural way* keeps a production process going that is wholly comparable with a purposeful *artisanal* production process.

b. Fertilization as the Activation of a Winding Mechanism (*Gener. anim.* II 1)

In *Generation of Animals* II 1, 733b23, Aristotle goes on to discuss what he calls "a major problem" (ἀπορία πλείων), that is: How do the new specimens

---

21. This point is insufficiently recognized in the article by L. A. Kosman, "Male and Female in Aristotle's *Generation of Animals*," in *Being, Nature, and Life in Aristotle. Essays in Honor of Allan Gotthelf*, ed. J. G. Lennox; R. Bolton (Cambridge: Cambridge University Press, 2010), 147–67.
22. Cf. *Gener. anim.* I 21, 729b33: μέγιστον δὲ σημεῖον.
23. This could raise the question whether Aristotle somehow used the Orphic theme of the World Egg in his cosmology.

of a plant or animal species issue from the semen of a father specimen? What is the efficient cause of this process?

First, he argues that it must be something in the semen and that it must be ensouled. Second, he notes that the parts of the new specimen are not produced simultaneously but *in succession*. How is this possible if the begetter (the carrier of the goal-oriented principle of motion) no longer has contact with the embryo?

The solution offered by Aristotle is the idea of *"passing on" a power*, as in the case (of a magnet, which passes on its power to rings which themselves then pass on this power; and as in the case) of an automaton, which *transmits* the power of the winding mechanism from one part to the next, so that such a winding mechanism seems as it were a living thing, because it executes goal-oriented movements on its own without an external cause of movement being manifest.

> And it is possible that one thing moves a second one, and the second a third, and that the process should be like that of the miraculous automata: the parts of these automata, even while at rest, have in them somehow or other a working power, and when some external agency sets the first part in movement, then immediately the adjacent part becomes active. The cases then are parallel; just as with the automaton in one way it is the external agency which is causing the thing's movement—viz. not by being in contact with it anywhere now, but by having at one time been in contact with it, so too that from which the semen originally came, or that which fashioned the semen [causes the embryo's movement], viz. not by being in contact with it still, but by having once been in contact with it at some point; in another way it is the movement resident within [which causes it to move], just as the activity of building causes the house to get built. (trans. A. L. Peck 1942, with changes)[24]

---

24. Cf. R. Ferwerda, *Aristoteles, Over Voortplanting, Vertaald, Ingeleid en van Aantekeningen Voorzien* (Groningen: Historische Uitgeverij, 2005), 80. Greek text: *Gener. anim.* II 1, 734b9–17: ἐνδέχεται δὲ τόδε μὲν τόδε κινῆσαι, τόδε δὲ τόδε, καὶ εἶναι οἷον τὰ αὐτόματα τῶν θαυμάτων. ἔχοντα γάρ πως ὑπάρχει δύναμιν τὰ μόρια ἠρεμοῦντα· ὧν τὸ πρῶτον ὅταν τι κινήσῃ τῶν ἔξωθεν εὐθὺς τὸ ἐχόμενον γίγνεται ἐνεργείᾳ, ὥσπερ οὖν ἐν τοῖς αὐτομάτοις τρόπον μέν τινα ἐκεῖνο κινεῖ οὐχ ἁπτόμενον νῦν οὐθενός, ἁψάμενον μέντοι· ὁμοίως δὲ καὶ ἀφ' οὗ τὸ σπέρμα ἢ τὸ ποιῆσαν τὸ σπέρμα, ἁψάμενον μέν τινος, οὐχ ἁπτόμενον δ' ἔτι· τρόπον δέ τινα ἡ ἐνοῦσα κίνησις ὥσπερ ἡ οἰκοδόμησις τὴν οἰκίαν. Cf. D. M. Balme, "Ἄνθρωπος ἄνθρωπον γεννᾷ. Human is Generated by Human' (1990), 23.

Reproduction is therefore the transmission of a special kind of power or motion, which is characterized as a "structure-plan-carrying" or "form-realizing" motion.[25] This motion is comparable with the motion of "house-building," which is the realization of architectural craft.[26]

But how can a structural plan be connected with a motion? In the sphere of human action this is only possible when a being with a practical intellect draws up a structural plan and summons *the will* to make it concrete, give it material shape. Aristotle took the entire natural process to be a process in which structural plans are materialized, not by a Demiurge or a craftsman, but by goal-orienting principles or "souls" as entelechies,[27] which are inextricably bound up with a body. However, the vital, productive power of these souls must have its Origin in the universal Power and Control Center of the transcendent Intellect.

We would tend to formulate the distinction between God as self-contained Intellect and his Power as the difference between God's thinking and his will. However, "will" is a highly anthropomorphic concept, and readily calls up associations with "needing something" and with changeability and caprice. Aristotle wants to exclude this at all costs, because the highest Principle must be absolutely unchanging. But he did distinguish two facets of God's existence. The Intellect is the masculine side of God. His Power must be interpreted as distinct from it, and as the feminine side of God so to speak. This is Aristotle's alternative to Plato's Demiurge from the *Timaeus*. We can conclude here that the criticism of Plato's Demiurge and his artisanal creation of the cosmos, and Aristotle's preference for the biotic metaphor of causing the cosmos as a form of "begetting," increased interest in the role of the male and the female partner in reproduction. Indeed, we could see Aristotle's hylomorphism as a byproduct of this change of focus.

His view of the divine design of the entire cosmos is therefore a view in which the entire order in the cosmos is "rational" and comes about κατὰ νοῦν—according to the principles of the Good and the Intellect—without

---

25. *Gener. anim.* II 1, 732a4; 735a1: "the movement of the instruments employed, which contain the *logos* of the art [ἡ κίνησις ἡ τῶν ὀργάνων ἔχουσα λόγον [τὸν] τῆς τέχνης]." There is a clear relationship here with the doctrine of Philo of Alexandria, who presented all form-principles in the cosmos as *dynameis* proceeding from the Logos of God.

26. II 1, 734b17–οἰκοδόμησις. Cf. *Gener. anim.* I 22, 730b6–8: "and to put it in general terms, the working or treatment of any material, and the ultimate movement which acts upon it, is in cases close by the material, e.g. the location of the activity of house-building is in the houses which are being built [ὅλως πᾶσα ἡ ἐργασία καὶ ἡ κίνησις ἡ ἐσχάτη πρὸς τῇ ὕλῃ οἷον ἡ οἰκοδόμησις ἐν τοῖς οἰκοδομουμένοις]."

27. On the problem of the meaning of *entelecheia* in Aristotle, see §10q below.

requiring an appraisal and choice of (one or more) alternatives.[28] The image presented in *On the Cosmos* 6, 400b13–31, that everything goes in the cosmos just as everything happens in the state (*polis*) by virtue of the Law,[29] is extraordinarily appropriate.

c. Transfer of Qualities in Reproduction

In this context, we also need to look at Aristotle's argument in *Generation of Animals* IV 3 on the transfer of qualities from one generation to the other. Aristotle sees the inheritance of characteristics as a phenomenon resulting from the power that is transmitted during fertilization. If this power is strong enough, the new specimen resembles his (male) begetter; if this is not the case, a female specimen is generated or a specimen with traits of a grandfather or a grandmother.[30]

In his cosmology, Aristotle uses the scheme of "closer" and "farther away" in relation to the Origin (see chapters 2 above and 9 below), and he employs the same scheme in explaining the 'likeness' between the begetter and his offspring.[31] According to Aristotle, just as we may sometimes recognize in a great-grandchild a quality of a great-grandfather, so we may recognize in the life of a spontaneously generated mussel the vital power of which God is the only source and begetter.

If the power of the begetter is too weak, it makes way for the powers of members of a previous generation, the grandfather or possibly the grand-

---

28. Cf. *Physics* II 8, 199a20–32, where Aristotle argues that ants and spiders, without possessing intellectual activity, make their webs and build their nests just as efficiently as if they were constructed by beings with biological expertise. This view was also formulated by Plotinus in his treatise "On Providence," *Enneads* III 2 [47], 1, 20–26. Cf. P. Boot, *Plotinus, Over Voorzienigheid. Enneade III 2-3 [47–48]. Inleiding—Commentaar—Essays* (Amsterdam: VU-Uitgeverij, 1984), 45–61.

29. Cf. G. Betegh and P. Gregoric, "Multiple Analogy in Ps. Aristotle, *De Mundo* 6," *Classical Quarterly* 64 (2014): 585–86. We find the same considerations in *Metaph.* Λ 10, 1075a11–25.

30. Cf. *Gener. anim.* IV 3, 767b20–3: "So that if this movement gains the mastery it will make a male and not a female, and a male which takes after its father, not after its mother; if however it fails to gain the mastery, whatever be the 'faculty' in respect of which it has not gained the mastery, in that 'faculty' it makes the offspring deficient [ὥστε κρατούσης μὲν ἄρρεν τε ποιήσει καὶ οὐ θῆλυ, καὶ ἐοικὸς τῷ γεννῶντι ἀλλ' οὐ τῇ μητρί· μὴ κρατῆσαν δὲ, καθ' ὁποίαν ἂν μὴ κρατήσῃ δύναμιν, τὴν ἔλλειψιν ποιεῖ κατ' αὐτήν]."

31. *Gener. anim.* IV 3, 767b27: "of the characteristics belonging to the generating parent, some are more closely, some more remotely his, qua procreator [τὰ μὲν ἐγγύτερον τὰ δὲ πορρώτερον ὑπάρχει τῷ γεννῶντι καθὸ γεννητικόν]."

mother.³² Aristotle makes a striking distinction here between "a deviation" and the phenomenon of "relapse." In the case of "deviation," the result switches to the opposite sex: the new specimen becomes female. If the fertilizing power relapses, powers of the grandfather or great-grandfather manifest themselves in the final product.³³

---

32. *Gener. anim.* IV 3, 768a14–6: "Now when it departs from type, it changes over into its opposites; the movements which are fashioning the embryo relapse, they relapse into those which stand quite near them [μεταβάλλει μὲν οὖν ἐξιστάμενον πρὸς τὰ ἀντικείμενα, λύονται δὲ αἱ κινήσεις αἱ δημιουργοῦσαι εἰς τὰς ἐγγύς]." Cf. A. M. Leroi, *The Lagoon* (2014), 216: "every little girl represents a failure in her father's semen"; see also M. Boylan, *The Origins of Ancient Greek Science: Blood—A Philosophical Study* (New York: Routledge, 2015), 68: "the normal or natural result of copulation is a male child. However, Aristotle cannot ignore the fact that some children take after their mother. The response is that females are 'regular' defects that occur."

33. *Gener. anim.* IV 3, 768a14–8b1. For a more extensive discussion of the problem of the relation between the male and the female factor, see §10.1 below.

7

Life Begins at the Moment of Fertilization

What was the greatest point of difference between Aristotle and his teacher Plato? One answer to this question, which was already given in Antiquity, is that their different view of "soul" predominated.[1] Plato had devoted to this

---

[1]. Cf. Ps.-Hippolytus, *Refutatio Omnium Haeresium* I 20, 3–4: "And overall he agrees with Plato on most matters, with the exception of the doctrine of soul. For according to Plato the soul is immortal, but according to Aristotle it survives and also disappears then by merging into the fifth element, which he assumes to exist alongside the other four—Fire and Earth and Water and Air—<but> more subtle, like *pneuma* [καὶ σχεδὸν τὰ πλεῖστα τῷ Πλάτωνι σύμφωνός ἐστιν πλὴν τοῦ περὶ ψυχῆς δόγματος· ὁ μὲν γὰρ Πλάτων ἀθάνατον, ὁ δὲ Ἀριστοτέλης ἐπιδιαμένειν < * > καὶ μετὰ ταῦτα καὶ ταύτην ἐναφανίζεσθαι τῷ πέμπτῳ σώματι, ὃ ὑποτίθεται εἶναι [μετὰ] τῶν ἄλλων τεσσάρων—τοῦ τε πυρὸς καὶ τῆς γῆς καὶ τοῦ ὕδατος καὶ τοῦ ἀέρος—λεπτότερον, οἷον πνεῦμα]" (ed. M. Marcovich 1986; see now also M. D. Litwa, *Refutation of All Heresies. Translated with Introduction and Notes* (Atlanta: SBL Press, 2015). Marcovich has proposed to delete the second μετά. In that case the translation would read: "which he assumes to be more subtle than the other four—. . .—, like *pneuma*." In both readings there is a relation between ether and *pneuma*, inasmuch as they are both fine-material. This relation is underscored by the proposition that *pneuma* dissolves into ether. This is possible only if *pneuma* is actually ether but in a mixed form. Once the mixture has been reversed, *pneuma* can once again show its original nature. (This text by Ps.-Hippolytus is not usually regarded as serious information about Aristotle's psychology. But it is hard to imagine why the author would attribute this view to Aristotle if he had no source material for it. Naturally Ps.-Hippolytus is wrong to report as Aristotelian the view that the soul is a *sôma* more subtle than the sublunary elements. This seems a Stoicizing interpretation. Aristotle will always have said that the soul itself is an entelechy, and not a body but something of a body (as in *Anim*. II 2, 414a20–1). At the same time, we need to recognize that *pneuma* in Aristotle is the agency by means of which psychic functions are realized. Ps.-Hippolytus's information is therefore incomplete in that he does not talk about the entelechy. But he does know about it, as we can infer from his statements in *Refutatio* VII 24, 1–2 about the Son of the Great World Archon in the doctrine of the Gnostic Basilides. This Son directs the Great Archon, just as the

theme his *Phaedo* and important parts of his *Phaedrus, Politicus* and *Timaeus*; Aristotle his dialogue *Eudemus*, which we know only from testimonies and fragments, and his lecture treatise *On the Soul*. To the question "What is a soul?" they gave completely disparate answers. Plato said, among other things: the soul is not material, but it *is* the principle of locomotion and can therefore set in motion bodies that do not possess motion by themselves.[2] Another task of the soul is "to take care" of everything that does not possess soul.[3] Aristotle gave a formulation that was almost a definition: "the soul is the first entelechy of a natural body which is *organikon*."[4] Yet he, too, maintained that the soul is nonmaterial.

They also gave very different answers to the question: "When is a body ensouled?"; and to the questions: "Do all living creatures have the same kind of soul? What is the cause of the differences in vital quality and capacity of humans and animals (and—in Aristotle—of plants)?"[5]

---

entelecheia uses its instrumental body according to Aristotle's definition of the soul. Plato talked about the soul's "fall" from its high celestial glory, in which it contemplated the Ideas, to an earthly sphere of transience. Aristotle distinguished between an Entelechy free of all corporeality and entelechies which as soul-principles had a guiding and organizing role in their instrumental body. Just as Platonists after Aristotle (starting with Xenocrates—cf. D. Thiel, *Die Philosophie des Xenokrates im Kontext der Alten Akademie* [München/Leipzig: K.G. Saur, 2006]) came to distinguish between a metacosmic Intellect and a World Soul or World Logos as the totality of all Ideas, which ensured that images of these eternal Ideas were realized throughout the visible cosmos, so Aristotle placed between the highest, divine Principle and the visible cosmos a level of entelechies (as *eidos*-bearing principles) and their instrumental bodies. It makes sense to see Aristotle's alternative to Plato's doctrine of Ideas as the necessary impulse for the Middle Platonist doctrine of the "Ideas in the divine Logos or Soul." In book VII Ps.-Hippolytus outlines the view of the Gnostic Basilides, whom he sees as a follower of Aristotle and not of Jesus Christ. To Basilides he attributed the position that the creation of the world was "the deposition of a World Seed"(!) by the highest God. See also Cicero, *De Natura Deorum* I 13, 33 = Arist. *Philos.* fr. 26 Ross; 25,1 Gigon: "multa turbat a magistro [Platone] uno dissentiens."

2. Plato, *Phaedrus* 245c7–9.

3. Cf. Pl. *Phaedr.* 246b6: "Soul, considered collectively, has the care of all that which is soulless [ψυχὴ πᾶσα παντὸς ἐπιμελεῖται τοῦ ἀψύχου]."

4. *Anim.* II 1, 412b5–6: ἐντελέχεια ἡ πρώτη σώματος φυσικοῦ ὀργανικοῦ (text A. Jannone and E. Barbotin 1966). Cf. 412a27–8: "the first entelechy of a natural body potentially possessing life [ἐντελέχεια ἡ πρώτη σώματος φυσικοῦ δυνάμει ζωὴν ἔχοντος]." In Aristotle's argument, the "usefulness" of the "natural body" witnesses to a much more positive view of the physical than Plato's outlook.

5. Plato is prepared to admit that plants also "participate in life" and that they should therefore rightly be called *zôia* ("living creatures"). But whereas humans and animals possess the same kind of soul (more or less degenerated), he believes that plants and trees possess only the "third soul-part" (*Tim.* 76e7–7c5) and do not possess locomotion. On the problems that this poses for Plato's doctrine of soul, see A. D. Carpenter, "Embodied Intelligent (?) Souls: Plants in Plato's *Timaeus*," *Phronesis* 55 (2010): 281–303.

Aristotle fully explains two points of his criticism in Book I (the "*Prolegomena*") of *On the Soul*. First, he formulates his objections to Plato's tenet that the soul, as the principle of motion, possesses motion and causes motion in all living creatures.[6] This leads him to conclude that the soul itself cannot possess motion, and that at most it moves with the motion of its vehicle or vessel,[7] which is accidental to the soul itself. Secondly, he opposes Plato's view that the soul enters a random body, as if the soul can accommodate itself to any random body.[8] This criticism also implies criticism of Plato's doctrine of reincarnation and transmigration. In this view, the soul of a human being who has lived below human standards may reincarnate as the soul of a woman and even as the soul of an animal. The problem here is that an evil human being never begets an animal, but that according to Plato he may reenter the world in an animal begotten by another living creature. For Plato, the measure of knowledge possessed by the soul determines the soul's quality of life in a body. This sojourn in a body is therefore always a form of punishment (*timôria*), but is also intended to "rehabilitate" the soul in a subsequent existence.[9]

Aristoteles counters that the soul presides over a specifically appropriate instrumental natural body that possesses a motion of its own. The big question, next, is what kind of natural body can possess such a motion of its own and can follow, as an instrument, the instructions of the soul as governing principle.[10] For a modern researcher, the question here is also in what way

---

6. *Anim.* I 3, 405b31–7b12.

7. Or its "lever," as we saw in *Physics* VIII 6 (§5e).

8. Cf. *Anim.* I 3, 407b13–26; II 2, 414a25–7. See also A. P. Bos, *The Soul and its Instrumental Body* (2003), 47–68.

9. This is already the purport of the "secret doctrine" to which Plato refers in *Phaedo* 62b2–9. This doctrine is usually assumed to be "Orphic." Cf. Plato, *Cratylus* 400c, where the same doctrine is attributed to "the followers of Orpheus." Cf. H. S. Long, *A Study of the Doctrine of Metempsychosis in Greece from Pythagoras to Plato* (PhD diss., Princeton University, 1948); R. Hackforth, *Plato's Phaedo, Translated, with Introduction and Commentary* (Cambridge: Cambridge University Press, 1955), 38. The soul's entry at the first breath after birth, which Aristotle, *Anim.* I 5, 410b27–30 ascribes to Orphic hymns, should therefore be seen as the beginning of the soul's sojourn in its institution for rehabilitation. See now R. G. Edmonds, *Redefining Ancient Orphism. A Study in Greek Religion* (Cambridge: Cambridge University Press, 2013).

10. His answer to this was: it is the astral element, ether, but in commixture with the sublunary elementary bodies, in varying degrees of purity, and referred to by Aristotle as *pneuma*. See A. P. Bos, "*Pneuma* as Quintessence of Aristotle's Philosophy," *Hermes* 141 (2013): 417–33. It is impossible that Aristotle took this to mean the entire, visible body of a living human being, animal or plant, as G. Heinemann, "*Sôma Organikon.* (Aristoteles, *De anima* 412b5–6)" recently argued in a contribution to *Organismus. Die Erklärung des Lebendigen*, ed. G. Toepfer and F. Michelini (Freiburg i.B.: Verlag Karl Alber, 2015). Thus also T. K. Johansen, *The Powers of Aristotle's Soul* (Oxford: Oxford University Press, 2012). On this, see more extensively chapters 12–14 below.

Aristotle's alternative took into account his previously expressed criticism of Plato's position.

a. Plato: The Soul Comes 'from Outside' into an Earthly Body at the Moment of Birth

Plato maintained that the World Soul was immaterial and moved perpetually and perfectly in a circular course; the World Body, consisting of fire, air, water, and earth, was built into it and was set and kept in motion by the World Soul.[11] The immortal, rational souls of the living creatures that are born were made by the Demiurge in a lower quality than the World Soul and then disseminated[12] over the planets as the "Instruments [*organa*] of Time," thence ending up in sublunary living creatures. The entry of a soul in such an earthly body with its digestive and perceptive processes had negative effects on the purity and perfection of the soul's circular course, which was thereby seriously disturbed.[13]

The question is: When do such imperfect souls end up in a sublunary living creature? Plato does not explicitly state this anywhere. However, he is

---

11. Plato, *Timaeus* 36d8–e5. The consequences of this connection of the World Soul with the World Body are unclear. Aristotle also criticizes this theory in *Cael.* II 1, 284a28–35: Plato makes the World Soul comparable with the unfortunate wheel-bound Ixion, because it perpetually moves the element Fire in a circular course, though this is not the natural motion of Fire. See also *Anim.* I 3, 407b3–5. In *Phaedrus* 245d8–e1 Plato observes that the motion of the World Soul prevents heaven and earth from colliding: "otherwise all the heavens and all the earth must fall in ruin and stop [ἢ πάντα τε οὐρανὸν πᾶσάν τε γῆν εἰς ἓν συμπεσοῦσαν στῆναι]." This led Aristotle to compare Plato's World Soul with the figure of the titanic Atlas, who shoulders the celestial globe and revolves it like a terrestrial axis. Cf. *Motu anim.* 3, 699a27–b11; *Cael.* II 1, 284a18–23. On this, see D. Lefebvre, "La Critique du Mythe d'Atlas *DMA*, 3, 699a27–b11" (2004), 115–36.

12. Cf. *Tim.* 41c8: σπείρας . . . παραδώσω and 42d4: ἔσπειρεν. The Demiurge is presented here as the soul-semen donor, while the male parent is presented in 90e ff. as the producer of body-semen.

13. Plato, *Tim.* 43a4–44d2. There is of course the problem of how Plato exactly conceived of the relation between the World Soul and the souls of individual living creatures. Plotinus saw a serious problem here and devoted three treatises to it (*Enneads* IV 3–5). His solution was that all soul is one and a part of the Soul as hypostasis, and that the World Soul and the souls of individual living creatures should be regarded as "sisters," differentiated only by the body in which they live. On this, cf. W. Helleman-Elgersma, *Soul-Sisters. A Commentary on* Enneads *IV 3 [27], 1–8 of Plotinus* (Amsterdam: Rodopi, 1980). There is also the problem of how a soul, if it is essential for it to move in a circular course, can remain a soul if its courses are disturbed. (The same problem occurs in Aristotle, when he asserts that *pneuma* [in the sublunary world] is an analogue of ether, which moves perpetually in a circular course.)

not likely to have connected the entry of the divine, immortal soul with the transfer of male semen. Nor does he link soul and semen anywhere.[14] He must have assumed that the independent functioning of a new living creature does not begin until the moment when this living creature starts to breathe, that is, immediately after birth.[15] The immortal soul, which has witnessed the supracelestial region and afterward traveled through the celestial spheres,[16] therefore enters the mortal body of a man "from outside,"[17] and in subsequent incarnations the body of a *woman* or animal. For Plato, the quality of the soul's knowledge and the extent to which it has contemplated the Ideas is decisive for the quality of its earthly existence,[18] but also for the quality and the organization of the visible body that it enters. How this correlation comes

---

14. In Pl. *Tim.* 73b1 ff. Plato does posit a special relationship between soul and marrow, with which he considers brain and semen to be connected. Cf. P. M. M. Geurts, *De Erfelijkheid in de Oudere Grieksche Wetenschap* (Nijmegen: Dekker & Van de Vegt, 1941), 75–79.

15. In *Anim.* I 2, 405b28–9, Aristotle observes that some of his predecessors took "the soul" to be related to "the cold," on account of the cooling that results from respiration: "those who identify it with cold maintain that soul is so called after the cooling process associated with respiration [οἱ δὲ τὸ ψυχρόν, διὰ τὴν ἀναπνοὴν καὶ τὴν κατάψυξιν καλεῖσθαι ψυχήν]" (W. S. Hett). In any case, the Atomists posited a necessary connection between life and respiration: 404a9–10 "Hence they consider also that respiration is the essential condition of life [Διὸ καὶ τοῦ ζῆν ὅρον εἶναι τὴν ἀναπνοήν]." This connection also seems to be indicated by Pl. *Tim.* 91d4–5: [and thereafter by bringing them to the light of the day accomplish the birth of the living creature [καὶ μετὰ τοῦτο εἰς φῶς ἀγαγόντες ζῴων ἀποτελέσωσι γένεσιν]." This implies that the embryo's movement in the mother's womb cannot be caused by the embryo's own soul. Yet, in *Laws* VII 789a ff., Plato does pay attention to the importance of prenatal care. In the controversial work *De Spiritu* the author attributes to a certain "Aristogenes" the view that respiration is the basis for the life and nutrition of a living being. In A. P. Bos and R. Ferwerda (2008), we argue that this view was held by Plato in the *Timaeus* and that the name "Aristogenes" refers to "the son begotten by Ariston," that is, Plato (op. cit. 23; 72).

16. Did the soul receive astral integuments there from the celestial gods in whose retinue it had travelled through the heavens? Cf. Plato, *Phaedrus* 246c4–7a7.

17. Cf. Plato, *Phaedrus* 248c5: βαρυνθεῖσα δὲ πτερορρυήσῃ τε καὶ ἐπὶ τὴν γῆν πέσῃ, as if there is a fixed correlation between the birth of new animals and humans and the availability of new souls from the air. Arist. *Anim.* I 5, 410b27–9 criticizes this view, which he knows from the Orphic poems, arguing that it fails to explain the life of fish and plants. His remark in I 1, 402b3 that contemporary discussions on the soul mainly concern the human soul certainly applies to Plato as well.

18. Plato never makes a connection with the moral quality of the begetter. Moreover, given his flirtation with the notion of the soul's reincarnation and transmigration, Plato does not recognize without exception the rule that "a human being begets a human being and a plant a plant." For him, crime and punishment are a matter of one and the same soul, extending even to a third and fourth generation.

about remains disappointingly vague in Plato's dialogues.[19] It is this problem which Aristotle critically targets. His proposition "A human being begets a human being," which occurs no fewer than fifteen times in his writings,[20] establishes a firm correlation between the soul-principle of a certain species of living creature and the instrumental body with which it is inextricably bound up. This thesis makes it impossible for a human soul to be matched with an animal soul-body. Aristotle's proposition that "only the intellect enters man 'from outside' "[21] is a correlate of this and a rejection of Plato's theory that the soul enters an embryo "from outside." The "Pythagorean myths" about the descent of a random soul into a random body, which Aristotle sharply rejects in *On the Soul* I 3, 407b22, should probably be identified with the mythical fabrications of the Pythagorean Timaeus of Locri, who according to Aristotle tells nonsensical stories about the soul's transmigration in Plato's eponymous dialogue.[22] Aristotle is constantly in discussion with contemporaries, some of whom had an affinity with Pythagoras. But Aristotle did not enter into a debate with Pythagoras himself.[23]

We should also consider this when he cites the doctrine of the Orphic hymns in *On the Soul* I 5, 410b27–11a2, according to which the soul enters a living being thanks to respiration, and is conveyed by the wind. As we observed above, it is likely that he regarded Plato as a supporter of this doctrine.

---

19. The simple postulate that the Ideas are "examples" for concrete living entities and that these concrete entities "share" in these "examples" is dismissed as "empty words and poetical metaphors" by Aristotle in *Metaph*. A 9, 991a20–22. It fails to answer the question: "For what is it that works, looking to the Ideas? [τί γὰρ ἐστι τὸ ἐργαζόμενον πρὸς τὰς ἰδέας ἀποβλέπον]"; 991a22–3. Aristotle's answer to this question was: ether is the agency that produces the sublunary cosmos, directed by the entelechy which God himself is; *pneuma* is the agency that produces every sublunary living creature, directed by the entelechy of the soul-principle in question, which is an analogue of the entelechy of ether. Cf. *Anim*. II 4, 416a13; *Spir*. 9, 485a28: "the vital heat which is the efficient principle in bodies [τὸ θερμὸν τὸ ἐργαζόμενον ἐν τοῖς σώμασι]." *Gener. anim*. II 3, 736a27; IV 1, 765b16; 4, 772a32; V 8, 789b8: "in fact it is probable that Nature makes the majority of her products by means of *pneuma* [ἐπεὶ καὶ τὸ τῷ πνεύματι ἐργάζεσθαι τὰ πολλὰ εἰκὸς ὡς ὀργάνῳ]." More on this in §10.1 below.

20. Cf. *Phys*. II 1, 193b6–7 and b12; 2, 194b13; 7, 198a24–7; III 2, 202a11–2; *Gener. corr*. II 6, 333b7–14; *Part. anim*. I 1, 640a25–6; II 1, 646a33; *Gener. anim*. II 1, 735a20–22; *Metaph*. Z 7, 1032a24–5; 8, 1033b30–2; Θ 8, 1049b24–6; Λ 3, 1070a5–8; 1070a26–8; 4, 1070b32–4; N 5, 1092a15–7; *Eudem. Eth*. II 6, 1222b15–8 and H. Bonitz, *Index Aristotelicus* 59b40 ff. E. Frank, "Das Problem des Lebens bei Hegel und Aristoteles," in *Deutsche Vierteljahrschrift für Literaturwissenschaft und Geistesgeschichte* 5 (1927): 616, with n. 2.

21. *Gener. anim*. II 3, 736b27–8. This passage is directly followed by the famous text on the correlation between the soul's working power and its pneumatic body, a text that is discussed below in §10a.

22. Plato, *Tim*. 41e–42d2; 90e6–92c1.

23. For more on Aristotle and the Pythagoreans, see §10h below.

We should assume the same for *On the Soul* I 5, 411a18–20, where Aristotle says: "so they are compelled to say that the soul also is homogeneous with its parts, if living creatures become possessed of soul because some part of the surrounding air is cut off and enclosed in them."[24] Aristotle implies there that if humans and animals are ensouled by inhaling the breath of life from outside, this life itself must also be a living being, and that it is strange that humans and animals possess very different capacities when they are formed, though they have inhaled the same breath of life.

b. Aristotle: There Is Life before Birth

Aristotle took a very different direction from Plato. It led him to posit that only the intellect comes "from outside";[25] the soul does not come "from outside," for it is always connected with a special material body and can only be transferred in combination with this fine-material pneumatic body. He had in fact become convinced that there is already life before birth. *For Aristotle, the beginning of the existence of a new living creature does not coincide with the moment of birth, but with the moment of fertilization.*[26] The soul is conjoined with its (instrumental) body from the moment of fertilization, because the soul is already present in animal semen and in the seeds of a tree or plant. Aristotle says as much in the chapter where he clarifies his definition of soul: *On the Soul* II 1, 412b25–6: "that which has the capacity to live is not the

---

24. *On the Soul* I 5, 411a18–20: ὥστ' ἀναγκαῖον αὐτοῖς λέγειν καὶ τὴν ψυχὴν ὁμοειδῆ τοῖς μορίοις εἶναι, εἰ τῷ ἀπολαμβάνειν τι τοῦ περιέχοντος ἐν τοῖς ζῴοις ἔμψυχα ζῷα γίνεται (trans. W. S. Hett [1936]). Cf. R. Polansky (2007), 135.

25. *Gener. anim.* II 3, 736b27: "It remains, then, that intellect alone enters in, as an additional factor, from outside, and that it alone is divine [λείπεται δὴ τὸν νοῦν μόνον θύραθεν ἐπεισιέναι καὶ θεῖον εἶναι μόνον]." Cf. also *Anim.* I 4, 408b19: "But the intellect seems to enter into us as an independent substance, and to be imperishable [Ὁ δὲ νοῦς ἔοικεν ἐγγίνεσθαι οὐσία τις οὖσα, καὶ οὐ φθείρεσθαι]."

26. Highly significant in this regard is *Anim.* II 5, 417b16–8: "In sentient creatures the first change is caused by the begetter and from the moment of conception the living thing is, in respect of sensation, at the stage which corresponds to the possession of knowledge [Τοῦ δ' αἰσθητικοῦ ἡ μὲν πρώτη μεταβολὴ γίνεται ὑπὸ τοῦ γεννῶντος, ὅταν δὲ γεννηθῇ, ἔχει ἤδη ὥσπερ ἐπιστήμην καὶ τὸ αἰσθάνεσθαι]." (E. Diamond, op. cit., 128 translates incorrectly "when the animal is born"). See also *Gener. anim.* II 1, 735a20: "Though it was generated by another thing bearing the same name [e.g., a man is generated by a man], it grows by means of itself [ἐγέννησε μὲν τοίνυν τὸ συνώνυμον οἷον ἄνθρωπος ἄνθρωπον, αὔξεται δὲ δι' ἑαυτοῦ]" (trans. A. L. Peck [1942]). Cf. *Eth. Nic.* I 12, 1102b1.

body which has lost its soul, but that which possesses its soul; so seed and fruit are such bodies potentially possessing life."[27]

Aristotle also argued at length that the soul of a living being is not yet actively present in male semen, but that, as regards its vegetative function, it becomes immediately productive and active as soon as the semen has combined with the menstrual fluid of a female.[28] A developing embryo develops thanks to its own vital principle and from that moment is no longer to be regarded as merely a part of the mother's body.

Aristotle understood that a living creature that starts to breathe after birth has already undergone months of intrauterine development, though it was not yet breathing then. Therefore, the life of an embryo does not just begin when a newly born starts to breathe, and it is not dependent on breath. Nor is the soul the helmsman of an adult human being only; it is already present in the prenatal phase as the guiding agency of the vegetative processes, owing to which a new living specimen comes into being. Lungs develop in an embryo under the direction of its own soul-principle, without respiration being activated. *Pneuma* is not dependent on *pneumôn* but vice versa. Respiration does not produce *pneuma*, but the heat of *pneuma* makes respiration necessary for some animals![29] This is

---

27. Ἔστι δὲ οὐ τὸ ἀποβεβληκὸς τὴν ψυχὴν τὸ δυνάμει ὂν ὥστε ζῆν, ἀλλὰ τὸ ἔχον· τὸ δὲ σπέρμα καὶ ὁ καρπὸς τὸ δυνάμει τοιονδὶ σῶμα. In his definition in II 1, 412a27, Aristotle had referred to the soul as "the first entelechy of a natural body potentially possessing life [σώματος φυσικοῦ δυνάμει ζωὴν ἔχοντος]." In 412b25, he wants to clarify this. What kind of natural body potentially possesses life? He explains it in the context of the question: What body is potentially capable of "seeing"? A material entity that seems to be an eye might be thought capable of seeing, but though a corpse has eyes, it can no longer see. Like a statue, it only has this possibility "in a homonymous way." If vital activity is to start manifesting itself, a "soul" must be present. (The use of the term ἀποβεβληκός is reminiscent of the discussion with the Megaric school in Arist. *Metaph.* Θ 3, 1047a1, where Aristotle emphasizes that a blind person is not potentially capable of seeing, in contrast to a sleeping person or a developing embryo. Cf. J. Beere, *Doing and Being: An Interpretation of Aristotle's Metaphysics Theta* (Oxford: Clarendon Press, 2009), 91–117.) Aristotle's conclusion: "semen and seeds are bodies of that sort [τὸ δὲ σπέρμα καὶ ὁ καρπὸς τὸ δυνάμει τοιονδὶ σῶμα]," does not mean that semen and seed have the potential to become ensouled. No, they *possess* soul and therefore they have the potential to display vital phenomena. Aristotle also explains this in *Gener. anim.* II 1, 735a4–26. See §5c above. For an opposite view, see G. Heinemann (2015), 67 with n. 17 and 74 with n. 41.

28. Both in *Anim.* II 1, 412b17–3a5 and in *Gener. anim.* II 1, 735a4–22, Aristotle reasons that semen not only contains soul, but also the respective "parts" of the soul, depending on the species of living creature. Cf. A. P. Bos, "The Soul and Soul-'Parts' in Semen" (2009). Hence, Aristotle can call semen in particular the "instrument of the soul." He does so as well in a part of the text of *On the Soul* II 4, 415b7: διόπερ τὸ σπέρμα τῶν ζῴων καὶ φυτῶν ὄργανόν ἐστι τῆς ψυχῆς, which has wrongly been left out of modern editions. Cf. A. P. Bos, "A Lost Sentence on Seed as Instrument of the Soul" (2010).

29. This fundamental change in the conceptual content of the word *pneuma* led to a profound ambivalence of the term in the later tradition. The same applies to the Latin equivalent *spiritus*.

the crucial insight that came to govern Aristotle's biology and psychology,[30] and he explicitly argued it in *On the Life-Bearing Spirit* (*De Spiritu*) 3–4.[31] He was led to postulate that plants and trees, like insects, fish, and molluscs, also possess "life" (even though they have no respiratory system), and that animals and humans always possess this lowest, purely vegetative level of life too. He adds the idea that respiration occurs only in living creatures of which the *pneuma* possesses a higher degree of heat than that of others and therefore requires cooling.[32]

In *On the Life-Bearing Spirit*, Aristotle consequently introduces the idea that the "life-bearing *pneuma*" is not breath but something else, which is present as life-bearing spirit in everything that lives, from the very first phase of growth and development.[33] This important proposition, which also forms the foundation of his other biological writings, was *never developed and argued anywhere else but in the treatise On the Life-Bearing Spirit*. It is thus highly unsatisfactory that precisely this work from the *Parva Naturalia* of the Aristotelian Corpus has been denied to Aristotle by scholars and all but ignored for almost a century since the much-quoted article by W. Jaeger (1913).[34] However, they did not recognize that Aristotle in *De Spiritu* 2, 481a29 referred to Plato with the name "Aristogenes" ("begotten by Ariston") just as Plato in his *Phaedrus* 251a2 referred to Aristotle by the word ἀρτιτελής ("he who is newly initiated").

---

30. See W. Jaeger, "Das *Pneuma* im Lykeion," *Hermes* (1913); repr. in id. *Scripta Minora* (Roma: Edizioni di Storia e Letteratura, 1960), 81: "Aristoteles hebt scharf hervor dass die Bildnertätigkeit des Pneuma bereits vor Bildung der Lunge einsetzt."

31. Cf. A. P. Bos and R. Ferwerda (2008), 91–112. Cf. also *Gener. anim.* II 6, 742a5: "others, which both breathe and get their articulation within the uterus, do not however breathe until their lungs have reached completion [τὰ δ' ἀναπνέοντα καὶ ἐν μήτρᾳ λαμβάνοντα τὴν διάρθρωσιν οὐκ ἀναπνεῖ πρὶν ἢ ὁ πνεύμων λάβῃ τέλος]."

32. On this theme, cf. J. G. Lennox, "Why Animals Must Keep Their Cool: Aristotle on the Need for Respiration (and other Forms of Cooling)," Paper for Conference on "Aristotle and his Predecessors on Heat, *Pneuma* and Soul," Prague, June 12–14, 2014. In *Gener. anim.* I 20, 728a17–30 Aristotle identifies difference in degree of heat as the reason why female menstrual fluid cannot develop into a new specimen of the same species without the semen of the male specimen. This is also why the parts of the visible body below the diaphragm are formed later and are less differentiated than the higher parts. Cf. *Gener. anim.* II 6, 741b27–31. For particularly these higher parts contain vital heat; cf. *Long.* 3, 465b2 and 6, 467a33.

33. The author of *On the Cosmos*, which we will discuss at length in ch. 9, also held this typically Aristotelian view, as can be gauged from the casual remark in 4, 394b9–12.

34. G. L. Duprat, "La Théorie du πνεῦμα chez Aristote," *Archiv für Geschichte der Philosophie* 12 (1898): 311 argued that *Spir.* is "suspect," since the work is never cited in the other, genuinely Aristotelian writings. Yet this claim itself is doubtful, because *Motu anim.* 10, 703a10—"How this innate *pneuma* is preserved has been set out elsewhere [τίς μὲν οὖν ἡ σωτηρία τοῦ συμφύτου πνεύματος, εἴρηται ἐν ἄλλοις]"—should certainly be taken as a reference to *Spir*. (But the authenticity of *Motu anim.* was also doubted until W. Jaeger's 1913 article!) *Spir.* is not even mentioned in A. L. Carbone, *Aristotele, L'Anima e il Corpo. Parva Naturalia. Introduzione, Traduzione e Note* (Milano: Bompiani, 2003) and in the new handbook by C. Rapp and K. Corcilius (2011).

This totally new approach means that Aristotle (much more than Plato) focuses his attention on semen and menstrual fluid, copulation and fertilization, the contribution of the male and the female, the differences between sexes within species and spontaneous generation. But the all-important question for him is how the species of a new specimen is determined from the moment of fertilization and how this new specimen is produced. His answer to this question is the concept of "entelechy," the goal-orienting, guiding principle.[35] Aristotle further explains the differences in quality of life by talking about an entelechy free of all materiality (*Anim.* II 1, 413a7) and entelechies that are connected with a soul-body (412b4–6). These entelechies may be "awake" or "asleep" (412a22–6), and in turn the "sleeping" entelechies may differ in vital quality through the quality of their instrumental body[36] (*Gener. anim.* II 3, 736b29–7a9) and its commixture with the sublunary elements, which differ in quality of life through their distance from the Origin, the Source of all Life (*Gener. anim.* III 11, 761b13–22). In Aristotle's dialogues these differences in the controlling capacity of guiding principles were placed in the Orphic framework of crime, alienation, and punishment, bondage, captivity, sleep, but also with the perspective of an awakening, liberation, return, and reunion. Though many scholars have presented the *Eudemus* as pervaded by a dualism that was even more pessimistic than that of Plato's *Phaedo*, we should realize that Aristotle used Platonic themes in this work in order to formulate a completely different philosophy.[37]

Recognition of vegetative processes as a form of ensouled life in plants but also as a basic function in all living beings, and the insight that these vegetative processes are present before birth and from the moment of fertilization, is *Aristotle's great innovation*. This radical change of perspective is summed up by Aristotle in his slogan: "A human being begets a human being." It drives his fundamental criticism of Plato. It also explains why he situates the entire process of generation within the sphere of nature and natural bodies and rejects the

---

35. See §10q below.

36. The difference in quality of the instrumental body of the human, animal, or vegetable soul is also indicated (without being noticed) in *Anim.* II 1, 412a28 and 2, 414a22. In both cases Aristotle means by τοιοῦτον a "specific," a "certain" body, differing for every major class of living beings, but so specific that it is usable and functional as an instrumental body for the soul of this category of creatures.

37. The discussion between Plato and Aristotle clearly shows that they made use of ancient Orphic myths, but constantly adapted and revised them to suit their own needs. The tragic poets had always done the same with Homeric motifs. Just so, the Gnostic authors would later use mythical themes to express philosophical notions. Cf. §18b below.

notion of the soul that enters nascent creatures "from outside." When Aristotle talks about "the body that receives the soul,"[38] he does not mean a concrete, newly born body into which the soul must descend as "vital breath" in order to produce a living being, but is referring to the female's menstrual fluid, which also contains *pneuma* in a mixture with other (sublunary) elements, as does the male's semen. This menstrual fluid is a somatic residue that is propelled by the *dynamis* of the male's semen into a lifelong vital process, which from that moment is no longer a process involving only the body of the female parent.

Furthermore, the fact that perception is always perception of phenomena in natural reality (vibrations of air that are heard and smelled, taste of moist substances, visual perception of light in air and water) led him to understand that perception is possible only thanks to the natural sensitive body of the soul.[39]

---

38. *Anim.* I 3, 407b21; II 2, 414a26.

39. Cf. §10e below and A. P. Bos, "The Soul's Instrument for Touching in Aristotle, *On the Soul* II 11, 422b34–3a21," *Archiv für Geschichte der Philosophie* 92 (2010): 89–102; "The Ears Are not the Subject of Hearing in Aristotle's *On the Soul* II 8, 420a3–12," *Philologus* 154 (2010): 171–86; "Perception as a Movement of the Instrumental Body of the Soul in Aristotle," *Rheinisches Museum für Philologie* 154 (2011): 22–42.

8

The Magnet as Model of a Mover at a Distance

So far we have described various aspects of Aristotle's philosophy, all of which express something of the relation between the cosmos and God. But they are hard to reconcile. The gap between an immaterial reality and the world of the elementary bodies and all that consists of them, which seemed unbridgeable in Plato, seems to remain a major problem in Aristotle too. Aristotle criticizes Plato for failing to make it clear in what way the immaterial Ideas can be "causes" of the concrete, visible entities that, in Plato's view, are "images" of the Ideas.[1] However, Aristotle has a comparable problem. He viewed all concrete living entities as realizations of intelligible forms; and he anchored the knowability of changeable reality in universal forms (*eidē*) that are present in matter. Did he succeed in offering a plausible solution for this?

He describes God as the absolutely transcendent, self-sufficient, and self-contained Intellect; and he repeatedly characterizes this divine Intellect as "separate" (κεχωρισμένος) from the cosmos and nature. As such, there is distance between God and all ensouled creatures, since every soul differs from intellect in being inextricably bound up with an instrumental body.

Yet Aristotle also talks about God (as Intellect, as Unmoved Mover, and as Ruler—κοίρανος):

> as the cause of the eternal motion of the ethereal spheres and,
> via them, of all that comes into being and passes away;

---

1. Arist. *Metaph.* A 9, 991a20–6 (cited in §7a above); 6, 987b13. See §10.1 below.

as the agency on which depend the being and life of all things in the cosmos, to a greater or lesser degree.

He talks about:

the "desire" for the eternal and for divinity in all mortal living reality;
the attraction that God exerts on all the celestial spheres;
the Power that proceeds from God and keeps the entire universe together;
the life of all ensouled entities as the possession of a goal-oriented power passed on in the process of reproduction, so that new carriers of this power constantly come into being;
living, ensouled creatures that do not just possess soul as entelechy, as animals and plants do, but also about living beings that potentially possess intellect and are predisposed to actualize this intellect.

How was Aristotle able to reconcile this with each other, and on what grounds did he believe himself capable of providing a more rational explanation of empirical phenomena than Plato?[2]

In my view, the answer to this question is as follows: Aristotle conceived of the transcendent Intellect, God, as *the Generator of goal-oriented Vital Power*. He presented this Power as:

- regulatively active and effective in all extra-divine reality;

- an intellectual power that manifests itself on a variety of levels as controlling power;[3]

- all-pervasive, without any detrimental reaction from the material reality that it pervades, and purposefully productive of life-forms;

- proceeding from and dependent on God without reciprocity. This Power acts on all cosmic reality, but not the other way round;

---

2. On this question, cf. P. Siwek SJ, "Comment le Premier Moteur meut l'Univers?," *Divinitas* 11 (1967): 377–92.

3. We said above that Aristotle introduced a strict separation between intellect and soul, in the sense that he reserves the term *intellect* for the driver of the team of horses in Plato's *Phaedrus*. However, he insists that although "the horses," like plants and all that lives, do not contain "intellects," they do have "guiding principles," "entelechies," "rein-holding principles," *logos*-realizing principles.

- conducive to life and existence;

- decreasing in effect as the distance from the Source of this Power increases;

- present and active in all levels of living entities, inasmuch as all entelechy-principles are rational principles that allow the practical realization of the production of new specimens of the everlasting specific forms that form part of the World Logos at the highest level;[4]

- a continuous chain of controlling principles; at the highest level rational ensouled (celestial) beings; at lower levels souls (entelechies) of human beings, with potential for rationality and intellect; and souls of animals and plants and products of spontaneous generation.

All these levels of life differ structurally from the divine Origin, but at the same time they are connected with the Origin through the unity of order and structure, which disappears into a "black hole" without the divine Intellect as Source. Aristotle took this concept of a Working Power, which proceeds from the transcendent, divine Intellect to material reality, from the sphere of magnetic phenomena. He was familiar with fragments of stone that without moving from their spot were able to attract and hold fast iron.[5] He knew Plato's *Ion*, in which the process of poetic inspiration and ecstasy was seen to result from a "divine Power," comparable with the power of a stone from Magnesia or Heracleia, cities in regions of present-day Turkey with large amounts of iron-bearing rock. He knew that this power does not cause damage to what it attracts, but also that this power could be transferred or passed on to other objects than the magnet itself. He was aware that this magnetic power was capable of moving other objects, holding them fast, drawing them to itself as to their goal, and suspending them from itself. This power differed from that of a block of stone that is thrown against another stone, because in a magnetic power the action does not provoke a comparable reaction. He

---

4. In this matter, Philo of Alexandria's doctrine of the divine *dynameis* that are present in the divine Logos was strongly influenced by Aristotle. Cf. A. P. Bos, "Philo of Alexandria: A Platonist in the Image and Likeness of Aristotle," *Studia Philonica Annual* 10 (1998): 66–86; "God as 'Father' and 'Maker' in Philo of Alexandria and its Background in Aristotelian Thought," *Elenchos* 24 (2003): 311–32.

5. The French expressively call the magnet *l'aimant*.

also knew that at the end of a series of iron rings this power finally became too weak to sustain the above effects.

In the following chapters of this book, I will argue that Aristotle explained all cosmic phenemona as results of the life-generating, life-transmitting, and life-structuring Power emanating from God. Although God and the divine Intellect are called "separate" (κεχωρισμένος) because they represent "a different kind" of being, there is certainly a "connection" between God as Origin and the cosmic reality that exists where God's Power of Thought manifests itself as a Guiding Power.

The entelechies or soul-principles as structuring, plan-realizing principles clearly show the connection with the Origin as Ultimate Goal, just as the magnetic power of the magnet is manifest in the iron rings suspended from it. An "entelechy" is the goal-pointing principle for a living entity and has an intrinsic relationship with the Origin, which is the ultimate Goal for all reality.[6]

This distinction between God as Unmoved Mover and his Guiding Power, which has an active guiding role in the special fine-material body of ether and *pneuma* as its vehicle, represents Aristotle's alternative to Plato's Demiurge, a concept that he considered internally contradictory because it stands for an Intellect that is contemplative on the one hand and productive and creative on the other. He needs the introduction of a special fine-material and divine body, ether and *pneuma,* because he holds that only this special body can be connected with a soul as guiding principle and can realize the "work" of the soul as "instrumental body." Aristotle's "dual physics" (see §5a above) is an essential element of Aristotle's "cybernetic vitalism," which was his alternative to the cosmo-theology of Plato's *Timaeus*.[7]

His arrival at the vague notion of "power" (δύναμις) follows from the fact that he characterized activities such as "willing," "striving," "being providentially aimed at," and "taking care of" as "psychic" functions and as belonging to the existence of living creatures burdened with (fine-) material bodies.

---

6. If Aristotle had known about the earth's magnetic field and its polar orientation, he could have neatly compared his concept of *entelecheia* with a compass needle, because it is always directed both at the form of the living being and at God as the comprehensive "for the sake of" or cause.

7. Aristotle's ontological view may therefore also be seen as a form of emanation doctrine. It differs from Plotinus's doctrine, which is traditionally characterized as a doctrine of emanation, in that Aristotle never referred to the Origin as "the One," or as "Being," but always as Intellect in act. Plotinus's doctrine of emanation remains structurally dependent on Plato's logicist doctrine of deduction, and regards all "beings" as participating in the One that is "beyond Being."

a. *On the Soul* I 2 on Thales of Miletus and the Power of a Magnet

Aristotle was aware that Thales of Miletus already knew about the phenomenon of magnetism. Thales lived in the sixth century BCE in the region of Magnesia and Heracleia, which gave their names to the phenomenon of magnetism in Antiquity. Aristotle says of him in the introductory passages of *On the Soul*:

> Thales, too, to judge from what is recorded of his views, seems to suppose that the soul is in a sense the cause of movement, since he says that the stone[8] has a soul because it causes movement to iron. (trans. W. S. Hett)[9]

This piece of information is known to anyone who has read an introduction to the earliest Greek philosophy. It also seems completely straightforward, until we consider that Antiquity usually held the difference between a living dog and a dead dog to be that a living dog itself possesses a soul and a dead one does not; and this is shown by the fact that a living dog can move its legs and other parts of the body. But these legs are not moved by something from outside! So why would Thales call the magnetic stone "ensouled" if the stone does not move itself but the iron object attracted by the magnet?

This could suggest that Aristotle may have held Thales's view of the soul as the principle of motion to be the same as the position set out in *On the*

---

[8]. Note that Aristotle's remark about Thales simply talks about "the stone" and says that it moves iron. So he sees no need to mention that the stone comes from Magnesia or elsewhere. Apparently, in Aristotle's time "the stone" was clear enough as a reference to the magnet with its special properties. Likewise in *Phys.* VIII 10, 267a2.

[9]. *Anim.* I 2, 405a19–21: ἔοικε δὲ καὶ Θαλῆς ἐξ ὧν ἀπομνημονεύουσι κινητικόν τι τὴν ψυχὴν ὑπολαβεῖν, εἴπερ τὴν λίθον ἔφη ψυχὴν ἔχειν, ὅτι τὸν σίδηρον κινεῖ. Cf. Diog. Laert. I 24: "Aristotle and Hippias affirm that, arguing from the magnet, and from amber, he attributed a soul or life even to inanimate objects [Ἀριστοτέλης δὲ καὶ Ἱππίας φασὶν αὐτὸν [sc. Thales] καὶ τοῖς ἀψύχοις μεταδιδόναι ψυχῆς, τεκμαιρόμενον ἐκ τῆς λίθου τῆς μαγνήτιδος καὶ τοῦ ἠλέκτρου]." This text suggests that Aristotle may have drawn his information from Hippias. Cf. P. Thillet, *Aristote, De l'Âme. Traduit du Grec. Édition établie, présentée et annotée* (Paris: Gallimard, 2005), 324. See also J. Mansfeld, "Aristotle and the Others on Thales, or the Beginning of Natural Philosophy" (1985), repr. in *Studies in the Historiography of Greek Philosophy* (Assen: van Gorcum, 1990), 126–46. Diogenes Laertius, V 26, notes that Aristotle wrote a separate book "On the Magnet." Cf. A. Radl, *Die Magnetstein in der Antike. Quellen und Zusammenhänge* (Stuttgart: Steiner Verlag Wiesbaden, 1988), 29.

Soul II 1, namely, that the soul as entelechy and as carrier of the form-principle (*eidos*) exerts an attraction as unmoved mover on the instrumental body of which the soul is the "goal-pointing" principle.[10] However, Aristotle has also just said that Anaxagoras identifies the Intellect as the agency that sets the cosmos in motion; and in *On the Soul* I 3 he will argue at length that the Intellect has nothing to do with motion, and the soul does not possess any motion of its own, but moves only accidentally, when its vessel or vehicle moves.

How should we interpret Thales's line of reasoning? Scholars often refer to the idea that Thales may have held there to be life in all visible reality, even in apparently lifeless fragments of stone. This would make Thales a representative of "hylozoism," a view of reality in which all material things are understood to be ensouled, alive, and the distinction between dead matter and living beings is not pronounced.[11] But a connection is readily made with another statement by Aristotle slightly farther on in the same book *On the Soul* I 5, 411a7–8:

> Certain thinkers say that the soul is intermingled in the whole universe, and it is perhaps for that reason that Thales came to the opinion that all things are full of gods.
>
> Καὶ ἐν τῷ ὅλῳ δέ τινες αὐτὴν μεμῖχθαί φασιν, ὅθεν ἴσως καὶ Θαλῆς ᾠήθη πάντα πλήρη θεῶν εἶναι.

If we may consider a link here, it would be that Thales, like Plato in the *Ion*, may have thought that the magnet's effect should be understood as

---

10. In *Motion of Animals* 4, Aristotle similarly explains the lines of Homer, *Iliad* 8, 18–27 as an expression of his own view of God as the agency on which everything depends. Note, too, that in *Metaph.* A 3, 983b20–4a3 Aristotle discusses Thales's proposition that the principle of all things is water and that the earth rests on water. Where did Thales get this notion from? Aristotle suggests: "Presumably he derived this assumption from seeing that the nutriment of everything is moist, and that *vital heat itself* is generated from moisture and depends upon it for its existence [λαβὼν ἴσως τὴν ὑπόληψιν ταύτην ἐκ τοῦ πάντων ὁρᾶν τὴν τροφὴν ὑγρὰν οὖσαν καὶ αὐτὸ τὸ θερμὸν ἐκ τούτου γιγνόμενον καὶ τούτῳ ζῶν]" (983b22–4 [H. Tredennick]). Aristotle thus seems to attribute arguments to Thales that he himself puts forward in *Gener. anim.* III 11, 762a18–32 (a text that will be quoted below). He adds: "and also from the fact that the seeds of everything have a moist nature, whereas water is the first principle of the nature of moist things [καὶ διὰ τὸ πάντων τὰ σπέρματα τὴν φύσιν ὑγρὰν ἔχειν· τὸ δ' ὕδωρ ἀρχὴ τῆς φύσεως ἐστι τοῖς ὑγροῖς]" (983b26–7). This argument assigned here to Thales also closely resembles Aristotle's own view in *Gener. anim.* II 2, 735b37–6a21.

11. This was a curious hypothesis. Surely there has never been a culture that did not treat the dead in an entirely different way from the living members of the group.

a "divine power" that can wholly pervade the iron of the iron rings and then draw it to the magnet. If this power can invisibly enter the iron, then obviously it can also enter the air between the magnet and the iron.

b. Everything Is Full of Psychic Heat
(*Gener. anim.* III 11, 762a19–21)

In connection with our subject, it is also important to note that Aristotle seems to refer to Thales without mentioning him when he says that "in earth water is present, and in water *pneuma* is present, and in all *pneuma* soul-heat is present, so that in a way all things are full of Soul."[12]

This text occurs in *Generation of Animals* after Aristotle has talked about all sexual reproduction. The importance of *pneuma* for this had already been demonstrated. Now Aristotle argues the same for all products of "spontaneous generation." To this end, he stresses that *pneuma* is present everywhere,[13] just as *pneuma* is necessary for the genesis of life in the region of aerial animals and quadrupeds. However, we might suspect that Aristotle relates the presence of *pneuma* in water and earth to a presence like that of the magnet's power in iron. We will give a further underpinning of this surmise in §9a in our treatment of the criticism that Aristotle levels at Thales's proposition, "Everything is full of gods," in *On the Cosmos* 6, 397b17, where Aristotle will posit that God himself is not present everywhere, but his Power does pervade everything.

Here we already note:

- For Aristotle, Thales's proposition "everything is water" is motivated by the observation that all living beings need water and that vital heat, too, consists of and exists through water;

---

12. *Gener. anim.* III 11, 762a19–21: ἐν γῇ μὲν ὕδωρ ὑπάρχειν ἐν δ' ὕδατι πνεῦμα, ἐν δὲ τούτῳ παντὶ θερμότητα ψυχικήν, ὥστε τρόπον τινὰ πάντα ψυχῆς εἶναι πλήρη. It seems to me crucial that here and in II 3, 736b29–7a1 Aristotle links vital heat to *pneuma* as an agency that is clearly distinct from the sublunary elements and is connected with the soul. From this fact it becomes clear that only *pneuma* and ether are bodies that can be used by soul as its instruments and can be called *empsycha*. However, J. Althoff, *Warm, Kalt, Flüssig und Fest bei Aristoteles. Die Elementarqualitäten in den Zoologischen Schriften* (Stuttgart: Franz Steiner Verlag, 1992), 195 n. 85 denies this importance and considers this passage to be refuted by *Anim.* I 5, 411a7ff.

13. It is useful to observe that according to this text *pneuma* is present in water, since this disqualifies the identification of *pneuma* with "air." The translation of *symphyton pneuma* as "connate air" is incorrect. There is no air in water. Cf. *Resp.* 2, 470b28 ff. and *Spir.* 2, 482a23. Cf. §10c below.

- he reinterprets Thales's proposition that "everything is full of gods," in *On the Cosmos* 6, as being correct only in the sense that "everything is full of God's Power";
- and he alludes to Thales in *Generation of Animals* III 11, 762a18–21 when he says that it would be right to say that "everything is full of soul," because "psychic heat" is present everywhere.

It becomes easier to combine all this if we may assume that for Aristotle *pneuma* is the analogue of the divine astral element (see §10a below) and as such carries the Power that proceeds from God, who is the "power station" of vital heat in the sublunary sphere. That is why I suspect that we may assume a connection between what Aristotle says about Thales's view of the magnet as "ensouled," about reality as "full of gods," and about water as basic matter, on the one hand, and on the other hand his own view of God's Power as pervading all reality and of *pneuma* as being present in all the sublunary elementary bodies and carrying the divine Vital Power and Vital Heat, which is his alternative to Plato's doctrine of the World Soul and the individual soul, and his view of the important role of semen as the carrier of a soul-principle.[14]

c. *Physics* VIII 10 on the Working of the Magnet

In *Physics* VIII 10, 267a2, Aristotle also talks about the magnet, now in relation to the question of how the eternal motion of the sphere of the fixed stars depends on and is caused by God.[15] For, in this context, he discusses the question of how something can continue to be moved when the agency that causes the movement does not have direct contact (anymore). At the end of *Physics* VIII 9, he had established that motion always exists and will exist; and what the principle of eternal motion is and the most primary motion, and which motion can be the only eternal motion. But finally, he also observes that the First Principle that causes motion is itself unmoved (9, 266a6–9). In chapter 10, he concludes this argument by proving that the First Unmoved Mover does not consist of parts (and therefore does not belong to material

---

14. The late Christian author Philoponus, in his work *De Aeternitate Mundi* (ed. Rabe, p. 230), in which he disputes Aristotle's doctrine of the eternity of the world and of ether as a divine element, repeatedly connects the way the rational soul-principles drive their astral vehicles and the effect of the magnet on iron particles. Cf. A. Radl, op. cit., 116 ff.
15. We already encountered this theme in *Cael.* I 9 in §2a.

reality). However, his argument also constantly witnesses to his concern with the "Power" which the First Principle exercises on the outer celestial sphere (as the first thing that moves through the effect of something else). In 10, 266a23 ff., we continually come across the term δύναμις in the sense of "power" (and not in the sense of "potency," "possibility," or "faculty"). Aristotle constantly talks about a "power" that "does" something (266a27).[16]

Aristotle starts from the proposition that everything that moves is moved by something else (10, 266b28–9), and then faces the question of how some things always continue to move, even when the agency that has set them in motion does not have contact anymore.[17] He first gives the example of a ball that is thrown.[18] Here, one may argue that the thrower not only sets the ball in motion, but also the air, which then continues to move the ball (b30–2);[19] or one may cite the principle of *periôsis* or *antiperistasis,* that is, the idea that the air that is pushed away by the projectile starts itself to push along the projectile from behind, because there cannot be empty space and the air needs to find a new place somewhere.[20] Aristotle argues against this that it remains impossible for the air to continue to move (and push the ball along) if the air no longer has contact with the thrower. Everything must be in motion together and must stop moving when the First Mover no longer makes contact.

---

16. Cf. §5d above. Sometimes he also talks about ἰσχύς (266a32). See also *Motu anim.* 3, 699a33; a34; b5; b6; b16.

17. We saw in §6b that Aristotle also drew attention to this problem in relation to reproduction, in which the power transferred by the semen of the male remains active after the actual copulation.

18. *Phys.* VIII 10, 266b30: οἷον τὰ ῥιπτούμενα. Cf. Plato, *Tim.* 80a1.

19. Aristotle links up here with his debate with the Atomists and Plato's *Tim.* 79a-e and 80a in *Physics* IV 8, 215a14–9: "Further, in point of fact things that are thrown move though that which gave them their impulse is not touching them, either by reason of mutual replacement, as some maintain, or because the air that has been pushed pushes them with a movement quicker than the natural locomotion of the projectile wherewith it moves to its proper place. But in a void none of these things can take place, nor can anything be moved save as that which is carried is moved [ἔτι νῦν μὲν κινεῖται τὰ ῥιπτούμενα τοῦ ὤσαντος οὐχ ἁπτομένου, ἢ δι᾽ ἀντιπερίστασιν, ὥσπερ ἔνιοί φασιν, ἢ διὰ τὸ ὠθεῖν τὸν ὠσθέντα ἀέρα θάττω κίνησιν τῆς τοῦ ὠσθέντος φορᾶς, ἣν φέρεται εἰς τὸν οἰκεῖον τόπον· ἐν δὲ τῷ κενῷ οὐδὲν τούτων ὑπάρχει, οὐδ᾽ ἔσται φέρεσθαι ἀλλ᾽ ἢ ὡς τὸ ὀχούμενον]" (R. P. Hardie and R. K. Gaye in J. Barnes, ed., 1984).

20. In *Timaeus* 79a5–e9 Plato had also used this principle to explain the motion of respiration, which he moreover took to be a motion throughout the visible body, and even held it to be responsible for the transport of food. In *De Spiritu* 3–5 Aristotle had radically disputed this account. He argued there that although the vital *pneuma* is present throughout the visible body, the inhaled air of respiration goes no farther than the lungs and is useful there for refrigeration of the heart. In this way, Aristotle postulated a clear distinction between the process of food transport to all parts of the visible body and the supply of air to the lungs.

This is also the case if, like the magnet, the First Mover is able to work on what he sets in motion in such a way that it in turn sets something else in motion. Aristotle is thinking here of a series of iron rings hanging from a magnet, which causes the magnetic power of attraction to be passed on to the next ring. But if the magnet is removed, all the rings drop from each other, too.[21]

To cope with these problems, Aristotle comes up with the proposal that the Power of the First Principle acts on an agency outside of this Principle, and enables this external agency to pass on the Power in turn, even when contact with the conveyor of this Power ceases.[22] This is what fascinated Aristotle in *winding mechanisms*: the fact that they enable the power of another, even when he is no longer in contact with them, to function efficiently and to pass from one part to the next. Only at the very end of a series of conveying agencies, in which the Power progressively diminishes, does this effect of passing on the motion stop.[23]

---

21. Arist. *Phys.* VIII 10, 266b33–7a2. Plato, *Tim.* 80c2 also talks about the "pulling power" of τῶν Ἡρακλείων λίθων, which he believes should be explained via the principle of *periôsis* too.

22. *Phys.* VIII 10, 267a5–7: "but this thing does not cease simultaneously to impart motion and undergo motion; it ceases to be in motion at the moment when its mover ceases to move it, but it still remains a mover [Ἀλλ' οὐχ ἅμα παύεται κινοῦν καὶ κινούμενον· ἀλλὰ κινούμενον μὲν ὅταν ὁ κινῶν παύσηται κινῶν, κινοῦν δὲ ἔτι ἐστίν]." Cf. §6b above.

23. For Aristotle, this progressive weakening manifests itself at the level of purely vegetative life, "spontaneous" generation, and the unensouled elementary bodies. He probably also used this concept to explain the diminished transfer of hereditary properties in the course of several generations. Cf. §6c.

9

God as Begetter of All Life According to *On the Cosmos*

In the foregoing chapters we have seen how everything in the cosmos "depends" on God, who exerts his "power of attraction" on the cosmos, and how all that lives is actuated by a natural "desire" for the divine and for immortality. We noted that Aristotle sometimes talks about a "love" (*erôs*) for God from subjects in the cosmos. We also established that according to Aristotle the supreme transcendent Principle is "unmoved" and therefore falls outside the category of material entities, but nevertheless should be considered to possess *energeia* and exercise "Power" (*Dynamis*) as the "Unmoved Mover" of all that moves in the cosmos. We also saw that Aristotle's concept of his transcendent Principle had to be more abstract than Plato's notion of a divine Demiurge, because he put more emphasis on its character as pure Intellect, and therefore denied to it all functions of "willing," "taking care of," "making," and "being providentially aimed at." He regarded these functions as *pathè* of a soul, but not as characteristic of an intellect. In Aristotle, the divine Origin is more transcendent than in Plato and absolutely unchanging and *apathès*. Hence, God does not "will." But he remains the central controlling cause. The "Power" proceeding from him is in fact of a different order from the power of a stick used for beating. This Power acts on a body that is different from and more divine than the so-called elements, and that is guided by this divine, goal-oriented, and goal-orienting power.

We now turn to the description of God's relationship with the cosmos and all that lives in it, in the short work *On the Cosmos*. This work has often been denied to Aristotle in the modern era.¹ Yet anyone who studies it against the background of the problems discussed in Aristotle's generally accepted works, especially his *Generation of Animals*, would have to conclude that the rejection of Aristotle's authorship is unwarranted.²

On the Cosmos describes how

---

1. The very title of this work has been seized upon to cast doubt on Aristotle's authorship. Cf. J. Mansfeld, "Περὶ Κόσμου. A Note on the History of a Title," *Vigiliae Christianae* 46 (1992): 391–411. He formulates his position on p. 400 as follows: "a Peripatetic philosopher of Platonic leanings using a Stoic book-title can hardly be dated earlier than the late first cent. BCE." See now J. C. Thom, ed., *Cosmic Order and Divine Power. Pseudo-Aristotle,* On the Cosmos. *Introduction, Text, Translation and Interpretive Essays* (Tübingen: Mohr Siebeck, 2014), 3: "an important example of the kind of eclectic popular philosophy found in the Hellenistic-Roman period." He takes over Mansfeld's position on p. 7 n. 35; 58 n. 1. But the title may well have been drawn from the work itself, which emphatically pays attention to the theme of "*cosmos*" (6, 397b11: περὶ κόσμου λέγοντας. 2, 391b9–12; 6, 397a7–8). Cf. J. C. Thom, op. cit., 112. And Stobaeus, who is held to be responsible for handing down a number of authentic fragments of the Pythagorean Philolaus, ascribes in *Ecloga* I 21, 7a [187, 14 Wachsmut] one of these fragments to a work by Philolaus entitled "Περὶ Κόσμου" (D.K. 44 B 2). On J. C. Thom (2014) see also my review in *Acta Classica* 58 (2015): 232–37.

2. The authorship of *On the Cosmos* has always been highly controversial. Cf. P. Moraux, *Der Aristotelismus bei den Griechen von Andronikos bis Alexander von Aphrodisias*, vol. 2 (Berlin: W. de Gruyter, 1984), 5–82; H. B. Gottschalk, "Aristotelian Philosophy in the Roman World from the Time of Cicero to the End of the Second Century," *Aufstieg und Niedergang der Römischen Welt*, vol. II 36, 2 (Berlin: W. de Gruyter, 1987), 1132–39. The discussion has been radically affected by the conclusion of J. Barnes (1977), in his review of G. Reale, *Aristotele. Trattato Sul Cosmo per Alessandro* (Napoli: Loffredo, 1974), that "the tract cannot be expropriated from Aristotle on purely doctrinal grounds, but he has neither stated nor examined the linguistic arguments for expropriation." Barnes considers the work's likely date to be before 250 BCE. D. M. Schenkeveld, "Language and Style of the Aristotelian *De Mundo* in Relation to the Question of its Inauthenticity," *Elenchos* 12 (1991): 221–55, argued for a date between 350–200 BCE. However, his dating of the work between 350 and 200 BCE on the basis of language and style raises a problem: Which anonymous and highly skilled author in this period would want to present his own ideas as Aristotelian in this way and why? One thing is certain: the text of *On the Cosmos* does not contain any overt reference to a person or event from the time after Aristotle. It therefore cannot have ended up accidentally between Aristotle's writings, but would have to be a deliberate imitation. In that case, however, why would such an author have been unable to avoid details that would show him up in the twentieth century? In the period after Aristotle's death, the author would not have mentioned Ecbatana and Susa as capitals of the Persian Empire, as we find in ch. 6, 398a14 and 34, but would have named Persepolis, whose role as the real capital only became known after the conquest of this city by Alexander the Great. For a survey of the modern debate, see G. Reale and A. P. Bos, *Il Trattato Sul Cosmo per Alessandro Attribuito ad Aristotele* (Milano: Vita e Pensiero, 1995), 369–411. C. Wildberg, in C. Rapp and K. Corcilius, eds., *Handbuch* (2011) 87, again accepts the first century as a probable date; T. Kukkonen, "On Aristotle's World," *Oxford Studies in Ancient Philosophy* 46 (2014): 326, situates the work in "the early imperial period." C. D. C. Reeve, *Action, Contemplation, and Happiness: an Essay on Aristotle* (Cambridge: Harvard University Press, 2012), 19 is not convinced that *On the Cosmos* is inauthentic.

- God is the "begetter" of all that lives in the cosmos;
- through the Power proceeding from him, and
- how all levels of reality depend on him; and
- how this dependence displays gradations corresponding to the distance from God.[3]

In passing, we find that the author involves Thales of Miletus in the discussion of these themes, but also the text of Homer, *Iliad* 8, 1–27, on the "Golden Rope." What it amounts to is that all kinds of crucial texts from Aristotle's generally accepted oeuvre return in *On the Cosmos* in an internally coherent and stylistically fine arrangement, which cannot be ascribed to an unknown and inferior imitator from the first century before Christ or later.

In the Introduction, the author dedicates the work to Alexander[4] (the Macedonian), whom he characterizes as "the best of world leaders."[5] In chapters 2–5 he then gives a fascinating description of the entire cosmos and all the phenomena it presents to us. However, in his Introduction he says that he does not just want to "talk" about all these matters, but wishes to "theologize."[6] He will do this in chapters 6–7. He starts there by saying that God is "the cause that holds the whole world together" and "that which is supreme in the cosmos."[7]

---

3. God / Celestial gods / Humans / Quadrupeds / Fish / Plants.

4. Arist. *Mu.* 1, 391a2.

5. *Mu.* 1, 391b6: ἡγεμόνων ἀρίστῳ. (For some time after the subjection of Greece in 338, Philip, and then Alexander, bore the title ἡγεμών. Cf. J. Lendering, *Alexander de Grote. De Ondergang van het Perzische Rijk* [Amsterdam: Athenaeum; Polak & van Gennep, 2004], 48–50. See also Plutarch, *Vita Alex.* XIV 671: ἡγεμὼν ἀνηγορεύθη.) The author also uses this term for God: 6, 399a30: ὁ πάντων ἡγεμών τε καὶ γενέτωρ and for the intellect in relation to the soul (1, 391a11–2). Cf. A. M. Leroi, *The Lagoon* (2014), 50: "In 335 Aristotle . . . returned to Athens, now under Macedonian hegemony."

6. *Mu.* 1, 391b3: "Let us, then, discuss, and, as far as it is possible let us theologize about all these things {Λέγωμεν δὴ ἡμεῖς καὶ, καθ' ὅσον ἐφικτόν, θεολογῶμεν περὶ τούτων συμπάντων]." For emphasis on this point, see also J. C. Thom (op. cit., 2014), 108–109.

7. *Mu.* 6, 397b9: περὶ τῆς τῶν ὅλων συνεκτικῆς αἰτίας, and b12: τὸ τοῦ κόσμου κυριώτατον. Cf. §2g above on *Polit.* VII 4, 1326a31–3: θείας γὰρ δὴ τοῦτο δυνάμεως ἔργον, ἥτις καὶ τόδε συνέχει τὸ πᾶν. T. Kukkonen (2014), 326–27 sees *On the Cosmos* as an alternative to Plato's *Timaeus* written by someone who had missed such a unified perspective on the cosmos in Aristotle's work. Thus, he can assert on p. 331: "the universe for Aristotle does not form a single teleologically oriented and ordered whole."

a. The Split in the Divine between God's Essence and His Power as a Criticism of Thales of Miletus

A fundamental aspect of the work is that the author introduces a unique and totally original distinction between God's Essence and his Power, and considers it necessary to react against the view of predecessors by means of it: "Some of the ancients were led to say that all the things of this world are full of gods."[8] The author refers here in any case to the view of Thales of Miletus,[9] which Aristotle had explicitly attributed to him in *On the Soul* I 5, 411a7–11. Aristotle there criticizes the Platonic doctrine of a World Soul: "Why does the soul when it resides in air or fire not form an animal, while it does so when it resides in mixtures of the elements?"[10] It is striking that Aristotle mentions the ancient philosopher there, when he states that "certain thinkers say that the soul is intermingled in the whole universe, and it is perhaps for that reason that Thales came to the opinion that all things are full of gods."[11]

In §8b above we saw that this theme was probably on Aristotle's mind when he said in *Generation of Animals* III 11, 762a19–21 that in a certain sense "everything is full of soul," owing to the presence of *pneuma* in all things.

It is crucially important to see that these two texts are connected. Each by itself might seem to be an isolated singularity in Aristotle's work. The text of *On the Cosmos* 6 on God's transcendent Essence and his all-pervading Power in the cosmos cannot be paralleled in Aristotle's generally acknowledged work; and very little attention is paid to the generally recognized text of *Generation of Animals* III 11. But the link between the two texts, the reference to Thales

---

8. *Mu.* 6, 397b16–7, cited below.

9. J. Dudley, "The Fate of Providence and Plato's World Soul in Aristotle," in *Fate, Providence, and Moral Responsibility in Ancient, Medieval and Early Modern Thought. Studies in Honour of C. Steel*, ed. P. D'Hoine and G. van Riet (Leuven: Leuven University Press, 2014), 61 mistakenly says: "Aristotle clearly appears to be giving approval to Thales," while referring to this text. See also §8a above. He may have attributed the same standpoint to Heraclitus. See §10p below.

10. Cf. Plato, *Laws* X 899B3–9, where, with regard to the celestial beings as contrivers of the seasons, Plato asks the question: ὅστις ταῦτα ὁμολογῶν ὑπομενεῖ μὴ θεῶν εἶναι πλήρη πάντα; Aristotle holds that bodies of perishable living creatures always contain at least portions of earth and water: *Meteor.* IV 4, 382a3–8; *Gener. corr.* II 8, 334b30–5a14.

11. *Anim.* I 5, 411a7–8: Καὶ ἐν τῷ ὅλῳ δέ τινες αὐτὴν μεμῖχθαί φασιν, ὅθεν ἴσως καὶ Θαλῆς ᾠήθη πάντα πλήρη θεῶν εἶναι. Cf. also *Metaph.* A 3, 983b22. Diogenes Laertius IX 7 attributes to Heraclitus the view that "all things are filled with souls and divinities [πάντα ψυχῶν εἶναι καὶ δαιμόνων πλήρη]." Perhaps, too, Thales was mentioned by Aristotle in connection with the question who "the seven Sages" were and who formulated the saying "Know thyself." Cf. Arist. *Philos.* 1, 2, 3 and 4 Ross; 709, 861, 28 and 29 Gigon.

of Miletus and to Plato's doctrine of soul, suggests strongly that Aristotle considered God's Power to be active throughout the cosmos, in the soul-principles or entelechy-principles, in combination with their instrumental bodies.

Aristotle proposes a radical change to the view of Thales and others: a fundamental distinction must be drawn between God's Essence (οὐσία) and his Power (δύναμις). God himself is not the "efficient cause" of everything in the cosmos and he is not the Demiurge or Creator. He is purely the controlling cause. The Power emanating from him, by using its special instrumental body, is the efficient cause.[12] The visible things are not full of God's Essence, but they are *full of God's Power*.[13] *On the Cosmos* emphasizes that this Power of God pervades the entire cosmos and is primarily connected with the divine celestial beings that consist of it[14] but also with the *pneuma* that permeates plants and animals in the sublunary sphere,[15] and that, according to *Generation of Animals* II 3, is an analogue of the astral element. *Pneuma* is mentioned only in passing in *On the Cosmos*,[16] but the refererence to Thales of Miletus is a sound argument for saying that the same psychology (and theology) connected this work and *Generation of Animals*.

This view could be called "dualistic," inasmuch as it clearly assumes a separation between God's Essence as transcendent and God's Power as immanent in the material cosmos. At the same time, Aristotle cuts across this dualism to the extent that God's Power certainly derives from God himself and apparently uses ether and the other four elements as its instruments and

---

12. We should consider here that Aristotle typifies Plato as someone who rejects the idea of an "efficient cause." Cf. §10.1 below. According to Aristotle, the "Demiurge" in Plato's *Timaeus* should not be regarded as "efficient cause," because as "intellect" he cannot produce, and as "soul" cannot be absolutely transcendent. Aristotle also repudiates Plato's theory of the World Soul and individual soul as principles of movement. A soul can only move along with the movement of its vehicle or instrumental natural body. The author of *On the Cosmos* deliberately avoids the use of technical philosophical terms, in accordance with his aim to reach an "educated, but non-specialist audience." On this, see the essay by C. Chandler, "Didactic Purpose and Discursive Strategies in *On the Cosmos*," in J. C. Thom, ed. (2014), 73. See also G. Betegh and P. Gregoric, "Multiple Analogy in Ps. Aristotle, *De Mundo* 6," *Classical Quarterly* 64 (2014): 574–91.

13. This is well spotted by A. Tzvetkova-Graser, "The Concepts of οὐσία and δύναμις in *De Mundo* and Their Parallels in Hellenistic-Jewish and Christian Texts," in: J. C. Thom, ed. (2014), 134: "For the author of *De Mundo* God is completely transcendent. It is his power, though, which is immanent in the world." See also p. 135: "δύναμις is clearly different from οὐσία, since the one is immanent and the other transcendent."

14. *Mu.* 6, 397b27–8a1.

15. *Mu.* 4, 394b9–12.

16. Cf. §9g below.

orders them into a beautiful whole (*cosmos*). If we must speak of "dualism," it is in any case a "moderate dualism": God's controlling Power can use matter as an "instrumental body." And if we put all the emphasis on the distinction between God's Essence and his Power, we could speak of a "split in the divine" in a monistic sense, which results in the ultimate duality of Intellect and material cosmos.

This is a very specific position that cannot be ascribed to any other known philosopher from Antiquity.[17] But the distinction between a supreme, transcendent God and a subordinate, productive divine agency became an extremely successful view. After Aristotle, no one ever went on to defend a "naïve" conception of a Creator-God such as the Demiurge in Plato's *Timaeus*.[18]

Again, this would be remarkable if the author were someone unknown to us, who pretended that his text had been produced by Aristotle. However, as we have seen in chapters 5 and 8 above, Aristotle himself certainly defended the position that God is transcendent to the entire cosmos, but acts on everything in the cosmos through his Power. Thus, it is very clear that Aristotle could no longer accept that the entire cosmos is "full of gods." He did maintain the idea that the cosmos depends completely on God and that "something" of God manifests itself in the cosmos. But this "something" is not identical with God. In the *Timaeus*, Plato had described the Demiurge as "good" and as the cause of all the good in the cosmos, but had to accept that the cosmos could only be made "as good as possible" by the Demiurge. Just so, Aristotle posits that the transcendent divine Intellect manifests itself in the cosmos through his controlling Power, which is always *clothed* in a cosmic covering, namely, ether in the divine part and *pneuma* in the sublunary part, and thus shares in the good, though to degrees of "more" and "less." Whereas Plato's *Timaeus* presents the Demiurge as one who personally carries out his plan, Aristotle makes a separation between the initiator and the executors or instruments, as between an architect and his builders, a doctor and the

---

17. Precisely Alexander of Aphrodisias, in his own work *On the Cosmos*, which has only been passed down in Arabic, fully accepted this distinction between God's Essence and his Power, as well as the authenticity of Aristotle's *On the Cosmos*. Cf. C. Genequand, *Alexander of Aphrodisias, On the Cosmos* (Leiden: Brill, 2001), 6; 17–19. Genequand himself follows P. Moraux and the modern tradition in talking about "the pseudo-Aristotelian *On the Cosmos*."

18. Worth mentioning here is the argument by J. Beere, *Doing and Being: An Interpretation of Aristotle's Metaphysics Theta* (Oxford: Clarendon Press, 2009), ch. 1 that Aristotle in *Metaphysics* Θ developed the two fundamental notions of *energeia* and *dynamis* in debate with Plato's *Sophistes* 246a ff., the "Gigantomachy." In this passage, late Plato is moving toward a connection between intelligible and sensible reality by introducing the notion of *dynamis* as a common property. Aristotle goes one better by positing that *energeia* lays the foundation for all *dynamis*.

prednisone he prescribes, a begetter and the genetic power of his semen. In this way, he introduces an intermediary between God and the cosmos that depends on him.

The theology of *On the Cosmos* displays a distinction resulting from Aristotle's strict separation of "intellect" and "soul." It shows which problems the author identified in the dialectical theology of Plato's *Timaeus*. In the fourth century BCE we see on the one hand a conviction that earthly life depends on God/the gods, but on the other a growing conviction of the Origin's absolute unchangeability and criticism of all too anthropomorphic conceptions of God. Plato's Demiurge falls short as a principle of Origin because he is not absolutely unchanging. He thinks first and acts subsequently. He considers various options and then chooses the best possible one. The reality of which he is the efficient cause is initially something unordered, on which he proceeds to impose order and form. As a craftsman, the Demiurge directly involves himself with bodies and matter. But he can only do so if he himself is also materially characterized.

Upholding the doctrine of God's absolute unchangeability meant that it was no longer possible to see God as efficient cause, as Maker, as providential creator, and as punisher of injustice.

Yet, at first sight there was no clear alternative. In the centuries after Plato no one still supported the naive theological mythology of the *Timaeus*. Its replacement led to various different proposals in the period after Aristotle, among Stoics, the Middle Platonists, Philo of Alexandria, Plotinus, and the Gnostics.

This choice by Aristotle in *On the Cosmos* means that God himself is not called the Creator or Maker of the cosmos and that there is a clear reason for saying that not the supreme, metacosmic God but a subordinate and dependent agency is the "Maker" or "Producer" of the cosmos.[19]

Aristotle's separation of "intellect" and "soul" following from his critical reflection on Plato's position has another, important consequence: a systematic separation between the spheres of sensory perception and thought. For Plato, the soul was immaterial, immortal, and of divine origin, and also a bearer of knowledge concerning the divine world through an *anamnesis* of its preexistence. For Aristotle, only the intellect is divine and the soul of mortal man is only capable of knowledge and memory of sensory, cosmic reality. This excludes implanted or natural knowledge of God. *On the Cosmos* 7, 401a12–3 underlines this by asserting that the many names of God are

---

19. This is insufficiently recognized by J. C. Thom (2014), 110, 115, 120.

designations of what his Power brings about, with the implication that no name is appropriate for the essence of God. Another reference to the absolute transcendence of the divine Intellect is surely found in the comparison of God's exaltedness with that of the Persian Great King, who is described in 6, 398a14 as "invisible to everyone" (παντὶ ἀόρατος). However, this also entails a postulation of "God's Unknowability" for earthly mortals. If *gnôsis* of God is not "innately" present in the soul, it can only be acquired by "revelation" through a person of superhuman stature (such as the demon Silenus in Aristotle's dialogue *Eudemus*), or through philosophy, as the activity of the contemplative intellect.[20]

The step taken by Aristotle here was extraordinarily influential and highly important for later theologies such as that of Philo of Alexandria, who introduced the Logos of God (the totality of all God's powers—*dynameis*) as the Creator of the World; of Arius of Alexandria, who in the Christian tradition presented Jesus Christ as the Logos and the Son of God, but not "of the same essence" as God the Father; of Basilides of Alexandria and of the Gnostics, who posited a transcendent, "unknown" God and opposite him understood created reality as the product of a fallen Sophia or of her son Yaldabaoth, the Evil World Creator.

b. God as Preserver and Begetter

God is immediately characterized by the author in a manner that forcefully shows how far he is removed from the Presocratic philosophers and Plato. "In saying this they used terms suitable to the power of God but not to his *ousia* (being/essence). For God is indeed the preserver (σωτήρ) of all things and the begetter (γενέτωρ)[21] of everything in this cosmos however it is brought to fruition, but he does not take upon himself the toil of a creature that works and labours for itself, but uses an indefatigable power, by means of which he

---

20. Cf. A. P. Bos, "Silenus als Bemiddelaar van Gnostische Kennis in Aristoteles' Dialoog *Eudemus* [Silenus as Mediator of Gnostic Knowledge in Aristotle's Dialogue *Eudemus*], in *Waar Haalden de Gnostici hun Wijsheid vandaan? Over de Bronnen, de Doelgroep en de Tegenstanders van de Gnostische Beweging*, ed. A. P. Bos and G. P. Luttikhuizen (Budel: Damon, 2016), 65–83 and 301–305.

21. *Mu.* 6, 397b21; 399a31. This term means that Aristotle strongly dissociates himself from Plato's description of God as "Demiurge." The cosmos is not God's "artifact," but "God's offspring" or "seedling."

prevails even over things that seem a great way off."[22] This theology, which, strikingly, avoids the term *Maker*, is a clear rejection of Plato's cosmogony, which presents the supreme God as being at the same time a practitioner of various crafts,[23] with lower gods as assistants. It may well be understood as a consequence of the fundamental correction that Aristotle applied to Plato's philosophy: his strict separation of "intellect" and "soul." "Making," "producing," and "organizing" are all terms for changes in the material sphere. They are therefore related to activity of the soul, which is not possible without a body (οὐκ ἄνευ σώματος or only μετὰ σώματος). But all soul is an immaterial and controlling principle in which God's Power manifests itself. On the other hand, the proposed alternative is certainly not Stoic, nor can it be connected with any other conception from after Aristotle's time. The author clearly supports the doctrine of five elements and considers the soul present in *pneuma* to be led by some principle of knowledge. Nor is there any trace of the Stoa's rejection of all spiritual reality.

By using the label *Begetter*, Aristotle postulates the fundamental relationship between God and the cosmos, but at the same time underlines the distinction between God as First Cause and his life-generating Power as Efficient Cause in the proper sense, as he had made plain in *Generation of Animals*. It characterizes this view as dominated by the Platonic problem of the distinction between an immaterial, spiritual reality and the world of physical bodies, and as a critique of Plato's solution to this problem.

---

22. *Mu.* 6, 397b16–24: Διὸ καὶ τῶν παλαιῶν εἰπεῖν τινες προήχθησαν ὅτι πάντα ταῦτά ἐστι θεῶν πλέα ... τῇ μὲν θείᾳ δυνάμει πρέποντα καταβαλλόμενοι λόγον, οὐ μὴν τῇ γε οὐσίᾳ. Σωτὴρ μὲν γὰρ ὄντως ἁπάντων ἐστὶ καὶ γενέτωρ τῶν ὁπωσδήποτε κατὰ τόνδε τὸν κόσμον συντελουμένων ὁ θεός, οὐ μὴν αὐτουργοῦ καὶ ἐπιπόνου ζῴου κάματον ὑπομένων, ἀλλὰ δυνάμει χρώμενος ἀτρύτῳ, δι' ἧς καὶ τῶν πόρρω δοκούντων εἶναι περιγίνεται. The term ἐπίπονος in combination with ζῷον is used by Aristotle to indicate the negative effects of an existence in the sphere of material reality and generation and decay. Cf. *Anim.* I 3, 407b2: "Again, the inescapable association of the mind with the body would be wearisome [ἐπίπονον δὲ καὶ τὸ μεμῖχθαι τῷ σώματι μὴ δυνάμενον ἀπολυθῆναι]" (W. S. Hett), in a critique of Plato's World Soul. See also *Cael.* II 1, 284a17, where Plato's World Soul is said to be as pitiable as the globe-shouldering Atlas. See also Arist. *Eudem.* fr. 6 Ross; 65 Gigon, where King Midas is called a descendant of a δαίμονος ἐπιπόνου, a product of the cosmic Archon. Human corporeality is associated with carrying a burden, toil, and lack of freedom.

23. Cf. L. Brisson, *Le Même et l'Autre dans la Structure Ontologique du Timée de Platon. Un Commentaire Systématique du Timée de Platon* (1974; 2nd revised ed. Sankt Augustin: Academia, 1994), 29–50.

c. God Compared with Zeus in Homer's Text on the "Golden Rope"

God is therefore not present in the cosmos. God's *ousia* is not cosmic. God's essence is just as superior as Zeus in Homer's *Iliad* 8, a highly laudatory comparison, which Aristotle himself had made in *Motion of Animals* 4.[24] In the words of the Poet, he is rightly called "the Supreme," having his throne on "the loftiest crest," that is, the vault of heaven.[25] By means of these quotations the author refers (in a way that Alexander of Macedonia would have recognized straightaway) to *Iliad* 8, 1–27, with a degree of subtlety that no imitator of Aristotle could have contrived but which is wholly plausible for Aristotle, given that he seemed to hear in Homer's words his own theology in *Motion of Animals* 4. God's power is the theme in *On the Cosmos* when the author refers to the text of *Iliad* 8, 1–27, and Aristotle alludes to the same power in *Motion of Animals* 4 as the cause of the bond between God and the cosmos.[26] The texts of Homer, *Iliad* 8, 1–29, Aristotle's *Motion of Animals* 4 and *On the Cosmos* 6 are like a three-stranded cord, by which Homer, Aristotle, and Alexander of Macedonia are joined together as by a golden rope that cannot be

---

24. Cf. §2e above and *Motu anim.* 4, 699b36: εὖ εἰρῆσθαι Ὁμήρῳ.

25. *On the Cosmos* 6, 397b24–7: Τὴν μὲν οὖν ἀνωτάτω καὶ πρώτην ἕδραν αὐτὸς ἔλαχεν, << ὕπατός >> τε διὰ τοῦτο ὠνόμασται, κατὰ τὸν ποιητὴν << ἀκροτάτῃ κορυφῇ >> τοῦ σύμπαντος ἐγκαθιδρυμένος οὐρανοῦ. Cf. G. Reale and A. P. Bos, *Il Trattato Sul Cosmo* (1995), 320–21. M. Sanz Morales, "Las Citas Homéricas Contenidas en el Tratado *De Mundo*, Atribuido a Aristóteles; Prueba de su Inautenticidad," *Vichiana* 4 (1993): 38–47, has argued that the author of *On the Cosmos* mentions "the Poet" three times with specific reference to Homer, whereas Aristotle's generally accepted writings also use this title when citing other authors. For Sanz, this is one reason for dating *On the Cosmos* to a later period. He also published *El Homero di Aristóteles* (Amsterdam: A. M. Hakkert, 1994). Certainly it is useful to consider every facet of a controversial work. And sometimes a small trace of DNA is sufficient evidence to overturn a murder conviction. The question is: What kind of argument is compelling enough in the case of a literary work? Also: What problems are caused by the hypothesis of an unknown, later imitator? In my view, Sanz's argument is too weak and the dedication of *On the Cosmos* to Alexander of Macedonia is reason enough to accept that Aristotle himself exclusively identified "the Poet" in that work with the author of the *Iliad* and the *Odyssey*, whom he had closely studied with Alexander in Mieza. See also F. Bakker, *Three Studies in Epicurean Cosmology* (Diss. Utrecht, 2010), 70–143, esp. 76 n. 204, who demonstrated that "the *De mundo* differs from Aristotle's *Meteorology* in its subdivisions of the subject matter, its omission of the Milky Way . . . and its inclusion of tides, volcanoes and poisonous exhalations."

26. Though the author of *Mu.* may have been referring to other texts in Hom. *Iliad* (1, 499; 5, 754), as J. C. Thom, op. cit., 63 n. 92 notes, the evidence for book 8, 1–27 seems compelling.

easily severed.[27] In a smooth transition, Aristotle modulates the Homeric image of the "Golden Rope" connecting the entire cosmos with God as Origin into the image of a golden "chain" of interlinking rings[28] attracted by the power of a magnet and into the image of a winding mechanism, of which the various parts are successively activated in a kind of chain reaction.[29]

d. God's Power Pervades All the Celestial Spheres and the Sublunary Sphere

The author of *On the Cosmos* presents the distinction between God's *ousia* and his Power as an important new theme. Whatever the author's identity, it seems that he can only have derived this distinction from his knowledge of magnetic phenomena. Had he projected the Sun as a source of light and heat, this

---

27. Did Rembrandt van Rijn know about this connection? One might be inclined to think so. The painter, in a stroke of genius, when asked by the Sicilian Antonio Ruffo to paint a portrait of a philosopher, represented "Aristotle Contemplating the Bust of Homer" (1653). Cf. J. Rosenberg, *Rembrandt*, II vols. (Cambridge: Harvard University Press, 1948), vol. 1 (Text), 167–68; J. Giltaij, *Ruffo en Rembrandt. Over een Siciliaanse Verzamelaar in de Zeventiende Eeuw die Drie Schilderijen bij Rembrandt Bestelde* (diss. Vrije Universiteit, Amsterdam, 1997), 35–77. I think that the great "golden chain" that Aristotle wears in the picture can be seen as a gift from Alexander the Great, whose portrait by Rembrandt (c.1665) seems to be connected with it. And there is a broad tradition that Aristotle initiated Alexander into the world of Homer's *Iliad*, although there is no record of such an unphilosophical present by Alexander to his teacher. (It may be that a misinterpretation of *On the Cosmos* 1, 391b5–8 plays a role here.) But we do know that Aristotle profoundly explained Homer's playful tale about the "golden chain" as a symbol of the creation's complete dependence on its metacosmic principle. In this way, Aristotle elevated the blind poet Homer to the status of a visionary philosopher. As a result, the motif of the "great chain of being" was widely disseminated. Cf. L. Edelstein, "The Golden Chain of Homer," in *Studies in Intellectual History*, ed. G. Boas and H. Cherniss (1953; repr. New York: Greenwood Press, 1968), 48–66 and L. Brisson, *Einführung in die Philosophie des Mythos. Antike, Mittelalter und Renaissance* (Darmstadt: Wissenschaftliche Buchgesellschaft, 1996), 53–54. Edelstein, p. 51 notes: "From the fifth century B.C. this passage seems to have been of singular importance to all allegorizers." And p. 59: "the *aurea catena Homeri* was established by the Middle Platonists as a figurative expression of the Scale of Being."

28. P. Lévêque, *Aurea Catena Homeri. Une Étude sur l'Allégorie Grecque* (Paris: Les Belles Lettres, 1959), 13–30. Cf. A. O. Lovejoy, *The Great Chain of Being. A Study in the History of an Idea* (Cambridge: Harvard University Press, 1936; repr. 1976). See also M. L. Kuntz and P. G. Kuntz, eds., *Jacob's Ladder and the Tree of Life. Concepts of Hierarchy and the Great Chain of Being* (New York: Lang, 1987).

29. Cf. E. Lesky (1950), 136.

would also have exemplified a dual unity allowing a clear distinction between Cause and Effect, but in that case the decrease in light and heat according to the distance from the Source would not have been obvious. As we have seen, for Aristotle the reduction in the effect of God's power was manifested by the lower degree of order and quality of life in the regions remote from the Origin.

God's Power is operative outside of God, from the outer celestial sphere, via all six intermediate spheres, down to the sphere of the Moon,[30] and from there down to the regions where humans and animals live. In the first place, God's Power therefore acts on the outer celestial sphere. However, like a magnet's power, God's power is passed on to following spheres.

As regards the celestial spheres, the author of *On the Cosmos* talks in 2, 392a18–30 about their *kykloi,* which may mean "spheres" or "circular courses," but was used in Plato's *Ion* for the (iron) "rings" hanging from a magnet. According to the author of *On the Cosmos,* the celestial or planetary spheres may well be seen as "rings" that "depend" on God because God's Power connects them with each other and with God.[31]

e. The Cosmic Winding Mechanism: Set in Motion by God

After illustrating the exalted status of God by describing the hierarchy and court of Persia's Great King, the author of *On the Cosmos* emphasizes that God does not depend on a large train of subordinates. He rules all things purely through his Power, which pervades the entire cosmos.[32] The Power therefore proceeds from God and remains God's Power throughout the cosmos. It is

---

30. The work follows the order of the planets that was assumed up till 300 BCE. This would be highly remarkable for a late imitator of Aristotle. In the subsequent period, Hermes and Venus were customarily situated between the Sun and the Moon.

31. See not so much 2, 392a13–6 as a18–20: "but the class of planets is organized in seven units, arranged in the same number of circles (rings) in a series [τὸ δὲ τῶν πλανήτων, εἰς ἑπτὰ μέρη κεφαλαιούμενον, ἐν τοσούτοις ἐστὶ κύκλοις ἐφεξῆς κειμένοις]" (P. Lévêque [1959], 21).

32. *On the Cosmos* 5, 396b27–9: "the whole of earth and sea, the aether, the sun, the moon and the whole heaven have been set in order by the single power which penetrates all things [γῆν τε πᾶσαν καὶ θάλασσαν αἰθέρα τε καὶ ἥλιον καὶ σελήνην καὶ τὸν ὅλον οὐρανὸν διεκόσμησε μία ἡ διὰ πάντων διήκουσα δύναμις]." 6, 397b33: "it is the nature of the Divine to penetrate to everything [ἐπὶ πᾶν διικνεῖσθαι πέφυκε τὸ θεῖον. 398a5: διήκουσα]." 6, 398b8: "while his power, penetrating the whole of the cosmos, moves the sun and moon and turns the whole of the heavens and is the cause of preservation for the things upon the earth [τὴν δὲ δύναμιν διὰ τοῦ σύμπαντος κόσμου διήκουσαν ἥλιόν τε κινεῖν καὶ σελήνην καὶ τὸν πάντα οὐρανὸν περιάγειν αἴτιόν τε γίνεσθαι τοῖς ἐπὶ τῆς γῆς σωτηρίας]."

important to stress this against those who believe that Aristotle's God does little more than snap his fingers. On lower levels, too, the (vital) power that works and is transmitted is the Power of God, responsible for the Order and the Forms of all that lives in the Cosmos. If this Power stops, a total cosmic blackout ensues.

The impressive thing about God's activity is that he is effortlessly the origin of all things through one single motion proceeding from him.[33] The author goes on to compare God's activity to that of constructors of winding mechanisms, just as in *Generation of Animals* II 1 he had compared the effect of the Power transmitted during copulation (whether or not via male semen) to the performance of a winding mechanism, and in *Motion of Animals* 7 the motor system of living beings to such devices.[34]

Aristotle used the comparison with winding mechanisms to express an essential point of his philosophy. There is an activity of thought that manifests itself in an instrument that carries out an efficient operation in which the designer's thought is recognizable and essential. However, the efficient movement of *pneuma* in semen is equally a movement that, on the level of biotic reality, executes a development that is aimed at adult vital activity and in which the *logos*, the plan, of a divine constructor is also recognizable.[35] The fundamental idea of Aristotelian philosophy is that there proceeds from the divine, transcendent Intellect, which forms the source of all forms of "life," a Power that provides itself with a (fine-material) body, which actively creates and organizes the world, and from which proceeds, at a farther remove from the Source, a vital power that provides itself with less-endowed (pneumatic) instrumental bodies. This vital power is always directed by an aim, both in the motion and locomotion of a human being and in the development of an embryo in his mother's womb. The implicit presupposition here is that this power provides itself on every level with the instrument (-al body) that it needs to achieve its aim. "Matter" and "corporeality" are not seen as negative in themselves here, but as that which makes production possible and is subservient to it. Visible

---

33. *On the Cosmos* 6, 398b13–6: "the most divine thing of all is to produce all kinds of results easily by means of a single motion [τοῦτο ἦν τὸ θειότατον, τὸ μετὰ ῥᾳστώνης καὶ ἁπλῆς κινήσεως παντοδαπὰς ἀποτελεῖν ἰδέας]."

34. Cf. §5j above; J. de Groot, "*Dynamis* and the Science of Mechanics: Aristotle on Animal Motion," *Journal of the History of Philosophy* 46 (2008); 43–68; P. Gregoric and M. Kuhar, "Aristotle's Physiology of Animal Motion: On *Neura* and Muscles," *Apeiron* 47 (2014): 99–100.

35. This is why Aristotle refers to the distinction between the "sleeping" soul and the "awakened" soul in *Anim.* II 1, 412a10–11 and a22–7 in terms of "science" and "contemplation." More on that in §10q.

reality is reality in which eternal forms of thought have been realized. For Aristotle, this is the basis for the scientific knowability of nature.[36]

The author talks there about μεγαλότεχνοι.[37] In any case he seems to refer to constructors of devices that perform various very different functions thanks to the string of a winding mechanism.[38] The divine Power therefore works in exactly the same way as the power that is transmitted during fertilization to the menstrual fluid of the female and that produces there one after the other part of the visible body, as we saw in §6b above.[39]

"So also the divine being, with a single movement of the first part distributes his power to the next and then to the more remote parts until it permeates the whole. One thing is moved by another and itself then moves a third in regular order."[40] Primarily, we should identify "the first part" here with the first part of the winding mechanism,[41] but in the second place with the outer celestial sphere, which is said to be "nearest to" God in 397b28.[42]

There is a certain irony in the fact that an ancient author, in a work that purports to be written by Aristotle (and that I believe was in fact written by Aristotle), presented a "mechanistic" worldview long before the time when, according to E. J. Dijksterhuis (1950), this view was developed in opposition to Aristotle.[43] For the author of *On the Cosmos*, but for Aristotle too, the cosmos works thanks to an instrument or mechanism. Remarkably, however, he does not say that this mechanism is "nothing but" a device that works purely under its

---

36. And for Aristotle, as Plato's pupil, this means that the eternal forms (*eidè*) are connected with God's thought. On this, see §10q below.

37. Or, according to W. L. Lorimer, *Aristotelis qui fertur Libellus De Mundo* (Paris: Les Belles Lettres, 1933), 85, μηχανότεχνοι; D. J. Furley (1955), 390, μηχανοποιοί.

38. *On the Cosmos* 6, 398b14–6: "just like the operators of machines, who produce many varied activities by means of the machine's single release-mechanism [ὥσπερ ἀμέλει δρῶσιν οἱ μεγαλότεχνοι, διὰ μίας ὀργάνου σχαστηρίας πολλὰς καὶ ποικίλας ἐνεργείας ἀποτελοῦντες]."

39. Cf. *Gener. anim.* II 1, 734b9–17.

40. *On the Cosmos* 6, 398b19–23: Οὕτως οὖν καὶ ἡ θεία φύσις ἀπό τινος ἁπλῆς κινήσεως τοῦ πρώτου τὴν δύναμιν εἰς τὰ συνεχῆ δίδωσι καὶ ἀπ' ἐκείνων πάλιν εἰς τὰ πορρωτέρω, μέχρις ἂν διὰ τοῦ παντὸς διεξέλθῃ· κινηθὲν γὰρ ἕτερον ὑφ' ἑτέρου καὶ αὐτὸ πάλιν ἐκίνησεν ἄλλο σὺν κόσμῳ. An obvious flaw in this extremely clever comparison is that a winding mechanism also needs to be "made."

41. See *Gener. anim.* II 1, 734b11, cited in §6b above. See also C. D. C. Reeve (2012), 19–21.

42. *On the Cosmos* 6, 397b27–30: "his power is experienced most of all by the body that is closest to him, less by the next, and so on down to the regions inhabited by us [μάλιστα δέ πως αὐτοῦ τῆς δυνάμεως ἀπολαύει τὸ πλησίον αὐτοῦ σῶμα, καὶ ἔπειτα τὸ μετ' ἐκεῖνο, καὶ ἐφεξῆς οὕτως ἄχρι τῶν καθ' ἡμᾶς τόπων]."

43. See §5a above.

own power and according to its own rules. The author of *On the Cosmos*, like Aristotle, sees the cosmos not as something that works under its own power, but as something that depends entirely on the power and intellectual activity of its designer. For Aristotle, every product of human technical skill refers to its designer, constructor, and maker. It is exactly the same with the system of the cosmos. In his book, E. J. Dijksterhuis describes an age-long progression of insight that finally led to a rejection of Aristotle's dual physics and psychico-physical worldview. Yet Aristotle could also well be described as the inventor of the "mechanistic" worldview. For him, it is impossible to imagine the existence of a mechanism or instrument without an intelligent human being who has contrived such an instrument or mechanism for a useful purpose or without an intelligent user of this instrument. To Aristotle, a "mechanistic" worldview in the modern sense would be self-contradictory. He would think it just as absurd to talk about a "natural law" without presupposing a lawgiver.[44]

Though the Power is passed on from a higher level to the next, the author of *On the Cosmos* considers it essential that God is the source of Power, which thus penetrates the entire cosmos. In this regard, God's vital Power can be compared to the power of a magnet, which is transmitted from one iron ring to the next. All manifestations of life and efficient power are thus interpreted by the author of *On the Cosmos* as products of the one source of Power. That is why he can describe all things in the cosmos as "the works of God who has power over the cosmos."[45] The many names that people have given to God are not in fact designations of his essence but of his works.

Chapter 1 of *On the Cosmos* is an introduction to the entire work. It describes philosophy as a discipline that tries to acquire an overall perspective on nature and the cosmos. To this end, the soul, taking the intellect as its guide, rises to a great height in order to contemplate divine reality with the divine eye of the soul (391a11–5). The description is reminiscent of texts in which Plato describes how the soul ascends to the world of Ideas. But Aristotle's focus is on the visible cosmos. Philosophy aims to reveal to human beings the truth about this cosmos. In 391b3 the author declares: "Let us therefore speak and, as far as possible, theologize about these matters [Λέγωμεν δὴ ἡμεῖς καί, καθ' ὅσον ἐφικτόν, θεολογῶμεν περὶ τούτων συμπάντων]." Seen in the light of 7,

---

44. See, in contrast, A. Gregory, *The Presocratics and the Supernatural: Magic, Philosophy, and Science in Early Greece* (London: Bloomberg Academic, 2013), 5, who describes his own position as that of "an outright rationalist" and "a sceptic in the strong modern sense": "Philosophically my view is quite straightforward. All that exists is natural. All that exists obeys natural laws."

45. Cf. *On the Cosmos* 6, 399b24–5: θεοῦ λέγοιτ' ἂν ὄντως ἔργα εἶναι τοῦ τὸν κόσμον ἐπέχοντος (trans. J. C. Thom [2014], 49).

401a12–3, this "theologizing" is not an exposition on "the essence" of God, but on everything that he accomplishes through his Power. It is therefore a "natural theology" in which the order and goal-orientedness of all things in the cosmos put the inquiring mind on the trail of the "Cause that holds all things together" (6, 397b9), though this cause itself is unnamed and unnameable. Thus, "theology" in this sense also means that the divine and eternal forms of the species of all living beings, their entelechies—see §10q below—are recognized as springing from the one Source of all divine order in the cosmos.

According to Aristotle, all talk about God comes "from below." People have no "memory" of a previous existence in freedom and divine perfection. They can only talk about their experience of cosmic reality. That is why all religion is a form of cosmic religiosity. God himself is the great "unknown God," until a human being achieves true *gnôsis* and thereby insight into the divinity of his own mind. Indeed, the author's criticism of Thales of Miletus proves here to be criticism of all previous philosophical theology.

On the basis of etymology the author even connects the most important name, "Zeus," and its derivative, "*Dia*," with "Him through whom we live."[46] Everything that lives and exists owes its life and existence to God as the indispensable center of vital heat and power. For Aristotle, living entities are not isolated monads but entities interconnected by the one Power that proceeds from God and is joined to the Source and the Goal.

According to Aristotle, the efficiency in all Nature can only be understood as the result of the active Power, which, connected with ether or *pneuma*, operates efficiently because it stays linked to the Intellect as Origin and Goal. Every entelechy in a living entity is a *logos* principle connected with ether or *pneuma*, a rational principle that carries out its particular plan.

Chapter 5 of *On the Cosmos* also contains an elaborate ode to the community (κοινωνία), agreement (ὁμολογία), and concord (ὁμόνοια) in the entire cosmos.

f. God's Power is Less Evident in Sublunary Reality

In the celestial spheres, consisting of the perfect divine element ether,[47] God's Power is therefore transmitted from the outer to the inner sphere, that of the

---

46. *On the Cosmos* 7, 401a13–5: "We call him both Zena and Dia, using the names interchangeably, as if we were to say 'Him through whom we live' [καλοῦμεν γὰρ αὐτὸν καὶ Ζῆνα καὶ Δία . . . ὡς κἂν εἰ λέγοιμεν δι' ὃν ζῶμεν]" (trans. D. J. Furley [1955], 405).
47. In *On the Cosmos* 2, 392a8–9. ether is referred to as "an element different from the four elements, pure and divine [στοιχεῖον . . . ἕτερον τῶν τεττάρων, ἀκήρατόν τε καὶ θεῖον]." See

Moon. However, in the sublunary sphere too, everything that lives is under the spell of the rings of the cosmic Archons[48] and there too this Power is passed on. It does not stop at the sphere of the Moon, and all sublunary reality is not totally deprived of the salutary effect of God's Power. The effects of this Power do diminish, though.

Aristotle had also said this in his discussion of "spontaneous generation" in *Generation of Animals* III 11, 761b14–22. There too he established an explicit correlation between distance from the Origin and quality of life.[49]

In *On the Cosmos* 6, 397b29–32 Aristotle says expressly that the benefit of God's Power diminishes as the distance increases, but that it still reaches our regions.

---

also 392a31–2: "After the aetherial and divine element, which is arranged in a fixed order, as we have declared, and is also unchangeable, unalterable and impassive [Μετὰ δὲ τὴν αἰθέριον καὶ θείαν φύσιν, ἥν τινα τεταγμένην ἀποφαίνομεν, ἔτι δὲ ἄτρεπτον καὶ ἀνετεροίωτον καὶ ἀπαθῆ]."

48. It is undeniable that the notion of the planetary powers as cosmic Archons, which became so important in the later tradition, derives from *On the Cosmos*. See 6, 398a18–35, where the author describes the hierarchy of the Persian Empire, which is transferred to the cosmos. It is quite clear that the court of the Persian Great King is modeled on Aristotle's theory of knowledge. In this theory, the intellect and the immaterial soul as entelechy form the central post where all information about the outside world gathered via the senses is brought together and from whence all directives for imperial government issue. This analogy may be reinforced by the words in 6, 398a18–9. After Aristotle has described how the Persian Great King has his seat in Ecbatana, "invisible to all," in his imposing palace, which is surrounded by strong walls and connected with gates and watch posts, he continues with the words: ἔξω δὲ τούτων, followed by an enumeration of his bodyguards, advisors, and other officials. These words are usually translated as "apart from these" (J. C. Thom). But it is possible to lay emphasis on these words and translate them, as D. J. Furley did, "outside these," which then suggest that no one can see God, not even his servants, who are ensouled beings, *and are therefore burdened with materiality*. In Aristotle's doctrine of perception it is essential that the soul can only perform its perceptive function via the soul's instrumental body. Cf. A. P. Bos, "Perception as a Movement of the Instrumental Body of the Soul in Aristotle" (2011); "The Soul's Instrument for Touching in Aristotle, *On the Soul* II 11, 422b34–3a21" (2010); "The Ears Are not the Subject of Hearing in Aristotle's *On the Soul* II 8, 420a3–12" (2010).

49. See *Gener. anim.* III 11, 761b13–21: "because we may say that plants belong to the earth, aquatic creatures to the water, and land-animals to the air, but the more and less and nearer and further make an amazingly great difference. As for the fourth tribe, we must not look for it in these regions, although there wants to be a kind corresponding to the position of fire in the series, since fire is reckoned as the fourth of the corporeal substances. . . . No, this fourth tribe must be looked for on the moon [τὰ μὲν γὰρ φυτὰ θείη τις ἂν γῆς, ὕδατος δὲ τὰ ἔνυδρα, τὰ δὲ πεζὰ ἀέρος· τὸ δὲ μᾶλλον καὶ ἧττον καὶ ἐγγύτερον καὶ πορρώτερον πολλὴν ποιεῖ καὶ θαυμαστὴν διαφοράν. τὸ δὲ τέταρτον γένος οὐκ ἐπὶ τούτων τῶν τόπων δεῖ ζητεῖν· καίτοι βούλεταί γέ τι κατὰ τὴν τοῦ πυρὸς εἶναι τάξιν· τοῦτο γὰρ τέταρτον ἀριθμεῖται τῶν σωμάτων . . . ἀλλὰ δεῖ τὸ τοιοῦτον γένος ζητεῖν ἐπὶ τῆς σελήνης]" (A. J. Peck [1942], 351–53). Cf. §3e above.

So the earth and the things that are on the earth, being at the greatest distance from the help of God, seem to be feeble and discordant and full of confusion and diversity.[50]

There is a cosmic "hierarchy," which Aristotle elaborately compares to that of the vast Persian Empire (with which Alexander of Macedonia had an account to settle!).[51] There too the Persian Great King is not personally active everywhere, but his control, via his subalterns, is noticeable to the farthest corners of the empire.

g. *Pneuma* Is the Carrier of God's Power in the Sublunary Sphere According to *On the Cosmos*

The cosmic theology of *On the Cosmos* thus contains the following elements:

- God is transcendent to the cosmos;
- God is the Origin of order and life in the cosmos;
- God is this Origin through the Power that proceeds from him;
- this Power pervades the entire cosmos;
- the effect of this Power is less strong in proportion to the distance from God, the generator of this Power;
- this Power does not change the carriers of the Power, but vitalizes them and creates order and life in them, in accordance with their capacity.

In an earlier section we surmised that Aristotle drew inspiration for this view from the phenomenon of magnetism: the magnet whose power penetrates iron rings and brings them to life, as it were. The question is: What is the carrier of this divine Power according to the author of *On the Cosmos*?

This question is easy to answer for the celestial spheres. The author says that they consist of a different, divine element: ether, which takes its name from

---

50. *On the Cosmos* 6, 397b29–32: καὶ ἐφεξῆς οὕτως ἄχρι τῶν καθ' ἡμᾶς τόπων. Διὸ γῆ τε καὶ τὰ ἐπὶ γῆς ἔοικεν, ἐν ἀποστάσει πλείστῃ τῆς ἐκ θεοῦ ὄντα ὠφελείας, ἀσθενῆ καὶ ἀκατάλληλα εἶναι καὶ πολλῆς μεστὰ ταραχῆς.

51. In the *Alcibiades Maior*, attributed to Plato, the vastness of the Persian Empire was also brought up in a conversation with the young and highly ambitious Alcibiades. In *Mu.*, which is dedicated to Alexander of Macedon, the aptness of this theme is conspicuous.

its continual motion (ἀεὶ θεῖν);⁵² and he says explicitly of the eight spheres (the outer celestial sphere and the seven planetary spheres) that they benefit from God's Power, one more than another.⁵³

But what about the region of the creatures that come into being and perish? The author of *On the Cosmos* says nothing about this. Are we to assume that God's Power permeates the sublunary elements, earth, water, air, and fire, just as it pervades the celestial spheres and beings? Or should we consider that a magnet influences iron, but not an earthenware jug? Does this mean that God's Power is not carried by earth, water, air, and fire, but by something else, which is receptive to (directives of) the soul as entelechy?⁵⁴

To answer this question, we need to look at one more relevant passage in *On the Cosmos*, though the author clearly has no intention of devoting a separate treatment to the subject. In a discussion of an entirely separate issue ("winds"—*pneumata*—the times in which they blow and the directions they come from), he adds the remark:

> "*Pneuma*" is used in a different sense with regard to the ensouled and generative substance which is found in plants and living creatures, pervading them totally; but with this we need not deal here.⁵⁵

The author talks here about *pneuma* as "the ensouled and generative substance which is found in plants and living creatures, pervading them

---

52. *Mu.* 2, 392a5–9; *Cael.* I 3, 270b22–4.
53. *Mu.* 6, 397b27–8a1.
54. As Aristotle postulates in *Anim.* I 3, 407b13–27 and *Gener. anim.* II 3, 736b29–7a1.
55. 4, 394b9–12: Λέγεται δὲ καὶ ἑτέρως πνεῦμα ἥ τε ἐν φυτοῖς καὶ ζῴοις <οὖσα> καὶ διὰ πάντων διήκουσα ἔμψυχός τε καὶ γόνιμος οὐσία, περὶ ἧς νῦν λέγειν οὐκ ἀναγκαῖον. The addition was proposed by D. Holwerda, "Textkritisches und Exegetisches zur pseudo-Aristotelischen Schrift Περὶ τοῦ κόσμου," *Mnemosyne* 46 (1993): 50. Cf. G. Reale and A. P. Bos (1995), 285–88. J. C. Thom doesn't read this addition and doesn't know the paper by Holwerda.
56. Some scholars have suggested that διὰ πάντων διήκουσα should be read as "which pervades all things." Thus, J. C. Thom, *Cosmic Order* (2014), 31. See also D. J. Furley (1955), 367. The objection to this is that *pneuma* would then also penetrate the entire ethereal sphere. See also *Spir.* 2, 481b17–9: "Moreover, respiration extends as far as the lungs, as they themselves say, but the innate *pneuma* is present throughout the living creature [ἡ μὲν ἀναπνοὴ μέχρι τοῦ πνεύμονος, ὥσπερ λέγουσιν αὐτοί, τὸ δὲ πνεῦμα δι' ὅλου τὸ σύμφυτον]" and 3, 482a33: "But the innate *pneuma* pervades the entire living creature [τὸ δὲ σύμφυτον πνεῦμα δι' ὅλου]." We emphasize here that in any case this passage ascribes to *pneuma* the remarkable property of wholly pervading the living bodies of plants and animals (and even all cosmic reality, according to D. J. Furley and J. C. Thom). This is no reason to assume Stoic influence in the text, since Aristotle also says in *Gener. anim.* III 11, 762a18–21 that *pneuma* is present in water, which in turn is present in earth, and that therefore everything is "full of soul" in a certain sense. It is, however, a reason for saying that *pneuma* is more akin to the divine ether than to the sublunary elements. See also ch. 10h below.

totally."⁵⁶ Though he does not want to expand on the subject, he clearly holds the Aristotelian view that *pneuma* is not identical with the "breath of life," as in Plato and the Hippocratics. Plants and trees also contain *pneuma* as a life-bearing and life-transmitting substance. And evidently *pneuma* "pervades" the visible bodies of these living entities throughout, just as God's Power "pervades" the entire cosmos.⁵⁷ In this regard, *On the Cosmos* is entirely in line

---

57. Cf. *On the Cosmos* 5, 396b27–9: γῆν τε πᾶσαν καὶ θάλασσαν αἰθέρα τε καὶ ἥλιον καὶ σελήνην καὶ τὸν ὅλον οὐρανὸν διεκόσμησε μία ἡ διὰ πάντων διήκουσα δύναμις. 6, 397b33: ἐπὶ πᾶν διικνεῖσθαι πέφυκε τὸ θεῖον. 398a5: διήκουσα. 6, 398b8: τὴν δὲ δύναμιν διὰ τοῦ σύμπαντος κόσμου διήκουσαν ἥλιόν τε κινεῖν καὶ σελήνην καὶ τὸν πάντα οὐρανὸν περιάγειν αἴτιόν τε γίνεσθαι τοῖς ἐπὶ τῆς γῆς σωτηρίας (already cited above).

58. As we argued in ch. 8 above, this means that we should also start from this position in *On the Cosmos* 5, 397a18: "From this all creatures breathe and take their life [Ἐκ τούτου πάντα ἐμπνεῖ τε καὶ ψυχὴν ἴσχει τὰ ζῷα]." So the reference there is not to a quasi-Orphic or quasi-Pythagorean view in which the soul is inhaled as vital breath. What the author means is that the air inhaled for the necessary cooling of the living creature, but also the soul, connected with the vital *pneuma*, originates from the cosmos in its totality. Note that the text is read in this way by W. L. Lorimer, *Aristotelis qui fertur Libellus De Mundo* 79, on the basis of three fourteenth- and fifteenth-century mss. The majority of mss, including some early ones, read ἐμπνεῖται instead of ἐμπνεῖ τε. It is natural to assume here that ἐμπνεῖται is a copyist's error for ἐμπνεῖ τε. In Greek, ἐμπνεῖται καὶ would have been unsightly. But ἐμπνεῖ (which does not otherwise occur in the Aristotelian Corpus; H. Bonitz, *Index Aristotelicus* does not even mention it) is surprising. It is mostly used in an active sense of "to breathe into," "to inspire," "to blow upon," "to blow (a whistle)." It may also mean "to breathe" and "to live." But see also Plato, *Apol.* 29d4: "and while I live and am able to continue, I shall never give up philosophy [καὶ ἕωσπερ ἂν ἐμπνέω καὶ οἷός τε ὦ, οὐ μὴ παύσωμαι φιλοσοφῶν]," and *Resp.* II 368c1. This usage never involves anything "from" which the breathing takes place. Interesting, too, is that, in the text as read by Lorimer, the author seems to connect the possession of soul with breathing. This in turn could suggest that the author, like Plato, sees the moment of birth and the first breath as the moment of the soul's entry. But precisely the author's emphatic assertion that breath and the soul come from the *kosmos* seems at odds with Plato's doctrine of soul. Also, the author of *On the Cosmos* has just casually remarked in 4, 394b9–12 that the soul is connected with *pneuma* and is present in plants. It is therefore worth considering that the word πνεῦμα was originally found in this text too, but has disappeared from it, as in *Motu anim.* 7, 701b16 (cf. O. Primavesi and K. Corcilius in their forthcoming edition with translation). If the original text read: Ἐκ τούτου πάντα πνε<ῦμα> τε καὶ ψυχὴν ἴσχει τὰ ζῷα, it is easy to understand how this led to a "correction" to ἐμπνεῖ and a further "improvement" to ἐμπνεῖται. Perhaps the text even originally read: Ἐκ τούτου πάντα ἔμ<φυτον> πνε<ῦμα> τε καὶ ψυχὴν ἴσχει τὰ ζῷα. In the sentence Ἐκ τούτου πάντα πνε<ῦμα> τε καὶ ψυχὴν ἴσχει τὰ ζῷα, the use of τε καὶ would also be more apt. In this form the sentence would fit neatly with *Metaph.* A 3, 983b26–7, where Aristotle says that "vital heat itself" comes from the moist and with *Gener. anim.* III 11, 762a18–21, where he says that *pneuma* is present in water and that therefore "in a certain sense everything is full of psychic heat."

with the treatment of all living entities in Aristotle's generally acknowledged biological writings, starting with *Generation of Animals*. This allows us to conclude that *On the Cosmos*, too, implies that *pneuma* is present throughout the sublunary sphere, as analogue of the astral element and as vehicle of vital power.[58] According to *On the Cosmos*, too, *pneuma* is exempt from the purely physical laws of action = reaction and does not have an "opposite" that brings about its destruction.[59]

Without this remark about the special meaning of the term *pneuma* it would be much harder to fathom the conception of the author of *On the Cosmos*. The almost casual addition of this remark strengthens my conviction that Aristotle regarded *pneuma* as the carrier of the soul-principle. But the very fact that the remark is so casual makes it once again improbable that *On the Cosmos* was written by a later imitator of Aristotle. Conversely, it is understandable that after Alexander of Aphrodisias had reinterpreted Aristotle's doctrine of soul, this passage in *On the Cosmos* was called into question.

Via the remarkable, casual statement about *pneuma* it is clear that *On the Cosmos*, like *Generation of Animals* II 3 (see §10b below), places *pneuma* more with ether than with the four sublunary elements. In *On the Cosmos*, too, *pneuma* should be understood as an analogue of the astral element. In this way the chain of divine entelechy-principles throughout the cosmos is assured of a suitable instrumental body. It is clear that the introduction of the fifth element (and of *pneuma*) is inextricably bound up with Aristotle's doctrine of the entelechy-principle, and that together they form his alternative to Plato's doctrine of soul.[60]

h. The Split between Intellect and Soul and between Philosopher and King in Mythical Guise

A salient feature of Aristotle's philosophy is the fundamental criticism that he levels against Plato's theory of soul. Aristotle's alternative was a consistent distinction of Intellect and Soul. *On the Cosmos* shows signs of this discussion when it talks about God's being as self-oriented and about a power of God that

---

59. Cf. *Long.* 2 and 3, and A. P. Bos, "'Fire Above': the Relation of Soul to its Instrumental Body in Aristotle's *De Longitudine et Brevitate Vitae* 2–3." Cf. §§5a above and 10k below.

60. See also §§10b and 10q below.

results in production and organization.[61] Aristotle's ethical writings described this distinction in terms of "theoretical intellect" and "practical intellect."[62] Plato had brought up the same subject in his great work *The Republic*, where he envisaged a personal union between the Philosopher and the King, but with the clear distinction that the Philosopher preferably engaged with immaterial reality and acquired knowledge of it through contemplation. Yet Plato insisted that the Philosopher, whom the state exempted for the study of science, should regularly "descend" to the sphere of everyday politics to give guidance and put the Idea of the Good into practice.[63] Plato, too, distinguished between the intellect and the soul, but not as sharply as Aristotle. In the *Phaedrus*, Plato argued that the intellect is the highest "part" of the immortal soul and that a continual struggle takes place between the intellect (the charioteer) and the lower soul-parts (the two horses), in particular the part of desire.[64] In Plato's

---

61. This is not just the case in the description of world government, but also in remarks about the individual human being. Cf. *Mu.* 1, 391a11–5: "the soul therefore by means of philosophy, taking the mind as its guide . . . and with the divine eye of the soul it comprehends the divine things [ἡ γοῦν ψυχὴ διὰ φιλοσοφίας, λαβοῦσα ἡγεμόνα τὸν νοῦν . . . καὶ θείῳ ψυχῆς ὄμματι τὰ θεῖα καταλαβομένη]" (J. C. Thom [2014], 21). In my view, Aristotle *Mu.* 1, 391b5–8 also upholds the distinction between Alexander as the "ruler" (who need not become a philosopher, but is exhorted to take an interest in the cosmos in its totality and its parts) and philosophy, which generously shares its insight with the most excellent among nonphilosophers. The Greek text reads: Πρέπειν δέ γε οἶμαι καὶ σοί, ὄντι ἡγεμόνων ἀρίστῳ, τὴν τῶν μεγίστων ἱστορίαν μετιέναι, φιλοσοφίᾳ τε μηδὲν μικρὸν ἐπινοεῖν, ἀλλὰ τοῖς τοιούτοις δώροις δεξιοῦσθαι τοὺς ἀρίστους. I believe this should be rendered as: "I think it is indeed fitting for you, as the best of world leaders, to obtain information about the greatest things, and for philosophy to focus on nothing small, but to welcome outstanding persons with such gifts." J. C. Thom, op. cit., 10, 13, 21, does see *On the Cosmos* as exhorting Alexander to philosophize. He translates: "I think it is indeed fitting for you . . . to pursue the study of the greatest things." See on this text also §9c above.

62. The "practical intellect" is emphatically a function of the rational *soul*, connected with its instrumental body. It is not a "separate" intellect.

63. Plato, *Respublica* VII 520c.

64. In the famous image of the myth in *Phaedrus* 246a5–b6 Plato compares "souls" to the combined power of a pair of winged horses and a charioteer—ἐοικέτω δὴ συμφύτῳ δυνάμει ὑποπτέρου ζεύγους τε καὶ ἡνιόχου. The charioteer is identified with "the mind, the pilot of the soul" (ψυχῆς κυβερνήτῃ νῷ). Human emotions and desires are compared with the two horses that draw the chariot in which the driver sits or stands. A discussion on the heavenly gods mentions Zeus as the great "leader," driving his winged chariot—246e4: "now the great leader in heaven, Zeus, driving a winged chariot, goes first, arranging all things and caring for all things [ὁ μὲν δὴ μέγας ἡγεμὼν ἐν τῷ οὐρανῷ Ζεύς, ἐλαύνων πτηνὸν ἅρμα, πρῶτος πορεύεται, διακοσμῶν πάντα καὶ ἐπιμελούμενος]." This image clearly shows that Plato introduces a separation within the unity of the soul. The intellect is characterized by a guiding motion and the two other soul-parts by a pulling motion. It is plain here that the driver's activity is essential to the performance of the chariot with its pair of horses, though it does not contribute to the vehicle's movement. The

theology of the *Timaeus* we see that the World Creator also displays two aspects: having contemplated the world of Ideas, he produces, after its example, the visible cosmos like a perfect craftsman.[65] He then withdraws and leaves the rest of the work to his assistants. In the *Timaeus*, Plato calls the Demiurge "Intellect," who produces the World Soul from several components. But the difference between Intellect and Soul remains unclear there.

In particular, Plato's Demiurge was utterly ambivalent for Aristotle. For although the Demiurge contemplates the Intelligible cosmos with his intellect, he is then, after a role reversal, turned to a world that he forms from the four material elements (which in turn are made up of regular triangles). Now the Demiurge must constantly find solutions to problems posed by this changeable and visible reality. In Aristotle's view, this second activity is in keeping not with

---

driver only gives direction. A particular feature of Aristotle's philosophy is that he pulled apart the trinity of Plato's mythical image and gave a specifically different interpretation of the intellect in relation to the soul. We will repeatedly return to the consequences of this move. Here we add that Aristotle may have reacted to this image from Plato's *Phaedrus*. The second-century Christian author Hermias referred to this text in his *Irrisio Gentilium Philosophorum* 11, in a discussion on the disagreement among Greek philosophers about the foundations of reality, by saying: "How would it be possible not to trust the philosopher who designed Zeus' chariot? [Πῶς γὰρ οὐ μέλλω πιστεύειν φιλοσόφῳ τῷ τοῦ Διὸς ἅρμα πεποιηκότι;]." He says this after reporting that Plato had posited the following three principles: God, matter, and the Intelligible Model. Hermias continues: "But behind him stands his pupil Aristotle, who tried to surpass the chariot-making of his master [κατόπιν δὲ αὐτοῦ μαθητὴς Ἀριστοτέλης ἕστηκε ζηλοτυπῶν τὸν διδάσκαλον τῆς ἁρματοποιίας]." He goes on to say that Aristotle postulated the active and the passive as fundamental principles. According to Aristotle, the active was the unchanging ether, but the passive has four properties: hot, cold, moist, and dry, and all things are formed through combinations of these. None of this would be easy to follow if we did not know more about Hermias's sources. But we possess another doxographical report, in the *Placita Philosophorum* by Pseudo-Plutarch I 881E-F (= Aetius, II 7, 32 H. Diels), which states: "Aristotle says that the highest god is a separate form, mounted on the sphere of the whole, which is an aetherial body, the one which he calls the fifth [Ἀριστοτέλης τὸν μὲν ἀνωτάτω θεὸν εἶδος χωριστὸν ἐπιβεβηκότα τῇ σφαίρᾳ τοῦ παντός, ἥτις ἐστιν αἰθέριον σῶμα, τὸ πέμπτον ὑπ' αὐτοῦ καλούμενον]" (trans. R. W. Sharples, "Aristotelian Theology after Aristotle," in *Traditions of Theology. Studies in Hellenistic Theology, its Background and Aftermath*, ed. D. Frede and A. Laks [Leiden: Brill, 2002], 15). This text says that Aristotle also imagined God, the Most High, as "standing on" the terrestrial globe as a charioteer stands in his chariot. We may support this by referring to *On the Cosmos* 6, 400b6-8: "And in general, what the helmsman is on a ship. and the driver in a chariot, and the leader in a chorus, and the law in a city, and a commander in an army, this God is in the cosmos [Καθόλου δὲ ὅπερ ἐν νηὶ μὲν κυβερνήτης, ἐν ἅρματι δὲ ἡνίοχος, ἐν χορῷ δὲ κορυφαῖος, ἐν πόλει δὲ νόμος, ἐν στρατοπέδῳ δὲ ἡγεμών, τοῦτο θεὸς ἐν κόσμῳ]" (J. C. Thom [2014], 53). While a general and a driver are still actively related to the army and the vehicle that they lead, the "law" is the most apt image for God's indispensability to the cosmos in that he is the Goal-Pointing System for all things in the cosmos. Cf. G. Betegh and P. Gregoric, "Multiple Analogy in Ps. Aristotle, *De Mundo 6*," *Classical Quarterly* 64 (2014): 574-91.

65. Plato, *Tim.* 29a2–31b3.

the activity of an Intellect, but with the activity of a soul (with an instrumental body). The same goes for the activity of Zeus in the *Phaedrus*, who "goes first, arranging all things and caring for all things," which includes taking the reins of the horses of his winged chariot. Aristotle fundamentally thought through and resolutely accepted the consequences of this criticism. However, this did not lead him to postulate a transcendent Intellect in splendid isolation and a dependent World Soul that arranges and orders everything. For all that lives is structurally connected with the supreme Principle.

There is ensouled reality, on a multiplicity of levels. But from the highest to the lowest level they participate in the divine controlling principle, inasmuch as every entelechy is an unmoved mover (of an ethereal or pneumatic body that serves it as an instrument). The soul of the divine celestial beings possesses reason and practical ingenuity, but it is as such connected with the eternal, divine being of the transcendent Intellect.[66] The soul of a human infant does not possess reason or practical ingenuity, but it is a (sleeping) entelechy-principle, which as unmoved mover guides the process of the infant's metabolism and perception.[67] And so it goes on, down to the level of the lowest animal and vegetable life.

For Aristotle, with his choice of an absolutely pure, transcendent Intellect as unchangeable Origin, the dependence of the entire cosmos on God was just as fundamental a conviction as it was for Plato. But he cannot pin this dependence on a divine "Willing," "Reasoning," "Speaking," or "Providence." Nor can he hold the supreme God responsible for the creation of natural bodies, in the way that Plato in the *Timaeus* had talked about the formation of physical bodies by the Demiurge, who limited unlimited spatiality through regular figures made up of equilateral and scalene triangles. Hence, Aristotle defended a much more positive view of corporeality, one in which this corporeality was presented as a female partner of practical, productive power and as desirous of form. Although this corporeality is a deformation (πήρωμα), it is also an indispensable part and principle of becoming and an instrument of the soul.

Moreover, he posited an indissoluble bond of all entelechy-principles with the Entelechy par excellence, and saw the extra-divine entelechy-principles as more and less equal to God himself. In this way, he could postulate that the entire cosmos existed "preserved by God and because of God."[68] Also, he

---

66. Its own entelechy is the "for the sake of which" *of* a living entity. God, as separate entelechy, is the "for the sake of which" *for* each living entity (*Anim.* II 4, 415b2–3; b20).

67. Cf. §10q below.

68. Cf. *Mu.* 6, 397b14: "all things have come into existence from God and because of God [ἐκ θεοῦ πάντα καὶ διὰ θεόν.'" See also 2, 391b11: "preserved by God and because of God [ὑπὸ θεοῦ τε καὶ διὰ θεὸν φυλαττομένη]."

could maintain that higher levels of reality participated "more" in the divine governance than lower levels. This gave rise to the broad doxographical tradition that R. W. Sharples called the "Non Sublunary Providence" theory (which held that Aristotle spoke of divine Providence for the supralunary spheres but not for sublunary reality).[69] A stumbling block in this theory must have been that Aristotle postulated cognitive principles that exist outside the absolute unity of the divine Intellect, and are (therefore?) clothed in a fine-material body. The same problem occurs at a lower level, where Aristotle says that the quality of psychic powers differs according to the quality of the *pneuma* with which they are connected.[70] Just as Plato assumed in all life the vitalizing effect of "souls," in different degrees of quality according to the degree in which they had acquired knowledge of the intelligible world, so Aristotle assumed in all life unmoved movers with varying degrees of effectivity, according to whether they were connected with an instrumental body of greater or lesser quality. But he also assumed the fundamental connection between the purely transcendent Entelechy of the whole cosmos and the materially bound entelechies of all living beings.

In his dialogue *The Statesman*, Plato developed this ambivalence of the Intellect in a different way by constructing a great mythical narrative about the two opposite conditions of the world. First there is the world period under Kronos as King of the World, when he governs the movement of the World and winds up its mechanism, as it were. Then comes the world time in which Kronos withdraws from world government, making way for the rule of Zeus, when the cosmos spirals into chaos, slowly but increasingly fast, in the opposite direction of movement and time, and under its own power (almost "mechanistically," in the modern sense).[71] Along traditional lines, Plato associated the period of Kronos with a restful, paradisal situation, and that of Zeus with an iron age of hard, strenuous labor and the struggle for life.

This Platonic motif too was drastically changed by Aristotle on the basis of his sharper distinction between Intellect and Soul. He presented Zeus as the transcendent, universal Intellect and Kronos as the World Archon. Though the World Archon is a divine figure, he is "bound" with the fine-material, eternal,

---

69. R. W. Sharples (2002), 13 ff. See 23: "The considerations that led to the attribution of N.S.P. to Aristotle must remain a matter of speculation." We must assume that the doxographical tradition used the standard word *pronoia* for Aristotle's well-considered alternative to Plato's idea of "providence." Cf. *Mu.* 6, 397b27: "The body closest to him has most benefit of his power [μάλιστα δέ πως αὐτοῦ τῆς δυνάμεως ἀπολαύει τὸ πλησίον αὐτοῦ σῶμα]."

70. Cf. §10j below.

71. Plato, *Politicus* 269a7–274e3. Cf. D. Thiel, *Die Philosophie des Xenokrates im Kontext der Alten Akademie* (München/Leipzig: K. G. Saur, 2006), 63–67. Aristotle was no doubt led to criticize this conception by his doctrine of God's absolute unchangeability.

and divine element of ether and has been placed into "custody," inasmuch as Aristotle depicted the entire cosmos as an "Underworld" compared with the perfect freedom of Zeus, the divine Intellect.[72]

Nevertheless, Aristotle sees the situation of Kronos and the celestial beings as divine and blessed, like the inhabitants of the "Isles of the Blessed."[73] Yet they do not possess the perfect bliss of Zeus. That is why Aristotle can compare the life of those who engage in the study of natural science and mathematics (the *enkyklios paideia*) to the situation of those who dwell on the "Isles of the Blessed,"[74] though he also suggests that an even higher form of bliss is conceivable: the condition of absolute transcendence and uniformity with the pure Intellect (the study of theoretical philosophy).[75]

In his great study *On the Nature of the Gods*, Cicero includes a lengthy argument, which he puts in the mouth of the Epicurean Velleius, who accuses

---

72. It is likely that Aristotle thus helped to consolidate a new meaning of the Greek term αἰών (*aiôn*) in the sense of "world." In the New Testament, *aiôn* is regularly used in the sense of "the world" in which people live, in contrast to the future "world" (cf. Mt. 13:22; 13:39; 13:40; 24:3; 28:20; Lk. 16:8; 20:34; Rom. 12:2; Gal. 1:4). A relevant text in this connection is Arist. *Cael.* I 9, 279a22–8, though it poses exegetical problems: "Indeed, our forefathers were inspired when they made this word, *aeon*. The total time which circumscribes the length of life of every creature, and which cannot in nature be exceeded, they named the *aeon* of each. By the same analogy also the sum of existence of the whole heaven, the sum which includes all time even to infinity, is *aeon*, taking the name from ἀεὶ εἶναι ('to be everlasting'), for it is immortal and divine [καὶ γὰρ τοῦτο τοὔνομα θείως ἔφθεγκται παρὰ τῶν ἀρχαίων. τὸ γὰρ τέλος τὸ περιέχον τὸν τῆς ἑκάστου ζωῆς χρόνον, οὗ μηθὲν ἔξω κατὰ φύσιν, αἰὼν ἑκάστου κέκληται. κατὰ τὸν αὐτὸν δὲ λόγον καὶ τὸ τοῦ παντὸς οὐρανοῦ τέλος καὶ τὸ τὸν πάντα χρόνον καὶ τὴν ἀπειρίαν περιέχον τέλος αἰών ἐστιν, ἀπὸ τοῦ αἰεὶ εἶναι εἰληφὼς τὴν ἐπωνυμίαν, ἀθάνατος καὶ θεῖος]." In this way, Aristotle may have introduced the distinction between the "transient" *aiôn*, to which man as a mortal being belongs, and which is ruled by Kronos, the cosmic Archon, and the other *aiôn*, to which man has access via his intellect. For an in-depth study of the concept of *aiôn*, cf. H. M. Keizer, *Life Time Entirety. A Study of Aiôn in Greek Literature and Philosophy, the Septuagint and Philo* (diss. University of Amsterdam, 1999). She discusses the use of the term αἰών in Aristotle on pp. 81–91, adding on pp. 97–101 that the expression *ex aiônos (atermonos) eis heteron aiôna*, in *Mu.* 5, 397a8–11 and 7, 401a13–6, suggests a post-Aristotelian date for the work. (But we must then assume that Stobaeus, *Ecloga* I 20, 2 [Wachsmut 172, 9] wrongly attributes to the ancient Pythagorean Philolaus a text in which ἐξ αἰῶνος καὶ εἰς αἰῶνα occurs twice—Diels-Kranz 44 B 21.) One hopes that this study will be followed up by an inquiry into the period starting from Philo, including Gnostic texts. See also G. Casadio, "From Hellenistic *Aiôn* to Gnostic *Aiônes*," in *Religion im Wandel der Kosmologien*, ed. D. Zeller (Frankfurt a. M.: P. Lang, 1999), 175–90 and I. Ramelli and D. Konstan, *Terms for Eternity:* Aiônios *and* Aïdios *in Classical and Christian Texts* (Piscataway, NJ: Gorgias Press, 2007).

73. For the information on this, see A. P. Bos, *The Soul and its Instrumental Body* (2003), 253–57.

74. Think for instance of the figure of Odysseus with Circe and of the sleeping Endymion. On the latter, see A. P. Bos, "Is the 'Greek King' in Aristotle's *Eudemus* fr. 11 (Ross) Endymion of Elis?," *The Modern Schoolman* 65 (1988): 79–96.

75. The model for this is of course Odysseus, when he is reunited with his beloved Penelope.

Aristotle of being vague and confusing.[76] The example he gives is that Aristotle sometimes proclaims the Intellect the only God, but other times mentions "another God," to whom he assigns the role of leading and preserving motion in the cosmos. Velleius must mean that Aristotle clearly distinguished between a supreme, transcendent Intellect, free from from any connection with materiality, and the Outer Celestial Sphere as the ensouled agency that brings about and preserves all motion in the cosmos. If we are to believe Tertullian,[77] Aristotle once referred to this figure as "the dreaming Kronos," that is to say, a being that differs from Zeus in that he sleeps and dreams. In a later period Plutarch offers a myth in which he talks about a god Kronos who sleeps and dreams, because he "has been shackled with the bonds of sleep" by Zeus.[78] In the same way, Aristotle may well have used Kronos as a symbol of the mind focused on practical activity and government. He is the one whom man resembles as a statesman and student of the *enkyklios paideia*.[79] Aristotle may have given such a mythical presentation of his philosophical reflections in his dialogues. In the text on Velleius, Cicero says that he drew his information from the third book of Aristotle's *On Philosophy*.[80] But this issue is also closely connected with the

---

76. Arist. *Philos.* fr. 26 Ross; 25, 1 Gigon = Cicero, *De Natura Deorum* I 13, 33.

77. Tertullian, *De Anima* 46, 10 = Arist. *Protr.* fr. 20; Ross; 979 Gigon. Cf. A. P. Bos, *Cosmic and Meta-cosmic Theology in Aristotle's Lost Dialogues* (Leiden: Brill, 1989); "The Distinction between 'Platonic' and 'Aristotelian' Dualism, Illustrated from Plutarch's Myth in *De Facie in Orbe Lunae*," in *Estudios sobro Plutarco. Misticismo y Religiones Mistéricas en la Obra de Plutarco*, ed. A. Pérez Jiménez and F. Casadesús Bordoy (Madrid/Malaga: Ediciones Clásicas, 2001), 57–70; "The Dreaming Kronos as World Archon in Plutarch's *De Facie in Orbe Lunae*," in *The Statesman in Plutarch's Work*, vol. I *Plutarch's Statesman and his Aftermath. Political, Philosophical, and Literary Aspects*, ed. L. de Blois et al. (Leiden: Brill, 2004), 175–87.

78. Plutarch, *De Facie in Orbe Lunae* 941F–942B. See also P. L. Donini, "Crono e Zeus nel Mito di Plutarco, *De Facie in Orbe Lunae*," in *Dignum Laude Virum. Studi di Cultura Classica e Musica offerti a Franco Serpa*, ed. F. Bottari, L. Casarsa, L. Cristante, and M. Fernandelli (Trieste: Edizioni Università di Trieste, 2011), 105–18. See also A. P. Bos, "Plutarch on the Sleeping Soul and the Waking Intellect and Aristotle's Double Entelechy Concept," in *Plutarch in the Religious and Philosophical Discourse of Late Antiquity*, ed. L. Roig Lanzillotta and Israel Muñoz Gallarto (Leiden: Brill, 2012), 25–42.

79. This is an interesting slant on the theme of "becoming like God" (*homoiôsis theôi*) familiarized by Plato. Cf. *Theaet.* 176a8–b1. See also L. Roig Lanzillotta, "A Way of Salvation: Becoming like God in Nag Hammadi." In the myth of the *Phaedrus*, Plato derives the different characters of people from the affinity of human souls with one of the eleven celestial gods who govern the cosmos under Zeus's guidance (but also assemble for banquets in Hestia's house at the crest of the heavenly vault—*Phaedrus* 246e4–7c2). On this basis, Plutarch, and probably Aristotle before him, made a division between people who become like the cosmic God and a small group of people who are able to rise to the level of the "unknown," transcendent God.

80. Cf. A. P. Bos, "*Exôterikoi Logoi* and *Enkyklioi Logoi* in the Corpus Aristotelicum and the Origin of the Idea of the *Enkyklios Paideia*," *Journal of the History of Ideas* 50 (1989): 179–98.

themes of the *Eudemus*.[81] We do not know exactly what the relationship was between the writings referred to by these two titles.

Kronos, the Titan, is a "shackled Intellect," but he is also an active World Creator and World Ruler. What about the human intellect? Aristotle argued that this intellect is "in many respects unfree," "bound,"[82] since a human intellect occurs only in a mortal earthly being with a perishable coarse-material body. Such a mortal being only starts to show signs of comprehension and possibly intellect a good while after he has come into being. How can this be explained? Aristotle's solution is that everything living in the sphere of generation and decay is guided by an entelechy as soul-principle, just as efficiently as if such an entity were guided by an intellect. These entelechies differ in quality through the quality of the *pneuma* with which they are connected (and its quality varies depending on its mixture with the sublunary elementary bodies). The entelechy of a plant or an animal is always a "sleeping" soul. The entelechy of a human being may become an "awakened" soul[83] when he has reached the age of discretion and comprehension. Such an entelechy then takes on the condition of "a sailor on his ship."[84]

Aristotle explicitly states that man may come to possess the knowledge that God himself possesses.[85] Nowhere does he indicate that the divine astral beings have the same possibility.[86] To solve this riddle, we should bear in mind that somewhere in the tradition of the Titanic meaning-perspective the myth of Dionysus (Zagreus) was introduced. This Dionysus was begotten by Zeus and lured away by the Titans, who then tore him apart and devoured him. Zeus only managed to save his heart, from which a new Dionysus was born. But the Titans were struck with lightning by Zeus and from their ashes

---

81. The demon Silenus, who revealed in the *Eudemus* that being born is a catastrophe ("*die Tragödie der Geburt*") and a punishment for the soul, which is subjected to a form of bondage, may well have spoken about the bondage of the intellect too.

82. Cf. *Metaph.* A 2, 982b31, where he talks about "human nature."

83. Cf. *Anim.* II 1, 412a23–7. This passage has always been wrongly explained too, because scholars believe that Aristotle is talking about "the belonging of the soul to something." But he is talking about "being soul," in which there is a difference between "sleeping" and "waking." For this, see more fully §10q.

84. See the famous/notorious sentence in *Anim.* II 1, 413a8–9. Man's ability to achieve even divine *theôria* always presupposes the presence of a divine *dynamis* in man.

85. *Metaph.* A 2, 982b31–3a11.

86. This is a mysterious matter which will play an important role in later Gnosticism. Indeed, Plotinus severely reproves the Gnostics on this count. I think that Basilides, with his doctrine of the three "Sonships," may have chosen a different approach to the fate of the celestial beings.

mankind was formed.[87] This mythical story also fits well with the theme of Aristotle's *Eudemus*.[88]

This typically Aristotelian outlook on the relationship body—soul—intellect involves a double "bond" of the intellect-principle with material reality: first, a bond with a fine-material pneumatic body that is an instrument for the soul as entelechy; and then, the covering of this body with a coarse-material visible body.[89] This representation also fits with a doctrine of "double liberation": (1) the liberation of the soul-principle from the visible body as a result of death. This then enables the human soul, because it consists of *pneuma* of the highest quality, to liberate the pneumatic soul-body completely from the effects of the sublunary elementary bodies and become purely ethereal. It thus regains its astral nature of the divine fifth element (the *quinta essentia*); (b) subsequently the casting off of the fine-material soul-covering and the achievement of complete "naked," "uncovered" unity with the world of the pure, transcendent intellect-principles.[90]

The famous story about Orpheus, who is allowed to fetch Eurydice from the Underworld, but must leave her behind at the very end of their climb, may have featured in Aristotle's dialogue *On Philosophy*, but fits equally well with the themes of his *Eudemus*, because this work seems to have represented that the intellect, on its climb out of its bat-like condition[91] up to the Light and those things that are by nature most knowable,[92] has first ascended with the soul to the world of the astral gods, but finally must leave his companion behind, because she is drawn down by the passions and memories of earthly life.[93]

In Aristotle's *Eudemus or On the Soul*, in which he distinguished more sharply between soul and intellect than Plato, the demon Silenus probably

---

87. The Hermetic text *Poimandres* has a comparable myth in which not Dionysus but a divine *Anthrôpos* assumes this role.

88. On the background to Dionysus Zagreus, cf. V. Yates, "The Titanic Origin of Humans: the Melian Nymphs and Zagreus," *Greek, Roman, and Byzantine Studies* 44 (2004): 183–98; R. G. Edmonds (2013), 296 ff.

89. Cf. A. P. Bos, "Aristotle on the Etruscan Robbers: a Core Text of 'Aristotelian' Dualism" (2003).

90. The theme of the dialogue *Eudemus* was that of "returning home." One would expect this to refer to the soul's return home, but the point of Aristotle's criticism of Plato leads him to state that the soul-body remains behind in the celestial sphere of the cosmos, while finally the intellect is freed and unites with the Transcendent. In other words: the soul becomes intellect. The female becomes male.

91. Cf. *Metaph.* α 1, 993b9–11.

92. Ibid., 993b11: τὰ τῇ φύσει φανερώτατα πάντων.

93. This is suggested by Plutarch, *De Facie in Orbe Lunae* 945A-B. Cf. A. P. Bos (2003), 276–81.

narrated not only the insight that being begotten is the greatest disaster for man, but also the story about Orpheus and Eurydice. In this way, Aristotle trumped Plato's narrative in the *Phaedo* about the soul's "being placed into custody" as the "secret doctrine" (of Orpheus).[94] But he thus also made it clear that he rejects the idea of the soul's "memory" (*anamnesis*) of a preexistent celestial glory that could put the soul "back" on the track to the divine world. According to Aristotle, "memory" always has to do with sensory experience of the visible world and is therefore only possible for the soul in combination with its instrumental body.

He probably also used the mythical motif of the Titans as divine beings who have been "imprisoned," placed into custody and chained.[95] In this way Aristotle may have made a plausible case for the distinction between the purely theoretical Intellect and a practical Intellect intent on creating and governing. Such a practical Intellect is always characterized by the will to accomplish something. In talking about God as the supreme and absolutely unchanging principle, Aristotle opted for the notion of God's "Power" (and not for God's "Will" or "Counsel"), to prevent any association with a "need," a "desire," or even a form of fickleness and changeability on the part of God. This is also the reason why the notion of God's "providence"—πρόνοια—and "care"—ἐπιμέλεια—for the cosmos are strikingly absent in *On the Cosmos*.[96] God is unwilling (because "willing" is a matter of the soul and its soul-body), but the unwilling God remains the Chief Intelligence Officer. For Aristotle, Will has become God's Law.

This notion of a divine Power of thought that is active in the cosmos seems to have been a source of inspiration for Philo of Alexandria, who conceives of God as an absolutely transcendent Intellect, but thinks of the Logos as the rationally creating and organizing agency that he has produced and which as the efficient cause brings forth the universe, thanks to the totality of its powers that are active as productive principles in all that lives. The distinction in John 1 between a supreme God and the Logos that proceeded from him and through which all things are created also seems to link up with this idea. In the *Poimandres* of the Hermetic Corpus we find the model of the celestial *Anthrôpos,* who as Son of God enters the material cosmos and becomes locked up in it.

---

94. Plato, *Phaedo* 62b.

95. This is indicated by the information that he saw the existence of humans on earth as a form of "penance" (τιμωρία). Cf. Arist. *Eudem.* fr. 6 Ross; 65 Gigon and *Protr.* fr. 10b Ross; 73 and 823 Gigon.

96. It would be remarkable if *On the Cosmos* was really produced in a later period influenced by the Stoa. Cf. R. Valdevit, "Note sulla Teologia dello Scritto Pseudo-Aristotelico de Mundo," *Studi Italiani di Filologia Classica* 3 (1986): 32–33.

Some in the Gnostic tradition[97] seem to have gone even farther by presenting the activity of a World Ruler and World Creator[98] as following from the fall of a Sophia figure. This Sophia is driven by the will to produce on her own. But because her action is described as driven by her "will," her *orexis*, the action is already characterized as psychic and corporeal. The materialization is the consequence of despiritualization, just as in Plotinus's devolution theory. The (imperfect) result of her action is the Demiurge, Yaldabaoth.[99] It is basically a similar aetiology, but with the aim of taking a further step in the "explanation" of ultimate Evil.

The Fall from Divinity

It is intriguing to see how philosophers and theologians in the period after Plato always explain the gulf between a spiritual and a material reality by referring to the factors of "desire" and "the female." In Aristotle, we established that he sets the utter self-sufficiency of the supreme Deity against a different reality, marked by an ontological "deficiency" or "desire," and compared it to "a mother" (*Phys.* I 9; cf. §3f above).

The Bible story of Genesis 3 figures two people, Adam and Eve, created by God after his image and likeness, who are tempted by the Snake in the Garden of Eden into eating the fruit of the tree of the knowledge of good and evil, which God had forbidden (2:17). Heeding the Snake therefore means breaking God's commandment. The Snake arouses Eve's desire for knowledge by promising that they both will be "like God" (3:5) (though they had already

---

97. Cf. G. P. Luttikhuizen, "Traces of Aristotelian Thought in the *Apocryphon of John*," in *For the Children, Perfect Instruction. Studies in Honor of H.-M Schenke*, ed. H. G. Bethge et al. (Leiden: Brill, 2002), 189: "It is my contention that Aristotle's disconnection of the supramundane God from the rule over the world provided the condition under which Gnostic mythmakers (or their pre-Gnostic forerunners in Hellenistic schools of philosophy) could contrast God with the cosmic rulers; this alteration of Plato's cosmology enabled them to speak highly of their true God, the Invisible Spirit, while at the same time uttering negative thoughts about the demiurgical God and his powers."

98. On the problems surrounding the World Archon in the Gnostic tradition, cf. P. Boyancé, "Dieu Cosmique et Dualisme: les Archontes et Platon," in *Le Origini dello Gnosticismo*, ed. U. Bianchi (Leiden: Brill, 1967), 340–56; J. Daniélou, "Le Mauvais Gouvernement du Monde d'après le Gnosticisme," in U. Bianchi (1967), 448–59; S. Pétrement, "Le Mythe des Sept Archontes Créateurs peut-il s'Expliquer à Partir du Christianisme?." in U. Bianchi (1967), 460–87; M. A. Williams, "The Demonizing of the Demiurge: The Innovation of Gnostic Myth," in *Innovation in Religious Traditions. Essays in the Interpretation of Religious Change*, ed. M.A. Williams (Berlin: Mouton De Gruyter, , 1992), 73–107, and *Rethinking "Gnosticism," An Argument for Dismantling a Dubious Category* (Princeton: Princeton University Press, 1996).

99. See especially the *Apocryphon of John*.

been created after God's image and likeness). In this story the fruit of the tree is also desirable (3:6) and both Eve and, at her instigation, Adam eat of the fruit of the tree. This results in the cycle of birth and death of their offspring.

Although the Bible story seems less about sexuality and reproduction than about the origin of evil and death, it does show a strong connection with the first theme. Adam and Eve, in their paradisal situation, seem to have lived like "angels in heaven" (Matt. 22:30; Mc 12:25) and had no sexual intercourse. Death is announced as punishment for their violation of God's commandment. But while the pronouncement of God's judgment does not allude to the end of the world or of the human race, the begetting of offspring does have a particular link with these motifs.

Plotinus talks about the (female) Soul who wants to be autonomous (*autexousios*) and destroys the original unity with her Origin (the Intellect). This step is also described as an act of *tolma*, pride or self-overestimation (*Enneads* V 1 [10] 1, 1–9), leading to loss of knowledge of the Origin and the self. Thus, Plotinus gives a philosophical exegesis of the motif from Plato's *Phaedrus* of the soul's loss of wings. As a result, the soul becomes less like to the divine and is attracted to the sphere of material reality, which she creates, as it were, through dissociation from the Origin.

The Gnostic *Apocryphon of John* (*Nag Hammadi Library* II 1, III 1, IV 1) relates the story of the unknowable divine Intellect and his partner Barbelo, who together produce a multitude of aeons in pairs of male and female partners. The last of the aeons, Sophia, is driven by the desire to bring forth reality, like the supreme Origin, but without the consent of her (male) partner. The result is a product of lower quality than the reality of the aeons, a zoomorphic deity, Yaldabaoth, who is so hideous that Sophia tries to hide him from view behind a cloud. In Yaldabaoth's reality, man will finally make his appearance as a mortal and sexually differentiated being, with part of the Power and the *pneuma* that Yaldabaoth had stolen from his mother, Sophia, and then breathed into his own creature, man.

Where Plotinus and the *Apocryphon* give "desire" a role in the process of alienation from the Origin, Aristotle emphasizes "desire" as the motive for returning to the Origin and the divine.

Plato has the theme of the soul's fall from the divine sphere due to the loss of its wings; Aristotle puts more emphasis on the dropping of all ballast (and what binds man to the body) in order to ascend and return to the divine Origin.

It seems that the transition from the Maker metaphor for the genesis of the cosmos to the Begetter metaphor caused, on the one hand, disqualification of the Demiurge as a lower and even evil demiurge and, on the other, an interest in sexual differentiation, so that the highest divine principle was presented as either male or as androgynous.[100]

---

100. Cf. R. Zimmermann, *Geschlechtermetaphorik und Gottesverhältnis. Traditionsgeschichte und Theologie eines Bildfeldes in Urchristentum und Antiker Umwelt* (Tübingen: Mohr Siebeck, 2001), 215–23.

10

Pneuma as the Vehicle of Divine Power in the Sublunary Region

Thus far, our analysis of the controversial work *On the Cosmos*. The question that really concerns us is how Aristotle understood the dependence of all things in the cosmos on God, and the fundamental desire of all life for God's eternity and immortality, which we described in chapters 2, 3, and 4. Could it be that God's Power does not just extend through the celestial spheres, but also to the regions where people live? Are, then, the elementary bodies of earth, water, air, and fire the vehicles of this vital power in the sublunary sphere? There are no indications for this in Aristotle's oeuvre. We will have to assume, as we noted in §9g, that in the heavenly spheres the divine vital power is connected with ether, the special divine element. In the sublunary sphere this divine vital power is carried by *pneuma*, which Aristotle calls an analogue of the celestial element.

It is a fact that introductions to Aristotle's philosophy or surveys of his work rarely deal with the theme of *pneuma*, if at all. The focus is usually on his logic, his "hylomorphism," the psychology of *De Anima*, his metaphysics, and his ethics. His biological writings and his doctrine of *pneuma* as the vehicle of vital functions are often disregarded and neglected. Modern scholars who do tackle the subject are uncomfortable with Aristotle's doctrine of *pneuma*. Some hold that Aristotle did entertain a theory of *pneuma*, but failed to sustain it and finally replaced this doctrine with the theory of *De Anima*, in which there is no place for a doctrine of *pneuma*. (Earlier writings like the *Historia Animalium* and the *De Motu Anmimalium*, in which *pneuma* played a role, were supposedly left unrevised.) Others consider an opposite hypothesis: at the end of his life he saw the need for a doctrine of *pneuma*, started to develop it, but lacked time to integrate it in his overall system.¹

---

1. D. E. Hahm, "The Fifth Element in Aristotle's *De Philosophia*: a Critical Re-examination," *Journal of Hellenic Studies* 102 (1982): 60–74, argued that Aristotle continued to hold a doctrine of four elements in *On Philosophy*; so already J. Longrigg, "Elementary Physics in the Lyceum and Stoa" (1975), 225, following D. J. Furley; J. Annas, *Hellenistic Philosophy of Mind* (Berkeley/Los Angeles: University of California Press, 1992), 20: "Aristotle has no overall coherent view of the biological role of *pneuma*; perhaps he would have developed one if he had lived longer." Cf. also D. Bronstein, *Ancient Philosophy* 26 (2006): 426: "The *De anima* definition focuses on the soul's relation to the visible body, while the biological works emphasize *pneuma*"; R. King, *Classical Review* 57 (2007): 323: "Now, there is hardly a whiff of *pneuma* in *De An.*" In a more general sense I. Düring, *Aristoteles. Darstellung und Interpretation seines Denkens* (Heidelberg: Carl Winter—Universitäts Verlag, 1966), 343–44: "Viele Gelehrten haben versucht, entweder eine aristotelische Theorie über die Lebenswärme oder eine über das Pneuma zu rekonstruieren. Keiner dieser Versuche hält eine Gegenüberstellung mit den vorliegenden Aussagen des Aristoteles stand, wahrscheinlich deshalb nicht, weil Aristoteles die Aufstellung einer konsequenten Theorie nie zu Ende geführt hat"; M. C. Nussbaum (1978), 143: "One of the thorniest exegetical problems confronting an interpreter of *MA* is the theory of the *symphyton pneuma*, or innate breath, presented in the treatise's penultimate chapter. The theory is internally obscure, one of a series of cryptic pointers towards a fuller account of this *pneuma* that Aristotle may have planned, or even composed, but which does not survive"; ibid., 161: "But in the absence of the detailed account of its operations that we suspect Aristotle at some point either wrote or planned, they strike us as a somewhat incredible promotional effort"; ibid., 163: "We had better regard the theory as one in the course of development and *pneuma* as a hypothetical gap-filler whose workings cannot be scrutinized too closely," with a reference to F. Solmsen, "Greek Philosophy and the Discovery of the Nerves," *Museum Helveticum* 18 (1961): 177; G. E. R. Lloyd, *Aristotelian Explorations* (Cambridge: Cambridge University Press, 1996), 46: "What little Aristotle has to say on the subject of *pneuma* is notoriously obscure and has occasioned protracted scholarly debate"; Lloyd, "*Pneuma* between Body and Soul," *Journal of the Royal Anthropological Institute* (N.S.) 13 (2007): 140–41; S. Berryman, "Aristotle on *Pneuma* and Animal Self-Motion," *Oxford Studies in Ancient Philosophy* 23 (2002): 93: "Nussbaum rightly argues that a new material, analogous to the *aithèr* . . . is introduced to perform a specific task that the four elements cannot perform"; K. Corcilius, *Streben und Bewegen. Aristoteles' Theorie der Animalischen Ortsbewegung* (Berlin: W. de Gruyter, 2008), 332: "Aristoteles' Äusserungen zum *symphyton pneuma* sind spärlich und zudem schwer unter einen Hut zu bringen"; R. Bees, "Rezeption des Aristoteles in der Naturphilosophie Zenons: die kosmische Lebenskraft im Rahmen der Gottesbeweise bei Cicero, *De Natura Deorum* 2.20–44," in *Was ist 'Leben'? Aristoteles' Anschauungen zur Entstehung und Funktionsweise von Leben*, ed. S. Föllinger (Stuttgart: Franz Steiner Verlag, 2010), 351: "Aus den weiteren Belegen zu einem 'angeborenen Pneuma' (σύμφυτον bzw. ἔμφυτον πνεῦμα) und zu einer 'angeborenen Wärme' (ἔμφυτον θερμόν) lässt sich kaum eine geschlossene Theorie ermitteln"; G. Freudenthal, *Aristotle's Theory of Material Substance. Heat and Pneuma, Form and Soul* (Oxford: Clarendon Press, 1995), 112: "Now, scholars are in general agreement that Aristotle never completely worked out the theory of connate *pneuma*. Therefore, the task which faces the interpreter is to make a plausible guess as to what Aristotle *intended* to accomplish by introducing the concept of *pneuma* into his physiology: What, we should ask, were the *problems* he sought to solve?" Freudenthal himself concludes, on p. 136: "Aristotle apparently groped toward a general theory of connate *pneuma*, which was to describe the physiology of all soul-functions"; see also p. 144: "Aristotle's theory of connate *pneuma* was

My starting point here is the fact that Aristotle never proposes *pneuma* as an extra, sixth element.² Nor is there any evidence that Aristotle ever assumed fewer than five elements. The distinction between an eternal and divine part of the cosmos and a noneternal, perishable, and changeable part of the cosmos, and Aristotle's "dual physics,"³ are not connected with an estimation of the volume of the astral world, as W. Jaeger suggested,⁴ but follow directly from Aristotle's criticism of Plato's cosmogony, in which a World Soul launches the celestial beings, composed of fire and earth, into an everlasting circular orbit. Aristotle's view that the immaterial soul cannot pass on a movement of its own to a material entity forced him to develop an alternative view of a rationally guiding principle that directs a special fine-material natural body.⁵ *Pneuma* should be understood within the framework determined by this five-element system, always regarded as highly typical of Aristotle. *Pneuma* is not identical to any of these five elements, but is more akin to the divine, fifth element than to the four sublunary elements. Just as a magnet cannot attract a potsherd or a piece of chocolate, but does pull an iron ring or a paperclip, so the vitalizing Power of God cannot work on just any elementary body. The doctrine of *pneuma* is not a completely isolated component of Aristotle's philosophy, but must be integrally linked to all other parts of his philosophy of life and the generation of living beings.

---

a grand, ambitious and perfectly sound project"; Freudenthal (2009), 249. In his line, see now F. Buddensiek, "Aristoteles' Zirbeldrüse? Zum Verhältnis von Seele und *Pneuma* in Aristoteles' Theorie der Ortsbewegung der Lebewesen," in *Body and Soul in Ancient Philosophy*, ed. D. Frede and B. Reis (Berlin/New York: W. de Gruyter, 2009), 311: "Das *Pneuma* ist, allgemein gesagt, das Instrument der Seele." See also D. Charles (2009), 304–307. C. D. C. Reeve (2012), provides in his chapter 1 on "The Transmission of Form" (pp. 1–24) an excellent overview of "The Role of Pneuma." E. Mendelsohn, *Heat and Life. The Development of the Theory of Animal Heat* (Cambridge: Harvard University Press, 1964), 1–26 gives a good introduction to the topic of "vital heat" in the history of biology.

2. Cf. T. Kouremenos, *Heavenly Stuff: the Constitution of the Celestial Objects and the Theory of Homocentric Spheres in Aristotle's Cosmology* (Stuttgart: Franz Steiner Verlag, 2010), 71.

3. See §5a above. Note too that the visible celestial gods consist of a soul and their instrumental body (made up of ether); mortal creatures have an instrumental body plus a mortal, visible body.

4. Cf. W. Jaeger, *Aristotle*, 154: "What first gave rise to it was obviously the new and precise calculations, undertaken by the school of Eudoxus and by Philip of Opus, about the size and distance of sun, moon, and the other heavenly bodies."

5. F. Wehrli, "Aristoteles in Neuer und Neuester Forschung," *Neue Zürcher Zeitung* 4, September 1966, repr. in *Theoria und Humanitas. Gesammelte Schriften zur Antiken Gedankenwelt* (Zürich: Artemis Verlag, 1972), 229: "Mit der Entelechielehre, der Annahme eines immanenten Formprinzips, welches vor allem in den Gebilden des organischen Lebens wirkt, hat Aristoteles die platonische Philosophie der Ideen . . . weit hinter sich gelassen."

An interesting point here is that the Neo-Platonists quite generally held a doctrine of *pneuma* as vehicle of the soul, which they said was developed by Plato and supported by Aristotle's writings.[6] Modern authors have vigorously opposed this idea. R. C. Kissling opened a discussion on the topic with the bold statement: "The theory of the ὄχημα—πνεῦμα, as met with in the Neo-Platonic writers, represents the reconciliation of Plato and Aristotle on a subject which the former never taught and the latter was incapable of defining intelligibly."[7] However, though such a modern contribution offers a robust point of view, it pays the price of disqualifying the philosophical judgment of the Neo-Platonist authors on this point, and it leaves unexplained who exactly introduced this theory of *pneuma* as vehicle of the soul in the time after Plato and Aristotle, and to which philosophical problems of his time the anonymous author wanted to give an answer with his new contribution.

On the other hand, if we recognize that Aristotle was forced by his criticism of Plato's theory of soul to define "soul" as the "first entelechy of a natural body possessing life potentially and serving the soul as its instrument," and we are prepared to consider that this "instrumental body" does not refer to the visible body, we will find it much less obvious than Kissling to say that Aristotle "was incapable of defining intelligibly" his *pneuma* doctrine. Rather, we will conclude that the modern debate has gone from a mistake to a wrong conclusion by starting from Alexander of Aphrodisias's anachronistic explanation of the *sôma organikon* and ending in the dismissal of Aristotle's dialogues as "early" and immature works.[8]

This may be readily understood if we take seriously the text of *Generation of Animals* II 3, where it is said that *pneuma* is the analogue of ether, that is to say, it performs the role that ether has in the supralunary sphere: that of *carrying the power that proceeds from God*.[9]

---

6. Cf. J. F. Finamore, *Iamblichus and the Theory of the Vehicle of the Soul* (Chico, CA: Scholars Press, 1985), 1, with the literature listed on 7 n. 1.

7. R. C. Kissling, "The Ὄχημα-Πνεῦμα of the Neo-Platonists and the *De Insomniis* of Synesius of Cyrene," *American Journal of Philology* 43 (1922): 318.

8. On this theme, cf. A. P. Bos, "The 'Vehicle of the Soul' and the Debate over the Origin of this Concept," *Philologus* 151 (2007): 31–50. See also M. Zambon, "Il Significato Filosofico della Dottrina dell' ὄχημα dell'Anima, "in *Studi sull'Anima in Plotino*, ed. R. Chiaradonna (Napoli: Bibliopolis, 2005), 305–35.

9. Cf. A. P. Bos, "*Pneuma* as Quintessence of Aristotle's Philosophy," *Hermes* 141 (2013): 417–34, from which this section is drawn.

a. *Generation of Animals* II 3, 736b29–7a1 on *Pneuma* in Semen

In *Generation of Animals* II 3, 736b29–7a1 Aristotle emphatically contrasts *pneuma* with the "so-called" elements and relates it to "a different kind of and more divine body":[10]

> However, the working power of every soul has to do with some body which is different from the so-called "elements" and more divine than they are. And as the souls differ from one another in the scale of value, so does that substance differ. For the semen of all (living entities) contains within itself that which causes that semen to be generative—what is known as "(vital) heat." This, however, is not fire nor a fire-like power, but the *pneuma* which is enclosed within the semen or foam-like stuff, and the nature which is in the *pneuma*; and this nature is analogous to the nature of the element of the stars.[11]

---

10. Aristotle's description of *pneuma* here occurs in a discussion of what semen is and contains. In *Anim.* II 4, 415b7, semen is called "an instrument of the soul," in a line that has not been included in any modern text edition but is certainly by Aristotle's own hand. Cf. A. P. Bos, "A Lost Sentence on Seed as Instrument of the Soul" (2010). Semen is a "natural body potentially possessing life," but not yet a living being. Cf. *Anim.* II 1, 412b25–7.

11. Πάσης μὲν οὖν ψυχῆς δύναμις ἑτέρου σώματος ἔοικε κεκοινωνηκέναι καὶ θειοτέρου τῶν καλουμένων στοιχείων· ὡς δὲ διαφέρουσι τιμιότητι αἱ ψυχαὶ καὶ ἀτιμίᾳ ἀλλήλων οὕτω καὶ ἡ τοιαύτη διαφέρει φύσις. πάντων μὲν γὰρ ἐν τῷ σπέρματι ἐνυπάρχει ὅπερ ποιεῖ γόνιμα εἶναι τὰ σπέρματα, τὸ καλούμενον θερμόν. τοῦτο δ' οὐ πῦρ οὐδὲ τοιαύτη δύναμίς ἐστιν ἀλλὰ τὸ ἐμπεριλαμβανόμενον ἐν τῷ σπέρματι καὶ ἐν τῷ ἀφρώδει πνεῦμα καὶ ἡ ἐν τῷ πνεύματι φύσις, ἀνάλογον οὖσα τῷ τῶν ἄστρων στοιχείῳ (text H. J. Drossaart Lulofs [1965], 61). The construction of the last-quoted sentence is a so-called comparatio compendiaria (a shortened comparison). Cf. A. Jori, *Aristoteles Über den Himmel, Übersetzt und Erläutert* (Darmstadt: Wissenschaftliche Buchgesellschaft, 2009), 233 n. 301. A. L. Peck (1942), 171–73; A. Platt, in J. A. Smith and W. D. Ross vol. 5 (1912); P. Louis, *Aristote, De la Génération des Animaux* (Paris: Les Belles Lettres, 1961), 61; A. Preus, "Science and Philosophy in Aristotle's *Generation of Animals*," *Journal for the History of Biology* 3 (1970): 35–38; R. Ferwerda (2005), 86. See also F. Solmsen, "The Vital Heat, the Inborn *Pneuma*, and the Aether," *Journal of Hellenic Studies* 77 (1957): 119–23; G. Freudenthal, *Aristotle's Theory of Material Substance* (1995), 107 ff., and A. P. Bos, "*Pneuma* and Ether in Aristotle's Philosophy of Living Nature," *The Modern Schoolman* 79 (2002): 255–76 and *The Instrumental Body of the Soul* (2003), 156–80. J. Althoff, *Warm, Kalt, Flüssig und Fest bei Aristoteles* (1992) regards this text of 736b29–7a7 as probably a later addition. See also his paper "Das Konzept der Generativen Wärme bei Aristoteles," *Hermes* 120 (1992): 181–93. On his entirely different approach to "hot and cold in Aristotle," see also §10n below.

Aristotle says there that "the working power (*dynamis*) of every kind of soul"[12] has something of a different kind of and more divine body, and that in proportion to the value and quality of a soul, that corporeal substance differs in value and quality too. The point of Aristotle's argument is not that the capacity of every soul in the sublunary sphere partakes in *pneuma* and that he refers to this as a "more divine element" within the sublunary sphere,[13] but that the capacity of every soul participates in ether through the agency of *pneuma*, though *pneuma* is not identical with ether. And the fact that the corporeal vehicle of the soul-principle may differ in functionality can only be explained by the hypothesis that this corporeal vehicle is never identical with one single substance, but is always the result of mixture.[14] Aristotle, in fact, is saying here that every soul has "a natural body" that is the "instrumental body" of the soul for its specific tasks, and in the case of those living beings that belong to the sphere of coming-to-be and passing-away, this natural body is *pneuma*.[15]

Because in the same *Generation of Animals* Aristotle also relates the difference between plants, fish, and quadrupeds to the difference in quality of earth, water, and air,[16] these two texts together warrant the conclusion that

---

12. In *Anim.* II 1, 412a6–11, Aristotle distinguishes between the *eidos* and the *hylè* of the soul and characterizes *hylè* there as the soul's *dynamis*. But we will first have to gain clarity on the soul's δύναμις before we can talk about the variety of the soul's δυνάμεις. T. K. Johansen, *The Powers of Aristotle's Soul* (Oxford: Oxford University Press, 2012) omits to do this. He discusses neither the text of *Anim.* II 1, 412a6–11 nor that of *Gener. anim.* II 3, 736b29–7a1. This last text should also be taken into account in the explanation of *Anim.* II 1, 412a6–11, because it shows, again, that Aristotle cannot be referring there to the "visible body" as the "matter" of the soul. J. Althoff, (1992), 183 translates the words in 736b29 as: "Die Wirkkraft nun jedes Seelenteiles," but the relationship with Aristotle's definition of the soul in *Anim.* II 1 becomes clearer if we understand Aristotle's real meaning in 736b29: every soul is always connected with a special "instrumental body."

13. *Pace* G. Freudenthal (1995) 37: "The substance in question is the vital heat." C. D. C. Reeve (2012), 6 follows him in this.

14. Cf. *Spir.* 9, 485b15–9, and A. P. Bos and R. Ferwerda, *Aristotle, On the Life-Bearing Spirit (De Spiritu)*, 181–82. *Pneuma* itself is not the product of mixture, but it is always present in a product of mixture with one or more sublunary elements. Cf. *Gener. anim.* III 11, 762a19–21.

15. Aristotle could not use the concept of *pneuma* in his definition of the soul in *Anim.* II, because he takes ether to be the "instrumental body" of the souls of the stars and planets. He was compelled to use a comprehensive term (σῶμα ὀργανικόν) that was applicable to both ether and *pneuma*, because he wanted to formulate the most general (412a5) definition of "soul," which could therefore also be applied to the souls of the astral living beings. Cf. ch. 14 below.

16. *Gener. anim.* III 11, 761b13–5: "We may say that plants belong to earth, aquatic creatures to water, and four-footed animals to air [τὰ μὲν γὰρ φυτὰ θείη τις ἂν γῆς, ὕδατος δὲ τὰ ἔνυδρα, τὰ δὲ πεζὰ ἀέρος]."

the *pneuma* present in every vital principle, from high to low, is not identical with one of the four sublunary elements. But nor can it be simply equated with the fifth element. *Pneuma* is therefore the fifth-element-in-its-connection-with-the-changeable-sublunary-elements, and differs in vital force and vital quality in accordance with its degree of connection with more or fewer sublunary elements, which differ in their potential for life. *Pneuma* does not exist separately, by itself, but exclusively within the sublunary sphere, and in combination with the sublunary elements.[17]

Pneuma, then, in Aristotle's view, is the fifth element in disguise, incognito. But it is of divine origin and quality, which manifests itself more or less, depending on whether it is more or less obstructed by the sublunary elements with which it has conjoined. Though unrecognizable in the sublunary sphere, ether appears to be pervasively present in that sphere. Therefore, Aristotle can talk about *pneuma* as a "body" (*sôma*) and a "power" (*dynamis*). However, he does imply that in *pneuma* the ether is not itself and that loss occurs wherever ether presents itself outside the sphere of the divine. For it makes a great difference how far the distance is from the Origin of all life.[18] It also makes a difference that whereas ether is unmixed in the supralunary sphere, *pneuma* does not occur unmixed in the sublunary sphere. For Aristotle, *pneuma* is the vehicle of vital potential and vital activity in the sphere of generation and decay,

---

17. S. Berryman, "Aristotle on *Pneuma* and Animal Self-Motion" (2002), 95, who mainly focused on the importance of *pneuma* for the locomotion of living beings, noted: "*Pneuma*, if it is indeed analogous to *aithèr* (*G.A.* 2. 3, 737a1), would literally be neither heavy nor light, i.e. have no tendency for upward or downward motion." In this regard, *pneuma* does not seem to belong to the sphere of "contraries," just as Aristotle states emphatically that the heavenly element is exempt from the sphere of contraries (*Cael.* I 3, 270a21). On p. 96, she continues: "*Pneuma* does not turn into one of the other elements, does not move other elements by means of its inherent upward or downward tendency, and,—we are told [in *Motion of Animals* 7 and 10]—can act on both light and heavy. The point seems to be that, unlike elements that change on expansion so as to become less capable of moving heavier bodies, *pneuma* retains its capacity for forcing other bodies aside. We do not get an explanation of how this works, just a stipulation of the task *pneuma* needs to perform."

18. Cf. §§3e and 9f above. The power active in the soul-body is of a higher quality according to the connection of *pneuma* with sublunary elements that are more or less suitable as vehicles of life. So it becomes clear here that plants merely possess vegetative life because their soul-body, which in any case contains *pneuma*, mainly contains earth besides. In fish, there is perception and a soul-body that in any case contains *pneuma* but also earth and water. And thus Aristotle relates quadrupeds to *pneuma* and (earth and water, but also) air. There is difference in quality of sublunary elements depending on whether their natural location is closer to or more distant from ether. The fact, too, that a soul only manifests itself as "first entelechy" or (in the case of rationally endowed beings) is capable of being active on the level of self-guiding, higher entelechies (see §10q below) depends on the quality of the *pneuma* as carrier of the divine, guiding power.

just as ether is the vehicle of vital activity in the celestial sphere. *Pneuma* is also different from the sublunary elements, because, like ether, it is a vehicle of *logos*, and as such is goal-oriented.[19]

Because *pneuma* is an "instrument of the soul" in the proper sense,[20] the presence of *pneuma* in living entities means that the sublunary elementary bodies may also function as "instruments of the soul." Hence, Aristotle can say that "all natural bodies are instruments of the soul."[21]

Being of divine origin, *pneuma* is also a vehicle of desire for eternity, which is characteristic of all that lives and comes into being. There is desire for eternity and immortality in all that comes into being and perishes, and there is something of a different and more divine element in all ensouled beings. This has to do with each other.[22] We could perhaps infer that Aristotle understood the life of all mortal creatures to depend on the activity of the power of the celestial, astral element in these creatures. But in these mortal sublunary creatures the heavenly, astral element is "incognito," unrecognizably disseminated, it is "in diaspora" there, "in dispersion," "in exile," as Aristotle expressed it in his comparison of the condition of the human soul with the fate of a prisoner of Etrurian pirates, who was bound to a corpse and left to his fate.[23] As the vehicle of "desire" for the divine and immortality, *pneuma* for Aristotle is the symbol of the soul with its sickness "for home," and for

---

19. For this reason, it seems right to me to talk about a "working power" in relation to the *dynamis* proceeding from God, because it is a power that performs a "work," analogous to the power of a craftsman and not to that of a falling boulder.

20. Vital heat or *pneuma* therefore also forms part of Aristotle's definition of the soul. This is underlined in *Gener. anim.* III 11, 762b16–18, where Aristotle says: "that portion of the soul-principle which gets enclosed or separated off within the *pneuma* makes a fetation and implants movement in it [τὸ δ' ἐναπολαμβανόμενον ἢ ἀποκρινόμενον ἐν τῷ πνεύματι τῆς ψυχικῆς ἀρχῆς κύημα ποιεῖ καὶ κίνησιν ἐντίθησιν]." I therefore reject the claim made by T. K. Johansen, *The Powers of Aristotle's Soul* 70: "There are lots of conditions necessary for an animal to live, for example, heat, which are no part of the definition of animal soul."

21. *Anim.* II 4, 415b18. The words *physical bodies*—φυσικὰ σώματα—in this text cannot be interpreted as "the bodies of living beings." The same is true in II 1, 412a11–3. Cf. A. P. Bos, "Aristotle on the Differences between Plants, Animals, and Human Beings" (2010), 826–31.

22. Of course this is similar to Plato's notion that every mortal creature contains a soul that longs for its original condition. But Aristotle's view differs essentially from Plato's.

23. Arist. *Protrepticus* fr. 10b Ross; C 106: 2 Düring; 823 Gigon (= Augustine, *Contra Julianum Pelagianum* IV 15, 78). This theme could well be placed in the dialogue the *Eudemus*. Cf. A. P. Bos, "Aristotle on the Etruscan Robbers" (2003), 289–306. The information in Cicero about a *quinta essentia* as substance of the soul according to Aristotle in *De Philosophia* fr. 27a-d (W. D. Ross) is another compelling reason to accept this doctrine of *pneuma* and reject Alexander of Aphrodisias's interpretation of Aristotle's psychology.

its essential concentrated condition. In Aristotle's dialogue the *Eudemus*, the protagonist Eudemus, who as an exile far from his homeland Cyprus probably engaged in practical politics, is himself a symbol of the soul.[24]

We might also consider that Aristotle presented his dialogue figure Eudemus as being "from Cyprus" (and not as a son of one the various kings, for instance, Themison, who ruled over one of the cities there), because the name of the island immediately calls up an association with Aphrodite Ourania, the goddess of love and desire. In that case, Aristotle may even have depicted Eudemus as a symbol of the soul that desires to become intellect again (by casting off its instrumental body). In his lost works Aristotle also paid attention to the Socratic exhortation "Know thyself." No doubt he also explained this in the sense that the human being who achieves self-knowledge realizes that he is fundamentally a divine intellect.

In the sublunary sphere, *pneuma* is the vehicle of vital force, as ether is in the supralunary sphere, and this vital force has its metaphysical Origin in the transcendent divine Intellect.[25]

The presence of *pneuma* on all levels of life allows Aristotle to explain the finality of all things in living nature. For, in his view, *pneuma* is the vehicle of goal-oriented action, comparable with that of a tool used expertly by a craftsman, and *pneuma* imparts this goal-orientedness to everything with which it is mixed.[26]

---

24. In this connection, the information is relevant that has been passed down by Ps.-Hippolytus, *Refutatio Omnium Haeresium* I 20, 3–4 and 6, which is not as strange as it has often seemed, but in fact is completely understandable. See on that §7 above.

25. Cf. Proclus, *In Platonis Timaeum* V 312C (ed. E. Diehl, vol. III 238, 19): "Before the younger gods produced this [visible] body they brought about the irrational soul together with another vehicle (*ochêma*), a pneumatic one, such as Aristotle accepted, that goes in and out together with our immortal [part of the soul], but nevertheless being mortal itself [οἱ νέοι θεοὶ παράγουσι πρὸ τοῦδε σώματος τὴν ἄλογον καὶ ὄχημα ἄλλο πνευματικόν, οἷον καὶ Ἀριστοτέλης ὑπέλαβε, συνεξίον τῷ ἀθανάτῳ τῷ ἐν ἡμῖν καὶ συνεισιόν, θνητὸν δὲ ὅμως ὄν]." Cf. A. J. Festugière, *Proclus, Commentaire sur le Timée, Traduction et Notes*, 5 vols (Paris: Vrin, 1966–68), vol. V, 104. See also Themistius, *In Arist. De an.* 19, 33: παρὰ Πλάτωνι μὲν τὸ αὐγοειδὲς ὄχημα ταύτης ἔχεται τῆς ὑπονοίας, παρὰ Ἀριστοτέλει δὲ τὸ ἀνάλογον τῷ πέμπτῳ σώματι ὃ φησιν ὑπάρχειν ἐν πάσαις σχεδὸν ταῖς τῶν ζῴων ψυχαῖς and cf. H. J. Blumenthal, *Aristotle and Neoplatonism in Late Antiquity. Interpretations of the De Anima* (London: Duckworth, 1996), 112.

26. For this motif, see *Spir.* 9, 485a35–b9; *Gener. anim.* V 8, 789b7–9: "So it is reasonable that nature should perform most of her operations using *pneuma* as its instrument [ἐπεὶ καὶ τὸ τῷ πνεύματι ἐργάζεσθαι τὰ πολλὰ εἰκὸς ὡς ὀργάνῳ]." *Anim.* I 3, 407b25–7: "each craft must employ its own tools, and each soul its own body [δεῖ γὰρ τὴν μὲν τέχνην χρῆσθαι τοῖς ὀργάνοις, τὴν δὲ ψυχὴν τῷ σώματι].

It is impossible to give Aristotle's teleological conception of nature an integrated place in his philosophy of nature as a whole unless we connect it with his doctrine of *pneuma* as bearer of an efficiently operative power, and therefore with his theology.[27] The fact that the prevailing interpretation of Aristotle's philosophy[28] has never been able to explain how Aristotle justified his teleological view of nature is a powerful argument for my alternative approach, in which the "instrumental body" of the soul is identified with *pneuma* and ether, and thus with God's guiding power.

b. *Pneuma* Is not a Sixth Simple Body

Some scholars have suggested that Aristotle abandoned the self-contained view of a cosmos consisting of 4 + 1 simple bodies and finally thought it necessary to add *pneuma* as a sixth simple body. *This is out of the question.* Aristotle never talks about the natural place or the natural movement of *pneuma*. In order to demonstrate that *pneuma* cannot be one of the sublunary elements, he could have easily used the arguments that he adduced in *On the Soul* I 3, 406a12 ff. to prove that the soul cannot possess its own natural movement. "If the soul moves upwards it will be fire, and if downwards, earth; for these two movements belong respectively to these two bodies; and the same will apply to movements intermediate between 'up' and 'down.'"[29]

Aristotle uses there the scheme that he employed in *On the Heavens* I 2–3 to underpin his theory of five elements, which he concluded by establishing that the number of simple bodies cannot possibly be more than five (3, 270b27–9). Aristotle is the one who introduced the doctrine of the fifth element as distinct from the four "ordinary" elements in the sphere of generation and decay and mortal living creatures, and nobody else ever defended this doctrine.[30] However, in his philosophy of nature, *pneuma* was essentially

---

27. On this, see §§10.o and q below.
28. For example P.-M. Morel, *De la Matière à l'Action. Aristote et le Problème du Vivant* (Paris: J. Vrin, 2007), 42 n. 1, who rejects the view that *pneuma* is "the instrumental body" from Aristotle's definition of soul with the remark: "Tout d'abord, le texte de *GA* II 3 n'a pas de lieu parallèle. Il ne peut donc être explicitement étayé que par lui-même." But note against this that *Gener. anim.* III 11, 762a18–22 strongly emphasizes the importance of *pneuma* for all genesis of life, such as all the passages that talk about "psychic heat" and "psychic fire."
29. *Anim.* I 3, 406a27–9: εἰ μὲν γὰρ ἄνω κινήσεται, πῦρ ἔσται, εἰ δὲ κάτω, γῆ· τούτων γὰρ τῶν σωμάτων αἱ κινήσεις αὗται. Ὁ δ' αὐτὸς λόγος καὶ περὶ τῶν μεταξύ. Cf. *Cael.* I 2, 269a17–8.
30. That point is emphasized by A. Falcon, *Aristotle's Science of Nature. Unity without Uniformity* (Cambridge: Cambridge University Press, 2005). She also stresses that the celestial bodies are materially different from the sublunary bodies (10, 121). She adds that "the celestial simple body

connected with this divine fifth element.³¹ This forces us to conclude that his doctrine of the special fifth element (and of *pneuma*) follows from his criticism of Plato's doctrine of soul. Everything is not "full of the World Soul," but "full of the instrumental body" that is dynamized by God's power.

He does not speak anywhere about the relation of *pneuma* to the four sublunary elements, which may for instance merge into each other because they have a common matter.³² They do not share this matter with ether or with *pneuma*.³³ This also helps to explain why "there cannot be an opposite to ether" and why "[i]t looks as if nature had providently abstracted from the class of opposites that which was to be ungenerated and indestructible, because generation and destruction take place among opposites."³⁴ Nowhere does Aristotle suggest that *pneuma* can be extinguished by water or can evaporate through fire. Nowhere is there any compelling reason for the hypothesis that Aristotle once entertained a *pneuma* doctrine without his theory of the divine fifth element, or his theory of ether without his doctrine of vital *pneuma*.

It is clear that *pneuma* played a very distinctive role *within* Aristotle's cosmology with its doctrine of 4 + 1 elements and in his biology, and is an

---

is the *first* element or the *first* body or the *first* substance because *it comes first in the order of explanation.*" "Aristotle thinks of the natural world as a very special causal system in which the direction of the explanation is from the celestial to the sublunary world only" (115). However, she concludes that "the celestial and the sublunary world form one single causal system which admits an important discontinuity within itself" (121). That is why "Aristotle's study of the soul is programmatically confined to the souls of the perishable living beings" (19, 91–93). She does not explain why a study of "the soul" could leave out an important category of souls. Nor does she ever mention Aristotle's use of *pneuma* and the way he saw it related with and dependent from the celestial element.

31. The thesis of A. Jori, *Aristoteles Über den Himmel* (2009) 236: "dass der Philosoph niemals eine einheitliche, feste und starr strukturierte Lehre von dem himmlischen Element aufbauen wollte," does not merit support. The doctrine of ether as a special divine element and of *pneuma* as its analogue is inextricably bound up with Aristotle's psychology and theology.

32. Cf. *Phys.* I 7, 190b8–9. In contrast to this, ether is called in *Cael.* I 3, 270b2 ἀναλλοίωτον καὶ ἀπαθές and in *Mu.* 2, 392a32: ἄτρεπτος.

33. Cf. Plotinus, *Enneads* II 5 [25] 3, 18: "Aristotle makes his Fifth Body immaterial [Ἀριστοτέλης φησὶ τὸ πέμπτον σῶμα ἄϋλον εἶναι]." Origen, *Contra Celsum* IV 56: "Aristotle and the Peripatetics, who think that the ether is immaterial and is composed of a fifth nature other than the four elements [Ἀριστοτέλει καὶ τοῖς ἀπὸ τοῦ Περιπάτου, ἄϋλον φάσκουσιν εἶναι τὸν αἰθέρα, καὶ πέμπτης παρὰ τὰ τέσσαρα στοιχεῖα αὐτὸν εἶναι φύσεως]" trans. H. Chadwick [1953], 230). However, *pneuma* itself can be called *hylè* for the soul. See §10.1 below.

34. *Cael.* I 3, 270a18–22: εἰ δὴ τούτῳ μηδὲν ἐναντίον ἐνδέχεται εἶναι ... ὀρθῶς ἔοικεν ἡ φύσις τὸ μέλλον ἔσεσθαι ἀγένητον καὶ ἄφθαρτον ἐξελέσθαι ἐκ τῶν ἐναντίων· ἐν τοῖς ἐναντίοις γὰρ ἡ γένεσις καὶ ἡ φθορά. In *Mu.* 2, 392a9, ether can therefore be called ἀκήρατος, in the sense of "invulnerable," "unassailable," in contrast to the sublunary sphere, which is said to be "destructible and perishable [φθαρτή τε καὶ ἐπίκηρη]" in 392a35.

important factor for the internal coherence of Aristotle's cosmology. We also have to conclude that for Aristotle *pneuma* is never present anywhere in isolation, but *always in combination with* one or more of the four sublunary elements. Precisely this "mixture" of *pneuma* with the four elements is the only possible explanation for the difference between ether and *pneuma*. Aristotle says that the nature present in *pneuma* is an analogue of the nature of the astral element and that the power of every soul therefore participates in an element more divine than the four sublunary elements. This can only be the case if *pneuma* represents ether *in an improper condition,* functioning in the sublunary region (where ether does not belong and cannot exist in a normal way) and denatured. In the doctrine of the five "natural" elements *pneuma* thus forms a kind of "improper" condition of the astral body.[35]

If in fact we may assume such a distinction between ether and *pneuma* in Aristotle's philosophy, and if we may view *pneuma* as the "covering or carrier of a soul-principle," such as ether, but always in the sublunary sphere of generation and decay, and always in combination with sublunary elements, it makes sense to ask in what way a soul connected with pure ether differs from a soul connected with *pneuma*. The text of *Generation of Animals* II 3, 736b29–7a1, which we discussed in §10a, suggests that there are degrees of quality of life based on the quality of the *pneuma* present. These gradations in quality of *pneuma* can only be explained by the connection of *pneuma* with the sublunary elements in their varying quality. But the question of the relation of *pneuma* to ether raises an analogous question: How does the quality of the soul connected with ether relate to the quality of souls connected with *pneuma*?[36]

Naturally, the primary opposition is that between immortality and mortality: the immortality of the ethereal beings and the mortality of living creatures that come into being (but also necessarily perish) in the sublunary sphere. In any case, this means being begotten and growing, like plants, in a naturally guided process that does not involve consciousness. For animals, it also means perception and motor activity, which is only realized at a later stage. And in

---

35. In *Timaeus* 41d4 ff., Plato describes how the Demiurge had sown the souls over the instruments of Time (the celestial gods [42d5]), after which they ended up in mortal bodies. Plato added that the circular motion proper to these souls by nature was seriously disturbed in this process. Aristotle seems to have talked about *logoi* (rational principles), whose ethereal covering, when they cross the boundary of the Moon sphere and enter the sphere of Coming-to-Be, is exchanged for or darkens into a lower quality of covering, namely, *pneuma*.

36. The next question is obvious too: What is the difference in quality between a soul connected with an instrumental body and a soul-principle free of any corporeality? And can there be any relation between a soul-principle free of corporeality and a soul that is connected with its instrumental body? On this, see §10q below.

the case of human life there is, finally, intellectual activity, with power of discernment, choices, and practical action. Here we see a goal-oriented activity of a higher order which does not manifest itself on the level of plants and animals. In this situation, sublunary life can be said to attain almost to the level of the astral divine beings, who are eternally active in a goal-oriented way.

Now, we read in *Generation of Animals* II 2, 736a1 the proposition "*pneuma* is hot air [τὸ δὲ πνεῦμα ἐστι θερμὸς ἀήρ]." If we had to conclude on this basis that *pneuma* is merely "air," with the difference that it is "hot," *pneuma* would simply be one of the so-called elements. But the subject in the passage is the composition of animal semen. Aristotle says there in II 2, 735b37–6a2: "Semen, then, is a compound of *pneuma* and water (*pneuma* being hot air), and that is why it is fluid in its nature; it is made of water."[37] For this position he makes reference to foam, olive oil, and even snow, and repeatedly mentions the *pneuma* they contain. Though he also uses the term air (*aēr*) five times,[38] the real question for him is how semen can have different properties from water. He finds the answer in the presence of *pneuma* in semen.[39] He thus anticipates his description two pages down, where *pneuma* is said to be the analogue of the astral element and necessarily connected with the *dynamis* of every soul.[40] We will therefore have to attribute the "heat" of the "hot air" in 736a1 to "vital heat" and certainly not to fire.[41] But if this vital heat cannot be traced down to one of the sublunary elements, it must come from the astral sphere.[42] We should note, too, that the topic here is

---

37. Ἔστι μὲν οὖν τὸ σπέρμα κοινὸν πνεύματος καὶ ὕδατος, τὸ δὲ πνεῦμα ἐστι θερμὸς ἀήρ· διὸ ὑγρὸν τὴν φύσιν ὅτι ἐξ ὕδατος (trans. A. L. Peck [1942]). The sentence is not a textbook example of lucid argumentation.

38. See II 1, 735b26; b29; b35; 6a1; a23.

39. The term *pneuma* occurs twelve times in this chapter.

40. *Gener. anim.* II 3, 736b29ff.

41. *Gener. anim.* II 3, 737a5–7. II 2, 735b33 says expressly that semen "contains a good deal of hot *pneuma* owing to the internal heat of the animals [ὑπὸ τῆς ἐντὸς θερμότητος πνεῦμα πολὺ ἔχον θερμόν]." In III 11, 762a18–21, which is cited in §10c below, Aristotle calls the heat of *pneuma* "psychic heat."

42. Cf. *Gener. anim.* II 3, 737a2–5: "the heat of the sun does effect generation, and so does the heat of animals [ἡ δὲ τοῦ ἡλίου θερμότης καὶ ἡ τῶν ζῴων ... ἔχει ... ζωτικὴν ἀρχήν]" (A. L. Peck [1942], 171). However, J. Althoff (1992), 183 wrongly claims: "Pneuma bedeutet dort [viz. in *Gener. anim.* II 2, 735a29 ff.], wie auch sonst bei Aristoteles, zunächst nichts anderes als Luft. . . . Sie unterscheidet sich nur dadurch, dass sie dem Lebewesen von Geburt an mitgegeben ist, von normaler Aussenluft." Here, he disregards the fact that *pneuma* is already active in the embryo from the moment of conception, and also in plants. But see his p. 184, where he takes the words ἡ ἐν τῷ πνεύματι φύσις to mean: as "(eine) Natur im Pneuma" and "nicht . . . als *Eigenschaft* einer Substanz . . . sondern ausnahmsweise als eine eigenständige Substanz. Andernfalls hätte er wohl formuliert ἡ τοῦ πνεύματος φύσις." On that, see §10n below.

the composition of semen in living creatures of higher species that reproduce through copulation and transfer of semen, and as such participate in *pneuma* of a higher and purer quality.[43]

It is certainly remarkable that Aristotle says nothing more about the relation of ether to *pneuma* in his extant work than that they possess an analogous nature and a heat that has nothing to do with fire, but generates and preserves life. However, this fact becomes less inhibiting when we consider that the term *instrumental body* in Aristotle's definition of "soul" also refers to *pneuma*.[44]

Note that *pneuma* is not visible. Whereas ether and astral beings consisting of ether are distinctly visible, the presence of *pneuma* can only be indirectly perceived through the presence or absence of a living entity's vital heat. *Pneuma* itself, however, cannot be considered a "visible body" (σῶμα αἰσθητόν).[45]

Moreover, the extant writings represent years of teaching activity at the Lyceum in Athens, while some of Aristotle's dialogues were probably available and known to many pupils. These dialogues did not propose a different doctrine, as many scholars have claimed.[46] They did sometimes offer a more comprehensive perspective than the lecture treatises, explaining why "being begotten" is the greatest catastrophe that can befall man and setting out the causes of the "bondage" of the human soul to a coarse-material body and of the human intellect to a fine-material instrumental body of the soul. No doubt they also painted the inviting prospect of being "liberated" from these bonds and "returning home," like Odysseus to his beloved Penelope. Cicero's repeated assurance that according to Aristotle the human soul consists of a *quinta essentia* must spring directly or indirectly from this source.

c. *Pneuma* Is Present Throughout the Sublunary Sphere

In *Generation of Animals* III 11, 762a18 Aristotle explains why plants and animals come into being on land and in seas and rivers. We find again there

---

43. In *Gener. anim.* III 11, 761b14, he had noted that the (soul-!) body of quadrupeds is connected with air.
44. Cf. ch. 14 below.
45. On this, see §10h below.
46. Cf. C. Wildberg, *John Philoponus' Criticism of Aristotle's Theory of Aether* (1988), 12; G. Freudenthal, *Aristotle's Theory of Material Substance* (1995), 101–105, on "The Roots of Aristotle's Vital Heat."

that *pneuma* is essential to all life and may even be described as the carrier of "psychic" heat:[47]

> Animals and plants come into being in earth and in liquids because there is water in earth, and *pneuma* in water and in all *pneuma* is psychic heat, so that in a sense all things are full of soul.[48]

The fact that *pneuma* is present in water demonstrates that it differs essentially from air. According to Aristotle, water does not contain air.[49] Fish do not have a respiratory system, but they do have "innate *pneuma*." And no matter how vital air is to higher animal species, Aristotle never identifies it as a carrier of "psychic heat." *Pneuma* does carry psychic heat, and is therefore immediately qualified to carry a soul-principle.[50] According to Aristotle, *pneuma* is also present in blood and determines its quality.

Without a process of copulation between living specimens, life may form spontaneously where an amount of *pneuma* is enclosed in a frothy bubble containing a mixture of water and earthy components.[51] Having already seen in the text discussed in §10a that *pneuma* is also the essential factor for all sexual reproduction, we can conclude that *pneuma* is indispensable to the presence of life and soul. Aristotle goes on there to talk about degrees in quality of life. These are due to the fact that the frothy bubble of the soul-principle

---

47. In *Anim*. III 12 and 13, he argued that no living creature can be formed from one simple body, but that this always requires a mixture of elements (434b8–10). He offers there his alternative to Plato's theory of soul, which held that living creatures could be formed in each of the cosmic regions, each with their own element (*Anim*. I 5, 411a7–11).

48. Γίνονται δ' ἐν τῇ γῇ καὶ ἐν ὑγρῷ τὰ ζῷα καὶ τὰ φυτὰ διὰ τὸ ἐν γῇ μὲν ὕδωρ ὑπάρχειν ἐν δ' ὕδατι πνεῦμα, ἐν δὲ τούτῳ παντὶ θερμότητα ψυχικήν, ὥστε τρόπον τινὰ πάντα ψυχῆς εἶναι πλήρη. This text was already brought up in §§8b and 9a, on account of its relation to Thales of Miletus.

49. Cf. *Spir*. 2, 482a23: "and we say further that no air is present in the moist substance [οὐδ' ἐνυπάρχειν ὅλως ἐν τῷ ὑγρῷ φαμεν ἀέρα]." Otherwise, animals with lungs would not need to surface in order to inhale air (*Resp*. 1, 470b22–3; 3, 471a31–b14). So there appears to be a conflict with *Gener. anim*. II 2, 736a1: "*pneuma* is hot air [τὸ δὲ πνεῦμά ἐστι θερμὸς ἀήρ]," cited in §10b above.

50. Obviously, this implies that *pneuma* as "matter" is the carrier of the entelechy as *eidos* of the soul. This text cannot be disregarded in the explanation of *Anim*. II 1.

51. *Gener. anim*. III 11, 762a22–4. Cf. also II 1, 735b8–15 and 736a13–8. In 736a18–21 Aristotle links "foam" (*aphros*) to the name of the Love goddess, just as Hesiod, *Theogonia* lines 191 and 197, did when he told the story of her birth in the sea near Cyprus.

not only encloses *pneuma* but other components too. And the main causes of the differences in mixture are the cosmic and geographical regions.[52]

This passage in III 11 forms a sound reason for concluding that *pneuma* is present throughout the sublunary sphere and all its various regions, and that it always occurs in combination with these sublunary components. This is in fact necessary for Aristotle's thesis that vital heat pervades the entire visible body from the center of the living being, and for his theory that the soul in the heart is the coordination center of perception, to which all perceptual images are transported via "tubes" (*poroi*) from the peripheral instruments of perception and from which impulses are given to the motor system.[53] Obviously, it cannot be that Aristotle designed a separate system of vital heat for the growth and procreation functions of a living entity, and another system as the material basis for perception, and a third system of *pneuma* that realizes the motor system. Motor activity is so closely connected with perception that Aristotle considered one and the same material instrument of the soul to be responsible for both.[54]

However, doesn't his doctrine of an all-pervasive *pneuma* conflict with his own theory that two bodies cannot be present in the same place?[55] This

---

52. *Gener. anim.* III 11, 762a26: "and the causes which determine this are the regions where the process takes place and the physical substance which is enclosed [τούτου δὲ καὶ οἱ τόποι αἴτιοι καὶ τὸ σῶμα τὸ περιλαμβανόμενον]." For these "regions," cf. 761b12 and 16, where Aristotle seems to suggest that they are the regions of the various elements. However, see also *Long.* 5, 466b16–7a5.

53. Cf. J. Dudley, "The Fate of Providence and Plato's World Soul in Aristotle," in *Fate, Providence, and Moral Responsibility in Ancient, Medieval, and Early Modern Thought. Studies in Honour of C. Steel*, ed. P. D'Hoine, and G. van Riet (Leuven: Leuven University Press, 2014), 62: "*pneuma* . . . something that is omnipresent." For the issue of perception, see now also R. Roreitner, "Perceptual *Pneuma* in Aristotle: What Happens Between the Individual Senses and the Central Organ?" Paper Prague Conference on "Aristotle and his Predecessors on Heat, *Pneuma*, and Soul," who argued that the system of blood vessels forms the material basis of perception.

54. Cf. *Problemata* VII 2, 886a34–6: "for that which causes recollection to occur is that which produces an impulse towards the imagined condition [τὸ γὰρ ποιῆσαν μνήμην εἶναι τὸ ἔχον ὁρμὴν πρὸς τὸ φαντασθὲν πάθος]."

55. For he says in *Anim.* I 5, 409b2: "For if the soul is present throughout the whole percipient body, there must, if the soul be a kind of body, be two bodies in the same place [Εἴπερ γάρ ἐστιν ἡ ψυχὴ ἐν παντὶ τῷ αἰσθανομένῳ σώματι, ἀναγκαῖον ἐν τῷ αὐτῷ δύο εἶναι σώματα, εἰ σῶμά τι ἡ ψυχή]." R. D. Hicks, *Aristotle, De Anima, with Translation, Introduction and Notes* (Cambridge: Cambridge University Press, 1907), 287 rightly notes for ἐν παντὶ τῷ αἰσθανομένῳ σώματι: "These words mean 'in every part of the sentient body,' not 'in every sentient body.'" See also II 7, 418b17: "for two bodies cannot be present in the same place [οὐδὲ γὰρ δύο σώματα ἅμα δυνατὸν ἐν τῷ αὐτῷ εἶναι]," and *Physics* IV 1, 209a6–7: "But the place cannot *be* body; for if it were, there would be two bodies in the same place [Ἀδύνατον δὲ σῶμα εἶναι τὸν τόπον· ἐν ταὐτῷ γὰρ ἂν εἴη δύο σώματα]."

problem returns in Stoic philosophy, which talks about the divine and creative Fire that pervades the entire cosmos and governs all things in the cosmos.[56] We could be inclined to compare Aristotle's theory of *pneuma* with what he says about "light" and "the transparent" in *On the Soul* II 7, 418b3–9a21: light is not a material body nor an emanation from a material body, but it can extend through air and water.[57]

If everything is full of *pneuma*, we can conclude that Aristotle considers pneumatic earth, pneumatic water, pneumatic air, and pneumatic fire to be possible, that is to say, combinations of the sublunary elements with something that has a divine, astral origin, but through its connection with the sublunary elements no longer has the nature of ether, but of something that Aristotle calls *pneuma*. In this way he links up with the Greek tradition in which *pneuma* (as "breath") is seen as the bearer of life. But Aristotle gives a whole new twist to this tradition by connecting the souls of plants (which have no form of respiration) with *pneuma* too,[58] and by explaining the process of respiration in higher living beings from the high heat of their "innate *pneuma*."[59]

That is why Aristotle can declare in III 11, 761b13–5 that plants are assigned to earth, aquatic animals to water, and quadrupeds to air. This is not the case because each of these species of animals consists of the element mentioned, but because their soul-principle is connected with *pneuma* in combination with earth, or with earth and water, or finally with earth, water, and air.

Aristotle is convinced that usefulness of the four elements for the quality of life of living beings is higher in proportion to their natural proximity to

---

56. Cf. L. Edelstein, *The Meaning of Stoicism* (Cambridge: Harvard University Press, 1966), 24. The fact that Aristotle says explicitly in *Gener. anim.* III 11, 762a18 that "in a sense all things are full of soul," because *pneuma* is present everywhere, is decisive for seeing the Stoa as being influenced by Aristotle in this matter and not the other way round, for instance by viewing *On the Cosmos* 4, 394b9–12 as Stoically contaminated. P. Gregoric and O. Lewis, "Pseudo-Aristotelian *De Spiritu*: A New Case against Authenticity," 162 with n. 14, opt once again for Stoic influence on the texts in *Spir.* and *Mu.*

57. *Anim.* II 7, 418b13–7: "We have thus described what the transparent is and what light is: it is neither fire, nor in general any body, nor an emanation from any body (for in that case too it would be a body of some kind), but the presence of fire or something of the kind in the transparent [τί μὲν οὖν τὸ διαφανὲς καὶ τί τὸ φῶς, εἴρηται, ὅτι οὔτε πῦρ οὔθ' ὅλως σῶμα οὐδ' ἀπορροὴ σώματος οὐδενός (εἴη γὰρ ἂν σῶμά τι καὶ οὕτως), ἀλλὰ πυρὸς ἢ τοιούτου τινὸς παρουσία ἐν τῷ διαφανεῖ]."

58. He does this in his generally acknowledged biological treatises, but in my opinion also in *De Spiritu*. Cf. A. P. Bos and R. Ferwerda (2007) and (2008). See also P. Macfarlane, *A Philosophical Commentary on Aristotle's* De Spiritu (diss. Duquesne University, 2007).

59. Cf. J. Lennox, "Why Animals Must Keep Their Cool," Paper for Conference Prague, June 12–14, 2014.

ether.[60] Flora and fauna differ through quality of life; that is an expression of the difference in quality of soul. But this soul can only function in a physical environment of *pneuma* in combination with earth, water, air, or fire.[61] As regards plants and animals, Aristotle declares that the vital heat is situated in the heart (or the analogue of the heart) in the center, but that at the same time all parts of a living entity and the body as a whole possess innate natural heat.[62] Aristotle always assumed a "central system of perception," with connections to the external organs of perception. Interpretations of some texts suggesting that the sensitive soul is located in the eye or in the ear are based on a misunderstanding.[63]

In individual living creatures, *pneuma* is also present throughout the entire living organism,[64] in contrast to the air of respiration. Whereas Plato in the *Timaeus* developed a theory in which inhaled air circulates through the entire body, Aristotle holds that the lungs are the end point of inhalation and responsible for the cooling required by living creatures with high vital heat.[65]

Another passage relevant in this context is *On the Cosmos* 4, 394b9–11, where Aristotle says: " '*Pneuma*' is also used in a different sense, of the

---

60. *Gener. anim.* III 11, 761b14–5: "the more and less and nearer and further make an amazingly great difference [τὸ δὲ μᾶλλον καὶ ἧττον καὶ ἐγγύτερον καὶ πορρώτερον πολλὴν ποιεῖ καὶ θαυμαστὴν διαφοράν]." Cf. §3e above.

61. On this correlation, see also §10e below. In §7a we already noted that Aristotle dismisses Plato's suggestion that a reduction in knowledge, due to the soul's loss of wings, was the cause of degeneration. Aristotle replaces this notion with the concept of distance from the Origin and reduction in the quality (heat and purity) of the *pneuma*.

62. *Iuv.* 4, 469b6–8: "Now all parts and indeed the whole body of living creatures contain within them some connate heat [πάντα δὲ τὰ μόρια καὶ πᾶν τὸ σῶμα τῶν ζῴων ἔχει τινὰ σύμφυτον θερμότητα φυσικήν]" (W. S. Hett). See also 469b14–7.

63. Cf. A. P. Bos, "The Soul's Instrument for Touching in Aristotle"; "The Ears Are not the Subject of Hearing in Aristotle's *On the Soul* II 8, 420a3–12." There is a similar misunderstanding in the explanation of *Sens.* 2, 438b8–10.

64. Cf. A. Preus, "Science and Philosophy in Aristotle's *Generation of Animals*" (1970), 27: "On the whole, in anatomical investigation, Aristotle does not find *pneuma* in any special location or reservoir, although he surely thinks that there is more *pneuma* in some parts than in others. But *pneuma* does become a part of the developing organism in this sense: the *pneuma* is there, in the organism. It is *everywhere* in the organism, and it is indistinguishable from the compounds into which it enters." A. Falcon (2005), 51 noted that ἀντιτυπία as characteristic of physical bodies was introduced by Epicurus.

65. *Spir.* 2, 481b17–9: "Moreover, respiration extends as far as the lungs, as they themselves say, but the innate *pneuma* is present throughout the living creature [ἡ μὲν ἀναπνοὴ μέχρι τοῦ πνεύμονος, ὥσπερ λέγουσιν αὐτοί, τὸ δὲ πνεῦμα δι' ὅλου τὸ σύμφυτον]." Cf. 3, 482a33: "But the innate *pneuma* pervades the entire living creature [τὸ δὲ σύμφυτον πνεῦμα δι' ὅλου]."

ensouled and generative substance which is found in plants and living creatures, and permeates them totally." The expression *and permeates them totally* [διὰ πάντων διήκουσα] refers to the plants and animals, in which *pneuma* is present throughout.[66]

This passage is supported by *Motion of Animals* 10, 703a9: "Now it is clear that animals do both possess connatural *pneuma* and derive force from this [πάντα δὲ φαίνεται τὰ ζῷα καὶ ἔχοντα πνεῦμα σύμφυτον καὶ ἰσχύοντα τούτῳ]."

A qualification of the above is the observation that Aristotle does not say in *Generation of Animals* III 11, 762a18 ff. that *pneuma* is also present in earth. According to Aristotle, earth is the least "viable" and least "plastic" element for nature's formative work. In individual creatures, the earthy parts, such as the bones, are not very "viable" either. They have no power of perception,[67] though there is growth in the skeleton. Bones have the function of giving robustness to the body and do not primarily serve the purpose of motion. This purpose is mainly fulfilled by the sinews, which do contain movement-actuating *pneuma*.[68] Plants do not have power of perception either, because they consist of earth.[69]

In this context, we should note that Aristotle repeatedly identifies the heart as the place where *pneuma* is more abundantly present than elsewhere in the body, and to which it contracts during sleep. Regarding the connection of sensory organs such as eyes and ears with the heart and the *sensus*

---

66. See §9g above. This casual remark makes it highly improbable that Aristotle is not the author of *On the Cosmos*. After all, *On the Cosmos* emphatically uses the framework of 4 + 1 elements. If the author of *On the Cosmos* is keen "to maintain the fiction of Aristotelian authorship," as J. C. Thom, *Pseudo-Aristotle*, On the Cosmos (2014), 8 claims, he would never have made such a remark were he not firmly convinced that Aristotle saw the framework of five elements and the doctrine of ensouled *pneuma* as belonging together. (But a forger would never have felt any need for such a casual remark about *pneuma*.)

67. Cf. *Anim*. III 13, 435a24–b1: "That is why we have no sensation by means of bones, hair, etc., because they consist of earth [Καὶ διὰ τοῦτο τοῖς ὀστοῖς καὶ ταῖς θριξὶ καὶ τοῖς τοιούτοις μορίοις οὐκ αἰσθανόμεθα, ὅτι γῆς ἐστιν]."

68. Cf. *Spir*. 8, 485a5–7: "In our view, it is not the bones which exist for the sake of movement, but rather the sinews or their analogues, the primary part containing the *pneuma* which causes movement [οὐκ ἂν δόξειε κινήσεως ἕνεκα τὰ ὀστᾶ, ἀλλὰ μᾶλλον τὰ νεῦρα ἢ τὰ ἀνάλογον, ἐν ᾧ πρώτῳ τὸ πνεῦμα τὸ κινητικόν]." Cf. A. P. Bos and R. Ferwerda (2008), 164–71. P. Gregoric and M. Kuhar, "Aristotle's Physiology of Animal Motion," show clearly that Aristotle's biological writings pay scant attention to muscles (which consist of flesh), and that sinews are identified as the binding and moving agency. The same view is found in *Spir*. 6–8.

69. *Anim*. III 13, 435b1–2: "So too plants, because they consist of earth, have no sensation [καὶ τὰ φυτὰ διὰ τοῦτο οὐδεμίαν ἔχει αἴσθησιν ὅτι γῆς εἰσιν]." But of course the presence of *pneuma* is also required. Cf. *Gener. anim*. III 11, 761b13.

communis, Aristotle talks about special tubes (πόροι) through which perceptions are conveyed.

A final question is why Aristotle used the name *pneuma* for this essential vehicle of life, since *pneuma* also had very different meanings: not just "wind," but also and importantly "breath." Aristotle's view of *pneuma* involved a radical break with Hippocratic and Platonic positions on *pneuma* as "breath of life," and undoubtedly Aristotle saw his own, new, and comprehensive view of *pneuma* as an evident correction of the older approach. Thus, he presents his alternative in *De Spiritu* as a correction of the position held by "Aristogenes," who could have been "the son begotten by Ariston," namely, Plato.

d. *Pneuma* as Instrumental Body of the Soul in Reproduction, Spontaneous Generation, and Regeneration

According to Aristotle's *Generation of Animals*, *pneuma* is connected with the *dynamis* of every soul. If we combine this with his statement that *pneuma* is present in the sublunary elements and that therefore, "in a sense all things are full of soul" (besides the assertion in *On the Cosmos* 4 that *pneuma* is an "ensouled substance" and entirely permeates plants and animals), we are forced to conclude that the *sôma organikon* in Aristotle's definition of soul in *On the Soul* II 1 refers to ether and *pneuma* as the "instrumental body" of the soul,[70] the former of the divine celestial beings and the latter of sublunary mortal living entities. Hence, wherever Aristotle talks about "the soul," he always means this very special combination of a nonmaterial soul as cybernetic principle or entelechy and a special soul-body as its instrument. The views on "life" in the undisputed writings *On the Soul* and *Generation of Animals* must have been set out by Aristotle from the same perspective and therefore together form a strong argument for reassigning *On the Cosmos* and *De Spiritu* to Aristotle, works that lost this status mainly due to the revision by Alexander of Aphrodisias.[71]

This means that all the activities and capacities that Aristotle attributes to "the soul" are primarily connected with *pneuma* as instrumental body, and

---

70. A modern reader, who usually has great trouble following the thread of *Anim.* II 1–2, may ask in exasperation: "So why doesn't he come out and say it?" But perhaps this would have surprised Aristotle: if you have absorbed the previous chapters of *Anim.* I, surely it is clear that the soul cannot set an entire visible body in motion! Nor, therefore, can the visible body be a body that "potentially possesses life." We should consider that *De Anima* only started to be studied long after Aristotle had died, and that in the time of Alexander of Aphrodisias a Platonist view was gaining ascendancy.

71. See ch. 12 below.

only secondarily with the visible body.[72] The unity of the soul with this instrumental body is explicitly postulated in *On the Soul* II 1, 412b6 and the unity of "the parts" of the soul with the same instrumental body in 412b17–3a5.[73] This supplementary passage on the indissoluble bond between the parts of the soul and the instrumental body forms the basis of Aristotle's conviction that a separate instrument of the soul cannot be situated in the abdomen for digestive purposes, and another instrument of the soul in the cardiac region for the purposes of perception, and yet another instrument of the soul in the head for the purpose of reasoning, as Plato had suggested.[74] There is only one instrumental body of the soul, which in an animal has a more complex function than in a plant, just as one iPhone may have more apps than another. In II 1, 413a8–9, Aristotle asks whether this instrumental body may relate to the soul like a "ship" to a "sailor."[75] Of the soul as compound *ousia* of entelechy and instrumental body, Aristotle says in *On the Soul* II 4, 415b7 that it is the "cause and principle" of the visible living body. In the traditional explanation, this passage seems entirely at odds with *On the Soul* I 3, where Aristotle forcefully rejects Plato's doctrine of the soul as the principle of movement. But it is wholly appropriate if taken to relate to the combination of the soul with *pneuma* as the carrier of vital power.

It is this instrumental body that Aristotle specifies in *Physics* VIII 6, 259b18–20 as the lever by which the soul moves itself, while being inside it.[76]

We can also put it this way: Aristotle split up the soul, which Plato had presented as a trinity of a charioteer and his two horses, into an (immaterial) operator and a (material) vehicle or vessel in motion.

---

72. Precisely because the "first," most basic function of the soul can be called γεννητική (II 4, 416a19; b24), it is clear that the visible body is a product of the soul with its instrumental body.

73. See §15a below.

74. See on this S. Broadie (2007), 244: "The *Timaeus* again and the Threptic Soul."

75. *Anim.* I 4, 408b14–5 gives an example of this. The text there reads: Βέλτιον γὰρ ἴσως μὴ λέγειν τὴν ψυχὴν ἐλεεῖν ἢ μανθάνειν ἢ διανοεῖσθαι, ἀλλὰ τὸν ἄνθρωπον τῇ ψυχῇ. R. Polansky (2007), 113 translates: "It is better perhaps not to say the soul pities or learns or thinks, but the human being due to the soul." "The *person* undergoes these with soul as cause. Aristotle speaks of humans so that intellectual operations can enter into consideration." But Aristotle is not referring here to what we call "the concrete human being." The activities mentioned here are activities guided by the human mind. "Man" is that by which a living being is distinct from an animal. He is the sailor of the ship, if he himself determines its course. When Aristotle says in *Metaph.* A 2, 982b29 that "in many respects human nature is unfree," he is referring to the intellect (cf. *Metaph.* α 1, 993b9–11). See also §10e below.

76. Cf. §5e above.

Note here that heat in itself (apart from the very special case of spontaneous generation) is not sufficient for the generation or preservation of life. Against the Presocratics who argued this, Aristotle counters in *On the Soul* II 4, 416a9–19 that heat without regulative principle never produces or preserves life. Heat is always a contributory cause (συναίτιον). Without soul there is no structural plan for a living being.[77]

In *On the Soul*, Aristotle calls the nutritive soul "the first and most widely shared capacity of the soul."[78] This vital activity is not just functional for humans and animals, but also for fish and for trees and plants. All that lives in the human environment has this basic soul-function. Next, as the specific activities of vital heat guided by the vegetative or nutritive soul, Aristotle goes on to mention procreation and digestion. "For this is the most natural of all functions among living entities . . . : (provided that they are perfect and not maimed, and do not have spontaneous generation): viz., to produce a new specimen like itself."[79]

It is remarkable that in his study of living nature Aristotle pays attention to reproduction through radical tubers, through bulb splitting, and through slipping[80] and grafting. Already unique in this regard, Aristotle connnects this aspect of life, too, with the necessary presence of *pneuma*.

However, this connection can only be understood if Aristotle's definition of "soul" refers to *pneuma* as the soul's "instrumental body," and not to the entire visible body as a "body equipped with organs." When a plant is slipped, a stalk is cut off and potted. This part of a plant may then develop into an entirely new plant. If we had to assume that the original plant possesses an entelechy, and if its visible body is the "instrumental body," it would be impossible to understand how Aristotle could think that a miniscule part of the plant could possess enough of the plant's entelechy to produce a new plant from the cutting. But if the plant is understood as the product of its inherent *pneuma* led by its entelechy principle, we can then compare the situation of a cutting with that of a seed, and conclude that the *pneuma* it contains[81] is always led

---

77. Cf. *Gener. anim.* II 1, 734b31–5a2. See also E. Lesky (1950), 143–44.
78. *Anim.* II 4, 415a24–5: πρώτη καὶ κοινοτάτη δύναμις ἐστι ψυχῆς καθ' ἣν ὑπάρχει τὸ ζῆν ἅπασιν. Cf. 416b25.
79. See §3a above and A. L. Peck (1942), Appendix B, 578–86.
80. We find the same theme in *Anim.* I 4, 409a9–10; 5, 411b19–27; II 2, 413b13–24.
81. Cf. *Gener. anim.* II 3, 736b33–5.

by the entelechy principle of the plant, and, if it is not obstructed, preserves the life and realizes the growth of the cutting.[82]

It is more problematic to understand how *pneuma* that is freely present in nature, and is not guided by a certain force or entelechy, may nevertheless, in certain circumstances, start to develop nutritive and sensitive activity in living beings that come into being and subsist "by themselves." We would expect something like this to occur mainly at the bottom of the *scala naturae*, and therefore chiefly on the purely vegetative level.[83] But Aristotle also sees spontaneous generation as a process that produces living beings (of a low order). Though these creatures are not guided by a formal principle that they transfer to female partners, as living beings they must possess *pneuma* guided by an entelechy. This remains a curious state of affairs.[84]

e. *Pneuma* as Instrumental Body of the Sensitive Soul

Aristotle not only posits that the soul as "first entelechy" is inseparably connected with a "natural body," but clarifies this by asserting that "the parts" (of the soul!) are also inextricably linked with this natural body.[85] While Plato assumed that "the three parts" of the soul are located in different places of the human body,[86] this is not an acceptable option for Aristotle. Aristotle holds that there is already soul and soul activity—and therefore an instrumental body to which the soul is joined—at a stage when different locations of a visible body

---

82. Cf. A. P. Bos, "Aristotle on the Dissection of Plants and Animals, and His Concept of the Instrumental Soul-Body," *Ancient Philosophy* 27 (2007): 95–106. See also D. Lefebvre, "L'Argument du Sectionnement des Vivants dans le *Parva Naturalia*: le Cas des Insectes," *Revue de Philosophie Ancienne* 20 (2002): 5–34.

83. This is in fact the case according to Aristotle in *Gener. anim.* I 1, 715b25–6a2, but he refers discussion of the matter to a separate place.

84. According to Aristotle, *pneuma* is also indispensable on this lowest level of vital activity. This casts doubt on the statement by M. E. M. P. J. Leunissen, *Explanation and Teleology in Aristotle's Science of Nature* (Cambridge: Cambridge University Press, 2010), 2, that "teleology operates among all nature, *from the level of the inanimate elements*, through that of living beings."

85. *Anim.* II 1, 412b17–3a6. Cf. A. P. Bos, "Het Gehele Lichaam dat Waarnemingsvermogen Bezit" (1999), 112–28.

86. Plato never states how this view relates to the soul's entry "from outside" during birth, nor how the relation of the three soul-parts to respiration should be understood. This is a point criticized by Aristotle in *Anim.* I 5, 411a16–24.

cannot yet be distinguished. For Aristotle, the fact that some simple animals, after being cut in half, may show vegetative and sensitive activity of life in both parts, like the original whole living creature, is a decisive argument for the position that although "parts" of the soul can be distinguished, they cannot be located in different places of the visible body and separately from each other.[87] He also rejects the possibility that higher soul-parts or soul-functions may be added later.[88] For him, it is clear that a living being with two or three soul-parts possesses all these parts from the moment of conception, when they are already connected with the "instrumental body" of the soul.

Aristotle's intentions can be summed up as follows. During fertilization (in most cases by means of semen), a power (*dynamis*) is transferred to the menstrual fluid of the female, a power that effects the vital movement proper to the species of the male and the female. As long as semen and menstrual fluid have not conjoined, the semen does contain water, air, and *pneuma* in reality, but not yet soul in act. It contains soul in potency. As soon as fertilization has taken place successfully, there is immediate vegetative activity of the soul in act, but the sensitive soul-part, though forming part of the soul-principle, is not operative in act, but only present potentially. For the sensitive soul is present from the moment of fertilization,[89] even though it does not yet function as such; and therefore the instrumental body functioning as carrier of all the senses (κοινὸν αἰσθητήριον) is also present from the moment of fertilization.[90] The sensitive soul-part is not added to the vegetative soul only when the instrumental parts for perception (eyes, ears) have developed. The various functions of the one soul develop one after the other, just as the parts of a winding mechanism are successively activated.

---

87. *Anim.* II 2, 413b13–24.

88. *Anim.* II 1 412b17–3a6; *Gener. anim.* II 1, 735a4–22; cf. A. P. Bos, "The Soul and Soul-'Parts' in Semen (*GA* II 1, 735a4–22)."

89. In *Anim.* II 5, 417b16–8 [cited in §7b above] Aristotle says: Τοῦ δ' αἰσθητικοῦ ἡ μὲν πρώτη μεταβολὴ γίνεται ὑπὸ τοῦ γεννῶντος, ὅταν δὲ γεννηθῇ, ἔχει ἤδη ὥσπερ ἐπιστήμην καὶ τὸ αἰσθάνεσθαι. Aristotle is not talking here about the moment of birth, as is suggested by the translations of W. S. Hett (1936), 99; W. D. Ross (1961), 234, "the first stage in the history of the capacity is the imparting of it by the parent to the child at birth," and J. A. Smith in J. Barnes, ed., vol. 1 (1984), 664, but about the moment of conception, as is made clear in A. Jannone and E. Barbotin (1966), 45, D. W. Hamlyn, *Aristotle's De Anima, Books II and III (with certain Passages from book I). Transl. with Introd. and Notes* (Oxford: Clarendon Press, 1968), 102, and P. Thillet (2005), 122.

90. This is what *Anim.* II 1, 412a24 refers to as τὸ ὅλον σῶμα τὸ αἰσθητικόν. It is impossible that Aristotle took this to mean "the visible body" and described it as "endowed with perception."

We saw in §10d above how *pneuma* and vital or psychic heat as instrumental body are indispensable to the vegetative soul-function. The sensitive soul-part, too, says Aristotle, depends entirely on an instrument through which the soul can develop its sensitivity. Aristotle states emphatically: "there is no possibility of perception without heat."[91] Essential here is Aristotle's starting point that the soul is situated in the center of the living being.[92] From this center, the soul must be connected with the parts of the body that allow perceptions coming from outside to reach the percipient. It is important to note that according to Aristotle it is not the eyes or the ears or the tongue that possess powers of perception, but the soul in an indissoluble tie with its instrumental body.[93] Aristotle's theory of perception is just as "monarchianist" as his theology.[94]

The fact that Aristotle posits in *On the Soul* that the soul is situated "within" the living being, in or near the heart, and that the control center of all vital activities is there, implies that this center must be connected with the external organs of perception via material substances. This means that *On the Soul* presupposes the information about the "tubes" (*poroi*) as we often find it in Aristotle's biological writings.[95]

---

91. *Anim.* III 1, 425a6: οὐθὲν γὰρ ἄνευ θερμότητος αἰσθητικόν. Cf. E. Lesky (1950), 143: "Sie [die angeborene Wärme] ermöglicht die Sinneswahrnehmungen." See also A. L. Peck (1942), Appendix B, 589–93; J. Longrigg, *Greek Rational Medicine. Philosophy, and Medicine from Alcmaeon to the Alexandrians* (London: Routledge, 1993), 173–74.

92. See *Sens.* 2, 439a1–3; *Somn.* 2, 455b34–6a4; *Insomn.* 3, 461a5–8; *Iuv.* 3, 469a5–12; 14, 474a25–b3; *Part. anim.* II 1, 647a24–31; II 10, 655b36–37; 656a27–9: ὅτι μὲν οὖν ἀρχὴ τῶν αἰσθήσεών ἐστιν ὁ περὶ τὴν καρδίαν τόπος, διώρισται πρότερον. III 3, 665a10–15; III 4, 665b10–6b1; *Gener. anim.* V 2, 781a20–22: οἱ γὰρ πόροι τῶν αἰσθητηρίων, ὥσπερ εἴρηται ἐν τοῖς περὶ αἰσθήσεως, τείνουσι πρὸς τὴν καρδίαν. *Motu anim.* 9, 702b20–25; *Probl.* III 30, 875b10.

93. Cf. *Part. anim.* III 4, 666a34–b1: "For the definitive characteristic of an animal is the possession of sensation; and the first sensory part is that which first has blood; that is to say the heart, which is the source of blood and the first of the parts to contain it [τὸ μὲν γὰρ ζῷον αἰσθήσει ὥρισται, αἰσθητικὸν δὲ πρῶτον τὸ πρῶτον ἔναιμον, τοιοῦτον δ' ἡ καρδία. καὶ γὰρ ἀρχὴ τοῦ αἵματος καὶ ἔναιμον πρῶτον]" (trans. W. Ogle [1984]).

94. If the traditional prejudices against Aristotle's authorship of *On the Cosmos* are set aside, it is obvious in that work (6, 398a18–35) that the author's description of the Persian Great King and his intelligence services represents a cosmic analogue of the human system of perception. The Persian King is situated in the control, coordination, and information center and receives, even from the far-flung corners of his empire, information via "listeners, messengers, superintendents of signal-fires, and undercover agents [ὠτακουσταί, σκοποί, ἀγγελιαφόροι φρυκτωρίων τε ἐπόπτηρες], so that, through their mediation, the King himself might see everything and hear everything and in this way knew the same day all that was news in Asia."

95. Cf. *Anim.* II 9, 422a3: τῶν φλεβῶν καὶ τῶν πόρων.

The basis of Aristotle's *Parva Naturalia* and his other biological writings is formed by *On the Soul* (cf. *Sens.* 1, 436a5). He constantly refers back to it (*Sens.* 1, 436a1; b10; b14; 2, 437a2).[96] So when he remarks in *On Sense* 1, 436b6: "That sensation is produced in the soul through the medium of a body is obvious [ἡ δ' αἴσθησις ὅτι διὰ σώματος γίγνεται τῇ ψυχῇ, δῆλον]," this should be understood as *On the Soul* explained it, that perception is a transfer of physical stimuli via physical *aisthètèria*, which form a natural unity with the sensitive soul.[97] In the case of taste, this is evident, given that Aristotle presents this sensation as a form of touch.[98]

In *On the Soul* I 4, 408b12–8, Aristotle makes it quite clear that the soul is the *unmoved principle* of all the affections and perceptions of a living creature: "To say that it is the soul which is angry is as if we were to say that it is the soul that weaves or builds houses. It is doubtless better to avoid saying that the soul pities or learns[99] or thinks, and rather to say that it is man who does this *with his soul*.[100] What we mean is not that the movement is in the soul,

---

96. Cf. G. E. R. Lloyd, "The Empirical Basis of the Physiology of the *Parva Naturalia*," in G. E. R. Lloyd and G. E. L. Owen, *Aristotle on the Mind and the Senses* (Cambridge, Cambridge University Press, 1978), 215.

97. The passage should therefore not be given a hylomorphistic or Platonistic explanation, in the sense that the visible body as a whole forms the substrate or matter of the (incorporeal) soul. Yet all the translators known to me assume that Aristotle is talking here about "the" body. Cf. J. I. Beare, in W. D. Ross ed. vol. 3 (1931): "through the medium of the body"; W. S. Hett (1936), 217: "through the medium of the body"; P. Gohlke (1947), 23: "durch den Leib"; J. Tricot (1951), 3: "par le moyen du corps"; E. Dönt (1997), 48: "mittels des Körpers"; A. L. Carbone (2002), 69: "attraverso il corpo." But see also *Sens.* 2, 438b4, where ἡ διὰ τούτου κίνησις refers to movement through light or air as intermediates.

98. Cf. *Sens.* 2, 438b30; *Anim.* III 13, 435a17–8, and A. P. Bos, "The Tongue Is not the Soul's Instrument for Tasting According to Aristotle, *On the Soul* II 10," *Hermes* 140 (2012): 375–85.

99. Aristotle says of 'learning' in *Sens.* 1, 437a11–9 that it particularly depends on hearing (the teacher's words). In *Gener. anim.* V 2, 781a26 ff., he explains in detail how the sensitive soul's *aisthètèrion* of hearing is involved here (and this *aisthètèrion* contains air, 781a23–4; *Sens.* 2, 438b20; *Anim.* II 8, 420a4–7), and how the innate *pneuma* is the entity that makes speech possible by causing vibrations in the windpipe and the vocal chords.

100. We can compare a sentence such as: "The organ played softly." This means that the organist sounding the instrument played softly. Similarly, the subject of anger or weaving is not the instrumental body or the hand, but the controlling entity. Aristotle is therefore not referring here to the concrete physical human being as the subject of pity and learning, but to man's practical intellect, which through discernment and judgment controls his sensitive experiences. The soul is now not "controlling," as in an embryo, but in the way that a sailor steers a ship (cf. *Anim.* II 1, 413a8–9). Man *is* that through which he differs from animals! In the *Protrepticus* Aristotle had portrayed Sardanapalus, the king who gave free rein to all his desires, as the type of "animal" man. See on that lost treatise D. S. Hutchinson and M. R. Johnson, "Authenticating Aristotle's *Protrepticus*," *Oxford Studies in Ancient Philosophy* 29 (2005): 193–294. G. Schneeweiss, "Die Überlieferungen von Themison und Sardanapall. Zur Datierung des aristotelischen Protreptikos,"

but that sometimes it *terminates in* the soul, and sometimes *starts from* it [ὁτὲ μὲν μέχρι ἐκείνης, ὁτὲ δ' ἀπ' ἐκείνης], sensation e.g. coming from without (and supplying stimuli *as far as* the soul), and reminiscence starting from the soul and terminating with the movements or states of rest in the *aisthètèria*." This is confirmed in *On Memory* 2, where Aristotle speaks at length of the "movements" that play a role in the process of calling something to mind. But in 2, 453a14, he declares that this process too is a σωματικὸν πάθος.[101]

Μέχρις ἀκοῆς in *On the Soul* II 8, 420a3 also indicates that the movement is solely a movement of the air, *as far as* the soul (μέχρι ἐκείνης), and not a movement *of the soul* itself.

According to Aristotle, the instrumental body of the soul is present in "tubes" (*poroi*), which connect the eyes, ears, nose, tongue, and skin, with the soul in the center.[102]

Aristotle says explicitly that all perception can only take place "through the body of the soul."[103] In *On Sleep and Waking* 1, 454a8–10, Aristotle provides us with something like a definition of "perception": "What is called sense-perception, as actuality, is a kind of movement *dia tou sômatos tès psychès* [ἡ δὲ λεγομένη αἴσθησις ὡς ἐνέργεια κίνησίς τις διὰ τοῦ σώματος τῆς ψυχῆς ἐστι]." Regrettably, this simple sentence has always been misread.[104] The text

---

Gymnasium 117 (2010): 531–57, takes 332 BCE as its *terminus post quem*. In a sentence such as "a human being begets a human being," Aristotle also refers to the entelechy as the guiding principle.

101. This line of reasoning also plays a role in *Phys.* VII 3, 247a5–12, as becomes particularly clear from a10: αἱ δ' ἐν τῇ μνήμῃ καὶ ἐν τῇ ἐλπίδι ἀπὸ ταύτης.

102. *Gener. anim.* V 2, 781a20–26: "For the passages of all the sensitive bodies, as it is stated in the treatise *Of Sensation*, run to the heart, or to the counterpart of it in animals which have no heart. Now the passage of the hearing, since the sensitive body of hearing consists of air, terminates at the point where the connate *pneuma* causes in some the pulsation, in others, the respiration [and inspiration]. This, too, is why we are able to understand what is said [οἱ γὰρ πόροι τῶν αἰσθητηρίων πάντων, ὥσπερ εἴρηται ἐν τοῖς περὶ αἰσθήσεως, τείνουσι πρὸς τὴν καρδίαν, τοῖς δὲ μὴ ἔχουσι καρδίαν πρὸς τὸ ἀνάλογον. ὁ μὲν οὖν τῆς ἀκοῆς, ἐπεί ἐστι τὸ αἰσθητήριον ἀέρος, ᾗ τὸ πνεῦμα τὸ σύμφυτον ποιεῖται ἐνίοις μὲν τὴν σφύξιν τοῖς δὲ τὴν ἀναπνοὴν καὶ εἰσπνοήν, ταύτῃ περαίνει· διὸ καὶ ἡ μάθησις γίγνεται τῶν λεγομένων]" (text H. J. Drossaart Lulofs [1965], 182, who puts it within brackets). See also M. Liatsi, *Aristoteles, De Generatione Animalium. Buch V. Einleitung und Kommentar* (Trier: Wissenschaftliche Verlag, 2000). Cf. also *Hist. anim.* I 9, 492a23: "Of creatures possessed of hearing, some have ears whilst others have none, but merely have the passages for ears visible [τῶν γὰρ ἐχόντων ἀκοὴν τὰ μὲν ἔχει ὦτα, τὰ δ' οὐκ ἔχει, ἀλλὰ τόν πόρον φανερόν]." And see A. P. Bos, "The Ears Are not the Subject of Hearing in Aristotle's *On the Soul* II 8, 420a3–12" (2010), 181–4.

103. Cf. A. P. Bos, "Perception as a Movement of the Instrumental Body of the Soul in Aristotle."

104. Cf. Sir David Ross (1955), 253: "perception as an activity is a movement of the soul through the body"; D. Gallop (1996), 63: "what is called perception, in the sense of exercise, is a certain movement of the soul by means of the body." However, their interpretation is flatly contradicted by *Anim.* I 3, 406a2: "it may be quite impossible that movement should be characteristic of the soul at all."

in *On Sleep* 1 must mean that perception is a movement through "the body *of the soul*." But what body can this be? This case, which clearly involves perception and the connected *aisthètèria* of the various forms of perception, strongly indicates that Aristotle is talking about the pneumatic (instrumental) body of the soul. In *On Sleep* 1, Aristotle calls perception a movement "through the body *of the soul*," or "through mediation of the body *of the soul*," and states emphatically that this movement continues "as far as" (μέχρις) the soul (and no farther).[105]

Another crucial element in Aristotle's theory of perception is that the perceptual stimuli of sound are transmitted through the air. Hence, the perceptive instrument of hearing must consist of (*pneuma*) and air.[106] But visual images, which reach the soul via the eye, require water: the pupil of the eye consists primarily of water. This means that the *aisthètèrion* of visual perception must also contain water.

In *De Sensu* 2, Aristotle suggests that the various instruments of perception (*aisthètèria*) correspond to the various elementary bodies.[107] The sense of touch requires that the instrumental body of the sensitive soul partakes in earth.

Important, too, is Aristotle's statement that the instruments of perception (*aisthètèria*) are *homoiomerè*. By contrast, eyes and ears are anhomoiomerous parts of the body. Eyes and ears are not present at the moment of fertilization. The soul and the sensitive part of the soul are present, however, and therefore so is the instrumental natural (homoiomerous) body that carries the soul.

In *Parts of Animals* II 1, Aristotle introduces his important distinction between homogeneous and heterogeneous parts of living beings. The hetero-

---

105. Cf. *Insomn.* 3, 461a30: "the movement which reaches the principle of sense comes from them [ἐκεῖθεν ἀφικνεῖσθαι τὴν κίνησιν πρὸς τὴν ἀρχήν]." Cf. C. H. Kahn, "Sensation and Consciousness in Aristotle's Psychology," *Archiv für Geschichte der Philosophie* 48 (1966): 44. This should be kept in mind also when we read *Phys.* VII 2, 244b11–2: "actual perception is a motion through body in the course of which the sense is affected in a certain way [ἡ γὰρ αἴσθησις ἡ κατ' ἐνέργειαν κίνησίς ἐστι διὰ σώματος πασχούσης τι τῆς αἰσθήσεως]." It is not the soul itself that is "being affected," but its instrumental, sensitive body. Cf. A. Hahmann, "Kann man Aristoteles' Philosophie der Wahrnehmung noch für Wahr Nehmen?," *Philosophisches Jahrbuch* 121 (2014): 12 n. 12, 30 n. 111.

106. *Anim.* II 8, 420a6–7: "the ensouled part which will be affected (by the acoustic vibrations) does not have air everywhere [οὐ γὰρ πάντῃ ἔχει ἀέρα τὸ κινησόμενον μέρος καὶ ἔμψυχον]."

107. See *Sens.* 2, 438b17–9: "if we must give an explanation and would have to connect each of the *aisthètèria* with one of the elements [εἰ δεῖ . . . προσάπτειν ἕκαστον τῶν αἰσθητηρίων ἑνὶ τῶν στοιχείων]." See also *Parts of Animals* II 1, 647a12–4: "the natural philosophers pair each of the *aisthètèria* with one of the elementary bodies [τῶν δ' αἰσθητηρίων ἕκαστον πρὸς ἕκαστον ἐπιζευγνύουσι τῶν στοιχείων, τὸ μὲν ἀέρα φάσκοντες εἶναι τὸ δὲ πῦρ]." On these texts, cf. A. P. Bos, "Perception as a Movement of the Instrumental Body of the Soul" (2011), 31–38.

geneous parts are instruments for activities (ἔργα) and operations (πράξεις) (646b12). For this reason they can also be called "instrumental parts" (ὀργανικὰ μέρη) (646b26). As examples Aristotle lists: eye, nose, face, finger, hand, and arm (646b13–14). But they do not include *aisthètèria*. "Instruments of perception" are always homogeneous (647a5).

Texts in *On the Soul* and in the *Parva Naturalia* where Aristotle might seem to attribute power of perception to the eye or the ear have been wrongly explained. Thus, *On the Soul* II 1, 412b17–3a5, on power of vision as the "soul" of the eye, where Aristotle is not talking about the eye as "part" of the body, but about the sensitive "part" of the soul![108]

Interesting, too, is how Aristotle talks about the relation between perception and the four sublunary bodies. These four bodies and their properties are, in any case, objects of perception. But with the exception of the element earth they also form part of the "instruments of perception" (*aisthètèria*).[109] As we saw above, this leads Aristotle to wonder whether the number of senses is related to the number of elements.[110]

---

108. Cf. A. P. Bos (2003), 103–109 and "The Soul and Soul-'Parts' in Semen (*GA* II 1, 735a4–22)," *Mnemosyne* 62 (2009), 378–400. W. D. Ross (1961), 211–15 also misconstrued this text. *On the Soul* II 1, 412b18–22 cannot be cited to prove that sight is located in the eye, though A. L. Carbone (2002), 295 does just that. Aristotle uses a counterfactual example there: "Suppose that the eye were an animal—sight would have been its soul." However, besides power of vision, a real living creature also has (a maximum of four) other powers of perception. That is why a living being has a physical substrate not only for seeing, but for all the senses of the soul. And "the whole sentient body" (τὸ ὅλον σῶμα τὸ αἰσθητικόν) (412b24–5) is also just "a part," that is, the sensitive part, of the instrumental body of the soul, which includes at least the nutritive part of the soul body (vital heat). In the passage concerned, Aristotle argues that all parts *of the soul* are inseparably connected with the one instrumental body of the soul, already in the seminal phase. In *Generation of Animals* II 1, 735a4–22 he makes exactly the same point. The proposition in this passage (412b20)—"the eye is the matter of vision, and if vision fails there is no eye, except in an homonymous sense [ὁ δ' ὀφθαλμὸς ὕλη ὄψεως, ἧς ἀπολειπούσης οὐκέτ' ὀφθαλμός, πλὴν ὁμωνύμως]"—underlines that the eye is indispensable, but that something else is the perceptive subject. *De Sensu* 2, 438b8–10: οὐ γὰρ ἐπὶ τοῦ ἐσχάτου ὄμματος ἡ ψυχὴ ἢ τῆς ψυχῆς τὸ αἰσθητικόν ἐστιν, ἀλλὰ δῆλον ὅτι ἐντός. W. D. Ross took this to indicate that Aristotle locates the soul on the inside of the eye. In doing so, Ross even goes against the view of Alexander. *On the Soul* II 8, 420a3–12: all modern translators explain this in the sense that Aristotle regards the ears as the seat of hearing. But we must conclude that there too he adheres to his doctrine that the center and principle of all perception is situated "inside."

109. *Anim.* III 13, 435a14–5: "Now except for earth, all the other elements would become *aisthètèria* [τὰ δὲ ἄλλα ἔξω γῆς αἰσθητήρια μὲν ἂν γένοιτο]."

110. Cf. *Sens.* 2, 437a19–20 and 439a4–5. See also A. P. Bos, "Perception as a Movement of the Instrumental Body of the Soul in Aristotle," 34–40, where I argue that these passages in *Sens.* 2 have always been wrongly understood and translated because scholars have always adopted the hylomorphistic view of Aristotle's psychology. Cf. also *Part. anim.* II 1, 647a12–4.

This problem also plays a role in *On the Soul* III 13. Aristotle begins this chapter by asserting that "the body of an animal cannot consist of a single element such as fire or air for without a sense of touch it is impossible to have any other sensation."[111] A relevant point there is that by "the body of an animal" Aristotle means "the natural instrumental body," which he has constantly been talking about since *On the Soul* II 1. The text of III 13 also takes up a theme from Aristotle's prolegomena to book I 5, where he already asked: "Why does not the soul make an animal when it is in air or in fire, but only when it is in a mixture of the elements?"[112] This shows once again, as we discussed in §10a, that the body with which the soul is connected does not consist of pure *pneuma*, but always of the "different and more divine body" mentioned in *Generation of Animals* II 3, in combination with other natural bodies. For the quality of this connection determines the quality of the life of living entities.[113]

Against the background of these considerations it is perhaps easier to understand the question that Aristotle poses in *On the Soul* II 5, 417a2–6, and which at first sight seems very peculiar: "Why there is no sensation of the senses themselves . . . although there is in them fire and earth and the other elements which excite sensation."[114] The question here of course is: What is Aristotle referring to in the words "although there is in them fire and earth and the other elements"? Where are this fire and this earth exactly located according to Aristotle? They cannot be in the "perceptions," but must be in the *aisthètèria* through which these perceptions are produced. These also have components of fire and earth, since the perceptive soul-body must be a mixture of all the natural bodies.

Another remarkable text is *On the Soul* II 5, where Aristotle talks about perception in a general sense. He presents perception there in the framework of his scheme "action ≈ reaction" or "acting upon ≈ undergoing." But he then uses this lengthy chapter II 5 to demonstrate that perception belongs to a different category and that sensory stimuli do act upon a perceiving subject, but not as fire brings water to the boil through its heat. If perception is taken as a form of change, it must be "a different kind of alteration."[115] This follows from the

---

111. *Anim.* III 13, 435a11–3: Ὅτι δ' οὐχ οἷόν τε ἁπλοῦν εἶναι τὸ τοῦ ζῴου σῶμα φανερόν. λέγω δ' οἷον πύρινον ἢ ἀέρινον. Ἄνευ μὲν γὰρ ἁφῆς οὐδεμίαν ἐνδέχεται ἄλλην αἴσθησιν ἔχειν.

112. *Anim.* I 5, 411a9–11: διὰ τίνα μὲν γὰρ αἰτίαν ἐν τῷ ἀέρι οὐ ποιεῖ ζῷον, ἐν δὲ τοῖς μικτοῖς.

113. Hence, Aristotle, simplifying matters, can also say in *Gener. anim.* III 11, 761b13–4 that a plant's body is made up of earth, a fish's body of water, and a quadruped's body of air.

114. *Anim.* II 5, 417a2–6: διὰ τί καὶ τῶν αἰσθήσεων αὐτῶν οὐ γίνεται αἴσθησις, ἐνόντος πυρὸς καὶ γῆς καὶ τῶν ἄλλων στοιχείων.

115. *Anim.* II 5, 417b7: ἕτερον γένος ἀλλοιώσεως. "A unique kind of alteration" (W. S. Hett). Cf. M. F. Burnyeat, "*De Anima* II 5," *Phronesis* 47 (2002): 28–90.

fact that perception is only possible thanks to "the different and more divine kind of body," which is the soul's instrument. Although Aristotle assumed a close connection between his psychology and his physics, his physics is not that of modern science, but a "dual physics" (cf. §5a above).

f. *Pneuma* as Instrumental Body of the Rational Soul

Essential to perception is that it is a movement passing through the body of the soul, which results in the reception of the percept's *eidos* (without matter) in the soul. But this movement of the soul's instrumental body also results in an "impression" of the perceptual image on the soul's instrumental body. This forms the basis for Aristotle's theory of memory. There is a necessary link between the activity of the discursive or rational soul, with the images proceeding from perception, and memory images, which are also supplied via the sensitive soul and its instrumental body. It is inconceivable that perceptual images, memory images, and the like could be imprinted in earth or water. This requires a "natural body" of higher quality.

In *On the Soul* II 11, 423a4 Aristotle uses the term *ensèmainô*—ἐνσημαίνω—"to make a (sensory) impression." In II 12, 424a1 ff., he explains that this involves the "impressing" of an *eidos* in the organ of perception, just as the impression of a signet ring is printed in wax.[116] Aging impairs the instrumental body and leads to loss of memory in *On the Soul* I 4, 408b27–8.[117] The example of the unity of wax and its form, which Aristotle uses in II 1, 412b6–7 to underline the unity of the soul and its instrumental body, is chosen on the basis of his theory of perception and his theory of memory. Perceptual stimuli, which have a physical nature, do not lead to a purely physical/chemical effect on the instrumental body, but have a psychic effect too.

The connection between the human mind and the vital heat of *pneuma* comes out in a passage in *Generation of Animals* II 6, 744a26–31. Aristotle discusses there why the bones in the skull of a human baby are relatively late in growing together. He explains this by pointing to the great fluidity of the

---

116. For the meaning of this, cf. *Mem.* 1, 450a27–b11 and D. Bloch, *Aristotle, On Memory and Recollection. Text, Translation, Interpretation, and Reception in Western Scholasticism* (Leiden: Brill, 2007), 30–31, 64 ff. Aristotle says emphatically there that the memory is the depository of these "impressions" and that it is located "in the soul and in the part of the body which possesses the soul" (450a29: δεῖ νοῆσαι τοιοῦτον τὸ γιγνόμενον διὰ τῆς αἰσθήσεως ἐν τῇ ψυχῇ καὶ τῷ μορίῳ τοῦ σώματος τῷ ἔχοντι αὐτήν). He also talks about "hardness" and "brittleness" of "that which receives the impressions," namely, the soul's instrumental body: διὰ σκληρότητα τοῦ δεχομένου τὸ πάθος οὐκ ἐγγίγνεται ὁ τύπος.

117. Cf. A. P. Bos, "*Pneuma* as Instrumental Body of the Soul in Aristotle's *De Anima* I 4, 408b18–30 on Afflictions of Old Age" (2013), 113–27.

human brain, which is caused by the fact that human beings possess the purest heat in the heart region. This is evidenced by their rational power.[118] That should be kept in mind also when we find Aristotle speaking about "the greater thinness and clarity" of blood as a cause of intelligence.[119]

g. *Pneuma* as Motive Principle Led by Desire or Will

Aristotle extensively studied the movement and interaction of water, earth, air, and fire in his *On the Heavens, On Coming-to-Be and Passing-Away,* and *Meteorologica*. But the question of how a human arm or leg or a bird's wing is moved belongs to a different order, since this always involves perception (via the sensitive part) of the soul, or a plan resulting from rational human deliberation.

How could a soul be the principle of motion if the soul itself did not possess movement, as Aristotle argues at length in *On the Soul* I, and the body consisted solely of water, earth, air, and fire? These four elements do not have the capacity to follow the instructions of the soul. And the soul is not the entelechy of a combination of sublunary elements, but of a matching instrumental body possessing community (*koinônia*) with the soul.

It is therefore significant that Aristotle introduces *pneuma* in *Motion of Animals* to explain this matter too. *Pneuma* is a natural body that reacts to guidance of the soul, expanding and contracting without changing in nature (it does not turn as regard its *hylè*, something the four sublunary elements can do).[120] In *Motion of Animals* 10, 703a20, *pneuma* is explicitly said to be the "instrument" (of the soul) for moving the visible body. In this chapter, Aristotle links up with his distinction between (1) an unmoved principle of

---

118. *Gener. anim.* II 6, 744a26–31: "The reason why this occurs especially in man is that in man the brain is more fluid and greater in volume than in any other animal, and the reason of this, in its turn, is that the heat in the heart is purest in man. The fineness of the blend in man is shown by his possession of intellect: there is no other animal which is so intelligent [αἴτιον δὲ τοῦ μάλιστ' ἐπὶ τῶν ἀνθρώπων τοῦτο συμβαίνειν ὅτι τὸν ἐγκέφαλον ὑγρότατον ἔχουσι καὶ πλεῖστον τῶν ζῴων, τούτου δ' αἴτιον ὅτι καὶ τὴν ἐν τῇ καρδίᾳ θερμότητα καθαρωτάτην. δηλοῖ δὲ τὴν εὐκρασίαν ἡ διάνοια· φρονιμώτατον γάρ ἐστι τῶν ζῴων ἄνθρωπος]" (trans. A. Peck [1942], 229). See also E. Lesky (1950), 143.

119. Cf. *Part. anim.* II 4, 650b20 ff. Cf. M. Boylan, *The Origins of Ancient Greek Science: Blood—a Philosophical Study* (New York: Routledge, 2015), 60–61.

120. *Motu anim.* 10, 703a25. Cf. *Phys.* I 7, 190b5–9: "Things which come to be without qualification, come to be in different ways . . . by alteration, as things which turn in respect of their matter [γίγνεται δὲ τὰ γιγνόμενα ἁπλῶς . . . τὰ δ' ἀλλοιώσει, οἷον τὰ τρεπόμενα κατὰ τὴν ὕλην]." The fact that this does not apply to *pneuma* is another indication of its affinity with ether, which is called ἀναλλοίωτον in *Cael.* I 3, 270a14.

motion, (2) a mover that is moved itself, and (3) something passive that is moved. He goes on to postulate that "desire" (*orexis*) belongs to category (2): for desire sets in motion after perception or deliberation has aimed it at an object to be pursued or avoided. And in ensouled bodies *orexis* must be a body that functions in this way.[121] It must be connected with the soul-part of perception and/or with the rational soul-part, and be capable of realizing the matching response of the visible body. For this, it needs to possess the necessary working power (*dynamis*) and strength (*ischys*) (703a6–9). "It is clear that all animals have connate *pneuma*, and derive their strength from this."[122] Because this chapter shows a direct relation between *pneuma* and the sensitive and rational soul-principle, and because the soul is located in the center of the living creature, it is clear that the innate *pneuma* is also situated in the center (and the heart): "Now since the origin is in some animals situated in the heart, in others in that which corresponds to the heart, it is therefore clear that the innate *pneuma* also is situated there."[123] But this special body is capable of expanding and contracting, and thereby attracting and pushing away other parts of the body; and as a "body" it has extension too.[124] But *pneuma* is not only brought up in *Motion of Animals* 10. In an entirely new critical text edition with German translation, O. Primavesi and K. Corcilius[125] now read in chapter 7, 701b14–6: αὐξανομένων <καὶ συστελλομένων> τῶν μορίων διὰ θερμότητα καὶ πνεῦμα καὶ ψῦξιν καὶ ἀλλοιουμένων, basing themselves on the reading of Parisinus 1853 (ms E) from the tenth century. The passage 10, 703a28–b2 is also relevant in this context. Aristotle emphasizes there that although the soul is present in the control center of the living being, the rest of the creature is alive because it forms a natural unity with this center and

---

121. *Motu anim.* 10, 703a4–6. Cf. the example given by A. M. Leroi, *The Lagoon* (2014), 328: "For the eagle to have opened its talons, some existing thing must have changed: the eagle's sensitive soul—the cognitive-motor system that perceived Aeschylus' head, considered its goals and desires, fired its *pneuma* and sprang its talons wide." See, however, also pp. 156–59.

122. *Motu anim.* 10, 703a9–10: πάντα δὲ φαίνεται τὰ ζῷα καὶ ἔχοντα πνεῦμα σύμφυτον καὶ ἰσχύοντα τούτῳ. The English translation quoted is by M. C. Nussbaum, from her brilliant study devoted to this work. Note the words that immediately follow this passage: "How the connate *pneuma* is maintained we have explained elsewhere [τίς μὲν οὖν ἡ σωτηρία τοῦ συμφύτου πνεύματος, εἴρηται ἐν ἄλλοις]." It seems very contrived to accept this passage in an authentic work and then reject *De Spiritu*, which deals with this subject, as spurious.

123. *Motu anim.* 10, 703a14–6: ἐπεὶ δ' ἡ ἀρχὴ τοῖς μὲν ἐν τῇ καρδίᾳ τοῖς δ' ἐν τῷ ἀνάλογον, διὰ τοῦτο καὶ τὸ πνεῦμα τὸ σύμφυτον ἐνταῦθα φαίνεται ὄν.

124. *Motu anim.* 10, 703a20: αὐξάνεσθαί τε δύνασθαι καὶ συστελλέσθαι. 703a22: ἑλκτικὴ καὶ ὠστική.

125. O. Primavesi and K. Corcilius, *Aristoteles De Motu Animalium. Kritische Neuedition des Griechischen Textes und Deutsche Übersetzung* (forthcoming).

this soul.[126] Without spelling it out, Aristotle implies that because *pneuma* pervades the entire living being, it forms the foundation of the "organic" unity of the living creature.

Pneuma, as we have seen, is also the "lever" (*mochlos*) by which the soul moves the visible body.[127]

In *On the Soul* III 10, 432b14–3a8, Aristotle denies emphatically that movement is produced by the soul itself or a part of the soul. Locomotion is a matter of "desire" or "striving" (*orexis*), and that which desires must "be corporeal" itself. Aristotle thus pursues the course struck out in *On the Soul* I 3–4: the soul itself is not a principle of motion, but guides something that has a movement of its own. "Striving" must be characteristic of a natural body that has a specific relation to the soul (because the "striving" or "desire" is excited by perceptual images that enter the sensitive soul). That body is *pneuma*. In Aristotle's view, all conation (*orexis*) is the movement of *pneuma* led by a soul-principle.[128] The fact that he does not explicitly mention *pneuma* in *On the Soul* III 10 is an insufficient basis for claiming that he had not yet developed a doctrine of *pneuma* or had abandoned that theory. Rather, it suggests that he used the concept of an instrumental natural body in *On the Soul* because the work included the theory of the celestial ensouled beings, who have an ethereal soul-body but not a pneumatic one. The celestial beings have an eternal circular course, not because the soul compels this, as Plato held, but because this circular course is proper to ether as a perfect natural body.

Pneuma being the "instrument" of the soul, all natural bodies in the sublunary sphere can also be instruments of the soul, seeing as they cooperate with *pneuma* in a cross-mixture (*Anim.* II 4, 415b18).[129]

On the Soul III 9–10 illustrates the iron consistency with which Aristotle maintained his criticism of Plato's doctrine of soul. Because the nonmaterial part of reality can only be the Intellect and guiding principle, it can never be connected with "movement." On the other hand, all reality that is not the perfect Intellect or guiding principle must be qualified by a striving (*orexis*)

---

126. *Motu anim.* 10, 703a37–b2: "the other parts live by their structural attachment to it and perform their own functions in the course of nature [τἄλλα ζῆν τῷ προσπεφυκέναι, ποιεῖν δὲ τὸ ἔργον τὸ αὑτῶν διὰ τὴν φύσιν]" (trans. E. S. Forster).

127. *Phys.* VIII 6, 259b18–20: "the body changes its place, so that that which is in the body changes its place also, i.e. that which moves itself by leverage [μεταβάλλει γὰρ τὸν τόπον τὸ σῶμα, ὥστε καὶ τὸ ἐν τῷ σώματι ὂν καὶ τῇ μοχλείᾳ κινοῦν ἑαυτό]" (text W. D. Ross [1950]). Cf. §5e above.

128. Cf. A. L. Peck (1942), Appendix B, 576–78. But see now K. Corcilius and P. Gregoric, "Aristotle's Model of Animal Motion," *Phronesis* 58 (2013): 52–97.

129. On the "mixture" of *pneuma* with the other sublunary elements, cf. *Spir.* 9, 485b17–8.

for the divine and eternal,[130] just as the female always desires the male. That is why this nondivine reality must always be materially characterized.

Summary of Results:

Aristotle's view on *pneuma* entailed that:

1. *pneuma* is an essential characteristic of the soul's instrumental body, which always consists of one or more sublunary elements besides;
2. *pneuma* cannot be identified with one of the ordinary elements, earth, water, air, or fire;
3. nor is *pneuma* identical with ether; but its nature is analogous to the nature of ether;
4. Aristotle does not indicate in any way that *pneuma* exists separately as an independent elementary body alongside earth, water, air, and fire, but *pneuma* pervades the entire sublunary sphere;
5. *pneuma* is present in the semen of a male and in the menstrual fluid of a female and in a residual substance from which new life springs through spontaneous generation;
6. *pneuma* is the essential factor for the generation of new specimens of living beings, either through copulation or through spontaneous generation;
7. *pneuma* wholly pervades plants and trees, aquatic animals, land animals, and human beings;
8. *pneuma* differs in its functionality through commixture with one or more of the sublunary elements, according to whether the souls of which it is the vehicle differ in quality; on the one hand, it is necessary that a soul-principle have an instrumental body suited to that principle; on the other hand, for the differences in quality, Aristotle offers no other explanation than the distance in relation to the Origin;
9. it is characteristic of *pneuma* as the vehicle of a soul-principle that it possesses "working power," in the sense that it may both possess this power latently and manifest it patently;

---

130. *Anim.* II 4, 415b1–8 and see §3a-c above.

10. because Aristotle never assumed fewer than five elements, nor more than five, the conclusion must be that *pneuma* is the sublunary veiled presence of the astral element.

h. Is *Pneuma* "All-Pervasive" because It Is "Nondivisible"? (*On the Heavens* I 1)

In §10c above, we drew attention to a major problem in Aristotle's doctrine of *pneuma*. It concerns the possible conflict between this doctrine and Aristotle's insistently repeated assertion that two bodies cannot be present in the same place.[131] Material entities can be mixed with each other and dissolve into each other, but they cannot occupy the same place at the same time. In *On the Soul* I 5, 409b2–4, Aristotle attacks Democritus's psychology by remarking that if the soul is material and present throughout the living body,[132] the soul-body and the other material components of the living body must be in the same place, since otherwise the vital atoms would only be present *between* the atoms of the living body, but would not be able to vitalize them. Although Aristotle situates the soul in the center of the living being and not throughout it, he does claim that the soul's instrumental body is present throughout the visible body.[133] The question therefore is whether he is criticizing Democritus for a problem that returns in a different form in his own view of living nature.

However, we should observe that a doctrine of a very special, fine-material, all-pervasive *pneuma* connected with life was also defended as a viable

---

131. Cf. *Anim.* I 5, 409b3; II 7, 418b17, and *Phys.* IV 1, 209a6–7, cited in §10c above.

132. See also *Anim.* I 2, 404a6–9: "It is the spherical atoms which they call the soul, because such shapes can most readily pass through anything [τούτων δὲ τὰ σφαιροειδῆ ψυχήν, διὰ τὸ μάλιστα διὰ παντὸς δύνασθαι διαδύνειν]."

133. Cf. *Gener. anim.* III 11, 762a19–20: διὰ τὸ ἐν γῇ μὲν ὕδωρ ὑπάρχειν ἐν δ' ὕδατι πνεῦμα, ἐν δὲ τούτῳ παντὶ θερμότητα ψυχικήν. *Spir.* 2, 481b17–9: "Moreover, respiration extends as far as the lungs, as they themselves say, but the innate *pneuma* is present throughout the living creature [ἡ μὲν ἀναπνοὴ μέχρι τοῦ πνεύμονος, ὥσπερ λέγουσιν αὐτοί, τὸ δὲ πνεῦμα δι' ὅλου τὸ σύμφυτον]"; and 3, 482a33: "But the innate *pneuma* pervades the entire living creature [τὸ δὲ σύμφυτον πνεῦμα δι' ὅλου]," which we already cited above in §9g. See also *Mu.* 4, 394b9–12: "'*Pneuma*' is used in a different sense with regard to the ensouled and generative substance which is found in plants and living creatures, permeating them totally; but with this we need not deal here [λέγεται δὲ καὶ ἑτέρως πνεῦμα ἥ τε ἐν φυτοῖς καὶ ζῴοις <οὖσα> καὶ διὰ πάντων διήκουσα ἔμψυχός τε καὶ γόνιμος οὐσία, περὶ ἧς νῦν λέγειν οὐκ ἀναγκαῖον]" (cf. §10c above). P. Gregoric et al., "The Substance of *De Spiritu*," *Early Science and Medicine* 20 (2015): 118 n. 37, state: "it is not clear that Aristotle thought the connate *pneuma* pervaded the whole body." But in fact they reject Aristotle's authorship of both *Mu.* and *Spir.*

theory by various authors in the centuries after Aristotle.[134] Aristotle may have considered whether it is possible to get around the problem. One option is that he did describe *pneuma* as a "material body," but not as "divisible." In that case *pneuma* would be continuous but "nondivisible," and this would also apply to the divine fifth element, so that, like the power of a magnet, *pneuma* can permeate and act on other bodies. In this way the proposition that two natural bodies cannot be present in the same place could be limited to the sublunary natural bodies, which would mean that the physics of the sublunary elements differs from the astrophysics of the astral element and *pneuma* as its analogue.

In this regard, *pneuma* would correspond to the soul as Plato had discussed it.[135] According to Plato, the soul is also present throughout the visible body and not just in the flesh or in the blood. Although Plato talked about "parts" of the soul and about "locations" of these soul-parts, the soul is just as present in a little toe as in an eye. If a jug is filled with water, it is impossible to get any air into it, but according to Aristotle this does not mean that *pneuma* is absent in the water. Did he, influenced by the debate since Plato on the vitalizing effect of the soul, assign a special quality to *pneuma*, which enabled him to oppose the psychology of the Atomists? And did he thus assign a much more positive role to this special body than Plato had done?[136]

This is worth considering on the basis of a striking sentence in *On the Heavens* I 1, 268a28–30. Aristotle writes there: "Magnitudes which are divisible are continuous. *Whether all continuous magnitudes are divisible has not emerged from the present inquiry* [ὅσα μὲν οὖν διαιρετὰ τῶν μεγεθῶν, καὶ συνεχῆ ταῦτα. εἰ δὲ καὶ τὰ συνεχῆ πάντα διαιρετά, οὔπω δῆλον ἐκ τῶν νῦν]." We cannot infer from the context why Aristotle here is led to add: "Whether all continuous magnitudes are divisible has not emerged from the present inquiry."

---

134. The Stoa also accepted the total permeation of matter by the Logos and the creative Fire. But it is much more plausible to assume that the Stoa was influenced here by Aristotle's work than to disqualify as non-Aristotelian all Aristotelian texts in which this theme occurs.

135. Plato, *Tim.* 30b3 had affirmed that intellect cannot be present in anything apart from soul: νοῦν δ' αὖ χωρὶς ψυχῆς ἀδύνατον παραγενέσθαι τῳ. διὰ δὴ τὸν λογισμὸν τόνδε νοῦν μὲν ἐν ψυχῇ ψυχὴν δ' ἐν σώματι συνιστὰς τὸ πᾶν συνετεκταίνετο ("that intellect cannot be present in anything apart from soul. In virtue of this reasoning, when he framed the universe, he fashioned intellect within soul and soul within body"). And soul, according to Plato has a rather complicated mixed constitution (*Tim.* 35a). Aristotle's triad of entelechy/instrumental body/visible body replaced Plato's triad of intellect/soul/body.

136. On various aspects of Plato's doctrine of soul, cf. R. Ferwerda, "The Meaning of the Word ΣΩΜΑ in Plato's Cratylus 400C," *Hermes* 113 (1985): 266–79.

Modern commentaries have long neglected to address the addition.[137] But in a thoroughgoing analysis C. Wildberg[138] has brought to light various new aspects of this chapter, and a valuable recent article has reconsidered the entire chapter and paid attention to the passage in question as well.[139]

Aristotle does not use a formulation such as: "this has been treated elsewhere." He makes out that the issue is still open and needs to be discussed.[140] And although his *Physics* talks about "continuity" and "divisibility," he does not talk about the celestial and divine element there. That only happens in *On the Heavens* I 2–3.

On the Heavens I 1 is a foundational chapter for Aristotle's physics, for it deals with the ontic status of physical reality, on which Aristotle held a radically different view from Plato.[141] Aristotle asserts here categorically that a physical body, because it has extension (διαστάσεις) in three directions, is "complete," "perfect" (τέλειον) in relation to the line and the plane, which are not "complete" in this sense (268b5–10). Thus, Aristotle emphatically dissociates himself from

---

137. W. K. C. Guthrie (1939), 7 note b: "'from the present inquiry,' because it has been demonstrated elsewhere, viz. in *Phys*. VI, 1"; O. Longo (1962), 298: "che il continuo escluda le parti indivisibili è dimostrato in *Phys*. Z 1." Likewise, A. Jori, *Aristoteles Über den Himmel* (2009), 380–81. But we should start by recording that the problem in *Cael*. I differs from that in *Physics* Z 1. The proposition that continua do not consist of indivisible minimal units does not imply that all continua are divisible. In 231a20, the chapter *Physics* Z 1 itself refers back to *Physics* E 3. If *On the Heavens* I 1 wanted to refer to these discussions of continuity and divisibility, the right place for this remark would be after 268b6–7, where Aristotle states with certainty: "Now a continuum is that which is divisible into parts always capable of subdivision [συνεχὲς μὲν οὖν ἐστὶ τὸ διαιρετὸν εἰς ἀεὶ διαιρετά]."

138. C. Wildberg, *John Philoponus' Criticism of Aristotle's Theory of Aether* (Berlin: W. de Gruyter, 1988), 9–38.

139. G. Betegh, F. Pedriali, and C. Pfeiffer, "The Perfection of Bodies: Aristotle's *De Caelo* I, 1," *Rhizômata* 1 (2013): 30–62.

140. Aristotle makes a comparable remark in *Anim*. II 1, 413a4–9 on "entelechy": οὐκ ἄδηλον . . . ."Ἔτι δὲ ἄδηλον εἰ οὕτως ἐντελέχεια τοῦ σώματος ἡ ψυχὴ ὥσπερ πλωτὴρ πλοίου. It seems here as if Aristotle also has "Aussparungen," just as some scholars have argued in the discussion of Plato's "unwritten doctrine" that Plato's written dialogues indicated by means of "Aussparungsstelle" that certain problems were saved for another occasion. Cf. Th. A. Szlezák, *Platon und die Schriftlichkeit der Philosophie. Interpretationen zu den frühen und mittleren Dialogen* (Berlin: W. de Gruyter, 1985), 303–25; id., "Platon und die neuzeitliche Theorie des platonischen Dialogs," *Elenchos* 10 (1989): 343: "Die bewusste Aussparung der tieferen Begründung ist eine konstitutiven Bestandteil des platonischen Dialogs. Der Dialog weist inhaltlich über sich selbst hinaus."

141. It is therefore surprising that C. Wildberg, op. cit., 28, after a searching and innovative discussion of *Cael*. I 1, answers the question of its significance as follows: "The answer is that the above propositions are almost entirely insignificant. Indeed, no argument rests on the premise that the solid is a complete magnitude, and the impression arises that at least the *content* of chapter 1 is surprisingly irrelevant. Once this is recognised it is only natural to assume that the importance of the present chapter . . . must lie in its *method*" (italics C. Wildberg).

142. Cf. *Anim*. I 2, 404b27–30 and I 4, 408b33 ff.

the doctrine of Plato (and at least Xenocrates too)[142] that physical corporeality can be deduced from mathematical reality, which is seen to be higher and (ontologically) "between" (μεταξύ) the Origin and material reality. For Aristotle, the line and the plane are not ontologically higher but in fact ontologically lower, since they are "less complete" than a physical body. Moreover, they exist only as abstractions of this physical body and have no independent existence.[143] In the sentence immediately following the one I have indicated to be problematic, Aristotle also stresses that "it is clear that no *metabasis eis allo genos* is possible,[144] such as from line to plane and from plane to body." For in that case the physical body would not be "complete," because such a deduction always leads to deficiency of being (ἔλλειψις).[145] Aristotle therefore expounds crucial views here,

---

143. Cf. *Metaph.* M 2, 1077a17–8; 26–9.

144. He also underlined this principle in *Anim.* I 1, 402a21–2: ἄλλαι γὰρ ἄλλων ἀρχαί, καθάπερ ἀριθμῶν καὶ ἐπιπέδων. This principle is shunted off both in a theory of emanation and in a theory of evolution.

145. Cf. §3a above. Aristotle, *On the Heavens* I 1, 268b3: "for the *ekbasis* necessarily goes hand in hand with a decrease of completeness [ἀνάγκη γὰρ γίγνεσθαι τὴν ἔκβασιν κατὰ τὴν ἔλλειψιν]." This text has always been wrongly taken to mean that Aristotle here rejects a transition of the three-dimensional body to a following (four-dimensional) magnitude. Thus, in A. Jori (2009), 22 and 129. Regrettably, G. Betegh et al. (2013), 47–49 also interpret it in this way, so that Aristotle is made to claim the opposite of what he means. On p. 47, Betegh states: "We suggest interpreting Aristotle's remarks here in the light of a possible dispute with a Platonic theory." But on p. 49 he concludes: "For he not only denies that there is a transition from body to another genus, but he apparently assumes that there *is* a transition from line to surface and surface to body." However, Aristotle rejects every *metabasis*. He dismisses Plato's explanation that physical reality must be deduced from nonphysical reality. He bases this on the proposition: "No *metabasis eis allo genos* is possible, such as from line to plane and from plane to body; for the result of such a *metabasis* would no longer be a complete magnitude [οὐκ ἔστιν εἰς ἄλλο γένος μετάβασις, ὥσπερ ἐκ μήκους εἰς ἐπιφάνειαν, εἰς δὲ σῶμα ἐξ ἐπιφανείας. οὐ γὰρ ἂν ἔτι τὸ τοιοῦτον τέλειον εἴη μέγεθος]." Aristotle does not assign a higher ontological status to mathematical entities than to physical ones, as Plato had done. He also repeatedly disputes the deduction of the physical elements from triangles, as Plato had proposed in the *Timaeus*. In Plato's system (cf. *Laws* X 894a) the physical and that which displays *dia-stasis* are always the result of loss of unity. Aristotle expresses this in his proposition: "for the *ekbasis* necessarily goes hand in hand with a decrease of completeness." See §3c above. It would be very peculiar if Aristotle here was rejecting the possibility of a four-dimensional magnitude. C. Wildberg, op. cit., 24 n. 66 rightly notes "that the general problem of a fourth spatial dimension does not occur to Aristotle." Aristotle's concern here is in fact his continual point of debate with Plato, who championed the logical deduction of physical reality from mathematical reality and ultimately from the One and the Indeterminate Dyad. Aristotle consistently rejects this philosophical position. (This is endorsed by C. Wildberg, op. cit., 25, with n. 68.) See J. J. Cleary, *Aristotle and Mathematics. Aporetic Method in Cosmology and Metaphysics* (Leiden: Brill, 1995), 73: "Plato is the intended target of Aristotle's firm rejection of the transition (μετάβασις) into another genus that is involved in generating planes out of lines or bodies out of planes" (quoted in §3c); L. Brisson, "Le Rôle des Mathématiques dans le *Timée* selon les Interprétations Contemporaines," in *Le Timée de Platon. Contributions à l'Histoire de sa Réception*, ed. A. Neschke-Hentschke (Louvain/Paris: Éd. Peeters, 2000), 302–303. I want to strengthen my position by arguing that the standard explanation of 268b1 would require this sentence to have the Greek word ὡς and not ὥσπερ of the textual tradition: μετάβασις, ὥσπερ ἐκ μήκους εἰς ἐπιφάνειαν. Cf. *Anim.* I 2, 404b10–1; *Gener. anim.* II 1, 735a8.

and he offers arguments of a sort in support of them. But most scholars remark that these arguments are wafer-thin for the load that Aristotle makes them bear. After all, the question is how Aristotle thinks about physical reality and how he sees this physical reality in relation to the purely spiritual Origin.[146]

This chapter of *On the Heavens* already intrigued me during my doctoral studies.[147] On reconsideration, I see that I did not yet fully understand all the important issues in this introductory chapter. I did recognize that Aristotle rejects here the deduction of physical bodies from mathematical objects and from meta-transcendent principles (the One and the Indeterminate Dyad) as taught by Plato. But it remained unclear what his alternative was.

In his discussion of principles in *Physics* I Aristotle does not explain how bodies depend on the divine principle of Origin, but only that, besides a formal principle, we also need to assume a material principle as a passive, "female" principle with a structural "desire" for the formal principle.[148] In this context, Aristotle had also described the "underlying" or material principle as a "non-being" in a merely accidental sense, but as "nearly a substance" (οὐσία πως) in the proper sense.[149] And in *On the Soul* he had called "matter" and "form" the two aspects of one genus *ousia*.[150] Whereas Plato had designated

---

146. However, we should consider that we have come to know Aristotle as a "moderate dualist" (see §3f above). In his view, matter is not the contradictory antipole of the Good, but a "quasi-substance" characterized by a desire for the Good. Matter relates to the Good as the female to the male. And precisely the doctrine of reproduction made Aristotle realize that the male may beget a female new specimen in a natural way. The female and the male are not two distinct genera, but are differences within one genus. Aristotle can therefore maintain that his view of "matter" (the female, "underlying"), as an alternative manifestation of the immaterial formal principle, does not commit the ontological error of *metabasis eis allo genos* of which he accuses Plato. The natural bodies may also serve as "instruments" of immaterial governing principles. Form and matter are two aspects of the one substance (*ousia*). This also allows us to understand Aristotle's agreement in *On the Cosmos* 7 with the Orphic conception that characterizes Zeus as "male and female."

147. Cf. A. P. Bos, *On the Elements. Aristotle's Early Cosmology* (Assen: Van Gorcum & Comp., 1973), 33–45.

148. See §3f above.

149. *Phys.* I 9, 192a4–6: "we hold that one of these, namely the matter, accidentally is not, while the privation in its own nature is not; and that the matter is nearly, in a sense *is*, substance [τούτων τὸ μὲν οὐκ ὂν εἶναι κατὰ συμβεβηκός, τὴν ὕλην, τὴν δὲ στέρησιν καθ' αὑτήν, καὶ τὴν μὲν ἐγγὺς καὶ οὐσίαν πως, τὴν ὕλην]." Cf. *Metaph.* M 2, 1077a31–2.

150. *Anim.* II 1, 412a6–9: "We describe one class of existing things as substance; and this we subdivide into three: (1) matter, which in itself is not an individual thing; (2) shape or form, in virtue of which individuality is directly attributed, and (3) the compound of the two [Λέγομεν δὴ γένος ἕν τι τῶν ὄντων τὴν οὐσίαν, ταύτης δὲ τὸ μὲν ὡς ὕλην, ὃ καθ' αὑτὸ μὲν οὐκ ἔστι τόδε τι, ἕτερον δὲ μορφὴν καὶ εἶδος, καθ' ἣν ἤδη λέγεται τόδε τι, καὶ τρίτον, τὸ ἐκ τούτων]" (W. S. Hett [1936], 67).

the physical side of visible reality as a product of nonbeing and therefore as unknowable, Aristotle took pains to place it within the sphere of being (*ousia*). This is a radical revaluation which also allowed him to regard the study of natural phenomena as a branch of science.

Yet this could explain why Aristotle never talks about the "principles" of material bodies.[151] If physical reality can be taken as an aspect or facet or component of being (*ousia*), then it is itself an aspect or component of the principle of all things. In that case, it is unnecessary to explain physical reality as resulting from a process of deduction, production, or emanation. "Formal principle" and "materiality" are then two sides of the same coin.

A persistent problem, however, is that Aristotle refers to the divine Intellect as absolutely transcendent and as "separate" from all material reality. Just as in *On the Cosmos* he emphatically calls God's essence "meta-cosmic," but God's working power "intra-cosmic." Now, in *Timaeus* 29e, Plato had postulated that the Demiurge is "good" and therefore does not wish to deprive anything of anything. It is therefore his *will* to make the cosmos as good as possible. Aristotle denies the divine Principle any changeability and any "will." But the power eternally proceeding from God must be a working power guided by mental activity, like the working power of a skilled craftsman.[152] In this way, Aristotle designs a cosmos and a nature that (without being produced by a Demiurge) is pervaded by a goal-oriented working power that manifests itself in suitable instruments and useful material. Aristotle's doctrine of God's working power (δύναμις) and his teleological view of nature, connected with his concept of entelechy, are Aristotle's alternative to Plato's notion of a divine Demiurge who orients himself to the intelligible world in order to create the material world.

God's working power is thus materially characterized (σωματικόν) in a structural way, just like the power of the winding mechanism that expresses the thought of the designer.

Two other matters escaped me back then.

In the first place, that Aristotle says in *On the Heavens* I 1, 268a4–6: "For physically constituted entities consist of (a) bodies and magnitudes, (b) beings possessed of body and magnitude, (c) the principles of the entities *which possess them* [τῶν γὰρ φύσει συνεστώτων τὰ μὲν ἐστι σώματα καὶ μεγέθη, τὰ δ' ἔχει σῶμα καὶ μέγεθος, τὰ δ' ἀρχαὶ τῶν ἐχόντων εἰσίν]" (cf. W. K. C.

---

151. E. Diamond, *Mortal Imitations of Divine Life* (2015), 22–23: "Aristotle never attempts to explain how or why the first principle produces what is other than it."

152. Remarkably, Aristotle often declared that craft imitates nature, while he interpreted nature after the model of human *technè*. Cf. S. Broadie, "Nature and Craft in Aristotelian Teleology," in *Aristotle and Beyond* (2007), 85–100.

Guthrie [1939], 5).[153] The question arising here is why Aristotle does not write "the principles of those entities" (ἀρχαὶ τούτων), but "the principles of the entities which possess them" (ἀρχαὶ τῶν ἐχόντων). For in this way he avoids speaking about the principles of bodies and magnitudes.[154]

"Beings possessed of body and magnitude" are all the things that exist thanks to nature or human craft. When Aristotle inquires into their "principles," he probably connects the things existing thanks to nature with the soul as the principle of the form, and the things existing thanks to craft with the rational design on which they are based; and furthermore with the matter of which they both consist. He talked about this in *Physics* I and partly also in *Physics* II.[155]

In the second place, he says at the very outset of his argument in 268b6–7: "The continuous may be defined as that which is divisible into parts which are themselves divisible to infinity, body is that which is divisible in all ways [συνεχὲς μὲν οὖν ἐστὶ τὸ διαιρετὸν εἰς ἀεὶ διαιρετά, σῶμα δὲ τὸ πάντῃ διαιρετόν]."[156] This contrasts with the passage that I have quoted from 268a28–30.[157] How can Aristotle say: "whether all continuous magnitudes are divisible has not emerged from the present inquiry," if he has already said in 268a6: "The continuous may be defined as that which is divisible into parts which are themselves divisible to infinity, body is that which is divisible in all ways"?

---

153. C. Wildberg, op. cit., arrives at a totally different interpretation of *Cael.* I 1 by starting from the position: "The emphasis . . . lies on (geometrical) solid rather than physical body" (20), whereas I believe Aristotle is concerned with the undeducibility of the physical body. (This is underlined by G. Betegh et al. [2013] in the title of their article.) Wildberg observes: "the Greek term is ambiguous, for it can mean both (physical) body and (geometrical) solid" (18). He therefore proposes to translate σώματα καὶ μεγέθη in 268a4 as "(geometrical) solids and magnitudes" (18). He then wants to accommodate "physical bodies" in the category τὰ δ' ἔχει σῶμα καὶ μέγεθος (19). However, Aristotle's concern here is not to postulate that a three-dimensional figure is "perfect" because there are no more than three dimensions (as Wildberg, 23, claims), but he argues that a physical body is "perfect" because it possesses three dimensions and is not deduced from purely spatial magnitudes.

154. In *Anim.* II 1, 412a11-3 Aristotle says of natural bodies: "for these are the principles of all other bodies [ταῦτα γὰρ τῶν ἄλλων ἀρχαί]."

155. Another particular feature of Aristotle's thought is that he also considers the soul, which is itself nonmaterial, to be "not without body," or "with body," as regards some of its "parts" (*Anim.* I 1, 403a6; a15–8).

156. The same assumption plays a role in *Phys.* I 2, 185b9–11: "If their One is one in the sense of continuous, it is many; for the continuous is divisible *ad infinitum* [εἰ μὲν τοίνυν συνεχές, πολλὰ τὸ ἕν· εἰς ἄπειρον γὰρ διαιρετὸν τὸ συνεχές]" (R. P. Hardie and R. K. Gaye, in J. Barnes, ed. [1984], vol. I, 317).

157. G. Betegh et al. (2013), 48 n. 38 have clearly recognized the problem, but conclude: "a satisfactory solution has not yet been proposed."

A second question that urges itself is: Can *pneuma* be a "body" if it is not "divisible in all ways"?

Could Aristotle have distinguished two kinds of "continuity":

1. the continuity of what is divisible in all ways [διαιρετὸν εἰς ἀεὶ διαιρετά], and

2. the continuity of what is not divisible [διαιρετόν], but an all-pervasive (almost immaterial) fluid?[158]

The first question that needs to be answered, of course, is why Aristotle thinks it relevant here in 268a29 to bring up this problem. If he did not discuss the problem in the extant writings, did he see it as an area of special attention belonging to "first philosophy"?[159] In the second place, however, we need to ask what he may have meant.

There is a further question, too: Why does Aristotle mention the Pythagoreans? For after positing that "magnitude divisible in one direction is a line, in two directions a surface, in three directions a body," he goes on to say:

> There is no magnitude not included in these; for three are all, and "in three ways" is the same as "in all ways," And then he refers to the Pythagoreans: "It is just as the Pythagoreans say, the whole world and all things in it are summed up in the number three; for end, middle and beginning give the number of the whole, and their number is the triad." (W. K. C. Guthrie [1939], 5)[160]

Who are the Pythagoreans that Aristotle cites here? Does he mean ancient Pythagoras and his followers, or contemporaries such as Timaeus of Locri, the

---

158. Could this be a reason why Aristotle talks about "divisibility" in relation to "visible" bodies in *Gener. corr.* I 2, 316b19–20?: "Every perceptible body is both divisible at any point whatsoever and undivided [Τὸ μὲν οὖν ἅπαν σῶμα αἰσθητὸν εἶναι διαιρετὸν καθ' ὁτιοῦν σημεῖον καὶ ἀδιαίρετον οὐδὲν ἄτοπον]." Aristotle does not say anywhere that *pneuma* is perceptible, like earth or fire. In *Mu.* 6, 399b14–5, "the soul" is called invisible (ἀόρατος). It is invisible as entelechy, but also as regards its instrumental *pneuma*.

159. As in *Phys.* II 2, 194b14–5 and I 9, 192a34–7.

160. *Cael.* I 1, 268a9–13: καὶ παρὰ ταῦτα οὐκ ἔστιν ἄλλο μέγεθος διὰ τὸ τὰ τρία πάντα εἶναι, καὶ τὸ τρὶς πάντῃ. καθάπερ γάρ φασι καὶ οἱ Πυθαγόρειοι, τὸ πᾶν καὶ τὰ πάντα τοῖς τρισὶν ὥρισται· τελευτὴ γὰρ καὶ μέσον καὶ ἀρχὴ τὸν ἀριθμὸν ἔχει τὸν τοῦ παντός, ταῦτα δὲ τὸν τῆς τριάδος. See now also G. Betegh (2013), 38–44. And see I 2, 268b25–6: "body was completed by the number three, and so is its motion [τό τε γὰρ σῶμα ἀπετελέσθη ἐν τρισὶ καὶ ἡ κίνησις αὐτοῦ]."

spokesman in Plato's eponymous dialogue,[161] Speusippus, Plato's direct successor as head of the Academy in 347, or Xenocrates, a pupil of Plato, who rejected the doctrine of Ideas and gave a primary position to the ideal numbers, and who had been head of the Academy since 339?

No other source mentions that this kind of claim was made by the ancient Pythagoreans. Nor is any indication for this found in Aristotle's own survey of the Pythagorean tradition before Plato in *Metaphysics* A 5. All he does there is formulate the notion that the number 1 is the origin of the numbers and that all other numbers fall into the categories *even* and *odd*.[162]

However, Aristotle may well be referring to Xenocrates, the man who was elected head of the Academy in 339 BC after the death of Speusippus (when Aristotle perhaps hoped that he could take charge of Plato's school). From this moment, Aristotle himself started to teach in an institution of his own, the Lyceum or Peripatos. Xenocrates had dissociated himself even more from Plato by abandoning the doctrine of Ideas and giving just as much priority to Numbers as the ancient Pythagoreans.[163] Thus, *Metaphysics* Λ 7, 1072b30 mentions "the Pythagoreans and Speusippus," and says that they did not situate "supreme beauty and goodness" in the beginning, but saw them as the end point of a development, just as the completeness of plants and animals forms the end of a long development.[164]

---

161. Cf. *Anim.* I 2, 404b16 ff., which cites ὁ Πλάτων ἐν τῷ Τιμαίῳ and Plato's doctrine of ideal numbers and says that Aristotle has pursued these matters in his dialogue *De Philosophia*. See also I 3, 407a6–10. But, particularly in *Anim.* I 3, 407b22, there is every reason to connect the "Pythagorean myths" with Plato. On the question of the relationship of Pythagoreans and Platonists in Aristotle's statements on "the Pythagoreans," see W. Burkert, *Weisheit und Wissenschaft. Studien zu Pythagoras, Philolaos und Platon* (Nürnberg: Verlag Hans Carl, 1962), 26–45; L. Zhmud, *Pythagoras and the Early Pythagoreans* (Oxford: Oxford University Press, 2012), 433–45; A. Gregory, *The Presocratics and the Supernatural* (2013), 127–48.

162. *Metaph.* A 5, 986a17–21. The Pythagoreans seem to have regarded the number ten as the complete, perfect number (5, 986a8). See also C. Wildberg, op. cit., 20, with n. 20.

163. Cf. L. Brisson, "Le Rôle des Mathématiques dans le *Timée*," 306–15, in which the author argues that *Anim.* I 2, 404b18–30 is not directed against Plato's *Timaeus* but against Xenocrates, who had tried to answer Aristotle's criticism of the mathematization of the cosmos. S. Broadie (2007), 237 ff. shows that Aristotle's polemic with Xenocrates is always pertinent in his debate with Platonism and the Platonists. See also D. Thiel, *Die Philosophie des Xenokrates im Kontext der Alten Akademie* (München/Leipzig: K.G. Saur, 2006). Diogenes Laertius V 3 has Aristotle saying: "It were base to keep silence and let Xenocrates speak [αἰσχρὸν σιωπᾶν, Ξενοκράτην δ' ἐᾶν λέγειν]" (although in that text sometimes the name of Isocrates is read).

164. *Metaph.* Λ 7, 1072b30–4: "Those who suppose, as do the Pythagoreans and Speusippus, that perfect beauty and goodness do not exist in the beginning (on the ground that whereas the first beginnings of plants and animals are causes, it is in the products of these that beauty and perfection are found) are mistaken in their views [ὅσοι δὲ ὑπολαμβάνουσι, ὥσπερ οἱ Πυθαγό-

At the close of book Lambda, Aristotle refers to the same "Pythagorean" theory that assigns ontic priority to Numbers and deduces from them other levels of reality (each with its own principle). He criticizes them there for holding a doctrine of Being that resembles a bad tragedy, with constantly new episodes and without a real principle of Unity.[165] Naturally, Aristotle did not carry on such a controversy with philosophers from the remote past, but with contemporaries. Xenocrates is certainly a suitable candidate for this role.

Following Plato, Xenocrates may have deduced Lines from Numbers, Planes from Lines, and, finally, three-dimensional Bodies as the phase in which this process is completed.[166] Although Aristotle concurs with Xenocrates's recognition of three-dimensional, physical reality as a "complete" reality, he explicitly rejects the notion that physical bodies represent a final stage in *On the Heavens* I 1. For Aristotle, physical reality is *teleion*, complete and perfect, not characterized by a deficiency of being like lines and planes, and not secondary.

In this connection, we can also note that Plato, in a rather ponderous text, mentions "the beginning and the end and the middle of all things that are."[167] He does this in *Laws* IV, 715e7–6a2: " 'Men,' we should say to them, 'God, as the ancient tradition says, holding the beginning and the end and the middle of all things that are, moves in a circular path in the course of nature, bringing them to fulfilment.' "[168] Aristotle knew this Platonic text well,

---

ρειοι καὶ Σπεύσιππος τὸ κάλλιστον καὶ ἄριστον μὴ ἐν ἀρχῇ εἶναι, διὰ τὸ καὶ τῶν φυτῶν καὶ τῶν ζῴων τὰς ἀρχὰς αἴτια μὲν εἶναι τὸ δὲ καλὸν καὶ τέλειον ἐν τοῖς ἐκ τούτων, οὐκ ὀρθῶς οἴονται]" (H. Tredennick). See also *Metaph.* M 2, 1077a18–20; 24–9. (C. Wildberg, op. cit., 25–26 seems to impute the position set out in this last passage to Aristotle. He describes it as a text "where Aristotle is indeed considering mathematical constructivism." But in fact Aristotle is criticizing Speusippus here.)

165. *Metaph.* Λ 10, 1075b37–76a4: "As for those who maintain that mathematical numbers is the primary reality, and so go on generating one substance after another and finding different principles for each one, they make the substance of the universe incoherent . . . and give us a great many governing principles. But the world must not be governed badly: 'The rule of many is not good; only one is the ruler' [οἱ δὲ λέγοντες τὸν ἀριθμὸν πρῶτον τὸν μαθηματικὸν καὶ οὕτως ἀεὶ ἄλλην ἐχομένην οὐσίαν καὶ ἀρχὰς ἑκάστης ἄλλας, ἐπεισοδιώδη τὴν τοῦ παντὸς οὐσίαν ποιοῦσιν . . . καὶ ἀρχὰς πολλάς· τὰ δὲ ὄντα οὐ βούλεται πολιτεύεσθαι κακῶς. 'οὐκ ἀγαθὸν πολυκοιρανίη· εἷς κοίρανος']." Cf. N 3, 1090b13–20.

166. Xenocrates was one of those who described the soul as "a number moving itself" (cf. *Anim.* I 2, 404b29). That could mean that the soul produced the physical, three-dimensional reality as ultimate and "complete" reality.

167. See also G. Betegh et al. (2013), 41 f.

168. Plato, *Leg.* IV, 715e7–6a2: Ἄνδρες', τοίνυν φῶμεν πρὸς αὐτούς, 'ὁ μὲν δὴ θεός, ὥσπερ καὶ ὁ παλαιὸς λόγος, ἀρχήν τε καὶ τελευτὴν καὶ μέσα τῶν ὄντων ἁπάντων ἔχων, εὐθείᾳ περαίνει κατὰ φύσιν περιπορευόμενος.

for he quotes it in full in *On the Cosmos* 7, 401b24-7, as the conclusion of the entire treatise, and expressly refers to his teacher as "the great Plato."[169]

The big question is what exactly Plato means in the text of *Laws* IV, but also to what "ancient tradition" he is referring. Scholars have often linked it to an Orphic theme.[170] This is quite plausible, given that an Orphic fragment cited by Aristotle in *On the Cosmos* says:

Zeus is the head, Zeus the centre, from Zeus comes all that is

Ζεὺς κεφαλή, Ζεὺς μέσσα, Διὸς δ' ἐκ πάντα τέτυκται.[171]

We might consider that this tradition also influenced the Pythagorean outlook and took on a specifically Pythagorean color there, as expressed in *On the Heavens* I 1. As for the author of *On the Cosmos*, however, we should bear in mind that he has already described God in 6, 397b9 as "the cause that holds the world together" (τῆς τῶν ὅλων συνεκτικῆς αἰτίας), and that he too refers to "an ancient idea, traditional among all mankind, that all things are from God and are constituted for the sake of God."[172] He explains this further in the theory of the Power that proceeds from God and gives life to the entire cosmos.

Perhaps we could get even closer to resolving these questions if we investigate what associations Aristotle had with the notions of "division" (διαίρεσις) and "extension" (διάστασις). Could it be that he saw the two terms in relation to the "disjunction" from the Origin?

---

169. *Mu.* 7, 401b26: ὁ γενναῖος Πλάτων. The only thing he changes in the quotation is the word περιπορευόμενος, which becomes πορευόμενος in *On the Cosmos*. This probably has to do with Aristotle's criticism of Plato's identification of the circular path with the movement of the soul or the intellect (*Anim.* I 3, 406b26-7b12). It is very doubtful whether a later imitator of Aristotle would make such a significant change to Plato's text. G. Betegh et al. (2013), 41 talk about "the Ps. Aristotelian *De Mundo*."

170. Cf. Pl. *Phdr.* 240c; *Phd.* 70c; *Epist.* VII 335a; O. Kern, *Orphicorum Fragmenta* 249, 7.

171. *Mu.* 7, 401a29. Precisely the Orphic poem quoted in *De Mundo* was long considered a reason for dating *De Mundo* to the period after Aristotle's life, because it was thought to display Stoic influences. This position was made untenable by the discovery of the Derveni papyrus in 1962, because it showed that the Orphic poem was already known and being commented on in 400 BCE. Cf. G. Reale and A. P. Bos (1995), 348-49; W. Burkert, *Babylon, Memphis, Persepolis. Eastern Contexts of Greek Culture* (Cambridge: Harvard University Press, 2004), 89-98. On the Derveni papyrus, see G. Betegh, *The Derveni Papyrus. Cosmology, Theology and Interpretation* (Cambridge, Cambridge University Press, 2004); T. Kouremenos et al., eds., *The Derveni Papyrus. Edited with Introduction and Commentary* (Florence: Leo S. Olschki Editore, 2006); R. G. Edmonds, *Redefining Ancient Orphism. A Study in Greek Religion* (Cambridge: Cambridge University Press, 2013) 59-62. In 2015, the Derveni papyrus was incorporated in the UNESCO Memory of the World Register.

172. *Mu.* 6, 397b13-5: "It is indeed an ancient idea, traditional among all mankind, that all things are from God and are constituted for the sake of God [Ἀρχαῖος μὲν οὖν τις λόγος καὶ πάτριός ἐστι πᾶσι ἀνθρώποις ὡς ἐκ θεοῦ πάντα καὶ διὰ θεὸν συνέστηκεν]."

From a twenty-first-century perspective, it is possible to inquire into what Aristotle said "On the Elements."[173] A problem here is that we tend to regard physical reality as the all-encompassing set of elements that have been discovered or conjectured and laid down in a periodic system. But this is anachronistic. Thus, Aristotle (let alone Plato) did not talk about "elements." Aristotle started by postulating a fundamental division in physical reality.[174] He then states of the one, supralunary part that it is divine and that it is perfectly rational to say that it is "immortal and closely linked with immortal."[175]

There is a problem here, too. Although Aristotle refers here to the popular tradition that imagined the heavens to be the abode of the immortal gods, as he also does in *On the Cosmos* 6, 400a7–19,[176] Homer was not a philosopher, and Aristotle was. For him, it was a puzzle how the immaterial, transcendent Origin can be related to the sphere of the divine fifth element, because an expression such as "closely linked with" (συνηρτημένον) is inappropriate here. As we saw in chapter 2 above, Aristotle does repeatedly use terms such as ἐξήρτηται (*Cael.* I 9, 279a29) and ἤρτηται (*Metaph.* Λ 7, 1072b14; *Motu anim.* 4, 700a6). But these are inspired by the metaphor of the "the golden rope," which Homer develops in *Iliad* 8, 1–28 and Aristotle eagerly exploits as an ancient allusion to his own theology of the Unmoved Mover.[177] Sometimes he also uses the term *to touch* (θιγγάνω), but this is just as inaccurate for a philosopher[178] who analyzed so exactly what "continuity," "touch," and "succession" mean (*Physics* VI 1). Aristotle's references to the Intellect as "separate" are too frequent to justify any talk about a "connection."

Although Aristotle keenly understood that "a transition to a different genus" must be rejected, he does postulate that a *working power* "proceeds" from the immaterial, unmoved (male) intellect and is clothed in an instrumental, matching (female) body. This working power brings about life and order to the very limits of the material cosmos.

Moreover, the fifth element is never an "element" by itself, but is always "ensouled," alive and divine. The fifth element is always subservient to a

---

173. Cf. the title of A. P. Bos (1973).

174. Cf. §5a above.

175. Cf. *Cael.* I 3, 270b6–9: "All men have a conception of gods, and all assign the highest place to the divine . . . supposing, obviously, that immortal is closely linked with immortal [πάντες τὸν ἀνωτάτω τῷ θείῳ τόπον ἀποδίδοασι . . . δῆλον ὅτι ὡς τῷ ἀθανάτῳ τὸ ἀθάνατον συνηρτημένον]."

176. See for instance 400a15: "and all ages bear witness to this fact, and allot the upper region to God [συνεπιμαρτυρεῖ δὲ καὶ ὁ βίος ἅπας, τὴν ἄνω χώραν ἀποδοὺς θεῷ]." See also *Mu.* 6, 397b25–7.

177. Cf. *Motion of Animals* 4, 699b32–700a6. Aristotle refers to the same theme in *On the Cosmos* 6, 397b24–7. Cf. G. Reale and A. P. Bos (1995), 319–20. Theophrastus, *Metaph.* 5b15 quotes from the same passage when he critically examines Aristotle's doctrine of the Unmoved Mover.

178. In *Anim.* I 3, 407a16–22 Aristotle accuses Plato of dealing negligently with this problem.

governing soul-principle. As such, it falls into the category of "complete bodies," in the sense of bodies of living beings that possess not just three but six "dimensions" (before/behind; under/above; left/right).[179]

Though the fifth element is a body, it is an "instrumental body," subservient to the soul that is its entelechy. Aristotle, we might say, distinguished between an "organic physics" and an "anorganic physics." For at the other end of the physical spectrum we do find an independent existence of the four sublunary elements, which, according to *Metaphysics* Z 16, 1040b5–16, are more like a "formless heap" (σωρός) than a living organism. Only after they have been incorporated by a living being into its nutritive system do they achieve the unity of a living being.[180]

This dichotomy in physics was strongly emphasized by Aristotle. The fifth element is "heterogeneous," in that it is eternal, divine, non-aging, unchangeable, impassive, and carries out a never-ending movement.

Now, if this fifth or first element is said to have its "place" between the sphere of the fixed stars and that of the Moon,[181] we may think that nothing of ether is left beyond the sphere of the Moon in the direction of the Earth. But this makes it hard to understand how *pneuma* can be present everywhere in the sublunary sphere, as an analogue of ether and possible bearer of life. If we stress that the fifth element is "impassive" and "unchanging," it would seem that "division" (and limitation) of the fifth element is impossible, since all division is the separation of portions of a substance by something of a different kind, a knife or a saw.[182] But clearly this is not easy in the case of a substance such as ether, which is impassive.[183] Therefore, the remark in I 1, 268a29–30 must refer ahead to the argument in I 2–3.[184]

---

179. *Cael.* II 2, 284b21–4. See also II 12, 292a20: "we ought to think of them as partaking of life and initiative [δεῖ δ' ὡς μετεχόντων ὑπολαμβάνειν πράξεως καὶ ζωῆς]" (W. K. C. Guthrie [1939], 207).

180. Cf. also *Metaph.* M 2, 1077a27–30.

181. *On the Cosmos* 2, 392a29: "and lastly the circle of the Moon—and there is the limit of the ether [τελευταῖος ὁ τῆς σελήνης, μέχρις ἧς ὁρίζεται ὁ αἰθήρ]" (E. S. Forster in J. Barnes [1984], vol. 1, 627).

182. Cf. *Phys.* VI 1, 231b4–6: "For that which is continuous has distinct parts, and these parts into which it is divisible are different in this way, i.e. spatially separate [τὸ γὰρ συνεχὲς ἔχει τὸ μὲν ἄλλο τὸ δ' ἄλλο μέρος, καὶ διαιρεῖται εἰς οὕτως ἕτερα καὶ τόπῳ κεχωρισμένα]."

183. To my knowledge, C. Wildberg, op. cit (1988), 23 is alone in having sensed that the sentence 268a29–30 in *Cael.* I 1 occupies a remarkable place, between the two main parts of the argumentation. He suspects that Aristotle thus wants to prevent an opponent from countering that if ether is just as divisible as all other continuous bodies, then ether and the celestial region are theoretically exposed to destruction. On p. 23 n. 63, he shows that Philoponus put forward such arguments against Aristotle in the sixth century CE. But Wildberg does not seem to assume that Aristotle himself had already taken this position.

184. I.e., not a reference back to *Phys.* VI 1.

Should we perhaps assume that *pneuma*, which manifests itself throughout the sublunary sphere, is nothing other than ether, which extends to the end of the cosmos, but cannot manifest itself in its pure nature because the four coarse-material elements prevent this?[185] It then becomes plain why Aristotle can say that the divine extends to our outer regions[186] and why there is continuity between the Source of all life and the sublunary sphere.[187] At the same time, there is a clear distinction between the divine that is "extended" but unchangeable, and the sublunary sphere, where the process of "extension" has entered a next phase of materiality that can even be entirely separate from the divine Origin.

In this extreme region, which he describes as "full of confusion and diversity" (πολλῆς μεστὰ ταραχῆς),[188] Aristotle situates the real Tartarus, the real Underworld. Here, the sphere of the Moon is the boundary between the sphere of (Life and) Death and the sphere of immortal life in the Isles of the Blessed.

Physical reality was thus viewed by Aristotle as that in which the productivity of the divine principle can manifest itself. It is the material side, which can never be seen separately from the formative divine working power that is active in it. For vital activity cannot show itself "without instrumental body" of the soul. The physical must always be seen in the light of the elements' subservience to vital activity ("all natural bodies are instruments of the soul").[189]

This makes it evident once again that Aristotle's physics is subordinate to his biological insights, as M. Furth has strongly underlined.[190] Clear, too, is that Aristotle was the one who explicitly introduced a theory of a fine-material

---

185. Could it be that the existence of the four elements follows from the necessity that noneternal living beings exist? If only divine, immortal beings existed, there would be no raison d'être for unensouled bodies and "dead matter."

186. *Mu.* 6, 397b32-4: "inasmuch as it is the nature of the divine to penetrate the whole universe [καθ' ὅσον ἐπὶ πᾶν διϊκνεῖσθαι πέφυκε τὸ θεῖον]."

187. In this connection, it is striking to see how P. Moraux, "*Quinta Essentia*," *P.W.-R.E.* 47 Halbbd (Stuttgart: Anton Hiersemann, 1963), 1171-263, cols. 1233-34, posits that the Stoic doctrine of the all-permeating creative fire was often presented as Aristotelian in later times: "Die Lehre von der Durchdringung des ganzen Kosmos durch das göttliche Feuer und die Auffassung von der Seele als einem Stück der göttlichen Gestirnsubstanz passen ebensowenig in den Geist des Aristotelismus hinein. Dennnoch hat die stoische Gleichsetzung des Äthers mit dem Feuer zweifellos dazu beigetragen, dass manche Züge des stoischen Systems von Eklektikern und Synkretisten auf die aristotelische Q.E.-Lehre zurückprojiziert oder gar mit ihr verwechselt würden."

188. *Mu.* 6, 397b32.

189. *Anim.* II 4, 415b18-9. But there remains a fundamental difference between ether and *pneuma* as "instrumental bodies" and the four sublunary elements as "material bodies," like the distinction between "organic" and "anorganic" physics.

190. M. Furth, *Substance, Form, and Psyche: An Aristotelean Metaphysics* (Cambridge: Cambridge University Press, 1988), 5.

substance, a *quinta essentia* (ether/*pneuma*) as carrier and vehicle of a guiding rational principle.

I would further like to mention information supplied by S. Berryman in an interesting article on a fragment of Eudemus of Rhodes.[191] She cites material there that can be found in Simplicius, *in Arist. Phys.* 879. 18–21 (= fr. 96 in F. Wehrli's edition of the fragments of Eudemus of Rhodes): "Eudemus, however, saw the organically fused as more unified than the continuous, and said that this was proper to natural things. 'This,' he said, 'is conceptually first and a principle. For on this follows continuity, being contiguous and being next. But organic fusion comes last in generation' [ὁ μέντοι Εὔδημος τὸ συμφυὲς τοῦ συνεχοῦς μᾶλλον ἡνωμένον θεασάμενος καὶ ἴδιον τῶν φυσικῶν αὐτὸ εἰπών· τοῦτο, φησί, κατὰ τὸν λόγον πρῶτον ἐστι καὶ ἀρχή· τούτῳ γὰρ ἕπεται τὸ συνεχὲς καὶ ἐχόμενόν τε καὶ ἐφεξῆς. κατὰ δὲ τὴν γένεσιν, φησί, τελευταῖον τὸ συμφυές]."[192]

Mrs. Berryman argues in her article that Eudemus's proposal "has merit in addressing a problem about degrees of unity and the implications these have for change."[193] In her view, "Eudemus proposes to treat *to symphyes* as a distinct class, more cohesive than things that are merely continuous."[194]

It is intriguing that Eudemus apparently awarded a high status to *to symphyes*, namely, that of "principle," and assigned (onto-)logical priority to it. Mrs. Berryman discusses Aristotle's use of the term *to symphyes* and the contrasting terms, such as *to suneches*.[195] She also mentions texts where Aristotle talks about *symphyes pneuma* or *symphyton pneuma*,[196] but she attaches no particular significance to this. She does cite the example from *De Incessu Animalium* 7, 707b2 ff., where Aristotle explains the fact that centipedes[197] can survive divi-

---

191. S. Berryman, "Continuity and Coherence in Early Peripatetic Texts," in *Eudemus of Rhodes*, ed. I. Bodnár and W. W. Fortenbaugh (New Brunswick: Transaction, 2002), 157–69.

192. Cf. *Simplicius: On Aristotle, Physics 5*, ed. R. Sorabji, trans. J. O. Urmson (London: G. Duckworth, 1996), 80. Cf. F. Wehrli, *Die Schule des Aristoteles* Heft VIII *Eudemos von Rhodos* (Basel: B. Schwabe & Co, 1955), 43. For a critical assessment of Wehrli's edition, see H. Baltussen, "Wehrli's Edition of Eudemus of Rhodes: The Physical Fragments from Simplicius' Commentary *On Aristotle's Physics*," in *Eudemus of Rhodes*, ed. I. Bodnár and W. W. Fortenbaugh (New Brunswick: Transaction, 2002), 127–56.

193. Art. cit., 158.

194. Ibid., 165.

195. She also discusses *Cael.* I 1, 268a30 (158).

196. Art. cit., 161.

197. *Inc. anim.* 7, 707a30: αἵ τε καλούμεναι σκολόπενδραι καὶ ἄλλα τῶν ἐντόμων καὶ προμηκῶν. Cf. *Anim.* I 5, 411b19–22.

sion into several parts by observing that the parts of such animals are *synechês* with each other, but not a natural unity (*symphyes*).[198] Berryman assumes that Eudemus of Rhodes's distinction serves to emphasize that the unity of a living organism is of a higher order than that of other entities.[199] However, in *Physics* V 3, on which Simplicius's text is a commentary, Aristotle himself also uses the terms σύμφυσις (2x) and συμπέφυκεν or συμφύσεται (227a23–7; cf. *Metaph.* K 12, 1068b30–1069a14), without emphatically distinguishing them from the term *continuous* (*syneches*).

Did Eudemus of Rhodes try to introduce a further terminological distinction in what Aristotle posited about the vital effect of ether and *pneuma*, as that which makes a "heap" (*sôros*) an organic unity (and thus a real *ousia*)?

One more remark may be added. In *On the Soul* I 3, 407a9–10 Aristotle concludes that Plato's view of the rotation of the celestial spheres as an expression of the divine Intellect's activity is untenable. Aristotle asserts there that the Intellect is one and continuous, like the activity of the Intellect. Thinking consists of thoughts. But the unity of these is one of succession, like that of numbers, whereas the unity of spatial magnitudes is not. His conclusion is: "So also the mind is not continuous in this sense, but it either has no parts, or at any rate is not continuous as a magnitude."[200]

j. Is the Quality of the Soul Dependent on the Quality of Its Instrumental Body or the Other Way Round?

In the discussion of *Generation of Animals* II 3, 736b29–7a1 in §10a above, we saw that Aristotle distinguishes between "value" and "lack of value" of souls (διαφέρουσι τιμιότητι αἱ ψυχαὶ καὶ ἀτιμίᾳ ἀλλήλων). Aristotle's various writings show that he rates most highly the souls of the outer celestial sphere

---

198. Art. cit., 163. *Inc. anim.* 7, 707b2: Αἴτιον δὲ τοῦ διαιρούμενα ζῆν ὅτι, καθάπερ ἂν εἴ τι συνεχὲς ἐκ πολλῶν εἴη ζῴων συγκείμενον, οὕτως ἕκαστον αὐτῶν συνέστηκεν.

199. Art. cit., 166, 168.

200. *Anim.* I 3, 407a6–10: "But mind is one and continuous in the same sense as the process of thinking; thinking consists of thoughts. But the unity of these is one of succession, like that of numbers, whereas the unity of spatial magnitudes is not. So also the mind is not continuous in this sense, but it either has no parts, or at any rate is not continuous as a magnitude [ὁ δὲ νοῦς εἷς καὶ συνεχὴς ὥσπερ καὶ ἡ νόησις· ἡ δὲ νόησις τὰ νοήματα· ταῦτα δὲ τῷ ἐφεξῆς ἕν, ὡς ὁ ἀριθμός, ἀλλ᾽ οὐχ ὡς τὸ μέγεθος· διόπερ οὐδ᾽ ὁ νοῦς οὕτω συνεχής, ἀλλ᾽ ἤτοι ἀμερὴς ἢ οὐχ ὡς μέγεθός τι συνεχής]."

and of the planets.²⁰¹ Next, the souls of the beings on the Moon, which are apparently higher in rank and quality than those of earthly mortals and which are connected with fire (as well as *pneuma*).²⁰² Then the souls of human beings; of quadrupeds; of fish; of living beings produced via spontaneous generation; and finally of plants and trees.

The text of *Generation of Animals* II 3, 736b29–7a1 also says that the body with which the working power of every soul is connected displays exactly the same differences. So there is a correspondence between the two series.

In *On the Soul* I 3, 407b13–27, Aristotle levels at his predecessors the criticism that they "associate the soul with and place it in the body, without specifying why this is so, and how the body is conditioned."²⁰³ According to Aristotle, this is absurd, because something only acts on something else through the "community" (*koinônia*) that exists between the two.²⁰⁴ A soul cannot be

---

201. An interesting question is whether Aristotle also assumed differences in quality within the sphere of the divine astral beings. In *On the Heavens* II 12, Aristotle connects the degrees of complexity in the movements of the planets with their differences in distance from the Origin (292a22–4; cf. 292b17–9). The same idea is important in *Mu.* 6, 397b27–8a1. The striking "light-names" assigned to the planets in *Mu.* 2, 392a23–31 also suggest degrees of luminosity.

202. See *Gener. anim.* III 11, 761b15–21; *Motu anim.* 4, 699b19.

203. *Anim.* I 3, 407b15–7: οὐθὲν προσδιορίσαντες διὰ τιν' αἰτίαν καὶ πῶς ἔχοντος τοῦ σώματος. (Cf. also II 2, 414a23: οὐθὲν προσδιορίζοντες ἐν τίνι καὶ ποίῳ.) This sentence may cause misunderstanding. Aristotle does not mean here that his predecessors, including Plato, should have explained why the soul must move into a body. They had done this. Empedocles seems to have talked about it, and Plato had spoken at length about the soul's "loss of wings" in his *Phaedrus* myth. Plato had thus merely indicated why there are souls that are not "perfect" but possess a lower quality of life and cognition. But he did not really explain how perception of the physical reality around us is possible for an immaterial soul within a living being. When Aristotle says here that it is necessary to explain why a soul must be connected with a body, he means that, in order for the soul to be capable of receiving external sensory stimuli, physical stimuli must be transmitted to it via a physically characterized instrumental body of the soul. In *Anim.* I 1, 403a5–7 he had already said that the soul cannot perceive or desire or be angry "without body." And in order to guide the process of development and growth of the body, the soul needs *pneuma* with its vital heat as instrumental body. However, as we established earlier (see ch. 7 above), Aristotle does not accept Plato's conception that when a new individual is born, the soul in itself descends into the newly born and makes life begin (as Plato in the *Timaeus* describes the "birth" of the cosmos when the world body is set in motion). According to Aristotle, the soul is already present from the moment of fertilization, conveyed by the vital Power of the Begetter.

204. Aristotle is therefore talking here about the necessity of a *koinônia* between the soul and its body. In *Gener. anim.* II 3, 736b30 he said that the working power of every soul seems to participate in (κεκοινωνηκέναι) "another and more divine body than the so-called elements." Cf. A. P. Bos, "The 'Instrumental Body' of the Soul in Aristotle's Ethics and Biology," *Elenchos* 27 (2006); 35–72. Obviously, this raises the question of what an immaterial soul and a material body can possess "in common." (In Plato there was a similar question regarding the "likeness" of visible things and the Ideas.) It seems natural to assume that this "community" consists in their divinity.

clothed in just any body. Aristotle ends this argument with the proposition: "each craft must employ its own tools and each soul its own body" (W. S. Hett [1936], 43).[205] This means that the "instrumental body" of the soul must be suitable for the "work" of the soul. Carpentry can do nothing with a flute, but comes into its own with a hammer or a saw. Coarse work requires coarse tools, but such a set of instruments is useless for more refined work.[206]

Yet we might still ask how the correlation between soul-principles and their instrumental bodies is to be explained: Does the quality of the soul depend on the soul's instrumental body, or the other way round? Is there a difference in quality of soul that "particularizes" itself in a different quality of instrumental body? Did Aristotle imagine principles of life whose vital functions decreased in quality and number, the lowest being the merely vegetative soul-principles of plants and trees, owing to the fact that they were connected with ethereal bodies and subsequently with fire, air, water, and earth, and thus became increasingly removed from the Origin? Or did he see the instrumental bodies as *resulting from* the departure of these vital principles, and as of less quality in proportion to the decrease in vital power of the soul-principles?

In this connection, it is also worth considering a remark that Aristotle made about Anaxagoras. In *Parts of Animals* IV 10, 687a6–b5 Aristotle cites Anaxagoras's view that man is the most intelligent of all creatures because a human being has hands instead of the front legs of quadrupeds. Aristotle objects that it is more rational to suppose the opposite: "But surely the reasonable point of view is that it is because he is the most intelligent animal that he has got hands."[207] In Aristotle's view, the fact that man is the most intelligent has to do with the high quality of his soul-principle and connected *pneuma*, which possesses a high degree of heat and purity, and which also promotes the quality and purity of the blood. In this line of argument, the usable quality of the parts of the visible body seems a side effect of the high soul capacity.[208]

---

205. *Anim.* I 3, 407b25–7: δεῖ γὰρ τὴν μὲν τέχνην χρῆσθαι τοῖς ὀργάνοις, τὴν δὲ ψυχὴν τῷ σώματι.

206. Aristotle thus seems to have rejected any possibility of a soul-principle transmigrating to a soul-body of non-matching quality. Clearly, the degradation of the soul from a human soul to the soul of a wolf or a swan is then out of the question. This does not make it clear whether Aristotle also ruled out every form of metempsychosis at the level of the same species. The final sentence of *Anim.* II 1, 413a8–9 seems to leave scope for reincarnation of human souls.

207. *Part. anim.* IV 10, 687a9–10: εὔλογον δὲ διὰ τὸ φρονιμώτατον εἶναι χεῖρας λαμβάνειν. According to Aristotle, it is more natural to give a flute to someone who possesses musical ability than to give musical ability to someone who possesses a flute (687a12–6)! Cf. W. Kullmann, *Aristoteles, Über die Teile der Lebewesen* (2007), 696–97. Art determines the instrument that can and must be used: *Anim.* I 3, 407b24–6 (cited above).

208. This is not at odds with the fact that philosophers tend to be all thumbs.

This might suggest that Aristotle gave priority to the capacity of the soul and that he regarded the material instrument for this soul as accidental.

We find a similar train of thought in *On Respiration* 13, which argues that the respiration of living beings is due to the larger quantity of vital heat possessed by some animals compared with animals that do not have lungs. The reason given for this is the higher value of the soul of these creatures.[209] Man, as a mortal being with relatively the largest amount of blood, which is also the purest, therefore has an erect gait.[210] Elsewhere, Aristotle explains man's stance by saying that "man is the only one of the animals known to us who has something of the divine in him, or if there are others, he has most."[211] Aristotle goes on to specify this divine element as the activity of the mind and reason. Animal locomotion impedes such activity.[212]

Of decisive importance is the starting point that the pure Intellect is not physically constituted and does not have conation or desire (*orexis*) either. Nor is the Power proceeding from God in the form of soul-principles (entelechies) physical, although it does have connection with a *sôma*. Everything constituted as soul does have "striving" and "willing" and is *therefore* also materially constituted (celestial beings by their ethereal bodies; mortal creatures by their pneumatic body and their visible material frame). This is the thrust of *On the Soul* III 9–10 and *Motion of Animals* 10. It seems natural to see the physical integument of guiding principles as a side effect of the differentiation between Intellect and soul-principles. The entire cosmos is the result of divine, guiding principles that enter physical-spatial bodies in the way that fertilization transfers a guiding power to the physically/spatially characterized menstrual fluid. This is also the basic idea in Plotinus's devolution theory and in the Gnostic doctrine about the "fall" of Sophia from the sphere of the eons.

I would like to add just one speculative remark. *On the Heavens* I 2 calls the circle a perfect figure (269a20) and the celestial element "more divine and prior" (269a31) on account of its circular course. The four sublunary elements are therefore of lower quality than the astral element.

---

209. *Resp.* 13, 477a15–7: "The answer to the first is that animals higher in the scale of nature have more heat; for they must at the same time have a higher form of soul [αἴτιον τοῦ μὲν ἔχειν ὅτι τὰ τιμιώτερα τῶν ζῴων πλείονος τετύχηκε θερμότητος· ἅμα γὰρ ἀνάγκη καὶ ψυχῆς τετυχηκέναι τιμιωτέρας]."

210. Cf. ibid., 477a17–25. Also *Part. anim.* II 7, 653a27–31; III 6, 669b1–6.

211. *Part. anim.* II 10, 656a7–13, with in a7: ἢ γὰρ μόνον μετέχει τοῦ θείου τῶν ἡμῖν γνωρίμων ζῴων, ἢ μάλιστα πάντων.

212. *Part. anim.* IV 10, 686a27–32; 687a6–8.

But they also differ among themselves, inasmuch as fire moves upward, away from the middle (of the cosmos), and the earthlike downward, to the center. Now, Aristotle often designates the element earth as the least viable and the least suitable for perception, and as associated with old age and loss of vital heat. The question therefore arises whether the difference in the sublunary elements' natural direction of movement is also affected by the presence of *pneuma*. In *On the Heavens*, too, Aristotle sees the criterion of proximity to God as determinative for the quality of life and being.[213] In *On the Cosmos* 6, Aristotle says: "That is why the earth and the things upon the earth, being farthest removed from the benefit which proceeds from God, seem feeble and incoherent and full of much confusion."[214]

In *Academica* I 7, 26,[215] Cicero seems to attribute to Aristotle the view that the elements air and fire have power of movement (*movendi vim et efficiendi*), and that water and earth possess mainly passivity (*accipiendi et quasi patiendi vim*).

Does this mean that, in Aristotle's view, the presence of *pneuma* in all sublunary reality also explains the endeavor of the four elements to achieve their own place? In *On the Heavens* I 2, 268b16, we read: "for nature, we say, is their principle of movement [τὴν γὰρ φύσιν κινήσεως ἀρχὴν εἶναι φαμεν αὐτοῖς]."[216] Just as the φύσις of living entities can be identified with the soul and the *pneuma* connected with the soul, so the φύσις of simple bodies can be seen to result from the continued effect of God's working power via *pneuma*. Someone who forcefully rejected Plato's doctrine of the soul as the principle of movement is likely to have come up with an alternative explanation for the

---

213. Cf. *Cael.* I 2, 269b15-7 "the superior glory of its nature is proportionate to its distance from this world of ours [τοσούτῳ τιμιωτέραν ἔχον τὴν φύσιν ὅσῳπερ ἀφέστηκε τῶν ἐνταῦθα πλεῖον]"; and I 9, 279a28-30: "From it derives the being and life which other entities, some more articulately but others feebly, enjoy [ὅθεν καὶ τοῖς ἄλλοις ἐξήρτηται, τοῖς μὲν ἀκριβέστερον τοῖς δὲ ἀμαυρῶς, τὸ εἶναί τε καὶ ζῆν]."

214. *Mu.* 6, 397b30-2: 'Διὸ γῇ τε καὶ τὰ ἐπὶ γῆς ἔοικεν, ἐν ἀποστάσει πλείστῃ τῆς ἐκ θεοῦ ὄντα ὠφελείας, ἀσθενῆ καὶ ἀκατάλληλα εἶναι καὶ πολλῆς μεστὰ ταραχῆς.

215. Arist. *Philos.* fr. 27a Ross; T 18, 1 Gigon.

216. Remarkably, it is only in relation to the fifth element that Aristotle talks about "moving in virtue of its own nature": I 2, 269a5-7, "it follows that there exists a simple body naturally so constituted as to move in a circle in virtue of its own nature [ἀναγκαῖον εἶναί τι σῶμα ἁπλοῦν ὃ πέφυκε φέρεσθαι τὴν κύκλῳ κίνησιν κατὰ τὴν ἑαυτοῦ φύσιν]" (W. K. C. Guthrie [1939], 13); and I 3, 270a8: "it would have been able to move either towards the centre in virtue of its own nature or away from the centre [ἢ γὰρ ἂν πρὸς τὸ μέσον ἢ ἀπὸ τοῦ μέσου ἠδύνατο φέρεσθαι κατὰ τὴν ἑαυτοῦ φύσιν]."

movement of the sublunary elements. The sublunary elements' "desire for their own place" could then be seen as the lowest variant of the "natural desire" with which everything in the cosmos is burdened. Plato's dogma of the all-pervasive World Soul was thus replaced by Aristotle's doctrine of ether and all-pervasive *pneuma* in the sublunary sphere.

k. Is *Pneuma* Perishable or Imperishable? (*De Longitudine Vitae* 2–3)

The working power (*dynamis*) of every soul therefore contains "vital heat" and *pneuma*. However, *pneuma* is not a body that is "more divine" than the four sublunary elements. Only ether, the astral element, is this. But through the connection with *pneuma*, the power of every soul "participates" in the astral element, because in the sublunary sphere *pneuma* is an analogue of the astral element. In *pneuma* and its vital power, the life-generating power of ether is passed on.

If the power of every soul "participates" in the astral body thanks to *pneuma*, then what happens to *pneuma* when the life of the plant, the animal, or the human being ends? Obviously, Aristotle must have given a different answer to this question compared with Plato. For Plato, it was clear that the immaterial soul was of a different order from the material body. And it followed that the soul survived after the death of a human being or animal.[217] Undoubtedly, Aristotle also assumed for the (immaterial) soul-by-itself (= the intellect) that it is immortal.[218] But the soul-in-connection-with-an-instrumental-body is quite a different matter. All the functions of this soul depend on the *pneuma* with which it is connected. But this *pneuma* is only present in the sublunary sphere. Indeed, according to *Generation of Animals* III 11, 762a18–21, it is present throughout the sublunary sphere. On the one hand, therefore, *pneuma* is simply sublunary. And *De Spiritu* 1 explains how a living being achieves an increase in *pneuma* during its development and growth by arguing that this probably happens through the intake of food. *Pneuma* is also contained in everything that is assimilated as food. And semen, in which *pneuma* plays a crucial role, is also a residue of the digestive process.[219] On the other hand,

---

217. Plato fails to clarify the situation of plants, which possess only the lowest (appetitive) soul-part and have no locomotive capacity.

218. Cf. *Anim.* II 2, 413b24–7. It is completely unclear from Aristotle's extant writings how we are to imagine the intellect's survival after the death of the individual person. A question, for instance, is whether there can be an immortal intellect of a human being who dies in infancy, or of an adult human being who has lived like a Midas or a Sardanapallus.

219. P. M. M. Geurts (1941), 127, calls Aristotle a supporter of a "trophic spermatology."

pneuma is special in that it does not form part of the group of four sublunary elements, but has something of the divine element.

This astral element falls outside the sphere of the "opposites"[220] and is not subject to generation and decay. By contrast, the four sublunary elements are the cause of each other's destruction.[221] The question is: What happens to *pneuma* when life comes to an end? For if it is one of the "opposites," it must perish through the agency of what is opposite to *pneuma*. But if it is not one of the "opposites," it belongs to the category of substances that includes ether, according to the passage in *On the Heavens* I 3 quoted above. And in that case, *pneuma* is immortal and imperishable.

A detail of this problem is touched upon in *On the Soul* I 4, 408b18–30, where Aristotle talks about old age. Old age is a matter of declining vital heat. Ageing occurs, not because the soul decays, but because of the damage suffered by that in which it resides.[222] This is apparently lost as a suitable vehicle and instrument of the soul. And decline of its quality also explains the occurrence of diseases in old age.

However, there is another text in the Corpus that possibly brings up an aspect of this problem, namely, *De Longitudine et Brevitate Vitae* 2–3. Aristotle asks there why some living beings live longer than others (the assumption being that no sublunary living being possesses eternal life). Aristotle also asks there, in what I believe to be the only possible reading, whether there is something of which "the perishable is imperishable." He mentions as example: "the fire above" (τὸ πῦρ ἄνω) (3, 465b2).[223]

In book 2, he starts an inquiry into what is perishable and what is not. He does this by emphatically distinguishing two levels: (1) the level of simple, natural bodies, and (2) the level of living entities:[224]

---

220. Cf. *Cael.* I 3, 270a20–2. Cf. A. Falcon (2005), 10, 16, 121.

221. *Long.* 2, 465a14–8.

222. *Anim.* I 4, 408b22 "The incapacity of old age is due not to an affection of the soul but of its vehicle, as occurs in drunkenness and disease [Ὥστε τὸ γῆρας οὐ τῷ τὴν ψυχήν τι πεπονθέναι, ἀλλ' ἐν ᾧ, καθάπερ ἐν μέθαις καὶ νόσοις]." See also b27: τουδὶ τοῦ ἔχοντος ἐκεῖνο. In b28–9 τοῦ κοινοῦ, ὃ ἀπόλωλεν refers to the (instrumental) body of the soul. Cf. A. P. Bos, "*Pneuma* as Instrumental Body of the Soul in Aristotle's *De Anima* I 4." Perhaps we should also use this passage in *Anim.* I 4 to explain *Anim.* III 9, 433a4–6, if the right translation of ὁ ἔχων τὴν ἰατρικὴν οὐκ ἰᾶται there is: "the man who knows medicine does not succed in healing his patient."

223. We already referred to this text in §5b above.

224. Aristotle had also started with this distinction in *On the Soul* II 1. There, he said that bodies seem in the first place to be *ousiai*, and of these especially the natural bodies—412a11–2. He emphatically distinguishes from these the compound *ousiai*, that is, those that have life—412a15–6.

(1) The natural elementary bodies, such as water and fire, destroy each other. And nonliving matters consisting of these elementary bodies decay in the same manner. Ice melts and evaporates through the action of fire (*Long.* 2, 465a14–9).

(2) Then Aristotle switches to a different level of *ousiai*. He is going to talk about living beings and humans, as carriers of health and knowledge. Health and knowledge are matters that may disappear without the carrier of health or knowledge ceasing to exist, but "when the animal dies, the health or knowledge resident in it passes away too."[225] For living entities are much more complex than simple bodies. They possess a body, but they are not a body. They are ensouled and this soul is the entelechy of a natural body that serves the soul as its instrument. And, if we can take *Generation of Animals* II 3, 736b29–7a1 seriously, *pneuma* also forms part of this instrumental body. According to *On the Soul* II 1, 412a15–6, the soul, together with its instrumental body, is "a substance of the compound type" (οὐσία συνθέτη). But what about the perishability of this instrumental body? Its situation is entirely different from that of ordinary, simple bodies. On the basis of these considerations Aristotle wants to talk about the soul's relation to the body. This relation is not the same as the relation of knowledge to the possessor of knowledge. But what is it then (465a27–32)?

In 3, 465b1–3, Aristotle then makes the intriguing remark: "Perhaps one might reasonably raise the question whether . . . ["Ἴσως δ' ἄν τις ἀπορήσειεν εὐλόγως, ἆρ' ἔστι οὗ ἄφθαρτον ἔσται τὸ φθαρτόν, οἷον τὸ πῦρ ἄνω, οὗ μὴ ἔστι τὸ ἐναντίον]." Here, the two occurrences of the word οὗ leave the interpreter with two difficult choices: should it be translated "of which" or "where"? There are three possibilities:

1. A common translation reads: "Is there (any place) *where* the destructible will be indestructible, like fire in the upper regions, *where* it (the fire) has no opposite (that could destroy it, though fire in itself is perishable)?"[226] (This translates the Greek words of the sentence, but it remains completely unclear what is meant and how this fits into the context of the argument.)

---

225. *Long.* 2, 465a25: φθειρομένων γὰρ τῶν ζῴων φθείρεται καὶ ἡ ἐπιστήμη καὶ ἡ ὑγίεια ἡ ἐν τοῖς ζῴοις.

226. Cf. L. Repici, "Aristotele, l'Anima e l'Incorruttibilità: Note su *De Longitudine et Brevitate Vitae, 1–3*," in *Attività e Virtù. Anima e Corpo in Aristotele*, ed. A. Fermani and M. Migliori (Milano: Vita e Pensiero, 2009), 432: "se ci sia un <luogo> dove il corruttibile sarà incorruttibile, come il fuoco in alto . . . dove non c'è contrario." In this way also I. Düring (1966), 569–70.

2. "Is there something *of which* the destructible will be indestructible, like fire in the upper parts (of a living being), *where* it (the fire) has no opposite?"
3. "Is there (any place) *where* the destructible will be indestructible, like fire in the upper parts (of a living being), *of which* (the fire) there is no opposite"?

In view of the fact that Aristotle is talking in this work about the life span of living entities, and the next passage (466b10–32) deals particularly with the "vital heat" (τὸ θερμόν) of animals and people and with the possibility that this vital heat "languishes" (for instance, due to a high outside temperature), I believe that we should interpret "the fire" (τὸ πῦρ) in 465b2 as "the natural fire," "the psychic fire," or vital heat.[227] His train of thought is thus that the vital fire, which forms part of a living substance, does not perish separately from this living substance. If a human being goes for a swim, there is no danger that his vital heat will be extinguished by the seawater.

Aristotle uses arguments here that can only be understood against the background of *On the Soul* II 1. He says: "But no opposite in a real substance is accidentally destroyed, because real substance is not predicated of any subject."[228] The striking expression "no opposite in a real substance," too, can only be understood against the background of Aristotle's argument in *On the Soul* II 1 about "physical bodies" as matters that "seem to be *ousiai*," and about ensouled bodies as "compound substances," of which the natural bodies form part. However, these natural bodies then no longer have their own nature, but have been employed by a soul-principle. The ordinary way in which a natural body is destroyed does not therefore apply to a natural body which is the substrate of a soul as entelechy![229]

This warrants the view that the soul-body, though fundamentally mortal in itself, does not necessarily have to perish in this combination of a body with

---

227. Cf. in the same work 6, 467a33: "the warmth resides in the upper parts [ἐν δὲ τῷ ἄνω τὸ θερμόν]"; and *Resp.* 15, 478a16: "their psychic fire [ψυχικὸν πῦρ]"; 8, 474b10–3: "the natural fire [τὸ φυσικὸν πῦρ]"; *Spir.* 9, 485a33: "the fire of nature [φύσεως πῦρ]." See also *Probl.* XXVII 6, 948a36, where fear is explained as "a draining of heat from the upper parts [ἔκλειψις ἐστι τὸ πάθος θερμοῦ ἐκ τῶν ἄνω τόπων]." Cf. 947b13; 948b8.

228. Cf. *Long.* 3, 465b5–7: κατὰ συμβεβηκὸς δ' οὐθὲν τῶν ἐν ταῖς οὐσίαις ἐναντίων φθείρεται, διὰ τὸ μηθενὸς ὑποκειμένου κατηγορεῖσθαι τὴν οὐσίαν. Cf. with this *Anim.* II 1, 412a16–9: "Now given that there are bodies of such and such kind, viz. having life, the soul cannot be a body; for the body is the subject or matter, not what is attributed to it [Ἐπεὶ δ' ἐστὶ καὶ σῶμα τοιόνδε, ζωὴν γὰρ ἔχον, οὐκ ἂν εἴη τὸ σῶμα ψυχή× οὐ γάρ ἐστι τῶν καθ' ὑποκειμένου τὸ σῶμα, μᾶλλον δ' ὡς ὑποκείμενον καὶ ὕλη]." Cf. also 412b6–9.

229. But cf. P. Gregoric et al., *E.S.M.* 20 (2015); 118: "if the connate *pneuma* is a part of the body, it must be subject to change and waste."

a soul-principle. But this is not acceptable to Aristotle, and he therefore comes up with a different approach. Something happens when an instrument is used for craft. A violin that is played with consummate skill takes on something of the artist's virtuosity. And a sculptor's chisel is able to carve an almost divine Hermes from a block of marble. But this does not make the violin and the chisel divine or immortal. This line of thought is followed by Aristotle in the argument of *De Longitudine Vitae*.

Vital heat is not imperishable (as we could already infer from the text in *On the Soul* I 4 discussed above). For vital heat acts on all food that is absorbed and also produces residues from it.[230] In this sense, there is an entity opposite to the vital heat, viz., the visible body that it maintains and sets in motion. This is a reason for assuming that a process of wear and tear and decay occurs,[231] and that the *pneuma* of a living entity finally merges back into the environment in which the entity lived and from which it was taken. Then the entelechy is no longer able to guide the *pneuma* and ceases to exist as the entelechy of the individual living being.

If this explanation of the reasoning in *De Longitudine Vitae* 2–3 is right, the conclusion must be that Aristotle treats "vital heat" as a "body," on a par with the four sublunary, simple bodies, but with the significant difference that this body has come to form part of a "compound substance," because it is subservient to a soul-principle. And precisely as "vital heat" he can also treat it as something that cannot possess independence, no more than "straightness" or "whiteness" can exist separately and independently.[232]

---

230. *Anim.* II 4, 416b28–9 also makes it clear that *pneuma* is regarded as belonging to the efficient cause: "that which produces digestion is heat [ἐργάζεται δὲ τὴν πέψιν τὸ θερμόν]." For more on this topic, see §10.1 below.

231. Cf. A. P. Bos, "'Fire Above': the Relation of Soul to its Instrumental Body in Aristotle's *De Longitudine et Brevitate Vitae* 2–3" (2002): 303–17; *The Soul and its Instrumental Body* (2003), 183–209; and L. Repici (2009) cited above. This author, art. cit., 419, finds a discrepancy between *Long.* and *Anim.* II 4 in that *Anim.* II 4, 416a9–18 does not identify Fire with "ensouled Fire," as *Long.* does. This forces her to hypothesize a different time of origin for the two writings. However, this hypothesis is completely superfluous, because *Anim.* II 4, 416b28–30, like *Long.*, talks about "vital heat," under the guidance of the soul, but most emphatically different from the sublunary element Fire.

232. Cf. *Long.* 3, 465b12–4; *Anim.* I 1, 403b7–15. In his dialogue the *Eudemus*, Aristotle also seems to have spoken about the question raised in Plato's *Phaedo*, whether the soul should perhaps be understood as the *harmonia* of the body. Philoponus, *In De Anim.* 141, 22–145, 25 (ed. Hayduck) appears to provide reliable information on this (cf. Arist. *Eudem.* fr. 7a Ross; 59 Gigon). Aristotle supposedly said there that "harmony" has an opposite, namely, "disharmony," but that nothing is opposite to the soul. In his *On the Soul* I 4, 407b27–8a30 Aristotle also discusses the option "soul = harmony," but does not use the argument from the *Eudemus* there. His own conception of the soul as "entelechy" also differs essentially from this disputed view.

1. Is *Pneuma* "Material Cause" or "Efficient Cause"?

The information that Aristotle provides on *pneuma* makes it difficult to determine where *pneuma* belongs among the four causes that he distinguishes.[233] These four causes are usually summed up as "material cause," "formal cause," "final cause," and "efficient cause." In *Metaphysics* A 3, 983a27–32, Aristotle briefly describes them: (1) the essence and the essential nature; (2) matter and the underlying; (3) the source of motion; (4) the purpose or "good" (as that at which the motion is aimed). He remarks that this has been sufficiently discussed in the expositions on Nature. In *Physics* II 3, 194b23–5a3, Aristotle targets the same four "causes." But he describes them differently. The material cause is there called: "That out of which a thing comes to be and which persists" (τὸ ἐξ οὗ γίγνεταί τι ἐνυπάρχοντος). The efficient cause is characterized as "the first principle of change and rest, for example the man who deliberated is a cause, the father is cause of the child, and generally what makes of what is made and what changes of what is changed."

Intriguingly, however, Aristotle adds in a further clarification: "But the seed and the doctor and the deliberator, and generally the maker, are all sources whence the change or rest originates."[234] This is striking, because 194b30 mentions "the father" as the efficient cause of a child, and this sentence "the seed." This brings us to an important facet of Aristotle's philosophy and his conflict with Plato. A child does not come into being without a father as begetter, but not without the father's semen either. Aristotle firmly holds that it is not the begetter who "brings about" or produces the child, but the working power that is transferred to the menstrual fluid by semen as the soul's instrument.[235]

Aristotle's doctrine of the "four causes" is aimed at clearly bringing out the difference between him and Plato. A conspicuous aspect of Aristotle's survey in *Metaphysics* A 3–9 outlining the development of philosophy up till his time is his assertion that Plato's philosophy had confined itself to two causes: a formal cause and a material cause.[236] Anyone who reads this claim

---

233. Cf. *Phys.* II 3, 194b23–5a3; *Metaph.* A 3, 983a24–b1; *Gener. anim.* I 1, 715a1–13. The word *cause* is somewhat unsuitable in this context, because Aristotle actually means something like "principle of explanation." But the term *cause* is now the accepted translation of Latin *causa*, which was used to render Greek αἰτία.

234. *Phys.* II 3, 195a21–3: τὸ δὲ σπέρμα καὶ ὁ ἰατρὸς καὶ ὁ βουλεύσας καὶ ὅλως τὸ ποιοῦν, πάντα ὅθεν ἡ ἀρχὴ τῆς μεταβολῆς ἢ στάσεως.

235. Cf. §§6b and 9a above.

236. *Metaph.* A 6, 988a8–10: "it is evident from what has been said that he used only two causes, that of the essence and the material cause [φανερὸν δ' ἐκ τῶν εἰρημένων ὅτι δυοῖν αἰτίαιν μόνον κέχρηται, τῇ τε τοῦ τί ἐστι καὶ τῇ κατὰ τὴν ὕλην]" (W. D. Ross). Cf. also A 9, 991a11 and a22–3. *Gener. corr.* II 1 has the same thrust and explicitly asks how Plato can explain coming-to-be with the help of Ideas and participation only.

is likely to object: "But what about the Demiurge in the *Timaeus*? Surely he was the 'Maker' of the World Soul and the World Body and of all second- and third-rate souls? And when Plato in the *Phaedrus* characterizes the soul as the 'principle of motion' that moves everything in the cosmos, surely this is also an 'efficient cause' on the level of individual things?"[237] Yet Aristotle asks very specifically in *Metaphysics* A 9: "For what is it that works, looking to the Ideas?"[238] The obvious reply here is: "The Demiurge, of course. Plato says so!" On closer consideration, it becomes clear that Aristotle almost uses the words of the *Timaeus* against its author: his concern is with concrete cases of coming-to-be in the sphere of living nature. Plato does sketch the origin of the cosmos as a whole, but he does not explain how living beings come into being.[239] That is precisely what Aristotle is interested in. This process requires an agency that possesses knowledge of the Form of a new creature, but also an agency that *does the work*, as "instrument" of the (creature's) soul. Aristotle plainly indicates here that Plato's talk about a world of Ideas as Patterns and about the "participation" of visible things in these Ideas does not explain anything about the way things proceed on the level of individual living entities.[240] Instead, he states that "the working power of every kind of soul has to do with some body which is different from the so-called 'elements' and more divine than they are."[241] There he calls this body vital heat or *pneuma*, which in the sublunary sphere is always combined with the sublunary elements. He says too that the soul is a first entelechy of an "instrumental body."

---

237. Cf. W. D. Ross, *Aristotle, Metaphysics*, vol. 1 (1924), 176–77.

238. *Metaph.* A 9, 991a22: τί γάρ ἐστι τὸ ἐργαζόμενον πρὸς τὰς ἰδέας ἀποβλέπον; For Aristotle, contemplation of the Ideas is a matter of the Intellect. But production is not, requiring as it does an ensouled, corporeal agency. What "works," according to Aristotle, is the instrumental body, which is guided by an entelechy as form-containing principle.

239. It is not far-fetched to argue that Aristotle takes the opposite approach. Starting from a new view on the generation of living beings, he designs an alternative cosmology.

240. *Metaph.* A 9, 991a20–2: "And to say that they are patterns and the other things share them is to use empty words and poetical metaphors [τὸ δὲ λέγειν παραδείγματα αὐτὰ εἶναι καὶ μετέχειν αὐτῶν τἆλλα κενολογεῖν ἐστι καὶ μεταφορὰς λέγειν ποιητικάς]." See 6, 987b13: "But what the participation or the imitation of the Forms could be they left an open question [τὴν μέντοι γε μέθεξιν ἢ τὴν μίμησιν ἥτις ἂν εἴη τῶν εἰδῶν ἀφεῖσαν ἐν κοινῷ ζητεῖν]." S. Broadie (2007) brilliantly discusses Aristotle's criticism of Plato's doctrine of Ideas in the *Timaeus*.

241. *Gener. anim.* II 3, 736b29–31: Πάσης μὲν οὖν ψυχῆς δύναμις ἑτέρου σώματος ἔοικε κεκοινωνηκέναι καὶ θειοτέρου τῶν καλουμένων στοιχείων. See §10a above. A striking feature is Aristotle's Platonic language in *Anim.* II 4, 415a29–b7, where he talks about τοῦ ἀεὶ καὶ τοῦ θείου μετέχειν and κοινωνεῖν τοῦ ἀεὶ καὶ τοῦ θείου, in connection with the desire of all things for likeness to God. But in Aristotle this desire (*orexis*) is a matter of the soul's instrumental body.

Moreover, he argues at length in *On the Soul* I 3, 405b31 and following that the soul cannot possess or cause motion. He explains all this with a view to the alternative presented in II 1 and following.

The development of philosophy as sketched by Aristotle seems to have described a strange curve. After people such as Anaxagoras and Empedocles, who recognized the necessity of an efficient cause, Plato appeared to revert to a system that admitted only a formal and a material cause, although in fact Plato's discovery of an intelligible reality had raised philosophy to an entirely different level.

These chapters 6 and 9 of *Metaphysics* A have caused a great deal of controversy. Scholars have talked about Aristotle's astonishing ignorance of crucial themes from his teacher's work, or about his unreliability and unkindness with regard to earlier colleagues. But the same chapters show that Aristotle is most certainly familiar with Plato's *Timaeus* and with his frequent discussions "on the soul."[242] The crux is that for Aristotle "the Demiurge" and "the soul" in Plato's writings are *internally contradictory* agencies. Aristotle argued against Plato that he should specify: Is the Demiurge Intellect or Soul?[243] And when talking about "the soul," Plato should also have made it clear whether he meant the intellect or that which is responsible for specifically psychic functions such as metabolism and perception and is connected with a natural body for this purpose.

In Aristotle's view, "the soul" is not a principle of self-motion, and therefore not a principle of motion for other agencies, either, in contrast to the soul as "entelechy in indissoluble unity with its instrumental body." However, in the latter situation it is actually a "compound" of a formal cause and an efficient cause, and as such it is at the same time a final cause, for the development it initiates is always aimed at the complete, adult specimen of the same kind. "For a human being begets a human being." Thus, in the sphere of sublunary creatures, three of the four "causes" coincide.[244] Aristotle underlines this in *On*

---

242. This also applies to *Gener. corr.* I 2, 315a29–32, where Aristotle blames Plato for talking about the coming-to-be of the elements, but not about the growth of flesh and bones etc. C. Mugler, *Aristote, De la Génération et de la Corruption. Texte Établi et Traduit* (Paris: Les Belles Lettres, 1966), 77 n. 1, suspects that Aristotle is mistaken here, because Plato discusses in detail the constitution of marrow in *Tim.* 73b. But this is certainly not a mistake on Aristotle's part. He radically rejects Plato's explanation.

243. Cf. §9h above. And *Anim.* I 3, 407a3–5. This was also a central theme in his dialogue the *Eudemus*. Cf. Themistius, *in De An.* 106. 29–107. 5 = fr. 2 Ross; 58 Gigon.

244. Cf. *Phys.* II 6, 198a24–6: "The last three often coincide; for the what and that for the sake of which are one, while the primary souce of motion is the same in species as these [Ἔρχεται δὲ τὰ τρία εἰς ἓν πολλάκις· τὸ μὲν γὰρ τί ἐστι καὶ τὸ οὗ ἕνεκα ἕν ἐστι, τὸ δ' ὅθεν ἡ κίνησις πρῶτον τῷ εἴδει ταὐτὸ τούτοις]." Aristotle does not mean that the three causes are identical. Cf. J. Rosen, "Essence and End in Aristotle," *Oxford Studies in Ancient Philosophy* 46 (2014): 73–107.

the Soul II 4, 415b9–6b31.²⁴⁵ And his proof that the soul is a "principle of change" leads to his proposition that all ensouled beings possess vital heat to effect digestion. His assertion in II 4, 416b28–9: "that which produces digestion is heat [ἐργάζεται δὲ τὴν πέψιν τὸ θερμόν]," is his answer to the question that he asked Plato: "For what is it that works, looking to the Ideas?" Aristotle states: *pneuma*, with its vital heat, is the efficient cause, and it is guided by the soul as (first) entelechy, as the agency that carries the Form in itself and that keeps the work of *pneuma* oriented to the goal.²⁴⁶

Wherever Aristotle talks about the "instrumental body" of the soul, he regards this soul-body as the *efficient cause* of the activity carried out. This is also the case where the origin of movement in a living being is situated in the instrument of *orexis* (*Anim.* III 10, 433b19–20). In *Motion of Animals* 10, 703a5 ff., he calls *pneuma* the instrument by which the soul effects the movement of limbs. In *Generation of Animals* II 6, 741b37, where Aristotle says that "the parts of animals are differentiated by means of *pneuma* [Διορίζεται δὲ τὰ μέρη τῶν ζῴων πνεύματι]," and in V 8, 789b7–9, where nature is said to perform most of its operations through *pneuma*, *pneuma* is the efficient cause, too. In his introduction to *Generation of Animals*, Aristotle also indicates explicitly that the entire work will be about (1) the generation of living beings and the (sexual) parts instrumental for this, and (2) the efficient cause by which this generation is realized.²⁴⁷ We should take this in the sense that Aristotle will speak about the role of the male as begetter and about semen and the *pneuma* it contains as transmitters of the procreative working power that makes new life possible.

Whereas we have seen that, for Aristotle, three kinds of "cause" come together in the concept of "soul," this is emphatically not the case with the "material cause." Yet Aristotle sometimes connects *pneuma* with "matter." Insofar as it is a body, we would apparently have to classify it as matter. And in *De Spiritu* 9, 485b6–7, Aristotle curiously says that nature not only uses *pneuma* as an instrument, but also as "matter":

---

245. First summarized in *Anim.* II 4, 415b9–12: "But the soul is equally the cause in each of the three senses we have distinguished; for it is the cause in the sense of being that from which motion is derived, in the sense of the purpose or final cause, and as being the substance of all bodies that have souls [Ὁμοίως δ' ἡ ψυχὴ κατὰ τοὺς διωρισμένους τρόπους τρεῖς αἰτία· καὶ γὰρ ὅθεν ἡ κίνησις αὕτη, καὶ οὗ ἕνεκα, καὶ ὡς ἡ οὐσία τῶν ἐμψύχων σωμάτων ἡ ψυχὴ αἴτιον]" (W. S. Hett). The rest of the chapter is devoted to a demonstration of this.

246. Cf. also *Spir.* 9, 485a28. In both cases Aristotle is talking about the heat of the instrumental body of the soul, *pneuma*.

247. For this, see ch. 6 above, with a critical note on the interpretation of this introduction proposed by D. M. Balme (1972).

But the crafts use fire solely as an instrument; nature, on the other hand, also uses it as matter.

ἀλλ' αἱ μὲν τέχναι ὡς ὀργάνῳ χρῶνται (sc. τῷ πυρί) ἡ δὲ φύσις ἅμα καὶ ὡς ὕλῃ.[248]

Also, insofar as *pneuma* is always connected with the working power of a soul, which implies that *pneuma* belongs to the body of the soul, we could establish on the basis of *On the Soul* II 1, 412a16–9 that *pneuma* must be regarded "as a substrate, that is, as matter" (ὡς ὑποκείμενον καὶ ὕλη) of the soul.[249]

In *On the Soul* I 1, 403a3–25, where Aristotle discusses the problem of the affections or emotions of the soul, such as anger, desire, loving, and hating, but also sensation generally, his conclusion is that all these affections (*pathè*) must be considered *logoi en hylei*—λόγοι ἐν ὕλῃ (a25). Because these "affections" of anger and sensation, etc. always involve *pneuma* and vital heat (τὸ θερμόν, 403b1), the term *hylè* there seems necessarily to include *pneuma*.[250]

Yet *De Longitudine Vitae* 2–3, which we discussed above §10k, makes it clear that *pneuma* does not belong to the simple bodies, which effect coming-to-be and passing-away for each other. Like ether, *pneuma* seems to fall outside the sphere of the elements, which possess opposite properties and can therefore

---

248. See also *Spir.* 9, 485b15–7: "But how are we then to explain the difference of the vital heat in each individual living creature, the heat taken as instrument or as matter or as both? For fire displays differences of more and less. This is much like mixed or unmixed. For pure fire is more fire [ἀλλὰ δὴ τίς ἡ διαφορὰ τοῦ καθ' ἕκαστον θερμοῦ, εἴθ' ὡς ὄργανον εἴθ' ὡς ὕλην εἴθ' ὡς ἄμφω; πυρὸς γὰρ διαφοραὶ κατὰ τὸ μᾶλλον καὶ ἧττον. τοῦτο δὲ σχεδὸν ὥσπερ ἐν μίξει καὶ ἀμιξίᾳ· τὸ γὰρ καθαρώτερον μᾶλλον]." Cf. A. P. Bos and R. Ferwerda (2008), 177–81.

249. Perhaps we can link this to the distinction in *Spir.* 8, 485a13–5 between upright bipeds, quadrupeds, and creatures with more than four feet. The latter are described there as: "whose matter is earthier and colder [ὅσοις ἡ ὕλη γεωδεστέρα καὶ ψυχροτέρα]." Because their vital principle is concerned, this must mean that their life-bearing *pneuma* is mixed with earth and is therefore colder. In *Gener. anim.* III 11, 761b13–4, Aristotle similarly associates plants with earth and fish with water, because these elements are dominant in them, in connections with the *pneuma* that is connected with all souls. In 762a24–6, Aristotle also makes the difference in quality of life depend on what has coalesced with the "psychic principle" (in cases of spontaneous generation). Cf. §10j above.

250. In *Anim.* I 1, 403a31–b1 Aristotle gives an example of a definition of "anger" as a natural philosopher might formulate it: "the former will describe it as a surging of the blood and heat around the heart [ὁ δὲ ζέσιν τοῦ περὶ τὴν καρδίαν αἵματος ἢ θερμοῦ]," where "heat" anticipates Aristotle's theory of vital *pneuma*. See also 403b10–2: "the natural philosopher's concern is with all the functions and affections of such a body, i.e. of matter in such a state [ἀλλ' ὁ φυσικὸς περὶ ἅπανθ' ὅσα τοῦ τοιουδὶ σώματος καὶ τῆς τοιαύτης ὕλης ἔργα καὶ πάθη]." On 403b1, see also R. Renehan, "Aristotle's Definition of Anger," *Philologus* 107 (1963): 61–74, who states on p. 68: "I conclude that ἢ θερμοῦ is an interpolation and should be deleted from the text."

dissolve into each other.[251] Chapter 3 of *De Longitudine Vitae* also shows that "the fire in the upper regions" acts on matter that is attracted as food and is converted to blood and residues.[252] We find there that the soul-body is on the side of the "efficient cause" and is not purely "matter."[253]

The special status of *pneuma* as instrument of the soul also seems to be underlined in *Motion of Animals* 10, 703a24–5. Aristotle says there: "Now that which is to initiate movement *without alteration* must be of the kind prescribed [δεῖ δὲ τὸ μέλλον κινεῖν μὴ ἀλλοιώσει τοιοῦτον εἶναι]." Perhaps Aristotle is here again separating *pneuma* from the four sublunary elements. For these four are generated from each other "by alteration, as things which turn in respect of their matter."[254] Aristotle does stress that all sensations that occasion self-motion are "changes in a certain sense,"[255] and these act on the *pneuma*. But he keeps *pneuma* itself outside these changes.

Pneuma does not structurally belong to the four sublunary elements, but is the representative of the astral element in the sublunary sphere. As such, *pneuma* belongs to the "moving cause," to which *Generation of Animals* pays special attention, as appears from chapter I 1. For the *pneuma* in semen is the "male" factor, which acts on the four elements as "the female" and "underlying."

Nevertheless, there is an added complication. Aristotle repeatedly declares that in the process of reproduction the male partner supplies the efficient cause (and no matter), while the female partner contributes the matter.[256] In the traditional interpretation this has often been taken to mean that the female

---

251. Cf. *Phys.* I 7, 190b5–9: "Things which come to be without qualification . . . by alteration, as things which turn in respect of their matter [Γίγνεται δὲ τὰ γιγνόμενα ἁπλῶς τὰ μὲν . . . τὰ δ' ἀλλοιώσει, οἷον τὰ τρεπόμενα κατὰ τὴν ὕλην]."

252. Cf. *Long.* 3, 465b11: "for everything which possesses matter must have a contrary in some sense [ἀδύνατον γὰρ τῷ ὕλην ἔχοντι μὴ ὑπάρχειν πῶς τὸ ἐναντίον]." Cf. also *Resp.* 8 on σβέσις and μάρανσις (474b14) of vital heat through extreme cold or extreme heat.

253. Cf. *Anim.* II 4, 416b28–9, cited in §10k above.

254. Cf. *Phys.* I 7, 190 b5–9, cited above.

255. Cf. on that *Anim.* II 5, 417b2–7 and §10e above.

256. *Gener. anim.* I 20, 727b31–3: "By now it is clear that the contribution which the female makes to generation is the *matter* used therein, and that this is to be found in the substance constituting the menstrual fluid, and finally that the menstrual fluid is a residue [Ὅτι μὲν οὖν συμβάλλεται τὸ θῆλυ εἰς τὴν γένεσιν τὴν ὕλην, τοῦτο δ' ἐστὶν ἐν τῇ καταμηνίων συστάσει, τὰ δὲ καταμήνια περίττωμα, δῆλον]." 729a28–31: "Thus, if the male is the active partner, the one which originates the movement, and the female . . . is the passive one, surely what the female contributes to the semen of the male will not be semen but material [εἰ οὖν τὸ ἄρρεν ἐστὶν ὡς κινοῦν καὶ ποιοῦν, τὸ δὲ θῆλυ [ᾗ θῆλυ] ὡς παθητικόν, εἰς τὴν τοῦ ἄρρενος γονὴν τὸ θῆλυ ἂν συμβάλλοιτο οὐ γονὴν ἀλλ' ὕλην]." 21, 730a24–7; 730b1; II 4, 738b20–4: "The female always provides the material, the male provides that which fashions the material into shape. . . . Hence, necessity requires that the female should provide the physical part, i.e. a quantity of material,

partner provides the material for the entire visible body. But this is total nonsense. In this context, Aristotle is always talking about the contributions of the male and the female to the embryo (*kyèma*), which is the first life-stage of the new living being.[257] To this embryo, the male supplies semen as carrier of the soul-principle; the female provides her menstrual fluid. Both components are residues of digested food and contain *pneuma*. But a curious situation arises here. The semen of the male possesses high-quality *pneuma*, because semen consists of blood that has been fully converted through the natural nuritive process of concoction. This high-quality *pneuma* is suitable as a carrier of the soul-principle. In contrast, one can tell from the menstrual fluid of the female partner that the concoction of blood has not completely succeeded. The *pneuma* it contains cannot produce a vital principle. The *pneuma* in the menstrual fluid is actually an unsuccessful (failed) product of nature.[258]

This is a point worth dwelling on. It means that the distinction between a male and a female creature results from a difference in the quality of the soul's instrumental body. So there is no distinction between a female and a male soul as entelechy. The soul as entelechy guides the process of life such that finally the *eidos* ("human" or "cat") is realized. But the male or female sex of the new specimen is not anchored in the soul as entelechy.[259]

On the other hand, it is true that nothing of the material substance of the semen remains in the embryo resulting from sexual intercourse.[260] The semen only transfers the power of the soul-principle to the *pneuma* of the

---

but not that the male should do so [ἀεὶ δὲ παρέχει τὸ μὲν θῆλυ τὴν ὕλην τὸ δ' ἄρρεν τὸ δημιουργοῦν.... ὥστε τὸ μὲν θῆλυ ἀναγκαῖον παρέχειν σῶμα καὶ ὄγκον, τὸ δ' ἄρρεν οὐκ ἀναγκαῖον]." These texts receive full attention in R. Mayhew, *The Female in Aristotle's Biology* (Chicago: University of Chicago Press, 2004), 38–43. But the author is very keen to challenge modern feminist slander against Aristotle, so that he fails to inquire into the systematic reason why the male partner does not supply "material" for the new specimen.

257. See *Gener. anim.* I 20, 727b31–3, cited above.

258. *Gener. anim.* II 3, 737a27–9: "The reason is that the female is as it were a deformed male; and the menstrual discharge is semen, though in an impure condition [τὸ γὰρ θῆλυ ὥσπερ ἄρρεν ἐστὶ πεπηρωμένον καὶ τὰ καταμήνια σπέρμα, οὐ καθαρὸν δέ]." I 20, 728a26: "for as we see, the menstrual fluid is semen, not indeed semen in a pure condition, but needed still to be acted upon [ἔστι γὰρ τὰ καταμήνια σπέρμα οὐ καθαρὸν ἀλλὰ δεόμενον ἐργασίας]." II 8, 748b31–4: "The male may occasionally generate (a) because the male is by nature hotter than the female, and (b) because the male does not contribute any corporeal ingredient to the mixture [ὁ δ' ἄρρεν ποτὲ γεννήσειεν ἂν διά τε τὸ θερμότερον εἶναι τοῦ θήλεος φύσει τὸ ἄρρεν καὶ διὰ τὸ μὴ συμβάλλεσθαι πρὸς τὴν μίξιν σῶμα μηδὲν τὸ ἄρρεν]." On this, see §§3a and 6a above. Cf. A. M. Leroi, *The Lagoon* (2014) 216: "every little girl represents a failure in her father's semen."

259. Perhaps we should conclude from this that, like the soul as entelechy, the *nous* (the intellect) is neither male nor female.

260. *Gener. anim.* II 3, 737a7–12.

female's menstrual fluid. All the matter of the embryo is therefore supplied by the female. The male, with his high-quality *pneuma*, does not even supply *pneuma* to the embryo, but only the vitalizing *logos*-containing power. (For fertilization can also take place without semen.)[261]

Here, we find the root cause of the ambivalence of *pneuma*: it can be an efficient cause in the case of the male's *pneuma*; it is a material cause where the female's *pneuma* is concerned.[262]

This very special approach to human and animal procreation, in which a power, using available material, supplies the essence and specific form of the new living specimen, seems to have been developed by analogy with Aristotle's theology, in which he presented God as the absolutely transcendent source of Power, thanks to which God can be called the (male!) "Begetter" of all that lives in the cosmos. This is connected with Aristotle's characterization of "the underlying," "the receiving" of "matter," as "mother," and as that which "desires" the good that provides the form-principle; and with Aristotle's positive valuation of matter or the underlying as "almost substance," as "close to substance," and even as "substance in a certain sense." I believe that there is also a link with Aristotle's quotation of an Orphic poem in *On the Cosmos* 7, 401b2 with the remarkable words: "Zeus is a man, Zeus an immortal maid [Ζεὺς ἄρσην γένετο, Ζεὺς ἄμβροτος ἔπλετο νύμφη]."

For the procreative power of the human begetter, semen is the instrumental body *par excellence*. For God's power, ether (and its analogue *pneuma*) is the instrumental body par excellence. In Aristotle's doctrine of procreation, this body is the carrier of the *logoi enhyloi* or *logoi spermatikoi* (*rationes seminales*), but also of the entelechies.

In other words, the male and the female are both necessary to procreation. But they are not equal. In Aristotle's way of thinking, a female specimen is an imperfect product (πήρωμα) of nature.[263] It is just so with the relation between the immaterial soul and its instrumental body. The soul differs qualitatively from the body with which it is connected, but cannot function without this material instrument. Finally, the same applies to God and the material world. As transcendent Intellect God is infinitely higher in value than the cosmos. But everything in the cosmos does form a manifestation of God's perpetual working power. The *plèrôma* (fullness of being) of the divine Intellect acts

---

261. On this, see §6a above.

262. *Gener. anim.* I 20, 729a32: "for the natural substance of the menstrual fluid is to be classed as 'prime matter' [κατὰ γὰρ τὴν πρώτην ὕλην ἐστὶν ἡ τῶν καταμηνίων φύσις]."

263. Cf. *Gener. anim.* II 3, 737a27–9 cited above. Cf. also IV 3, 767b6–12. And *Anim.* II 4, 415a26–8, where it is said that the production of new life is characteristic of "perfect" living beings, and "failed specimens" (πηρώματα) are excluded from this. See E. Lesky (1950), 150.

on the *pèrōma* (deficiency of being) of material reality. This view is typical of Aristotle's moderate dualism.²⁶⁴

m. Is *Pneuma* Always "Ensouled"?

Pneuma, as the carrier of soul-principles and as the carrier of vital power, can be called "ensouled."²⁶⁵ We need to take into account here the fact that the soul does not pervade *pneuma* in its entirety the way *pneuma* itself pervades the entire visible body of a living being (on this, see §10c above). Aristotle often stresses that the soul of a living being is located in the center and is not itself present everywhere. But *pneuma*, too, is highly present in the center and there it receives the directives of the soul. Sometimes, Aristotle also talks about "psychic fire"²⁶⁶ and "psychic heat." But it is typical of the sublunary condition of *pneuma* that life and soul can be "potentially" present in it. Just as a wound-up automaton is not yet "active," but can "come into action" straightaway, so the *pneuma* in semen is not yet "active," but does meet all the conditions for coming into action as soon as it has been connected with the menstrual fluid.

In the same way, Aristotle argued that semen is an instrument of the soul,²⁶⁷ and that it possesses soul only "potentially."²⁶⁸ It possesses soul really, but semen in itself is not a living being; at most it is "vital moisture"—ὑγρότης ζωτική.²⁶⁹ However, a soul-principle functions only after a fertilization. Hence,

---

264. See also §3f above.
265. Cf. *Mu.* 4, 394b11: "Ensouled . . . substance" (ἔμψυχος . . . οὐσία). See also *Gener. anim.* III 11, 762a19–21. Cf. also *Spir.* 1, 481a16: "For that which is connected with the soul is purer [καθαρώτερον γὰρ ὃ τῇ ψυχῇ συμφυές]," and 9, 485b12: "And the case is just as remarkable with the soul. For it is present in them [ἔτι δὲ τοῦτο θαυμαστὸν καὶ περὶ ψυχῆς· ἐν τούτοις γὰρ ὑπάρχει]."
266. Cf. *Resp.* 15, 478a16.
267. Cf. *Anim.* II 4, 415b7 and *Gener. anim.* I 22, 730b19–23. See also A. P. Bos, "A Lost Sentence on Seed as Instrument of the Soul" (2010): 276–87.
268. Cf. A. P. Bos, "The Soul and Soul-'Parts' in Semen" (2009).
269. Cf. *Motu anim.* 11, 703b23. This is a thorny problem for Aristotle. He is talking here about involuntary movements of members, such as erections and reflexes. Plato was able to see these as instances where a lower soul-part fails to obey the orders of a higher soul-part. For Aristotle, who followed Plato in distinguishing several soul-parts, but did not locate them in different places, it was harder to explain how the one entelechy of the living being can manifest itself in internally contradictory ways of functioning. He solved this problem in *Anim.* III 9–10 by connecting *orexis* not with the soul as entelechy, but with the instrumental body of the soul. He did not explain the problem of insufficient self-control as a conflict between two different parts of the one soul, as Plato had done, but as an opposition between the soul as entelechy and the instrumental body of the soul.

Aristotle can say that *pneuma* possesses "*psychic* heat."[270] This heat differs radically from the heat of fire. It is the heat that, like the heat of the Sun, causes seeds and embryos to develop everywhere as carriers of soul-principles.[271]

Aristotle rejected Plato's doctrine of a World Soul that permeates the entire cosmos. Like Plato, he holds that the astral sphere and the celestial gods are ensouled beings. But in his view the entire sublunary sphere is permeated by *pneuma*, as the carrier of divine vitality. That is why life can spontaneously flourish in the sublunary sphere, even in places and times where one does not expect it. *Pneuma* is therefore the carrier of potential for life and, wherever the conditions for vital activity are met, the carrier and instrument of soul.[272]

Aristotle needs the theory of *pneuma* to explain phenomena that characterize the sphere of generation and decay, in particular, the fact that seeds of plants and trees contain germinative power that does not come into "action" before the appropriate season has arrived and the required temperature, boosted by the Sun, has been reached. (This seems a subject that Aristotle certainly would have treated in his work *De Plantis*, which he repeatedly announced[273] but may not have completed.)

Likewise, there is the fact that semen of animals and humans contains soul that only becomes active after successful copulation. That is what Aristotle means in his definition of soul in *On the Soul* II 1, 412a28: "a natural body having life potentially." These words refer only to male semen and female menstrual fluid and germinative seeds, and not to any other substance. The reason is that they contain *pneuma*.

Also, in animals and humans some soul-functions stay latent longer than others and only the nutritive function is immediately operative, even though other functions are present from the moment of fertilization, too.[274]

Finally, *pneuma*, though material, is carrier of the human soul with its rational function and therefore also carrier of the passive intellect.

---

270. *Gener. anim.* III 11, 762a20.

271. *Gener. anim.* II 3, 737a1–5.

272. Cf. Aristotle's special interest in the "slipping" of plants and the regeneration of animals such as rainworms after they have been cut in two (*Anim.* I 5, 411b19–27; II 2, 413b16–24). See §10d above and A. P. Bos, "Aristotle on the Dissection of Plants" (2007): 95–106.

273. For example, in *Long.* 6, 467b4–5. In *Gener. anim.* I 22, 731a30, Aristotle says: "Plants, however, have been dealt with in another treatise [ἀλλὰ περὶ μὲν φυτῶν ἐν ἑτέροις ἐπέσκεπται]." It seems natural to assume a connection with the study *On Nutrition* which Aristotle also cited (*Somn.* 3, 456b6) and announced several times (e.g., in *Anim.* II 4, 416b30–1; *Spir.* 3, 482b12–3), but which may not have been written either. See A. P. Bos and R. Ferwerda (2008), 100.

274. Cf. *Anim.* II 1, 412b17 ff.; 5, 417b16–8 and §15 below.

However, in §10d above we already indicated a problem to which Aristotle never provided a solution. The *pneuma* in semen, which Aristotle calls "instrument of the soul," is governed by the soul of the begetter. Only after being united with the menstrual fluid of a female partner is the *pneuma* of the embryo guided by the entelechy of the new conspecific specimen. But what about the *pneuma* present everywhere in the sublunary sphere? Is it ensouled too?

1. Is it guided by a soul as (first) entelechy in the case of (plants and) living beings that are generated spontaneously? Insofar as such animals have a digestive process and minimal sensory perception, this seems all but inevitable. In describing *generatio spontanea, Generation of Animals* III 11, 762a26 also mentions "the embracing of the psychic principle." But because *pneuma* must be completely indifferent before it is enclosed in a frothy bubble, it seems incapable of being led by any entelechy.

2. A second question to be asked is: What about the *pneuma* that every living entity integrates via nutrition? Is the specific quality of this *pneuma* guaranteed? After all, Aristotle had strongly emphasized that the cognitive and vital quality of souls differs in value, as does, by analogy, the quality of the carrier of the soul.[275] Is *pneuma* that is absorbed in a living creature via nourishment assimilated to the *pneuma* present and active in the creature, just as the *pneuma* in the menstrual fluid of a female is assimilated to the *pneuma* in the semen of the male?

n. Vital Heat as a Property of *Pneuma*

In the foregoing, we have frequently seen that Aristotle talks about *pneuma* as something present in living beings and in semen and menstrual fluid. But often we also saw him speaking about "natural fire," "natural (vital) heat" or "psychic (vital) heat," and even simply about "heat."[276]

---

275. Cf. *Anim.* I 3, 407b13–27; *Gener. anim.* II 3, 736b29–33.

276. Aristotle calls this instrumental body the ἔμφυτον or σύμφυτον πνεῦμα or "vital heat," ἔμφυτος θερμότης, ψυχικὴ θερμότης (*Gener. anim.* II 1, 732a18; III 2, 752a2; 11, 762a20), φυσικὴ θερμότης (*Meteor.* IV 3, 380a20), ζωτικὴ θερμότης (*Iuv.* 12 (6) 473a9); τὸ θερμόν (*Anim.* II 4, 416b29; *Spir.* 9, 485a28), τὸ φυσικὸν θερμόν (*Meteor.* IV 3, 380a22), ψυχικὸν πῦρ (*Resp.* 15, 478a16), ἔμψυχος οὐσία (*Mund.* 4, 394b11), φυσικὸν πῦρ (*Resp.* 8, 474b10–3), etc. P. Gregoric, O. Lewis, and M. Kuhar, "The Substance of *De Spiritu*" (2015), 113–14, assume, wrongly in my view, a distinction in *Spir.* 9 between "heat/fire," which they believe plays an "instrumental role" in the realization of the various parts of a living body, and *pneuma*, whose role is "to secure the right balance of heat in the mixture." In my opinion, this role belongs exclusively to the soul or the entelechy or *physis*, as *Spir.* 9, 485b7–15 puts it.

We have been able to infer from the text of *Generation of Animals* II 3, 736b29–7a1 (see §10a above) that, according to Aristotle, what is known as "(vital) heat" (τὸ καλούμενον θερμόν, b34–5) is identical with "*pneuma* . . . and the nature which is in the *pneuma*." Aristotle goes on straightaway to emphasize the essential difference between the "vital heat" of *pneuma*[277] and the heat spread by fire. *Pneuma* is a body and possesses (vital) heat as a property by which it acts on its environment. (Vital) heat is not a body,[278] but an essential quality of *pneuma*. This essential difference between "ordinary" fire and vital heat is underlined by Aristotle in *On the Soul* II 4, 416a9–19. Against some of the earlier philosophers who identified fire as the cause of nutrition and growth, Aristotle argues that fire goes on without limit, but vital heat is led by the soul-principle as entelechy, and as a result teeth or feet grow, but there is also a limit to their increase. The soul as entelechy determines the *logos* of the developing body and therefore the effect of the vital heat. Vital heat is an instrument of the soul and psychic in character. Ordinary fire is not.[279]

This means that all the passages where Aristotle talks about "heat" or "the hot" in living creatures presuppose his doctrine of *pneuma*. We can therefore no longer say that this doctrine does not occur in *On the Soul*. For his discussion there of anger and of growth and reproduction makes emphatic mention of "(vital) heat," which is clearly shown to be governed by the (sensitive or vegetative) soul.[280]

There is a causal chain that runs from the (immaterial) soul, for instance from the *phantasia* of the soul, to the vital heat or *pneuma* with which the soul (as soul) is inextricably bound up, and from there to the parts of the concrete human being, who is guided by the soul. That is what Aristotle means in *Motion*

---

277. Aristotle connected the heat of *pneuma* with the heat of the Sun as astral celestial being.

278. Cf. *Long.* 3, 465b12: "Qualities such as heat or straightness may be present in anything, but nothing can consist solely of heat, straightness, or whiteness [παντὶ μὲν γὰρ ἐνεῖναι τὸ θερμὸν ἢ τὸ εὐθὺ ἐνδέχεται, πᾶν δ᾽ εἶναι ἀδύνατον ἢ θερμὸν ἢ εὐθὺ ἢ λευκόν]" (reading παντὶ with W. D. Ross [1955]).

279. Cf. J. Beere (2009), 76, 146.

280. Cf. *Anim.* I 1, 403a31–b1: "a surging of the blood and heat around the heart [ζέσιν τοῦ περὶ τὴν καρδίαν αἵματος ἢ θερμοῦ]." (But see also on this text R. Renehan [1963].) II 4, 416b29: διὸ πᾶν ἔμψυχον ἔχει θερμότητα. But see also I 3, 407b21: τοῦ δεξομένου σώματος. I 4, 408b25: ἄλλου τινὸς ἔσω. b27: τοῦ ἔχοντος ἐκεῖνο, en I 1, 403a4: τοῦ ἔχοντος. II 8 420b20: τὴν θερμότητα τὴν ἐντός. III 10, 433b19–20: ᾧ δὲ κινεῖ ὀργάνῳ ἡ ὄρεξις, ἤδη τοῦτο σωματικόν ἐστιν. *Gener. anim.* II 1, 734b31; *Spir.* 9, 485a28; a31. The same applies to *Metaph.* A 3, 983b23, where Aristotle, in connection with Thales, says that "vital heat itself [αὐτὸ τὸ θερμόν] is generated from moisture and depends upon it for its existence."

of Animals 8, 702a17–9: "For the affections suitably prepare the instrumental parts, desire the affections, and *phantasia* the desire."²⁸¹

The *Problems* have been passed down under Aristotle's name, but we do not know which parts were written by Aristotle himself. Book XXVII contains a number of questions relating to "fear" and "courage" that cannot be denied to Aristotle on obvious grounds and in fact show a close affinity to positions in his recognized writings.²⁸² The first question there is: 947b12 Διὰ τί οἱ φοβούμενοι τρέμουσιν; ἢ διὰ τὴν κατάψυξιν; ἐκλείπει γὰρ τὸ θερμὸν καὶ συστέλλεται· διὸ καὶ αἱ κοιλίαι λύονται τοῖς πολλοῖς.²⁸³ Note that συστέλλεται here stands for "contraction" of the vital heat.²⁸⁴ This heat does not leave people who grow afraid, but withdraws from the external parts of the body and thus can no longer function with maximum effect there.²⁸⁵ As a result, phenomena such as "goose pimples," "trembling," and "knocking knees" occur. The fact that people sometimes soil themselves²⁸⁶ is an indication that vital heat and *pneuma* play a regulating role in digestive processes, including defecation.

---

281. M. C. Nussbaum (1978), 46: τὰ μὲν γὰρ ὀργανικὰ μέρη παρασκευάζει ἐπιτηδείως τὰ πάθη, ἡ δ' ὄρεξις τὰ πάθη, τὴν δ' ὄρεξιν ἡ φαντασία. Nussbaum, 156–64, continues to have problems with this Aristotelian view. Like A. L. Peck, she has been unable to make the connection with *On the Soul* II 1.

282. H. Flashar (1962), 693 notes: "Die für fast alle Probleme gültige Erklärung ist die in der hippokr. Wärmelehre verwurzelte und bei Ar. geläufige Theorie, dass Abkühlung Furcht, Angst und Schrecken, innere Wärme aber Tapferkeit bedeuten." Cf. P. Louis (1993), vol. 2, 226. On pp. 223–25, this author gives reasons suggesting that the author was a physician at the end of the third century BCE. See now also W. W. Fortenbaugh, "On *Problemata* 27: Problems Connected with Fear and Courage," in *The Aristotelian* Problemata Physica. *Philosophical and Scientific Investigations*, ed. R. Mayhew (Leiden: Brill, 2015), 311–20.

283. W. S. Hett, vol. 2 (1937), 117, translates: "Why do the frightened tremble? Is it owing to their being chilled? For the heat leaves them and is contracted; this is also why the bowels become loose with many people." Likewise P. Louis, *Aristote, Problèmes*, vol. 2 (1991–94), 226; J. Beets et al., *Aristoteles, Problemen. 415 Vragen over Melancholie, Wijn, Muziek, Liefde etc.* (Budel: Damon, 2010), 158: "For the heat is then insufficient and contracts. Hence the bowels empty themselves with many people."

284. In *Motion of Animals* 10, 703a20–1, Aristotle states emphatically: "the instrument of movement has to be capable of expanding and contracting. And this is just the nature of *pneuma* [δεῖ τὸ ὄργανον αὐξάνεσθαί τε δύνασθαι καὶ συστέλλεσθαι. τοιαύτη δ' ἐστὶν ἡ τοῦ πνεύματος φύσις]."

285. This is stated explicitly in *Probl.* XXVII 2, 947b16: "Or are the chilling and warmth in different parts, the former being on the surface, which the heat has left, while the latter is inside, so that it warms this part? [ἢ οὐκ ἐν ταὐτῷ τόπῳ ἡ κατάψυξις καὶ ἡ θερμότης, ἀλλ' ἡ μὲν ἐν τῷ ἐπιπολῆς, ἔνθεν ἐκλείπει τὸ θερμόν, ἡ δὲ ἐν τῷ ἐντός, ὥστε ἐκθερμαίνει]" (W. S. Hett).

286. A splendid example is King Belshazzar from the story in Daniel 5:6, whose bladder and bowels failed ("were loosened") when he did not know how to "loosen" the riddle of the writing on the wall of his banquet hall. Cf. A. M. Wolters, "Belshazzar's Feast and the Cult of the Moon God Sîn," *Bulletin for Biblical Research* 5 (1995): 199–206.

In *Problemata* XXVII 3, we find further specifications. The author observes that the states of both anger and fear involve contraction of the vital heat. In people who are angry this heat centers around the heart and in the upper part of the chest,[287] but in people who are fearful the movement of blood and vital heat is downward: hence the spontaneous loosening of the bowels.

The fact that blood and vital heat and *pneuma* are mentioned in combination clearly indicates that *pneuma* cannot be translated "breath" here, as W. S. Hett does. *Pneuma* is identical here with vital heat and present *in* blood.[288]

It is interesting that the author goes on to mention the "beating" (ἡ πήδησις) of the heart. Again, there is a difference here for angry and frightened people (3, 947b29). Aristotle also discusses the beating of the heart in *On the Life-Bearing Spirit* 4, 483a1–5. The occasion there is his proposition that breath and pulsation (of the *pneuma* in the blood) have nothing to do with each other. The pulsation stays the same whether we breathe regularly or quickly and deeply. But it becomes irregular and agitated owing to certain physical disorders and in stressful situations caused by panic attacks or hopeful expectations of the soul.[289]

Here, Aristotle connects matters such as fear and hope with the soul, while emphasizing the quickened pulsation of the *pneuma* in the blood, which thus reacts to a perception of the sensitive soul.

---

287. *Probl.* XXVII 3, 947b25: "In the case of the angry it is the heart which is affected, which is the reason why they are courageous, flushed and full of *pneuma*, but in the case of the frightened the blood and the heat escape downwards [τοῖς μὲν ὀργιζομένοις περὶ τὴν καρδίαν, διὸ καὶ θαρρητικοὶ καὶ ἐν ἐρυθήματι καὶ πνεύματος πλήρεις, ἄνω τῆς φορᾶς οὔσης, τοῖς δὲ φοβουμένοις κάτω]." P. Louis (1993), vol. 2, 226: "Quand on est en colère il s'agit de la partie qui entoure le coeur (c'est pourquoi on a de l'assurance, on est rouge et plein de souffle, le déplacement de la chaleur se faisant vers le haut.)"

288. Cf. also 947b35: "owing to the upward passage of the *pneuma* and heat [διὰ τὴν ἀναφορὰν τοῦ πνεύματος ἅμα καὶ θερμοῦ]."

289. *Spir.* 4, 483a1–5: "when someone breathes rapidly or evenly, and when he breathes heavily or lightly, the pulsating movement is the same and unchanged, but an irregular and agitated pulse occurs during some bodily ailments and in the case of fears, hopeful expectations, and afflictions of the soul [ἐάν τε γὰρ πυκνὸν ἐάν τε ὁμαλὸν ἐάν τε σφοδρὸν ἢ ἀραιὸν ἀναπνέῃ τις, ὅ γε σφυγμὸς ὅμοιος καὶ ὁ αὐτός, ἀλλ' ἡ ἀνωμαλία γίνεται καὶ ἐπίτασις ἔν τε σωματικοῖς τισι πάθεσι καὶ ἐν τοῖς τῆς ψυχῆς φόβοις, ἐλπίσιν, ἀγωνίαις]." Cf. A. P. Bos and R. Ferwerda (2008), 108–109, and Plato, *Tim.* 70c. See also II 26, 869a6: "and the man who is nervous is affected not by fear and chill but by the future prospect [καὶ ὁ ἀγωνιῶν οὐ διὰ φόβον καὶ διὰ ψύξιν πάσχει, ἀλλὰ διὰ τὸ μέλλον]" (trans W. S. Hett). *Probl.* XXVII 4, 948a23 gives an example of a similar phenomenon that is caused by pneumonia or insanity: "So those who are suffering from pneumonia and the insane crave for wine [οἱ ἐν τῇ περιπνευμονίᾳ καὶ οἱ μαινόμενοι ἀμφότεροι ἐπιθυμοῦσιν οἴνου]."

In *Parts of Animals* III 6, 669a18, Aristotle observes that palpitations mainly occur in human beings: "The jumping of the heart is almost exclusively found in man, because he has hopes and expectations for the future [τὸ τῆς πηδήσεως διὰ τὸ μόνον ἐν ἐλπίδι γίνεσθαι καὶ προσδοκίᾳ τοῦ μέλλοντος]." These hopes and expectations are possible only thanks to perception, memory, and reasoning, all three of which are matters of the human soul, in the center of the living person. For these functions, the soul already requires connections with the external senses. But a reaction of this living being also requires a connection of the soul with all parts of the living being. For this, too, Aristotle postulated *pneuma* or vital heat.

In *Problems* XXVII 4, 948a18–9, Aristotle states that in some cases "the presentiment of danger"[290]—φαντασία τοῦ δεινοῦ—leads to cooling of the chest region and to palpitations. Brave men are less affected by this, because their chest is full of blood.

The fatal flaw in the article on "Animal Motion" by K. Corcilius and P. Gregoric[291] is that they talk about a "mechanism" of heating and cooling, whereas Aristotle puts forward the soul/entelechy as the director and controller of this "instrument." My proposition is therefore: wherever Aristotle talks about "vital heat," he is talking about the life-generating action of *pneuma* under the guidance of an entelechy. Nowhere is confusion with "heat" of fire or anything else unavoidable.

We would further like to draw attention here to J. Althoff's study on the role of the four elementary properties hot, cold, dry, and moist in Aristotle's thought.[292] As is to be expected, the author also talks about the notion of the "vital heat" of *pneuma*. He does this in an excursus entitled "Die Rolle des Pneuma bei Aristoteles und in der Stoa."[293] With regard to Aristotle's position he concludes:

> Überschaut man schliesslich die Stellen, an denen Aristoteles dem Pneuma eine Rolle bei physiologischen Prozesse zuspricht, so kann man folgendes feststellen. Pneuma spielt bei der Wahrnehmung, bei

---

290. J. Beets et al. (2010), 158: "images of something that is frightening."
291. K. Corcilius and P. Gregoric, "Aristotle's Model of Animal Motion," *Phronesis* 58 (2013): 52–97. See also P. Gregoric and O. Lewis, "Pseudo-Aristotelian *De Spiritu*: a New Case against Authenticity," *Classical Philology* 110 (2015): 165–66.
292. J. Althoff, *Warm, Kalt, Flüssig und Fest bei Aristoteles* (1992).
293. Op. cit., 283–91. See also "Das Konzept der Generativen Wärme bei Aristoteles," *Hermes* 120 (1992): 181–93.

> der Bewegung der Tiere und bei der Zeugung bzw. Embryonalgenese eine Rolle. Die meisten Stellen haben den Charakter späterer Einfügungen, die allerdings in den meisten Fällen wohl von Aristoteles selbst stammen werden. Oftmals werden Vorgänge erneut angegriffen, die bereits befriedigend mit Hilfe der Elementärqualitäten erklärt worden sind. Meist ist nicht mit letzter Klarheit zu sagen, welche Rolle das Pneuma spielt. Es scheint von daher verfehlt, von einer aristotelischen "Pneumalehre" zu sprechen. Man gewinnt vielmehr den Eindruck, dass es sich überwiegend um späte Gedanken des Aristoteles handelt, die nur noch sehr unvollkommen in die bereits bestehenden Texte eingefügt sind, die aber Anstösse zur weiteren Ausarbeitung gegeben haben. Inhaltlich ist zunächst festzustellen, dass Pneuma bei Aristoteles wohl immer einfach "Luft" bedeutet, die mit den Qualitäten warm und feucht versehen ist.[294]

Althoff fails to see in his book that *pneuma* has a privileged connection with the soul in Aristotle. He does mention that *pneuma* is linked to the astral, divine element (195) and recognizes that this cancels the identification of *pneuma* with "air," but on page 196, Althoff relates the connection with the astral element exclusively to vital heat and not to *pneuma*. The author is also inclined to take the entire passage *Generation of Animals* II 3, 736b29–7a7 as a later addition.[295] Obviously, this cannot be upheld if we can assume that Aristotle's definition of "soul" refers to *pneuma* (and ether) as a "*sôma organikon*." Althoff believes that Aristotle did not distinguish "eine spezifische organische Wärme, die ihrer Wirkung und wohl auch ihrer Beschaffenheit nach von der bei anorganische Prozesse wirksame Wärme verschieden sei" (279). In general, Althoff does not consider Aristotle to be a consistent philosopher and scientist. He is willing to accept that Aristotle adopted internally contradictory views of predecessors and that, in the course of his teaching activities, he added other views, which in turn clashed with these standpoints. He regards this as a "Zeichen eines flexiblen, sich in der Auseinandersetzung mit den Erscheinungen entwickelnden Denkens, dem dogmatische Starre wesentlich fremd ist" (271).

It is clear, in my view, that the four elements with their four properties cannot possibly be guided and "used" by the soul as *eidos* and entelechy if there is no mediation by *pneuma* as the instrumental body of the soul. And *pneuma* cannot possibly be identical with air.

---

294. J. Althoff (1992), 285–6; "Das Konzept," 183.
295. J. Althoff, *Warm, Kalt, Flüssig und Fest bei Aristoteles* (1992), 197 n. 74; see also 274: "Dies scheint ein sehr spät entwickeltes Konzept zu sein, das sich sonst in den zoologischen Schriften nicht belegen lässt."

Althoff does try to do justice to a difference between *pneuma* and the four ordinary, sublunary elements in his article from 1992.[296] He says of the generative heat that Aristotle talks about in *Generation of Animals* II 3, 736b29 ff.:

> Diese Wärme ist aber nicht mit normaler, etwa durch Feuer entstehenden Wärme zu vergleichen, sondern stellt eine besondere "Natur" des Pneuma dar, die dem Sternenelement analog ist. Auch wenn es nicht ausdrücklich gesagt ist, wird hier das Attribut der Göttlichkeit vom Pneuma, dem es zunächst zukam, auf diese besondere Wärme übertragen. Dass Aristoteles von einer "Natur im Pneuma" (ἡ ἐν τῷ πνεύματι φύσις) spricht, macht es wahrscheinlich, dass die Wärme hier nicht, wie sonst bei Aristoteles, als *Eigenschaft* einer Substanz aufgefasst wird, sondern ausnahmsweise als eine eigenständige Substanz. Andernfalls hätte er wohl formuliert ἡ τοῦ πνεύματος φύσις.

The objection to this explanation is that it once again makes *pneuma* identical to Air. And the relation between the substance of generative heat and the substance of *pneuma* therefore remains unclear. But Althoff is right to point out that Aristotle's way of talking here is exceptional. Aristotle may have chosen this phraseology because for him "the nature in *pneuma*" was the same as "the nature in ether."

Aristotle did have a problem in that *pneuma* is also a common Greek word for "wind" and for "breath." And it was plain to him that heat is essential to all processes of growth and that loss of heat heralds death. This explains why in talking about processes of growth and digestion he often does not use the notion of *pneuma* but terms such as "concoction" and "natural heat," "*symphyton* heat," "natural fire." and "*symphyton* fire."[297] When the subject is the movements of arms and legs, he explicitly speaks about *pneuma* and "such a body."

But of course the vital heat that, guided by the soul, attracts and concocts food and uses it to produce the parts of the living entity, cannot be any other instrument of the soul than the *pneuma*, which passes on sensations to the soul as the center of sensation, and of course the movements with which

---

296. "Das Konzept," 184.

297. Cf. *Anim.* II 4, 416b28–9: "that which produces digestion is heat; therefore everything which has a soul has heat [ἐργάζεται δὲ τὴν πέψιν τὸ θερμόν· διὸ πᾶν ἔμψυχον ἔχει θερμότητα]" (W. S. Hett). But see also *Gener. anim.* II 6, 741b37: "Now the parts of animals are differentiated by means of *pneuma* [Διορίζεται δὲ τὰ μέρη τῶν ζῴων πνεύματι]" (A. L. Peck).

a living being reacts to sensation must be situated in the same instrumental body of the soul.[298]

o. Two Kinds of Motion of Physical Bodies: Goal-Oriented and Random

Via our inquiry into *pneuma* in Aristotle we have concluded that Aristotle's criticism of Plato's doctrine of soul was focused on the fact that Plato attributed motion to the immaterial soul and even made soul the principle of all motion. Aristotle was convinced that motion is always a property of a body.[299] That is why he also considered all "psychic" functions to be impossible unless they are the work of an (immaterial) soul-principle *plus* a corporeal, instrumental soul-body. But in the category of "the bodies," Aristotle drew a fundamental distinction between a divine, astral body and four corruptible, sublunary bodies. Into this he inserted his theory of *pneuma*. *Pneuma*, in the sphere of the sublunary bodies, is the analogue of ether, inasmuch as *pneuma*, like ether, is a carrier of a *different kind of* movement. The motion of the astral celestial beings is rational and goal-oriented. The movement of *pneuma*, though nonrational, is nevertheless functional, like that of a tool used or programmed by a skillful craftsman. The gap in Plato's *Timaeus* (47e–48a) between "the works of the Intellect" and "the works of Necessity" is relocated by Aristotle within the cosmos. The factor of Necessity he situates in the four sublunary elements,

---

298. See also *Anim.* II 4, 416a13; *Spir.* 9, 485a28: "the vital heat which is the efficient principle in bodies [τὸ θερμὸν τὸ ἐργαζόμενον ἐν τοῖς σώμασι]." *Gener. anim.* I 21, 729b28; II 3, 736a27; IV 1, 765b16; 4, 772a32; V 8, 789b8: "in fact it is probable that Nature makes the majority of her products by means of *pneuma* [ἐπεὶ καὶ τὸ τῷ πνεύματι ἐργάζεσθαι τὰ πολλὰ εἰκὸς ὡς ὀργάνῳ]." *Gener. anim.* II 1, 734b31: "As for hardness, softness, toughness, brittleness and the rest of such qualities which belong to the parts that have soul in them—heat and cold may very well produce these [σκληρὰ μὲν οὖν καὶ μαλακὰ καὶ γλίσχρα καὶ κραῦρα καὶ ὅσα ἄλλα τοιαῦτα πάθη ὑπάρχει τοῖς ἐμψύχοις μορίοις, θερμότης καὶ ψυχρότης ποιήσειεν ἄν]"; and 734b37–735a4: "Heat and cold make the iron soft and hard, but the movement of the tools that contains the essential form of craft makes this into a sword. For craft is the origin and the form of the object that is made, but it lies in something else; by contrast, the movement of nature lies in the thing itself, though it comes from a different nature which possesses the form in actuality [σκληρὸν μὲν γὰρ καὶ μαλακὸν σίδηρον ποιεῖ τὸ θερμὸν καὶ τὸ ψυχρόν, ἀλλὰ ξίφος ἡ κίνησις ἡ τῶν ὀργάνων ἔχουσα λόγον τὸν τῆς τέχνης· ἡ γὰρ τέχνη ἀρχὴ καὶ εἶδος τοῦ γιγνομένου, ἀλλ' ἐν ἑτέρῳ· ἡ δὲ τῆς φύσεως κίνησις ἐν αὐτῷ ἀφ' ἑτέρας οὖσα τῆς ἐχούσης τὸ εἶδος ἐνεργείᾳ]."
299. Cf. *Cael.* I 9, 279a15: "But in the absence of natural body there is no movement [κίνησις δ' ἄνευ φυσικοῦ σώματος οὐκ ἔστιν]."

which in themselves do not possess life and goal-orientedness. The factor of the Intellect he sees manifesting itself in the work of living nature, which, though "not without body" (and therefore not identical with pure Intellect), works rationally and produces all its works functionally, as beings endowed with intellect do. In the sublunary world, *pneuma* is a representative of the astral sphere. There, though mixed throughout the sphere of the sublunary bodies, and therefore not ether, it does operate functionally, with a different kind of movement from that of the four sublunary elements.

This distinction is the soundly Aristotelian basis for the doxographical tradition that often ascribed to Aristotle a doctrine of "limited Providence."[300] In this doctrine, the system and order in the heavenly spheres results from the direct action of God's working power, whereas the sublunary sphere is ruled by the working power of the stars and planets. and only indirectly by the working power of the supreme God.

Just as Aristotle saw all facets of adult human behavior as being led by the intellect, so he saw all purposeful activity of humans, animals, and plants as being led by God's thought. God aims all that lives at a goal, on a wide range of levels. He is the *entelechos* of the cosmos, just as a charioteer is the *hèniochos* (ἡνίοχος) of the pair of horses that he drives.[301] God directs all activity in the cosmos, just as a magnet orients and attracts all the iron particles around it. In this way God, in his unassailable transcendence, exercises power over the cosmos, is connected through this power with the cosmos, like Homer's Golden Rope, and is its absolute Ruler (κοίρανος). It is unthinkable that Aristotle would call God the great ruler and that this rule and government would not proceed from God in any way. When he asks in *Metaphysics* Λ 10 in what sense "the Good" is present in the cosmos, and leaves open two options, (1) it is something by itself, separate, or (2) it is in the cosmos as the order of the cosmos, he chooses *both* options: "Probably in both senses, as an army

---

300. Cf. A. P. Bos, *Providentia Divina. The Theme of Divine* Pronoia *in Plato and Aristotle* Inaugural Lecture, Vrije Universiteit, Amsterdam (Assen: Van Gorcum, 1976); R. W. Sharples, "Aristotelian Theology after Aristotle," in *Traditions of Theology. Studies in Hellenistic Theology, Its Background and Aftermath*, ed. D. Frede and A. Laks (Leiden: Brill, 2002), 22.

301. Cf. §9h above; *Mu.* 6, 400b7 and Ps.-Plut. *Placita* I 881E-F: Ἀριστοτέλης τὸν μὲν ἀνώτατω θεὸν εἶδος χωριστὸν ἐπιβεβηκότα τῇ σφαίρᾳ τοῦ παντός, ἥτις ἐστὶν αἰθέριον σῶμα. On this text see J. Mansfeld, "Aristotle in the Aëtian *Placita*," in *Brill's Companion to the Reception of Aristotle in Antiquity*, ed. A. Falcon (Leiden: Brill, 2016), 303. See also §10q below. (Perhaps, however, we should consider associating the word ἐπιβεβηκότα not with a charioteer standing on his wagon, but with the "treading" of a female bird by a cock. The sphere of "the All" should in that case be understood as the ὕλη or ὑποκείμενον, the "underlying," for the life-generating Form Principle.)

does; for the efficiency of an army consists partly in the order and partly in the general [ἢ ἀμφοτέρως ὥσπερ στράτευμα; καὶ γὰρ ἐν τῇ τάξει τὸ εὖ καὶ ὁ στρατηγός, καὶ μᾶλλον οὗτος]" (1075a13–5). But God can only be compared to an army leader if his unchangeability is guaranteed.[302] It cannot be the case that God ever *starts* to rule.

p. "Gods are Here as well"—A Quotation from Heraclitus

The view on the concept of *pneuma* in Aristotle's philosophy developed in the foregoing prompts us to take another look at the meaning of what Aristotle says in *Parts of Animals* I 5. In that chapter he compares the eternal divine beings in the celestial spheres and the area of the "higher element," on the one hand, with the region of everything that lives in the sublunary sphere on the other. Very emphatically, he underlines the difference in value (*timiotès*) of the two main regions of the cosmos. He concludes that knowledge about the divine world, which is so much higher in value than the world around us, must naturally be much higher in value too. If we could only reach out to that divine world just a little with our knowledge, we would prefer to do that rather than study everything around us, just as we would prefer a glimpse of our beloved[303] to many other things that we could observe fully and clearly.

But we, mortals in the sublunary sphere, cannot acquire this knowledge, or only to a very limited extent. We can, however, gain abundant knowledge of the living nature around us. After all, we are suckle brothers of all scratching animals here on earth.[304] If only we are not too particular in choosing our fields of research.

In all that lives around us there is certainly much that can excite our admiration and wonder (645a17: θαυμαστόν).[305] Aristotle underlines this by means of a famous quotation from Heraclitus, who on a cold winter's day was

---

302. Cf. *Mu.* 6, 397b22–4; 400b11–15.

303. *Part. anim.* I 5, 644b34: τῶν ἐρωμένων. There is clearly a relationship with *Metaph.* Λ 7, 1072b3—"it produces motion by being loved [κινεῖ δὲ ὡς ἐρώμενον]"—that we discussed in §4a above.

304. Cf. *Part. anim.* I 5, 644b29: "living as we do in their midst [διὰ τὸ σύντροφον εἶναι]."

305. The term θαυμαστόν brings to mind that *Metaph.* A 2, 983a11–21, after describing "first philosophy" or "theology" as the science that is most divine and highest in value (ἡ γὰρ θειοτάτη καὶ τιμιωτάτη; 983a5), notes that man does not possess this science ready to hand, like God, but is led toward it through wonder. For Aristotle, wondering is the beginning of wisdom (and wisdom is the end of wondering).

warming himself at the oven in the kitchen and called out to visitors reluctant to join him: "Feel free to come on in, there are gods here too."[306] Heraclitus was probably referring to his doctrine of the eternal Fire as the principle of all things, even of Water, into which it can turn. In this way, Heraclitus may have wanted to emphasize that there is no good reason to avoid and ignore certain parts of reality. For the effect of the divine, all-permeating, and vitalizing Fire can be observed everywhere.

Aristotle may have used this quotation because he was convinced that all forms of life in the sublunary sphere, through their connection with *pneuma* as an analogue of ether, contained something of the divine.[307] Like study of the soul, study of the sublunary sphere can point man toward a view of the ways in which the divine manifests itself, not only in the sphere of the celestial regions, but also, in an analogous, concealed manner, in the sublunary sphere. P. Gregoric[308] rightly observes: "The wonderful thing is, of course, the purposefulness which pervades the whole natural world and which is the counterpart of the beautiful (τὸ καλόν) in things of art." But for Aristotle this purposefulness is inextricably bound up with the soul and with *pneuma* as its instrument in the sublunary sphere of mortal living beings. Aristotle would have probably wanted to apply the same correction to Heraclitus as to Thales: God himself is not present in the sublunary sphere, but the Power of God is present there in *pneuma* as the carrier of this Power.[309]

An interesting point of reference here is Raphael's depiction of Plato and Aristotle in his great painting *The School of Athens*. Plato, with his *Timaeus* under

---

306. *Part. anim.* I 5, 645a17–21: "There is a story which tells how some visitors once wished to meet Heraclitus, and when they entered and saw him in the kitchen, warming himself at the stove, they hesitated; but Heraclitus said, 'Come in; don't be afraid; there are gods even here' [Ἡράκλειτος λέγεται πρὸς τοὺς ξένους εἰπεῖν τοὺς βουλομένους ἐντυχεῖν αὐτῷ, οἳ ἐπειδὴ προσιόντες εἶδον αὐτὸν θερόμενον πρὸς τῷ ἰπνῷ ἔστησαν (ἐκέλευσε γὰρ αὐτοὺς εἰσιέναι θαρροῦντας· εἶναι γὰρ καὶ ἐνταῦθα θεούς)]" (A. L. Peck [1937], 101). On this story and its various interpretations, see P. Gregoric, "The Heraclitus Anecdote: De Partibus Animalium i 5, 645a17–23," *Ancient Philosophy* 21 (2001): 73–85. It is not far-fetched to hear an allusion here to Thales's dictum "Everything is full of Gods," which had gained an almost proverbial status (see §9a).

307. W. Kullmann, *Aristoteles, Über die Teile der Lebewesen* (2007), 353, comments: "Mit Recht hebt Aubenque 1962, 502 hervor, dass Aristoteles sich hier gegen das Dogma der Astraltheologie von den Trennung des Irdischen und des Göttlichen wendet." Note, though, that in the same chapter Aristotle fully endorses this "cosmic theology," but crucially adds that an analogue of the astral element is active in the sublunary sphere. Cf. P. Aubenque, *Le Problème de l'Être chez Aristote* (Paris: Presses Universitaires de France, 1962), 485–505.

308. Art. cit. (2001), 83.

309. See §9a above.

one arm, points upward; Aristotle, with his *Ethics*, points obliquely downward. This has often been taken to mean that Raphael represents the Stagirite above all as an empiricist, whereas Plato urges the viewer to seek the divine world of Ideas. A better interpretation perhaps is that the painter sees both Plato and Aristotle urging us to pursue the divine, but that for Aristotle a mortal can only follow this path via earthly reality here and now. Aristotle had dismissed Plato's idea of a soul that descends into a body with a (vague) memory of what it had contemplated in heavenly reality. In his view, memory can only be based on sensory perception of the visible world. Direct knowledge of God's essence is therefore not granted to man. A human being can, however, observe the effects of God's working power in all that excites wonder.[310] This wonder may encourage him to track down the causes of these astonishing matters.

q. Entelechy as Rei(g)ning Principle of *Pneuma*

In *On the Soul* II 1, Aristotle makes it clear that the soul, in its specifically "psychic" functions, is necessarily connected with a body. As we established earlier, Aristotle takes this to be a consequence of his position that a soul does not possess movement of its own and can only be moved *per accidens*. This position follows from his strict distinction between intellect and soul, as a correction of Plato's psychology.

In II 1, 412a27 and b6, Aristotle specifies this body connected with the soul as the "instrumental body" (σῶμα ὀργανικόν) of the soul, which is the "first entelechy." He further describes this body as "matter" (ὕλη), as "the underlying" (ὑποκείμενον), as "fitting" (οἰκεία), but also as "*dynamis*" (δύναμις) of the soul and as "potentially possessing life" (δυνάμει ζωὴν ἔχον).[311] He had also said that the soul must possess "community" (κοινωνία) with its body. The soul uses this body as a craftsman uses his tools.[312] And with the help of this instrumental body it performs its "works" (ἔργα) and its (psychic) activities (ἐνέργειαι).

If all this is said of the soul's body, what does this mean for the soul as "entelechy"? How can the soul use its instrument without moving it?

---

310. In the Letter to the Romans 1:19–21, the apostle Paul also remarks that since the creation man has known God's "eternal *power* and divine nature" only from his works.

311. See *Anim.* II 1, 412a7; 412a19–20; 412a27–8; 412a8: Ἔστι δ' ἡ μὲν ὕλη δύναμις. II 2, 414a26.

312. Cf. *Anim.* I 3, 407b13–27.

The words *first entelechy* in II 1, 412a27 are commonly translated as "first actuality" or "first grade of actuality."[313] But this is completely *un-Aristotelian*. Aristotle holds that one and the same thing or entity can exist "in potency" or "in act."[314] It is unthinkable that the body of the soul is "the potency" of something of which the soul itself is the "actuality." Therefore, the body with which the soul is inextricably bound up (for the realization of psychic functions) both "potentially possesses life" and "actually posesses life" (that is, the menstrual fluid of a female specimen possesses life "in potency" until the moment of successful copulation and then possesses life "in act"). And it is one and the same dog that has the potential to bark when asleep and which barks when awake.

In any case the concept of "entelechy" is crucial to Aristotle's psychology. He must have considered it well known, for he never explains it in detail.

---

313. In the "Introduction" to his commentary on *On the Soul* (1961), 10, W. D. Ross brings up the concept of "entelechy" in his discussion on the three phases that should be distinguished in Aristotle's philosophy according to the author (following F. J. C. J. Nuyens 1939; 1948). The first phase is described as a strongly Platonistic and dualistic period. All Aristotle's works that he himself released for distribution are said to have been written in this period. In a transitional phase, Aristotle assumed a more positive relation between soul and body and situated the soul in the center of a living being. The third and last phase covers *On the Soul*, "where we hear no longer of a location of the soul in any one part of the body, but it is described as the ἐντελέχεια of the whole body. 'If, then, we have to give a general formula applicable to all kinds of soul, we must describe it as the first grade of actuality (ἐντελέχεια ἡ πρώτη) of a natural organized body. That is why we can dismiss as unnecessary the question whether the soul and the body are one; it is as meaningless as to ask whether the wax and the shape given to it by the stamp are one, or generally the matter of a thing and that of which it is the matter. Unity and being have many senses but actuality is the meaning which belongs to them by the fullest right (412b4–9).' In contrast with the importance attached to the heart in the biological works and the *Parva Naturalia*, in none of the four passages in which the heart is mentioned in the *De Anima* is any primary importance attached to it, although in 403a31, 408b8, and 432b31 it is still treated as the seat of anger and fear." Ross continues his study with a survey of all the passages in which the term ἐντελέχεια occurs in Aristotle (10 ff.). On p. 15 he states: "The word ἐντελέχεια is, so far as we know, a coinage of Aristotle's own. It is probably derived from the phrase τὸ ἐντελὲς ἔχον, 'having completeness.' The thought, then, which it conveys is that soul is not a substance separate from the body, but an added condition of body, a condition which not all bodies have. When he comes to define soul (in 412a27), he says that it is the *first* ἐντελέχεια of a natural (i.e. not manufactured) body which potentially has life, i.e. which without soul potentially has life, and with soul actually has life." M. E. M. P. J. Leunissen, *Explanation and Teleology in Aristotle's Science of Nature* (Cambridge: Cambridge University Press, 2010), 55 has "the first actuality of a natural body that is instrumental." L. A. Kosman, *The Activity of Being* (2013), 46, prefers "realization" as a translation of Aristotle's ἐντελέχεια.

314. Cf. *Somn.* 1, 454a8: "an activity is the activity of something potentially capable of it [οὗ γὰρ ἡ δύναμις, τούτου καὶ ἡ ἐνέργεια]," and A. P. Bos, "Perception as a Movement of the Instrumental Body of the Soul in Aristotle" (2011), 30–31.

Also, he introduces a distinction between a "first entelechy" and some other entelechy, without specifying anywhere how one condition passes into the other. But he does not just bring up the term *entelechy* in his definition of the soul. In *On the Soul* I 1, 402a25–6, he already mentions the term when starting to list all the questions that need to be answered to gain clarity on the theme of "soul": "does soul belong to the class of potential existents, or is it rather some sort of entelechy? For this makes no small difference [πότερον τῶν ἐν δυνάμει ὄντων ἢ μᾶλλον ἐντελέχειά τις. διαφέρει γὰρ οὐ μικρόν]."[315]

Apparently, it makes no small difference whether the soul belongs to the class of potential existents or is, rather, an entelechy. We can infer at least two things from this: first, that the concept of "entelechy" is assumed to be familiar by Aristotle when he composes *On the Soul*; secondly, that an entelechy is something that does not itself belong to "the class of potential existents" (τὰ ἐν δυνάμει ὄντα). In view of the very accurate and systematic construction of *On the Soul* as a whole, there is no reason to play down this remark in *On the Soul* I 1 and dismiss it as irrelevant to the explanation of II 1.[316]

Anticipating, we can clarify here that Aristotle uses the distinction "in potency" versus "in act" in relation to things in material reality. A sensory organ such as an eye can be closed and does not perceive anything in this state. And the vocal cords of a sleeping dog may be suddenly activated. But the perceiving soul of a living being is never soul "in potency." And the soul by itself is always in act, but in different ways. It is therefore impossible that Aristotle took the soul to be the "actuality" of the body that potentially possesses life. This raises the question: Why did scholars get the explanation of *On the Soul* II 1 so terribly wrong? And what is the right explanation of the definition of soul that Aristotle gives there?

The reason why the explanation of *On the Soul* II 1 has gone so wrong will be discussed in chapters 12 and following. Here, we will concentrate on

---

315. This question is clearly answered by *Anim.* II 1, 412a21–2: the soul is "entelechy." It does *not* itself belong to the class of potential existents (τὰ ἐν δυνάμει ὄντα). Cf. II 2, 414a27–8. But its instrumental body does: 413a2 τὸ δὲ σῶμα τὸ δυνάμει ὄν. Therefore, we have to reject the position of A. M. Leroi, *The Lagoon* (2014), 158, who translates Aristotle's definition of "the soul" as "the first actuality of a natural body with organs," and explains: "The key word here is 'actuality'—*entelekheia*. . . . He often uses it in opposition to 'potentiality'—'*dynamis*.'" This leads him to state on p. 159: "he means that the forms of unfertilized seed are mere potentials, and that these forms when realized in growing embryos and functioning adults are souls."

316. I agree with R. Polansky (2007), x, that Aristotle's work can be shown to be "remarkably systematic and to display meticulous organization. From start to finish he is in control of his material," and, "Design can thus be seen to govern every aspect of Aristotle's treatment of soul." Cf. also P. Thillet (2005) 9: "Le traité *De l'âme* est l'un des traités du Corpus aristotélicien qui présente le plus d'unité." In the same sense, T. K. Johansen (2012), ch. 2.

what has gone wrong. We start by observing that Aristotle refers to the body with which the soul is connected as the substrate (ὑποκείμενον) or "the underlying" of "the compound substance" of the soul and its body.[317] This body is a body that is guided and used by the soul as an instrument for the activities performed by the soul: the vegetative activity of concocting and causing to grow; the sensitive activity of perception[318] (with at least one and at most five sensory functions); and rational activity (as the place where sensory and conceptual images are stored, a function that depends strongly on the capacity of the soul-body for storing and recovering these images).[319]

Yet this body is also presented by Aristotle as a *dynamis*.[320] What did Aristotle mean by that?

It is useful here to recall the important text of *Generation of Animals* II 3, 736b29–7a1, discussed in §10a above, where Aristotle also talks about "the power (*dynamis*) of every kind of soul" and says that it "has to do with some physical body which is different from the so-called 'elements' and more divine than they are." There, Aristotle also seems to distinguish between the soul in itself and its *dynamis,* and to emphasize that this *dynamis* is materially characterized.[321] In the philosophical lexicon of *Metaphysics* Δ 12 Aristotle gives the first meaning of δύναμις as "a source of movement or change, which is in another thing or in the same thing *qua* other."[322] And in §10.1 above, we established that *pneuma* functions in particular as an efficient cause. This goes well with the theme of the vital *power* that is transferred to the menstrual fluid in the process of fertilization.[323] In this context we noted that Aristotle compared "the *dynamis* for vital activity" to the "power" that is present in the parts of a winding mechanism, even when the parts of the mechanism are in abeyance.[324] But here we should also consider that the most fundamental

---

317. Cf. *Anim.* II 1, 412a15–6.

318. See in this connection *Anim.* II 8, 420a8: ἀέρα . . . ἔμψυχον.

319. Cf. §10d-f above.

320. *Anim.* II 1, 412a9–10: "Ἔστι δ' ἡ μὲν ὕλη δύναμις, τὸ δ' εἶδος ἐντελέχεια.

321. In that context, it would be wholly inappropriate to translate *dynamis* as "potency." Aristotle must be talking there about the substrate of the soul.

322. *Metaph.* Δ 12, 1019a15–7: "We call a capacity a source of movement or change, which is in another thing or in the same thing *qua* other, e.g. the art of building is a capacity which is not in the thing built [Δύναμις λέγεται ἡ μὲν ἀρχὴ κινήσεως ἢ μεταβολῆς ἢ ἐν ἑτέρῳ ἢ ᾗ ἕτερον, οἷον ἡ οἰκοδομικὴ δύναμίς ἐστιν ἢ οὐχ ὑπάρχει ἐν τῷ οἰκοδομουμένῳ]." The example, house-building, is once again drawn from a goal-oriented, artisanal activity. See also T. K. Johansen (2012), 19 ff.

323. Cf. §6a above.

324. *Gener. anim.* II 1, 734b7–13. See §6b above.

distinction in *On the Cosmos* 6 is the distinction between God's being (*ousia*) and his *dynamis*, which pervades the entire cosmos.[325]

Aristotle's philosophy displays a parallelism between theology and anthropology similar to that proposed by Plato (which has also been referred to as "the macro-micro-cosmos theme"), insofar as he contrasts God in himself, as *ousia*, with the working power (*dynamis*) that proceeds from him throughout the ether and the sublunary sphere (as *pneuma*), just as he contrasts the immaterial soul as *ousia* or *eidos* with its instrumental body as its *dynamis*, which permeates the entire visible body.

This means that the role that God plays as the Goal for everything that is brought about in the cosmos by his *dynamis* is also played by the soul for everything that is realized by its *dynamis*. The soul, as *eidos* and *entelecheia*, directs its instrumental body (which is the "principle of motion"), as the "goal-pointing principle,"[326] aimed in the first place at the goal of the living being of which it is the soul-principle, but aimed in the second place at the Goal, which everything in the cosmos desires, the being and the divinity and immortality of God himself. The term *entelecheia* should therefore be explained as the *goal-pointing principle*, that is to say, the principle that points to the goal of the concrete living being, but also in a higher sense to "the Goal of all things." That is why Aristotle can cryptically say at various places in his work: "the for the sake of which has a double sense." Aristotle says no fewer than five times that we need to distinguish in nature, where everything is guided by a goal, between τὸ οὗ ἕνεκα τινός and τὸ οὗ ἕνεκα τινί.[327] Several scholars have puzzled their heads over this *zweifache Telos*.[328] Recently, M. R. Johnson has again marked out these passages as "central to resolving the problems of Aristotle's teleology."[329]

---

325. This was discussed in §9a above.

326. T. K. Johansen (2012), 9, 11, mistakenly proposes to translate *entelecheia* as "fulfillment." See below for more on the meaning of *entelecheia*.

327. Note that Aristotle varies in his terminology, sometimes using διττόν (*Anim.* II 4, 415b2) other times διχῶς. Also, he alternates between τὸ οὗ ἕνεκα τινός (*Metaph.* Λ 7, 1072b2–3) and οὗ ἕνεκα οὗ (*Anim.* II 4, 415b3; b20), and between τὸ οὗ ἕνεκα τινί and οὗ ἕνεκα ᾧ.

328. See K. Gaiser, "Das Zweifache Telos bei Aristoteles," in *Naturphilosophie bei Aristoteles und Theophrast*, ed. I. Düring (Heidelberg: Lothar Stiehm, 1969), 97–113; W. Kullmann, "Different Concepts of the Final Cause in Aristotle," in *Aristotle on Nature and Living Things*, ed. A. Gotthelf (Pittsburgh: Mathesis Publications, 1985), 170–75. Cf. A. Graeser, "Aristoteles' Schrift 'Über die Philosophie' und die Zweifache Bedeutung der 'Causa Finalis,'" *Museum Helveticum* 29 (1972); 44: "Was es aber mit dieser Unterscheidung auf sich gehabt hatte, scheint bis heute noch ungeklärt." M. R. Johnson, *Aristotle on Teleology* (2005), 65, holds nonetheless that "this central distinction has received little attention."

329. M. R. Johnson (2005), 65. See also 1.

My alternative to the standard perspective on these problems can be summarized under the following five points:

1. Misinterpretation of the term *entelecheia*' is the cause or consequence of a misreading of the passages in *On the Soul* II 1, 412a10–11 and a21–27, in which Aristotle talks about a twofold *entelecheia*.
2. It has led to a misunderstanding of what "first" and what "second" *entelecheia* is.
3. It has led to a misunderstanding of Aristotle's own conception of the *goal-orientedness* in nature. According to all modern scholars, this goal-orientedness is an essential part of his outlook on nature. But everyone goes on to add that Aristotle has neglected to argue this position.
4. Because the concept of *entelecheia* has been wrongly treated, Aristotle's repeated references to a "twofold goal" have also been misconstrued.
5. The upshot is a failure to understand Aristotle's three-part cosmology: God => ether (as instrumental body) => matter (consisting of the four sublunary elements) and its parallel in: soul => *pneuma* (as instrumental body) => visible body.

A. Aristotle's Teleological View of Nature

Aristotle has left a body of works on living nature that has often been described as "teleological." W. Kullmann opens his study on this subject as follows: "Mit dem Begriff der Teleologie (oder der Finalität) verbinden wir die Vorstellung, dass bestimmte Bewegungsabläufe, insbesondere bestimmte technische oder organische Prozesse zielgerichtet sind. Diese Vorstellung ist vor allem von Aristoteles stark geprägt worden."[330] But nobody has been able to explain why Aristotle developed such a teleological framework for his philosophy of nature. W. Wieland[331]

---

330. W. Kullmann, *Die Teleologie in der Aristotelischen Biologie. Aristoteles als Zoologe, Embryologe und Genetiker* (Heidelberg: Winter, 1979), 7. Cf. also W. Theiler, *Zur Geschichte der Teleologischen Naturbetrachtung bis auf Aristoteles* (Zürich / Leipzig, 1925; repr. Berlin: W. de Gruyter, 1965); M. E. M. P. J. Leunissen, *Explanation and Teleology in Aristotle's Science of Nature* (2010).

counted Aristotle's teleological view of nature among "den wirkungsmächtigsten Lehrstücken der aristotelische Philosophie überhaupt." He also comments: "*Wie* teleologische Zusammenhänge in der Natur nun eigentlich gesteuert werden, darüber gibt Aristoteles keine Auskunft." I. Düring noted in his extensive study on Aristotle's work: "Sobald Bedingungszusammenhänge vorliegen, betont er, dass das Naturgeschehen von teleologischer Formbestimmtheit gesteuert wird; wie es gesteuert wird, sagt er *nie*."[332] Allan Gotthelf[333] comments on Aristotle's teleological thinking in general: "One would expect to find, somewhere in the vast Aristotelian corpus, a thorough analysis and explicit definition of this notion. Surprisingly, it is not there to be found. Readers of the corpus will search in vain for a detailed analysis of what it is to be (or come to be) for the sake of something. The longest continuous passages on final causality, *Physics* II 8 and (sections of) *Parts of Animals* I 1, while containing much that eventually proves helpful, do not address themselves directly to this issue. In each case, the purpose is to argue for the applicability to nature of a conception of final causality whose precise meaning and statement is largely taken for granted." D. Sedley recently remarked: "Pretty well everything in nature has a purpose, despite the fact that no intelligence either conceived that purpose or administers it."[334]

There can be no doubt that Aristotle saw all Nature as "guided by a goal." But he did not regard Nature as goal-oriented. Bees and ants build nests and honeycombs as if they had carefully contrived how to do this in the most efficient and profitable way, yet Aristotle denies that they take part in any form of deliberation. "Nature produces nothing that does not fulfil a purpose," Aristotle says repeatedly. But he denies that Nature is on a par with

---

331. W. Wieland, *Die Aristotelische Physik. Untersuchungen über die Grundlegung der Naturwissenschaft und die Sprachlichen Bedingungen der Prinzipienforschung bei Aristoteles* (Göttingen: Vandenhoeck und Ruprecht, 1961; 2e Auflage 1970), 255; see also 274. Wieland notes on p. 256: "Im Bewusstsein der modernen Forschung gilt die teleologischen Naturbetrachtung des Aristoteles als ein im günstigsten Fall interessanter und vielleicht sogar historisch begreiflicher Irrtum, der im übrigen jedoch die Schuld trägt, den Fortschritt der Naturwissenschaft um zwei Jahrtausende aufgehalten und die angeblich viel fruchtbareren Ansätze Demokrits unterdrückt zu haben."

332. I. Düring, *Aristoteles* (1966), 552.

333. Allan Gotthelf, "Aristotle's Conception of Final Causality," *Review of Metaphysics* 30 (1976): 226–54; repr. with addition in A. Gotthelf and J. G. Lennox, eds., *Philosophical Issues in Aristotle's Biology* (Cambridge: Cambridge University Press, 1987), 204.

334. D. Sedley, "Teleology, Aristotelian and Platonic" (2010), 6. Cf. A. Gotthelf, *Teleology, First Principles, and Scientific Method in Aristotle's Biology* (Oxford: Oxford University Press, 2012), 390: "How can development be *aimed* at a result when there's no mind or consciousness to do the aiming?"; S. Broadie, "Nature and Craft in Aristotelian Teleology" (2007), 85–100; D. Charles, "Teleological Causation," in *The Oxford Handbook of Aristotle* ed. C. Shields (Oxford: Oxford University Press, 2012), 228, 235: "To his critics, these claims appear wholly mysterious." Cf. A. Falcon (2005), 13, with n. 31.

a planning and reflecting Demiurge. The fact that acknowledged experts have failed to recognize the structural embedment of this central element in Aristotle's philosophy of nature implies once again a fundamental misconstruction of this philosophy. We should therefore investigate whether the notion of the Power proceeding from God provided Aristotle with the connection between the transcendent divine Intellect and all entelechy principles in the cosmos.

B. The Soul as "Entelechy"

Aristotle's definition of "soul" makes it urgent for us to know what an "entelechy" actually is. Basically every translator and commentator since Antiquity has given the impression that he knows what Aristotle means, though it is easy to advance objections to every proposed interpretation.[335] According to the current view as expressed by W. D. Ross (cited above), the term *entelechy* "derives from the phrase τὸ ἐντελὲς ἔχον, 'having completeness.' The thought which it conveys, then, is that soul is not a substance separate from the body, but an added condition of body, a condition which not all bodies have."[336]

---

335. Certainly we must reject the proposition of G. A. Blair, "The Meaning of '*Energeia*' and '*Entelecheia*' in Aristotle," *International Philosophical Quarterly* 7 (1967): 102, 110, that "entelechy" is in every respect equivalent to the term *energeia*. For it is out of the question that the term *entelecheia* could be replaced by *energeia* in the definition of the soul. And in the proposition of *Metaphysics* Λ 7, 1072b26 that "the *energeia* of the Intellect is life," we cannot possibly replace *energeia* by *entelecheia*. In the distinction of "a twofold entelechy" in *On the Soul* II 1, 412a10 and a22–3, it would also be difficult to present *energeia* as an equivalent of *entelecheia*. See also S. Makin, *Aristotle, Metaphysics* Θ. *Translated with an Introduction and Commentary* (Oxford: Oxford University Press, 2006), xxvii–xxx. On the problems with the interpretation of *energeia*, cf. J. Beere, *Doing and Being: An Interpretation of Aristotle's Metaphysics Theta* (2009), 153–67; L. A. Kosman (2013), vii–x and 240.

336. W. D. Ross (1961), 15. The question that urges itself is whether the Greek language lacked words for this meaning and why Aristotle felt the need to introduce a neologism. Moreover, the term ἐντελής is used only once in the Aristotelian Corpus. Alexander of Aphrodisias, *Anim.* 16, 6 gave as derivation: ὡς τοῦ ἐν τῷ τέλει εἶναι τὸ πρᾶγμα οὗ ἐστιν οὖσαν αἰτίαν, and rather often replaced the term ἐντελέχεια by τελειότης. Cf. G. A. Blair (1967), who on p. 110 presents as an alternative: "having an end within"; id. (1992), 81: "having its end within it"; L. Couloubaritsis, "La notion d'Ἐντελέχεια dans la *Métaphysique*," in *Aristotelica. Mélanges offerts à Marcel de Corte* (Bruxelles: Ousia, 1985), 129–55; D. W. Graham, "The Etymology of Ἐντελέχεια," *American Journal of Philology* 110 (1989): 73–80; G. A. Blair, *Energeia and Entelecheia: "Act" in Aristotle* (Ottawa: University of Ottawa Press, 1992) and (1993); A. P. Bos (2003), 132–35. Blair (1992) 1 notes the following alternatives used in English translations: "actuality," "fulfillment," "complete reality." M. Furth (1988), 147 used "completedness." C. V. Mirus, "The Metaphysical Roots of Aristotle's Teleology," *Review of Metaphysics* 57 (2003–04): 699, opts for "actuality" in the sense of "form, or first actuality, and activity, or second actuality." P.-M. Morel (2007), 12 translates "réalisation."

Though this view is broadly accepted, it has problematic aspects too. In this way, the connection with a body is made a condition for being soul, whereas Aristotle argues at length in *On the Soul* I 1, 403a3 ff. that "what is peculiar" (*to idion*) to the soul is "separate" and is not something of a body. And in chapter II 1, where the definition of the soul is formulated, Aristotle states that there may be entelechies that are not an entelechy of any body: διὰ τὸ μηθενὸς εἶναι σώματος ἐντελεχείας (II 1, 413a7).[337]

Second, the expression "having completeness" may give rise to misunderstanding. It seems to designate the end point of a development. But this is not true of the soul as entelechy. Things that develop, develop from a phase in which they possess a certain potency to the realization of this potency: these are all things that are ἐν δυνάμει. The soul-body first has the "potency" for perception, and then possesses perception-in-act. But the sensitive soul is always present and in action. And in his introductory discussion Aristotle had announced his intention to determine: "does soul belong to the class of potential existents, or is it rather an entelechy? Our answer to this question is of the greatest importance."[338] This problem is indicated as the second in a long series there, and its importance is underlined. The soul as entelechy is the *eidos* of the ensouled (instrumental) body, and it receives as subject of perception the *eidè* of perceived objects (without their matter)—*Anim.* II 12, 424a18—and as subject of theoretical knowledge has knowledge of the intelligible objects of science. As *eidos* of the instrumental body, it also determines the degree of growth and the quality of flesh and bones of the visible body, etc.[339] But this takes us no farther toward an explanation of the technical term *entelechy*, which Aristotle uses for "the soul." And we must constantly bear in mind that according to Aristotle the soul itself is not a body or corporeal, and that only contemplation (θεωρεῖν) is a matter of the soul by itself (the intellect).[340]

---

337. See also *Metaph.* Λ 8, 1074a35–6: "But the primary essence has no matter; for it is *entelecheia* [τὸ δὲ τί ἦν εἶναι οὐκ ἔχει ὕλην τὸ πρῶτον· ἐντελέχεια γάρ]." W. D. Ross (1961) notes on p. 21 that Aristotle in *Anim.* II 1, 413a7 is hinting at "the doctrine of the νοῦς ποιητικός expressed in III 5." Cf. also A. Jannone and E. Barbotin (1966), 31 n. 2: "Réserve qui prépare la thèse de l'intellect 'séparé'; *infra*, III, 4"; and K. Corcilius, in C. Rapp and K. Corcilius, eds. (2011), 91. M. Boylan, *The Origins of Ancient Greek Science: Blood—a Philosophical Study* (New York: Routledge, 2015), 57, calls this text an "enigmatic passage" and translates *entelecheia* as "[controlling] actuality."

338. *Anim.* I 1, 402a25–b1: ἔτι δὲ πότερον τῶν ἐν δυνάμει ὄντων ἢ μᾶλλον ἐντελέχειά τις· διαφέρει γὰρ οὐ μικρόν, already cited above in this section.

339. Cf. *Anim.* II 4, 416a14–8; *Gener. anim.* II 1, 734b28–5a4.

340. Cf. *Anim.* II 2, 414a20.

A third problem is that to speak about the soul present in seed or an embryo as "(first) actuality," "complete reality," "réalisation" does not seem to make sense, because at that stage nothing of the new specimen is realized or actual.

Nor is it all clear in what way an entelechy, in the sense of "having completeness," can use its body, as Aristotle says in *On the Soul* I 3, 407b25–7.

I therefore want to take a new look at "entelechy" as component of the definition of the soul in *On the Soul* II 1. Let me start by noting that in *On the Soul* II 1, 412a9–11 and a19–28 Aristotle distinguishes between "a twofold entelechy," which he clarifies by comparing them to "knowledge" and "theorizing." In II 1, 412a9–11 Aristotle says: "Matter is *dynamis*, while form is entelechy, and that [the word *entelechy*] is used in two senses, in one sense as 'knowledge' and in an other sense as 'theorizing.'"[341]

After Aristotle has then specified the soul as *eidos* and entelechy of a body with certain qualities, he again addresses this theme of "a twofold entelechy": "But that word [*entelechy*] has two senses, corresponding to 'knowledge' and 'theorizing.' Clearly we intend 'entelechy' in the sense of 'corresponding to knowledge.' For *en tôi hyparchein tèn psychèn* there is sleep and waking, and waking is analogous to theorizing, sleep to its possession without exercising it. And in relation to the same subject [entelechy analogous to] knowledge comes first in the order of becoming."[342]

This is an important statement. But it is not easy to explain. A major problem is that a transition from potency to act seems to be attributed here to the soul as entelechy, although the soul as entelechy *has no materiality*; and the "theorizing" mentioned here is an activity of the soul by itself, that is, of the intellect. Also, it is very remarkable that Aristotle does not seem to explain anywhere

---

341. *Anim.* II 1, 412a9–11: Ἔστι δ' ἡ μὲν ὕλη δύναμις, τὸ δ' εἶδος ἐντελέχεια, καὶ τοῦτο διχῶς, τὸ μὲν ὡς ἐπιστήμη, τὸ δ' ὡς τὸ θεωρεῖν.

342. *Anim.* II 1, 412a22–6: Αὕτη δὲ λέγεται διχῶς, ἡ μὲν ὡς ἐπιστήμη, ἡ δ' ὡς τὸ θεωρεῖν. Φανερὸν οὖν ὅτι ὡς ἐπιστήμη· ἐν γὰρ τῷ ὑπάρχειν τὴν ψυχὴν καὶ ὕπνος καὶ ἐγρήγορσίς ἐστιν, ἀνάλογον δ' ἡ μὲν ἐγρήγορσις τῷ θεωρεῖν, ὁ δ' ὕπνος τῷ ἔχειν καὶ μὴ ἐνεργεῖν· προτέρα δὲ τῇ γενέσει ἐπὶ τοῦ αὐτοῦ ἡ ἐπιστήμη. For the grammatical construction, cf. *Anim.* I 4, 408b22: Ὥστε τὸ γῆρας οὐ τῷ τὴν ψυχήν τι πεπονθέναι, ἀλλ' ἐν ᾧ and II 1, 413a6: διὰ τὸ μηθενὸς εἶναι σώματος ἐντελεχείας. R. Kühner and B. Gerth, *Ausführliche Grammatik der Griechischen Sprache*, 2 vols. (4 Auflage. Leverkusen: Gottschalksche Verlagsbuchhandlung, 1955) vol. 2, 38 (§478, 3): "Wenn zu dem Infinitive, mag er als Subjekt oder als Objekt stehen, ein Subjekt und Prädikatsbestimmungen treten, so tritt, wie beim Infinitive ohne Artikel, sowohl jenes als diese in den Akkusativ," with reference to Xenophon, *Cyrop.* 5, 4, 19: τὸ ἁμαρτάνειν ἀνθρώπους ὄντας οὐδὲν οἶμαι θαυμαστόν. Greek can also connect a dative with the infinitive, as in *Anim.* II 1, 412b13: τὸ πελέκει εἶναι and II 7, 414a9: τοῦτο γὰρ ἦν αὐτῷ τὸ χρώματι εἶναι.

in *On the Soul* how soul as first[343] entelechy changes into soul as second (?) or ultimate (?) entelechy. It is striking too that, though Aristotle seems to be trying to clarify the concept, the text in which he does so admits of three different interpretations. And in any case we will have to consider carefully that with the terms ἐπιστήμη and θεωρεῖν Aristotle refers to two matters that he connects in the next chapter with the soul by itself (and not with the body of the soul).[344]

C. Different Ways of Explaining Aristotle's Distinction of a "Twofold Entelechy"

The first explanation takes "sleep" and "waking" literally, and concludes that Aristotle emphasizes here that a living being that sleeps possesses soul just as much as a living being that is awake.[345]

---

343. J. K. Johansen (2012), 16 has proposed: "The distinction between first and second fulfilment is correspondingly to be read in terms of the degree with which the soul realizes the body's potential: in the activity of contemplating, perceiving, taking nourishment, the body's potential is more fully realized than in merely having the capacity to do these things." But we will certainly have to associate "first entelechy" with the "sleeping soul" and contrast it with the "awakened soul." Another problem neglected by commentators here is that this text gives the impression that there are two kinds of entelechy, and that one precedes (πρότερα) the other in the order of becoming. In that case the choice of ἐντελέχεια ἡ πρώτη in 412a27 and b5 is striking, to say the least, and raises the question why Aristotle did not talk about ἐντελέχεια ἡ πρότερα. F. D. Miller (2012), 316 notes on these lines: "Alternatively (at II 1, 412a22–7) he distinguishes two levels of actualization: possessing knowledge, e.g., of a grammatical rule (call this *first level actualization*) and exercising that knowledge, e.g., recognizing that a sentence is ungrammatical (call this *second level actualization*)."

344. Cf. *Anim.* II 2, 414a4–12. He has just underlined in II 2, 413b24–7 that the intellect and the theoretical working power can be called "a separate genus" of soul because they can function without instrumental body. The point is therefore the contrast between the function of the intellect in two different conditions.

345. Cf. R. D. Hicks, *Aristotle, De Anima* (1907) 51: "for sleep, as well as waking, implies the presence of soul"; cf. J. A. Smith, in W. D. Ross, ed. (1931), vol. 3: "for both sleeping and waking presuppose the existence of soul"; W. S. Hett (1936), 69: "for both sleep and waking depend upon the presence of soul"; P. Siwek, *Aristoteles, De Anima, Libri Tres, graece et latine*, 3 vols. (Romae: Apud Aedes Pont. Univ. Gregorianae, 1954), vol. 2, 93: "nam sive somnus sive vigilia tunc tantum adesse posset, quando adest anima"; J. Tricot (1959), 67: "le sommeil aussi bien que la veille impliquent la présence de l'âme"; W. D. Ross (1961), 211: "for both sleep and waking involve existence of soul." Likewise, in J. Barnes, ed. (1984), vol. 1, 656. In the same way I. J. M. van den Berg (1953), 94; G. Movia (1979), 138; M. Furth (1988), 150; G. A. Blair (1992), 87: "sleep and waking belong to the soul"; M. Durrant (1993), 21: "for sleep, as well as waking, implies the presence of soul"; R. Bodéüs (1993), 137: "la présence de l'âme implique sommeil et éveil," with n. 1: "Cette affirmation vaut évidemment pour tous les animaux. Elle ne s'applique pas, comme telle, aux végétaux"; H. Seidl (1995), 61: "mit dem Dasein des Seele gibt es auch Schlaf und Wachen"; B. Schomakers (2000), 219: "Waar ziel is, komen ook slaap en waken voor [where there is soul, sleep and waking exist too]" (but see also p. 381); G. Patzig (2009), 257: "denn Schlaf und Wachen setzen beide das Vorhandensein der Seele voraus." This explanation also seems the choice of H. Bonitz, *Index Aristotelicus* 279b25–7.

Objection: This cannot possibly be right. According to Aristotle, plants do have a soul as (first kind of) entelechy, but do not sleep, because sleep is the nonactive state of the perceptive soul-part, which plants do not possess (*Somn.* 1, 454b27–9). But the distinction, which Aristotle introduces here, applies to *every soul* in the sense that every soul is either a "sleeping" entelechy or a "waking" entelechy. The soul of a plant is certainly at least a "first kind of entelechy." Therefore, we should assume that Aristotle is using the notions of "sleep" and "waking" metaphorically here. He is not talking about the sleeping or waking of a human being or animal, but he is explaining something *of the soul* as such.

A much more likely translation is therefore that of A. Jannone and E. Barbotin (1966), 30: "Car le fait d'être animé comporte les deux états de veille et de sommeil."[346] In that case, Aristotle is referring to the possibility that soul may be present in an ensouled body, of a plant just as much as of an animal, even if it does not manifest itself in activity. If this was Aristotle's meaning, he is emphasizing that a grain of corn or a chestnut not yet sown or planted is in a state of germinative dormancy, which he represents as a "sleep" of (the vegetative part of) the soul, and that the sensitive soul-part of a sleeping dog is "asleep," just as the rational soul-part of a human embryo is "asleep." All these cases involve functions of "parts" of the soul that the soul cannot perform "without body," and in all these cases the potency is the potency of the soul's instrumental body, and the activity the activity of the same instrumental body.

Objection: This explanation faces the same objection as the traditional explanation of "having life potentially" in Aristotle's definition of the soul. A visible living body of a human or an animal may not have actualized various functions, but it cannot "have life potentially," for it necessarily has "life"

---

346. Cf. P. Gohlke (1947), 56: "Denn in der Beseelung liegt sowohl Schlafen wie Wachen"; W. Theiler (1959), 24: "Mit dem Dasein der Seele ist auch Schlaf und Wachen gegeben" (with an explanation on p. 107); P. Thillet (2005), 103: "dans le fait d'avoir une âme, il y a sommeil et veille"; R. Polansky, *Aristotle's De Anima* (2007), 158: "sleeping pertains to what has soul as does being awake"; L. A. Kosman, *The Activity of Being* (2013), 201: "The soul is, as he puts it, the principle of both sleeping and waking life (*De Anima* 2.1, 412a24–25)." It seems that E. Diamond, *Mortal Imitations of Divine Life* (2015), 44, reads the vexed line in a comparable way: "For both sleep and waking are in the belonging to soul." On p. 46 he takes the lines *Anim.* II 1, 412b25–413a3 as providing an example, which he explains: "Here we have the seed or embryo as the first potentiality prior to the living activity (body), the first actual realization of life and the first activity as soul when sleeping, and the exercise of the activities latent in sleep as the waking state." It is a pity that Diamond in his, really innovative, argument has missed Aristotle's true intention in the crucial text of 412a23–4. For it leads him to view the nutritive function as the "first entelechy of a natural body possessing life potentially" (47). Diamond follows the lead of J. Hübner, "Die Aristotelische Konzeption der Seele als Aktivität in *De Anima* II 1," *Archiv für Geschichte der Philosophie* 81 (1999): 3: "denn innerhalb der Präsenz der Seele treten sowohl Schlaf als auch Wachen auf."

actually. It is just so with something that possesses soul, in the case of a concrete living being. When it is asleep or at rest, this does not mean that its ensouledness has been switched off. In *Physics* VIII 2 and 6, Aristotle explains at length that locomotion of a living being is only possible thanks to various functions of the instrumental body active under the soul's guidance, such as respiration, pulsation of the blood, and digestion.[347]

Moreover, in this interpretation Jannone and Barbotin talk about a twofold condition of what is "ensouled," not about a twofold condition of "soul." They read ὑπάρχειν as "to belong to," as if it is followed by a dative and as if the text had ἐν γὰρ τῷ <τινι> ὑπάρχειν τὴν ψυχήν[348] and as if *something that possesses soul* has the two conditions of "sleeping" and "waking." But ὑπάρχειν is not followed by a dative here and is used at least as often by Aristotle as an equivalent of εἶναι.[349]

The sentence in question should therefore be read as:

For in being soul there is sleep and waking.[350]

That is to say, the soul is "entelechy" in two conditions,[351] that of a sleeping entelechy and that of an awakened entelechy.[352] But in both situa-

---

347. Cf. §5d above. M. Furth (1988), 158 noted: "the whole question of threptic continuity is complicated by the difficulty of distinguishing in the threptic case between first and second actualization. . . . The problem is that threptically, anything that is alive at all seems to be always 'awake'—what would threptic 'sleep' be like?"

348. As in I 1, 402a10: "and others seem to belong to living things also, by virtue of the soul [τὰ δὲ δι' ἐκείνην καὶ τοῖς ζώοις ὑπάρχειν]," and *Phys.* VIII 4, 254b8–10: κατὰ συμβεβηκὸς μὲν (κινεῖ καὶ κινεῖται) οἷον ὅσα τε τῷ ὑπάρχειν τοῖς κινοῦσιν ἢ κινουμένοις (κινεῖ καὶ κινεῖται), and in the *Analytics—passim*.

349. Cf. H. Bonitz, *Index Aristotelicus* 788b43 ff. and *Anim.* III 5, 430a13: "these distinct elements must be present in the soul also [ἀνάγκη καὶ ἐν τῇ ψυχῇ ὑπάρχειν ταύτας τὰς διαφοράς]," and II 5, 417b25: "the presence of the object is essential [ἀναγκαῖον γὰρ ὑπάρχειν τὸ αἰσθητόν]." II 7, 418b8: τις φύσις ὑπάρχουσα ἡ αὐτή. III 12, 434a31: "For all provisions of nature are means to an end [Ἕνεκά του γὰρ ἅπαντα ὑπάρχει τὰ φύσει]." *Metaph.* Γ 2, 1004a4: ὑπάρχει γὰρ εὐθὺς γένη ἔχον τὸ ὄν. *Spir.* 9, 485b14. See also H. G. Liddell, R. Scott. And H. S. Jones, *A Greek-English Lexicon* (Oxford: Clarendon Press, 1961), *s.v.* B3 and 4.

350. The translation by Jannone and Barbotin would then have to be corrected to: "Car le fait d'être âme comporte les deux états de veille et de sommeil."

351. That is also the intention of 412a10: καὶ τοῦτο διχῶς. Τοῦτο there refers exclusively to ἐντελέχεια.

352. One could suitably introduce here the contrast between "latent" and "patent" as renderings of "sleeping" and "waking." The opposition "in potency" and "in actuality" does not apply to the soul itself (to the intellect). The essence of the intellect is *energeia*. Aristotle comes close here to the discussion of Plato's *Phaedo*, but gives it an entirely different twist. Plato compares

tions the soul as entelechy must use its instrumental body. For this reason, I propose as the translation of *entelechy*: "goal-pointing system" (G.P.S.), or "goal-marker."³⁵³ Such a reading of this passage has never been considered, neither in Antiquity nor in the modern era. In combination with the wrong explanation of the term *organikon,* this has led scholars to misinterpret the foundation of Aristotle's philosophy of living nature. For they have failed to understand that Aristotle's teleology has a basis in his psychology. The soul of plants and animals is "entelechy," just like the soul of humans, but with the important difference that the soul of plants and animals is always "on automatic pilot."³⁵⁴ By contrast, humans can, in time,³⁵⁵ switch "out of automatic pilot" to self-steering, as in the work of a skilled craftsman. Aristotle's teleology is therefore an anthropomorphist view of biology and zoology.³⁵⁶

D. Differences in Conditions of Souls

We are dealing with a highly intriguing set of problems here. Not only does Aristotle use the difference between "sleeping" and "waking" in the notion

---

the incarnated existence of the soul to "sleeping" and the existence free of a mortal body to "being awake." Aristotle describes the situation of the soul from the embryonic phase (until the development of a person's rational and purposeful activity) as "being asleep" and "first entelechy." Cf. *Phd.* 71c1: "Well then, said Socrates, is there anything that is the opposite of living, as being awake is the opposite of sleeping? [Τί οὖν; ἔφη, τῷ ζῆν ἐστί τι ἐναντίον, ὥσπερ τῷ ἐγρηγορέναι τὸ καθεύδειν]."

353. In §10.o above we suggested that the term *entelecheia* may be associated with *hèniocheia* (ἡνιοχεία), "to hold the reins." In this way an *entelecheia* is the agency that "keeps the goal in sight." A. M. Leroi, *The Lagoon* (2014), 176: "Many scholars, struggling to convey what Aristotle meant by the soul, have described it as a 'cybernetic system.' The metaphor is consciously anachronistic, but plausible." These scholars were, in my opinion, closer to Aristotle's actual intentions than Leroi could accept.

354. For a recent, differently oriented explanation, cf. C. D. C. Reeve, who starts his book *Action, Contemplation, and Happiness: An Essay on Aristotle* (Cambridge: Harvard University Press, 2012) with a chapter 1 on "Transmission of Form" and the role of *pneuma* in this.

355. Every human being starts his existence like a plant and an animal. Only gradually does he reach the "age of discretion." The development of his capacity for rational discernment and action is always a phase after infancy and adolescence. The addition in 412b26: "in relation to the same subject (entelechy analogous to) knowledge comes first in the order of becoming" is meaningful if Aristotle is referring to the said distinction, but less relevant if he is thinking of the general distinction between a function in potency and the same function in act, comparable with "sitting" and "standing," as in *Anim.* II 5.

356. He does recognize the difference between the soul-principles of humans and those of animals and plants. But while he blames his contemporaries for relating their psychology to human souls only (*Anim.* I 1, 402b4), his own view of the soul as *entelecheia* is also strongly anthropomorphist.

of soul/entelechy, he also introduces a distinction between "what is peculiar" to the soul (the intellect; I 1, 403a7) and "the soul in connection with an instrumental body," and he recognizes entelechies that are the entelechy of a natural body and entelechies which "are not an entelechy of any body" (II 1, 413a7: διὰ τὸ μηθενὸς εἶναι σώματος ἐντελεχείας; quoted above. It does, in fact, seem as if "entelechies which are not the entelechy of any body" refers to the intellect (which needs no instrumental body; *Anim.* III 4, 429a24–6). The fact is, Aristotle never calls the combination of guiding principle with instrumental body "soul," but always exclusively the guiding principle. This is shown not only by the definition of "soul" in *On the Soul* II 1, but also by II 2, 414a14–28.[357] It is thus clear that Aristotle talks about "soul" to refer to what in itself belongs to the category of "intellect" but differs from it through the connection with an instrumental body, from which the intellect is structurally free. But how does this square with the distinction between a "sleeping" and an "awakened" soul? What did Aristotle mean by this distinction? Does it refer to the same distinction between (A1) souls in their connection with an instrumental soul-body and (A2) the intellect, which is free of any instrumental body?[358] Or does it involve a distinction *within the category of souls connected with a natural body,* that is, between (B1) souls, which are active in a purpose-guided but unconscious way (in plants and animals), and (B2) souls of human beings who have developed their rational faculty and act with deliberate purpose?

If we go for option (B), this would mean that Aristotle did not distinguish two but *three* kinds of "entelechy," viz:

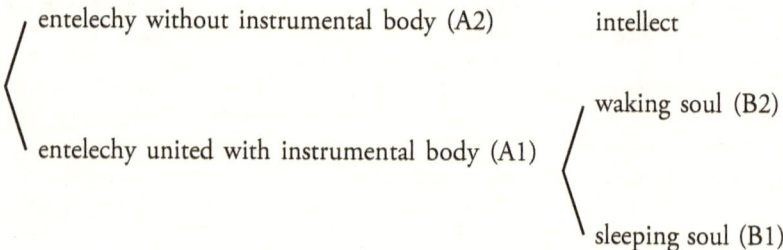

---

357. That is why the conclusion in II 2, 414a27–8 is so important: "From all this it is clear that the soul is a kind of entelechy and defining principle (*logos*) of what has the capacitiy of being such entity [Ὅτι μὲν οὖν ἐντελέχειά τίς ἐστι καὶ λόγος τοῦ δύναμιν ἔχοντος εἶναι τοιούτου, φανερὸν ἐκ τούτων]."

358. I have defended that position in A. P. Bos, "Plutarch on the Sleeping Soul and the Waking Intellect and Aristotle's Double Entelechy Concept" (2012), 25–42.

I have now come to the conclusion that the text of *On the Soul* II 1 must mean that, for Aristotle, both the "sleeping" and the "waking" soul are an entelechy of a body, and therefore an entelechy forming part of a "composite *ousia*" (412a15–6).[359] In that case, the distinction "analogous to knowledge" (ὡς ἐπιστήμη) versus "analogous to theorizing" (ὡς τὸ θεωρεῖν) seems to denote the distinction between the soul as φύσις ("natural principle of life") and the soul as rational faculty and practical intellect. As guiding principles they can both be present in man and function analogously, as Aristotle notes in *On the Soul* II 4, 415b15–7: "It is manifest that the soul is also the final cause. For nature, like intellect, always does whatever it does for the sake of something, which something is its end [Φανερὸν δ' ὡς καὶ οὗ ἕνεκεν ἡ ψυχὴ αἰτία· ὥσπερ γὰρ ὁ νοῦς ἕνεκά του ποιεῖ, τὸν αὐτὸν τρόπον καὶ ἡ φύσις, καὶ τοῦτ' ἔστιν αὐτῆς τέλος]."

Obviously, the transcendent Intellect is an *entelecheia* in a different sense from the soul of a celestial being or a human being or a plant. The soul of a plant keeps its instrumental body directed to the goal of that plant. This is true of man too, although man's mind also enables him to be consciously goal-oriented. The divine Intellect is an entelechy or "goal-directing principle" insofar as it *is* the goal itself and directs all other reality to itself.

But because, for Aristotle, the supreme, purely transcendent Intellect is completely immaterial, and there are also mortal beings that possess a capacity for intellectual activity, Aristotle may well have distinguished between:

1. Intellect, pure in itself and immaterial (third entelechy);

2. intellect of a soul as "awakened" entelechy in immortal ensouled beings of the ethereal sphere of the cosmos (second entelechy);

3. intellect as potency for rational activity and goal-oriented activity in the pneumatic sphere of sublunary living beings (second entelechy);

4. "sleeping" entelechy as a goal-guided principle in humans, animals and plants (first entelechy).

---

359. In particular, the passage 412a19–27 seems to support this choice. Aristotle says there that the soul is *ousia*. And then: "But the *ousia* is entelechy, and thus soul is the entelechy of a body as above characterized. Now there are two kinds of entelechy ['Η δ' οὐσία ἐντελέχεια. Τοιούτου ἄρα σώματος ἐντελέχεια. Αὕτη δὲ λέγεται διχῶς.]." Αὕτη in 412a22 could refer to ἐντελέχεια by itself. But it seems more natural to connect it with Τοιούτου ἄρα σώματος ἐντελέχεια.

On levels 2 through 4, an intelligent principle is clothed in a (fine-)material covering and the level of knowledge decreases according to the diminishing quality of this covering.[360]

An indication of this seems to be expressed in the well-known passage of *Metaphysics* A 2, 982b29–30: "for in many ways human nature is in bondage [πολλαχῇ γὰρ ἡ φύσις δούλη τῶν ἀνθρώπων ἐστίν]." For although man's "essence" is his intellect, there is little evidence of it during a long period from his conception till his student days. There is only the human soul, which by means of its pneumatic instrumental body leads the vegetative, sensitive, and motor functions. Only in the long term does man arrive at rational insight and technical and scientific knowledge and thus at goal-directed activity. Very few succeed in turning away from natural reality to the understanding that the First Cause of the entire cosmos is transcendent. Only through this insight does "man" perceive his bat-like condition as regards knowledge (cf. *Metaph*. α 1, 993b9–11).

We could reconstruct Aristotle's argument by means of the following propositions:

1. *There is a sleep of the intellect,* which refers to an intelligent principle bound with "the bond of sleep" and with an instrumental body. Such an intelligent principle has lost its own nature and its identity with the transcendent Intellect, and becomes alienated from it because of the connection with a natural body. Such an intelligent principle has become a soul-principle. This is the condition of the astral beings and of all sublunary living human beings.[361] They remain characterized by a controlling, goal-driven activity, but their connection with the source of all intellectuality is not manifest but latent.

2. *There is a sleep of the soul,* which occurs wherever a soul-principle operates within the sublunary sphere. This soul-principle regulates the vegetative and animal functions. But human beings can achieve rational insight and goal-oriented activity and can themselves become goal-oriented, "awakened,"

---

360. This principle is formulated in *Generation of Animals* II 3, 736b29–33: "However, the power of every kind of soul has to do with some physical body which is different from the so-called 'elements' and more divine than they are. *And as the souls differ from one another in the scale of value, so does that substance differ.*" On this crucial text, cf. A. P. Bos "*Pneuma* as Quintessence of Aristotle's Philosophy" and "Aristotle on the Differences between Plants, Animals, and Human Beings" (2010), 823–25 and §10a above. *Anim.* I 3, 407b12–27 implies the same correspondence between the soul and its instrumental body.

361. Plutarch, *De Facie in Orbe Lunae* 941F uses the expression "bound with the bonds of sleep," when he says that the sleeping God Kronos was fettered by Zeus with the chains of sleep: τὸν γὰρ ὕπνον αὐτῷ μεμηχανῆσθαι δεσμὸν ὑπὸ τοῦ Διός. Doubtless Kronos here represents the cosmic gods, who differ from the transcendent God (who never sleeps or slumbers, *Metaph.* Λ 9, 1074b18; cf. L. A. Kosman, *The Activity of Being*, 201) by being clothed in a fine-material body.

guide their lives, and choose their goals in life.[362] Only at the very last does human intellect gain insight into the "First Causes" and turn away from the natural world.

Against this background, we can accommodate the various stories about "sleeping" and "waking" in Aristotle's *Eudemus* to the information from the Corpus Aristotelicum.[363] Only man, who has gained rational insight and actualized his "practical intellect," can be regarded as an "entelechy" in the manner of a "sailor on his ship."[364] The sailor heads the ship toward its goal, for as long as he is at sea. When a sailor keeps his ship on course at sea, this compares with the situation in which the vegetative part of man's soul continues to aspire to health (much like sailing as the ship's goal), but in which the rational soul-part promotes health through long walks or wholesome food supplements.

My proposal boils down to this: the term *entelechy* was introduced by Aristotle as a bridge between the notions of "intellect" and "soul." Soul and intellect are both "entelechy." Soul is "first[365] entelechy" and "sleeping" entelechy and, as φύσις, present in every living entity in natural reality. But the soul can also be "awakened" entelechy, as rational mind and practical intellect,[366] though only (finally, after a long development) in man and in beings of comparable or higher order.[367] The notion of "completion," "fulfilment," "realization," or "actuality" as a translation of *entelechy* needs to be discarded.

---

362. Man can then for instance, as a physician, devise dietary or medicinal prescriptions for the benefit of his own health. Also, he is then able to regulate the effects of emotions and urges through self-control.

363. For example, the stories about the dreaming god Kronos; the "Greek King" (of Elis?) who prophesied a tsunami (*Eudem.* fr. 11a Ross); the dream of the protagonist Eudemus during a serious illness; and cf. also the story about living prisoners tied to corpses by Etrurian pirates.

364. *Anim.* II 1, 413a8–9: "But it is still uncertain whether the soul is an entelechy of its body as the sailor is of his ship [Ἔτι δὲ ἄδηλον εἰ οὕτως ἐντελέχεια τοῦ σώματος ἡ ψυχὴ ὥσπερ πλωτὴρ πλοίου]." This sentence, which W. D. Ross (1961), 214–15 and many others believe to be completely out of place at the end of *On the Soul* II 1, has a meaningful function in my explanation. Aristotle rightly says that he has not yet made it clear whether the soul can also be entelechy like a sailor on a ship. But he indicates that he will explain this later. It is unthinkable that in the crucial chapter II 1 of *On the Soul* Aristotle wrote down (and never deleted) a sentence that he did not mean seriously. K. Corcilius, in C. Rapp and K. Corcilius eds., (2011), 91, still sees no satisfactory solution to this problem. L. A. Kosman (2013) does not deal with the passage.

365. The consequence of my hypothesis is that in plants and animals there can be no transition from an "earlier" to a "later" entelechy. This may be why Aristotle opted for the ordinal number πρώτη, which we should translate "entelechy of the first kind."

366. This crucial theme was Aristotle's alternative to Plato's theme of the "sowing" of "second-" and "third-rate" souls among the stars and planets as their vehicles (*ochèmata*). Pl. *Tim.* 41d4–42a2.

367. Cf. *Anim.* II 3, 414b18.

In *On the Soul* II 1, 412a27, Aristotle can say: "That is why the soul is an entelechy of the first kind of a natural body having life potentially in it [Διὸ ἡ ψυχή ἐστιν ἐντελέχεια ἡ πρώτη σώματος φυσικοῦ δυνάμει ζωὴν ἔχοντος]," and in 412b6: "That is why we can dismiss as unnecessary the question whether the soul and its body are one [Διὸ καὶ οὐ δεῖ ζητεῖν εἰ ἓν ἡ ψυχὴ καὶ τὸ σῶμα]," but he can also maintain that there are entelechies that are not the entelechy of a body. What he means is that pure intellect is entelechy not bound in any way to an instrumental body.

We could express Aristotle's intention by saying: the soul as first entelechy is a goal-pointing system like a computer program, an automatic pilot, or a route planner;[368] the soul as awakened entelechy does the same as the designer of the route planner or a living driver.[369]

E. The Intellect as "a Different Genus of Soul"

In *On the Soul* II 1, Aristotle argues first that the soul is inseparable from its instrumental body, and then explains that this also applies to "the parts" *of the soul*.[370] In chapter II 2, however, he leaves room for freedom from an instrumental body. First, he emphasizes there the unity and connection of all "parts" of the soul burdened with an instrumental body. They do not occur separately from each other if together they form part of the soul of a living creature. But in 413b24–7, he emphatically makes an exception for the intellect and the potential for theoretical activity. That seems to be "a different kind of

---

362. D. Quarantotto, "Che Cosa Fa da una Forma un'Anima?—l'Organizzazione Anatomo-fisiologica dei Viventi e la Sede della *Psyche*," in *Attività e virtù. Anima e corpo in Aristotele*, ed. A. Fermani and M. Migliori (Milano: Vita e Pensiero, 2009), 368 uses the term *organizzazione dinamica*.

369. J. M. Cooper, "Aristotle on Natural Teleology," in *Language and Logos. Studies in Ancient Greek Philosophy*, ed. M. Schofield and M. Craven Nussbaum (Cambridge: Cambridge University Press, 1982), 221, summed up his interpretation of Aristotle's teleological view of nature as follows: "Aristotle, unlike other teleologists of nature (Plato, the medievals, Leibniz), finds goal-directedness in natural processes without feeling any need at all to find intentions (whether God's or, somehow or other, nature itself's) lying behind and explaining it." This is also the position of W. Wieland (1961), 268, 274, and M. R. Johnson (2005), 271 ff.

370. This passage has always been incorrectly explained. The point for Aristotle is not that "the parts" of the body, such as the eye, are ensouled, but that for instance the sensitive part of the soul cannot function without an instrumental body and that therefore the *pneuma* in semen is also a vehicle of these various soul-functions. Cf. also *Gener. anim.* II 1, 735b4–22, and A. P. Bos, "The Soul and Soul-'Parts' in Semen (*GA* II 1, 735a4–22)," *Mnemosyne* 62 (2009): 378–400 and §15a below.

soul" (ἔοικε ψυχῆς γένος ἕτερον εἶναι),³⁷¹ because this function/activity *can* exist separately, by itself—καὶ τοῦτο μόνον ἐνδέχεται χωρίζεσθαι,³⁷² καθάπερ τὸ ἀΐδιον τοῦ φθαρτοῦ.³⁷³ This necessarily implies in Aristotle that in reality, too, this function/activity once existed by itself and one day will exist by itself. According to Aristotle, the intellect is something imperishable in a mortal living creature. We should connect this with the remark in *On the Soul* I 1, 402a21–2, where he affirms that one field of inquiry (e.g., arithmetic) has different principles from the other (geometry). Aristotle believes firmly that switching from one genus to another is impermissible.³⁷⁴ If the soul does in fact involve two kinds of genus, it will also require two kinds of discipline to know the soul.³⁷⁵ Aristotle affirms this in *On the Soul* I 1, 403a27–9: the

---

371. This theme was anticipated in I 1, 402b2: εἰ δὲ μὴ ὁμοειδής, πότερον εἴδει διαφέρουσα ἢ γένει; The unpleasant consequence is that Aristotle's definition of "soul" in *Anim.* II 1 does not apply to this different kind of "soul." R. Polansky (2007), 181 suggests as an alternative to the translation given above: "another kind *than* soul," and adds, "which fits even better the view that mind is not intrinsically part of soul but something divine." J. Dillon, "How does the Soul direct the Body, after all? Traces of a Dispute on Mind-Body Relations in the Old Academy," in *Body and Soul in Ancient Philosophy*, ed. D. Frede and B. Reis (Berlin/New York: W. de Gruyter, 2009), 354 n. 10, also tends toward this interpretation. But this runs up against problems with regard to the Greek text here and in I 1, 403a10–1. Cf. II 5, 417b7: ἕτερον γένος ἀλλοιώσεως. Aristotle's position is special precisely because he presents the soul as the product of a *katabasis eis allo genos* of the *nous*. And he saw the *nous* in its condition of potency of a soul as an *allogenes*, "stranger," "sojourner." This forms the connection between *On the Soul* and the *Eudemus*.

372. On the problem of the intellect's "separation," as Aristotle talks about it here and in III 4–5, R. Bodéüs, *Aristote, De l'Âme* (1993), 52 says: "Nul interprète, jusqu'à ce jour, n'a entièrement réussi à faire la lumière sur la signification exacte et les implications précises de ce langage qui fait état de la 'séparation' de l'intelligence ou d'une forme d'intelligence. Le texte du *DA*, à l'endroit le plus crucial, pourrait avoir souffert lors de sa transmission."

373. This clearly implies that, for Aristotle, the vegetative, sensitive, and dianoetic soul-parts are not immortal in the proper sense (which does not rule out a postmortal existence of the soul).

374. Cf. *Anal. Post.* I 7, 75a38: "Hence it is not possible to prove a fact by passing from one genus to another—e.g. to prove a geometrical proposition by arithmetic [Οὐκ ἄρα ἔστιν ἐξ ἄλλου γένους μεταβάντα δεῖξαι, οἷον τὸ γεωμετρικὸν ἀριθμητικῇ]."

375. Cf. also *Part. Anim.* I 1, 641a32–b10. Aristotle asks there in 641a33: "whether it is the business of natural science to treat of soul in its entirety or of some part of it only [πότερον περὶ πάσης ψυχῆς τῆς φυσικῆς ἐστι τὸ εἰπεῖν ἢ περί τινος]." The answer must be: the natural philosopher talks about the soul as a sleeping and waking entelechy, the first philosopher about the soul as a "separate" entelechy. Cf. b9: "because it is not soul in its entirety that is an animal's 'nature,' but some part or parts of it [οὐδὲ γὰρ πᾶσα ψυχὴ φύσις, ἀλλά τι μόριον αὐτῆς ἓν ἢ καὶ πλείω]." This distinction is also behind the remark in *Anim.* I 1, 402a4–6: 'Moreover this investigation seems likely to make a substantial contribution to the whole body of truth, and particularly to the study of nature'—Δοκεῖ δὲ καὶ πρὸς ἀλήθειαν ἅπασαν ἡ γνῶσις αὐτῆς μεγάλα συμβάλλεσθαι, μάλιστα δὲ πρὸς τὴν φύσιν. The contrast is therefore between first philosophy as the study of separate being and natural philosophy as the study of all physically characterized entities.

physikos has the soul as his field of inquiry, inasmuch as the soul is connected with a physical body. If something of the soul also exists "separately," this is the domain of the "first philosopher" (403b9–16; cf. also II 3, 415a11–2 and *Phys.* II 2, 194b14–5). He had already suggested this possibility in *On the Soul* I 1, 402a16: "but if there is no one common method of finding the essential nature [εἰ δὲ μὴ ἔστι μία καὶ κοινὴ μέθοδος περὶ τὸ τί ἐστιν]."

But this also indicates that the connection of an intellect with the soul of a mortal living being *is not an original situation*. This connection must be due to the "descent" (*katabasis*) of a principle "of a different genus" into an environment of mortality,[376] which prevents the intellect from functioning properly. For Aristotle, the visible body is not a "tomb," a "casket" for the soul, as Plato had suggested, but the soul-body is the "bond" of the intellect.[377] To enter the sphere of coming-to-be (*genesis*) necessarily entails loss of being for an intelligent principle, because it can only "come to itself" at the end of a protracted natural development. This is what the demon Silenus revealed to King Midas in the *Eudemus*: "Not to be born is (for human beings) best of all."[378]

This does raise the question why there are also countless living creatures with a soul that does not have something of "a different kind," in contrast to human beings, who do possess it as a potency. The only explanation which Aristotle supplies in his extant writings is the reference to "pure" *pneuma* as distinct from "less pure" *pneuma*, and the difference in quality of the four sublunary natural bodies with which *pneuma* becomes mixed.[379] Reason (*dianoia*)

---

376. This is Aristotle's reinterpretation of Plato's words in *Phaedrus* 246c2: "but the soul which has lost its wings is borne along until it gets hold of something solid [ἡ δὲ πτερορρυήσασα φέρεται ἕως ἂν στερεοῦ τινος ἀντιλάβηται]."

377. Cf. E. Barbotin, *La Théorie Aristotélicienne de l'Intellect d'après Théophraste* (Louvain/Paris: Publications Universitaires, 1954), 220: "En somme, le schisme intérieur qui divisait le composé humain chez Platon subsiste chez son disciple, mais subit une transposition progressive: au lieu d'opposer le σῶμα à la ψυχή, celui-ci oppose finalement la ψυχή au νοῦς; dans la hiérarchie des principes constitutifs de l'homme, le dualisme s'est déplacé de bas en haut."

378. Cf. Ps.-Plutarch, *Consol. ad Apollon.* 115B-E = Arist. *Eudem.* fr. 6 Ross; 65 Gigon. Cf. A. P. Bos, "Silenus als Bemiddelaar van Gnostische Kennis in Aristoteles' Dialoog *Eudemus*" (Silenus as Mediator of Gnostic Knowledge in Aristotle's Dialogue *Eudemus*) (2016), 65–83, 301–305.

379. In *Anim.* III 13, 435b1–2, Aristotle explains the difference between vegetable and animal existence by positing that plants consist "of earth," that is, the matter that receives a plant-soul and can be used by the plant-soul as its instrument consists of vitalizing *pneuma* plus earth. It is tempting to surmise that Aristotle's dialogue *Eudemus* represented the demon Silenus, faithful companion of the god Dionysus, after his imprisonment by King Midas, as one who "revealed" the crime of the Titans, being that they lured the young god Dionysus with attractive presents, then ripped him apart and devoured him. This led to the generation of human beings as mortal beings with a pure divine component.

in potency can only be connected with a soul-body of the highest quality and purity. This suggests that the origin of different levels of life and differences in quality of soul may have been explained in a kind of psychogonic myth, for example, told by the demon Silenus, as the result of a gradual decline in the vitalizing Power proceeding from the Principle of Origin, together with an increase in Ignorance (*Agnoia*), which is to say an obscuration of *gnôsis*.

S. Broadie, in a splendid article on "Nature and Craft in Aristotelian Teleology,"[380] has raised the question: "Is a non-psychological teleology as intelligible as Aristotele evidently takes it to be?" My argument in the foregoing was aimed at showing that Aristotle does not find a "non-psychological teleology" anywhere in nature, though it is true that on the level of animals and plants there is no question of *phronèsis*, as there is with a craftsman. Yet in plants and animals too, Aristotle defends a "psychological teleology." But talk about "being-soul" needs to be more differentiated. The soul of a plant and an animal (and of a human being in his first phase of development) uses its instrumental body just as effectively as a craftsman uses his instrument, even though this soul has not yet been "awakened" to intellectuality. In *Metaphysics* A 2, 982b22–3a11, Aristotle refers to the connection between the divine Intellect and the human intellect. Here, in *On the Soul* II 1, he shows how he sees the connection between man's intellect and the entelechy of nonreflective creatures. It is this text that provided Aristotle with the solid foundation for his teleological view of nature.

Finally, I want to formulate the results of the enquiry so far as follows:

> Aristotle described "the soul" as: "the entelechy of a natural body that is *organikon*."
> It has become clear enough now that the rendering of this definition as "the actuality of the visible body as it is equipped with organs" is completely un-Aristotelian because:
> a. The "natural body" must be "instrumental" for the soul.
> b. That is why it can only be (ether and, in the sublunary sphere) *pneuma*.
> c. For only this special body can function as carrier of the power that is transferred as soul-principle and entelechy to the menstrual fluid of a female partner during fertilization (usually via semen).
> d. In almost all living beings the soul functions as "sleeping" soul under whose direction the development of a plant, animal, or

---

380. In *Aristotle and Beyond. Essays on Metaphysics and Ethics* (2007), 85.

human being proceeds functionally in the manner of a winding mechanism.
e. Only human beings, whose *pneuma* is of the highest quality and degree of heat, can experience the "awakening" of their entelechy, when they reach the age of discretion.

This conception of Aristotle results throughout from his criticism of Plato's doctrine of the immortal and immaterial soul that descends from outside when a new human being or animal is born. Through his unhistorical interpretation, Alexander of Aphrodisias read back a Platonist psychology into the text of Aristotle's *On the Soul* and into the words that Aristotle used there.

Additional Note: *On the Soul* II 5 on "Science" and "Being a Scientist"

The heart of the above argument was in §10q, that Aristotle presents the soul as the *eidos* of a natural body that is used as an instrument by the soul (*Anim.* II 1, 412a19–21). He then stipulates that two modes can be distinguished. The soul can be *eidos* as "science" (ἐπιστήμη) or as "being a scientist" (θεωρεῖν) (*Anim.* II 1, 412a22–3). The choice of the two terms *science* and *being a scientist* establishes a link with the intellect. The soul as entelechy is present in all living entities as *eidos* of the instrumental body, but directs this instrumental body like a program in a scientific textbook, or like an intellect in act. The first case (the scientific textbook) involves only the "thoughts" (*noèmata*) of an Intellect. In the second case, the Intellect itself has a directing role. In the discussion of this, I drew attention to Aristotle's implication that plants and animals can only have a soul as "first" entelechy, which functions as a scientific textbook for the development of a life. Only human beings are able to reach the other condition of soul, in which their intellect takes control.

We also noted that Aristotle does not explicitly say how this change of condition in human beings can come about. He used for this the metaphor of the intellect's "awakening."

We should consider that *On the Soul* II 5, 417a21 ff. raises issues that are highly relevant to the discussions in II 1, but also essentially different.[381] The subject there is perception and "being sensitive," but also science and

---

381. L. A. Kosman, *The Activity of Being* (2013), 57–68 and 201 explains II 1, 412a21–7 from the perspective of II 5, 417a21 ff., and so misses an important point.

being a scientist. The essential difference is that he is not talking there about "every soul," but about the human soul with sensitive and intellectual powers or "soul-parts." Man belongs to the kind of beings that are *epistèmôn* and "possess science" (II 5, 417a24). And man also possesses hearing when asleep (417a11) and also has "cognitive power" when still an embryo.

In *On the Soul* II 5, Aristotle wants to make the difference clear between the change by which a person acquires "hearing" and "cognitive power," to wit, the simple fact of his generation (II 5, 417b17), and the change that occurs because hearing is activated by external stimuli, or because someone who possesses science starts to pursue science. These are two different kinds of "change" (417b7).[382] In this connection, Aristotle notes in II 5, 417b5: "that which merely possesses knowledge comes to exercise it [θεωροῦν γὰρ γίνεται τὸ ἔχον τὴν ἐπιστήμην]." This is illuminating for what we have seen in II 1, but the point is a very different one. In II 5, it becomes clear that man (and only man) has the possibility of leaving behind the condition of plants and animals and attaining the activity of intellect. But the point in II 1 was that every living being develops under the direction of its *eidos*, its specific form, the externalization of the *noèmata* of the Intellect.[383]

---

382. Cf. M. F. Burnyeat, "*De Anima* II 5" (2002), 28–90.

383. We might consider that II 5, 417b16–9 refers back to what Aristotle said in II 1 about "science" and "being a scientist," especially if we follow manuscript V: ὅταν δὲ γεννηθῇ, ἔχει ἤδη ὥσπερ ἐπιστήμην [καὶ τό] αἰσθάνεσθαι. Καὶ τὸ κατ' ἐνέργειαν δὲ ὁμοίως λέγεται τῷ θεωρεῖν ["When it is begotten the subject has sensation in the sense of possession of knowledge. Again, actual sensation corresponds to the exercise of knowledge"].

11

Desire as a Form of Nostalgia for the Origin

How can we explain the presence of an *orexis* in the entire cosmos, as we discussed in chapter 3 for Aristotle's entire work?

The answer is that it must be related to Aristotle's talk about *pneuma*, a natural body that is connected with the working power of every soul and that has something of "a different and more divine body" than the four sublunary elements. With its vital heat, *pneuma* makes seeds germinative (*gonima*) and thus brings about the process of *genesis*, for living entities incapable of possessing eternity. There is desire for eternity and immortality in all that lives, and according to *Generation of Animals* II 3, 736b29 ff., there is something of a different and more divine element in all that possesses soul. *These two things must be interrelated.* But the astral element itself is not present in the sublunary sphere.[1]

This suggests that Aristotle saw the life of all mortal creatures as dependent on the effect of the working power of the divine, astral body.

But in these mortal sublunary creatures the divine astral element is "incognito," disseminated beyond recognition, it is "in diaspora" there, "scattered," "in exile," as Aristotle wanted to show in his comparison of the human soul's condition to the fate of prisoners of Etrurian pirates, who were bound to a corpse and left to die. It seems likely that Aristotle represented *pneuma* as that which harbors the desire for divinity and immortality, because it has itself an immortal origin. The *orexis* that is active in all ensouled and repro-

---

1. Obviously this is akin to Plato's idea that every mortal creature contains an immortal soul that longs for its original condition. But Aristotle's view differs essentially from Plato's.

ductive beings and that manifests itself on the level of human existence in the "desire for knowledge" (*Metaph.* A 1, 980a1) was regarded by Aristotle as an ontic "shortcoming," a "deficiency" (and as an alternative to Plato's theory that every soul contains a trace "memory" [*anamnesis*] of the eternal and divine). As a carrier of "desire" for divinity and immortality, *pneuma* for Aristotle is the symbol of the soul with its sickness "for home," for times past, and for its original concentrated condition. In Aristotle's dialogue the *Eudemus*, the protagonist Eudemus himself is a symbol of the soul.[2] This *pneuma* is the manifestation of ether in the sublunary sphere. It is natural to assume that the essence of *pneuma*, like the answer to the question of how an immortal intellect came to be connected to a mortal living being, was revealed by Silenus in his exposition to King Midas;[3] the very name Silenus identifies him as a Lunar being, one of the demonic beings that resides on the boundary of the corruptible and the incorruptible. He reveals everything about "being born/begotten" to Eudemus of Cyprus, whose island of origin immediately brings to mind Aphrodite, who was born in the sea off Cyprus from the foam (*aphros*) of the genitals of Ouranos, cut off by the Titan Kronos.

We should add that, according to Aristotle, there is also "desire" for the higher, perfect reality in the divine, astral sphere. For, as we saw in §4a above, the everlasting motion of the heavenly living beings is caused by their "love" (*erôs*) for God. The supreme divine Principle, which itself has no desire or love for anything,[4] is the agency that exerts a perpetual attraction on all extra-divine reality.[5]

This needs to be seen against the background of what Aristotle says in *Physics* I 9.[6] There, he distinguishes between something that is divine and worthy of desire in itself, and another side of reality that strives and longs for this highest principle, like the female for the male. And he does not disqualify the

---

2. A. Preus, "Science and Philosophy in Aristotle's *Generation of Animals*" (1970), 39 had a sense of this when he wrote: "Aristotle puts a considerable weight on the fateful theory that *pneuma* is a special material. . . . There is something of the myth-maker about Aristotle here; he seems to bring the gods, or at least the divine, down to earth in order to explain that which he finds otherwise inexplicable."

3. Cf. O. Gigon, "Der Menschliche und der Absolute Geist bei Aristoteles," *Hegel-Jahrbuch* 29 (1981–82): 32.

4. Cf. Simplicius, *in De Caelo* 288, 28–289, 15 = Arist. *De Philosophia* fr. 16 Ross; 30 Gigon.

5. Theophrastus had made comments on this in his *Metaphysics* 2, 5b10–7, which have been dealt with in §2e above.

6. Cf. §3f above.

female as nonbeing or as a contradiction of being, but describes it positively as "in a sense substance."[7]

In the important text of *Generation of Animals* II 1, 732a2–3, we read that "it will surely be for the sake of generation that 'the male' and 'the female' are present *in all that exists*."[8]

This seems to produce a framework in which all caused reality is the result of a female (material) principle that receives being thanks to the form-giving power emanating from the male, higher Principle. This causation takes place on the level of eternal astral reality and, next, on the level of the living beings that come into being and pass away.

When *On the Cosmos* 7, 401b2 quotes the profound words,

Zeus is a man, Zeus an immortal maid

Ζεὺς ἄρσην γένετο, Ζεὺς ἄμβροτος ἔπλετο νύμφη

these could be taken as an allusion to the Orphic tradition in which Zeus swallowed the goddess Mêtis and then gave birth to the goddess Athene from his head.[9]

---

7. *Phys.* I 9, 192a6. Cf. *Anim.* III 5, 430a10: "Since in every class of objects, just as in the whole of nature, there is something which is their matter . . . and something else which is their cause or agent in that it makes them all [Ἐπεὶ δ' ὥσπερ ἐν ἁπάσῃ τῇ φύσει ἐστί τι τὸ μὲν ὕλη ἑκάστῳ γένει . . . ἕτερον δὲ τὸ αἴτιον καὶ ποιητικόν, τῷ ποιεῖν πάντα]" (trans. W. S. Hett [1936]).

8. *Gener. anim.* II 1, 732a2–3: ἕνεκα τῆς γενέσεως ἂν εἴη τὸ θῆλυ καὶ τὸ ἄρρεν ἐν τοῖς οὖσιν. The Greek text of the manuscripts has 'ἐν τοῖς οὖσιν' here. H. J. Drossaart Lulofs, *Aristotelis De Generatione Animalium* (Oxford: Clarendon Press, 1965; repr. 2005), 47, corrects this to: ἔχουσιν. He therefore proposes to read: "in all <those> beings <that possess sexual differentiation>." He is followed by R. Mayhew, *The Female in Aristotle's Biology* (2004), 38. But there is no good reason for this textual change and we should assume that Aristotle wrote "in all that exists." Interestingly, however, this reading is also undermined by a text in Philo of Alexandria, *De Opificio Mundi* 8, where Philo emphasizes Moses's keen insight into the absolute necessity that the beings contain both an active and a passive principle: ἔγνω δή, ὅτι ἀναγκαιότατόν ἐστιν ἐν τοῖς οὖσι τὸ μὲν εἶναι δραστήριον αἴτιον τὸ δὲ παθητόν. Philo does this in an exposition that, completely in line with Aristotle's theology, sets out a doctrine of the principles of being. Cf. A. P. Bos, "Philo on God as *Archê Geneseôs*," *Journal of Jewish Studies* 60 (2009): 34–36, 40–42.

9. Cf. L. Brisson (2008), 90–91, cited in §3f above.

12

Why Doesn't *Pneuma* Play an Important Role in Ancient and Modern Interpretations of Aristotle?

As we have seen, there are many passages in Aristotle's own writings that show that Aristotle regarded *pneuma* as the natural body that, from the very beginning of a living creature's existence, whether it results from sexual reproduction or from spontaneous generation, is inextricably linked to the soul as entelechy and regulatory principle. All the information on this subject compels the view that Aristotle's definition of "soul" refers to *pneuma* as the *sôma organikon* of the soul of mortal beings (as well as to ether as the instrumental body of the astral souls).

However, this view was never held, neither in Antiquity nor in the Modern Era.

Introductions to Aristotle's philosophy or surveys of his work rarely deal with the theme of *pneuma,* if at all. The focus is usually on his logic, his hylomorphism, the psychology of *On the Soul,* his metaphysics, and his ethics. His biological writings and his doctrine of *pneuma* as the vehicle of vital functions are often disregarded and neglected.

Moreover, scholars who have dealt with the subject are uncomfortable with Aristotle's doctrine of *pneuma.* Some hold that Aristotle did entertain a theory of *pneuma,* but failed to sustain it and finally replaced this doctrine with the theory of *On the Soul,* in which there is no place for a doctrine of *pneuma.* (Earlier writings, in which *pneuma* did play a role, were supposedly left unrevised.) Others consider an opposite hypothesis: at the end of his life he saw the need for a doctrine of *pneuma*, started to develop it, but lacked time to integrate it in his overall system.[1]

What is the reason for this?

In the first place, we should mention the fact that Alexander of Aphrodisias, appointed to an imperial chair in Athens, launched his interpretation of Aristotle's *On the Soul*, which involved a radically unhistorical explanation and also a drastic revision of Aristotle's doctrine of soul.[2] At least since 200 CE, scholars have accepted the view that Aristotle interpreted the soul as "the first entelechy of a natural body *equipped with organs*."[3] Alexander introduced

---

1. Cf. A. P. Bos, "*Pneuma* as Quintessence of Aristotle's Philosophy" (2013), 417–18, and §10 above.

2. Cf. F. A. J. de Haas, "Late Ancient Philosophy," in *The Cambridge Companion to Greek and Roman Philosophy*, ed. D. Sedley (Cambridge: Cambridge University Press, 2003), 266: "Alexander rejects any kind of immortality of the individual soul—a consequence of his Aristotelian view that the human soul is nothing but the form of the human body and has to perish with it. This 'hylomorphic' (as it is now called) conception of soul and body dominated the Peripatetic tradition after Alexander, whereas before Alexander interpreters of Aristotle had rather identified the *pneuma* ('breath'), not the human body as a whole, as the instrument of the soul"; R. W. Sharples, *Peripatetic Philosophy 200 BC–AD 200. An Introduction and Collection of Sources in Translation* (Cambridge: Cambridge University Press, 2010), xi: "it has increasingly come to be realised that many doctrines which have for nearly two millennia been regarded by students *and critics* of Aristotle as central to his philosophy are in fact interpretations by Alexander of Aphrodisias, and only questionably held by Aristotle himself." L. A. Kosman (2013), 103. However, P.-M. Morel, *De la Matière à l'Action. Aristote et le Problème du Vivant* (2007), 23 states: "Enfin le fait que les *PN* ne formulent pas expressément la thèse hylémorphiste ne signifie évidemment pas qu'ils n'y souscrivent pas." He again on p. 12 translates Aristotle's definiton of the soul as "l'âme est la 'réalisation première' d'un corps naturel déjà organisé ou pourvu d'organes."

3. Cf. Alexander of Aphrodisias, *Anim.* 16, 11 (ed. I. Bruns, 1887): "For an *organikon sôma* is a body that has several and different parts that are subservient to the powers of the soul [ἔστι γὰρ ὀργανικὸν σῶμα τὸ ἔχον πλείω τε καὶ διαφέροντα μέρη ψυχικαῖς δυνάμεσιν ὑπηρετεῖσθαι δυνάμενα]." See also M. Bergeron and R. Dufour, *Alexandre d'Aphrodise, De L'Âme. Texte Grec Introduit, Traduit et Annoté* (Paris: Librairie Philosophique J. Vrin, 2008), 89–91. *Quaest.* 54, 9–11. Because Aristotle states in *Hist. anim.*VII (IX) 3, 583b15–28 that a male foetus is still "unarticulated" (ἄναρθρον, ἀδιάρθρωτον) during its first forty days, scholars later concluded that such a foetus does not yet contain a soul. Cf. G. Jerouschek, *Lebensschutz und Lebensbeginn. Kulturgeschichte des Abtreibungsverbot* (Stuttgart: Ferdinand Enke Verlag, 1988), 14–16, 41; and L. G. M. Spruit, *Religie en Abortus. Interactiemodellen ter Verklaring van de Houding tegenover Abortus* (Nijmegen: Instituut voor Toegepaste Sociale Wetenschappen, 1991), 68. D. A. Jones, *The Soul of the Embryo. An Enquiry into the Status of the Human Embryo in the Christian Tradition* (London: Continuum, 2004), 21–32 is much more accurate. But Aristotle does not say such a thing anywhere. Indeed, it would clash with his views in *Gener. anim.* II 1 and *Anim.* II 1, 412b27 and 5, 417b16–8, where he explicitly declares the soul to be present in semen. If Aristotle had really wanted to talk about "a body that possesses differentiated parts," he would have written σῶμα διηρθρωμένον. But to effect this differentiation, the soul always needs an "instrumental body." Aristotle's remarks in *Anim.* III 12, 434b4–5; 434a13 and II 7, 418b9 should also have counted more significantly against Alexander of Aphrodisias's interpretation.

a Platonizing revision of Aristotle's psychology, primarily in order to keep Aristotle as far as possible from Stoic materialism.

This trend started by Alexander of Aphrodisias has influenced the tradition and even the textual transmission.[4]

---

4. For the role played by Alexander of Aphrodisias in the constitution of the transmitted text, see also O. Primavesi, "Aristotle, *Metaphysics* A. A New Critical Edition with Introduction," in *Aristotle's* Metaphysics *Alpha. Symposium Aristotelicum, with a New Critical Edition of the Greek Text by O. Primavesi*, ed. C. Steel (Oxford: Oxford University Press, 2012), 385–516.

13

The Dubious Lines of *On the Soul* II 1, 412b1–4

We will doubtless have to concur with R. Bolton, F. Ricken, and R. W. Sharples that lines II 1, 412b1–4 gave modern scholars cause to read *organikon* in the transmitted text as "equipped with organs."[1] For after Aristotle has introduced the term ὀργανικόν for the first time, the Greek text continues as follows:

> 412b1–4: The parts of plants are instruments too, though very simple ones: e.g., the leaf protects the pericarp, and the pericarp protects the seeds [*karpos*]; the roots are analogous to the mouth, for both these draw in food. (W. S. Hett [1936], 69, with changes)

---

1. R. Bolton, "Aristotle's Definition of the Soul. *De Anima*, II 1–3," *Phronesis* 23 (1978); 275 n. 6; and F. Ricken SJ, *Theologie und Philosophie* 80 (2005): 426, in his review of A. P. Bos (2003): "Die traditionelle Interpretation versteht unter *soma organikon* einen Körper, der mit Organen ausgestattet ist. An allen anderen Stellen, die der Index von Bonitz bringt, hat *organikon* nach B. jedoch nicht diese Bedeutung; es wurde vielmehr gebraucht für Dinge die instrumental sind, d.h., die als Mittel oder Werkzeug dienen. Das mag zutreffen, schließt jedoch nicht aus, daß Aristoteles das Wort in *De anima* II 1 anders gebraucht. Daß das der Fall ist, wird aus den unmittelbar folgenden Zeilen (412b1–4) deutlich." See also M. D. Boeri, "Μήτ' ἄνευ σώματος εἶναι μήτε σῶμά τι ἡ ψυχή (Aristóteles, *De anima* B 2, 414a19–20). A Propósito del Alcance de las Interpretaciones Funcionalistas de la Psicología Aristotélica y del Carácter Causal del Alma," *Elenchos* 30 (2009): 62–63 with n. 15; and R. W. Sharples, "The Hellenistic Period: What Happened to Hylomorphism?" in *Ancient Perspectives on Aristotle's* De Anima, ed. G. van Riel and P. Destrée (Leuven: Leuven University Press, 2009), 159 n. 23: "A major difficulty to Bos's interpretation of Aristotle is that 412b1–4 need to be deleted as a mistaken gloss."

Ὄργανα δὲ καὶ τὰ τῶν φυτῶν μερή, ἀλλὰ παντελῶς ἁπλᾶ, οἷον τὸ φύλλον περικαρπίου σκέπασμα, τὸ δὲ περικάρπιον καρποῦ. αἱ δὲ ῥίζαι τῷ στόματι ἀνάλογον. ἄμφω γὰρ ἕλκει τὴν τροφήν.

This passage undoubtedly persuaded many later readers that σῶμα ὀργανικόν must refer to the body of a plant with its leaves and fruit as an instrument/organ for protecting the seeds, and likewise to the bodies of animals and humans with their various bodily parts.

Although the content of lines 412b1–4 is soundly Aristotelian, they cannot be accepted as having been written by Aristotle himself in the place where they now stand.[2] In the argument that he has set out so far, Aristotle cannot yet talk about plants and about bodies with instrumental parts. Aristotle's talk about "the body of the soul" in *On the Soul* II 1 should be understood against the backdrop of his extensive refutation of Plato's doctrine of soul. If Aristotle here was simply speaking about the visible body with which the soul is connected, the entire critical argument in book I 2–3 would have no relevance at all. Also, we should emphasize that for Aristotle the starting point of a new life is the moment of fertilization, not the moment of birth.[3] As a consequence, Aristotle must assume that the soul is present from the moment of fertilization, if inextricably bound up with its *sôma organikon*. But semen and a grain of corn and an animal or human embryo (*kyèma*) can only contain a *sôma organikon* that is homogeneous. For all genesis starts with the presence of homogeneous components (*homoiomerè*) on the basis of the four sublunary elementary natural bodies. That is what his argument has been about up till now. We need to stress, too, more than is usual, that Aristotle's *On the Soul* has the soul as its subject and not "the living being."

Lines 412b1–4 must therefore have been added by a reader or commentator who supported the psychological view of Alexander of Aphrodisias.[4]

The fact that there were such readers emerges from the famous manuscript E (Parisinus gr. 1853, from the tenth century), which is the oldest manuscript in which *On the Soul* has been passed down, but which contains in many

---

2. G. Picht, *Aristoteles, De Anima* (Stuttgart: Klett-Cotta, 1987), 325, already noted: "Der Satz über die Organe der Pflanzen ist lediglich eine eingeschobene Anmerkung, die zeigen soll, das und warum der Begriff 'organischer Körper' auch auf die Pflanzen angewendet werden kann. Vermutlich handelt es sich um eine jener eingeschobenen Randnotizen, wie sie uns im Text des Aristoteles öfter begegnen."

3. Cf. §7b above.

4. Cf. A. P. Bos, "Aristotle's Definition of the Soul: Why Was It Misunderstood for Centuries? The Dubious Lines *Anim.* II 1, 412b1–4," *Museum Helveticum* 69 (2012): 140–55.

parts an intriguingly different reading of the Greek text compared with the majority of some eighty manuscripts. In discussing this textual matter we will have to bear in mind that according to M. C. Nussbaum the text of *On the Soul* is "unusually corrupt."[5]

A. Torstrik[6] states that this manuscript (fol. 187 bis, l. 15) contains a note explaining the word *organikon* in the text of 412b1. The note reads:

> For the soul is not the first entelechy of fire; I mean the calorific power, even if that is also a natural body. But, because it is not furnished with organs, the soul is not its entelechy. *Organikon* is what possesses organs, via which the vital functions manifest themselves.

οὐ γὰρ ἡ πρώτη τοῦ πυρὸς ἐντελέχεια ψυχή· λέγω δὴ ἡ θερμαντικὴ δύναμις· καίτοι καὶ τοῦτο φυσικόν ἐστι σῶμα· ἀλλ' ἐπεὶ οὐκ ὀργανικόν, οὐκ ἔστιν ἡ πρώτη αὐτοῦ ἐντελέχεια ψυχή· ὀργανικὸν δέ ἐστι τὸ ἔχον ὄργανα δι' ὧν αἱ κατὰ τὸ ζῆν ἐνέργειαι γίνονται.

That is to say: this reader considered that Aristotle's words "natural body" could be linked to an elementary body, and specifically to heat. But he himself believes that Aristotle must be referring to a body "equipped with organs." He therefore states that τοιοῦτον in 412a28 is not a modifying demonstrative pronoun, but a limiting one. In his view, Aristotle means a "natural body," which must also be *organikon,* and therefore is not a simple body, but a body "furnished with organs." He thus rejects the option that the words σῶμα ὀργανικόν in Aristotle refer to "fire" or "heat" by giving ὀργανικόν a meaning the word never had or could have in Aristotle.[7] He seems to be led here by the text

---

5. M. C. Nussbaum, "The Text of Aristotle's *De Anima*," in *Essays on Aristotle's* De Anima, ed. M. C. Nussbaum and A. Oksenberg Rorty (Oxford: Clarendon Press, 1992), 2; For the manuscript tradition, see A. Förster, *Aristotelis De Anima libri tres* (Budapestini: Typis Societatis Franklinianae, 1912); M. de Corte, "Études sur les Manuscrits du Traité *De l'Âme* d'Aristote," *Revue de Philologie* 59 (1933): 141–60, 261–81, 355–67; P. Siwek, *Les Manuscrits Grecs des* Parva Naturalia *d'Aristote* (Rome: Desclée et Cie, 1961), and *Le "De Anima" d'Aristote dans les Manuscripts Grecs* (Città del Vaticano: Biblioteca Apostolica Vaticana, 1965); A. Jannone and E. Barbotin (1966), xxiv–xlv (who were not yet able to use P. Siwek [1965], but do sharply criticize the treatment of the manuscript tradition by W. D. Ross [1961], xxv). See now P. Thillet, *Aristote, De l'Âme* (2005), 11–16, who was able to do more justice to the work of P. Siwek (1965).

6. A. Torstrik, *Aristotelis De Anima, libri tres* (Berlin: Weidmannsche Buchhandlung, 1862; repr. Hildesheim: G. Olms, 1970), 134.

7. Cf ch. 14 below.

of Aristotle's *On the Soul*, but gives it a fundamentally different meaning from the one intended by Aristotle and cancels out everything that Aristotle in his biological works had argued about the genesis of living beings.

The words that he uses, "organs, via which the vital functions manifest themselves [ὄργανα δι' ὧν αἱ κατὰ τὸ ζῆν ἐνέργειαι γίνονται]," can be clearly recognized as non-Aristotelian and in the style of Alexander of Aphrodisias.[8] Note, too, that lines 412b1–4, which have been passed down in all the manuscripts, can easily be read as a continuation of the lines quoted above from the margin of the text, and as the refutation of a possible objection against Alexander of Aphrodisias's reinterpretation of Aristotle's psychology, underlining that plants, like animals and human beings, have bodies "equipped with organs."

If we purge lines 412b1–4 from the text of *On the Soul* II 1 and observe that these are typically a consequence of misinterpretation of the word *organikon* in 412a28, we can also see that by τοιοῦτον δέ in 412a28, Aristotle means: "But in a very specific sense, namely that which is instrument for the soul."[9] This creates room for his proposition in *Generation of Animals* II 3, 736b31–3 that the quality of the soul differs according to the difference in quality of its instrumental body.[10] He had anticipated this thesis in *On the Soul* I 3, 407b13–27, where he argued that a particular work of the soul requires a specific tool/instrumental body.

Because Alexander of Aphrodisias, and many after him, directly associated *organikon* with "(bodies) equipped with organs," and therefore with bodies of sublunary, mortal living creatures, the addition in *On the Soul* II 1, 412a14— "by life we mean the capacity for self-sustenance, growth, and decay [ζωὴν δὲ λέγω τὴν δι' αὑτοῦ τροφήν τε καὶ αὔξησιν καὶ φθίσιν]"—also seems to be the result of Alexander's interpretation. After all, II 2, 413a23–5 shows that Aristotle takes "life" in a much broader sense than in the sentence of 412a14–5.

---

8. Cf. Alexander of Aphrodisias, *Mantissa* 104, 15: "'That which potentially possesses life' is that which is capable of living, i.e., that which has instruments subservient to vital activities, and 'that which potentially possesses life' is equivalent to '*organikon*' [ἔστιν τὸ δυνάμει ζωὴν ἔχον τὸ δυνάμενον ζῆν, τουτέστιν τὸ ἔχον ὄργανα πρὸς τὰς κατὰ τὸ ζῆν ἐνεργείας καὶ ἔστιν ἴσον τὸ 'δυνάμει ζωὴν ἔχον' τῷ 'ὀργανικόν']." Cf. R. W. Sharples, *Alexander of Aphrodisias, Supplement to On the Soul, Translated* (London: Duckworth, 2004), 19. Cf. also *Anim.* 16, 2–4: "for of a body, and specifically of a natural body; not of an artificial body like that of a statue, and not of a simple body like that of fire, but of a compound body that is *organikon* [σώματος γάρ, καὶ σώματος φυσικοῦ. οὐ γὰρ τεχνικοῦ, ὡς τὸ τοῦ ἀδριάντος. καὶ φυσικοῦ οὐχ ἁπλοῦ ὡς τὸ πυρός, ἀλλὰ συνθέτου τε καὶ ὀργανικοῦ]." 24, 6: "and for activities corresponding with this it needs the instrumental parts of the body [πρὸς δὲ τὰς κατὰ ταύτην ἐνεργείας χρῆται τοῖς ὀργανικοῖς μέρεσι τοῦ σώματος]." For a critique of the position of Alexander in Simplicius (?), *In De Anim. Comm.* cf. M. Perkams, "Doppelte Entelecheia. Das Menschenbild in 'Simplikios' Kommentar zu Aristoteles' *De Anima*," *Elenchos* 24 (2003): 57–91.

9. Τοιούτῳ has the same meaning in *Anim.* II 2, 414a22.

10. Cf. §10a above.

14

Why Can't the Words *Sôma Organikon* in Aristotle's Definition of the Soul Refer to the Visible Body?

We have established that there is no sound basis for the position that the term *organikon* in Aristotle's definition of "soul" means "equipped with organs," as W. D. Ross claimed. In effect, this would boil down to a translation of the term *organikon* as "equipped with instrumental parts."

Aristotle was probably the first to use the term *organikon* as a neologism. He used this term twenty-nine times,[1] where it consistently means "instrumental," "possessing and performing the function of an instrument." Most of these cases involve "parts" with a certain function, for instance, the legs as parts of a living being that are specifically suitable to be used for walking.[2]

However, it is evident that in chapter II 1 of *On the Soul* Aristotle is talking about "a body" that is *organikon*, and not about "a part of the body." This might suggest that Aristotle is in fact referring to the *entire*, visible, concrete body of a plant, animal, or human being, and that he sees this entire body as

---

1. Cf. *Anim.* III 9, 432b18: "some part instrumental towards this movement [μόριον ὀργανικόν]" (transl. W.S. Hett [1936], 183); and b25: "parts instrumental to progression [τὰ ὀργανικὰ μέρη τῆς πορείας]." H. Bonitz, *Index Aristotelicus* 521a20–49, mentions twenty-three passages. To these might be added six more: *Anim.* III 9, 432b18; *Hist. anim.* I 6, 491a26; *Part. anim.* II 1, 647a2; *Inc. anim.* 3, 705b2; *Gener. anim.* II 6, 742b2; b10.

2. Cf. *Gener. anim.* II 1, 734b28; *Part. anim.* II 1, 647b23.

the one "instrument" of the soul. That is the view of R. W. Sharples[3] and of C. Brockmann in his contribution "Organe" to the *Aristoteles-Handbuch* of 2011.[4] After a lengthy discussion of everything that Aristotle has to say about members with a specific function, Brockmann remarks: "Auch der Körper selbst wird als *organon* verstanden. So wie jeder seiner Teile um eines bestimmten Zweckes willen besteht, so ist auch der gesamte Organismus auf ein Ziel ausgerichtet (*De part. anim.* I 1, 642a11–14)." Slightly farther on, Brockmann refers to *Parts of Animals* I 5, 645b16–7: "it is evident that the body as a whole must exist for the sake of some . . . action [φανερὸν ὅτι καὶ τὸ σύνολον σῶμα συνέστηκε πράξεώς τινος ἕνεκα πολυμεροῦς]."[5]

---

3. R. W. Sharples, *Peripatetic Philosophy 200 BC–AD 200* (2010), 246: "Bos indeed argues not only that the more natural meaning of the word [*organikon*] is 'serving as an instrument,' but also that Aristotle himself in the definition was referring not to the whole body of the animal, as has been supposed at least since Alexander, but to the *pneuma* functioning as soul's instrument, and that the absence from Hellenistic discussion of the hylomorphic account of soul in Aristotle as now generally understood is not so much evidence of a lack of interest in Aristotle's position as a reflection of the fact that this account was not in fact Aristotle's at all. However, the point about the understanding of the term 'organic' is independent of these further issues, for the whole body, too, might reasonably be seen as itself the instrument of soul." This claim by Sharples is all the more remarkable because Sharples himself has repeatedly expressed his surprise that the "hylomorphism" ascribed to Aristotle by the tradition played no role in the scientific discussion in the first centuries after Aristotle's death.

4. In C. Rapp and K. Corcilius, eds., *Handbuch* (2011), 286–92; cf. G. Heinemann (2015), 67–68; K. Corcilius and P. Gregoric, in "Aristotle's Model of Animal Motion" (2013), 54, also state that Aristotle "could advocate the hylomorphic view that the soul is the form of the whole body."

5. Text P. Louis (1956), 20. He translates: "en vue d'un action complexe." The problem here is that πολυμεροῦς is read in only one ms, P (fourteenth or fifteenth century). All the others have πολυρους (the oldest, E, tenth century) or πλήρους. D. M. Balme (1972) chooses πλήρους and translates: "for the sake of a full activity" (19). He adds on p. 124: "complete and comprehensive, i.e. the coordinated activity of the animal as a whole organism, not merely the aggregation of the activities of the parts (hence the variant πολυμεροῦς is wrong)." G. Heinemann (2015), 67–68 also defends the reading πλήρους and translates: "dasz der ganze Körper zwecks einer vollständigen Tätigkeit gebildet ist." J. G. Lennox, "ΒΙΟΣ, ΠΡΑΞΙΣ, and the Unity of Life," in *Was ist "Leben"? Aristoteles' Anschauungen zur Entstehung und Funktionsweise von Leben*, ed. S. Föllinger (Stuttgart: Franz Steiner Verlag, 2010), 253, defends the vulgate reading πλήρους ("full, complete, whole"). Cf. L. A. Kosman (2013), 103. J. Gelber, "Aristotle on Essence and Habitat," *Oxford Sudies in Ancient Philosophy* 48 (2015): 267, reads "a certain complete action," following J. G. Lennox. It is hard to imagine what the one function of the entire body could be. Nowhere else such a function is mentioned. Perhaps we should also enlist *Part. anim.* II 10, 655b37–6a6 to explain this text. Aristotle says there of plants that "they do not exhibit a great variety of non-uniform substances; they have few actions [πράξεις] to perform, and therefore but few instruments are needed to perform them. . . . But with creatures that not only live but also have the power of sensation, the formations are more varied [πολυμορφοτέραν . . . ἰδέαν] and there is more diversity in some than in others, the greatest variety [πολυχουστέραν . . . ἰδέαν] being found

However, Brockmann goes on to note: "Diese Auffassung wird auch in den berühmten allgemeine Definitionen der Seele in *De anima* deutlich. . . . Der beseelte natürliche Körper ist also wie ein Mittel oder werkzeughaft; er kann Funktionen ausführen."[6]

Brockmann is familiar with the criticism of the traditional explanation of *organikon*, but believes that the view of the visible body as the "instrument" of the soul does not clash with the conception that this body consists of many smaller units, each of which has its own instrumental function. This would mean that a central term in Aristotle's definition of soul was misinterpreted and mistranslated for centuries, but that this had no adverse consequences otherwise.[7] It could also mean that Aristotle makes a fundamental error in his definition of "soul" by saying that "the soul is the first entelechy of an ensouled body."

However, the point of my argument in chapters 7 and 10 was that the visible body is something secondary in Aristotle's view, and that he is wholly focused on explaining how the visible body with all its very different but species-specific parts is produced by the soul and its instrumental body, which precede the visible body. The visible body of a plant, animal, or human being *cannot possibly be identified with* the *sôma organikon* from Aristotle's definition of soul for the following five reasons:[8]

1. The visible body of a living entity is not a "physical body" (σῶμα φυσικόν).

2. Nor is it a "body potentially possessing life" (σῶμα δυνάμει ζωὴν ἔχον).

3. It is not "the body that receives the soul," as stated in *On the Soul* I 3, 407b21 and II 2, 414a24.

4. It cannot be used by the (immaterial) soul itself as an instrument.

---

in those creatures which in addition to living have the capability of living the good life, as man has" (trans. A. L. Peck [1939], with changes). In *Cael.* II 12, 292b2-3, Aristotle notes: "For on our earth it is man that has the greatest variety of actions [καὶ γὰρ ἐνταῦθα αἱ τῶν ἀνθρώπου πλεῖσται πράξεις]." Another relevant text in this connection is Arist. *Protrepticus* B 65 ed. I. Düring (1961), where man's *ergon* is identified as the highest activity of the highest soul-part.

6. C. Brockmann, art. cit., 289a.

7. The same criticism applies to G. Heinemann (2015).

8. Cf. also A. P. Bos, "Aristotle's Definition of the Soul: Why Was It Misunderstood for Centuries?" (2012), 142–44 for more reasons.

5. Aristotle presented the visible body in itself as a corpse, as we find in the comparison of the soul's condition with the situation of living prisoners of Etrurian robbers, who bound them to dead bodies.

Sub (1): In *On the Soul* II 1, 412a12–22, Aristotle starts from "natural bodies" and says that some of these possess life and others do not.[9] In the rest of the argument, he shows how living bodies are compounds of a body plus a soul-principle. In Aristotle's view, therefore, a concrete living body of a plant, animal, or human being is always an "ensouled" body and not a basic "natural body." There is not a single example in Aristotle's work in which he calls a living dog or human being a "natural body."[10] Aristotle made an emphatic distinction between that which is a body and that which has a body.[11]

Aristotle introduces here a fundamental distinction between "natural bodies" that do not possess life and "natural bodies" that do. He does this at the very beginning of his exposition on "the Soul." The only distinction preceding it is that between "two kinds of *ousia*" (II 1, 412a6–11), *viz.*, *ousia* as "matter" and *ousia* as "form," and the combination of these two as "compound *ousia*" (412a16). In his important study on *Substance, Form and Psyche*, M. Furth emphasizes that this last distinction is not dealt with in the work *Categoriae*. Nevertheless, he is convinced that only Aristotle can have written the *Categoriae*.[12] We could also take this to suggest that Aristotle could only fully elaborate his doctrine of *ousia* after setting out his doctrine of the soul as the entelechy of a "natural body" that is used and guided by this entelechy.

---

9. *Anim.* II 1, 412a13–5: "But of natural bodies some have life and some have not; by life we mean the capacity for nutrition, growth and decay by itself [τῶν δὲ φυσικῶν τὰ μὲν ἔχει ζωήν, τὰ δ' οὐκ ἔχει· ζωὴν δὲ λέγω τὴν δι' αὑτοῦ τροφήν τε καὶ αὔξησιν καὶ φθίσιν]."

10. Nevertheless C. Shields, in C. Rapp and K. Corcilius eds., *Handbuch* (2011), 313a, in his contribution on "Seele" also has: "Die Seele ist die erste Wirklichkeit eines natürlichen organischen Körpers (De an. II 1, 412b4–6)."

11. Cf. *Cael.* I 1, 268a4–6: "For the sum of physically constituted entities consist of (a) bodies and magnitudes, (b) beings possessed of body and magnitude, (c) the principles of the entities which possess them [τῶν γὰρ φύσει συνεστώτων τὰ μὲν ἐστι σώματα καὶ μεγέθη, τὰ δ' ἔχει σῶμα καὶ μέγεθος, τὰ δ' ἀρχαὶ τῶν ἐχόντων εἰσίν]" (cf. W. K. C. Guthrie [1939], 5).

12. M. Furth, *Substance, Form, and Psyche: An Aristotelean Metaphysics* (Cambridge: Cambridge University Press, 1988), 38–39 n. 12: "My belief in the Aristotelean authorship of the *Categories* is indeed based chiefly on the unlikelihood that there should have been a second person having so deep and exact a comprehension of Aristotelean metaphysics as to be able to write an introductory text to it that everywhere comes precisely to the edge of what can be rounded off in a plausible way without toppling off into the depths of the *Metaphysics*—and that we should know nothing else whatsoever about him . . ."

For it is only with the help of his doctrine of the soul as entelechy that he can plausibly show why the "natural bodies" in themselves have more the character of an aggregate (a *sôros*) than of a structured whole, such as a living plant or animal.[13] The four sublunary "simple" natural bodies are the necessary conditions (*archai*—412a13) for all visible living entities, but only as suppliers of matter. For the life of plants and animals, something else of a radically different order is needed: the soul as entelechy.[14]

This fundamental difference between sublunary "natural bodies" and living substances is a compelling reason not to identify the words *sôma physikon* in the definition of the soul in *On the Soul* II 1 with the living, structured body of a human being, animal, or plant, but with a "natural body" that becomes "matter" and "instrument" for the soul and is structured by it.[15]

Sub (2): Nor is a concrete living body of a plant, animal, or human being a body that potentially possesses life. It must necessarily possess life, otherwise it would at most be "life-possessing" in a homonymous way.[16] Though a sleeping dog can be said to have potency for barking, a sleeping dog cannot be said to have (merely) "potency for life."

---

13. Cf. ibid., 50–52.

14. Aristotle wants to assess Plato's theory of Ideas positively, if *eidê* are assumed of all that lives in nature (and not even of "flesh" or "head" in itself). Cf. *Metaph.* Λ 3, 1070a13–20.

15. According to G. A. Lucchetta, *Scienza e Retorica in Aristotele. Sulle Radici Omeriche delle Metafore Aristoteliche* (Bologna: Il Molino, 1990), 69–95, Aristotle borrowed the term *hyle* from Homer, where it still simply means "firewood," "timber."

16. This is well pointed out by T. K. Johansen, *The Powers of Aristotle's Soul* (2012), 13: "How can it be true to say that the body only *potentially* has life? For surely the body of which the soul is the fulfilment has life not just potentially, but actually. If it didn't have life actually it wouldn't be a living body, but if it wasn't a living body, then, Aristotle underlines, it would only be a body homonymously." On p. 15, the author formulates the problem (which is fictitious, in my view) even more clearly: "But this still leaves us with a question of what it means for the body of the fully formed living being to be *potentially* alive." The author solves the problem by claiming that Aristotle "means to deny that the body is sufficient on its own or as such to be alive or to have life. The body as such only potentially has life and it is the presence of soul that fulfils this potentiality." I don't think this is a correct solution to the problem. It is one and the same body that potentially possesses life and that lives (at a later stage). The point is that there are phases in which the soul's natural instrumental body is not active: for instance, in seed and in a fruit (412b25–7), just as power is already present in a winding mechanism that is not yet working (*Gener. anim.* II 1, 734b10–11). Aristotle would never want to say this about the visible body of a plant or animal. Hence, this description of the body as "potentially possessing life" is a compelling argument for the position that Aristotle is referring here to *pneuma* as the "instrumental body" of the soul. Johansen op. cit., 14 also has the wrong end of the stick when he states: "the seed is potentially a body that potentially has life." In 412b27, which he cites, Aristotle is emphatically saying that semen and fruits have soul, but that their vital activity has not yet been activated.

Sub (3): When Aristotle argues in *On the Soul* I 3, 407b21 that a soul can only enter a matching, kindred body,[17] he is talking about the menstrual fluid of a female. This female may receive semen and thus form a living germ cell of which the vegetative soul-function is directly actualized. But copulation between a stallion and a bitch does not produce a viable result because the menstrual fluid of the bitch is not suitable for the activity of a stallion's soul. In Aristotle's view, however, a complete visible body of a neonate cannot possibly breathe in a soul at its birth. It must have had a vegetative soul in act for nine months, a soul that realized the formation of lungs, among other parts.

Sub (4): However, the greatest objection is that the idea that the visible body is the "instrument of the soul" renders completely superfluous Aristotle's criticism of the Platonic doctrine of the soul as the principle of motion. The soul that Aristotle describes in *On the Soul* is immaterial and possesses no motion of its own. Nor can it ever set in motion a material body consisting of earth, water, air, and fire. It can only be the *telos*-indicating principle (entelechy) of a special natural body that is able to be its instrument, by analogy with the celestial element that serves the astral living beings as their instrumental body.

Sub (5): We should also consider that in one of his lost dialogues (probably the *Eudemus*) Aristotle compared the woeful fate of the human soul with the condition of a *living* prisoner of war whom Etrurian robbers had bound to a corpse. This comparison differs significantly from Plato's remark about the body as the "grave" of the soul. It is an indication that Aristotle regarded the visible body as an external burden for the soul in conjunction with its soul-body and, considered on its own, as a corpse.[18] L. Edelstein has defended that the change in attitude toward human dissection among learned men and philosophers in Alexandria was due to philosophical teachings that began to take practical effect not long after Aristotle's death.[19]

---

17. Cf. *Anim.* II 2, 414a24.

18. Arist. *Protrepticus* 10b Ross; 73 and 823 Gigon; B 106–107 Düring. However, this text is better assigned to the *Eudemus*. Cf. A. P. Bos, "Aristotle on the Etruscan Robbers: a Core Text of 'Aristotelian' Dualism" (2003) and §18b below.

19. See on this interesting but controversial topic, O. and C. L. Temkin, eds., *Ancient Medicine. Selected Papers of Ludwig Edelstein* (Baltimore: Johns Hopkins University Press, 1967), 278; and J. Longrigg, *Greek Rational Medicine. Philosophy and Medicine from Alcmaeon to the Alexandrians* (London: Routledge, 1993), 185 ff.

15

Collateral Damage of the Hylomorphistic Explanation of Aristotle's Psychology

What has gone wrong with the explanation of Aristotelian texts as a result of Alexander of Aphrodisias's misinterpretation of Aristotle's view of the soul? I start with a brief enumeration of the most salient facts.[1]

a. Consequences for Reading *On the Soul* II 1

1. The term *natural body* (σῶμα φυσικόν) in *On the Soul* II 1 has been explained in the sense that it should be identified with a living, ensouled body furnished with organs, though this meaning does not occur anywhere else in Aristotle's work.

2. From 200 to 1980, in the context of the definition of "soul" in *On the Soul* II 1, 412a27 and 412b6, the term *organikon* has always been taken to mean "furnished with organs." However, ὀργανικόν never means "furnished with organs" in Aristotle, but always "instrumental," "serving as an instrument." It is out of the question that only in the definition of soul has the word ὀργανικόν been given a meaning which it has nowhere else.[2]

---

1. Cf. A. P. Bos, "Aristotle's Definition of the Soul: Why Was It Misunderstood for Centuries?" (2012), 142–44.

2. Cf. C. Shields, "The Priority of Soul in Aristotle's *De Anima*: Mistaking Categories?," in *Body and Soul in Ancient Philosophy*, ed. D. Frede and B. Reis (Berlin/New York: W. de Gruyter, 2009), 282–83: "The word has this meaning nowhere in Aristotle." In his new commentary *Aristotle, De Anima. Translation with an Introduction and Commentary* (Oxford: Oxford University Press, 2016), he chooses the translation "organic." See L. A. Kosman, "Animals and Other Beings in Aristotle," in *Philosophical Issues in Aristotle's Biology*, ed. A. Gotthelf and J. G. Lennox (Cambridge: Cambridge University Press, 1987), 376.

3. Owing to the interpretation of *organikon* as "furnished with organs," scholars have also attributed to Aristotle the beginner's error of providing a definition of "soul" in which the term to be defined is already incorporated in the definition. Whereas Aristotle says that the soul is the first entelechy of a natural body that potentially possesses life and that is *organikon*, the standard interpretation accepts that he is talking about "a natural body that is already ensouled," because a natural body "furnished with organs" or "organic" or "organized" is necessarily a living body, and the definition thus amounts to a statement in the sense of "the soul is the first entelechy of an ensouled body."[3]

4. The lines in *On the Soul* II 1, 412b1–4 on "the parts of a plant" were incorporated into the text long after Aristotle had written the chapter, and should be regarded as a displaced marginal note by a later reader who took Alexander of Aphrodisias's interpretation entirely for granted.[4]

5. The text of *On the Soul* II 1, 412b17–3a7 was also completely misinterpreted because scholars took "the parts" in 412b16 to be "parts" of the visible body, though the term clearly refers to "parts" *of the soul* and Aristotle wants to explain there that "the parts" of the soul are just as inextricably tied up with the instrumental body as the soul in its entirety. Aristotle is in fact talking there about the soul-"part" of perception. This error may have been promoted by the insertion of lines 412b1–4.[5]

The unique remark about the necessary unity of the "parts" of the soul with the instrumental body of the soul in II 1, 412b17–3a7 means that the

---

3. Cf., for example, J. J. Cleary, *Aristotle and Mathematics* (1995), 457: "the soul may be defined as the first actuality of an animate body"; A. M. Leroi, *The Lagoon* (2014), 159: "the soul is associated with the presence of organs, which means that it is a functional property of living things." See also P.-M. Morel (2007), 12–13: "Ainsi l'âme est la 'réalisation première' d'un corps naturel déjà organisé ou pourvu d'organes c'est-à-dire déjà animé au sens où il est disposé à vivre." He adds on p. 13 n. 1 that the "définition, ou esquisse de définition . . . est formellement défectueuse, puisqu'elle semble placer le *definiendum* dans le *definiens*." While rejecting the solutions suggested by R. Brague, S. Menn, and A. P. Bos, he sticks to his hylomorphistic interpretation and even adds: "Néanmoins le caractère circulaire de cette pseudo-définition, paradoxe souligné par de nombreux commentateurs, *présente cet avantage qu'il exprime très bien la radicalité et l'aspect originel de l'unité hylémorphique*" (italics A. P. B.). Cf. ibid., 42 n. 1. It seems unlikely that Aristotle would have appreciated these words of praise, which at the same time accuse him of violating the basic rules of logic.

4. Cf. ch. 13 above.

5. Cf. A. P. Bos, "Het Gehele Lichaam dat Waarnemingsvermogen Bezit" (1999): 112–28. For a related problem to do with "parts" of the soul, see "The Soul and Soul-'Parts' in Semen (*GA* II 1, 735a4–22)," *Mnemosyne* 62 (2009): 378–400.

rational soul-part, too, is inextricably tied to the soul-body from the moment of fertilization. Although Aristotle argues that the activity of the intellect is not a materially characterized activity, and the intellect comes "from outside" (*Gener. anim.* II 3, 736b27–9), he also argues that the "intellect of the soul" or the practical intellect is already transferred as "part" of the soul during fertilization (*Gener. anim.* II 3, 737a9–11). But it still needs to be "awakened" and then turned away from cosmic reality to transcendent and immaterial reality.[6]

6. The expression "potentially possessing life" (δυνάμει ζωὴν ἔχον) has been incorrectly explained and connected with a living entity "furnished with organs" instead of with *pneuma* and with semen of animals and seeds of plants and trees.[7]

7. The term *entelecheia* has always been wrongly explained. The term stands for "the goal-orienting principle." It is usually the controlling principle of an ethereal or a pneumatic soul-body. The "twofold entelechy" in 412a10–11 and a22–7 has also been completely misunderstood, and scholars have failed to see that there is a third kind of entelechy, which is not the entelechy of a body.[8]

8. The final sentence of *On the Soul* II 1 has been misconstrued. Scholars have generally accepted that the sentence mentioning "the sailor on his ship" (413a8–9) was not seriously intended by Aristotle and was only left there by mistake.[9] However, Aristotle indicates there that a human soul is not just present as "sleeping entelechy" (in the embryonic phase and early youth), but may also be active as "awakened entelechy" of a human being with a practical mind,[10] and finally, when it has achieved theoretical intellectuality, may even

---

6. T. K. Johansen, "Parts in Aristotle's Definition of the Soul: *De Anima* Books I and II," in *Partitioning the Soul: Debates from Plato to Leibniz*, ed. K. Corcilius and D. Perler (Berlin: De Gruyter, 2014), 39–61, who on pp. 56–60 tries to undergird the "unity of the soul" in Aristotle's psychology, could have benefited greatly from a correct appraisal of this passage in *Anim.* II 1, 412b17–3a5.

7. Cf. *Gener. anim.* II 1, 735a4–7 and II 3, 737a16–8: "We have now determined in what sense fetations and semen have Soul and in what sense they have not. They have Soul *potentially*, but not *in actuality* [Περὶ μὲν οὖν ψυχῆς πῶς ἔχει τὰ κυήματα καὶ ἡ γονὴ καὶ πῶς οὐκ ἔχει διώρισται· δυνάμει μὲν γὰρ ἔχει, ἐνεργείᾳ δ' οὐκ ἔχει]."

8. Cf. §10q above, and A. P. Bos, "Plutarch on the Sleeping Soul and the Waking Intellect and Aristotle's Double Entelechy Concept" (2012), 25–42. See now P. Jackson, *Aristotle on the Meaning of Man. A Philosophical Response to Idealism, Positivism, and Gnosticism* (Bern: P. Lang, 2016), 28 n. 21.

9. Cf. Sir David Ross, *Aristotle, De Anima* (1961), 214–15; P. Thillet (2005), 340. F. D. Miller, "Aristotle on the Separability of Mind," in *The Oxford Handbook of Aristotle*, ed. C. Shields (Oxford: Oxford University Press, 2012), 312. R. Polansky (2007), 168–69 comes close to a satisfactory solution.

leave behind its instrumental body, just as a passenger may leave his ship on reaching safe harbor.

9. In *On the Soul* II 1, 412a5, Aristotle says explicitly that he is searching for "the most general possible account" (κοινότατος λόγος αὐτῆς) of "soul." Therefore, this definition must include the soul of celestial living beings, something the tradition has generally denied.[11]

b. Consequences for Reading the Rest of *On the Soul*

10. The passage on "all natural bodies" in II 4, 415b18 has fared just as badly as that on the "natural body" in II 1, 412a11, and following. Aristotle can say in *On the Soul* II 4, 415b18 that all "natural bodies" are instruments of the soul, in reference to the four sublunary elements, which play an important role in his theory of perception, in combination with *pneuma*.[12]

11. The text on semen as "instrument" of the soul has disappeared from the transmitted text of *On the Soul* II 4, 415b7,[13] probably because it sat uneasily with the hylomorphistic explanation of Aristotle's psychology. After all, if one assumes with Alexander of Aphrodisias that only a body "furnished with organs" can be the *sôma organikon*, then obviously semen cannot be an instrument of the soul.

---

10. Cf. *Anim.* II 1, 412a13–5 and §10q above.

11. This intention also seems to be expressed in I 1, 402b7, where Aristotle asks whether we should consider a possible difference in kind of soul for horse, dog, human being, or god. The same intention appears to underlie the use of the word *sphaira* in III 11, 434a13, which seems to point to a celestial sphere (cf. E. Diamond, *Mortal Imitations of Divine Life* (2015), 240–47; but this text is highly controversial). The view that Aristotle's definition of "soul" in II 1 was meant to include astral psychology became problematic when *organikon* in II 1, 412a28 came to be interpreted as '"equipped with organs." The astral beings do not have "organs." But their ethereal body may well have been referred to as "an instrumental body." A remaining problem is II 1, 412a14–5, where "life" seems to be confined to entities with a nutritive soul-function (though Aristotle attributes "life" to the transcendent Intellect, too). Earlier we established that this passage is superfluous to the argument and may have been inserted later, after Alexander of Aphrodisias.

12. This passage has usually also been interpreted in a hylomorphistic sense, as if Aristotle is talking there about "living bodies" of plants, animals, and human beings. See A. P. Bos, "Aristotle on the Differences between Plants, Animals, and Human Beings" (2010), 826–31.

13. On this passage, which has been wrongly excluded from the modern editions of *On the Soul*, cf. A. P. Bos, "A Lost Sentence on Seed as Instrument of the Soul" (2010), 276–87. See also *Motu anim.* 11, 703b25: "there flows from it the seminal potency, itself a kind of living creature [ἐξέρχεται ἐξ αὐτοῦ ὥσπερ ζῷόν τι ἡ τοῦ σπέρματος δύναμις]."

12. All places that talk about "the soul" and "the body" need to be reexamined to find out what body Aristotle is referring to.[14]

13. There are many misunderstandings about the role of the soul's instrumental body for perception, though Aristotle explicitly assigns a role here to *pneuma* in "tubes" that extend to the heart, and in *De Somno* 1, 454a9–10 explicitly defines sensation as "motion through the body of the soul."

c. Other Problems Resulting from Alexander's Misunderstanding

14. It is strange that the ancient alternative interpretations of Aristotle's definition of "soul," as found in Pseudo-Hippolytus, *Refutatio Omnium Haeresium*

---

14. Cf. *Anim.* III 10, 433b19–21 and *Motu anim.* 10, 703a4–11; *Sens.* 1, 436a1–b3; *Somn.* 1, 454a7–11. This applies in particular to texts in which Aristotle talks about "'blending" (*krasis*), "mixing" (*mixis*), or "symmetry" (*symmetria*) of "the body" or "the bodies." There is good reason to suspect that many of these are primarily concerned not with the "visible body" as a whole, but with the relation of vital heat or *pneuma* to other components of a plant or animal. See A. L. Peck, *Aristotle, Historia Animalium*, in three volumes (London: W. Heinemann, 1965), vol. 1, lxxv–lxxvii. Cf. *Hist. anim.* VII (VIII) 2, 589b22: "Those that are water animals in the second way, that is because of their bodily blend and their life [ἔνυδρα δ' ἐστὶ τὸν ἕτερον τρόπον, διὰ τὴν τοῦ σώματος κρᾶσιν καὶ τὸν βίον]." Cf. 590a13: "and since the animals have been divided into aquatic and terrestrial triply—and by taking in air or water, and by their bodily blend, and thirdly by their feeding [διῃρημένων δὲ τῶν ζῴων εἰς τὸ ἔνυδρον καὶ πεζὸν τριχῶς, τῷ τε δέχεσθαι τὸν ἀέρα ἢ τὸ ὕδωρ, καὶ τῇ κράσει τῶν σωμάτων]." Because these texts deal with the differences in quality of life between different kinds of creatures, the instrumental body of the soul, that is, *pneuma*, is always involved. We have repeatedly observed that *Gener. anim.* III 11, 761b13–6 connects plants with earth, fish with water, etc., because these elements, alongside the *pneuma* they always possess, are dominant and determine the quality of their life. In *Spir.* 8, 485a13–5, Aristotle explains the difference between humans and quadrupeds by stating that "matter is earthier and colder" for the latter (ἡ ὕλη γεωδεστέρα καὶ ψυχροτέρα). In *Spir.* 9, 485b15–9, he makes it clear that one and the same creature has bones of varying kinds of hardness due to differences in the "mixture" (*mixis*) of vital heat and earth. Cf. also *Part. anim.* II 4, 650b28–30: "At the same time too great an excess of water makes animals timorous. For fear chills the body; so that in animals whose heart contains so watery a mixture the way is prepared for the operation of this emotion [Δειλότερα δὲ τὰ λίαν ὑδατώδη. Ὁ γὰρ φόβος καταψύχει· προωδοποίηται οὖν τῷ πάθει τὰ τοιαύτην ἔχοντα τὴν ἐν τῇ καρδίᾳ κρᾶσιν]." *Gener. anim.* II 6, 744a29–30: "the heat in man's heart is purest. His intellect shows how well he is tempered [τὴν ἐν τῇ καρδίᾳ θερμότητα καθαρωτάτην. δηλοῖ δὲ τὴν εὐκρασίαν ἡ διάνοια]." *Eth. Nic.* VII 14, 1154b11–3: "melancholics by nature always need relief; for even their body is ever in torment owing to its special blending, and they are always under the influence of violent desire [οἱ δὲ μελαγχολικοὶ τὴν φύσιν δέονται ἀεὶ ἰατρείας· καὶ γὰρ τὸ σῶμα δακνόμενον διατελεῖ διὰ τὴν κρᾶσιν, καὶ ἀεὶ ἐν ὀρέξει σφοδρᾷ εἰσίν]." Here it is questionable whether "the body" refers to the visible body. The very fact that they are driven by *orexis* suggests that Aristotle is talking about *pneuma*.

VII 24, 1–2, Plutarch, *Quaestiones Platonicae* 8,[15] and Diogenes Laertius V 33, have never played any part in modern commentaries.[16]

15. R. W. Sharples has repeatedly emphasized how curious it is that the view that we nowadays call "Aristotelian hylomorphism" is never attributed to Aristotle in Antiquity, nor discussed as an important theme by people belonging to the Aristotelian tradition.

16. Also, it is totally unclear from what moment the soul is present as ἐντελέχεια. For at the moment of fertilization there is no question yet of "a body furnished with organs for the exercise of its faculties." This would mean that the soul only enters a *kyèma* in a later phase of the development of the *kyèma*. But Aristotle never talked about this in his oeuvre. He did establish in *On the Soul* II 1, 412b27 that semen of animals and fruits of plants already possess soul. And in *Generation of Animals* II 1, 735a20–2, he established that directly after fertilization the *kyèma* grows and develops thanks to the vegetative function of its own soul.[17]

17. An urgent question for the traditional view is, What principle leads the development of an embryo from the moment of copulation to the situation in which the embryo can be characterized as "furnished with organs"?

---

15. Cf. A. P. Bos, "Plutarch's Testimony to an Earlier Explanation of Aristotle's Definition of the Soul," in *Plutarco, Platón y Aristóteles. Actas del V Congreso Internacional de la I.P.S.*, ed. A. Pérez Jiménez, J. García López, R.M. Aguilar (Madrid-Cuenca, 4–7 de Mayo de 1999) (Madrid: Ediciones Clásicas, 1999), 535–48.

16. But see now R. W. Sharples, *Peripatetic Philosophy 200 BC–AD 200* (2010) 34: "The definition of 'instrumental' at the end of [Diog. Laertius, V 28–34] is to be contrasted with Alexander's later, influential and arguably incorrect interpretation of the term as 'furnished with organs.'"

17. Alexander of Aphrodisias and his Platonizing followers simply explained the passage in 412b27–8 in the sense that semen of animals and seeds of plants only "potentially possess soul" (because semen and seeds do not yet contain "instrumental parts"), but this goes entirely against the flow of the argument. For Aristotle, semen and seeds are precisely what his definition refers to. They have soul and they consist of *pneuma* plus earth and/or water, air and fire as the "instrumental body" of the soul, and semen contains not only visual perception as a real possibility, but, even more comprehensively, "the entire (instrumental) body of perception" (412b24: τὸ ὅλον σῶμα τὸ αἰσθητικόν), that is, the instrumental body of the sensitive soul.

16

Resulting Damage to the Assessment of *On the Cosmos* and *On the Life-Bearing Spirit* (*De Spiritu*)

If we can conclude that for Aristotle *pneuma* has a crucial significance, in which cosmology, biology, and theology are interconnected, there is good reason to reconsider the work *On the Cosmos*. This work is generally regarded as inauthentic and dated centuries after Aristotle's death. But precisely in this work the basic structure is a doctrine of five elements, and though the author of the work does not deal separately with the theme of *pneuma* and its importance for the study of living nature, he adds, in a discussion of an entirely separate issue (namely, the various conditions of weather and the twelve wind directions that go with them—*pneumata*), the remark: "'*Pneuma*' is used in a different sense with regard to the ensouled and generative substance which is found in plants and living creatures, pervading them totally; but with this we need not deal here."[1]

On the Cosmos also has a theology that is striking in its criticism of any demiurgic conception of God. A description of God as "Father and Maker," which Plato used in his *Timaeus* is lacking, and instead we find the salient term *Begetter* (6, 397b21; 399a31).[2]

---

1. *Mu.* 4, 394b9–12.
2. Cf. A. P. Bos, "Aristotle on God as Principle of Genesis" (2010), 368–70; "Aristote sur Dieu en tant qu'*Archê Geneseôs* en opposition au Démiurge de Platon," *Revue de Philosophie Ancienne* 27 (2009): 39–57 and §9a, b above.

Entirely in accordance with this, and with the theory of procreation in *Generation of Animals*, is that *On the Cosmos* explains in detail that everything living and existing in the cosmos is the result of the operative power (*dynamis*) proceeding from God (6, 397b20–8a1).[3] God's being (οὐσία) transcends the cosmos; his Power (δύναμις) pervades the entire cosmos.[4]

On the Cosmos is also unique in the tradition of Greek theology in that, via a quotation of Orphic verses, it distinguishes two aspects of God's existence, namely, a male and a female aspect (7, 401b2).[5] The philosophy of *On the Cosmos* should be regarded as authentically Aristotelian and as highly influential on the Stoa.[6]

However, according to the passage in *On the Cosmos* 4, as in the acknowledged Aristotelian writings, *pneuma* is present in all that lives, including plants and fish, and in everything that has potency for life (such as semen and seed). In warm and moist locations it may even lead to spontaneous generation of simple living beings.

This *pneuma* is therefore strikingly different from the *pneuma* recognized by Plato and the pre-Socratic physicians. They had mainly discussed it as "vital breath" and as such attached great importance to it. Aristotle puts his own, very specific complexion on this tradition by connecting the soul of plants (which have no form of respiration) with *pneuma*, and by explaining the process of respiration as a result, in higher creatures, of the great heat of their "innate *pneuma*." Aristotle also keenly saw that in creatures with respiration this system of respiration must develop in an embryonic phase in which there is no breath and respiration, but in which there must be a vital principle (as entelechy) and an instrumental body of this soul. He set this out systematically in his work *On the Life-Bearing Spirit* (*De Spiritu*), especially in chapters 2–4, which forms part of the *Parva Naturalia*.[7]

---

[3]. It would be most remarkable if a forger or imitator emphasized central themes from Aristotle's *Generation of Animals*, even though Aristotle's biological writings had long been neglected.

[4]. Just so, Aristotle distinguishes between the οὐσία of the soul, which is located in the center of a living being, and its δύναμις, which pervades the entire living being: *Anim.* II 1, 412a15–21 and *Gener. anim.* II 3, 736b29–33.

[5]. In *Phys.* I 9, 192a14–25, Aristotle compares the principles of Form and Matter with the duality of the male and the female. (He thus confuses a subject-object relation with an intersubject relation.)

[6]. Pace J. C. Thom, ed., *Cosmic Order and Divine Power. Pseudo-Aristotle,* On the Cosmos (2014).

[7]. W. Jaeger and other modern authors have wrongly dated *Spir.* almost a hundred years after Aristotle. In *Spir.*, the *symphyton pneuma* is said to be connected with the soul in a natural unity (1, 481a17), and is called the soul's instrument in chapter 9, 485b1–10. Cf. A. P. Bos and

I give a short overview of the positions which the author of *De Spiritu* himself holds:[8]

> He is convinced that the concoction of food consumed by a living creature not only produces building materials for the parts of the visible body but always residues (*perittômata*) as well: 1, 481a19–20, 2, 481b27–28.
>
> The respiration of living creatures is not characteristic of all living entities and not even of all animals, and therefore is not the central and most fundamental vital process, but serves to cool living creatures with high vital heat: 2, 482a16; 3, 482a31; b1; 5, 483b6; 484a9–10.
>
> A related position is that insects (which have no respiration) do have a cooling system, but one which works via their diaphragm: 2, 482a17.
>
> Water does not contain air (and so fish cannot have a respiratory system): 2, 482a23.
>
> The pulsatory motion noticeable in many living creatures is not a phenomenon connected with respiration and the inhaled *pneuma*, but of the blood in the heart region: 4, 482b36.
>
> All living creatures, including those which possess no respiratory system, have a principle of vital heat. That is why they need an opposite principle that provides the right balance in temperature: 5, 484a7.
>
> Everything that is moved starts from a state of rest: 7, 484b19.
>
> Bones have a glutinous fluid surrounding them which can be regarded as blood that has not been fully concocted. They do not receive their nutriment via respiration or the *artèriai*: 6, 484a32.
>
> In natural inquiry it is most useful to determine accurately what a thing's final cause is: 8, 485a4–6.

R. Ferwerda (2007) and (2008). See also P. Macfarlane (2007). A new refutation of Aristotle's authorship is offered by P. Gregoric, O. Lewis, and M. Kuhar, "The Substance of *De Spiritu*," *Early Science and Medicine* 20 (2015), 101–24; P. Gregoric and O. Lewis, "Pseudo-Aristotelian *De Spiritu*: a New Case against Authenticity," *Classical Philology* 110 (2015): 159–67; O. Lewis and P. Gregoric, "The Context of *De Spiritu*," *Early Science and Medicine* 20 (2015): 125–49. See also P. Gregoric and M. Kuhar, "Aristotle's Physiology of Animal Motion" (2014).

8. Cf. A. P. Bos and R. Ferwerda (2008), 18–21.

An interesting detail is that the author of *De Spiritu* states in 8, 485a21 that shellfish do have feet, but not for the purpose of movement but to support their weight, as *De incessu animalium* 19, 714a14 also argues.

A fundamental starting point in natural inquiry is: comparable effects have the same causes in the same way: 2, 482a10–11; 482a24–25; 6, 484b7–8; 8, 485a11–12.

All these are positions that Aristotle defended, like the position on "the soul" held in *De Spiritu*.

In 1, 481a16, he asks: Can *pneuma* arise from nutriment, if it is itself primary (*prôton*)? Because that which is connected with the soul is "purer" (481a17), one would not expect it to arise from something like nutriment. This already sheds light on the view, underlying the entire work, that *pneuma* is a *sôma* that is connected with the soul in a very special way and is the instrument of this soul.

In 2, 481b15–17, he opposes "Aristogenes" when the latter states that breath derives its heat from the motion of the lungs. The author objects that in that case the vital breath is not "the primary moving cause." Clearly for the author *pneuma* does constitute "the primary moving cause" (directed by the soul-principle).

In 4, 483a3, the author distinguishes somatic disorders from fears, hopes, and tensions of the soul, which affect the frequency of the pulsatory motion of the blood in the heart. To anyone familiar with Aristotle's biological works, this passage makes it clear that in *De spiritu*, too, he posits a close relation between the soul and a *sôma*, not, however, the visible, coarse-material body, but the fine-material soul-*sôma*, or *pneuma*, that forms an indissoluble unity with the soul. This soul-*sôma* is also the "prime mover" of all vital activity, including the pulsatory motion.

In 5, 483a23–27, the soul comes up in a discussion on perception. The author states that, according to his opponents, only the *artèria* possesses perception. He asks whether this is due to the inhaled air that flows through the *artèria*, or whether his opponents see the inhaled air as subordinate and serviceable to the soul, and so really regard the soul as the subject of perception. The starting point of this question seems to be Aristotle's own theory of perception as a matter of the soul assisted by its instrumental *pneuma*.

In 483a27–30, he raises the issue that, besides the nutritive activity of the soul, there are also its rational and conative activities. The underlying question here seems to be: What guarantees the unity of the soul? This is a question that Aristotle often poses as a challenge to Plato.

In 483b10, he talks about inhaled air in the view of his opponents as "that which is the primary vehicle of the soul." Again, he uses his own terminology here and concludes that such a substance would have to be of the finest quality.

In chap. 9, the author finishes off the opponents whose theory he contests throughout *De Spiritu*. He states there that nature uses vital heat to produce living creatures (485b6–9). The soul is active in vital heat or *pneuma*. And it can be viewed as forming a unity with *pneuma* (485b13–15). It is the theory of the soul and its instrumental body which Aristotle uses extensively in *Generation of Animals* II 1, as in all his biological writings.

In both *On the Cosmos* and *De Spiritu* the very presence of the *pneuma* doctrine gave interpreters from the time after Alexander of Aphrodisias reason to assume that the works must be later and influenced by the Stoa.

17

Damage to the View of the Unity of Aristotle's Work

A century-old article by W. Jaeger has contributed strongly to the elimination of *De Spiritu* as a genuinely Aristotelian work.[1] In this paper, Jaeger first argues, against V. Rose (1854), that *Motion of Animals* was undoubtedly written by Aristotle himself: like the *Parva Naturalia*, it refers back to *On the Soul*, and it develops the doctrine of innate *pneuma* as the originator of the locomotion of a living creature, in line with *On the Soul* III 10.[2] Jaeger regards this doctrine of innate *pneuma* (to be distinguished from the *pneuma* inhaled from outside by higher animal species) as soundly Aristotelian.[3] In *Motion of Animals*, the doctrine is used to explain "den rätselhaften Übergang der psychischen in physiologische oder rein mechanische Energie." In chapters 6–10, Aristotle unfolds "die eigentliche Lehre von dem psychischen Anteil an der organischen Körperbewegung." The innate *pneuma* is also crucial to the Stagirite's thought on the generation of living beings.[4] However, Jaeger goes on to argue in detail that *De Spiritu* cannot be attributed to Aristotle because it is full of anti-Aristotelian polemic.[5] Since then, this work has played no

---

1. W. Jaeger, "Das *Pneuma* im Lykeion" (1913); quoted after the reprint in *Scripta Minora* (Roma: 1960), 57–102.

2. Ibid., 59–70.

3. Ibid., 74: "Alle Lebewesen besitzen angeborenes Pneuma, in ihm wurzelt ihre Lebenskraft," and "Der Zweck unsrer Schrift [*Motu anim.*—APB] ist erfüllt mit dem Nachweis, dass das Pneuma das Organ sei, wodurch der Wille—bei den fertig ausgebildeten Lebewesen—der Körper zu dem Ziele, das ihm vorschwebt, bewegt." On p. 83 Jaeger even talks about "die Mittlerrolle als Seelenorgan die er als Naturforscher dem Pneuma zuweist."

4. Ibid., 70–83.

5. Ibid., 83–102. See especially 76.

significant role in the scientific debate and has been unable to function as an antidote to the standard view.[6]

This had an important side effect. In the following years, W. Jaeger closely studied the fragments of Aristotle's lost works. In 1923, this resulted in the publication of his revolutionary book on Aristotle's three-phase development. Jaeger introduced a view of Aristotle's philosophy that had never been defended before. It was eagerly accepted by the academic world because the information about Aristotle's lost works was hard to reconcile with the standard view of Aristotle's psychology.

Instead of being used to show that the standard view of Aristotle had been wrong for 1,700 years, this information became the foundation of *a new, completely unhistorical approach* to an ancient oeuvre. It is astonishing how successful W. Jaeger was in disseminating his development-historical approach, despite the fact that its foundation was totally unsound.[7] Apart from that, the past few decades have seen a trend in which hardly any attention is paid to the fragments of Aristotle's lost works, as if they cannot yield reliable knowledge.[8]

"Exoteric" and "Esoteric"

If we may conclude that there were not two (or even more) philosophical conceptions, we must also accept that Aristotle never meant some of his writ-

---

6. Ibid., 76 also dismisses E. Zeller's claim that *Motu anim.* 10, 703a10, "How this innate *pneuma* is preserved, has been set out elsewhere [τίς μὲν οὖν ἡ σωτηρία τοῦ συμφύτου πνεύματος, εἴρηται ἐν ἄλλοις]," refers to *Spir.* 1, 481a1: "The innate *pneuma*, how does it maintain itself and grow? [τίς ἡ τοῦ ἐμφύτου πνεύματος διαμονὴ καὶ τίς ἡ αὔξησις]." On the topic of σωτηρία in Aristotle, cf. M. Rashed, "La Préservation (σωτηρία) Objet des *Parva Naturalia* et Ruse de la Nature," *Revue de Philosophie Ancienne* 20 (2002): 35–59.

7. Cf. A. P. Bos, *The Soul and its Instrumental Body* (2003), 374–77; "'Development' in the Study of Aristotle" (2006). A. M. Leroi, *The Lagoon* (2014), 346 remarked: "His scheme, brilliant and a little mad, enchanted Aristotelians until the 1960s. Since then it has been unpicked so that little of it remains." But then he continues: "Yet this way of reading Aristotle [emphasizing the unity of Aristotle's thought] conceals as much as it illuminates. After all, two facts are indisputable: that he began his intellectual life as a student of Plato, writing Platonic dialogues on Platonic themes, and that it ended having developed a system of thought that, whatever its debt to his predecessors, contained the elements of natural science." However, although Aristotle did begin as a student of Plato, it has never been proved that he wrote "Platonic dialogues."

8. This sometimes means that those who do pay attention to these fragments (and to those of all pre-Socratic philosophers, who are only known from fragments) are not taken seriously. Cf. W. Kullmann, *Aristoteles, Über die Teile der Lebewesen* (2007), 155: "Düring hat darauf hingewiesen, dass man aus methodischen Gründen nicht Aussagen des *Dialogs* auf eine Stufe mit den Thesen einer Lehrschrift stellen dürfe und in Dialogäusserungen nicht die eigene Auffassung des Aristoteles finden könne. Dies gilt auch für den Versuch einer Uminterpretation des aristotelischen Seelenlehre durch A.P. Bos, soweit sie auf einer entsprechenden Interpretation des *Eudemos* aufbaut."

ings to have a different kind of content than others. Hence, it is out of the question that Aristotle himself intended some of his works to target a broader audience and to be less serious or scientific than others.[9]

When, therefore, Aristotle himself employs the term *exôterikoi logoi* (without using a contrasting term), we will first have to search for a meaning of the term that conveys something about the content of these discourses. Just as *physikoi logoi* and *èthikoi logoi* are treatises on physical and ethical subjects respectively, so *exôterikoi logoi* will have to be taken as treatises "on that which lies (more) outside (our experiential reality)." It cannot be that Aristotle himself would have used this term to denote texts intended for people "outside" the inner circle, and that in them he presented generally accepted opinions, *but not his own views*. Alexander of Aphrodisias could only defend this belief after attributing to Aristotle a philosophy at odds with what Aristotle had argued in his dialogues.

Writings "not intended for the real pupils" but for "outsiders" have never been ascribed to any authors other than Aristotle.[10]

The same applies to the expression *enkyklioi logoi*, which Aristotle uses a few times. This expression, too, has been repeatedly explained as referring to writings that circulated in the coterie of Aristotle's trusted pupils.[11] We should consider here that Aristotle introduced the theory of the *enkyklion sôma* (ether), and in his *Eudemus* probably contrasted the *enkyklios paideia* with "true philosophy." Here, *enkyklios* always has the sense of "moving in a circular course" and "surrounding." The *enkyklioi logoi* could also well be interpreted as dissertations on the empirical reality around us.

If the title *ta metaphysika* was also used by Aristotle, it will certainly have said something about the content of certain writings, and nothing about the order of scrolls on a library shelf. In any case, *metaphysika* may be interpreted as "treatises on that which is connected with physical reality," such as the soul and all living nature, of which Aristotle regularly says that it cannot exist without body (οὐκ ἄνευ of μετὰ σώματος φυσικοῦ).

---

9. Cf. F. Egermann, "Platonische Spätphilosophie und Platonismen bei Aristoteles," *Hermes* 87 (1959): 133–42. In contrast, cf. A. P. Bos, "*Exôterikoi Logoi* and *Enkyklioi Logoi*" (1989), 179–98.

10. Cf. A. P. Bos, "Why Is Aristotle Treated so Differently from Other Greek Philosophers?" *Elenchos* 29 (2008): 145–65.

11. See, for example, A. Jori, *Aristoteles Über den Himmel* (2009), 410: "Mit dem Ausdruck ἐγκύκλια φιλοσοφήματα (279a30–31) bezieht sich Aristoteles ohne Zweifel auf die ἐξωτερικοὶ λόγοι, d.h. auf seine mehrheitlich dialogischen veröffentlichen Schriften."

18

Intellect, Soul, and Entelechy
The Golden Rope

a. How Did Aristotle See the Connection between Intellect, Soul, and Entelechy?

We have concluded that Aristotle's philosophy follows from his critical analysis of Plato's views.[1] Where Plato talks about (1) "the soul" and (2) the divine Demiurge as World Maker, Aristotle proposes (1) a doctrine of an intellect plus a doctrine of an instrumental body guided by an entelechy, and (2) a theology of a divine Intellect as Leader (κοίρανος), General, and Ruler of the entire cosmos. He adds a theory of ether as a divine astral body clothing the divine celestial beings and serving as the instrumental body of their souls; and a theory of *pneuma* as the instrumental body of all mortal souls.

Whereas the souls of the celestial beings are eternal souls endowed with mind, the souls of beings living under the moon have merely a guiding role in the case of plants and animals, but the situation of human beings is special: initially, and for a long time, they are led by their soul as "first entelechy," but they may achieve rationality and a condition in which their intellect leads the way, like a sailor on his ship.[2]

---

1. See ch. 7 and §9h above.
2. Their souls have then achieved the condition of "awakened" souls (*Anim.* II 1, 412a23–4). See §10q above.

In the preceding chapters, we have seen that the traditional interpretation of Aristotle's philosophy is incorrect, because it interprets the term *organikon* as "equipped with organs," and subsequently misconstrues the notion of "entelechy" as "actuality," and moreover as actuality of the visible body. This obscures the essential role of *pneuma* in Aristotle's philosophy, and at the same time no longer recognizes the connection of every entelechy (as guiding principle) with the divine Intellect as Original Entelechy. Our inquiry is aimed at the rehabilitation of *pneuma* in Aristotle's philosophy, and of the entelechy as connected with all entelechies and with the divine Intellect. Aristotle's teleological view of the cosmos and all that lives in it can only be understood by recognizing the relation between the divine Intellect as Origin and all the entelechy-principles in all that lives, which principles are embodied in the special natural body of ether or *pneuma*.[3] However, crucial elements of Aristotle's alternative view are not clearly set out in the lecture treatises. Five may be mentioned:

1. the notion of "entelechy";[4]

2. the question of how an immaterial entelechy (soul) can be or become connected with a material instrumental body;

3. the question of how it is possible that a human being arrives at rational insight (and finally even at knowledge of the Transcendent);

4. the question of how it is possible that a plurality of intellects exists; and

5. the relation of intellect and soul.[5]

---

3. The study by M. E. M. P. J. Leunissen, *Explanation and Teleology in Aristotle's Science of Nature* (Cambridge: Cambridge University Press, 2010), does not solve the problems existing with regard to this subject, because it (1) gives teleology a role even on the level of the "inanimate elements"; (2) fails to recognize the necessary link between Aristotle's teleological view of nature and his talk about *pneuma* (and ether) as the "instrumental body" of the soul; and (3) has not understood the crucial significance of *Anim.* II 1, 412a23–4 on "the twofold entelechy."

4. C. V. Mirus, "The Metaphysical Roots of Aristotle's Teleology" (2003–04), 701 noticed: "It seems that nowhere in Aristotle's writings does he even give an informal general explanation of what he means by τέλος or τὸ οὗ ἕνεκα." See §10q above.

5. Aristotle calls the intellect "a different genus of soul" in *Anim.* II 2, 413b26.

More than once, for an explanation of the theme of the intellect, Aristotle refers to other discourses, sometimes described as a higher kind of discipline, "first philosophy."[6]

Yet we have been able to note a number of significant details which his extant works do contain:

- "man's nature is in many respects 'unfree' ";[7]

- there is a difference between a soul's "sleeping" and "awakened" state;[8]

- man's intellect comes from "outside";[9]

- man's intellect may possess the same knowledge that God possesses;[10]

- but man is only capable of this for a very short time;[11]

- man's capacity to know may be compared to a bat in relation to sunlight;[12]

- but the most significant point is that the soul (of a human being, like every other soul) is inextricably linked to an instrumental body, whereas the intellect (God's and man's) is not.[13]

---

6. Cf. *Phys.* II 2, 194b9–15. Perhaps also *Anim.* I 2, 404b19. Aristotle mentions in *Anim.* I 1, 402a21–2 that different genera of beings have different principles. Cf. E. Diamond, *Mortal Imitations of Divine Life* (2015), 10–11: "the indepth investigation of the nature of divine activity belongs to first philosophy (metaphysics or theology, while psychology belongs to the study of nature)."

7. *Metaph.* A 2, 982b29–30. δούλη should not be translated as "slavish," as C. Steel does in *Aristoteles, De Eerste Filosofie. Metaphysica Alpha, vertaald, ingeleid en van aantekeningen voorzien* (Groningen: Historische Uitgeverij, 2002), 47.

8. Cf. *Anim.* II 1, 412a23–4. Cf. §10q above.

9. Cf. *Gener. anim.* II 3, 736b27–8.

10. *Metaph.* A 2, 983a4–11.

11. *Metaph.* Λ 7, 1072b24–6.

12. *Metaph.* α 1, 993b9–11. The comparison of human souls to bats goes back to Homer, *Odyssey* 24, 1–9.

13. *Anim.* I 1, 403a7–11; II 2, 413b24–9.

b. Did the Dialogue *Eudemus* Provide a More Comprehensive View?

In his dialogue *Eudemus or On the Soul*, Aristotle talked about the soul and the soul's relation to the intellect, and about the question whether the soul is immortal. He also argued there that the greatest disaster for human beings, men and women alike, is "to be born."[14] In this connection he probably compared the condition of the human soul to the wretched situation of living prisoners who were tied to corpses by Etruscan robbers and abandoned to their fate.[15] This suggests that what Plato called "soul" was presented by Aristotle as an instrumental body governed by a (*nous*-principle as) entelechy, which drags around a coarse-material body for the term of its life until death follows.

In the *Eudemus*, Aristotle did not refer talk about the intellect to a discussion of a different, higher order. He may well have regarded the more comprehensive discourse on intellect and soul in the *Eudemus* as "first philosophy," in the sense that this discourse also treated the "exo"-terical perspective of transcendent/nonphysical reality. In that case, Aristotle may also have elucidated, through the demon Silenus as mouthpiece, why "being born" is the greatest disaster for man and how this process of being begotten and born should be understood and explained.

Though we cannot talk about this with absolute certainty, we must try to discuss the subject, in view of our fundamental conviction that there was only one Aristotelian philosophy, and not three or more, as W. Jaeger argued with regrettable success in 1923.[16]

We will, then, have to assume that Aristotle explained in the *Eudemus* how God in his being is utterly pure, transcendent Intellect; and that everything existing outside of God is permeated by the working power (*dynamis*) that proceeds from him. This working power manifests itself in materiality, which it uses as its instrument. The divine fine-material ether is the clothing that covers the divine working power in the sphere closest to God, and consequently the celestial beings are not perfect intellects like God, but intellects "shackled by the bonds of sleep," in other words, rational souls connected with an instrumental

---

14. Cf. Ps.-Plutarch, *Consolatio ad Apollonium* 115B-E = Arist. *Eudem.* fr. 6 Ross; 65 Gigon and A. P. Bos, "Silenus als Bemiddelaar van Gnostische Kennis in Aristoteles' Dialoog *Eudemus*" (Silenus as Mediator of Gnostic Knowledge in Aristotle's Dialogue *Eudemus*) (2016).

15. Cf. Arist. *Protrepticus* 10b Ross; 73 and 823 Gigon. And see A. P. Bos, "Aristotle on the Etruscan Robbers: a Core Text of 'Aristotelian' Dualism" (2003).

16. Jaeger's scientific hypothesis was in turn the result of Alexander of Aphrodisias's reinterpretation of Aristotle's philosophy. Cf. A. P. Bos, "'Development' in the Study of Aristotle" (2006).

body that possesses the highest degree of purity. The fine-material *pneuma* is the clothing that covers the divine working power in the sphere farther away from God, and differs in purity and quality depending on the extent to which it is more or less mixed with fire, air, water, or earth.

The difference in quality of the instrumental bodies that clothe the astral entelechies and the entelechies of mortal beings explains the difference in the effect of the working power that emanates from God. This helps us understand the thesis often found in later authors, that Aristotle took the Providence of God to be directly operative in the astral sphere alone, and only indirectly in the sublunary sphere.[17]

Plato had presented the living beings in the cosmos as products of the divine Demiurge, who intended to bring forth not just immortal but also mortal living beings, and to this end used a "mixed" substance for the souls, of the highest purity for the souls of the celestial beings and of a second- or third-rate quality for the souls of mortal creatures.[18] Aristotle indicated much more strictly than Plato that the difference between the divine Intellect and all entelechies of ensouled beings is based on the fact that ensouled beings "are clothed in a natural body,"[19] not a natural body that is alien to this guiding principle, but a body that possesses "community" with the guiding principle, like the female, "underlying" (*hypokeimenon*), with the male.

As in Plato's *Timaeus*, God himself is the cause of the existence of "serial eternity" in the sphere of mortal living creatures.[20] Generation requires both the male and the female principle.[21] But the male supplies only the *dynamis*. As the "underlying" and the matter, the female receives life, order, and form through this power.

Because God is pure Intellect, he is beyond conation (*orexis*), desire, and will. Everything outside of him, characterized by psychic reality, is always driven by *orexis*.

c. A Titanic Meaning-Perspective

Aristotle's philosophy clearly displays a hierarchy of levels of being and knowledge, whose apex is formed by God as transcendent Intellect. Did Aristotle

---

17. The "Non-Sublunary Providence (N.S.P.) doctrine," as R. W. Sharples (2002), 22 calls it.
18. Pl. *Tim.* 34b10–42e3.
19. In this theory, Aristotle thinks through Plato's proposition in *Phaedrus* 246b6: "all soul has the care for all that which is soulless [ψυχὴ πᾶσα παντὸς ἐπιμελεῖται τοῦ ἀψύχου]." Plato could never have said this about the intellect!
20. Cf. *Gener. Corr.* II 10, 336b27–34 and §3e above.
21. Cf. *Gener. anim.* II 1, 732a1–3.

make an attempt to explain the existence of extra-divine reality? We have established that extra-divine reality is connected with God because he is the cause of being in the sphere of generation and decay.[22] But it is equally clear that, for Aristotle, extra-divine reality cannot be the result of God's creative will: God cannot be a Creator and he has no Will because "to will" belongs to the instrumental body of a (rational) soul but not to an intellect.[23]

In Aristotle's view, an instrumental body and, on an even lower level, a mortal, coarse-material body is a negative, or even a crippling burden. He therefore talked in terms of "unfreedom," "being shackled by the bonds of sleep," "eclipse of the mind," loss of divinity and perfection and consequently a desire (*orexis*, in the sense of "nostalgia," the desire to return home)[24] for true being and divinity.

Although Aristotle talked about the "*nous* of the soul" as a human potential for achieving full knowledge of God and perfect bliss, he also talked about the difference between God and mortals—with their precarious potential—in terms harking back to the Orphic myth of Kronos and the Titans. The ancient anthropomorphic conceptions of the gods and their relationships were always about the power of the supreme divine king and the loss of this power due to revolution. The upshot was always loss of divine status and incarceration in Tartarus, the abode of Death, where immortal gods are eternally tormented by their yearning for a return of absolute hegemony and the divine bliss of old.

In this way Aristotle discussed:

1. Intellect in absolute freedom and purity;

2. Intellect of a divine astral being fettered by an ethereal instrumental body;

3. Human intellect shackled by a pneumatic instrumental body and by a coarse-material body;

4. Vegetable or animal guiding principle chained by an inferior pneumatic instrumental body and a coarse-material mortal body

---

22. Cf. again *Gener. corr.* II 10, 336b27–34 and §3e above.

23. *Anim.* III 10, 433b19–20. There is no jealousy or envy in God either (*Metaph.* A 2, 983a2–3). Plato, *Tim.* 29e says the same about the Demiurge and finds the explanation for this in God's goodness. Aristotle's denial is based on his position that jealousy and feelings in general are impossible without a fine-material body (*Anim.* I 1, 403a16–7). Cf. E. Diamond, *Mortal Imitations of Divine Life* (2015), 22–23 hits the mark by saying: "Aristotle never attempts to explain how or why the first principle produces what is other than it, but rather assumes the existence of the world and all its distinctions and simply tries to account for how it is governed by this principle."

24. Cf. G. Méautis, "L'Orphisme dans l'*Eudème* d'Aristote," *Revue des Études Anciennes* 57 (1955): 254, 261.

that as first entelechy (autopilot) organizes the life of plants and animals.

In Silenus's revelation on why "being born" is the greatest catastrophe for man, he probably talked about the difference between God and all extra-divine levels participating in the divine. Here, he will have used the Hesiodic motif (also a favorite theme in Plato) that crime is always followed by punishment.[25] The blame is never on God, but always on the creatures who break out of the intimate unity with the Origin by endeavoring but failing to imitate or equal God, and that consequently become alienated from God's essence, though they continue to participate in their original divine nature.

The great difference between the celestial beings and man must also have to do with the crime of the divine beings who, on the level of rational celestial beings, were attracted by the coarse-material world that the cosmic archons produced.

Such a mythical story may well have provided insight into a cosmic hierarchy. But Silenus cannot have explained the existence of a reality covering or shackling divine intelligent beings who withdrew from the divine fullness of being. For this implies the existence alongside and outside God of a less divine, fine–material reality that seduces divine beings through attraction and thus entangles them in a desire (which itself possesses a [fine-] material nature, according to Aristotle).

The internal contradiction is obvious: a purely intellectual being is exclusively oriented to pure intelligible reality and cannot be attracted by an extra-divine reality, because desire and conation cannot be connected with a transcendent Intellect,[26] but always presuppose a form of materiality, which implies a degeneration of intellectuality. However, there cannot exist a fine-material reality outside God of which God himself is not the cause.

This means that the contradiction can be removed only to a certain extent if it is ultimately located in the Origin itself. That is the "split in the divine," which caused much controversy in the later tradition. It is what Aristotle did in *Physics* I 9 by presenting matter as the female and "underlying" and as the principle aimed at the formal cause, and what the author of *On the Cosmos* 7 did by quoting an Orphic poem in which Zeus is conceived of as androgynous.

However, the same philosopher always presented the female as a defective product (πήρωμα) of male procreativity. That is why, although the androgyny

---

25. Cf. Pl. *Phaedrus* 248c6–9d2; *Leges* X, 904c6–e4.

26. It is interesting to see that E. Diamond at the end of the "Conclusion" of his intriguing new book *Mortal Imitations of Divine Life. The Nature of the Soul in Aristotle's De Anima* (2015), 251 52 adds an Appendix entitled "A Qualification about the Desire of Theoretical Mind," in which he touches on this ultimate problem.

of the Principle of Origin is necessary for realizing a complete imitation of the spiritual *plèrôma*, androgyny is not held up as an ideal, but remains something to be transcended in Aristotle's conception, as a form of *elleipsis* and as the result of *pèrôsis*. In later times this is expressed as "the female must become male."

19

Aristotle on Life-Bearing *Pneuma* and on God as Begetter of the Cosmos

Brief Survey of Results

a. The Word *Organikon* as Crowbar and Lever for Changing our View of Aristotle's Philosophy

In this book, I present the results of a project that I started twenty years ago, when I suddenly realized that the words *sôma organikon* (σῶμα ὀργανικόν) in Aristotle's definition of "the soul" should not be explained as "body equipped with organs," but as "instrumental body."[1] This proposal by L. A. Kosman[2] has been accepted by a growing number of experts and today the traditional translation is no longer defended. As far as I know, all the translations and commentaries published after 2000 translate *sôma organikon* as "an instrumental body," "a body that is the instrument (of the soul)."[3]

The text of this chapter was, with small changes, presented as paper at the Worldcongress "Aristotle—2400 Years," held in Thessaloniki, Greece, May 2016.

1. On that occasion, I added to the proofs of G. Reale and A. P. Bos, *Il Trattato Sul Cosmo per Alessandro Attribuito ad Aristotele* (Milano: Vita e Pensiero, 1995), 288, the remark: "Forse possiamo trarre addirittura la conclusione—almeno come ipotesi—che la definizione dell'anima in *De Anima* II 1, 412b5 . . . debba essere interpretata come segue: l'anima è l' <<entelechia>> del <<pneuma>> che è l'organo dell'anima."

2. He made this suggestion in his "Animals and Other Beings in Aristotle" (1987), 376.

3. Cf. S. Menn, "Aristotle's Definition of Soul and the Programme of the *De Anima*," *Oxford Studies in Ancient Philosophy* 22 (2002): 110 n. 40; L. P. Gerson, *Aristotle and Other Platonists*

There are still people who fail to attach major consequences to this correction and continue to assume that Aristotle describes the soul as the first entelechy of the visible body. For me, however, this insight meant that Aristotle's definition of soul, already from the days of the famous commentator Alexander of Aphrodisias, had been misinterpreted in the context of an unhistorical interpretation of Aristotle's entire philosophy. We often say that the early commentators were closer to Aristotle's Greek, and that Alexander of Aphrodisias was an "orthodox" Aristotelian. But on this point he was demonstrably mistaken and predecessors came closer to the truth about Aristotle's view of the soul.

From that time, I developed into an anti-Jaegerian and an antidevelopmentalist and started to investigate whether "instrumental body" in Aristotle may in fact refer not to the visible body, but to a different kind of body. And I started to suspect that the criticism that Aristotle levels in *On the Soul* I against Plato's doctrine of soul as the principle of self-motion was in fact the preparation for this challenging proposition.

b. *Pneuma* as Instrumental Natural Body of the Soul

Because Aristotle's definition talks about a "natural body" that is the soul's instrument, I began to investigate whether Aristotle may have been alluding to *pneuma*, which in any case several of his writings closely connect with soul and with living and ensouled creatures. The reason that Aristotle avoided mentioning the word *pneuma* in his definition of "soul" and instead used the description *instrumental body of the soul* may have been that "ether" is also an instrumental body of the soul (in the sphere of the divine celestial beings). *Pneuma* holds this position in the sphere of entities living under the moon. It

---

(Ithaca: Cornell University Press, 2005), 136; R. Polansky, *Aristotle's De Anima* 161; K. Corcilius, *Streben und Bewegen.* (2008), 31: "werkzeughaft"; F. Buddensiek, "Aristoteles' Zirbeldrüse?," 311; T. K. Johansen, *The Powers of Aristotle's Soul*, 9, 12, 120; C. Shields, "The Priority of Soul in Aristotle's *De Anima*: Mistaking Categories?," 282–83: "The word has this meaning [i.e., 'equipped with organs'] nowhere in Aristotle"; R. W. Sharples, *Peripatetic Philosophy 200 BC–AD 200. An Introduction and Collection of Sources in Translation* (2010), xi: "[I]t has increasingly come to be realised that many doctrines which have for nearly two millennia been regarded by students *and critics* of Aristotle as central to his philosophy are in fact interpretations by Alexander of Aphrodisias, and only questionably held by Aristotle himself."

may also be designated as "ship" (πλοῖον),[4] as "vehicle" (ὄχημα)[5] of the soul in the two meanings of "chariot" and "ship," but also as "lever" (μοχλός)[6] for moving the visible body, and as "winding mechanism" (αὐτόματον).[7]

Next, the hypothesis that the instrumental body of the soul refers to *pneuma*, which Aristotle repeatedly describes as an "instrument" (*organon*) of nature or of the soul and as the carrier of psychic heat, guided me toward an intensive study of Aristotle's doctrine on the reproduction of human beings, animals, and plants.

c. The Crucial Role of *Pneuma* in Reproduction and Spontaneous Generation

The most striking aspect of *pneuma* is that, according to Aristotle, it must be necessarily present in the semen of male animals belonging to higher species and in the menstrual fluid of females. It also plays an essential role in the processes of reproduction and spontaneous generation, not just in animals but also in the world of plants and trees, where Aristotle also speaks of "life" and "being ensouled."

It is therefore significant that he draws attention in On the Soul II 1, 412b27 to "semen and seed" (σπέρμα καὶ καρπός) as instruments of the soul and possessors of soul (including the soul-*parts*, in the case of animal or human semen), though they do not yet possess life in reality but "in power." For the standard interpretation of Aristotle's theory of soul, the remark about "semen and seeds" as "possessing soul" was absurd because in semen the soul cannot possibly be connected with "a body equipped with organs." For those who question or reject the standard interpretation, it is a strong indication that Alexander of Aphrodisias's hylomorphistic explanation was incorrect. This radical change of perspective is summed up by Aristotle in his slogan "A human being begets a human being."[8] From the moment of fertilization, the *eidos* (as intelligible plan) is present in *pneuma*, which is receptive to it.

---

4. Cf. *Anim.* II 1, 413a9.
5. Cf. *Motu anim.* 7, 701b4; b 11: τὸ ἁμάξιον.
6. Cf. *Phys.* VIII 6, 259b18–20.
7. Cf. *Motu anim.* 7, 701b2; b10; *Gener. anim.* II 1, 734b10; b13.
8. *Phys.* II 1, 193b6–7 and b12; 2, 194b13; 7, 198a24–7; III 2, 202a11–2; *Gener. corr.* II 6, 333b7–14; *Part. anim.* I 1, 640a25–6; II 1, 646a33; *Gener. anim.* II 1, 735a20–22; *Metaph.* Z 7, 1032a24–5; 8, 1033b30–32; Θ 8, 1049b24–26; Λ 3, 1070a5–8; 1070a26–8; 4, 1070b32–4; N 5, 1092a15–7; *Eudem. Eth.* II 6, 1222b15–8.

d. *Pneuma* Is not Breath but the Life-Bearing Spirit in Animals and Plants

By drawing attention to the semen of animals and seeds of plants and trees, Aristotle makes it clear that he also attributes "life" to plants and trees and regards them as ensouled beings; and that he sees similarities between plants and animals as regards digestion, nutrition, and reproduction. This means that, for Aristotle, life and being ensouled do not begin when a living creature is born, but before that, when fertilization takes place. Animal semen and vegetable seed, but also the resulting plants and animals (even in their embryonic phase) and fish (which Aristotle believes do not possess a respiratory system), therefore contain soul *and* an instrumental body of the soul. However, this implies that in Aristotle's biological writings the notion of *pneuma*, because it is an essential component of semen and seeds, and because it is the carrier of vital heat and even of "psychic" heat, does not (exclusively or preferably) have the meaning "breath," but has been expanded into the notion of "life-bearing *pneuma*" and "vital heat" and "psychic heat." Respiration does not produce *pneuma*, but the heat of *pneuma* makes respiration necessary for some animals!

e. Aristotle's Innovative View of *Pneuma* Substantiated in His *De Spiritu*

Given that nobody before Aristotle had defended such a view of *pneuma*, and given that Plato's dialogues, especially the *Timaeus*, indicated the moment of birth as the moment of the soul's entry, and respiration as the basic process of all vital functions, it was essential for Aristotle to conduct a debate with his teacher on what can be called the real carrier of life and soul. He did this in the treatise *De Spiritu*, a discussion with Plato and his predecessors on *pneuma* as the instrumental body of the soul.[9] Unfortunately, this brief work has been denied to Aristotle in the later tradition, because it is presented as a debate with one "Aristogenes."[10] In my view, however, this figure is to be identified

---

9. Cf. A. P. Bos and R. Ferwerda, *Aristotle, On the Life-Bearing Spirit (De Spiritu)* (2008).

10. Cf. W. Jaeger, "Das *Pneuma* im Lykeion" (1913). In A. L. Carbone, *Aristotele, L'Anima e il Corpo. Parva Naturalia.* (2003), and in the new handbook by C. Rapp and K. Corcilius (2011) it is not even mentioned. See now P. Gregoric, O. Lewis, and M. Kuhar, "The Substance of *De Spiritu*" (2015); P. Gregoric and O. Lewis, "Pseudo-Aristotelian *De Spiritu*: A New Case against Authenticity" (2015), 159–67; O. Lewis and P. Gregoric, "The Context of *De Spiritu*" (2015), 125–49.

with "the son begotten by Ariston," that is, Plato. In the same playful way Plato himself had used the word *artitelès* (ἀρτιτελής) in the *Phaedrus* 251a2 to hint at young Aristotle.

f. Semen Is the Carrier of a Guiding Power (*Dynamis*)

Semen, therefore, plays a role in reproduction; and, according to Aristotle, semen must contain *pneuma*. Indeed, *pneuma* is indispensable even in "spontaneous" generation. But in his great treatise *Generation of Animals*, Aristotle also insists that reproduction is not about *pneuma* but about the power (δύναμις) that it transfers. In reproduction, the male does not contribute a material substance to the embryo but only a power.[11] This is a very special feature of Aristotle's theory of reproduction, that he views the role of the male partner in the process of reproduction as the transmission of a life-generating power (*dynamis*) to the menstrual fluid of the female partner. Male semen is only and exclusively an instrument for passing on this life-generating power, also specified as the soul-principle. The material substance constituting semen has no participation in the growing embryo.

But the begetter plays no further role, either. The development of the new specimen (of the same species as the male and female) is solely activated by the power transferred to the menstrual fluid of the partner. Aristotle applied this ground-breaking insight to all that lives and functions in the sublunary sphere, from the highest living beings to the lowly products of spontaneous generation. It means that the reproductive process conveys an (immaterial) operative rational form-principle to a form-less but form-desiring substance appropriate to this operative force.

g. Not the Moment of Birth but the Moment of Fertilization Is Crucial

We have already indicated one important point here on which Aristotle criticized his teacher: new life is not formed by the entry of an immaterial soul in a baby that starts to breathe. No, new life is formed at the moment when menstrual fluid is fertilized. From this moment it is clear what the result of

---

11. Cf. J. G. Lennox, "Teleology, Change, and Aristotle's Theory of Spontaneous Generation" (1982), 221.

this fertilization will be: a new specimen of the same species as the begetter and his female partner. And in the embryo, from this moment of fertilization, the soul is active as power and guides its instrumental body, the vital heat of *pneuma*. However, the soul is not the principle of motion for this new living creature, but the principle that *controls* the motion of the instrumental body. For the soul uses its instrumental body as a craftsman uses his tools.[12]

h. Aristotle's Strict Separation between Intellect and Soul

So far, we have determined that the generation of a new living being is explained by Aristotle as the result of a power (*dynamis*) that is transferred to the *pneuma* of the female's menstrual fluid, and which then uses this *pneuma* as an instrument for realizing the *eidos*, the blueprint for the new specimen, and allowing this new specimen to function. According to Aristotle, the soul itself is not a body, but it is always connected with a body, and it is the entelechy of this instrumental body, but also a power (*dynamis*). How are we to understand this notion of soul as power (*dynamis*)?

This is best approached as the second point of criticism that Aristotle urged against Plato. Aristotle believed that Plato's concept of "soul" was profoundly ambivalent and internally contradictory.[13] According to Aristotle, what Plato considers to be most important in "the soul" is not "soul" but "intellect." And what Aristotle calls "soul" is (although in itself immaterial and immortal, as Plato said) always inextricably bound up with a "natural body" and, as regards animals and plants, mortal. A meaningful, rational philosophy ought to distinguish between intellect on the one hand and soul on the other. Not the soul "knows" or "contemplates" the Ideas, but the intellect.[14] However, matters such as perception and setting in motion are not possible for something immaterial; they are possible only for a principle that is connected with a (special) body.

But how is the relation of the intellect to the soul? In Plato, in his myth of the *Phaedrus*, this is a *guiding* influence of the charioteer who stands *still* on a chariot that is *moved* by two horses. Aristotle attributed a *guiding power*

---

12. *Anim.* I 3, 407b25–7. That is why translations of *entelecheia* as "actuality," "activity," "realization," 'réalisation,' "verwezenlijking," "fulfillment," "complete reality," "verwerkelijking," "having its end in itself," "Wirklichkeit," etc. are misleading.

13. Cf. Ps.-Hippolytus, *Adversus Omnes Haereses* I 20, 3–6. Arist. *On Philosophy* fr. 26 Ross; 25, 1 Gigon, where I read, "*multa turbat a magistro* uno *dissentiens.*"

14. Aristotle argued in his dialogue *Eudemus* fr. 2 Ross; 58 Gigon that Plato's arguments for the immortality of the soul should rather be understood as arguments for the immortality of the intellect.

to the intellect and to the soul as entelechy. The soul as entelechy uses its body by guiding it as its instrument. Just as the charioteer guides his horses via the reins that he holds, so the soul leads its pneumatic body by keeping it oriented to its goal. Aristotle's neologism *entelecheia* is his alternative to Plato's "chariot-driving" (*hèniocheia/* ἡνιοχεία). It should be understood as "Goal-Pointing System" (G.P.S.).

The introduction of the fifth element (and with it the introduction of *pneuma* in the sublunary sphere) as a body to be used by the soul/entelechy is the consequence of Aristotle's fundamental criticism of Plato's doctrine of the soul as the principle of (loco-) motion and his doctrine of respiration as the basic process of life.

Now, the notorious chapter II 1 of Aristotle's *On the Soul* contains a sentence about the twofold meaning of "entelechy." This sentence has always been misunderstood. Aristotle meant this sentence to express: "for in being soul there is sleep and waking."[15] This implies that in a plant and an animal the soul works as "first" entelechy, that is to say, in "sleeping" mode, as if on automatic pilot. But in an adult human being, the soul works as "waking" intellect, because this soul, in rationality, makes choices and directs the existence of the living being. However, all souls, in both conditions, direct their instrumental bodies, because all are distinguishing and deciding and leading principles, and in this regard show a greater or lesser resemblance to the Intellect.[16]

i. Aristotle's Theology of the All-Governing Intellect

So far, we have mainly looked at Aristotle's innovations in the fields of psychology and biology. But what was his view of the cosmos, and what role does God play in it? Another question that urges itself: Why didn't Aristotle ever

---

15. *Anim.* II 1, 412a22–3: ἐν γὰρ τῷ ὑπάρχειν τὴν ψυχὴν καὶ ὕπνος καὶ ἐγρήγορσίς ἐστιν. Cf. §10q above.

16. *Anim.* II 4, 415b16–7. This is the foundation of Aristotle's teleological view of nature. On its basis, we may overcome the pessimism of D. Sedley, "Teleology, Aristotelian and Platonic," 6: "Pretty well everything in nature has a purpose, despite the fact that no intelligence either conceived that purpose or administers it"; Allan Gotthelf, "Aristotle's Conception of Final Causality," repr. with addition in *Philosophical Issues in Aristotle's Biology*, ed. A. Gotthelf and J. G. Lennox (1987), 204: "One would expect to find, somewhere in the vast Aristotelian corpus, a thorough analysis and explicit definition of this notion. Surprisingly, it is not there to be found. Readers of the corpus will search in vain for a detailed analysis of what it is to be (or come to be) for the sake of something"; I. Düring, *Aristoteles* (1966), 552: "Sobald Bedingungszusammenhänge vorliegen, betont er, dass das Naturgeschehen von teleologischer Formbestimmtheit gesteuert wird; wie es gesteuert wird, sagt er *nie*."

produce a great alternative to Plato's *Timaeus*? Here, first of all, we need to point to the obvious fact that during his lifetime Aristotle wrote magnificent dialogues that have been lost.[17] But in his extant writings it is also clear that he presented God as pure Intellect and as the source of all power, which preserves the cosmos and all that lives.[18] The notion of the "dependence" of all things on a first Principle is underlined by Aristotle in *Motion of Animals* 4, 699b32–700a6, with a reference to the famous passage in *Iliad* 8 on "the Golden Rope," which ends with the words: "if it depends from an Origin which is unmovable [εἰ ἐξ ἀκινήτου ἤρτηται ἀρχῆς]."[19] This Intellect is free of all corporeality, it is unmoved and unchanging. Yet it is the great Governor, the Ruler and Leader of all things. God is un-willing (because "willing" is a matter of the soul and its soul-body), but nevertheless God remains the Chief Intelligence Officer. For Aristotle, will has been replaced by rational law.

j. God as Begetter of Life through his Life-Generating Power

In my view, Aristotle's blueprint for human, animal, and vegetable reproduction also covers God's relationship with the cosmos, over which he wields absolute dominion. In Aristotle, God is the great leader (κοίρανος) and *oikonomos* of the universal system, who preserves the dependent cosmos through his all-pervading Power.

How is this to be understood? A work we could consult here is *On the Cosmos* (*De Mundo*). Recently someone has said that this work was composed by an obscure author from the early imperial age to make up for the lack of an Aristotelian equivalent to Plato's *Timaeus*![20] It is clear in this work that

---

17. Cf. A. P. Bos, *Cosmic and Meta-cosmic Theology in Aristotle's Lost Dialogues* (1989). Alexander of Aphrodisias voiced the opinion that Aristotle's dialogues did not represent his own philosophy! For W. Jaeger, they represented a Platonizing and immature philosophy.

18. See also *Polit.* VII 4, 1326a31–3: "But a very great multitude cannot be orderly: to introduce order in such a number is the work of a divine power—of such a power as holds together the universe [ὁ δὲ λίαν ὑπερβάλλων ἀριθμὸς οὐ δύναται μετέχειν τάξεως· θείας γὰρ δὴ τοῦτο δυνάμεως ἔργον, ἥτις καὶ τόδε συνέχει τὸ πᾶν]." Cf. §2g above.

19. See also *Cael.* I 9, 279a28–30; *Metaph.* Λ 7, 1072b13; Γ 2, 1003b16–7. Cf. M. Matthen, "The Holistic Presuppositions of Aristotle's Cosmology," *Oxford Studies in Ancient Philosophy* 20 (2001): 171–99. In a passage from *On the Cosmos*, a work addressed to Alexander of Macedonia (with whom Aristotle had read Homer's *Iliad* in Mieza, near the "Cave of the Nymphs"), Aristotle compares the cardinal importance of God for the cosmos with that of the Persian Great King for his empire, and in using the words *the supreme* and *on the highest peak* refers subtly to this text from *Iliad* 8, which Alexander must have relished.

20. Cf. T. Kukkonen, "On Aristotle's World," 326–27.

the author rejects Plato's concept of the Demiurge.[21] Instead, he posits the divine, self-sufficient Intellect on the one hand and the Power (*Dynamis*) that emanates from him and pervades the entire cosmos on the other. This aspect of *On the Cosmos* agrees entirely with Aristotle's very special theory about the controlling power in the process of reproduction.[22] And, significantly, the author avoids the names of "Demiurge" and "Father" there, choosing instead the term *Begetter* (γενέτωρ). The distinction between God and his efficient Power is the result of Aristotle's criticism of Plato's doctrine of the World Soul and of the world-creating Demiurge.

He compares the power emanating from God with the power operative in a winding mechanism that carries out its constructor's plan. This comparison connects the cosmo-theology of *On the Cosmos* with the theory of procreation in *Generation of Animals*, where the power functional in an embryo is compared to the drive mechanism of an automaton.[23] Once we have properly understood the structure of Aristotle's theory of reproduction in *Generation of Animals*, we can no longer maintain that the doctrine of God as the "Begetter" of all life through his all-pervasive Power, as found in *On the Cosmos*, is un-Aristotelian.[24]

k. "Everything Full of Soul"

There is a remarkable connection between two texts from acknowledged Aristotelian writings and one from the controversial work *On the Cosmos*. In *On the Soul* I 5, 411a7–9, Aristotle refers to Plato's doctrine of the World Soul in the *Timaeus*, according to which the soul is intermingled in the entire universe. Aristotle repudiates this, because it would mean that the Intellect is also

---

21. According to Aristotle, Plato's Demiurge is wrongly modeled on the image of a human craftsman, who first draws up a plan and then introduces order into material available to him. Cf. *Cael.* I 10, 279b32–80a10. Consequently, the Demiurge does not satisfy Aristotle's doctrine of the absolute unchangeability of the Principle of Origin.

22. Interestingly, Alexander of Aphrodisias in his own work *On the Cosmos*, passed down only in Arabic, fully accepted this distinction between God's essence and power, as he did the authenticity of Aristotle's *On the Cosmos*. Cf. C. Genequand, *Alexander of Aphrodisias, On the Cosmos* (2001), 6, 17–19. Genequand himself follows P. Moraux and the modern tradition by speaking of "the pseudo-Aristotelian *On the Cosmos*."

23. *Gener. anim.* II 1, 734b4–17.

24. M. Wilson, *Structure and Method in Aristotle's* Meteorologica: *A More Disorderly Nature* (2013), 73, concluded: "One of the most remarkable developments of the last thirty years in scholarship on Aristotle has been the successful reintegration of his biological works into the mainstream of his corpus." This "development" should be completed by recognizing the link between Aristotle's biology and his theology.

intermingled in the entire cosmos, and because something immaterial cannot be "mingled" with natural bodies. (Aristotle is convinced that the soul is always located in the center of a living being.) In this context, he says that Thales of Miletus was thinking of something similar when he said that "everything is full of gods." In *Generation of Animals* III 11, 762a18–21, Aristotle alludes to this theme. He says there that earth contains water and water contains *pneuma* and all *pneuma* contains psychic heat, so that in a certain sense "everything is full of soul." That is to say, in explaining his alternative to Plato's doctrine of soul, Aristotle puts forward his doctrine of *pneuma*, which can be controlled and used by the soul. This *pneuma* pervades all things by being "mixed" with other natural bodies[25] in the sublunary sphere. The soul itself, however, is not mixed with earth and water, but is the "controller" of the *pneuma* appropriate to it.[26]

Precisely, the author of *On the Cosmos* 6, 397b16–20 cites one of the ancients as saying that "everything is full of gods." Thales's maxim is called to mind there in order to be fundamentally corrected: not God's essence is everywhere, but God's power (*dynamis*). We are then told that this power of the divine Intellect manifests itself in the divine element of the stars and in the *pneuma* of all sublunary living beings.

For an openminded observer, Aristotle's criticism of Plato's soul doctrine thus led to an immaterial principle that has a controlling effect on a receptive instrumental body (ether in the astral sphere and *pneuma* in the sublunary sphere). The quality of the guiding principles is correlate to the quality of their instrumental bodies. But the guiding principles are connected with the transcendent Intellect, just as the power of a magnet is connected with the source of this power.

1. Aristotle on the Male and the Female

If we look back from a certain distance at Aristotle's philosophy as a whole, it must strike us that he speaks much more positively about material reality than Plato. For Plato, there was always a world of Ideas and another, constantly changing, non-scientifically knowable, material reality. Sometimes he characterized this material reality as a "prison," an abode of custody for the soul; and sometimes as an object of its attention and care.[27]

In his surviving works, Aristotle never explains to what the natural bodies owe their existence. But he calls them "complete" (*teleion*) and judges their

---

25. *Spir.* 9, 485b18.
26. *Motu anim.* 10, 703a36–b2.
27. In *Alcibiades* I 130a, it is said that the soul "uses" the body! But this dialogue has often been denied to Plato.

quality so positively that they are "usable" (*organikon*) for soul-principles. At the highest level, Aristotle will always talk about the divine Intellect, "separate from" and "free of" corporeality. However, he introduces a continuous chain of guiding principles in all that lives, as the form-giving, male soul-principles or entelechies, as opposed to the female "underlying" principles of matter.[28]

Everything that exists below the divine Intellect is characterized by "desire" (*orexis*), just as the female desires the male.[29] The divine Intellect is so utterly self-sufficient that it does not have any "desire." Yet, all the "female" depends on the Intellect.

We should therefore note that Aristotle praises the natural complementarity of the female and the male and considers them both to be equally necessary as "principles of generation" in all that exists.[30] Against this background, it is understandable that *On the Cosmos* 7, 401b2 approvingly cites an Orphic poem with the remarkable words:

Zeus is a man, Zeus an immortal maid

Ζεὺς ἄρσην γένετο, Ζεὺς ἄμβροτος ἔπλετο νύμφη.[31]

Nevertheless, the fact remains that the male takes precedence. It is the symbol of the fullness of being (*plèrôma*). The female is characterized by a "deficiency" (*pèrôma*). Ultimately, the soul must transcend itself toward the intellect; the female must become male.[32]

---

28. *Phys.* I 9, 192a31: "For my definition of matter is just this—the first underlying of each thing [λέγω γὰρ ὕλην τὸ πρῶτον ὑποκείμενον ἑκάστῳ]." For Aristotle, there is always a sexual metaphor in the term "the subject," "the underlying." The Latin translation *material materies* has retained this connotation.

29. *Physics* I 9, 192a13–9.

30. *Gener. anim.* II 1, 732a1–3. On this text, see A. P. Bos, "Aristotle on God as Principle of Genesis," 373–74.

31. In the same work, *On the Cosmos* 5, 396b7–11, the author, who in any case wants to appear Aristotelian, has a strikingly positive appreciation of the conjunction of opposites. He sees it as evidence of the "harmonious community" (*homonoia*) in nature and the cosmos: "It may perhaps be that nature has a liking for contraries and evolves harmony out of them and not out of similarities (just as she joins the male and the female together and not members of the same sex), and has devised the original harmonious community by means of contraries and not similarities [Ἴσως δὲ τῶν ἐναντίων ἡ φύσις γλίχεται καὶ ἐκ τούτων ἀποτελεῖ τὸ σύμφωνον, οὐκ ἐκ τῶν ὁμοίων, ὥσπερ ἀμέλει τὸ ἄρρεν συνήγαγε πρὸς τὸ θῆλυ καὶ οὐχ ἑκάτερον πρὸς τὸ ὁμόφυλον, καὶ τὴν πρώτην ὁμόνοιαν διὰ τῶν ἐναντίων συνῆψεν, οὐ διὰ τῶν ὁμοίων]" (trans. E. S. Forster, in J. Barnes [1984], vol. 1, 633).

32. Cf. *Gospel of Thomas* logion 114, and M. W. Meyer, "*Gospel of Thomas* Logion 114 Revisited," in *For the Children, Perfect Instruction. Studies in Honor of H.-M. Schenke*, ed. H.-G. Bethge, a.o. (Leiden: Brill, 2002), 101–11.

Bibliography

Ackrill, J. L. "Aristotle's Definitions of *Psyche*." *Proceedings of the Aristotelian Society* 73 (1972–73): 119–33.
Alexandri Aphrodisiensis, Quaestiones, De Fato, De Mixtione. Edited by I. Bruns. *C.A.G.* Supplem. 2, 2. Berolini: Typis Georgii Reimer, 1892.
Alexandri Aphrodisiensis Scripta Minora. De Anima liber cum Mantissa. Edited by I. Bruns. *C.A.G.* Supplem. 2, 1. Berolini: Typis Georgii Reimer, 1887.
Alexandri in Librum De Sensu Commentarium. Edited by P. Wendland. *C.A.G.* 3, 1. Berolini: Typis Georgii Reimer, 1901.
Althoff, J. "Das Konzept der Generativen Wärme bei Aristoteles." *Hermes* 120 (1992): 181–93.
———. *Warm, Kalt, Flüssig, und Fest bei Aristoteles. Die Elementarqualitäten in den Zoologischen Schriften*. Stuttgart: Franz Steiner Verlag, 1992.
Anagnostopoulos, A. *A Companion to Aristotle*. Malden, MA: Wiley-Blackwell, 2009.
Anderson, Ø. "Aristotle on Sense Perception in Plants." *Symbolae Osloenses* 51 (1976): 81–85.
Annas, J. *Hellenistic Philosophy of Mind* Berkeley/Los Angeles: University of California Press, 1992.
Apelt, O. *Aristoteles De Anima libri III*, recognovit G. Biehl (1896). Editio tertia. Leipzig: B.G. Teubner, 1926.
Apostle, H. G. *Aristotle's Physics, Translated with Commentaries and Glossary*. Grinnell, IA: The Peripatetic Press, 1969.
Aubenque, P. *Le Problème de l'Être chez Aristote*. Paris: Presses Universitaires de France, 1962.
Bakker, F. *Three Studies in Epicurean Cosmology*. Dissertation, University of Utrecht, 2010.
Balme, D. M. "'Ἄνθρωπος ἄνθρωπον γεννᾷ. Human is Generated by Human." In *The Human Embryo. Aristotle and the Arabic and European Traditions*, edited by G. R. Dunstan, 20–31. Exeter: University of Exeter Press, 1990.
———. *Aristotle's De Partibus Animalium I and De Generatione Animalium I (with Passages from II, 1–3)*. Translated with Notes. Oxford: Clarendon Press, 1972.
———. "The Development of Biology in Aristotle and Theophrastus: Theory of Spontaneous Generation." *Phronesis* 7 (1962): 91–104.

Baltussen, H. "Wehrli's Edition of Eudemus of Rhodes: The Physical Fragments from Simplicius' Commentary *On Aristotle's Physics*." In *Eudemus of Rhodes* edited by I. Bodnár and W. W. Fortenbaugh, 127–56. New Brunswick, NJ: Transactions Publishers, 2002.

Barbotin, E. *La Théorie Aristotélicienne de l'Intellect d'après Thnéophraste*. Louvain/Paris: Publications Universitaires, 1954.

Barnes, J. "Review of G. Reale, *Aristotele. Trattato Sul cosmo per Alessandro* (1974)." *Classical Review* 27 (1977): 40–43.

———. "Review of S. Everson (1997)." *Classical Review* 49 (1999): 120–22.

———, ed., *The Complete Works of Aristotle. The Revised Oxford Translation*. 2 vols. Princeton: Princeton University Press, 1984.

M. Bastit. "Qu'est-ce qu'une Partie de l'Âme pour Aristote?" In *Corps et Âme. Sur le De Anima d'Aristote*, edited by C. Viano, 13–35. Paris: J. Vrin, 1996.

Beere, J. *Doing and Being: An Interpretation of Aristotle's Metaphysics Theta*. Oxford: Clarendon Press, 2009.

Bees, R. "Rezeption des Aristoteles in der Naturphilosophie Zenons: die kosmische Lebenskraft im Rahmen der Gottesbeweise bei Cicero, *De Natura Deorum* 2.20–44." In *Was ist 'Leben'? Aristoteles' Anschauungen zur Entstehung und Funktionsweise von Leben*, edited by S. Föllinger, 339–66. Stuttgart: Franz Steiner Verlag, 2010.

Beets, J., R. Ferwerda, and B. Schomakers. *Aristoteles, Problemen. 415 Vragen over Melancholie, Wijn, Muziek, Liefde etc.* Budel: Damon, 2010.

Berg, I. J. M. van den. *Aristoteles' Verhandeling over de Ziel*. Utrecht/Nijmegen: Dekker & Van de Vegt, 1953.

Bergeron, M., and R. Dufour. *Alexandre d'Aphrodise, De L'Âme. Texte Grec Introduit, Traduit et Annoté*. Paris: Librairie Philosophique J. Vrin, 2008.

Berryman, S. "Ancient Automata and Mechanical Explanation." *Phronesis* 48 (2003): 344–69.

———. "Aristotle on *Pneuma* and Animal Self-Motion." *Oxford Studies in Ancient Philosophy* 23 (2002): 85–97.

———. "Continuity and Coherence in Early Peripatetic Texts." In *Eudemus of Rhodos*, edited by I. Bodnár and W. W. Fortenbaugh, 157–69. New Brunswick, NJ: Transactions Publishers, 2002.

Berti, E. *La Filosofia del "Primo" Aristotele*. Padova: Cedam, 1962; 2a edizione Milano: Vita e Pensiero, 1997.

Besnier, B. "*De Mundo*. Tradition Grecque. Aristote de Stagire." In *Dictionaire des Philosophes Antiques*, edited by R. Goulet, 475–80. Paris: CNRS Éditions, 1989–2005. Supplément 2003.

Betegh, G. *The Derveni Papyrus. Cosmology, Theology and Interpretation*. Cambridge: Cambridge University Press, 2004.

———, and P. Gregoric. "Multiple Analogy in Ps. Aristotle, *De Mundo* 6." *Classical Quarterly* 64 (2014): 574–91.

Betegh, G., F. Pedriali, and C. Pfeiffer. "The Perfection of Bodies: Aristotle's *De Caelo* I, 1." *Rhizômata* 1 (2013): 30–62.

Biehl, G. *Aristotelis De Anima libri III* (1896). Editio tertia curavit O. Apelt. Leipzig: Teubner, 1926.
Blair, G. A. "Aristotle on Ἐντελέχεια. A reply to Daniel Graham." *American Journal of Philology* 114 (1993): 91–97.
———. *Energeia and Entelecheia: "Act" in Aristotle*. Ottawa: University of Ottawa Press, 1992.
———. "The Meaning of '*Energeia*' and '*Entelecheia*' in Aristotle." *International Philosophical Quarterly* 7 (1967): 101–17.
Bloch, D. *Aristotle, On Memory and Recollection. Text, Translation, Interpretation, and Reception in Western Scholasticism*. Leiden: Brill, 2007.
Block, I. "The Order of Aristotle's Psychological Writings." *American Journal of Philology* 82 (1961): 50–77.
Blumenthal, H. J. *Aristotle and Neoplatonism in Late Antiquity. Interpretations of the De Anima*. London: Duckworth, 1996.
Blyth, D. *Aristotle's Ever-turning World in Physics 8: Analysis and Commentary*. Leiden: Brill, 2015.
Bodéüs, R. "Âme du Monde ou Corps Céleste? Une Interrogation d'Aristote." In *Corps et Âme*, edited by C. Viano, 81–88. Paris: J. Vrin, 1996.
———. *Aristote, De l'Âme. Traduction inédite, Présentation, Notes, et Bibliographie*. Paris: Éd. Flammarion, 1993.
———. *Aristote, Éthique à Nicomaque*. Paris: Éd. Flammarion, 2004.
———. *Aristote et la Théologie des Vivants Immortels*. Québec: Éd. Bellarmin, 1992.
———. "La Prétendue Intuition de Dieu dans le *De Caelo* d'Aristote." *Phronesis* 35 (1990): 245–57.
———. *Aristotle and the Theology of the Living Immortals*. Albany: State University of New York Press, 2000.
Bodnár, I. M. "Movers and Elemental Motions in Aristotle." *Oxford Studies in Ancient Philosophy* 15 (1997): 81–117.
Boer, S. W. de. *Soul and Body in the Middle Ages. A Study of the Transformations of the Scientia de Anima c. 1260–c. 1360*. Dissertation. Nijmegen, 2011.
Boeri, M. D. "Μήτ' ἄνευ σώματος εἶναι μήτε σῶμά τι ἡ ψυχή (Aristóteles, *De anima* B 2, 414a19–20). A Propósito del Alcance de las Interpretaciones Funcionalistas de la Psicología Aristotelica y del Carácter Causal del Alma." *Elenchos* 30 (2009): 53–97.
Bolton, R. "Aristotle's Definition of the Soul. *De Anima*, II 1–3." *Phronesis* 23 (1978): 258–78.
———. "Perception Naturalized in Aristotle's *De Anima*." In *Metaphysics, Soul, and Ethics in Ancient Thought. Themes from the Work of Richard Sorabji*, edited by R. Salles, 209–44. Oxford: Clarendon Press, 2005.
Bonitz, H. "Aristotelische Studien." In *Sitzungsberichte der Philosophisch-Historische Classe der Kaiserlichen Akademie der Wissenschaften* 39 (1862), 41 (1863), 42 (1863), 52 (1866), 55 (1867). Reprint Hildesheim: Georg Olm, 1969.
———. *Index Aristotelicus*. Berlin: Königliche Preussische Akademie der Wissenschaften, 1870. Reprint Graz: Akademische Druck- und Verlagsanstalt, 1955.

Boot, P. *Plotinus, Over Voorzienigheid. Enneade III 2–3 [47–48]. Inleiding—Commentaar—Essays*. Amsterdam: VU-Uitgeverij, 1984.

Bos, A. P. "Aristote sur Dieu en tant qu'*Archê Geneseôs* en opposition au Démiurge de Platon." *Revue de Philosophie Ancienne* 27 (2009): 39–57.

———. *Aristoteles, Over de Kosmos. Ingeleid, Vertaald en van Verklarende Aantekeningen Voorzien*. Meppel: Boom, 1989.

———. "'Aristotelian' and 'Platonic' Dualism in Hellenistic and Early Christian Philosophy and in Gnosticism." *Vigiliae Christianae* 56 (2002): 273–91.

———. "Aristotle on God as Principle of Genesis." *British Journal for the History of Philosophy* 18 (2010): 363–77.

———. "Aristotle on the Differences between Plants, Animals, and Human Beings and on the Elements as Instruments of the Soul (*Anim*. II 4, 415b18)." *Review of Metaphysics* 63 (2010): 821–41.

———. "Aristotle on the Dissection of Plants and Animals, and his Concept of the Instrumental Soul-Body." *Ancient Philosophy* 27 (2007): 95–106.

———. "Aristotle on the Etruscan Robbers: A Core Text of 'Aristotelian' Dualism." *Journal of the History of Philosophy* 41 (2003): 289–306.

———. "Aristotle's *De Anima* II 1: The Traditional Interpretation Rejected." In *Aristotle and Contemporary Science*, vol. 2, edited by D. Sfendoni-Mentzou, 187–201. New York: P. Lang, 2001.

———. "Aristotle's Definition of the Soul: Why Was It Misunderstood for Centuries? The Dubious Lines *Anim*. II 1, 412b1–4." *Museum Helveticum* 69 (2012): 140–55.

———. "Aristotle's *Eudemus* and *Protrepticus*: Are They Really Two Different Works?" *Dionysius* 8 (1984): 19–51.

———. "Aristotle's Psychology: Diagnosis of the Need for a Fundamental Reinterpretation." *American Catholic Philosophical Quarterly* 73 (1999): 309–31.

———. *Cosmic and Meta-cosmic Theology in Aristotle's Lost Dialogues*. Leiden: Brill, 1989.

———. *De Ziel en Haar Voertuig. Aristoteles' Psychologie Geherinterpreteerd en de Eenheid van zijn Oeuvre Gedemonstreerd*. Leende: Damon, 1999.

———. "'Development' in the Study of Aristotle." Valedictory lecture, Amsterdam, Free University, 2006.

———. "Die Prägung des Gnostizismus durch den Aristotelischen Dualismus." In *Philosophische Religion. Gnosis zwischen Philosophie und Theologie*, edited by P. Koslowski, 37–55. München: Wilhelm Fink Verlag, 2006.

———. "The Distinction between 'Platonic' and 'Aristotelian' Dualism, Illustrated from Plutarch's Myth in *De Facie in Orbe Lunae*." In *Estudios sobro Plutarco. Misticismo y Religiones Mistéricas en la Obra de Plutarco*, edited by A. Pérez Jiménez and F. Casadesús Bordoy, 57–70. Madrid/Malaga: Ediciones Clásicas, 2001.

———. "The Divine '*Monarchia*' and the System of World-Government in Aristotle's *De Mundo*." In *Polis and Cosmopolis: Problems of a Global Era*, edited by K. Boudouris, 51–68. Athens: Ionia Publications, 2003.

———. "The Dreaming Kronos as World Archon in Plutarch's *De Facie in Orbe Lunae*." In *The Statesman in Plutarch's work*, vol. I, *Plutarch's Statesman and his*

Aftermath. Political, Philosophical, and Literary Aspects, edited by L. de Blois et al., 175–87. Leiden: Brill, 2004.

———. "The Ears Are not the Subject of Hearing in Aristotle's *On the Soul* II 8, 420a3–12." *Philologus* 154 (2010): 171–86.

———. "*Exôterikoi Logoi* and *Enkyklioi Logoi* in the Corpus Aristotelicum and the Origin of the Idea of the *Enkyklios Paideia*." *Journal of the History of Ideas* 50 (1989): 179–98.

———. "'Fire Above': The Relation of Soul to Its Instrumental Body in Aristotle's *De Longitudine et Brevitate Vitae* 2–3." *Ancient Philosophy* 22 (2002): 303–17.

———. "God as 'Father' and 'Maker' in Philo of Alexandria and Its Background in Aristotelian Thought." *Elenchos* 24 (2003): 311–32.

———. "Hagar and the '*Enkyklios Paideia*' in Philo of Alexandria." In *Abraham, the Nations, and the Hagarites. Jewish, Christian, and Islamic Perspectives on Kinship with Abraham*, edited by M. Goodman, G. H. van Kooten, and J. T. A. G. M. van Ruiten, 163–75. Leiden: Brill, 2010.

———. "Het Gehele Lichaam dat Waarnemingsvermogen Bezit (Aristoteles, *De Anima* II 1, 412b24–25)." *Algemeen Nederlands Tijdschrift voor Wijsbegeerte* 91 (1999): 112–28.

———. *In de Greep van de Titanen. Inleiding tot een Hoofdstroming van de Griekse Filosofie*. Amsterdam: Buijten & Schipperheijn, 1991.

———. "The 'Instrumental Body' of the Soul in Aristotle's Ethics and Biology." *Elenchos* 27 (2006): 35–72.

———. "Is the 'Greek King' in Aristotle's *Eudemus* fr. 11 (Ross) Endymion of Elis?" *The Modern Schoolman* 65 (1988): 79–96.

———. "La *Metafisica* di Aristotele alla Luce del Trattato *De Mundo*." *Rivista di Filosofia Neo-scolastica* 85 (1993): 425–54.

———. "La *Metafisica* di Aristotele alla Luce del Trattato *De Mundo*." In *Aristotele. Perché la Metafisica?*, edited by A. Bausola and G. Reale, 289–318. Milano: Vita e Pensiero, 1994.

———. "A Lost Sentence on Seed as Instrument of the Soul in Aristotle, *On the Soul* II 4, 415b7." *Hermes* 138 (2010): 276–87.

———. "*Manteia* in Aristotle, *De Caelo* II 1." *Apeiron* 21 (1988): 29–54.

———. "Notes on Aristotle's *De Mundo* Concerning the Discussion of its Authenticity." *Philosophical Inquiry* 1 (1979): 141–53.

———. *On the Elements. Aristotle's Early Cosmology*. Assen: Van Gorcum, 1973.

———. "Perception as a Movement of the Instrumental Body of the Soul in Aristotle." *Rheinisches Museum für Philologie* 154 (2011): 22–42.

———. "Philo of Alexandria: A Platonist in the Image and Likeness of Aristotle." *Studia Philonica Annual* 10 (1998): 66–86.

———. "Philo on God as *Archê Geneseôs*." *Journal of Jewish Studies* 60 (2009): 32–47.

———. "Plutarch on the Sleeping Soul and the Waking Intellect and Aristotle's Double Entelechy Concept." In *Plutarch in the Religious and Philosophical Discourse of*

Late Antiquity, edited by L. Roig Lanzillotta and Israel Muñoz Gallarto, 25–42. Leiden: Brill, 2012.

———. "Plutarch's Testimony to an Earlier Interpretation of Aristotle's Definition of the Soul." In *Plutarco, Platón y Aristóteles*, edited by A. Pérez Jiménez, 535–48. Madrid: Ediciones Clásicas, 1999.

———. "*Pneuma* and Ether in Aristotle's Philosophy of Living Nature." *The Modern Schoolman* 79 (2002): 255–76.

———. "*Pneuma* as Instrumental Body of the Soul in Aristotle's *De Anima* I 4." *Philotheos. International Journal for Philosophy and Theology* (Beograd) 13 (2013): 113–27.

———. "*Pneuma* as Quintessence of Aristotle's Philosophy." *Hermes* 141 (2013): 417–34.

———. *Providentia Divina. The Theme of Divine* Pronoia *in Plato and Aristotle*. Inaugural Lecture, Vrije Universiteit, Amsterdam. Assen: Van Gorcum, 1976.

———. "Review of J. C. Thom, ed., *Cosmic Order and Divine Power. Pseudo-Aristotle,* On the Cosmos. *Introduction, Text, Translation, and Interpretive Essays*." *Acta Classica* 58 (2015): 232–37.

———. "Silenus als Bemiddelaar van Gnostische Kennis in Aristoteles' Dialoog *Eudemus* [Silenus as Mediator of Gnostic Knowledge in Aristotle's Dialogue *Eudemus*]." In A. P. Bos and Luttikhuizen, *Waar Haalden de Gnostici hun Wijsheid vandaan? Over de Bronnen, de Doelgroep en de Tegenstanders van de Gnostische Beweging*, 65–83, 301–305. Budel: Damon, 2016.

———. *The Soul and Its Instrumental Body. A Reinterpretation of Aristotle's Philosophy of Living Nature*. Leiden: Brill, 2003.

———. "The Soul and Soul-'Parts' in Semen (*GA* II 1, 735a4–22)." *Mnemosyne* 62 (2009): 378–400.

———. "The Soul's Instrument for Touching in Aristotle, *On the Soul* II 11, 422b34–3a21." *Archiv für Geschichte der Philosophie* 92 (2010): 89–102.

———. "Teologia Cosmica e Metacosmica nella Filosofia Greca e nello Gnosticismo." *Rivista di Filosofia Neo-scolastica* 84 (1992): 369–82.

———. "The Tongue Is not the Soul's Instrument for Tasting According to Aristotle, *On the Soul* II 10." *Hermes* 140 (2012): 375–85.

———. "The 'Vehicle of the Soul' and the Debate over the Origin of this Concept." *Philologus* 151 (2007): 31–50.

———. "Why the Soul Needs an Instrumental Body According to Aristotle (*Anim.* I 3, 407b13–26)." *Hermes* 128 (2000): 20–31.

———, and R. Ferwerda. *Aristotle, On the Life-Bearing Spirit (De Spiritu). A Discussion with Plato and his Predecessors on Pneuma as the Instrumental Body of the Soul. Introduction, Translation, and Commentary*. Leiden: Brill, 2008.

———. "Aristotle's *De Spiritu* as a Critique of the Doctrine of *Pneuma* in Plato and His Predecessors." *Mnemosyne* 60 (2007): 565–88.

Boyancé, P. "Dieu Cosmique et Dualisme: les Archontes et Platon." In *Le Origini dello Gnosticismo*, edited by U. Bianchi, 340–56. Leiden: Brill, 1967.

Boylan, M. *The Origins of Ancient Greek Science: Blood—a Philosophical Study*. New York: Routledge, 2015.

Braque, R. *Aristote et la Question du monde. Essai sur le Contexte Cosmologique et Anthropologique de l'Ontologie*. Paris: Presses Universitaires de France, 1988.
Brennan, T. "Stoic Souls in Stoic Corpses." In *Body and Soul in Ancient Philosophy*, edited by D. Frede and B. Reis, 389–407. Berlin/New York: W. de Gruyter, 2009.
Brisson, L., *Einführung in die Philosophie des Mythos. Antike, Mittelalter und Renaissance.* Darmstadt: Wissenschaftliche Buchgesellschaft, 1996.
———. *Le Même et l'Autre dans la Structure Ontologique du Timée de Platon. Un Commentaire Systématique du Timée de Platon*. 2nd revised ed. (1974). Sankt Augustin: Academia, 1994.
———. "Le Rôle des Mathématiques dans le *Timée* selon les Interprétations Contemporaines." In *Le Timée de Platon. Contributions à l'Histoire de sa Réception*, edited by A. Neschke-Hentschke, 295–315. Louvain/Paris: Éd. Peeters, 2000.
———. *Le Sexe Incertain: Androgynie et Hermaphrodisme dans l'Antiquité Gréco-romaine*. Paris: Les Belles Lettres, 2008.
Broadie, S., *Aristotle and Beyond. Essays on Metaphysics and Ethics*. Cambridge: Cambridge University Press, 2007.
———. "Why no Platonistic Ideas of Artefacts?" In *Maieusis: Essays in Ancient Philosophy in Honour of Miles Burnyeat*, edited by D. Scott, 232–52. Oxford: Oxford University Press, 2007.
Brockmann, C. "Organe." In *Aristoteles-Handbuch: Leben, Werk, Wirkung*, edited by C. Rapp and K. Corcilius, 286–92. Stuttgart: J. B. Metzler, 2011.
Bronstein, D. "Review of A. P. Bos (2003)." *Ancient Philosophy* 26 (2006): 422–27.
Buchheim, T. *Aristoteles, Über Werden und Vergehen. Übersetzt und Erläutert*. Darmstadt: Wissenschaftliche Buchgesellschaft, 2010.
Buddensiek, F. "Aristoteles' Zirbeldrüse? Zum Verhältnis von Seele und *Pneuma* in Aristoteles' Theorie der Ortsbewegung der Lebewesen." In *Body and Soul in Ancient Philosophy*, edited by D. Frede and B. Reis, 309–29. Berlin/New York: W. de Gruyter, 2009.
Burkert, W. *Babylon, Memphis, Persepolis. Eastern Contexts of Greek Culture*. Cambridge: Harvard University Press, 2004.
———. *Weisheit und Wissenschaft. Studien zu Pythagoras, Philolaos und Platon*. Nürnberg: Verlag Hans Carl, 1962.
Burnyeat, M. F. "*De Anima* II 5." *Phronesis* 47 (2002): 28–90.
Busche, H. *Die Seele als System. Aristoteles' Wissenschaft von der Psyche*. Hamburg: Felix Meiner Verlag, 2001.
Byl, S. "Le Toucher chez Aristote." *Revue de Philosophie Ancienne* 9 (1991): 123–32.
———. "Note sur la Polysémie d'*Organon* et les Origines du Finalisme." *L'Antiquité Classique* 40 (1971):121–33.
———. *Recherches sur les Grands Traités Biologiques d'Aristote: Sources Écrites et Préjugés*. Bruxelles: Palais des Académies, 1980.
Calder III, W. C., ed. *Werner Jaeger Reconsidered*. Atlanta: Scholars Press, 1992.
Cannarsa, M. "Una Lacuna Platonica. Il Problema della Relazione Anima-Corpo nella Prima Accademia Antica." In *Attività e Virtù. Anima e Corpo in Aristotele*, edited by A. Fermani and M. Migliori, 43–82. Milano: Vita e Pensiero, 2009.

Capelle, W. "Das Problem der Urzeugung bei Aristoteles und Theophrast und in die Folgezeit." *Rheinisches Museum* 98 (1955): 150–80.

Carbone, A. L. *Aristotele, L'Anima e il Corpo. Parva Naturalia. Introduzione, Traduzione e Note.* Milano: Bompiani, 2003.

Carpenter, A. D. "Embodied Intelligent (?) Souls: Plants in Plato's *Timaeus*." *Phronesis* 55 (2010): 281–303.

Carteron, H. *Aristote, Physique. Texte Établi et Traduit.* Paris: Les Belles Lettres, vol. 1 (3rd ed.) 1961; vol. 2 (2nd ed.) 1956.

Casadio, G. "From Hellenistic *Aiôn* to Gnostic *Aiônes*." In *Religion im Wandel der Kosmologien*, edited by D. Zeller, 175–90. Frankfurt a. M.: P. Lang, 1999.

Caston, V. "The Spirit and the Letter: Aristotle on Perception." In *Metaphysics, Soul, and Ethics in Ancient Thought. Themes from the Work of Richard Sorabji*, edited by R. Salles, 245–320. Oxford: Clarendon Press, 2005.

———. "Was es heißt, die Form ohne die Materie aufzunehmen. Wahrnehmung, Vorstellung und Denken bei Aristoteles." In *Wissen und Bildung in der antiken Philosophie*, edited by C. Rapp and T. Wagner, 179–98. Stuttgart/Weimar: J. B. Metzler, 2006.

Centrone, B. "ΜΕΛΑΓΧΟΛΙΚΟΣ in Aristotele e il *Problema* XXX 1." In *Studi sui* Problemata Physica *Aristotelici*, edited by B. Centrone, 309–39. Napoli: Bibliopolis, 2011.

———, ed. *Studi sui* Problemata Physica *Aristotelici*. Napoli: Bibliopolis, 2011.

Chandler, C. "Didactic Purpose and Discursive Strategies in *On the Cosmos*." In *Cosmic Order and Divine Power. Pseudo-Aristotle,* On the Cosmos. *Introduction, Text, Translation, and Interpretive Essays*, edited by J. C. Thom, 69–87. Tübingen: Mohr Siebeck, 2014.

Charles, D. "Aristotle on Desire and Action." In *Body and Soul in Ancient Philosophy*, edited by D. Frede and B. Reis, 291–307. Berlin/New York: W. de Gruyter, 2009.

———. "Teleological Causation." In *The Oxford Handbook of Aristotle*, edited by C. Shields, 227–66. Oxford: Oxford University Press, 2012.

Chroust, A. H. *Aristotle. New Light on His Life and on Some of His Lost Works*, 2 vols. London: Routledge & Kegan Paul, 1973.

Clark, S. R. L. *Aristotle's Man. Speculations upon Aristotle's Anthropology.* Oxford: Clarendon Press, 1975.

Cleary, J.J. *Aristotle and Mathematics. Aporetic Method in Cosmology and Metaphysics.* Leiden: Brill, 1995.

———. "Mathematics and Cosmology in Aristotle." In *Aristotle's Philosophical Development. Problems and* Prospects, edited by W. Wians, 193–228. Lanham/London: Rowman, 1996.

Cohoe, C. "Why the Intellect Cannot Have a Bodily Organ: *De Anima* 3.4." *Phronesis* 58 (2013): 347–77.

Coles, A. "Animal and Childhood Cognition in Aristotle's Biology and the *Scala Naturae*. In *Aristotelische Biologie. Intentionen, Methoden, Ergebnisse*, edited by W. Kullmann and S. Föllinger, 287–323. Stuttgart: Franz Steiner Verlag, 1997.

———. "Biomedical Models of Reproduction in the Fifth Century BC and Aristotle's *Generation of animals.*" *Phronesis* 46 (1995): 48–88.

Cooper, J. M. "Aristotle on Natural Teleology." In *Language and Logos. Studies in Ancient Greek Philosophy*, edited by M. Schofield and M. Craven Nussbaum, 197–222. Cambridge: Cambridge University Press, 1982.

———. "Metaphysics in Aristotle's Embryology." In *Biologie, Logique, et Métaphysique chez Aristote*, edited by D. Devereux and P. Pellegrin, 55–84. Paris: Éditions du Centre National de la Recherche Scientifique, 1990.

Corcilius, K. "Akrasia bei Aristoteles. Die erste Aporie." In *Beiträge zur Aristotelischen Handlungstheorie*, edited by K. Corcilius and C. Rapp, 143–72. Stuttgart: Frans Steiner Verlag, 2008.

———. *Streben und Bewegen. Aristoteles' Theorie der Animalischen Ortsbewegung*. Berlin: W. de Gruyter, 2008.

———, and P. Gregoric. "Separability vs Difference: Parts and Capacities of the Soul in Aristotle." *Oxford Studies in Ancient Philosophy* 39 (2010): 81–119.

———. "Aristotle's Model of Animal Motion." *Phronesis* 58 (2013): 52–97.

Corcilius, K., and D. Perler, eds. *Partitioning the Soul: Debates from Plato to Leibniz*. Berlin: De Gruyter, 2014.

Corte, M. de. "Études sur les Manuscrits du Traité *De l'Âme* d'Aristote." *Revue de Philologie* 59 (1933): 141–60, 261–81, 355–67.

Couloubaritsis, L. "La notion d'Ἐντελέχεια dans la *Métaphysique*." In *Aristotelica. Mélanges offerts à Marcel de Corte*, 129–55. Bruxelles: Ousia, 1985.

Crowley, T. J. "Aristotle's 'So-Called Elements.'" *Phronesis* 53 (2008): 223–42.

———. "On the Use of *Stoicheion* in the Sense of 'Element.'" *Oxford Studies in Ancient Philosophy* 29 (2005): 367–94.

Cumont, F. *Recherches sur le Symbolisme Funéraire des Romains*. 1942; repr. Paris: Librairie Orientaliste, 1966.

Dalimier, C., and P. Pellegrin. *Aristote, Traité du Ciel. Texte et traduction*. Paris: G. F. Flammarion, 2004.

Dancy, R. M. "Keeping Body and Soul Together: On Aristotle's Theory of Forms." In *Aristotle's Philosophical Development. Problems and Prospects*, edited by W. Wians, 249–87. Lanham/London: Rowman, 1996.

Daniélou, J. "Le Mauvais Gouvernement du Monde d'après le Gnosticisme." In *Le Origini dello Gnosticismo*, edited by U. Bianchi, 448–59. Leiden: Brill, 1967.

Denniston, J. D. *The Greek Particles*. Oxford: Oxford University Press, 1934; second ed. 1954.

Diamond, E. *Mortal Imitations of Divine Life. The Nature of the Soul in Aristotle's De Anima*. Evanston: Northwestern University Press, 2015.

Dierauer, U. *Tier und Mensch im Denken der Antike. Studien zur Tierpsychologie, Anthropologie und Ethik*. Amsterdam: Grüner, 1977.

Dillon, J. "Come fa l'Anima a dirigere il Corpo? Tracce di una Disputa sulla Relazione Corpo-Anima nell'Antica Accademia." In *Interiorità e Anima. La "Psychè" in Platone*, edited by M. Migliori, L. M. Napolitano Valditara, and A. Fermani, 51–57. Milano: Vita e Pensiero, 2007.

———. "How Does the Soul Direct the Body, After All? Traces of a Dispute on Mind-Body Relations in the Old Academy." In *Body and Soul in Ancient Philosophy* edited by D. Frede and B. Reis, 349–56. Berlin/New York: W. de Gruyter, 2009.

Dirlmeier, F. *Aristoteles, Nikomachische Ethik*. Darmstadt: Wissenschaftliche Buchgesellschaft, 1956.
Dönt, E. *Aristoteles, Kleine Naturwissenschaftliche Schriften, übersetzt und herausgegeben*. Stuttgart: Philipp Reclam jun., 1997.
Donini, P. L. "Aristotele: a Chi e Che Cosa Serve una Tragedia." In *Anthropine Sophia. Studi di Filologia e Storiografia Filosofica in Memoria di Gabriele Giannantoni*, edited by F. Alesse et al., 351–77. Napoli: Bibliopolis, 2008.
———. "Crono e Zeus nel Mito di Plutarco, de Facie in Orbe Lunae." In *Studi di Cultura Classica e Musica offerti à Franco Serpa*, edited by F. Bottari, L. Casarsa, L. Cristante, and M. Fernandelli, 105–18. Edizioni Università di Trieste, 2011.
Dowd, J. "Does Aristotle Believe in Essentially-Ensouled Matter?" *Ancient Philosophy* 35 (2015): 97–111.
Drachmann, A. G. *The Mechanical Technology of Greek and Roman Antiquity. A Study of the Literary Sources*. Copenhagen: Munksgaard, 1963.
Drossaart Lulofs, H. J. *Aristoteles, De Insomniis et De Divinatione per Somnum. A New Edition of the Greek Text with the Latin Translation*. Leiden: E. J. Brill, 1947.
———. *Aristotelis De Generatione Animalium*. Oxford: Clarendon Press, 1965; repr. 2005.
———. *Aristotelis De Somno et Vigilia liber adiectis Veteribus Translationibus et Theodori Metochitae Commentario*. Leiden: Burgersdijk & Niermans, 1943.
———. *De Ogen van Lynceus*. Leiden: Brill, 1967.
Dudley, J. "The Fate of Providence and Plato's World Soul in Aristotle." In *Fate, Providence, and Moral Responsibility in Ancient, Medieval, and Early Modern Thought. Studies in Honour of C. Steel*, edited by P. D'Hoine, and G. van Riet, 59–73. Leuven: Leuven University Press, 2014.
Düring, I. *Aristoteles. Darstellung und Interpretation seines Denkens*. Heidelberg: Carl Winter-Universitäts Verlag, 1966.
———. *Aristotle's De Partibus Animalium. Critical and Literary Commentaries*. Göteborg: Elanders Boktryckeri, 1943.
———. *Aristotle's Protrepticus. An Attempt at Reconstruction*. Göteborg: Almquist & Wiksell, 1961.
Duhot, J. J. "Aristotélisme et Stoicisme dans le Περὶ κόσμου pseudo-aristotélicien." *Revue de Philosophie Ancienne* 8 (1990): 191–228.
Dunstan, G. R., ed. *The Human Embryo. Aristotle and the Arabic and European Traditions*. Exeter: University of Exeter Press, 1990.
Duprat, G. L. "La Théorie du πνεῦμα chez Aristote." *Archiv für Geschichte der Philosophie* 12 (1898): 305–21.
Durrant, M., ed. *Aristotle's De Anima in Focus*. London: Routledge, 1993.
Dijksterhuis, E. J. *De Mechanisering van het Wereldbeeld*. Amsterdam: Meulenhof, 1950.
———. *The Mechanization of the World Picture*. Oxford: Oxford University Press, 1969.
Easterling, H. J. "A Note on *De Anima* 413a8–9." *Phronesis* 11 (1966): 159–62.
———. "Quinta Natura." *Museum Helveticum* 21 (1964): 73–85.
Edelstein, L. *Ancient Medicine. Selected Papers of Ludwig Edelstein*. Edited by O. and C. L. Temkin. Baltimore: Johns Hopkins University Press, 1967.

———. "The Golden Chain of Homer." In *Studies in Intellectual History*, edited by G. Boas and H. Cherniss, 48–66. 1953; repr. New York: Grenwood Press, 1968.
———. *The Meaning of Stoicism*. Cambridge: Harvard University Press, 1966.
Edmonds, R. G. *Redefining Ancient Orphism. A Study in Greek Religion*. Cambridge: Cambridge University Press, 2013.
Effe, B., *Studien zur Kosmologie und Theologie der Aristotelischen Schrift "Über die Philosophie."* München: C.H. Beck, 1970.
Egermann, F. "Platonische Spätphilosophie und Platonismen bei Aristoteles." *Hermes* 87 (1959): 133–42.
Eijk, P. J. van der. *Aristoteles, Over het Geheugen, de Slaap en de Droom, vertaald, ingeleid en van aantekeningen voorzien*. Groningen: Historische Uitgeverij, 2003.
———. *Aristoteles, Over Melancholie, vertaald, ingeleid en van aantekeningen voorzien*. Groningen: Historische Uitgeverij, 2001.
El Murr, D. "Hesiod, Plato, and the Golden Age: Hesiodic Motifs in the Myth of the *Politicus*." In *Plato and Hesiod*, edited by G. R. Boys-Stones and J. H. Haubold, 276–97. Oxford: Oxford University Press, 2010.
Eustathii Commentarii ad Homeri Iliadem pertinentes Y. Vol. 2. Edited by M. van der Valk. Leiden: Brill, 1976.
Everson, S. *Aristotle on Perception*. Oxford: Clarendon Press, 1997.
Falcon, A. *Aristotle's Science of Nature. Unity without Uniformity*. Cambridge: Cambridge University Press, 2005.
———. "The Scope and Unity of Aristotle's Investigation of the Soul." In *Ancient Perspectives on Aristotle's* De Anima, edited by G. van Riel and P. Destrée, 167–81. Leuven: Leuven University Press, 2009.
———, ed., *Brill's Companion to the Reception of Aristotle in Antiquity*. Leiden: Brill, 2016.
Feola, G. "*De An*. A 1: L'Aporia sulle 'Parti' dell'Anima e la Struttura Dialettica del Trattato *De Anima*." *Elenchos* 27 (2006): 123–39.
Fermani, A., and M. Migliori, eds. *Attività e Virtù. Anima e Corpo in Aristotele*. Milano: Vita e Pensiero, 2009.
Ferrini, M. F. *Aristotele, Problemi, introd. Traduzione*. Milano: Bompiano, 2002.
Ferwerda, R. *Aristoteles, Over Dieren, Vertald, Ingeleid en van Aantekeningen Voorzien*. Groningen: Historische Uitgeverij, 2000.
———. *Aristoteles, Over Voortplanting, Vertaald, Ingeleid en van Aantekeningen Voorzien*. Groningen: Historische Uitgeverij, 2005.
———. "The Meaning of the Word ΣΩΜΑ in Plato's Cratylus 400C." *Hermes* 113 (1985): 266–79.
Festugière, A. J. *Proclus, Commentaire sur le Timée, Traduction et Notes*. 5 vols. Paris: Vrin, 1966–68.
Finamore, J. F. *Iamblichus and the Theory of the Vehicle of the Soul*. Chico, CA: Scholars Press, 1985.
Flashar, H. *Aristoteles, Fragmente zu Philosophie, Rhetorik, Poetik, Dichtung, übersetzt, und erläutert*. Darmstadt: Wissenschaftliche Buchgesellschaft, 2006.

———. *Aristoteles, Problemata Physica, übersetzt und erläutert*. Darmstadt: Wissenschaftliche Buchgesellschaft, 1962.

———. "Urzeugung und/oder Spontane Entstehung." In *Was ist "Leben"? Aristoteles' Anschauungen zur Entstehung und Funktionsweise von Leben*, edited by S. Föllinger, 331–37. Stuttgart: Franz Steiner Verlag, 2010.

Föllinger, S. "Das Problem des Lebens in Aristoteles' Embryologie." In *Was ist "Leben"? Aristoteles' Anschauungen zur Entstehung und Funktionsweise von Leben*, edited by S. Föllinger, 225–36. Stuttgart: Franz Steiner Verlag, 2010.

———, ed. *Was ist "Leben"? Aristoteles' Anschauungen zur Entstehung und Funktionsweise von Leben*. Stuttgart: Franz Steiner Verlag, 2010.

Ford, A. *Aristotle as Poet: The Song for Hermias and Its Contexts*. Oxford: Oxford University Press, 2011.

Förster, A. *Aristotelis De Anima libri tres*. Budapestini: Typis Societatis Franklinianae, 1912.

Fortenbaugh, W. W. "On *Problemata* 27: Problems Connected with Fear and Courage." In *The Aristotelian* Problemata Physica. *Philosophical and Scientific Investigations*, edited by R. Mayhew, 311–20. Leiden: Brill, 2015.

Fraenkel, J. M. *Aristoteles' Zielkunde, met een Inleiding, Korte Overzichten en Verklarende Aanteekeningen*. Groningen: J. B. Wolters, 1919.

Frank, E. "Das Problem des Lebens bei Hegel und Aristoteles." *Deutsche Vierteljahrschrift für Literaturwissenschaft und Geistesgeschichte* 5 (1927): 609–43.

Frede, D. "Theodicy and Providential Care in Stoicism." In *Traditions of Theology. Studies in Hellenistic Theology*, edited by D. Frede and A. Laks, 85–117. Leiden: Brill, 2002.

———, and B. Reis, eds. *Body and Soul in Ancient Philosophy*. Berlin/New York: W. de Gruyter, 2009.

Freeland, C. "Aristotle on the Sense of Touch." In *Essays on Aristotle's De Anima*, edited by M. C. Nussbaum and A. Oksenberg Rorty, 227–48. Cambridge: Clarendon Press, 1992.

Freeland, C. A., ed. *Feminist Interpretations of Aristotle*. University Park: The Pennsylvania State University Press, 1998.

Freudenthal, G. *Aristotle's Theory of Material Substance. Heat and Pneuma, Form and Soul*. Oxford: Clarendon Press, 1995.

———. "The Astrologization of the Aristotelian Cosmos: Celestial Influences on the Sublunar World in Aristotle, Alexander of Aphrodisias, and Averroes." In *New Perspectives on Aristotle's* De Caelo, edited by A. C. Bowen and C. Wildberg, 239–81. Leiden: Brill, 2009.

Fronterotta, F. "Οὐ μνημονεύομεν δέ . . . Su Aristotele, *De Anima* Γ 5, 430a23–35." In *Attività e Virtù. Anima e Corpo in Aristotele*, edited by A. Fermani and M. Migliori, 179–207. Milano: Vita e Pensiero, 2008.

Furley, D. J. *Aristotle, On Sophistical Refutations; On Coming-to-Be and Passing-away; On the Cosmos*. London: W. Heinemann, 1955.

———. "Self Movers." In *Aristotle on Mind and the Senses*, edited by G. E. R. Lloyd and G. E. L. Owen, 165–79. Cambridge: Cambridge University Press, 1978;

repr. in *Self-Motion. From Aristotle to Newton*, edited by M. L. Gill and J. G. Lennox, 3–14. Princeton: Princeton University Press, 1994.

Furth, M. *Substance, Form, and Psyche: An Aristotelean Metaphysics*. Cambridge: Cambridge University Press, 1988.

Gaiser, K. "Das Zweifache Telos bei Aristoteles." In *Naturphilosophie bei Aristoteles und Theophrast*, edited by I. Düring, 97–113. Heidelberg: Lothar Stiehm, 1969.

———. "Die Elegie des Aristoteles an Eudemus." *Museum Helveticum* 23 (1966): 84–106.

———. "Ein Gespräch mit König Philipp: zum 'Eudemos' des Aristoteles." In *Aristoteles. Werk und Wirkung. Paul Moraux Gewidmet*, edited by J. Wiesner, 457–84. Berlin: W. de Gruyter, 1985.

Gallop, D. *Aristotle on Sleep and Dreams. A Text and Translation with Introduction, Notes, and Glossary*. Warminster: Aris and Philips, 1991.

Gätje, H., *Das Kapitel über das Begehren aus dem Mittleren Kommentar des Averroes zur Schrift Über die Seele*. Amsterdam: North-Holland, 1985.

Gelber, J. "Aristotle on Essence and Habitat." *Oxford Sudies in Ancient Philosophy* 48 (2015): 267–93.

Genequand, C. *Alexander of Aphrodisias, On the Cosmos*. Leiden: Brill, 2001.

Gerson, L. P. *Aristotle and Other Platonists*. Ithaca: Cornell University Press, 2005.

Geurts, P. M. M. *De Erfelijkheid in de Oudere Grieksche Wetenschap*. Nijmegen: Dekker & Van de Vegt, 1941.

Gigon, O. *Aristoteles, Vom Himmel; Von der Seele; Von der Dichtkunst*. München: Deutscher Taschenbuch Verlag, 1983.

———. *Aristoteles, Von der Seele*. München: Deutscher Taschenbuch Verlag, 1950; repr. 1960, 1996.

———. *Aristotelis Opera liber III. Deperditorum Librorum Fragmenta*. Berlin: W. de Gruyter, 1987.

———. "Der Menschliche und der Absolute Geist bei Aristoteles." *Hegel-Jahrbuch* 29 (1981–82): 19–38.

Gill, M. L. "Aristotle on Self-Motion." In *Self-Motion. From Aristotle to Newton*, edited by M. L. Gill and J. G. Lennox, 15–34. Princeton: Princeton University Press, 1994.

———. *Aristotle on Substance. The Paradox of Unity*. Princeton: Princeton University Press, 1989.

———. "First Philosophy in Aristotle." In *A Companion to Ancient Philosophy*, edited by M. L. Gill and P. Pellegrin, 347–73. Oxford: Blackwell, 2006.

———. "The Theory of the Elements in De Caelo 3 and 4." In *New Perspectives on Aristotle's De Caelo*, edited by A. C. Bowen and C. Wildberg, 139–61. Leiden: Brill, 2009.

Giltaij, J. *Ruffo en Rembrandt. Over een Siciliaanse Verzamelaar in de Zeventiende Eeuw die Drie Schilderijen bij Rembrandt Bestelde*. Dissertation. Vrije Universiteit, Amsterdam, 1997.

Gohlke, P. *Aristoteles, Kleine Schriften zur Seelenkunde*. Paderborn: F. Schöningh, 1947.

———. *Aristoteles, Probleme*. Paderborn: F. Schöningh, 1961.

———. *Aristoteles, Über die Seele*. Paderborn: F. Schöningh, 1947.

Gotthelf, A. "Aristotle's Conception of Final Causality." *Review of Metaphysics* 30 (1976): 226–54; repr. with addition in *Philosophical Issues in Aristotle's Biology*, edited by A. Gotthelf and J. G. Lennox, 204–42. Cambridge: Cambridge University Press, 1987.

———. "Teleology and Spontaneous Generation in Aristotle: A Discussion." *Apeiron* 22 (1989): 181–93.

———. *Teleology, First Principles, and Scientific Method in Aristotle's Biology*. Oxford: Oxford University Press, 2012.

———, ed. *Aristotle on Nature and Living Things*. Pittsburgh: Mathesis Publications, 1985.

Gottschalk, H. B. "Aristotelian Philosophy in the Roman World from the Time of Cicero to the End of the Second Century." In *Aufstieg und Niedergang der Römischen Welt*, vol. II 36, 1132–92. Berlin: W. de Gruyter, 1987.

Graeser, A. "Aristoteles' Schrift 'Über die Philosophie' und die Zweifache Bedeutung der 'Causa Finalis." *Museum Helveticum* 29 (1972): 44–61.

Graham, D. W. "The Etymology of Ἐντελέχεια," *American Journal of Philology* 110 (1989): 73–80.

Granger, H. "The Scala Naturae and the Continuity of Kinds." *Phronesis* 30 (1985): 181–200.

Gregoric, P. *Aristotle on the Common Sense*. Oxford: Oxford University Press, 2007.

———. "The Heraclitus Anecdote: *De Partibus Animalium* i 5, 645a17–23." *Ancient Philosophy* 21 (2001): 73–85.

———. "The Pneumatic Theory of *De Spiritu*." Paper for Conference on "Aristotle and His Predecessors on Heat, *Pneuma* and Soul." Prague, June 12–14, 2014.

———, and M. Kuhar. "Aristotle's Physiology of Animal Motion: on *Neura* and Muscles." *Apeiron* 47 (2014): 94–115.

Gregoric, P., and O. Lewis. "Pseudo-Aristotelian *De Spiritu*: a New Case against Authenticity." *Classical Philology* 110 (2015): 159–67.

Gregoric, P., O. Lewis, and M. Kuhar. "The Substance of *De Spiritu*." *Early Science and Medicine* 20 (2015): 101–24.

Gregory, A. *The Presocratics and the Supernatural: Magic, Philosophy, and Science in Early Greece*. London: Bloombury Academic, 2013.

Groot, J. de. "*Dynamis* and the Science of Mechanics: Aristotle on Animal Motion." *Journal of the History of Philosophy* 46 (2008): 43–68.

Guthrie, W. K. C. *Aristotle, On the Heavens, with an English Translation*. London: William Heinemann, 1939; repr. 1960.

———. *A History of Greek Philosophy*. 6 vols. Cambridge: Cambridge University Press, 1981.

Gutiérrez-Giraldo, D. Ψυχή and Genotype." In *Aristotle and Contemporary Science*, vol. 2, edited by D. Sfendoni-Mentzou, 163–72. New York: P. Lang, 2001.

Haas, F. A. J. de. "Late Ancient Philosophy." In *The Cambridge Companion to Greek and Roman Philosophy*, edited by D. Sedley, 242–70. Cambridge: Cambridge University Press, 2003.

Hackforth, R. *Plato's Phaedo, Translated, with Introduction and Commentary*. Cambridge, Cambridge University Press, 1955.

Hahm, D. E. "The Fifth Element in Aristotle's *De Philosophia*: A Critical Re-examination." *Journal of Hellenic Studies* 102 (1982): 60–74.
Hahmann, A. "Kann man Aristoteles' Philosophie der Wahrnehmung noch für Wahr Nehmen?" *Philosophisches Jahrbuch* 121 (2014): 3–32.
Halfwassen, J. "Der Demiurg: seine Stellung in der Philosophie Platons und seine Deutung im Antiken Platonismus." In *Platos Timaios. Beiträge zu seiner Rezeptionsgeschichte*, edited by A. Neschke-Hentschke. Louvain: Peeters, 2000.
Hamlyn, D. W. *Aristotle's De Anima, Books II and III (with certain Passages from book I). Transl. with Introd. and Notes*. Oxford: Clarendon Press, 1968.
Hardie, W. F. R. "Aristotle's Treatment of the Relation between the Soul and the Body." *Philosophical Quarterly* 14 (1964): 53–72.
Harris, W. V. *Dreams and Experience in Classical Antiquity*. Cambridge: Harvard University Press, 2009.
Heinemann, G. "*Sôma Organikon*. Zum ontologischen Sinn des Werkzeugvergleichs bei Aristoteles." In *Organismus. Die Erklärung des Lebendigen*, edited by G. Toepfer and F. Michelini, 63–80. Freiburg i.B.: Verlag Karl Alber, 2016.
Helleman-Elgersma, W. E. *Soul-Sisters. A Commentary on* Enneads *IV 3 [27], 1–8 of Plotinus*. Amsterdam: Rodopi, 1980.
Henry, D. M. "Generation of Animals." In *A Companion to Aristotle*, edited by A. Anagnostopoulos, 368–83. Malden MA: Wiley-Blackwell, 2009.
———. "Organismal Natures." In *Aristotle on Life*, edited by J. Mouracade (= *Apeiron* vol. 41 [2008]): 47–74.
Hett, W. S. *Aristotle, On the Soul, Parva Naturalia, On Breath, with an English Translation*. London: W. Heinemann, 1936.
———. *Aristotle, Problems, with an English Translation*. 2 vols. London: W. Heinemann, 1926–1937.
Hicks, R. D. *Aristotle, De Anima, with Translation, Introduction, and Notes*. Cambridge: Cambridge University Press, 1907.
Hilt, A. *Ousia—Psyche—Nous. Aristoteles' Philosophie der Lebendigkeit*. Freiburg-München: Alber Symposion, 2005.
Hinton, B. "Generation and the Unity of Form in Aristotle." *Apeiron* 39 (2006): 359–80.
Holwerda, D. "Textkritisches und Exegetisches zur pseudo-Aristotelischen Schrift Περὶ τοῦ κόσμου." *Mnemosyne* 46 (1993): 46–55.
Horn, H.-J. *Studien zum Dritten Buch der Aristotelischen Schrift* De Anima. Göttingen: Vandenhoeck & Ruprecht, 1994.
Hübner, J. "Die Aristotelische Konzeption der Seele als Aktivität in *De Anima* II 1." *Archiv für Geschichte der Philosophie* 81 (1999): 1–32.
Hutchinson, D. S. "Aristotle and the Spheres of Motivation: *De Anima* III 11." *Dialogue* 29 (1990): 7–20.
———. "Restoring the Order of Aristotle's *De Anima*." *Classical Review* 37 (1987): 373–81.
———, and M. R. Johnson. "Authenticating Aristotle's *Protrepticus*." *Oxford Studies in Ancient Philosophy* 29 (2005): 193–294.

———. "Protreptic Aspects of Aristotle's *Nicomachean Ethics*." In *The Cambridge Companion to Aristotle's Nicomachena Ethics*, edited by R. Polansky, 383–409. Cambridge: Cambridge University Press, 2014.

Jackson, P. *Aristotle on the Meaning of Man. A Philosophical Response to Idealism, Positivism, and Gnosticism*. Bern: P. Lang, 2016.

Jaeger, W. *Aristoteles. Grundlegung einer Geschichte seiner Entwicklung*. Berlin: Weidmannsche Buchhandlung, 1923; repr. 1955.

———. *Aristotelis De Animalium Motione et De Animalium Incessu; Pseudo-Aristotelis de Spiritu Libellus*. Edited by V. G. Jaeger. Leipzig: Bibliotheca Teubneriana, 1913.

———. *Aristotle. Fundamentals of the History of his Development*. Translated, with the author's corrections and additions, by R. Robinson. Oxford: Oxford University Press, 1934; 2nd ed. 1948; repr. 1962.

———. "Das *Pneuma* im Lykeion." *Hermes* 48 (1913): 29–74; repr. in id. *Scripta Minora*. Roma: Edizioni di Storia e Letteratura, 1960.

Jannone, A., and E. Barbotin. *Aristote, De l'Âme*. Paris: Les Belles Lettres, 1966.

Jerouschek, G. *Lebensschutz und Lebensbeginn. Kulturgeschichte des Abtreibungsverbot*. Stuttgart: Ferdinand Enke Verlag, 1988.

Joachim, H. H. *Aristotle. The Nicomachean Ethics. A Commentary*. Edited by D. A. Rees. Oxford: Clarendon Press, 1951.

Jones, D. A. *The Soul of the Embryo. An Enquiry into the Status of the Human Embryo in the Christian Tradition*. London: Continuum, 2004.

Johansen, T. "The Soul as an Inner Principle of Change: The Basis of Aristotle's Psychological Naturalism." In *Maieusis: Essays in Ancient Philosophy in Honour of Miles Burnyeat*, edited by D. Scott, 276–99. Oxford: Oxford University Press, 2007.

Johansen, T. K. *Aristotle on the Sense-Organs*. Cambridge: Cambridge University Press, 1997.

———. "From Plato's *Timaeus* to Aristotle's *De Caelo*: the Case of the Missing World Soul." In *New Perspectives on Aristotle's* De Caelo, edited by A. C. Bowen and C. Wildberg, 9–28. Leiden: Brill, 2009.

———. "Parts in Aristotle's Definition of the Soul: *De Anima* Books I and II." In *Partitioning the Soul: Debates from Plato to Leibniz*, edited by K. Corcilius and D. Perler, 39–61. Berlin: De Gruyter, 2014.

———. *The Powers of Aristotle's Soul*. Oxford: Oxford University Press, 2012.

Johnson, M. R. *Aristotle on Teleology*. Oxford: Clarendon Press, 2005.

Johnston, R. "Aristotle's *De Anima*: On Why the Soul Is not a Set of Capacities." *British Journal for the History of Philosophy* 19 (2011): 185–201.

Jori, A. *Aristoteles Über den Himmel, Übersetzt und Erläutert*. Darmstadt: Wissenschaftliche Buchgesellschaft, 2009.

Kahn, C. H. "Sensation and Consciousness in Aristotle's Psychology." *Archiv für Geschichte der Philosophie* 48 (1966): 43–81; repr. in J. Barnes, M. Schofield, and R. Sorabji, eds., *Articles on Aristotle*. London: Duckworth, 1979, vol. 4, 1–31.

Karamanolis, G. E. *Plato and Aristotle in Agreement? Platonists on Aristotle from Antiochus to Porphyry*. Oxford: Clarendon Press, 2006.

Keizer, H. M. *Life Time Entirety. A Study of Aiôn in Greek Literature and Philosophy, the Septuagint, and Philo*. Dissertation, University of Amsterdam, 1999.
Kelsey, S. "Hylomorphism in Aristotle's *Physics*." *Ancient Philosophy* 30 (2010): 107–24.
King, H. R. "Aristotle without *Prima Materia*." *Journal of the History of Ideas* 17 (1956): 370–89.
King, R. A. H., ed. *Common to Body and Soul. Philosophical Approaches to Explaining Living Behaviour in Greco-Roman Antiquity*. Berlin: W. de Gruyter, 2006.
King, R. "The Concept of Life and the Life-Cycle in *De Juventute*." In *Was ist "Leben"? Aristoteles' Anschauungen zur Entstehung und Funktionsweise von Leben*, edited by S. Föllinger, 171–87. Stuttgart: Franz Steiner Verlag, 2010.
———. "Review of A. P. Bos (2003)," *Classical Review* 57 (2007): 322–23.
Kissling, R. C. "The Ὄχημα-Πνεῦμα of the Neo-Platonists and the *De Insomniis* of Synesius of Cyrene." *American Journal of Philology* 43 (1922): 318–30.
Kosman, L. A. *The Activity of Being. An Essay on Aristotle's Ontology*. Cambridge: Harvard University Press, 2013.
———. "Animals and Other Beings in Aristotle." In *Philosophical Issues in Aristotle's Biology*, edited by A. Gotthelf and J. G. Lennox, 360–91. Cambridge: Cambridge University Press, 1987.
———. "Male and Female in Aristotle's *Generation of Animals*." In *Being, Nature, and Life in Aristotle. Essays in Honor of Allan Gotthelf*, edited by J. G. Lennox and R. Bolton, 147–67. Cambridge: Cambridge University Press, 2010; repr. in id., *Virtues of Thought. Essays on Plato and Aristotle*. Cambridge: Harvard University Press, 2014, 204–26 and 312.
Kouremenos, T. *Heavenly Stuff: The Constitution of the Celestial Objects and the Theory of Homocentric Spheres in Aristotle's Cosmology*. Stuttgart: Franz Steiner Verlag, 2010.
———, et al., eds. *The Derveni Papyrus. Edited with Introduction and Commentary*. Florence: Leo S. Olschki Editore, 2006.
Kühner, R., and B. Gerth. *Ausführliche Grammatik der Griechischen Sprache*. 2 vols. 4 Auflage. Leverkusen: Gottschalksche Verlagsbuchhandlung, 1955.
Kukkonen, T. "On Aristotle's World." *Oxford Studies in Ancient Philosophy* 46 (2014): 311–51.
Kullmann, W. *Aristoteles, Über die Teile der Lebewesen, übersetzt und erläutert*. Darmstadt: Wissenschaftliche Buchgesellschaft, 2007.
———. *Die Teleologie in der Aristotelischen Biologie. Aristoteles als Zoologe, Embryologe und Genetiker*. Heidelberg: Winter, 1979.
———. "Different Concepts of the Final Cause in Aristotle." In *Aristotle on Nature and Living Things*, edited by A. Gotthelf, 170–75. Pittsburgh: Mathesis Publications, 1985.
———. "Übergänge zwischen Unbeseeltheit und Leben bei Aristoteles." In *Was ist "Leben"? Aristoteles' Anschauungen zur Entstehung und Funktionsweise von Leben*, edited by S. Föllinger, 115–35. Stuttgart: Franz Steiner Verlag, 2010.
Kuntz, M. L., and P. G. Kuntz, eds. *Jacob's Ladder and the Tree of Life. Concepts of Hierarchy and the Great Chain of Being*. New York: Lang, 1987.

Laks, A., and M. Rashed, eds. *Aristote et le Mouvement des Animaux. Dix Études sur le* De Motu Animalium. Villeneuve d'Ascq: Presses Universitaires du Septentrion, 2004.

Lameere, W. "Au Temps où Franz Cumont s'interrogeait sur Aristote." *L'Antiquité Classique* 18 (1949): 279–324.

Lanza, D., and M. Vegetti. *Aristotele, Opere Biologiche*. Torino: Editrice Torinese, 1971.

Laurent, J. "La Voix Humaine (*De Anima* II, 8, 420b5–421a3)." In *Corps et Âme. Sur le De Anima d'Aristote*, edited by C. Viano, 169–87. Paris: J. Vrin, 1996.

Lee, H. D. P. *Aristotle,* Meteorologica *with an English Translation*. London: W. Heinemann, 1952.

Lefebvre, D. "La Critique du Mythe d'Atlas *DMA*, 3, 699a27–b11." In *Aristote et le Mouvement des Animaux. Dix Études sur le* De Motu Animalium, edited by A. Laks and M. Rashed, 115–36. Villeneuve d'Ascq: Presses Universitaires du Septentrion, 2004.

———. "L'Argument du Sectionnement des Vivants dans le *Parva Naturalia*: le Cas des Insectes." *Revue de Philosophie Ancienne* 20 (2002): 5–34.

Lefèvre, C. " '*Quinta Natura*' et Psychologie Aristotélicienne." *Revue Philosophique de Louvain* 69 (1971): 5–43.

———. *Sur l'Évolution d'Aristote en Psychologie*. Louvain: Éd. de l'Institut Supérieur de Philosophie, 1972.

Lendering, J. *Alexander de Grote. De Ondergang van het Perzische Rijk*. Amsterdam: Athenaeum; Polak & van Gennep, 2004.

Lennox, J. G. "Aristotle's Biology and Aristotle's Philosophy." In *A Companion to Ancient Philosophy*, edited by M. L. Gill and P. Pellegrin, 292–315. Oxford: Blackwell, 2006.

———. *Aristotle's Philosophy of Biology: Studies in the Origins of Life Science*. Cambridge: Cambrdige University Press, 2001.

———. "ΒΙΟΣ, ΠΡΑΞΙΣ and the Unity of Life." In *Was ist "Leben"? Aristoteles' Anschauungen zur Entstehung und Funktionsweise von Leben*, edited by S. Föllinger, 239–59. Stuttgart: Franz Steiner Verlag, 2010.

———. "*De Caelo* 2.2 and its Debt to *De Incessu Animalium*." In *New Perspectives on Aristotle's* De Caelo, edited by A. C. Bowen and C. Wildberg, 187–214 Leiden: Brill, 2009.

———. "Kinds, Forms of Kinds, and the More and the Less in Aristotle's Biology." In *Philosophical Issues in Aristotle's Biology*, edited by A. Gotthelf and J. G. Lennox, 339–59. Cambridge: Cambridge University Press, 1987.

———. "Teleology, Change, and Aristotle's Theory of Spontaneous Generation." *Journal of the History of Philosophy* 20 (1982): 219–38.

———. "Why Animals Must Keep Their Cool: Aristotle on the Need for Respiration (and other Forms of Cooling)." Paper for Conference on "Aristotle and his Predecessors on Heat, *Pneuma*, and Soul." Prague, June 12–14, 2014.

———, and R. Bolton, eds. *Being, Nature and Life in Aristotle. Essays in Honor of Allan Gotthelf*. Cambridge: Cambridge University Press, 2010.

Leroi, A. M. *The Lagoon. How Aristotle Invented Science*. London: Bloomsbury Circus, 2014.

Lesky, E. *Die Zeugungs- und Vererbungslehren der Antike und ihr Nachwirken*. Wiesbaden: Steiner, 1950.
Leunissen, M. E. M. P. J. *Explanation and Teleology in Aristotle's Science of Nature*. Cambridge: Cambridge University Press, 2010.
Lévêque, P. *Aurea Catena Homeri. Une Étude sur l'Allégorie Grecque*. Paris: Les Belles Lettres, 1959.
Lewis, O. "Heat in *De Spiritu*." Paper for Conference on "Aristotle and his Predecessors on Heat, *Pneuma*, and Soul." Prague, June 12–14, 2014.
———, and P. Gregoric. "The Context of *De Spiritu*." *Early Science and Medicine* 20 (2015): 125–49.
Liatsi, M. *Aristoteles, De Generatione Animalium. Buch V. Einleitung und Kommentar*. Trier: Wissenschaftliche Verlag, 2000.
Liddell, H. G., R. Scott, and H. S. Jones. *A Greek-English Lexicon*. Oxford: Clarendon Press, 1961.
Litwa, M. D. *Refutation of All Heresies. Translated with Introduction and Notes*. Atlanta: SBL Press, 2015.
Lloyd, G. E. R. *Aristotelian Explorations*. Cambridge: Cambridge University Press, 1996.
———. "The Empirical Basis of the Physiology of the *Parva Naturalia*." In G. E. R. Lloyd and G. E. L. Owen, *Aristotle on the Mind and the Senses*, 215–39. Cambridge: Cambridge University Press, 1978.
———. "*Pneuma* between Body and Soul." *Journal of the Royal Anthropological Institute* (N.S.) 13 (2007): 135–46.
Long, H. S. *A Study of the Doctrine of Metempsychosis in Greece from Pythagoras to Plato*. PhD dissertation, Princeton University, 1948.
Longo, O. *Aristotele, De Caelo. Introduzione, Testo Critico, Traduzione e Note*. Firenze: Sansoni, 1962.
Longrigg, J. "Elementary Physics in the Lyceum and Stoa." *Isis* 66 (1975): 211–29.
———. *Greek Rational Medicine. Philosophy and Medicine from Alcmaeon to the Alexandrians*. London: Routledge, 1993.
———. "A Seminal 'Debate' in the Fifth Century BC?" In *Aristotle on Nature and Living Things. Philosophical and Historical Studies presented to D. M. Balme*, edited by A. Gotthelf, 277–87. Bristol: 1985.
Lorimer, W. L. *Aristotelis qui fertur Libellus De Mundo*. Paris: Les Belles Lettres, 1933.
Louis, P. *Aristote, De la Génération des Animaux*. Paris, Les Belles Lettres, 1961.
———. *Aristote, Les Parties des Animaux, Texte Établi et Traduit*. Paris: Les Belles Lettres, 1956.
———. *Aristote, Problèmes. Texte Établi et Traduit*. 3 vols. Paris: Les Belles Lettres, 1991–94.
Lovejoy, A. O. *The Great Chain of Being. A Study of the History of an Idea*. Cambridge: Harvard University Press, 1936.
Lucchetta, G. A. "Perché agli Ubriaconi Piace il Sole? (*Problemata* III 32). Attività vitale, virtù del corpo ed effetti del vino." In *Attività e Virtù. Anima e Corpo in Aristotele*, edited by A. Fermani and M. Migliori, 179–95. Milano: Vita e Pensiero, 2009.

Luchte, J. *Pythagoras and the Doctrine of Transmigration. Wandering Souls.* London: Continuum I.P.G., 2009.
Luttikhuizen, G. P. "Traces of Aristotelian Thought in the *Apocryphon of John*." In *For the Children, Perfect Instruction. Studies in Honor of H.-M Schenke*, edited by H.-G. Bethge et al., 181–202. Leiden: Brill, 2002.
Macfarlane, P. *A Philosophical Commentary on Aristotle's* De Spiritu. PhD Thesis, Duquesne University, 2007.
———, and R. Polansky. "God, the Divine, and the ΝΟΥΣ in Relation to the *De Anima*." In *Ancient Perspectives on Aristotle's* De Anima, edited by G. van Riel and P. Destrée, 107–23. Leuven: Leuven University Press, 2009.
Makin, S. *Aristotle, Metaphysics* Θ. *Translated with an Introduction and Commentary.* Oxford: Oxford University Press, 2006.
Mansfeld, J. "Aristotle and the Others on Thales, or the Beginning of Natural Philosophy." In *Studies in the Historiography of Greek Philosophy*, 126–46. Assen: van Gorcum, 1990.
———. "Aristotle in the Aëtian *Placita*." In *Brill's Companion to the Reception of Aristotle in Antiquity*, edited by A. Falcon, 299–318 Leiden: Brill, 2016.
———. "Περὶ Κόσμου. A Note on the History of a Title." *Vigiliae Christianae* 46 (1992): 391–411.
Manuwald, B. *Das Buch H der Aristotelischen Physik. Eine Untersuchung zur Einheit und Echtheit.* Meisenheim am Glan: Verlag Anton Hain, 1971.
Marcovich, M. *Hippolytus, Refutatio Omnium Haeresium.* Berlin/New York: W. de Gruyter, 1986.
Marmodoro, A. *Aristotle on Perceiving Objects.* Oxford: Oxford University Press, 2014.
Martineau, E. "*Aiôn* chez Aristote 'De Caelo' 1.9: Théologie Cosmique ou Cosmo-théologie?" *Revue de Métaphysique et de Morale* 84 (1979): 32–69.
———. "Réponse à M. Denis O'Brien (À propos d'Aristote, 'De Caelo' 1.9)." *Revue de Métaphysique et de Morale* 85 (1980): 519–28.
Matthen, M. "The Holistic Presuppositions of Aristotle's Cosmology." *Oxford Studies in Ancient Philosophy* 20 (2001): 171–99.
Maudlin, T. "*De Anima* III 1: Is Any Sense Missing?" *Phronesis* 31 (1986): 51–67.
Mayhew, R. *The Female in Aristotle's Biology.* Chicago: University of Chicago Press, 2004.
———, ed. *The Aristotelean* Problemata Physica. *Philosophical and Scientific Investigations.* Leiden: Brill, 2015.
———, and D. C. Mirhady. *Aristotle, Problems, Edited and Translated.* 2 vols. London: W. Heinemann, 2011.
Méautis, G. "L'Orphisme dans l'*Eudème* d'Aristote." *Revue des Études Anciennes* 57 (1955): 254–67.
Mendelsohn, E. *Heat and Life. The Development of the Theory of Animal Heat.* Cambridge: Harvard University Press, 1964.
Menn, S. "Aristotle's Definition of Soul and the Programme of the *De Anima*." *Oxford Studies in Ancient Philosophy* 22 (2002): 83–139.
———. "Aristotle's Theology." In *The Oxford Handbook of Aristotle*, edited by C. Shields, 422–64. Oxford: Oxford University Press, 2012.

Meyer, M. W. "*Gospel of Thomas* Logion 114 Revisited." In *For the Children, Perfect Instruction. Studies in Honor of H.-M. Schenke*, edited by H.-G. Bethge et al., 101–11. Leiden: Brill, 2002.

Michaelis Ephesii In Aristotelis Parva Naturalia. Edited by P. Wendland. *C.A.G.* XXII, 1. Berlin: G. Reimer, 1903.

Migliori, M. "L'Anima in Aristotele. Una concezione polivalente e al contempo aporetica." In *Attività e Virtù. Anima e Corpo in Aristotele* edited by A. Fermani and M. Migliori, 227–60. Milano: Vita e Pensiero, 2009.

Miller, F. D. "Aristotle on the Separability of Mind." In *The Oxford Handbook of Aristotle*, edited by C. Shields, 306–39. Oxford: Oxford University Press, 2012.

Miller, M. G., and A. E. Miller. "Aristotle's Dynamic Conception of the *Psychè* as Being-Alive." In *Was ist "Leben"? Aristoteles' Anschauungen zur Entstehung und Funktionsweise von Leben*, edited by S. Föllinger, 55–88. Stuttgart: Franz Steiner Verlag, 2010.

Mirus, C. V. "The Metaphysical Roots of Aristotle's Teleology." *Review of Metaphysics* 57 (2003–04): 699–724.

Modrak, D. K. W. *Aristotle. The Power of Perception.* Chicago: University of Chicago Press, 1987; repr. 1989.

Moraux, P. *Aristote, Du Ciel. Texte Établi et Traduit.* Paris: Les Belles Lettres, 1965.

———. *Der Aristotelismus bei den Griechen von Andronikos bis Alexander von Aphrodisias.* Vol. 2. Berlin: W. de Gruyter, 1984.

———. "*Quinta Essentia.*" *P. W.-R. E.* 47 Halbbd. Stuttgart: Anton Hiersemann, 1963, 1171–263.

Morel, P.-M. *Aristote, Petits Traités d'Histoire Naturelle (Parva Naturalia), Traduction inédite, Introduction, Notes, et Bibliographie.* Paris: GF Flammarion, 2000.

———. "'Common to Soul and Body' in the Parva Naturalia (Aristotle, *Sens.* 1, 436b1–12)." In *Common to Body and Soul. Philosophical Approaches to Explaining Living Behaviour in Greco-Roman Antiquity*, 121–39. edited by R. A. H. King, Berlin: W. de Gruyter, 2006.

———. *De la Matière à l'Action. Aristote et le Problème du Vivant.* Paris: J. Vrin, 2007.

Morsink, J. *Aristotle on the Generation of Animals.* Washington, DC: University Press of America, 1982.

Movia, G. *Aristotele, L'Anima. Traduzione, Introd. e Commento.* Napoli: L. Loffredo, 1979.

Mugler, Ch. *Aristote, De la Génération et de la Corruption. Texte Établi et Traduit.* Paris: Les Belles Lettres, 1966.

Mugnier, R. *Aristote, Petits Traités d'Histoire Naturelle. Texte Établi et Traduit.* Paris: Les Belles Lettres, 1953.

———. "La Filiation des Manuscripts des *Parva Naturalia* d'Aristote." *Revue de Philologie* 78 (1952): 36–46.

Murphy, D. "Aristotle on Why Plants Cannot Perceive." *Oxford Studies in Ancient Philosophy* 29 (2005): 295–339.

Needham, J. *A History of Embryology.* 1934; 2nd ed. Cambridge: Cambridge University Press, 1959.

Neuhäuser, J. *Aristoteles' Lehre von dem Sinnlichen Erkenntnisvermögen und Seinen Organen.* Leipzig: E. Koschny, 1878.

Niederbacher, B., and E. Runggaldier, eds. *Die Menschliche Seele. Brauchen wir den Dualismus?* Frankfurt a. M.: Ontos, 2006.

Nothstein, R.-R. *Seele und Wahrnehmung. Eine Einführung in das Zweite Buch des Aristotelischen Werkes "De Anima."* Regensburg: Roderer Verlag, 1998.

Nussbaum, M. C. *Aristotle's De Motu Animalium. Text with Translation, Commentary, and Interpretive Essays.* Princeton, Princeton University Press, 1978.

———. "The Text of Aristotle's *De Anima*." In *Essays on Aristotle's* De Anima, edited by M. C. Nussbaum and A. Oksenberg Rorty, 1–6. Oxford: Clarendon Press, 1992.

Nuyens, F. *L'Évolution de la Psychologie d'Aristote.* Louvain: Éd. de l'Institut Supérieur de Philosophie, 1948.

Nuyens, F. J. C. J. *Ontwikkelingsmomenten in de Zielkunde van Aristoteles. Een Historisch-Philosophische Studie.* Nijmegen/Utrecht: Dekker & Van de Vegt, 1939.

O'Brien, D. "Aristote et l' 'Aiôn': Enquête sur un Critique Récente." *Revue de Métaphysique et de Morale* 85 (1980): 94–108; 87 (1982): 557–58.

———. "Life Beyond the Stars: Aristotle, Plato and Empedocles (*De Caelo* I 9, 279a11–22)." In *Common to Body and Soul. Philosophical Approaches to Explaining Living Behaviour in Greco-Roman Antiquity*, edited by R. A. H. King, 49–102. Berlin: W. de Gruyter, 2006.

Odzuck, S. *The Priority of Locomotion in Aristotle's Physics.* Göttingen: Vandenhoeck and Ruprecht, 2014.

Oehler, K. "Der Entwicklungsgedanke als Heuristisches Prinzip der Philosophiehistorie." *Zeitschrift für Philosophische Forschung* 17 (1963): 606–15; repr. in id., *Antike Philosophie und Byzantinisches Mittelalter. Aufsätze zur Geschichte des Griechischen Denkens*, 38–47. München: C. H. Beck, 1969.

———. "'Ein Mensch Erzeugt einen Menschen.' Über den Missbrauch der Sprachanalyse in der Aristotelesforschung." In *Einsichten. Gerhard Krüger zum 60 Geburtstag*, edited by K. Oehler and R. Schaeffler, 230–88. Frankfurt a. M.: Klostermann, 1962; repr. in id., *Antike Philosophie und Byzantinisches Mittelalter. Aufsätze zur Geschichte des Griechischen Denkens*, 121–45. München: C. H. Beck, 1969.

Palmer, J. A. "Aristotle on the Ancient Theologians." *Apeiron* 33 (2000): 181–205.

Patzig, G. "Körper und Geist bei Aristoteles—zum Problem des Funktionalismus." In *Body and Soul in Ancient Philosophy*, edited by D. Frede and B. Reis, 249–66. Berlin/New York: W. de Gruyter, 2009.

Peck, A. L. *Aristotle, Generation of Animals, with an English Translation.* London: W. Heinemann, 1942.

———. *Aristotle, Historia Animalium, in Three Volumes.* London: W. Heinemann, 1965.

———. *Aristotle, Parts of Animals; Movement of Animals; Progression of Animals, with an English Translation.* London: W. Heinemann, 1937.

Perkams, M. "Doppelte Entelecheia. Das Menschenbild in 'Simplikios' Kommentar zu Aristoteles' *De Anima*." *Elenchos* 24 (2003): 57–91.

Pétrement, S. "Le Mythe des Sept Archontes Créateurs peut-il s'Expliquer à Partir du Christianisme?" In *Le Origini dello Gnosticismo*, edited by U. Bianchi, 460–87. Leiden: Brill, 1967.

Philip, J. "The 'Pythagorean' Theory of the Derivation of Magnitudes." *Phoenix* 20 (1966): 32–50.
Picht, G. *Aristoteles, De Anima*. Stuttgart: Klett-Cotta, 1987.
Piquemal, J. "Sur une Métaphore de Clément d'Alexandrie: les Dieux, la Mort, la Mort des Dieux." *Revue Philosophique de la France* 88 (1963): 191–98.
Polansky, R. *Aristotle's De Anima*. Cambridge: Cambridge University Press, 2007.
Preus, A. "Man and Cosmos in Aristotle's *Metaphysics* Λ and the Biological works." In *Biologie, Logique et Métaphysique chez Aristote*, edited by D. Devereux and P. Pellegrin, 471–90. Paris: Éd. C.N.R.S, 1990.
———. "Science and Philosophy in Aristotle's *Generation of Animals*." *Journal for the History of Biology* 3 (1970): 1–52.
Primavesi, O. "Aristotle, *Metaphysics* A. A New Critical Edition with Introduction." In *Aristotle's* Metaphysics *Alpha. Symposium Aristotelicum, with a New Critical Edition of the Greek Text by O. Primavesi*, edited by C. Steel, 385–516. Oxford: Oxford University Press, 2012.
———. "Ein Blick in den Stollen von Skepsis: Vier Kapitel zur Frühen Überlieferung des Corpus Aristotelicum." *Philologus* 151 (2007): 51–77.
———, and K. Corcilius. *Aristoteles De Motu Animalium. Kritische Neuedition des Griechischen Textes und Deutsche Übersetzung*. Forthcoming.
Quarantotto, D. *Causa Finale, Sostanza, Essenza in Aristotele*. Napoli: Bibliopolis, 2005.
———. "Che Cosa Fa da una Forma un'Anima?—l'Organizzazione Anatomo-fisiologica dei Viventi e la Sede della *Psyche*." In *Attività e virtù. Anima e corpo in Aristotele*, edited by A. Fermani and M. Migliori, 367–81. Milano: Vita e Pensiero, 2009.
Raalte, M. van, *Theophrastus, Metaphysics, with an Introduction, Translation, and Commentary*. Leiden: Brill, 1993.
Rackham, H. *Aristotle, The Nicomachean Ethics, with an English Translation*. London: W. Heinemann, 1926.
Radice, R. *La Filosofia di Aristobulo e i Suoi Nessi con il De Mundo attribuito ad Aristotele*. Milano: Vita e Pensiero, 1994.
Radl, A. *Die Magnetstein in der Antike. Quellen und Zusammenhänge*. Stuttgart: Steiner Verlag Wiesbaden, 1988.
Ramelli, I., and D. Konstan, *Terms for Eternity:* Aiônios *and* Aïdios *in Classical and Christian Texts*. Piscataway, NJ: Gorgias Press, 2007.
Rapp, C., and K. Corcilus, eds. *Aristoteles-Handbuch: Leben, Werk, Wirkung*. Stuttgart: J. B. Metzler, 2011.
Rashed, M. *Aristote, De la Génération et la Corruption*. Nouvelle édition. Paris: Les Belles Lettres, 2005.
———. *Essentialisme. Alexandre d'Aphrodise entre Logique, Physique et Cosmologie*. Berlin: W. de Gruyter, 2007.
———. "La Préservation (σωτηρία) Objet des *Parva Naturalia* et Ruse de la Nature." *Revue de Philosophie Ancienne* 20 (2002): 35–59.
———, *L'Héritage Aristotélicien. Textes Inédits de l'Antiquité*. Paris: Les Belles Lettres, 2007.
Reale, G. *Aristotele. Trattato Sul Cosmo per Alessandro*. Napoli: Loffredo, 1974.

———, and A. P. Bos. *Il Trattato Sul Cosmo per Alessandro Attribuito ad Aristotele. Monografia Introduttiva, Testo Greco con Traduzione a Fronte, Commentario, Bibliografia Ragionata e Indici.* Milano: Vita e Pensiero, 1995.

Reeve, C. D. C. *Action, Contemplation, and Happiness: An Essay on Aristotle.* Cambridge: Harvard University Press, 2012.

Renehan, R. "Aristotle's Definition of Anger." *Philologus* 107 (1963): 61–74.

Repici, L. "Aristotele, l'Anima e l'Incorruttibilità: Note su De Longitudine et Brevitate Vitae, 1–3." In *Attività e Virtù. Anima e Corpo in Aristotele*, edited by A. Fermani and M. Migliori, 413–48. Milano: Vita e Pensiero, 2009.

Ricken SJ, F. "Review of A. P. Bos (2003)." *Theologie und Philosophie* 80 (2005): 425–27.

———. "Zur Methodologie von Aristoteles, De anima B 1–3," *Bijdragen* 59 (1998): 391–405.

Rist, J. M. *The Mind of Aristotle. A Study in Philosophical Growth.* Toronto: University of Toronto Press, 1989.

———. "On Greek Biology, Greek Cosmology, and Some Sources of Theological Pneuma." *Prudentia* (Supplem. vol.) (1985): 27–47; repr. in id., *Man, Soul and Body. Essays in Ancient Thought from Plato to Dionysius.* Aldershot: Variorum, 1996.

Rodier, G. *Aristote, Traité de l'Âme. Traduit et Annoté.* 2 vols. Paris: Ernest Leroux Éd., 1900; repr. 1985.

Roig Lanzillotta, L. "A Way of Salvation: Becoming like God in Nag Hammadi." *Numen* 60 (2013): 71–102.

Rolffs, E. *Aristoteles, Kleine Naturwissenschaftliche Schriften.* Leipzig: Felix Meiner, 1924.

Romeyer-Dherbey, G. "La Construction de la Théorie Aristotélicienne du Sentir." In *Corps et Âme. Sur le De Anima d'Aristote*, edited by C. Viano, 127–47. Paris: J. Vrin, 1996.

———. "Voir et Toucher. Le Problème de la Prééminence d'un Sens chez Aristote." *Revue de Métaphysique et de Morale* 96 (1991): 437–54.

Roreitner, R. "Perceptual *Pneuma* in Aristotle: What Happens Between the Individual Senses and the Central Organ?" Paper Prague Conference on "Aristotle and his Predecessors on Heat, *Pneuma* and Soul." Prague, June 12–14, 2014.

Roselli, A. [*Aristotele*] *De Spiritu*. Pisa: Ets. Editrice, 1992.

Rosen, J. "Essence and End in Aristotle." *Oxford Studies in Ancient Philosophy* 46 (2014): 73–107.

Rosenberg, J. *Rembrandt.* II vols. Cambridge: Harvard University Press, 1948.

Ross, Sir David. *Aristotle, De Anima, Edited, with Introduction and Commentary.* Oxford: Clarendon Press, 1961.

———. *Aristotle, Parva Naturalia.* Oxford: Clarendon Press, 1955.

Ross, W. D. *Aristotelis De Anima, Recognovit Brevique Adnotatione Instruxit.* Oxford: Clarendon Press, 1956.

———. *Aristotelis Fragmenta Selecta, Recognovit Brevique Adnotatione Instruxit.* Oxford: Clarendon Press, 1955; repr. 1969.

———. *Aristotelis Physica, Recognovit Brevique Adnotatione Critica Instruxit.* Oxford: Clarendon Press, 1950.

---. *Aristotle's Metaphysics. A Revised Text with Introduction and Commentary.* II vols. Oxford: Clarendon Press, 1924.
---. *Aristotle's Physics. A Revised Text with Introduction and Commentary.* Oxford: Clarendon Press, 1936.
---. "The Text of the *De Anima*." In *Autour d'Aristote. Recueil d'Études . . . offert à A. Mansion*, 207–15. Louvain: Publications Univ. de Louvain, 1955.
---, ed. *The Works of Aristotle.* Vol. 3. Oxford: Clarendon Press, 1931.
---, ed. *The Works of Aristotle.* Vol. 7. Oxford: Clarendon Press, 1927.
Runia, D. T. "Plato's *Timaeus*. First Principle(s), and Creation in Philo and Early Christian Thought." In *Plato's* Timaeus *as Cultural Icon*, edited by G. J. Reydams-Schils, 133–51. Notre Dame: University of Notre Dame Press, 2003.
Sachs, J. *Aristotle's Physics. A Guided Study.* New Brunswick: Rutgers University Press, 1995.
Saffrey, H. D. *Le ΠΕΡΙ ΦΙΛΟΣΟΦΙΑΣ d'Aristote et la Théorie Platonicienne des Idées Nombres.* Leiden: Brill, 1955.
Sanz Morales, M. *El Homero di Aristóteles.* Amsterdam: A. M. Hakkert, 1994.
---. "Las Citas Homéricas Contenidas en el Tratado *De Mundo*, Atribuido a Aristóteles; Prueba de su Inautenticidad." *Vichiana* 4 (1993): 38–47.
Schenkeveld, D. M. "Language and Style of the Aristotelian *De Mundo* in Relation to the Question of its Inauthenticity." *Elenchos* 12 (1991): 221–55.
Schneeweiss, G. *Aristoteles' Protreptikos: Hinführung zur Philosophie, rekonstruiert, übersetzt und kommentiert.* Darmstadt: Wissenschaftliche Buchgesellschaft, 2005.
---. "Die Überlieferungen von Themison und Sardanapall. Zur Datierung des Aristotelischen Protreptikos." *Gymnasium* 117 (2010): 531–57.
Schomakers, B. *Aristoteles, De Ziel.* Leende: Damon, 2000.
---. *Aristoteles, Over Poëzie.* Leende: Damon, 2000.
Schütrumpf, E., *Praxis und Lexis. Ausgewählte Schriften zur Philosophie von Handeln und Reden in der Klassischen Antike.* Stuttgart: Franz Steiner Verlag, 2008.
---. "Werner Jaeger Reconsidered." *Illinois Classical Studies* Supplement 3 (1992): 309–25.
Sedley, D. *Creationism and Its Critics in Antiquity.* Berkeley: University of California Press, 2007.
---. "Is Aristotle's Teleology Anthropocentric?" *Phronesis* 36 (1991): 179–96.
---. "*Metaphysics* Λ 10." In *Aristotle's* Metaphysics Lambda, edited by M. Frede and D. Charles, 327–50. Oxford: Clarendon Press, 2000.
---. "Teleology, Aristotelian and Platonic." In *Being, Nature, and Life in Aristotle. Essays in Honor of A. Gotthelf*, edited by J. G. Lennox and R. Bolton, 5–29. Cambridge: Cambridge University Press, 2010.
---. "Teleology, Aristotelian and Platonic." In *La Scienza e le Cause a Partire dalla Metafisica di Aristotele*, edited by F. Fronterotta, 313–49. Napoli: Bibliopolis, 2010.
---, ed. *The Cambridge Companion to Greek and Roman Philosophy.* Cambridge: Cambridge University Press, 2003.

Seidl, H. *Aristoteles, Über die Seele mit Einleitung, Übersetzung* (nach W. Theiler) *und Kommentar*. Hamburg: Felix Meiner Verlag, 1995.

Sharples, R. W. *Alexander of Aphrodisias, Supplement to On the Soul, Translated*. London: Duckworth, 2004.

———. "Aristotelian Theology after Aristotle." In *Traditions of Theology. Studies in Hellenistic Theology, Its Background and Aftermath*, edited by D. Frede and A. Laks, 1–40. Leiden: Brill, 2002.

———. "Common to Body and Soul: Peripatetic Approaches After Aristotle." In *Common to Body and Soul. Philosophical Approaches to Explaining Living Behaviour in Greco-Roman Antiquity*, edited by R. A. H. King, 165–86. Berlin: W. de Gruyter, 2006.

———. "The Hellenistic Period: What Happened to Hylomorphism?" In *Ancient Perspectives on Aristotle's* De Anima, edited by G. van Riel and P. Destrée, 155–66. Leuven: Leuven University Press, 2009.

———. *Peripatetic Philosophy 200 BC . . . AD 200. An Introduction and Collection of Sources in Translation*. Cambridge: Cambridge University Press, 2010.

———. "Philo and Post-Aristotelian Peripatetics." In *Philo of Alexandria and Post-Aristotelian Philosophy*, edited by F. Alesse, 55–73. Leiden: Brill, 2008.

———, and A. Sheppard, eds. *Ancient Approaches to Plato's* Timaeus. London: Institute of Classical Studies, 2003.

Shields, C. "The Aristotelian *Psuchê*." In *A Companion to Aristotle*, edited by G. Anagnostopoulos, 292–309. Chichester/Malden, MA: Wiley-Blackwell, 2009.

———. *Aristotle*. London: Routledge, 2007.

———. *Aristotle, De Anima. Translation with an Introduction and Commentary*. Oxford: Oxford University Press, 2016.

———. *Order in Multiplicity. Homonymy in the Philosophy of Aristotle*. Oxford: Oxford University Press, 1999.

———. "The Priority of Soul in Aristotle's *De Anima*: Mistaking Categories?" In *Body and Soul in Ancient Philosophy*, edited by D. Frede and B. Reis, 267–90. Berlin/New York: W. de Gruyter, 2009.

———. "Substance and Life in Aristotle." In *Aristotle on Life*, edited by J. Mouracade, 129–51. Kelowna, BC: Academic Printing and Publishing, 2008.

———, ed. *The Oxford Handbook of Aristotle*. Oxford: Oxford University Press, 2012.

Siwek SJ, P. *Aristoteles, De Anima, Libri Tres, graece et latine*. 3 vols. Romae: Apud Aedes Pont. Univ. Gregorianae, 1954.

———. *Aristotelis Parva Naturalia, Graece et Latine, edidit, versione auxit, notis illustravit*. Romae, Desclée et Cie, 1963.

———. "Comment le Premier Moteur meut l'Univers?" *Divinitas* 11 (1967): 377–92.

———. *Le "De Anima" d'Aristote dans les Manuscripts Grecs*. Città del Vaticano: Biblioteca Apostolica Vaticana, 1965.

———. *Les Manuscrits Grecs des* Parva Naturalia *d'Aristote*. Rome: Desclée et Cie, 1961.

Skemp, J. B. "The Activity of Immobility." In *Études sur la Métaphysique d'Aristote* (Actes du VIe Symposium Aristotelicum) 1978, 229–245.

Slakey, T. J. "Aristotle on Sense Perception." *Philosophical Review* 70 (1961): 470–84.

Smith, J. A., and W. D. Ross, eds. *The Works of Aristotle*. Vol. 5. Oxford: Clarendon Press, 1912.
Solmsen, F. "Greek Philosophy and the Discovery of the Nerves." *Museum Helveticum* 18 (1961): 150–97; repr. in id., *Kleine Schriften*. Hildesheim: Georg Olms, 1968.
———. "The Vital Heat, the Inborn *Pneuma*, and the Aether." *Journal of Hellenic Studies* 77 (1957): 119–23.
Sophoniae in Libros Aristoteles De Anima Paraphrasis. Edited by M. Hayduck. *C.A.G.* XXIII Pars 1. Berolini: Typis G. Reineri, 1883.
Sorabji, R. "Body and Soul in Aristotle." *Philosophy* 49 (1974): 63–89.
———. "Intentionality and Physiological Processes: Aristotle's Theory of Sense-Perception." In *Essays on Aristotle's* De Anima, edited by M. C. Nussbaum and A. Oksenberg Rorty, 195–225. Oxford: Clarendon Press, 1992.
Spoerri, W. "Inkommensurabilität, Automaten und Philosophisches Staunen im Alpha der 'Metaphysik.'" In *Aristoteles, Werk und Wirkung. Paul Moraux gewidmet* Bd. 1, edited by J. Wiesner, 239–72. Berlin: W. de Gruyter, 1985.
Spruit, L. G. M. *Religie en Abortus. Interactiemodellen ter Verklaring van de Houding tegenover Abortus*. Nijmegen: Instituut voor Toegepaste Sociale Wetenschappen, 1991.
Steel, C. *Aristoteles, De Eerste Filosofie. Metaphysica Alpha, Vertaald, Ingeleid en van Aantekeningen Voorzien*. Groningen: Historische Uitgeverij, 2002.
Szlezák, Th. A. "Platon und die neuzeitliche Theorie des platonischen Dialogs." *Elenchos* 10 (1989): 337–57.
———. *Platon und die Schriftlichkeit der Philosophie. Interpretationen zu den frühen und mittleren Dialogen*. Berlin: W. de Gruyter, 1985.
Theiler, W. *Aristoteles, Werke in Deutscher Übersetzung* Band 13: *Über die Seele*. Darmstadt: Wissenschaftliche Buchgesellschaft, 1959; Zweite Auflage 1966.
———. *Zur Geschichte der Teleologischen Naturbetrachtung bis auf Aristoteles*. Zürich/Leipzig, 1925; repr. Berlin: W. de Gruyter, 1965.
Thiel, D. *Die Philosophie des Xenokrates im Kontext der Alten Akademie*. München/Leipzig: K. G. Saur, 2006.
Thillet, P. *Aristote, De l'Âme. Traduit du Grec. Édition Établie, Présentée et Annotée*. Paris: Gallimard, 2005.
Thom, J. C. "The Power of God in Pseudo-Aristotle's *De Mundo*: An Alternative Approach." In *The World Soul and Cosmic Space: New Readings on the Relation of Ancient Cosmology and Psychology*, edited by C. Helmig and C. Markschies. Forthcoming.
———, ed. *Cosmic Order and Divine Power. Pseudo-Aristotle*, On the Cosmos. *Introduction, Text, Translation, and Interpretive Essays*. Tübingen: Mohr Siebeck, 2014.
Thorp, J. J. "The Luminousness of the Quintessence." *Phoenix* 36 (1982): 104–23.
Toelner, R. "Urzeugung." *Historisches Wörterbuch der Philosophie* Bd 11, 490–96. Basel: Schwabe & Co, 2001.
Toepfer, G., and F. Michelini. *Organismus: Die Erklärbarkeit des Lebendigen*. Freiburg/München: K. Alber, 2016.

Torstrik, A. *Aristotelis De Anima, libri tres*. Berlin: Weidmannsche Buchhandlung, 1862; repr. Hildesheim: G. Olms, 1970.

Tracy SJ, T. J. "Heart and Soul in Aristotle." In *Essays in Ancient Greek Philosophy*, vol. 2, edited by J. P. Anton and A. Preus, 321–39. Albany: State University of New York Press, 1983.

———. "The Soul as Boatman of the Body, Presocratics to Descartes." *Diotima* 7 (1979): 195–99.

———. "The Soul/Boatman Analogy in Aristotle's *De Anima*." *Classical Philology* 77 (1982): 97–112.

Tricot, J. *Aristote, De l'Âme, Traduction Nouvelle et Notes*. Paris: J. Vrin, 1959.

———. *Aristote, Parva Naturalia suivi du Traité Ps. Aristotélicien De Spiritu, Traduction Nouvelle et Notes*. Paris: J. Vrin, 1951.

Tuominen, M. *The Ancient Commentators on Plato and Aristotle*. Stocksfield: Acumen, 2009.

Tzvetkova-Graser, A. "The Concepts of οὐσία and δύναμις in *De Mundo* and Their Parallels in Hellenistic-Jewish and Christian Texts." In *Cosmic Order and Divine Power. Pseudo-Aristotle, On the Cosmos. Introduction, Text, Translation, and Interpretive Essays*, edited by J. C. Thom, 133–52. Tübingen: Mohr Siebeck, 2014.

Untersteiner, M. *Aristotele, Della Filosofia. Introduzione, Testo, Traduzione e Commento Esegetico*. Roma: Edizioni di Storia e Letteratura, 1963.

Urmson, J. O. *Simplicius: On Aristotle, Physics 5*. Edited by R. Sorabji. London: G. Duckworth, 1996.

Valdevit, R. "Note sulla Teologia dello Scritto Pseudo-Aristotelico *de Mundo*." *Studi Italiani di Filologia Classica* 3 (1986): 29–41.

Vallejo Campos, A. *Aristóteles, Fragmentos*. Introducción, Traducción y Notas. Madrid: Editorial Gredos, 2005.

Viano, C., ed. *Corps et Âme. Sur le De Anima d'Aristote*. Paris: J. Vrin, 1996.

Vinci, T., and J. S. Robert. "Aristotle and Modern Genetics." *Journal of the History of Ideas* 66 (2005): 201–21.

Voigt, U. "Von Seelen, Figuren und Seeleuten. Zur Einheit und Vielfalt des Begriffs des Lebens (ζωή) bei Aristoteles." In *Was ist "Leben"? Aristoteles' Anschauungen zur Entstehung und Funktionsweise von Leben*, edited by S. Föllinger, 17–33. Stuttgart: Franz Steiner Verlag, 2010.

Vuillemin-Diem, G. "Anmerkungen zum Pasikles-Bericht und zu Echtheitszweifeln am grösseren und kleineren Alpha in Handschriften und Kommentaren." In P. Moraux et al., *Zweifelhaftes im Corpus Aristotelicum. Studien zu Einigen Dubia*, 157–192. Berlin: W. de Gruyter, 1983.

Wagner, H. *Aristoteles, Physikvorlesung*. Darmstadt: Wissenschaftliche Buchgesellschaft, 1967.

Warrington, J. *Aristotle's Ethics*. London: Everyman's Library, 1963.

Webb, Ph. "Bodily Structures and Psychic Faculties in Aristotle's Theory of Perception." *Hermes* 110 (1982): 25–50.

Wehrli, F. "Aristoteles in Neuer und Neuester Forschung." *Neue Zürcher Zeitung*, 4 September 1966; repr. in *Theoria und Humanitas. Gesammelte Schriften zur Antiken Gedankenwelt*. Zürich: Artemis Verlag, 1972.
———. *Die Schule des Aristoteles* Heft VIII *Eudemos von Rhodos*. Basel: B. Schwabe, 1955.
Whiting, J. "Living bodies." In *Essays on Aristotle's De Anima*, edited by M. C. Nussbaum and A. Oksenberg Rorty, 75–91. Oxford: Clarendon Press, 1992.
———. "Locomotive Soul: The Parts of Soul in Aristotle's Scientific Works." *Oxford Studies in Ancient Philosophy* 22 (2002): 141–200.
Wians, W., ed. *Aristotle's Philosophical Development. Problems and Prospects*. Lanham/London: Rowman, 1996.
Wicksteed, P. H., and F. M. Cornford. *Aristotle, The Physics, with an English Translation*. 2 vols. London: W. Heinemann, 1929–1934.
Wieland, W. *Die Aristotelische Physik. Untersuchungen über die Grundlegung der Naturwissenschaft und die sprachlichen Bedingungen der Prinzipienforschung bei Aristoteles*. Göttingen: Vandenhoeck und Ruprecht, 1961; 2e Auflage 1970.
Wilberding, J. "The Revolutionary Embryology of the Neoplatonists." *Oxford Studies in Ancient Philosophy* 49 (2015): 321–61.
Wildberg, C. *John Philoponus' Criticism of Aristotle's Theory of Aether*. Berlin: W. de Gruyter, 1988.
Williams, C. J. F. *Aristotle's De Generatione et Corruptione, Translated with Notes*. Oxford: Clarendon Press, 1982.
Williams, M.A. "The Demonizing of the Demiurge: the Innovation of Gnostic Myth." In *Innovation in Religious Traditions. Essays in the Interpretation of Religious Change*, edited by M. A. Williams, 73–107. Berlin: Mouton De Gruyter, 1992.
———. *Rethinking "Gnosticism." An Argument for Dismantling a Dubious Category*. Princeton: Princeton University Press, 1996.
Wilson, M. *Structure and Method in Aristotle's Meteorologica: a More Disorderly Nature*. Cambridge: Cambridge University Press, 2013.
Witt, C. "Form, Normativity, and Gender in Aristotle. A Feminist Perspective." In *Feminist Interpretations of Aristotle*, edited by C. A. Freeland, 118–37. University Park: The Pennsylvania State University Press, 1998.
Wolters, A. M. "Belshazzar's Feast and the Cult of the Moon God Sîn." *Bulletin for Biblical Research* 5 (1995): 199–206.
Woodruff, P. "Aristotle's *Poetics*: The Aim of Tragedy." In *A Companion to Aristotle*, edited by A. Anagnostopoulos, 612–27. Malden MA: Wiley-Blackwell, 2009.
Wootton, D. *The Invention of Science. A New History of the Scientific Revolution*. London: Allen Lane, 2015.
Yates, V. "The Titanic Origin of Humans: The Melian Nymphs and Zagreus." *Greek, Roman and Byzantine Studies* 44 (2004): 183–98.
Zambon, M. "Il Significato Filosofico della Dottrina dell' Ὄχημα dell'Anima." In *Studi sull'Anima in Plotino*, edited by R. Chiaradonna, 305–35. Napoli: Bibliopolis, 2005.
Zekl, H. G. *Aristoteles' Physik / Vorlesung über Natur* Griechisch-Deutsch. Hamburg: Felix Meiner Verlag, 1987–88.

Zhmud, L. *Pythagoras and the Early Pythagoreans*. Oxford: Oxford University Press, 2012.
Zierlein, S. *Aristoteles, Historia Animalium Buch I und II, Übersetzt, Eingeleitet und Kommentiert*. Berlin: Akademie Verlag, 2013.
Zimmermann, R., *Geschlechtermetaphorik und Gottesverhältnis. Traditionsgeschichte und Theologie eines Bildfeldes in Urchristentum und Antiker Umwelt* (Tübingen: Mohr Siebeck, 2001).

Index of Modern Names

Althoff, J., 93, 135, 136, 143, 205–207
Annas, J., 132
Aubenque, P., 211

Bakker, F., 106
Balme, D. M., 64, 65, 70, 194
Barbotin, E., 220, 223, 232, 247
Barnes, J., 98
Beere, J., 82, 102, 202, 219
Bees, R. 132
Beets, J., 203
Berg, I. J. M. van den, 222
Bergeron, M., 242
Berryman, S., 132, 137, 180
Betegh, G., 72, 101, 119, 168, 169, 172, 173, 175
Blair, G. A., 219
Bloch, D., 161
Blumenthal, H. J., 139
Blyth, D., 53, 54
Bodéüs, R., 2, 222, 231
Bodnár, I. M., 55
Boeri, M. D., 245
Bolton, R., 245
Bonitz, H., 80, 116, 222, 224, 249
Boot, P., 72
Boyancé, P., 127
Boylan, M., 73, 162, 220
Brague, R., 256
Brisson, L., 38, 105, 107, 169, 174, 239

Broadie, S., 5, 24, 68, 151, 171, 174, 218, 233
Brockmann, C., 250, 251
Bronstein, D., 132
Buchheim, T., 35
Buddensiek, F., 133, 280
Burkert, W., 174, 176
Burnyeat, M. F., 160, 235

Calder, W. C., 6
Carbone, A. L., 83, 159, 282
Carpenter, A. D., 76
Carteron, H., 54
Casadio, G., 122
Chandler, C., 101
Charles, D., 133, 218
Cleary, J. J., 31, 169, 256
Cohoe, C., 30
Coles, A., 16, 30
Cooper, J. M., 230
Corcilius, K., 23, 26, 45, 50, 53, 54, 57, 59, 116, 132, 163, 164, 205, 220, 229, 250, 280, 282
Corte, M. de, 247
Couloubaritsis, L., 219
Crowley, T. J., 46

Daniélou, J., 127
Diamond, E., 11, 21, 25, 30, 36, 68, 81, 171, 223, 258, 273, 276, 277
Dijksterhuis, E. J., 47, 110, 111

Dillon, J., 231
Donini, P. L., 123
Drachmann, A. G., 54
Drossaart Lulofs, H. J., 34, 65, 239
Dudley, J., 100, 146
Düring, I., 132, 188, 218, 285
Dufour, R., 242
Duhot, J. J., 19
Duprat, G. L., 83
Durrant, M., 222

Easterling, H. J., 44
Edelstein, L., 107, 147, 254
Edmonds, R. G., 77, 125, 176
Egermann, F., 269

Falcon, A., 46, 140, 148, 187, 218
Ferwerda, R., 7, 70, 79, 83, 135, 136, 147, 149, 167, 195, 200, 204, 263, 282
Festugière, A. J., 139
Finamore, J. E., 134
Flashar, H., 203
Förster, A., 247
Fortenbaugh, W. W., 203
Frank, E., 80
Frede, D., 2
Freudenthal, G., 132, 136, 144
Furley, D. J., 110, 113
Furth, M., 179, 219, 224, 252

Gaiser, K., 216
Gallop, D., 157
Gelber, J., 250
Genequand, C., 102, 287
Gerson, L. P., 279
Geurts, P. M. M., 79, 186
Gigon, O., 238
Giltaij, J., 107
Gohlke, P., 223
Gotthelf, A., 218, 285
Gottschalk, H. B., 98
Graeser, A., 216
Graham, D. W., 219

Gregoric, P., 7, 45, 50, 54, 57, 59, 72, 101, 109, 119, 147, 149, 164, 166, 189, 201, 205, 211, 263, 282
Gregory, A., 111, 174
Groot, J. de, 60, 109

Haas, F. A. J. de, 242
Hackforth, R., 77
Hahm, D. E., 132
Hahmann, A., 158
Hamlyn, D. W., 152
Heinemann, G., 77, 82, 250, 251
Helleman-Elgersma, W., 78
Hicks, R. D., 146, 222
Holwerda, D., 115
Hübner, J., 223
Hutchinson, D. S., 156

Jackson, P., 257
Jaeger, W., 1, 6, 7, 13, 83, 133, 262, 267, 274, 282, 286
Jannone, A., 220, 223
Jerouschek, G., 242
Johansen, T. K., 53, 54, 77, 136, 138, 214, 216, 222, 253, 257, 280
Johnson, M. R., 25, 156, 216, 230
Jones, D. A., 242
Jori, A., 13, 31, 135, 141, 269

Kahn, C. H., 158
Keizer, H. M., 122
King, R. A. H., 132
Kissling, R. C., 134
Konstan, D., 122
Kosman, L. A., 15, 29, 41, 46, 53, 66, 69, 213, 219, 223, 229, 234, 242, 250, 255, 279
Kouremenos, T., 133, 176
Kuhar, M., 109, 149, 201, 263, 282
Kukkonen, T., 98, 99, 286
Kullmann, W., 13, 183, 211, 217, 268
Kuntz, M. L., 107
Kuntz, P. G., 107

Lefebvre, D., 57, 78, 153
Lendering, J., 99
Lennox, J. C., 64, 83, 147, 250, 283
Leroi, A. M., 66, 73, 99, 163, 197, 214, 225, 256
Lesky, E., 67, 107, 152, 155, 162, 198
Leunissen, M. E. M. P. J., 153, 213, 217, 272
Lévêque, P., 16, 107, 108
Lewis, O., 7, 147, 201, 263, 282
Liatsi, M., 157
Lloyd, G. E. R., 132, 156
Long, H. S., 77
Longrigg, J., 47, 132, 155
Lorimer, W. L., 110, 116
Louis, P., 203
Lovejoy, A. O., 16, 107
Lucchetta, G. A., 253
Luttikhuizen, G. P., 127

Macfarlane, P., 7, 263
Makin, S., 219
Mansfeld, J., 91, 98, 209
Martineau, E., 12
Matthen, M., 286
Mayhew, R., 68, 197, 239
Méautis, G., 276
Mendelsohn, E., 133
Menn, S., 2, 256, 279
Meyer, M. W., 289
Miller, F. D., 222, 257
Mirus, C. V., 219, 272
Moraux, P., 6, 19, 31, 98, 179
Morel, P. M., 66, 140, 219, 242, 256
Morsink, J., 24
Mugler, Ch., 193

Needham, J., 64
Nussbaum, M. C., 16, 17, 45, 132, 163, 203
Nuyens, F. J. C. J., 59, 213

O'Brien, D., 12, 31
Odzuck, S., 53

Oehler, K., 6

Patzig, G., 222
Peck, A. L., 152, 155, 164, 259
Pedriali, F., 168
Perkams, M., 248
Pétrement, S., 127
Pfeiffer, C., 168
Philip, J., 7, 31
Picht, G., 246
Polansky, R., 22, 81, 151, 214, 223, 231, 257, 280
Preus, A., 135, 148, 238
Primavesi, O., 16, 58, 116, 163, 243

Quarantotto, D., 230

Raalte, M. van, 17
Radl, A., 91, 94
Ramelli, I., 122
Rapp, C., 83
Rashed, M., 6, 24, 47, 268
Reale, G., 6, 17, 98, 106, 115, 176, 177, 279
Reeve, C. D. C., 98, 110, 133, 225
Renehan, R., 195, 202
Repici, L., 188, 190
Ricken SJ, F., 245
Roig Lanzillotta, L., 25, 123
Roreitner, R., 146
Rose, V., 267
Rosen, J., 193
Ross, W. D., 2, 22, 157, 213, 249, 257

Sanz Morales, M., 106
Schenkeveld, D. M., 98
Schneeweiss, G., 156
Schomakers, B., 222
Seidl, H., 222
Sedley, D., 28, 218, 285
Sharples, R. W., 39, 119, 121, 209, 242, 245, 248, 260, 275, 280
Shields, C., 252, 255
Siwek SJ, P., 88, 222

Skemp, J. B., 35
Solmsen, F., 132, 135
Spoerri, W., 60
Spruit, L. G. M., 242
Steel, C., 273
Szlezák, Th. A., 168

Theiler, W., 217, 223
Thiel, D., 76, 121, 174
Thillet, P., 91, 154, 214, 223, 247, 257
Thom, J. C., 6, 38, 98, 103, 115, 118, 149, 262
Torstrik, A., 247
Tzvetkova-Graser, A., 101

Untersteiner, M., 13

Valdevit, R., 126

Wehrli, F., 133
Whiting, J. E., 2
Wieland, W., 218, 230
Wildberg, C., 31, 98, 144, 168, 169, 172, 174, 175, 178
Williams, C. J. F. 46
Williams, M. A., 127
Wilson, M., 287
Wolters, A. M., 203
Wootton, D., 47

Yates, V. 125

Zambon, M., 134
Zeller, E., 268
Zhmud, L., 174
Zierlein, S., 48
Zimmermann, R., 129

Index of Ancient Names

Academy, 174
Adam, 127, 128
Alcibiades, 114
Alexander of Aphrodisias, 4, 7, 17, 59, 64, 102, 106, 117, 150, 234, 242, 243, 248, 255, 260, 265, 269, 280, 281, 286, 287
Alexander of Macedon, 17, 99, 107, 114, 286
Anaxagoras, 50, 92, 183, 193
Aphrodite (Ourania), 139
Aristogenes, 7, 79, 83, 150, 282
Ariston, 79, 83, 150, 283
Aristobulus, 32
Arius, 104
Asia, 155
Athene, 239
Atlas, 78

Basilides of Alexandria, 75, 76, 104, 124
Belshazzar, 203

Cambyses, 17
Cicero, 122, 123, 144
Circe, 25, 122
Cyprus, 145, 238

Darius, 17
Dionysus (Zagreus), 124, 232
Diotima, 25

Ecbatana, 98, 113
Elea, 37
Elis, 229
Empedocles, 193
Endymion, 122
Etruscans, 138, 229, 237, 254, 274
Eudemus of Cyprus, 139, 238
Eudemus of Rhodos, 180–181
Eurydice, 125
Eustathius, 16
Eve, 127, 128

Gnostics, 84, 103, 104, 124, 127

Heracleia, 18, 89, 91
Heraclitus, 100
Hermes, 108, 190
Hermias, 119
Hesiod, 145, 277
Hippocratics, 116, 150
Homer, 16, 106, 177, 209

Ithaca, 25, 53
Ixion, 78

Kronos, 58, 121, 122, 123, 124, 228, 229, 238, 276

Lyceum, 5, 144, 174

Magnesia, 18, 89, 91
Mètis, 239
Midas, 104, 186, 232, 238
Mieza, 17, 286

Neo-Platonists, 134

Odysseus, 25, 53, 122, 144
Orpheus, 125, 126
Orphics, 69, 77, 79, 80, 84, 176, 198, 239, 262, 276, 289
Ouranos, 238

Paul, 212
Penelope, 25, 122, 144
Peripatos, 1, 174
Persepolis, 98
Persia, 104, 108, 113, 114, 155
Phaeacians, 53
Philip of Macedon, 99
Philo of Alexandria, 32, 71, 89, 103, 104, 122, 126
Philolaus, 98
Philoponus, 94, 98, 178
Platonists (Middle), 76, 103, 156
Plotinus, 30, 90, 103, 124, 127, 128, 184
Plutarch, 123
Presocratics, 3, 104, 152, 262
Pythagoreans, 80, 173, 174, 175, 176

Sardanapallus, 156, 186
Silenus, 124, 125, 126, 232, 233, 238, 274, 277
Simplicius, 181
Sophia, 104, 127, 128, 184
Speusippus, 32, 174
Stobaeus, 98
Stoics, 103, 179, 205, 243, 262, 265
Susa, 98

Tartarus, 276
Tertullian, 123
Thales of Miletus, 91–94, 99, 100, 101, 112, 202, 211, 286
Themison, 139
Theophrastus 17
Timaeus of Locri, 80, 173
Titans, 58, 124, 126, 232, 238, 276

Velleius, 122, 123
Venus, 108

Xenocrates, 169, 174, 175
Xerxes, 17

Yaldabaoth, 104, 127, 128

Zeus, 58, 112, 118, 121, 122, 124, 228, 239

Index of Texts

Alexander of Aphrodisias
  De Anima (16, 11), 242
  Mantissa (101, 15), 248
Aristotle
  Analytica Posteriora
    I (7, 75a38), 231
  De Generatione Animalium
    I (20, 727b31–33), 196, 197
    I (21, 729a20–1), 68
    I (21, 729b4–8), 65
    I (21, 729b22–3a28), 69, 71, 208
    I (22, 730b19–22), 27, 63, 64
    I (22, 731a30), 200
    I (23, 731a31–b4), 22
    II (1, 731b24–2a3), 33, 69
    II (1, 732a1–4), 24, 33, 34, 65, 71, 239, 275, 289
    II (1, 732a18), 201
    II (1, 734b9–17), 64, 70, 71, 110, 215, 253, 287
    II (1, 734b28–5a4), 208, 220
    II (1, 735a4–22), 81, 257, 260
    II (1, 735a20), 81
    II (1, 735b4–22), 230
    II (2, 735b37–6a21), 92, 143
    II (2, 735b33), 143
    II (3, 736a27), 80
    II (3, 736b27–7a7), 14, 48, 80, 115, 134–140, 142, 143, 152, 181, 182, 188, 192, 197, 200, 201, 202, 206, 207, 215, 228, 237, 248, 262, 273
    II (3, 736b27–8), 12, 80, 81, 257
    II (3, 737a7–11), 65, 257
    II (3, 737a16–18), 257
    II (4, 738b20–24), 196
    II (6, 741b37), 194, 207
    II (6, 742a5), 83
    II (6, 744a26–31), 161, 162
    II (8, 748b31–34), 197
    III (2, 752a2), 201
    III (4, 755a20), 48
    III (11, 761b13–22), 14, 28, 35, 84, 113, 136, 144, 147, 148, 195, 259
    III (11, 762a18–3a25), 24, 93, 94, 100, 115, 116, 136, 144, 145, 146, 149, 166, 186, 200, 201, 288
    III (11, 762b14), 67
    III (11, 762b16–18), 138
    IV (1, 765b16), 80
    IV (3, 767b6–12), 198
    IV (3, 767b20–7), 72
    IV (3, 768a14–b1), 73
    IV (4, 772a32), 80
    V (2, 781a23–24), 156, 157
    V (8, 789b8), 80, 139, 194, 208
  De Incessu Animalium
    (3, 705b2), 249
    (7, 707a30–b2), 180, 181

Aristotle *(continued)*
  Ethica Nicomachea
    VII (14, 1154b11–13), 259
  Fragments of Lost Works
    Eudemus, 274–278
      fr. 1, 238
      fr. 2, 27, 193, 284
      fr. 5, 25
      fr. 6, 44, 105, 126, 232, 238, 274
      fr. 7a, 190
      fr. 11a, 229
    On Philosophy
      fr. 1–4, 100
      fr. 16, 30, 33, 238
      fr. 26, 76, 123, 284
      fr. 27a–d, 43, 138, 185
    Protrepticus
      fr. 10b, 126, 138, 254, 274
      fr. 20, 123
      fr. B 65 (Düring), 251
  History of Animals
    I (9, 492a23), 157
    I (17, 496a4), 48
    I (17, 496a17), 48
  Mechanical Problems, 55
  Metaphysics
    A (1, 980a1), 238
    A (2, 982b22–3a11), 233, 273
    A (2, 983a2), 33, 276
    A (2, 982b29–3a11), 124, 151, 228, 273
    A (2, 983a11–21), 210
    A (3, 983a27–32), 191
    A (3, 983b20–4a3), 92, 100, 116
    A (6, 987b13), 87
    A (6, 988a8–10), 191
    A (9, 991a20–22), 30, 80, 87, 192
    A (9, 991a11), 191
    α (1, 993b9–11), 125, 151, 228, 273
    Γ (2, 1003b16–17), 15, 286
    Δ (12, 1019a15–17), 215
    Z (7, 1032a24–25), 281
    Z (16, 1040b5–16), 178
    K (12, 1068b30–9a14), 181
    Λ (1, 1069a30–3), 41
    Λ (3, 1070a18), 26, 253
    Λ (7, 1072a26), 51, 57, 58, 281
    Λ (7, 1072b3), 41, 216
    Λ (7, 1072b13), 14, 286
    Λ (7, 1072b14), 15, 177
    Λ (7, 1072b26), 219, 273
    Λ (7, 1072b29), 29, 174
    Λ (8, 1074a35–6), 220
    Λ (10, 1075a13–15), 209–210
    Λ (10, 1075b37–6a4), 175
    Λ (10, 1076a4), 32
    M (2, 1077a17–29), 169, 178
    N (3, 1090b19), 32, 175
  Motion of Animals, 55–58
    (3, 699a27–b11), 78
    (4, 699b32–700a6), 15, 106, 177
    (7, 701b2–11), 281
    (7, 701b15), 58, 116, 163
    (8, 702a17–19), 203
    (10, 703a4–9), 36, 51, 58, 163, 259
    (10, 703a9–11), 59, 83, 163, 268
    (10, 703a20), 162, 163, 203
    (10, 703a24–25), 162, 196
    (10, 703a28–b2), 163, 164
    (11, 703b23), 199, 258
  On Dreams (3, 461a30), 158
  On Generation and Corruption
    I (2, 315a29–32), 193
    I (2, 316b19–20), 173
    II (10, 336a16–8), 46
    II (10, 336b17), 46
    II (10, 336b27–7a7), 28, 34, 35, 275, 276
  On Length and Shortness of Life
    (2–3), 48, 117, 186–190, 195
    (3, 465b2), 83, 187, 188
    (3, 465b11–12), 196, 202
    (6, 467a33), 48, 88
  On Memory
    (1, 450a27–b11), 161
    (2, 453a14), 157

On Respiration
  (2, 470b28), 93
  (13, 477a15–25), 184
  (15, 478a16), 48, 201
On Sense
  (1), 156
  (1, 436a1–b3), 259
  (2), 158
  (2, 438b30), 156
  (2, 439a1–5), 155, 159
On Sleep
  (1, 454a8–10), 157, 213
  (1, 454b27–29), 223
On the Cosmos, 1, 2, 6, 7, 8, 19, 68, 97–117, 261–262, 286–287
  (1, 391a11–15), 118
  (1, 391b3–12), 99, 107, 118
  (2, 391b14–2a10), 14, 56, 112, 115, 141
  (2, 392a18–34), 108, 141, 178
  (4, 394b9–12), 83, 101, 115, 147, 148, 166, 199, 201, 261
  (5, 396b7–11), 38, 289
  (5, 396b27–29), 108, 116
  (5, 397a8–11), 122
  (5, 397a18), 116
  (6, 397b9), 19, 176
  (6, 397b11), 98
  (6, 397b14), 120, 176
  (6, 397b17), 93, 100, 288
  (6, 397b21–24), 104, 105, 210
  (6, 397b24–27), 106
  (6, 397b27–30), 110, 113, 114, 115, 121, 185
  (6, 397b33), 17, 22, 101, 108, 179
  (6, 398a5), 116
  (6, 398a14), 104
  (6, 398a18–35), 113
  (6, 398b8), 108, 116
  (6, 398b13–23), 109, 110
  (6, 399a31), 104
  (6, 399b14–15), 173
  (6, 399b24–25), 111
  (6, 400a7–19), 14, 177
  (6, 400b6–8), 119, 209
  (6, 400b13–31), 72, 210
  (7, 401a12–13), 103
  (7, 401a13–15), 112, 123
  (7, 401a29), 176
  (7, 401b2), 24, 34, 38, 170, 198, 239, 289
  (7, 401b24–27), 176
On the Heavens
  I (1), 166–181
  I (1–3), 46
  I (1, 268a4–6), 252
  I (1, 268a9–b10), 31, 32, 173
  I (2, 268b25–26), 173
  I (2, 269a5–7), 185
  I (2, 269b13–17), 13–15, 185
  I (3, 270a14), 162
  I (3, 270a18–22), 36, 46, 137, 141
  I (3, 270b2), 141
  I (3, 270b20), 14
  I (3, 270b22–24), 115
  I (3, 270b27–29), 140
  I (4, 271a33), 36
  I (9, 279a15), 208
  I (9, 279a18–30), 11–13, 122, 286
  I (10, 279b31–80a10), 61
  II (1, 284a18–35), 78
  II (2, 284b21–24), 178
  II (12, 292a20), 178
  II (12, 292b2–3), 251
On the Soul
  I (1, 402a4–6), 231
  I (1, 402a10), 234
  I (1, 402a16), 232
  I (1, 402a21–22), 231, 273
  I (1, 402a25–b1), 220
  I (1, 402b3), 79, 225, 231
  I (1, 402b7), 258
  I (1, 403a3–25), 172, 195, 182, 220, 273
  I (1, 403a27–29), 231
  I (1, 403a31–b1), 195
  I (1, 403b7–15), 190
  I (2, 404a6–10), 79, 166

Aristotle, *On the Soul* (continued)
- I (2, 404a25–b6), 50
- I (2, 404b16), 174
- I (2, 404b19), 273
- I (2, 404b27–30), 168, 175
- I (2, 405a13–9), 50
- I (2, 405a19–21), 91
- I (2, 405b28–9), 79
- I (3, 405b31–6b25), 45, 53, 77, 140, 193
- I (3, 407a3–5), 193
- I (3, 407a9–10), 181
- I (3, 407a16–22), 177
- I (3, 407b3–5), 78
- I (3, 407b13–26), 77, 85, 115, 139, 174, 182, 183, 201, 212, 221, 248, 251, 254
- I (3, 407b22), 80
- I (4, 407b27–8a30), 190
- I (4, 408b12–18), 151, 156
- I (4, 408b19), 81, 187
- I (4, 408b27–28), 161
- I (4, 408b33), 168
- I (5, 409b2–4), 146, 166
- I (5, 410b27–11a20), 79, 80
- I (5, 411a7–8), 92, 100, 287
- I (5, 411a18–20), 81, 153
- I (5, 411b19–20), 180, 200
- II (1, 412a5), 258
- II (1, 412a8), 212
- II (1, 412a9–11), 8, 109, 126, 215, 217, 219, 221, 224, 257
- II (1, 412a12–22), 138, 172, 187, 252, 258
- II (1, 412a14–16), 30, 215, 227, 248, 252, 262
- II (1, 412a19–28), 8, 76, 82, 84, 200, 213, 214, 220, 221, 227, 230, 234, 258, 273
- II (1, 412a22–6), 84, 109, 124, 154, 212, 214, 217, 221, 234, 255, 257, 271, 285
- II (1, 412b1–4), 245–248, 256
- II (1, 412b4–6), 12, 76, 151, 153, 161, 212, 230, 255
- II (1, 412b17–3a5), 14, 43, 82, 135, 151, 153, 154, 159, 200, 223, 253, 256, 260
- II (1, 412b27), 64, 242, 260, 281
- II (1, 413a4–7), 43, 84, 220
- II (1, 413a8–9), 44, 124, 151, 156, 183, 239, 257
- II (2, 413a22), 31, 248
- II (2, 413b13–24), 152, 154, 200
- II (2, 413b24–7), 44, 186, 230, 272, 273
- II (2, 413b33), 28
- II (2, 414a20–1), 75, 84, 248
- II (2, 414a25–7), 77, 85, 214, 226, 251, 254
- II (3, 414b1), 28
- II (3, 414b19–5a1), 21, 229
- II (3, 415a11–12), 232
- II (4, 415a24–b6), 21–28, 33, 51, 63, 152, 165, 192, 216
- II (4, 415b7), 21, 63, 82, 135, 151, 258
- II (4, 415b9–6b31), 194
- II (4, 415b15–17), 36, 45, 227, 258, 285
- II (4, 415b18), 138, 179
- II (4, 415b26–30), 27
- II (4, 416a9–19), 152, 230
- II (4, 416a13), 80
- II (4, 416b28–29), 194, 207
- II (5, 417a2–6), 160
- II (5, 417a11), 235
- II (5, 417a21), 234
- II (5, 417b7), 160
- II (5, 417b16–8), 81, 154, 200, 235, 242
- II (7, 418b3–9a21), 147, 242
- II (8, 420a3–7), 156, 157, 158, 215
- II (8, 420b20), 202
- II (9, 422a3), 155
- II (11, 423a4), 161
- II (12, 424a18), 220
- III (1, 425a6), 155
- III (5, 430a10), 239

III (9, 432b18–25), 249
III (9, 432b14–3a8), 164, 187, 194, 259
III (10, 433b19–21), 27, 36, 44, 51, 58, 194, 202, 276
III (11, 434a13), 258
III (12–13), 22
III (12, 434b4–5), 242
III (13, 435a11–13), 160
III (13, 435a17–18), 156
III (13, 435a24–b1), 149, 232
On the Spirit, 2, 7, 8, 262–265, 282–283
  (1), 163, 186
  (1, 481a1), 268
  (1, 481a16), 199, 262
  (2, 481a29), 83
  (2, 481b17–19), 115, 148, 166
  (2, 482a23), 93, 145
  (3–4), 83
  (3, 482a33), 115, 148
  (4–5), 23, 52, 53
  (4, 483a1–5), 204
  (8, 485a5–7), 149, 263
  (8, 485a13–15), 259
  (9, 485a28), 80, 194, 208
  (9, 485a35–b9), 139, 262
  (9, 485b6–7), 194, 201
  (9, 485b12), 199
  (9, 485b15–19), 136, 164, 195, 259
On Youth (4, 469b6–8), 148
Parts of Animals
  I (1, 641a32–b10), 231
  I (1, 642a11–14), 250
  I (5, 654a17–21), 210–211, 250
  II (1), 155, 158
  II (1, 647b23), 249
  II (4, 650b20), 162
  II (7, 653a27–31), 184
  II (10, 655b37–6a6), 250
  II (10, 656a7–13), 184
  II (10, 656a27–29), 155
  III (4, 666a34–b1), 155
  III (6, 669a18), 205

III (6, 669b1–6), 184
IV (10, 687a6–b5), 183
Physics
  I (2, 185b9–11), 172
  I (7, 190b5–9), 141, 162, 196
  I (9), 37–39, 173
  I (9, 192a4–6), 179, 239
  I (9, 192a13–23), 32, 33, 262, 289
  I (9, 192a31), 289
  II (2, 194b9–15), 173, 232, 273
  II (3, 194b23–5a3), 191
  II (3, 195a21–23), 191
  II (6, 198a24–26), 193
  III (1, 201a23–7), 49
  III (2, 202a7, a8), 49
  IV (8, 215a14–19), 95
  VI (1, 231b4–6), 178
  VIII (1, 250b11–3), 50
  VIII (1, 252a11), 45
  VIII (2 + 6), 23, 52–4, 224
  VIII (2, 253a11–12), 50, 52–53
  VIII (4, 254b8–10), 224
  VIII (5, 256b24–7), 50
  VIII (5, 257b23), 49
  VIII (6, 258b25), 49
  VIII (6, 259b1–20), 50, 51, 53–54, 151, 164, 281
  VIII (10, 266a10), 49
  VIII (10, 266b33–7a2), 96
  VIII (10, 267a2–7), 94, 96
  VIII (10, 267a23), 49, 55
  VIII (10, 267b5–9), 12
Politics VII (4, 1326a31–3), 19, 286
Problems
  II (26, 869a6), 204
  VII (2, 886a34–36), 146
  XXVII (1, 947b12–16), 203
  XXVII (3, 947b29), 204
  XXVII (4, 948a18–19), 205
  XXVII (6, 948a36), 189

Bible
  Daniel (5:6), 203
  Gnostic Gospels
    Apocryphon of John, 127, 128

Bible, Gnostic Gospels *(continued)*
    Gospel of Thomas (logion 114),
        289
    Luke (1:35), 68
    Letter to the Romans (1:19–21), 212

Eudemus of Rhodes
    fr. 96, 180

Hermeticum Corpus
    Poimandres, 125
Hermias
    Irrisio (11), 119
Hesiod
    Theogonia (191–197), 145
Hippolytus (Ps-?)
    Refutatio Omnium Haeresium
        I (20, 3–4), 75, 139, 284
        VII (24, 1–2), 75, 76, 259–260
Homer
    Iliad
        (2, 140), 25
        (2, 204), 32
        (8, 20–22), 16
    Odyssea
        (9, 29), 25
        (10, 483–4), 25
        (24, 1–9), 273

Origenes
    Contra Celsum IV (56), 141

Plato
    Apologia (29d4), 116
    Cratylus (400c), 77
    Epistola VII (335a), 176
    Ion
        (533d1–e5), 18
        (534d2), 18
    Laws
        IV (715e7–6a2), 175
        VII (789a), 79
        X (894a–e), 31, 277

Phaedo
    (62b2–9), 77, 126
    (70c), 176
    (71c1), 225
Phaedrus, 4
    (240c), 176
    (245d8–e1), 78
    (245e7–9), 76
    (246a), 45, 118
    (246b6), 76
    (246c4–7a7), 79, 123
    (248c–e), 68, 79, 277
    (251a2), 283
Politicus
    (269a7–274e3), 121
Republic
    VI (506b2–11e4), 31
    VI (509b), 14
    VI (520c), 118
Symposium (207d–9e), 25
Theaetetus (176a–b), 25, 123
Timaeus
    (28b6–7), 60
    (29a2–31b3), 119, 167, 276
    (34b10–42e3), 273
    (36d8–e5), 78
    (41c–42d), 27, 78, 80, 142,
        229
    (42d4), 78
    (43a4–44d2), 78
    (47e–48a), 208
    (53c4–55c6), 32
    (70c), 204
    (73b1), 79
    (76e7–7c5), 76
    (79a5–e9), 95
    (80c2), 18, 96
    (90e), 68, 80
    (91d4–5), 79
Ps.-Plato
    Alcibiades
        I, 114
        I (130a), 288

Plotinus
  Enneads
    I (6 [1] 8, 16), 26
    II (5 [25] 3, 18), 141
    III (2 [47]), 72
    III (8 [30] 8, 15–6), 30
    IV (3 [27]), 78
    V (1 [10] 1, 1–9), 128
Plutarch of Chaeronea
  De Facie in Orbe Lunae
    (941F), 228
    (942A), 59, 123
    (945A–B), 125
  Quaestiones Platonicae (8), 260
  Vita Alexandri XIV (671), 99
Ps.-Plutarch
  Placita I (881E–F), 119, 209
Proclus
  In Platonis Timaeum V (312C), 139
Themistius
  In Arist. De anim. (19, 33), 139
Theophrastus
  Metaphysics (2, 5b10–17), 16, 238

www.ingramcontent.com/pod-product-compliance
Lightning Source LLC
Chambersburg PA
CBHW030009240426
43672CB00007B/877